Handbooks in Health, Work, and Disability

Series Editors
Robert J. Gatchel, Arlington, TX, USA
Izabela Z. Schultz, Vancouver, BC, Canada

More information about this series at
http://www.springer.com/series/8766

Reuben Escorpizo • Sören Brage • Debra Homa •
Gerold Stucki
Editors

Handbook of Vocational Rehabilitation and Disability Evaluation

Application and Implementation of the ICF

Springer

Editors
Reuben Escorpizo
Department of Rehabilitation and Movement Science
University of Vermont
Burlington, Vermont
USA

Sören Brage
Research Unit
Directorate for Labour and Welfare
Oslo, Oslo
Norway

Debra Homa
Department of Rehabilitation and Counsel
University of Wisconsin-Stout
Menomonie, Wisconsin
USA

Gerold Stucki
Department of Health Sciences and Health Policy
University of Lucerne
Lucerne, Luzern
Switzerland

ISSN 2198-7084 ISSN 2198-7092 (electronic)
ISBN 978-3-319-08824-2 ISBN 978-3-319-08825-9 (eBook)
DOI 10.1007/978-3-319-08825-9
Springer Cham Heidelberg New York Dordrecht London

Library of Congress Control Number: 2014954133

Printed on acid-free paper

Springer is part of Springer Science+Business Media (www.springer.com)

Foreword

Promoting the right of persons with disabilities and their full inclusion in all sectors of society on an equal basis with others is a policy goal in many countries around the world, following the entry into force of the UN Convention on the Rights of Persons with Disabilities (UNCRPD) in May 2008. The UNCRPD highlights the right of persons with disabilities to access general health, education, habilitation and rehabilitation, and vocational and training services and their right to decent and productive work and employment in the open labour market, on an equal basis with others. Whether their disability dates from birth or an early age, or whether they acquired their disability in the course of their working lives, States that have ratified UNCRPD are required to promote and protect these rights, among others, through a range of measures, including prohibition of discrimination on the basis of disability and ensuring reasonable accommodation is made. It is not immediately clear to States what measures will be effective in transforming the vision the UNCRPD represents into a reality for persons with disabilities around the world. It is thus important to draw attention to those that have been tried and tested, examining their impact on health, education, training, and employment outcomes.

For a long time, it was assumed that exclusion or marginalization of persons with disabilities was closely interrelated to, and in fact the unavoidable consequence of, the physical and mental impairments of the persons concerned. It is now increasingly recognized that many of the disadvantages they face leading to their exclusion from employment and other sectors of society are not due to individual impairments but rather a result of how society reacts and caters to those impairments. The WHO's International Classification of Functioning, Disability and Health (ICF) is key in promoting this understanding of disability, which underlies the provisions of the UNCRPD.

Taking the right to work and employment as an example, countries are seeking to tackle the low employment rates and low rates of participation in the labour market, which is the situation of persons with disabilities of working-age everywhere, and to address the pattern that, when in employment, workers with disability are more likely to be in low-paid jobs with poor career prospects and working conditions than workers without disability. This situation has negative impacts at many levels for the estimated 780 million persons with disabilities of working age. Many are counted among the working poor, and many more rely on social security benefits or charity, trapping them in a vicious cycle associated with widespread poverty for both themselves and their households. As a consequence, employers do not fully benefit from the unique and substantial contribution persons with disabilities can make in the workplace. From a national and global perspective, there are significant economic losses arising from high unemployment and lost productivity of women and men with disabilities – estimated at between 3 % and 7 % of Gross Domestic Product in a pilot study conducted by the International Labour Organization (ILO) of ten low and middle-income developing countries. Thus, effectively implementing the right to work and employment will have benefits across the board, and the ICF can be used to promote this right more effectively, through possible and innovative new approaches to vocational assessment, workplace disability evaluation and disability management.

This publication, *Handbook of Vocational Rehabilitation and Disability Evaluation – Application and Implementation of the ICF,* is timely in that it addresses pressing issues and themes of relevance to enabling persons with disabilities to work effectively and to reaching their full potential and participate in all sectors of society. Apart from the immediate audience of researchers, academicians and students in the field of work and employment, it is of broader relevance to policy-makers and service providers, as they move to implement the provisions of the UNCRPD. By highlighting good and emerging practice in these areas and more broadly, through the use of the ICF as a conceptual model and classification system, it will make an important contribution to improving the quality of life of persons with disabilities worldwide, and enabling societies to benefit from the valuable contribution that persons with disabilities can make in their communities.

Conditions of Work and Equality Department,
International Labour Office, Geneva,
Switzerland

Barbara Murray

Acknowledgements

We would like to express our profound gratitude to all the authors, collaborators and colleagues who have spent their precious time and shared their expertise that made this book a success. Without the generous contributions of these individuals and the support of their institutions, the book that we now enjoy reading would not have been possible. We would like to thank Melissa Selb, our coordinator extraordinaire who made sure that everything was on task and on time.

We would like to thank our institutions and its leaders who believed in us and made sure that we can do our work to serve our community in vocational rehabilitation and disability evaluation.

We would like to thank Janice Stern and all the wonderful and supportive people at Springer: Joe Quatela, Christina Tuballes, Nishantini Dayalan, Sarvani Rao, Srinivasa Rao, Elumalai Balamurugan and their staff. The direction and planning of this book were guided by our brilliant series editors- Bob Gatchel and Izabela Schultz- thank you very much! Our sincerest appreciation goes to our families and friends who have been supportive and understanding of the times when we were away from them – focused on our mission of completing this book!

Finally, our endless gratitude goes to all our stakeholders in the realm of vocational rehabilitation and disability evaluation for making us understand that they matter, and writing a book about them is the least we can do to advocate for their cause. Nothing can summarize it better than the words of Professor Stephen Hawking, *...it is very clear that the majority of people with disabilities in the world have an extremely difficult time with everyday survival, let alone productive employment and personal fulfillment... this century will mark a turning point for the inclusion of people with disabilities in the lives of their societies...*

Contents

Part I
Introduction

Chapter 1
Conceptual Framework: Disability Evaluation and Vocational Rehabilitation

Gerold Stucki, Soren Brage, Debra Homa, and Reuben Escorpizo

1.1 Introduction

Disability represents a major challenge that societies worldwide have to address [1, 2]. First, from an individual perspective, persons with disabilities have the right to "full and effective participation and inclusion in the society." Second, from a societal perspective, the society has the ethical and legal obligation to include them in all aspects of life. Third, from an economic perspective, the society is interested that persons with disabilities contribute to the community either in the form of tangible or intangible productivity [3].

For most people, work is a major aspect of life. When any type of disability affects a person, work disability may occur and contribute to negative consequences not just on the individual but for the society as well. If all attempts for remedying

G. Stucki
Swiss Paraplegic Research, Nottwil, Switzerland

ICF Research Branch of the WHO CC FIC in Germany (DIMDI), Nottwil, Switzerland

Department of Health Sciences and Health Policy, University of Lucerne, Lucerne, Switzerland

S. Brage
Research Unit, Directorate for Labour and Welfare, Oslo, Norway

D. Homa
Department of Rehabilitation and Counseling, University of Wisconsin-Stout, Menomonie, WI, USA

R. Escorpizo (✉)
Swiss Paraplegic Research, Nottwil, Switzerland

ICF Research Branch of the WHO CC FIC in Germany (DIMDI), Nottwil, Switzerland

Department of Rehabilitation and Movement Science, The University of Vermont, Burlington, VT 05405, USA
e-mail: escorpizo.reuben@gmail.com

R. Escorpizo et al. (eds.), *Handbook of Vocational Rehabilitation and Disability Evaluation*, Handbooks in Health, Work, and Disability, DOI 10.1007/978-3-319-08825-9_1

work disability still result in a persons' inability to work in full or optimal capacity, then income replacement in the form of disability benefits is an alternative to help ensure that persons with disabilities have the economic means for "attaining and maintaining maximum independence" and participation in other major aspects of life [1].

When any type of disability affects a person, work disability may occur and contribute to negative consequences not just on the individual but for the society as well.

1.2 Disability Evaluation

The assessment of a person's work disability is among the key features of *disability evaluation* (DE). Disability evaluation is instrumental in assigning persons with disabilities (henceforth *claimants*) to appropriate *return-to-work* (RTW) programs, medical rehabilitation, and provision of assistive devices or medical devices. Providing the appropriate intervention for a particular person at the right time increases the cost-effectiveness of selected interventions, or, in other words, the chances for a successful outcome, namely, RTW [4]. *RTW programs* can be understood interchangeably with the term *vocational rehabilitation* (VR), which will be presented later in this chapter. An RTW program is in principle a process of VR for those who have previously worked with the ultimate goal of undertaking work duties in the long term. In the context of RTW, work disability can be understood as the inability to work due to an illness or injury in light of influencing contextual factors.

Disability evaluation is also crucial to determine a claimant's eligibility for disability benefits as well as to establish appropriate levels of benefits. In addition, DE provides the necessary information to determine if the claimant should participate in an RTW program before receiving disability benefits. While there are differing definitions of disability evaluation toward eligibility determination for benefits [5–7], we refer to the *"Medical Subject Headings"* (MeSh) definition of DE: *DE* is the "determination of the degree of a person's physical, mental, or emotional [disability]. The diagnosis is applied to legal qualification for benefits and income under disability insurance and to eligibility for Social Security and workers' compensation benefits" [8]. In the context of eligibility determination for benefits, work disability is a legal concept with varying definitions among social security laws of different countries [9]. However, work disability usually refers to a person's inability to work due to an illness or injury without considering the influence of contextual factors.

1.3 Requirements for Disability Evaluation

Disability evaluations should fulfill fundamental requirements to provide a just assignment to RTW programs as well as fair eligibility determination for disability benefits. The evaluations should be comparable in terms of content validity and inter-rater reliability between the medical experts who perform the assessments [10, 11]. This could be achieved with the introduction of standards in the disability evaluation process [12].

It is also essential that disability evaluation be documented in a transparent way [13, 14] and address how functional limitations at work are affected by the claimant's health condition or by contextual factors. Moreover, the documentation should be plausible and comprehensible for all those involved in the disability evaluation process, including the medical experts, the claimants themselves, the legal system, and the disability insurance systems. To provide transparency, professional guidance on disability evaluation advises medical experts to capture a comprehensive picture of the claimants in their medical reports [15]. Such transparent documentations provide claimants with a basis for formally appealing eligibility decisions they deem as unwarranted.

> Disability evaluations should fulfill fundamental requirements to provide a just assignment to RTW programs as well as fair eligibility determination for disability benefits.

1.4 Functioning Assessment in Disability Evaluation

Although different countries organize disability evaluation in varying ways, the key information in the evaluation usually refers to functioning and disability. Therefore, *functioning assessments* are a core element of disability evaluation [9] and provide important information for evaluating work disability. Functioning assessment in the context of disability evaluation address the claimant's ability to perform activities relevant for executing physical or cognitive work tasks such as lifting or focusing attention. There are differences in functioning assessments depending on whether the sole purpose for the disability evaluation is determining eligibility for benefits, considering RTW, or both. Toward facilitating RTW, functioning assessments in disability evaluation focus on the appraisal of the *performance* of the claimant. The assessment of functional limitations or abilities and influencing contextual factors, such as the claimant's living conditions or the job market situation, is the basis for selecting appropriate RTW programs to enhance the claimant's potential to perform work tasks and subsequent work participation. Functioning assessment in the context of determining eligibility for benefits is geared toward an objective statement about the claimant's functional *capacity* in a standardized environment without considering the influence of contextual factors. The functioning assessment provides key information on the relationship between impairments and functional limitations and thus ascertains a claimant's work disability.

The functioning assessment provides key information on the relationship between impairments and functional limitations and thus ascertains a claimant's work disability.

1.5 Work Disability and Vocational Rehabilitation

When a worker becomes ill or develops a health condition or disease, work disability may result which can prevent the individual from continuing to work. Work disability may be associated with personal suffering, limitations in functioning, loss of income, high medical costs, and strained relationships of the individual with others. In addition, work disability may lead to diminished productivity for the individual as a member of society.

Work disability poses a great burden and challenge to both developing [16] and developed nations [17, 18], with indirect cost making up the bulk of the burden in industrialized countries (approximately 80 %) [19]. The challenge is to find ways to mitigate work disability-related burden and how to sustain optimal work participation.

Vocational rehabilitation is defined as *"a multi-professional evidence-based approach that is provided in different settings, services, and activities to working age individuals with health-related impairments, limitations, or restrictions with work functioning, and whose primary aim is to optimize work participation"* [20]. This general definition is based on the International Classification of Functioning, Disability, and Health (ICF) [21] to indicate the breadth and complexity of factors that are relevant to vocational rehabilitation. This conceptual definition considers the aspects of vocational rehabilitation based on the components of the ICF: *Body Functions* and *Body Structure*, *Activities And Participation*, and the contextual factors [21].

The primary goal of vocational rehabilitation is both RTW and sustained RTW. In some cases, it may be that an individual did not work before (i.e., does not have any work history). Rather than returning to work, the individual in this situation wants to engage in work, which still falls within the context of vocational rehabilitation (e.g., a person who just graduated from high school and had an accident resulting in spinal cord injury, who now wants to work). In this case, vocational rehabilitation is designed to ensure that the person is able to participate in employment despite the disability.

1.6 The ICF: A Standard for Disability Evaluation and Vocational Rehabilitation

Because the key information in disability evaluation refers to functioning and disability, standards for functioning assessment are instrumental in ensuring comparability, transparency, and fairness in disability evaluation, and the ICF can help facilitate this process. The framework of the ICF conceptualizes human functioning as a dynamic interplay between *body functions* and *body structures, activities and participation*, as well as contextual factors, i.e., *environmental factors* and *personal factors*. In disability evaluation, the *ICF* allows for a comprehensive description of a claimant's functioning and can facilitate a standardized and comprehensible documentation [22]. Thus, it could ensure comparability of functioning assessment in terms of inter-rater reliability. Moreover, the ICF could contribute to a transparent illustration of how impairments affect a claimant's work activities, work participation, and work disability [23] and point to the role of contextual factors in the process [24]. Finally, the ICF can be used to standardize reporting of work disability, which in turn could facilitate comparison of functioning assessment across countries [25].

Study Questions

1. What is disability evaluation and how is it related to work disability?

   Answer: Disability evaluation is the determination of the degree of a person's physical, mental, or emotional [disability]. The diagnosis is applied to legal qualification for benefits and income under disability insurance and to eligibility for Social Security and workers' compensation benefits. In the context of eligibility determination for benefits, work disability is a legal concept with varying definitions among social security laws of different countries. However, work disability usually refers to a person's inability to work due to an illness or injury without considering the influence of contextual factors.

2. What is functioning assessment?

   Answer: Functioning assessment is a core element of disability evaluation and provides important information for evaluating work disability. Functioning assessment in the context of disability evaluation address the claimant's ability to perform activities relevant for executing physical or cognitive work tasks such as lifting or focusing attention. There are differences in functioning assessments depending on whether the sole purpose for the disability evaluation is determining eligibility for benefits, or considering RTW, or both.

3. What is vocational rehabilitation?

Answer: Vocational rehabilitation is a multi-professional evidence-based approach that is provided in different settings, services, and activities to working age individuals with health-related impairments, limitations, or restrictions with work functioning and whose primary aim is to optimize work participation.

Glossary

Disability Evaluation The assessment of the extent of a person's work disability is among the key features of *disability evaluation* (DE). DE is instrumental to assign persons with disabilities (i.e., claimants) to the most appropriate *return-to-work* (RTW) programs, medical rehabilitation, and/or provision of assistive devices. DE is also crucial to determine claimants' eligibility for disability benefits, to establish appropriate levels of benefits, and provides the necessary information whether assignment to an RTW program is required before receiving disability benefits.

Eligibility Determination for Benefits *DE in the context of eligibility determination for benefits* is the "determination of the degree of a person's physical, mental, or emotional [disability]. The diagnosis is applied to legal qualification for benefits and income under disability insurance and to eligibility for Social Security and workers' compensation benefits."

Functioning Assessments *Functioning assessments* (FA) are core elements of DE across countries [2] and provide useful information for evaluating work disability. FA in the context of DE address the claimant's ability to perform activities relevant for executing physical or cognitive work tasks such as lifting or focusing attention. There are differences in FA depending on whether the sole purpose for the DE is determining eligibility for benefits or also, respectively, exclusively considering RTW. Toward facilitating RTW, FA in DE focuses on the appraisal of the claimant's *functional performance*. Assessments of functional limitations or abilities and influencing contextual factors such as the claimant's living conditions or the situation on the job market are the basis for selecting appropriate RTW programs to enhance the claimant's functioning at work and, finally, work participation. FA in DE toward eligibility determination for disability benefits are geared toward an objective statement on the claimant's *functional capacity* in a standardized environment without considering the influence of contextual factors. The assessments provide key information for the determination of the relationship between impairments and functional limitations and, thus, for establishing a claimant's work disability.

Return-to-Work Programs and Vocational Rehabilitation *Return-to-work (RTW) programs* can be understood interchangeably with the term *vocational rehabilitation* (VR). Escorpizo et al. [19] defined VR as "a multi-professional evidence-based approach that is provided in different settings, services, and activities to working age individuals with health-related impairments, limitations, or restrictions with work functioning, and whose primary aim is to optimize work participation." An RTW program is in principle VR of those who have previously worked with the ultimate goal of undertaking work duties long term. RTW programs encompass services such as job counseling, job placement, job matching, job coaching, skills development and retraining, provision of products and technology, work conditioning, or workplace modification.

Work Disability In the context of RTW, work disability is defined as a claimant's inability to work due to an illness or injury in the light of influencing contextual factors.In the context of eligibility determination for disability benefits, work disability is seen as a legal concept with varying definitions among social security laws of different countries. However, work disability usually refers to a person's inability to work due to an illness or injury without considering the influence of contextual factors.

References

1. United Nations. Convention on the rights of persons with disabilities. Geneva: United Nations; 2006.
2. World Health Organization, World Bank. World report on disability. Geneva: WHO Press; 2011.
3. Community Support Network Inc. Employment. Available from: www.csni.org/fpg/Volume%20I%20Employment.pdf (2013). Accessed 18 Jun 2013.
4. Eisenberg JM, Power EJ. Transforming insurance coverage into quality health care: voltage drops from potential to delivered quality. JAMA. 2000;284(16):2100–7.
5. de Boer W, Besseling J, Willems J. Organisation of disability evaluation in 15 countries. Pratiques et organisation des soins. 2007;38:205–17.
6. Slebus FG, Sluiter JK, Kuijer PP, Willems JH, Frings-Dresen MH. Work-ability evaluation: a piece of cake or a hard nut to crack? Disabil Rehabil. 2007;29(16):1295–300.
7. Waddell G, Aylward M. The scientific and conceptual basis of incapacity benefits. Norwich: TSO; 2005.
8. National Library of Medicine. Medical Subject Headings (MeSH). http://www.nlm.nih.gov/cgi/mesh/2013/MB_cgi (2013). Accessed 18 Jun 2013.
9. Anner J, Schwegler U, Kunz R, Trezzini B, de Boer W. Evaluation of work disability and the international classification of functioning, disability and health: what to expect and what not. BMC Public Health. 2012;12:470.
10. Demeter SL, Andersson GBJ, Smith GM, editors. Disability evaluation. St. Louis: Mosby and the American Medical Association; 1996.
11. Rudbeck M, Fonager K. Agreement between medical expert assessments in social medicine. Scand J Public Health. 2011;39(7):766–72.
12. Matheson LN, Kane M, Rodbard D. Development of new methods to determine work disability in the United States. J Occup Rehabil. 2001;11(3):143–54.

13. Meershoek A, Krumeich A, Vos R. Judging without criteria? Sickness certification in Dutch disability schemes. Sociol Health Illn. 2007;29(4):497–514.
14. Stöhr S, Bollag Y, Auerbach H, Eichler K, Imhof D, Fabbro T, et al. Quality assessment of a randomly selected sample of Swiss medical expertises – a pilot study. Swiss Med Wkly. 2011;141:w13173.
15. Hesse B, Gebauer E. Disability assessment for the statutory benefits insurance: significance, need for research, and opportunities. Rehabilitation (Stuttg). 2011;50(1):17–24.
16. Chan CC, Zhuo DH. Occupational rehabilitation in twenty-first century Asia Pacific: facilitating health and work: an introduction. J Occup Rehabil. 2011;21 Suppl 1:S1–4.
17. Stubbs J, Deaner G. When considering vocational rehabilitation: describing and comparing the Swedish and American systems and professions. Work. 2005;24(3):239–49.
18. Organisation for Economic Co-operation and Development Directorate for Employment, Labour and Social Affairs. Sickness, disability and work: keeping on track in the economic downturn (background paper). May 2009. Report No.: High-Level Forum, Stockholm.
19. Dagenais S, Caro J, Haldeman S. A systematic review of low back pain cost of illness studies in the United States and internationally. Spine J. 2008;8(1):8–20.
20. Escorpizo R, Reneman MF, Ekholm J, Fritz J, Krupa T, Marnetoft SU, et al. A conceptual definition of vocational rehabilitation based on the ICF: building a shared global model. J Occup Rehabil. 2011;21(2):126–33.
21. World Health Organization. International classification of functioning, disability and health (ICF). Geneva: World Health Organization; 2001.
22. Schwegler U, Anner J, Boldt C, Glässel A, Lay V, De Boer WEL, et al. Aspects of functioning and environmental factors in medical work capacity evaluations of persons with chronic widespread pain and low back pain can be represented by a combination of applicable ICF Core Sets. BMC Public Health. 2012;12(1):1088.
23. Baron S, Linden M. The role of the "International Classification of Functioning, Disability and Health, ICF" in the description and classification of mental disorders. Eur Arch Psychiatry Clin Neurosci. 2008;258 Suppl 5:81–5.
24. Sanderson K, Nicholson J, Graves N, Tilse E, Oldenburg B. Mental health in the workplace: using the ICF to model the prospective associations between symptoms, activities, participation and environmental factors. Disabil Rehabil. 2008;30(17):1289–97.
25. Brage S, Donceel P, Falez F. Development of ICF core set for disability evaluation in social security. Disabil Rehabil. 2008;30(18):1392–6.

Chapter 2
Conceptual Framework: Functioning and Disability

Reuben Escorpizo

Abbreviations

DOT	Dictionary of Occupational Titles
FCE	Functional capacity evaluation
ICF	International Classification of Functioning, Disability and Health
MGS	Minimal generic set
RTW	Return to work
VR	Vocational rehabilitation
WHO	World Health Organization
WHO DAS 2.0	World Health Organization-Disability Assessment Schedule version 2.0
WHS	World Health Survey
WORQ	Work Rehabilitation Questionnaire

2.1 Introduction

In 1916, John Collie in his seminal paper presented the challenging issue of return to work for those individuals who have had injuries (or health conditions) that prevent them from working. His paper provided what could be one of the early publications on the challenges and difficulties encountered by the worker, one of

R. Escorpizo (✉)
Department of Rehabilitation and Movement Science, The University of Vermont, Burlington, VT 05405, USA

Swiss Paraplegic Research, Nottwil, Switzerland

ICF Research Branch of the WHO CC FIC in Germany (DIMDI), Nottwil, Switzerland
e-mail: escorpizo.reuben@gmail.com

R. Escorpizo et al. (eds.), *Handbook of Vocational Rehabilitation and Disability Evaluation*, Handbooks in Health, Work, and Disability, DOI 10.1007/978-3-319-08825-9_2

which being the worker not only *recovering* from the ill effects of injury or a health condition which prevents engaging with work but also being able to sustain that recovery [1]. About a century later, return to work as a process has greatly evolved and has become what we now understand as a multifactorial process with outcomes that are complex and often interrelated. This increasing complexity is coupled with the need for fair and true disability or work disability evaluation so as to inform effective vocational rehabilitation or other appropriate programmes.

This chapter will introduce the readers to the International Classification of Functioning, Disability and Health (ICF) [2] model of the World Health Organization (WHO) and discuss how the ICF model can help us to understand and examine the broader context of work disability in an effort to evaluate disability. This chapter will also provide the readers with an overview of the role of the ICF in vocational rehabilitation and disability evaluation.

2.2 ICF

2.2.1 The ICF as a Conceptual Model

In 2001, the World Health Assembly endorsed the ICF [2] as a common framework and language to describe the different aspects of human functioning and disability (disability denotes a negative state, while "functioning" a positive state).[1] The ICF is a conceptual model and also a classification system with applications for providing clinical care and conducting research, developing health and social policy, and conducting population surveys for various reasons. The ICF can be used to understand health and health-related domains and can serve as a common language of disability, in effect serving as a basis to compare disability data across different countries [2]. Hence, the ICF can be used independent of the setting, culture, and context.

As a conceptual model, the ICF illustrates the interrelationship and association between a health condition (disease or injury) and its impact on the individual's body (as depicted by body functions component and body structure component), and its impact on the individual's participation in the society (as depicted by activities and participation component). These different components represent the "functioning" aspect of the ICF with the notion that functioning may be influenced by contextual factors (environmental factors and personal factors), which can worsen, improve, or maintain the level of disability of an individual (see Fig. 2.1).

[1] Portions of this section of the chapter has been excerpted and used with some modification from Escorpizo et al. [21] (including Supplement Material), with kind permission of the American Physical Therapy Association (APTA).

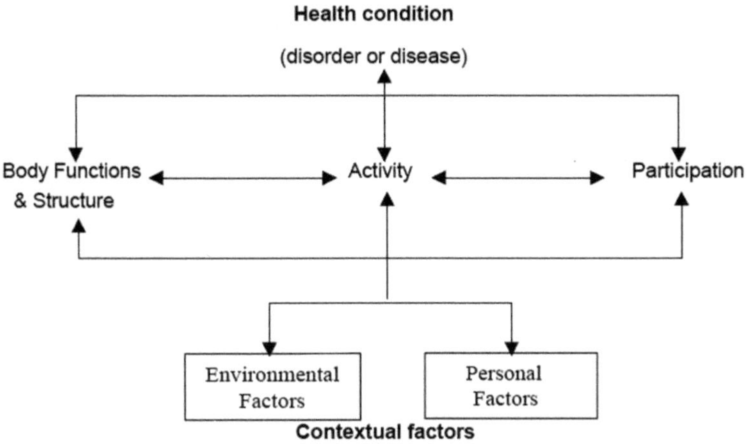

Fig. 2.1 The International Classification of Functioning, Disability and Health (ICF) model of the WHO

Disability refers to either impairment of the body structure and function, limitation of activities, or restriction in participation. Hence, functioning and disability can be illustrated using a sliding scale depending on the positive or negative direction that functioning and disability may take in light of a health condition (Fig. 2.2).

> The ICF illustrates the interrelationship and association between a health condition (disease or injury) and its impact on the individual's body (as depicted by body functions component and body structure component) and its impact on the individual's participation in the society (as depicted by activities and participation component).

2.2.2 *The ICF as a Classification System*

In the ICF, there are different components of human functioning (and disability): *body functions* and *body structures* classify functions and structures at the organ system level respectively. An example of *body function* would be "muscle power function" and "structure of the shoulder region" would be *body structure*. *Activities and participation* classify the full range of actions, tasks, and social or life roles such as reading, carrying out daily routine, walking, and remunerative employment. *Body function*, *body structure*, and *activities and participation* can be influenced by characteristics of the person (*personal factors*) such as coping and his or her physical, social, and attitudinal environment (*environmental factors*) such as physical accessibility of a building, attitude of family members, and support from health

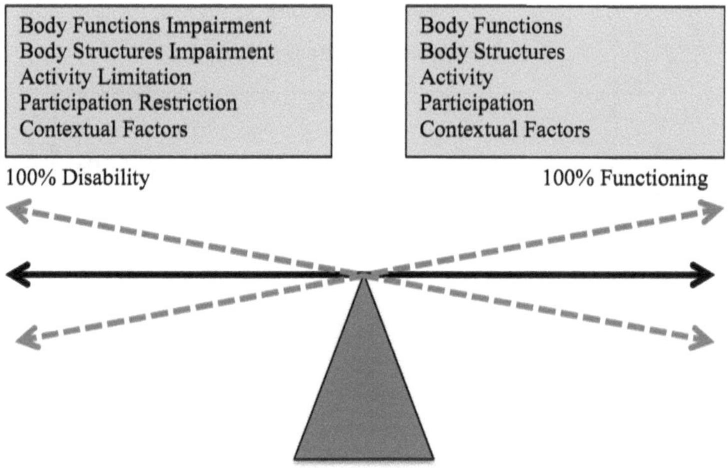

Fig. 2.2 Functioning and disability as depicted in a scale. Impairment, limitation, and restriction in any of the ICF components weigh the scale towards disability; the level of disability is influenced by contextual factors (environment and personal factors)

professionals. Each ICF component, except for *personal factors*, is assigned a letter code: "b" for *body functions*, "s" for *body structures*, "d" for *activities and participation*, and "e" for *environmental factors*. *Personal factors* while defined as the "... background of an individual's life and living, and comprise features of the individual that are not part of a health condition or health states" [2] are not classified (which means no codes) at this time.

Each ICF component consists of different chapters or domains (e.g. in *body functions* the chapters include mental functioning, sensory functions, functions of the cardiovascular, haematological, immunological, and respiratory system, etc.), and each chapter is made up of several alphanumerically coded *ICF categories* which are the specific units of a domain. Each ICF category is given a distinct alphanumeric code that identifies the component (b, s, d, or e), chapter (number), and level (specific domains) in the hierarchical structure. The classification and coding structure is presented in Fig. 2.3.

As previously said, each ICF category is assigned a component letter and numerical code which makes each category unique. The hierarchical arrangement is illustrated below under *body functions* within the domain "pain":

ICF component	b	Body function
Chapter/first level	b2	Sensory functions and pain
2nd level category	b280	Sensation of pain
3rd level category	b2801	Pain in body part
4th level category	b28010	Pain in head and neck

Below is an example of the hierarchy of codes under *body structure* within the domain "structure of lower extremity":

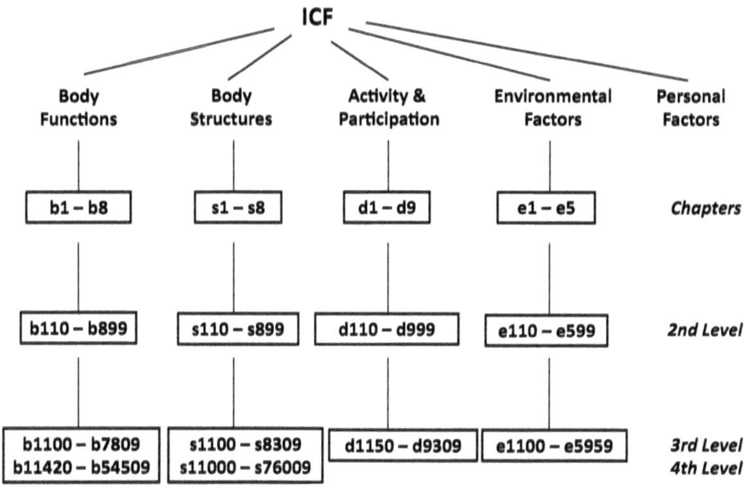

Fig. 2.3 The hierarchical structure of the ICF: from chapter level down to 4th level ICF category specification. For example, "b1–b8" means that there are eight chapters to *body functions*, i.e. chapter b1, b2, b3, etc., "b110–b899" is a collection of codes from b110 to b899

ICF component	s	Body structure
Chapter/first level	s7	Structures related to movement
2nd level category	s750	Structure of lower extremity
3rd level category	s7500	Structure of thigh
4th level category	s75001	Hip joint

In some cases, 4th level categories are not available for some domains. Here is an example for *activities and participation*:

ICF component	d	Activities and participation
Chapter/first level	d8	Major life areas
2nd level category	d850	Remunerative employment
3rd level category	d8500	Self-employment
4th level category	*no code*	

In the case of d850, other 3rd level ICF categories include d8501 part-time employment and d8502 full-time employment.

Below is an example of the hierarchy of codes under *environmental factors* within the domain "products and technology":

ICF component	e	Environmental factors
Chapter/first level	e1	Products and technology
2nd level category	e135	Products and technology for employment
3rd level category	e1351	Assistive products and technology for employment

As illustrated above, 3rd and 4th level categories are specifications of the more general and higher levels, namely, the 2nd and 1st levels. In the entire ICF, there are 30 chapters in total and 1,424 separate categories distributed across the four ICF components (*body function*, *body structure*, *activities and participation*, and *environmental factors*).

2.2.3 ICF Contents in Detail

Table 2.1 illustrates the depth and breadth of coverage of the ICF at the chapter level. There are eight chapters for *body functions* ranging from mental functions to integumentary functions and also eight chapters for *body structures* (covering all body organ systems). *Activities and participation* has nine chapters ranging from the simple, person level (learning and applying knowledge) to the more complex, societal level (community, social, and civic life) of interaction. Finally, *environmental factors* cover the entire physical, human-built, technological, attitudinal, and social and political world which are divided into five chapters (Table 2.1).

Table 2.2 illustrates the specification of a chapter, e.g. on mental functions under the *body functions* component, where the two parts of the chapter relate to global mental functions, e.g. consciousness and intellectual function, and to specific mental functions, e.g. perceptual and higher-level cognitive functions.

Table 2.3 illustrates the specification of a chapter, Chap. 4 Mobility of the *Activities and Participation* component in this case. From this table, mobility is categorized into several mobility-relevant descriptions such as those of body position, handling objects, walking, and using transportation. Each category is defined in the ICF handbook, and inclusion and exclusion criteria for each are also provided to make the distinction between and among seemingly similar ICF categories. Readers are referred to the ICF handbook for the detailed description of ICF categories [2].

2.2.4 The ICF Qualifier

The previous section of this chapter provided what domains of functioning and disability are to be assessed in light of health condition. In this section, a way of assessing the problem in a given ICF category will be discussed using "ICF qualifiers" (rating scale). The ICF *qualifiers* can be used to rate the severity or magnitude of the impairment of *body functions* or *body structures*, limitation in *activity*, and restrictions in *participation*. The ICF also provides qualifiers to indicate the extent of an *environmental factor* being a barrier or a facilitator of functioning. Without these qualifiers, an ICF code would not be meaningful in terms of the information that it conveys.

Table 2.1 Components and chapters of the ICF

Body functions (Chapters b1–b8)	
Chapter 1 Mental functions	Chapter 5 Functions of the digestive, metabolic, and endocrine systems
Chapter 2 Sensory functions and pain	Chapter 6 Genitourinary and reproductive systems
Chapter 3 Voice and speech functions	Chapter 7 Neuromusculoskeletal and movement-related functions
Chapter 4 Functions of the cardiovascular, haematological, immunological, and respiratory systems	Chapter 8 Functions of the skin and related structures
Body structures (Chapters s1–s8)	
Chapter 1 Structures of the nervous system	Chapter 5 Structures related to the digestive, metabolic, and endocrine systems
Chapter 2 The eye, ear, and related structures	Chapter 6 Structures related to genitourinary and reproductive systems
Chapter 3 Structures involved in voice and speech	Chapter 7 Structures related to movement
Chapter 4 Structures of the cardiovascular, immunological, and respiratory systems	Chapter 8 Skin and related structures
Activities and participation (Chapters d1–d9)	
Chapter 1 Learning and applying knowledge	Chapter 6 Domestic life
Chapter 2 General tasks and demands	Chapter 7 Interpersonal interactions and relationships
Chapter 3 Communication	Chapter 8 Major life areas
Chapter 4 Mobility	Chapter 9 Community, social, and civic life
Chapter 5 Self-care	
Environmental factors (Chapters e1–e5)	
Chapter 1 Products and technology	Chapter 4 Attitudes
Chapter 2 Natural environment and human-made changes to environment	Chapter 5 Services, systems, and policies
Chapter 3 Support and relationships	

There are different levels of the ICF qualifier. In this chapter, we will simplify and focus on the first-level qualifier and, as for the other levels, see the ICF handbook for details. The first-level qualifier is a generic rating scale from 0 to 4, with 0 = no problem, 1 = mild problem, 2 = moderate problem, 3 = severe problem, and 4 = complete problem. Two additional options can be used: 8 (not specified)[2] and 9 (not applicable).[3] On the other hand, the ICF qualifier for the *environmental factors* has nine response options ranging from 4 (complete barrier) to +4 (complete facilitator), with a zero value indicating neither a facilitator nor a barrier. Three additional options for environmental factors can be used: 8 (barrier,

[2] When there is not enough or insufficient information to rate an ICF category.

[3] When rating an ICF category is not applicable, e.g. assessing d830 higher education in an individual who is still in high school.

Table 2.2 Chapter on "mental functions" and its 2nd-level categories

Global mental functions	b110 Consciousness functions
	b114 Orientation functions
	b117 Intellectual functions
	b122 Global psychosocial functions
	b126 Temperament and personality functions
	b130 Energy and drive functions
	b134 Sleep functions
	b139 Global mental functions, other specified and unspecified
Specific mental functions	b140 Attention functions
	b144 Memory functions
	b147 Psychomotor functions
	b152 Emotional functions
	b156 Perceptual functions
	b160 Though functions
	b164 Higher-level cognitive functions
	b167 Mental functions of language
	b172 Calculation functions
	b176 Mental function of sequencing complex movements
	b180 Experience of self and time functions
	b189 Specific mental functions, other specified and unspecified
	b198 Mental functions, other specified
	b199 Mental functions, unspecified

not specified), +8 (facilitator, not specified), and 9 (not applicable) using the same principles of definition stated earlier [2]. For each ICF qualifier, the WHO also provides a corresponding range of percentage. See Table 2.4 for a summary of the ICF qualifiers.

So, for example, an ICF code with qualifier of "b134.1" means that there is a mild (or between 5 % and 24 % level of) impairment of sleep functions. The "b134" refers to the ICF code on sleep functions and the "1" refers to the ICF qualifier for mild impairment. ICF categories belonging to *activities and participation* require a performance and capacity qualifier which means at least two first qualifiers. An example is "d4300.32" which means that there is a severe (50–95 %) difficulty with performance in lifting (d4300) and moderate (25–49 %) difficulty with capacity in lifting. The first of the two qualifiers refers to performance and the second to capacity. The concept of performance refers to what an individual does in his or her *current environment or actual context* in which they live; performance involves the influence of environmental factors. Capacity qualifier refers to an individual's ability tested in a standard or uniform environment (i.e. adjusted for environment) [2].

For *environmental factors*, a plus sign is used to denote that that environmental factor is a facilitator and no sign to denote a barrier. So, for example, a code of e330.+4 means that support and relationship with "people in positions of

Table 2.3 Chapter on "mobility" and its 2nd-level categories

Changing and maintaining body position	d410 Changing basic body position
	d415 Maintaining a body position
	d420 Transferring oneself
	d429 Changing and maintaining body position, other specified and unspecified
Carrying, moving, and handling objects	d430 Lifting and carrying objects
	d435 Moving objects with lower extremities
	d440 Fine hand use
	d445 Hand and arm use
	d449 Carrying, moving, and handling objects, other specified and unspecified
Walking and moving	d450 Walking
	d455 Moving around
	d460 Moving around in different locations
	d465 Moving around using equipment
	d469 Walking and moving, other specified and unspecified
Moving around using transportation	d470 Using transportation
	d475 Driving
	d480 Riding animals for transportation
	d489 Moving around using transportation, other specified and unspecified
	d498 Mobility, other specified
	d499 Mobility, unspecified

authority" (i.e. e330) is a complete (96–100 %) facilitator, while a code of e330.4 means that the support is a complete barrier.

Readers are advised to consult the ICF handbook for more details on the ICF qualifiers.

2.3 Work Disability

2.3.1 Work Disability

Work or employment is a major area in people's lives. You or somebody you know has worked at some point in their lives. Work contributes to a person's well-being and health; hence, it is a significant aspect of daily activities. However, when a worker suffers from the effects of a health condition, illness, or disease, work disability may result which can prevent that individual from working (hence, work disability). Other additional health conditions or comorbidities can occur as a result of work disability. Work disability may be associated with personal suffering, limitations in functioning, loss of income, high medical costs, and

Table 2.4 ICF qualifiers with corresponding percentage values provided by the WHO. ICF qualifiers are designed to rate how much problem there is with a particular item, i.e. the higher the number or percentage, the worse is the problem. In the case of environmental factors, ICF qualifiers are used to rate how much of a barrier or facilitator (annotated with a *plus sign*) an environmental item is, i.e. the higher the number, the more of a facilitator (with *plus*) or barrier that environmental factor is

ICF qualifier	Equivalent percentage (%)
Body functions, body structures, and activities and participation	
0 NO problem (none, absent, negligible. . .)	0–4
1 MILD problem (slight, low. . .)	5–24
2 MODERATE problem (medium, fair. . .)	25–49
3 SEVERE problem (high, extreme. . .)	50–95
4 COMPLETE problem (total. . .)	96–100
Environmental factors	
+4 Complete facilitator	96–100
+3 Substantial facilitator	50–95
+2 Moderate facilitator	25–49
+1 Mild facilitator	5–24
0 Neither barrier nor facilitator	0–4
1 Mild barrier	5–24
2 Moderate barrier	25–49
3 Severe barrier	50–95
4 Complete barrier	96–100

strained relationships of the individual with others. In addition, work disability may lead to diminished productivity and increase in societal costs.

Work disability poses a great burden and challenge to both developing [3] and developed nations [4, 5], with indirect cost like loss of productivity, making up the bulk of the burden in industrialized countries (approximately 80 %) [6]. The challenge is to find ways to mitigate work disability-related burden and to sustain optimal work participation. One proven way to address work disability is through vocational or work rehabilitation.

2.3.2 Vocational Rehabilitation

Vocational rehabilitation is defined as *a multi-professional evidence-based approach that is provided in different settings, services, and activities to working-age individuals with health-related impairments, limitations, or restrictions with work functioning, and whose primary aim is to optimize work participation* [7]. This general definition is based on the ICF to indicate the breadth and complexity of factors that are relevant to vocational rehabilitation. This conceptual definition considers the aspects of vocational rehabilitation within the context of the ICF:

body functions and *body structure*, *activities and participation*, and the contextual factors.

The primary goal of vocational rehabilitation is both return to work (RTW) and sustained RTW. In some cases, it may be that an individual did not work before (i.e. does not have any work history), and hence in this situation is not really returning to work but engaging in work but still within the scope of vocational rehabilitation. For example, a person who just graduated from high school and had a car accident, which resulted in spinal cord injury, and now wants to work. In this case, vocational rehabilitation is designed to ensure that the person is able to participate in employment despite the disability. The process of vocational rehabilitation explicitly involves disability evaluation as part of the overall work disability management. Even post-vocational rehabilitation, disability evaluation remains as an important component to enhance lifelong functioning of an individual.

2.3.3 Disability Evaluation

Disability is a result of an interaction of several components of functioning based on the ICF. Hence, disability is an outcome of varying extents of impairment in body function and body structures, limitation in performing activities, and restriction in participation. Disability level needs to be assessed and evaluated so proper intervention or rehabilitation can occur – this is particularly important in clinical decision making and return-to-work coordination. In the case of work disability, an individual needs to be evaluated so appropriate RTW management or approach can be developed and implemented. An appropriate disability evaluation must be performed to fairly determine whether RTW or other nonwork alternative (such as disability pension) is the appropriate solution for the worker.

2.3.4 Why Integrate ICF and Work

The biopsychosocial perspective of the ICF has been recently used in the definition of vocational rehabilitation (see definition above) [7]. This is a first step in aligning a conceptual definition that is based on the ICF with current and future research and practice in the field of vocational rehabilitation and disability evaluation. Laying out this conceptualization would contribute to the pursuit and better understanding of the operationalization and application of the ICF in vocational rehabilitation, disability evaluation, and RTW strategies.

The experience of work and employment, in one form or another, is universal in that it is a common experience regardless of the country and nationality and culture. Work disability, hence, also becomes a universal experience when an individual's disability prevents him or her from working. The ICF was intended by the WHO to be a universal language when describing functioning and can be applied in the work context. The breadth of the ICF is evident by way of its comprehensive set of functioning domains, which can address the multifactorial nature and complexity of vocational rehabilitation and RTW. The ICF can be used in selecting which domains are relevant to vocational rehabilitation and which domains can be used as measures of successful RTW.

> The breadth of the ICF is evident by way of its comprehensive set of functioning domains, which can address the multifactorial nature and complexity of vocational rehabilitation and RTW.

2.4 ICF Application to Vocational Rehabilitation and Disability Evaluation

2.4.1 The Minimal Generic Set

The Minimal Generic Set is a list of essential ICF domains that have been tested and can be applied across healthcare settings and health conditions [11]. This list consists of the following domains that can be evaluated and potential targets for intervention: energy and drive functions (b130), emotional functions (b152), sensation of pain (b280), carrying out daily routine (d230), walking (d450), moving around (d455), and remunerative employment (d850). These domains can be used as a simple checklist to initiate vocational rehabilitation and determine disability.

2.4.2 The ICF Core Sets

The ICF Core Set consists of carefully selected short lists of ICF categories that makes the hundreds of categories contained in the ICF practical and useable. A Core Set is designed to be applicable to a specific health condition or health-related event or to a specific setting that can describe the most salient aspects of the disability experience for that health condition or setting. There are multiple Core Sets that are available for different health conditions or settings. Each ICF Core Set is a product of extensive expert input and validation studies and is data-driven, multi-perspective, and consensus-based [8]. The general methodology for Core Set development involves a structured set of processes that include preparatory studies: systematic review of the literature, an expert survey, cross-sectional study, and qualitative patient interviews. Each study seeks to identify those ICF categories that are most relevant to a specific health condition or setting. The final selection of ICF categories for inclusion in the Core Set is culminated in a multistage consensus process.

2.4.3 The Comprehensive and Brief ICF Core Sets

There are two versions of a Core Set. A Core Set can be *comprehensive* or *brief* [8]. A comprehensive Core Set (with more ICF categories) is usually utilized in multidisciplinary assessment and has as few categories as possible to still be practical but as many as necessary to capture the full spectrum of variables specific to a health condition or health-related event. A brief Core Set (with fewer ICF categories than the comprehensive), on the other hand, contains the minimum number of categories to be included in studies or trials on a health condition and can be used by a single discipline in a clinical encounter, for example. In a multidisciplinary setting such as that in hospitals, a variety of health professionals can use the comprehensive Core Set as functioning domains, while in a private outpatient clinic, a healthcare practitioner may find it more convenient to use the brief version which already provides the minimum number of ICF categories to be assessed. As a general rule, clinicians and researchers can always use additional ICF categories not already included in the Core Set, if they feel that those categories are essential for their purpose and setting.

2.4.4 The ICF Core Set for Vocational Rehabilitation

In light of the ICF Core Set development, the ICF Core Set for vocational rehabilitation was aimed to develop a list of relevant ICF categories that can be used to describe the functioning of individuals who are undergoing vocational rehabilitation [9]. Table 2.5 contains the comprehensive ICF Core Set for vocational rehabilitation with the brief ICF Core Set written in bold.

2.4.5 The ICF Core Set for Social Security Evaluation

In addition to using vocational rehabilitation-centric ICF Core Sets, one other option of using the ICF in disability evaluation towards the later stage of the work disability management process is by using the ICF Core Set for Social Security Evaluation, which captures those domains to be assessed to determine disability pension and sick leave benefits. To look at the overlap and gap, a table comparing the contents of the ICF Core Set for vocational rehabilitation and the ICF Core Set for social security evaluation is presented in Table 2.6. This table highlights those domains that can be used to assess functioning within the

Table 2.5 Comprehensive ICF core set for vocational rehabilitation, $N = 90$. Brief ICF core set for vocational rehabilitation in bold, $N = 13$. A short description is included which is only an excerpt. For more details, consult the ICF handbook

ICF code	Title	*Short description*
Activities and participation		
d155	**Acquiring skills**	*Developing basic and complex competencies in integrated sets of actions or tasks so as to initiate and follow through with the acquisition of a skill, such as manipulating tools or playing games like chess*
d160	Focusing attention	*Intentionally focusing on specific stimuli, such as by filtering out distracting noises*
d163	Thinking	*Formulating and manipulating ideas, concepts, and images, whether goal oriented or not, either alone or with others, such as creating fiction, proving a theorem, playing with ideas, brainstorming, meditating, pondering, speculating, or reflecting*
d166	Reading	*Performing activities involved in the comprehension and interpretation of written language (e.g. books, instructions or newspapers in text or Braille), for the purpose of obtaining general knowledge or specific information*
d170	Writing	*Using or producing symbols or language to convey information, such as producing a written record of events or ideas or drafting a letter*
d172	Calculating	*Performing computations by applying mathematical principles to solve problems that are described in words and producing or displaying the results, such as computing the sum of three numbers or finding the result of dividing one number by another*
d175	Solving problems	*Finding solutions to questions or situations by identifying and analyzing issues, developing options and solutions, evaluating potential effects of solutions, and executing a chosen solution, such as in resolving a dispute between two people*
d177	Making decisions	*Making a choice among options, implementing the choice, and evaluating the effects of the choice, such as selecting and purchasing a specific item or deciding to undertake and undertaking one task from among several tasks that need to be done*
d210	Undertaking a single task	*Carrying out simple or complex and coordinated actions related to the mental and physical components of a single task, such*

(continued)

Table 2.5 (continued)

ICF code	Title	*Short description*
		as initiating a task; organizing time, space, and materials for a task; pacing task performance; and carrying out, completing, and sustaining a task
d220	Undertaking multiple tasks	*Carrying out simple or complex and coordinated actions as components of multiple, integrated, and complex tasks in sequence or simultaneously*
d230	Carrying out daily routine	*Carrying out simple or complex and coordinated actions in order to plan, manage, and complete the requirements of day-to-day procedures or duties, such as budgeting time and making plans for separate activities throughout the day*
d240	**Handling stress and other psychological demands**	*Carrying out simple or complex and coordinated actions to manage and control the psychological demands required to carry out tasks demanding significant responsibilities and involving stress, distraction, or crises, such as driving a vehicle during heavy traffic or taking care of many children*
d310	Communicating with – receiving – spoken messages	*Comprehending literal and implied meanings of messages in spoken language, such as understanding that a statement asserts a fact or is an idiomatic expression*
d315	Communicating with – receiving – nonverbal messages	*Comprehending the literal and implied meanings of messages conveyed by gestures, symbols, and drawings, such as realizing that a child is tired when she rubs her eyes or that a warning bell means that there is a fire*
d350	Conversation	*Starting, sustaining, and ending an interchange of thoughts and ideas, carried out by means of spoken, written, sign, or other forms of language, with one or more people one knows or who are strangers, in formal or casual settings*
d360	Using communication devices and techniques	*Using devices, techniques, and other means for the purposes of communicating, such as calling a friend on the telephone*
d410	Changing basic body position	*Getting into and out of a body position and moving from one location to another, such as getting up out of a chair to lie down on a bed and getting into and out of positions of kneeling or squatting*

(continued)

Table 2.5 (continued)

ICF code	Title	*Short description*
d415	Maintaining a body position	*Staying in the same body position as required, such as remaining seated or remaining standing for work or school*
d430	Lifting and carrying objects	*Raising up an object or taking something from one place to another, such as when lifting a cup or carrying a child from one room to another*
d440	Fine hand use	*Performing the coordinated actions of handling objects, picking up, manipulating, and releasing them using one's hand, fingers, and thumb, such as required to lift coins off a table or turn a dial or knob*
d445	Hand and arm use	*Performing the coordinated actions required to move objects or to manipulate them by using hands and arms, such as when turning door handles or throwing or catching an object*
d450	Walking	*Moving along a surface on foot, step-by-step, so that one foot is always on the ground, such as when strolling, sauntering, walking forwards, backwards, or sideways*
d455	Moving around	*Moving the whole body from one place to another by means other than walking, such as climbing over a rock or running down a street, skipping, scampering, jumping, somersaulting, or running around obstacles*
d465	Moving around using equipment	*Walking and moving around in various places and situations, such as walking between rooms in a house, within a building, or down the street of a town*
d470	Using transportation	*Using transportation to move around as a passenger, such as being driven in a car or on a bus, rickshaw, jitney, animal-powered vehicle, or private or public taxi, bus, train, tram, subway, boat, or aircraft*
d475	Driving	*Being in control of and moving a vehicle or the animal that draws it, travelling under one's own direction or having at one's disposal any form of transportation, such as a car, bicycle, boat, or animal-powered vehicle*
d530	Toileting	*Planning and carrying out the elimination of human waste (menstruation, urination, and defecation) and cleaning oneself afterwards*

(continued)

Table 2.5 (continued)

ICF code	Title	*Short description*
d540	Dressing	*Carrying out the coordinated actions and tasks of putting on and taking off clothes and footwear in sequence and in keeping with climatic and social conditions, such as by putting on, adjusting, and removing shirts, skirts, blouses, pants, undergarments, saris, kimono, tights, hats, gloves, coats, shoes, boots, sandals, and slippers*
d570	Looking after one's health	*Ensuring physical comfort, health, and physical and mental well-being, such as by maintaining a balanced diet and an appropriate level of physical activity, keeping warm or cool, avoiding harms to health, following safe sex practices, including using condoms, getting immunizations, and regular physical examinations*
d710	Basic interpersonal interactions	*Interacting with people in a contextually and socially appropriate manner, such as by showing consideration and esteem when appropriate or responding to the feelings of others*
d720	**Complex interpersonal interactions**	*Maintaining and managing interactions with other people, in a contextually and socially appropriate manner, such as by regulating emotions and impulses, controlling verbal and physical aggression, acting independently in social interactions, and acting in accordance with social rules and conventions*
d740	Formal relationships	*Creating and maintaining specific relationships in formal settings, such as with employers, professionals, or service providers*
d820	School education	*Gaining admission to school, education, engaging in all school-related responsibilities and privileges, and learning the course material, subjects, and other curriculum requirements in a primary or secondary education programme, including attending school regularly; working cooperatively with other students, taking direction from teachers; organizing, studying, and completing assigned tasks and projects; and advancing to other stages of education*
d825	Vocational training	*Engaging in all activities of a vocational programme and learning the curriculum material in preparation for employment in a trade, job, or profession*

(continued)

Table 2.5 (continued)

ICF code	Title	*Short description*
d830	Higher education	*Engaging in the activities of advanced educational programmes in universities, colleges, and professional schools and learning all aspects of the curriculum required for degrees, diplomas, certificates, and other accreditations, such as completing a university bachelor's or master's course of study, medical school, or other professional school*
d840	Apprenticeship (work preparation)	*Engaging in programmes related to preparation for employment, such as performing the tasks required of an apprenticeship, internship, articling, and in-service training*
d845	**Acquiring, keeping and terminating a job**	*Seeking, finding, and choosing employment; being hired and accepting employment; maintaining and advancing through a job, trade, occupation, or profession; and leaving a job in an appropriate manner*
d850	**Remunerative employment**	*Engaging in all aspects of work, as an occupation, trade, profession, or other form of employment, for payment, as an employee, full-time or part-time, or self-employed, such as seeking employment and getting a job, doing the required tasks of the job, attending work on time as required, supervising other workers or being supervised, and performing required tasks alone or in groups*
d855	**Non-remunerative employment**	*Engaging in all aspects of work in which pay is not provided, full-time or part-time, including organized work activities, doing the required tasks of the job, attending work on time as required, supervising other workers or being supervised, and performing required tasks alone or in groups, such as volunteer work, charity work, working for a community or religious group without remuneration, working around the home without remuneration*
d870	Economic self-sufficiency	*Having command over economic resources, from private or public sources, in order to ensure economic security for present and future needs*
Environmental factors		
e1101	Drugs	*Any natural or human-made object or substance gathered, processed, or manufactured for medicinal purposes, such as allopathic and naturopathic medication*

(continued)

Table 2.5 (continued)

ICF code	Title	*Short description*
e115	Products and technology for personal use in daily living	*Equipment, products, and technologies used by people in daily activities, including those adapted or specially designed, located in, on or near the person using them*
e120	Products and technology for personal indoor and outdoor mobility and transportation	*Equipment, products, and technologies used by people in activities of moving inside and outside buildings, including those adapted or specially designed, located in, on, or near the person using them*
e125	Products and technology for communication	*Equipment, products, and technologies used by people in activities of sending and receiving information, including those adapted or specially designed, located in, on, or near the person using them*
e130	Products and technology for education	*Equipment, products, processes, methods, and technology used for acquisition of knowledge, expertise, or skill, including those adapted or specially designed*
e135	Products and technology for employment	*Equipment, products, and technology used for employment to facilitate work activities*
e150	Design, construction, and building products and technology of buildings for public use	*Products and technology that constitute an individual's indoor and outdoor human-made environment that is planned, designed, and constructed for public use, including those adapted or specially designed*
e155	Design, construction, and building products and technology of buildings for private use	*Products and technology that constitute an individual's indoor and outdoor human-made environment that is planned, designed, and constructed for private use, including those adapted or specially designed*
c225	Climate	*Meteorological features and events, such as the weather*
e240	Light	*Electromagnetic radiation by which things are made visible by either sunlight or artificial lighting (e.g. candles, oil, or paraffin lamps, fires, and electricity) and which may provide useful or distracting information about the world*
e250	Sound	*A phenomenon that is or may be heard, such as banging, ringing, thumping, singing, whistling, yelling, or buzzing, in any volume, timbre, or tone, and that may provide useful or distracting information about the world*

(continued)

Table 2.5 (continued)

ICF code	Title	*Short description*
e260	Air quality	*Characteristics of the atmosphere (outside buildings) or enclosed areas of air (inside buildings), and which may provide useful or distracting information about the world*
e310	**Immediate family**	*Individuals related by birth, marriage, or other relationship recognized by the culture as immediate family, such as spouses, partners, parents, siblings, children, foster parents, adoptive parents, and grandparents*
e320	Friends	*Individuals who are close and ongoing participants in relationships characterized by trust and mutual support*
e325	Acquaintances, peers, colleagues, neighbours, and community members	*Individuals who are familiar to each other as acquaintances, peers, colleagues, neighbours, and community members, in situations of work, school, recreation, or other aspects of life and who share demographic features such as age, gender, religious creed, or ethnicity or pursue common interests*
e330	**People in positions of authority**	*Individuals who have decision-making responsibilities for others and who have socially defined influence or power based on their social, economic, cultural, or religious roles in society, such as teachers, employers, supervisors, religious leaders, substitute decision-makers, guardians, or trustees*
e340	Personal care providers and personal assistants	*Individuals who provide services as required to support individuals in their daily activities and maintenance of performance at work, education, or other life situation, provided either through public or private funds, or else on a voluntary basis, such as providers of support for home-making and maintenance, personal assistants, transport assistants, paid help, nannies, and others who function as primary caregivers*
e355	Health professionals	*All service providers working within the context of the health system, such as doctors, nurses, physiotherapists, occupational therapists, speech therapists, audiologists, orthotist-prosthetists, medical social workers*

(continued)

Table 2.5 (continued)

ICF code	Title	*Short description*
e360	Other professionals	*All service providers working outside the health system, including social workers, lawyers, teachers, architects, and designers*
e430	Individual attitudes of people in positions of authority	*General or specific opinions and beliefs of people in positions of authority about the person or about other matters (e.g. social, political, and economic issues) that influence individual behaviour and actions*
e450	Individual attitudes of health professionals	*General or specific opinions and beliefs of health professionals about the person or about other matters (e.g. social, political, and economic issues) that influence individual behaviour and actions*
e460	Societal attitudes	*General or specific opinions and beliefs generally held by people of a culture, society, subcultural, or other social group about other individuals or about other social, political, and economic issues that influence group or individual behaviour and actions*
e465	Social norms, practices, and ideologies	*Customs, practices, rules, and abstract systems of values and normative beliefs (e.g. ideologies, normative world views, and moral philosophies) that arise within social contexts and that affect or create societal and individual practices and behaviours, such as social norms of moral and religious behaviour or etiquette, religious doctrine and resulting norms and practices, norms governing rituals, or social gatherings*
e525	Housing services, systems, and policies	*Services, systems, and policies for the provision of shelters, dwellings, or lodging for people*
e535	Communication services, systems, and policies	*Services, systems, and policies for the transmission and exchange of information*
e540	Transportation services, systems, and policies	*Services, systems, and policies for enabling people or goods to move or be moved from one location to another*
e550	Legal services, systems, and policies	*Services, systems, and policies concerning the legislation and other law of a country*
e555	Associations and organizational services, systems, and policies	*Services, systems, and policies relating to groups of people who have joined together in the pursuit of common, noncommercial interests, often with an associated membership structure*

(continued)

Table 2.5 (continued)

ICF code	Title	*Short description*
e565	Economic services, systems, and policies	*Services, systems, and policies related to the overall system of production, distribution, consumption, and use of goods and services*
e570	Social security services, systems, and policies	*Services, systems, and policies aimed at providing income support to people who, because of age, poverty, unemployment, health condition, or disability, require public assistance that is funded either by general tax revenues or contributory schemes*
e580	**Health services, systems, and policies**	*Services, systems, and policies for preventing and treating health problems, providing medical rehabilitation, and promoting a healthy lifestyle*
e585	Education and training services, systems, and policies	*Services, systems, and policies for the acquisition, maintenance, and improvement of knowledge, expertise, and vocational or artistic skills. See UNESCO's International Standard Classification of Education (ISCED-1997)*
e590	**Labour and employment services, systems, and policies**	*Services, systems, and policies related to finding suitable work for persons who are unemployed or looking for different work or to support individuals already employed who are seeking promotion*
Body functions		
b117	Intellectual functions	*General mental functions, required to understand and constructively integrate the various mental functions, including all cognitive functions and their development over the life span*
b126	Temperament and personality functions	*General mental functions of constitutional disposition of the individual to react in a particular way to situations, including the set of mental characteristics that makes the individual distinct from others*
b130	**Energy and drive functions**	*General mental functions of physiological and psychological mechanisms that cause the individual to move towards satisfying specific needs and general goals in a persistent manner*
b134	Sleep functions	*General mental functions of periodic, reversible, and selective physical and mental disengagement from one's immediate environment accompanied by characteristic physiological changes*

(continued)

Table 2.5 (continued)

ICF code	Title	*Short description*
b140	Attention functions	*Specific mental functions of focusing on an external stimulus or internal experience for the required period of time*
b144	Memory functions	*Specific mental functions of registering and storing information and retrieving it as needed*
b152	Emotional functions	*Specific mental functions related to the feeling and affective components of the processes of the mind*
b160	Thought functions	*Specific mental functions related to the ideational component of the mind*
b164	**Higher-level cognitive functions**	*Specific mental functions especially dependent on the frontal lobes of the brain, including complex goal-directed behaviours such as decision making, abstract thinking, planning and carrying out plans, mental flexibility, and deciding which behaviours are appropriate under what circumstances, often called executive functions*
b210	Seeing functions	*Sensory functions relating to sensing the presence of light and sensing the form, size, shape, and colour of the visual stimuli*
b230	Hearing functions	*Sensory functions relating to sensing the presence of sounds and discriminating the location, pitch, loudness, and quality of sounds*
b235	Vestibular functions	*Sensory functions of the inner ear related to position, balance, and movement*
b280	Sensation of pain	*Sensation of unpleasant feeling indicating potential or actual damage to some body structure*
b455	**Exercise tolerance functions**	*Functions related to respiratory and cardiovascular capacity as required for enduring physical exertion*
b730	Muscle power functions	*Functions related to the force generated by the contraction of a muscle or muscle groups*
b740	Muscle endurance functions	*Functions related to sustaining muscle contraction for the required period of time*
b810	Protective functions of the skin	*Functions of the skin for protecting the body from physical, chemical, and biological threats*

Table 2.6 Title and description of ICF categories [2] in the ICF core set for vocational rehabilitation [11] brief version ($n = 13$ categories) and the ICF core set for disability evaluation in social security [12] ($n = 20$ categories). ICF categories denoted by ** are included in the Minimal Generic Set

ICF code and title	Title and definition	ICF core set for vocational rehabilitation	ICF core set for disability evaluation in social security
b130 Energy and drive functions**	General mental functions of physiological and psychological mechanisms that cause the individual to move towards satisfying specific needs and general goals in a persistent manner	✓	
b164 Higher-level cognitive functions	Specific mental functions especially dependent on the frontal lobes of the brain, including complex goal-directed behaviours such as decision-making, abstract thinking, planning and carrying out plans, mental flexibility, and deciding which behaviours are appropriate under what circumstances, often called executive functions	✓	✓
b280 Sensation of pain**	Sensation of unpleasant feeling indicating potential or actual damage to some body structure	*	✓
b455 Exercise tolerance functions	Functions related to respiratory and cardiovascular capacity as required for enduring physical exertion	✓	✓
b710 Mobility of joint functions	Functions of the range and ease of movement of a joint		✓
b730 Muscle power functions	Functions related to the force generated by the contraction of a muscle or muscle groups	*	✓
d110 Watching	Using the sense of seeing intentionally to experience visual stimuli, such as watching a sporting event or children playing		✓
d115 Listening	Using the sense of hearing intentionally to experience auditory stimuli, such as listening to a radio, music, or lecture		✓
d155 Acquiring skills	Developing basic and complex competencies in integrated sets of actions or tasks so as to initiate and follow through with the acquisition of a skill, such as manipulating tools or playing games like chess	✓	✓

(continued)

Table 2.6 (continued)

ICF code and title	Title and definition	ICF core set for vocational rehabilitation	ICF core set for disability evaluation in social security
d177 Making decisions	Making a choice among options, implementing the choice, and evaluating the effects of the choice, such as selecting and purchasing a specific item or deciding to undertake and undertaking one task from among several tasks that need to be done	*	✓
d220 Undertaking multiple tasks	Carrying out simple or complex and coordinated actions as components of multiple, integrated, and complex tasks in sequence or simultaneously	*	✓
d240 Handling stress and other psychological demands	Carrying out simple or complex and coordinated actions to manage and control the psychological demands required to carry out tasks demanding significant responsibilities and involving stress, distraction, or crises, such as driving a vehicle during heavy traffic or taking care of many children	✓	✓
d399 Communication, unspecified			✓
d410 Changing basic body position	Getting into and out of a body position and moving from one location to another, such as getting up out of a chair to lie down on a bed and getting into and out of positions of kneeling or squatting	*	✓
d415 Maintaining a body position	Staying in the same body position as required, such as remaining seated or remaining standing for work or school	*	✓
d430 Lifting and carrying objects	Raising up an object or taking something from one place to another, such as when lifting a cup or carrying a child from one room to another	*	✓

(continued)

Table 2.6 (continued)

ICF code and title	Title and definition	ICF core set for vocational rehabilitation	ICF core set for disability evaluation in social security
d440 Fine hand use	Performing the coordinated actions of handling objects, picking up, manipulating, and releasing them using one's hand, fingers, and thumb, such as required to lift coins off a table or turn a dial or knob	*	✓
d445 Hand and arm use	Performing the coordinated actions required to move objects or to manipulate them by using hands and arms, such as when turning door handles or throwing or catching an object	*	✓
d450 Walking**	Moving along a surface on foot, step by step, so that one foot is always on the ground, such as when strolling, sauntering, walking forwards, backwards, or sideways	*	✓
d470 Using transportation	Using transportation to move around as a passenger, such as being driven in a car or on a bus, rickshaw, jitney, animal-powered vehicle, or private or public taxi, bus, train, tram, subway, boat, or aircraft	*	✓
d720 Complex interpersonal interactions	Maintaining and managing interactions with other people, in a contextually and socially appropriate manner, such as by regulating emotions and impulses, controlling verbal and physical aggression, acting independently in social interactions, and acting in accordance with social rules and conventions	✓	✓
d845 Acquiring, keeping, and terminating a job	Seeking, finding, and choosing employment; being hired and accepting employment; maintaining and advancing through a job, trade, occupation, or profession; and leaving a job in an appropriate manner	✓	

(continued)

Table 2.6 (continued)

ICF code and title	Title and definition	ICF core set for vocational rehabilitation	ICF core set for disability evaluation in social security
d850 Remunerative employment**	Engaging in all aspects of work, as an occupation, trade, profession, or other form of employment, for payment, as an employee, full-time or part-time, or self-employed, such as seeking employment and getting a job, doing the required tasks of the job, attending work on time as required, supervising other workers or being supervised, and performing required tasks alone or in groups	✓	
d855 Non-remunerative employment	Engaging in all aspects of work in which pay is not provided, full-time or part-time, including organized work activities, doing the required tasks of the job, attending work on time as required, supervising other workers or being supervised, and performing required tasks alone or in groups, such as volunteer work, charity work, working for a community or religious group without remuneration, working around the home without remuneration	✓	
e310 Immediate family	Individuals related by birth, marriage, or other relationship recognized by the culture as immediate family, such as spouses, partners, parents, siblings, children, foster parents, adoptive parents, and grandparents	✓	
e330 People in positions of authority	Individuals who have decision-making responsibilities for others and who have socially defined influence or power based on their social, economic, cultural, or religious roles in society, such as teachers, employers, supervisors, religious leaders, substitute decision-makers, guardians, or trustees	✓	

(continued)

Table 2.6 (continued)

ICF code and title	Title and definition	ICF core set for vocational rehabilitation	ICF core set for disability evaluation in social security
e580 Health services, systems, and policies	Services, systems, and policies for preventing and treating health problems, providing medical rehabilitation, and promoting a healthy lifestyle	✔	
e590 Labour and employment services, systems, and policies	Services, systems, and policies related to finding suitable work for persons who are unemployed or looking for different work or to support individuals already employed who are seeking promotion	✔	

*Included in the comprehensive version ($n = 90$ ICF categories) of the ICF core set for vocational rehabilitation [11]

continuum of vocational rehabilitation and disability evaluation. By doing so, the appropriate service and appropriate level of care can be implemented.

2.5 Measurement Based on the ICF

2.5.1 ICF Contents of Existing Questionnaires

There are many patient-reported and clinician-administered (or interviewer-administered) questionnaires or measures available. A simple way of integrating ICF concepts would be to look at the ICF contents (i.e. ICF categories) of those questionnaires and see what ICF categories were included from the ICF Core Set for vocational rehabilitation and social security and what ICF domains in general are covered by the questionnaires. In the past, questionnaires have been linked to the ICF using published linking rules [10] where items of the questionnaires are linked to the corresponding ICF category that best fits its content. For example, questionnaires on worker productivity that assess presenteeism (at work productivity loss) in arthritis and musculoskeletal population were linked to the ICF [12]. The authors found that there was not only a broad range of ICF categories represented in these questionnaires but also their contents also greatly varied despite having a similar purpose, which is assessing presenteeism. Through ICF linking, one is able to identify gaps in existing instruments and to guide in selecting instruments fit for the purpose of the user. Linking also allows comparison of those ICF categories identified in the questionnaires used in vocational rehabilitation with the categories in the ICF Core Set for vocational rehabilitation.

2.5.2 The ICF Can Be Used in Questionnaire Development

The first step in developing an ICF Core Set-based questionnaire is to define the purpose of the questionnaire and the context in which the questionnaire is intended for use. ICF Core Sets can be used as a basis to develop new questionnaires or measurement instruments should there be a need for such development. One example of a patient-reported questionnaire which was developed based on the ICF Core Set for vocational rehabilitation is the Work Rehabilitation Questionnaire (WORQ) [14] (www.myworq.org; see Chap. 23 for WORQ development).

2.5.3 Added Value of the ICF

In summary, the ICF can provide a conceptual framework to understand, describe, and assess the impact and burden of disease on an individual worker and his or her work using the broad, holistic, and biopsychosocial perspective of the ICF in addition to the traditionally used biomedical model (pathology-aetiology model). With the ICF, we have a classification system that would be able to capture and measure the complex functioning domains of vocational rehabilitation and disability evaluation. Having done so not only would the ICF help in the thought process of understanding work-related burden but it would guide clinical decision-making and ultimately push for effective clinical and non-clinical care in the context of work and employment.

Study Questions

1. What is the ICF?

   Answer: The ICF is a conceptual model and classification system to understand health and health-related domains and to serve as a common language of disability. The ICF illustrates the interrelationship and association between a health condition (disease or injury) and its impact on the individual's body (as depicted by body functions component and body structure component), and its impact on the individual's participation in the society (as depicted by activities and participation component). Disability refers to either impairment of the body structure and function, limitation of activities, or restriction in participation under the ICF and may be influenced by contextual factors, namely, environmental factors and personal factors.

2. What are the different ways by which the ICF can be used in work disability and disability evaluation?

   Answer: Ways include the use of the Minimal Generic Set and ICF Core Sets which can be used in vocational rehabilitation and disability evaluation settings. These ICF-based sets can be used to examine ICF concepts in existing measures or instruments and to develop a new measure or instrument.

3. What is an ICF Core Set?

   Answer: The ICF Core Set consists of carefully selected short lists of ICF categories that makes the hundreds of categories contained in the ICF practical and useable. A Core Set is designed to be applicable to a specific health condition or health-related event or to a specific setting that can describe the most salient aspects of the disability experience in that health condition or setting. There are two versions of a Core Set. A Core Set can be comprehensive or brief. A comprehensive Core Set (with more ICF categories) is usually utilized in multidisciplinary assessment and has as few categories as possible to still be practical but as many as necessary to capture the full spectrum of variables specific to a health condition or health-related event. A brief Core Set (with fewer ICF categories than the comprehensive) contains the minimum number of categories to be included in studies or trials on a health condition and can be used by a single discipline in a clinical encounter.

References

1. Collie J. Return to work-legal and other impediments. Br Med J. 1916;2(2918):757–9.
2. World Health Organization. International classification of functioning, disability and health. Geneva: World Health Organization; 2001.
3. Chan CC, Zhuo DH. Occupational rehabilitation in twenty-first century Asia Pacific: facilitating health and work: an introduction. J Occup Rehabil. 2011;21 Suppl 1:S1–4.
4. Stubbs J, Deaner G. When considering vocational rehabilitation: describing and comparing the Swedish and American systems and professions. Work. 2005;24(3):239–49.
5. Organisation for Economic Co-operation and Development Directorate for Employment, Labour and Social Affairs. Sickness, disability and work: keeping on track in the economic downturn (background paper). May 2009. Report No.: High-Level Forum, Stockholm.
6. Dagenais S, Caro J, Haldeman S. A systematic review of low back pain cost of illness studies in the United States and internationally. Spine J. 2008;8(1):8–20.
7. Escorpizo R, Reneman MF, Ekholm J, Fritz J, Krupa T, Marnetoft SU, et al. A conceptual definition of vocational rehabilitation based on the ICF: building a shared global model. J Occup Rehabil. 2011;21(2):126–33.
8. Cieza A, Ewert T, Üstün B, Chatterji S, Kostanjsek N, Stucki G. Development of ICF core sets for patients with chronic conditions. J Rehabil Med (Suppl). 2004;36(44):9–11.
9. Escorpizo R, Ekholm J, Gmuender HP, Cieza A, Kostanjsek N, Stucki G. Developing a core set to describe functioning in vocational rehabilitation using the international classification of functioning, disability, and health (ICF). J Occup Rehabil. 2010;20(4):502–11.
10. Cieza A, Geyh S, Chatterji S, Kostanjsek N, Ustun B, Stucki G. ICF linking rules: an update based on lessons learned. J Rehabil Med. 2005;37(4):212–8.

11. Cieza A, Oberhauser C, Bickenbach J, Chatterji S, Stucki G. Towards a minimal generic set of domains of functioning and health. BMC Public Health. 2014;14:218. doi:10.1186/1471-2458-14-218.
12. Escorpizo R, Cieza A, Beaton D, Boonen A. Content comparison of worker productivity questionnaires in arthritis and musculoskeletal conditions using the international classification of functioning, disability, and health framework. J Occup Rehabil. 2009;19(4):382–97.
13. Escorpizo R, Stucki G, Cieza A, Davis K, Stumbo T, Riddle DL. Creating an interface between the international classification of functioning, disability and health and physical therapist practice. Phys Ther. 2010;90(7):1053–63.
14. Finger ME, Escorpizo R, Bostan C, De Bie R. Work Rehabilitation Questionnaire (WORQ): development and preliminary psychometric evidence of an ICF-based questionnaire for vocational rehabilitation. J Occup Rehabil. 2014;24(3):498–510.

Chapter 3
ICF from a Population Health Perspective: The Impact of Chronic Disease on Work Participation and Its Consequences for Intervention and Treatment

Alex Burdorf

3.1 Changing Ideas About Health

For more than 50 years, the WHO definition of health, formulated in 1948, has served well to describe health as 'a state of complete physical, mental and social well-being and not merely the absence of disease or infirmity'. The paradigm shift introduced by this definition was its integral attention to health and its consequences in terms of disability, functioning, and quality of life. In recent years, attention has shifted from disease and limitations in activities and participation towards a person's capacity and ability to actively manage their life, despite the presence of a medical condition. Several researchers have challenged the classical definitions of health, such as provided by WHO, and argue for a definition of health as a dynamic process of adaptation and self-management [1].

These changing ideas about health are also reflected in the discussions about outcome measures within the framework of the World Health Organization's International Classification of Functioning, Disability, and Health (ICF). The adverse consequences of chronic disease are traditionally assessed by measuring disease activity, structural damage, and loss of function, especially in clinical studies. These outcome measures are well represented in the ICF domains. However, social participation is increasingly recognised as a core outcome measure among persons with chronic disease, in particular participation in paid employment [2]. Being out of the workforce due to disability and unemployment is one of the most important determinants of health inequalities in society [3]. From a perspective of population health, the interplay between chronic disease and work participation should be a central theme in decisions on treatment and rehabilitation.

A. Burdorf (✉)
Department of Public Health, Erasmus MC, University Medical Center Rotterdam, P.O. Box 2040, 3000 CA, Rotterdam, The Netherlands
e-mail: a.burdorf@erasmusmc.nl

R. Escorpizo et al. (eds.), *Handbook of Vocational Rehabilitation and Disability Evaluation*, Handbooks in Health, Work, and Disability, DOI 10.1007/978-3-319-08825-9_3

This chapter will primarily focus on the importance of work participation within the ICF framework. As a starting point, some descriptive information will be presented on the impact of ill health in maintaining paid employment. Subsequently, studies on rheumatoid arthritis will be used to illustrate how a chronic disease may interfere with being productive at work. Next, the influence of the social and physical work environment on optimal work participation will be discussed. This chapter will conclude with some recommendations for researchers, policymakers, and health professionals.

3.2 The Importance of Health for Labour Force Participation

In our ageing society, there is a clear need to increase work participation and sustain a productive workforce because of decreasing birth rates and increased life expectancy in most industrialised countries. Many countries are developing policies to stimulate labour force participation, particularly to encourage older workers to remain at work for a longer period. In this development of working longer at older age, workers with existing or emerging health problems are a vulnerable group. Ill health plays an important role in loss of paid employment, particularly due to disability pension and, to a lesser extent, unemployment [4]. On the individual level, loss of paid employment will not only increase financial and social problems, it may also contribute to onset of new health problems or to aggravation of existing health problems.

The importance of ill health on work participation can be illustrated in the Survey on Health and Ageing in Europe (SHARE study) [5]. This longitudinal study among citizens aged 50 years and older in various European countries has collected information by interview on different measures of health, for example: (i) the European version of self-perceived health, whereby the answers 'very bad', 'bad', and 'fair' can be used to define ill health, (ii) occurrence of at least one chronic disease as diagnosed by a physician, (iii) presence of clinically relevant symptoms indicating depression, based on at least four affirmative answers on the EURO-D 12 items scale of depression, and (iv) mobility problems based on the presence of at least one physical limitation with mobility, arm function, or fine motor function lasting longer than 3 months, derived from a limitative list of ten items, such as walking 100 meters, climbing stairs without resting, and reaching with arms above shoulder level. Figure 3.1 shows the associations of these four measures of health on the likelihood of becoming work disabled or unemployed during the 2-year follow-up period. A less-than-good self-perceived health had the strongest effect on becoming disabled (OR = 4.56, 95 % CI 2.88–7.22) or unemployed (OR = 2.09, 95 % CI 1.39–3.13). Interestingly, the presence of a chronic disease had comparable effects on disability and unemployment, but depressive symptoms and mobility problems had substantially less influence on exit from paid employment. These findings clearly suggest that different measures of health may exert a different influence on a worker's ability to remain in paid employment and that perceptions of one's own health may be more important than limitations in activities [4].

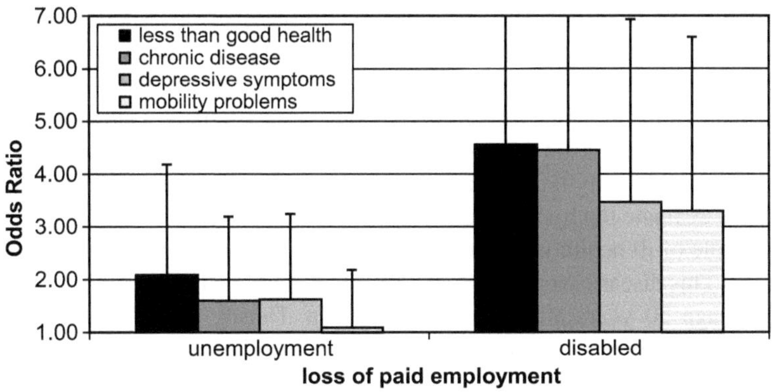

Fig. 3.1 The effects of different measures of ill health in 2004 on unemployment and work-related disability in 2006 in 11 European countries, expressed by adjusted odds ratios (Based on Ref. [4])

In Western countries, ill health is an important determinant of becoming or staying unemployed. Ill health is largely responsible for displacement from the labour force due to disability. Loss of paid employment may cause chronic disease, such as depression and cardiovascular disease.

The SHARE study clearly demonstrates the importance of health for labour force participation. However, an increased risk of displacement from the labour market during the 2-year follow-up period does not present sufficient insight into the consequences of ill health on paid employment during the life course of a person. In the past few years, new approaches have been developed that capture the long-term consequences of ill health for a sustained working life. One of the most promising new metrics is the work life expectancy (WLE) measure, which reflects how many years a person at a given age is expected to work in a paid job. A linked measure is the number of working years lost due to being out of paid employment, for example, due to work-related disability. A recent study on the Norwegian disability pension registry estimated that subjects with a permanent disability benefit lost about 15 years of their working life. Mental disorders contributed most to the total working years lost (33.8 %), followed by musculoskeletal disorders (29.4 %). Individuals with a mental disorder were awarded a disability benefit on average at much younger age than individuals awarded for a musculoskeletal disorder (46 years vs. 55 years, respectively) [6]. In a Canadian study, it was reported that working life of individuals with arthritis was reduced with about 4 years among men and 3 years among women [7].

Working life expectancy equals the number of years a person at a given age is expected to work in a paid job. Working years lost equal number of years out of paid employment. Individuals with arthritis will lose 3–4 years of paid employment due to their disease. Individuals with mental disorder may lose up to 15 years of paid employment.

The metric WLE can be adapted to construct a disease-work participation model that describes for each age, stratified by sex, the transitional probabilities from paid employment to disability and unemployment and the particular contribution of ill health to this displacement from the work force. Such models are extremely useful to estimate the total loss of working years across the life course of the workforce and the relative contribution of ill health to the working years lost. The aforementioned SHARE study was used to evaluate the hypothetical impact of health promotion by assuming that the particular role of ill health in the displacement from the workforce can be completely eliminated. This disease-work participation model starts with a reference population of persons at age 50 years all in paid employment. During the 2-year follow-up, the proportion of workers with paid employment is calculated for each following year, stratified by age and sex, as well as the proportion of workers who exit paid employment through possible exit routes such as work-related disability, unemployment, retirement, and becoming homemaker. Subsequently, the relative contribution to ill health to disability and unemployment can be calculated by the population attributable fraction of ill health. This analysis was conducted for one definition of ill health (less than good health), without taking into account possible additional effects of other measures of ill health, such as presence of chronic disease or limitations in activities in daily life. Figure 3.2 presents the potential impact of prevention of ill health on labour force participation among men. For women a similar pattern was observed. It is estimated that the average age of quitting paid employment could increase from 60.4 to 61.5 years (13.2 months) among men and from 59.2 to 60.5 years (16.2 months) among women. Thus, tackling ill health among workers may prolong WLE by at least 1 year [8]. This example illustrates that new metrics, such as working life expectancy and working years lost, may convey a powerful message to stakeholders, such as policymakers and health professionals, about the need to develop interventions and policies that support workers to remain in paid employment and delay unwanted health-related retirement.

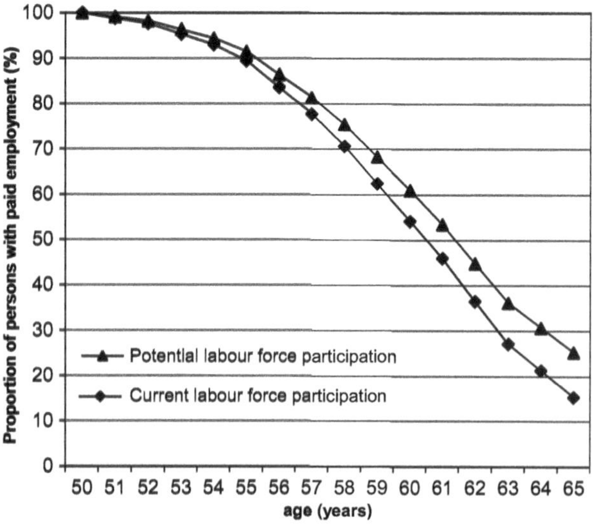

Fig. 3.2 Theoretical effect of elimination of health problems through preventive efforts aimed at important health determinants on the labour force participation among men who have paid employment at the age of 50 year (Based on Ref. [8])

3.3 Consequences of Chronic Disease for Optimal Participation at Work

An important consequence of having a chronic disease is disability, ranging from limitations in executing a simple task to restrictions in societal roles. As stated before, there is a growing interest in the influence of chronic disease on the performance of social roles, i.e. participation, and especially paid employment. Restriction in work participation strongly represents the indirect costs of illness, defined by productivity losses of a person due to sickness absence or less productivity at work because of health problems. This domain is not covered in the ICF, whereas it is very important in cost-effectiveness evaluations. Traditionally, studies among persons with chronic diseases have focused on work-related disability, but comparability across countries is hampered by the strong influence of legal and socio-economic determinants on eligibility for a disability benefit. In recent years, sickness absence has received more attention as a key parameter of restriction in work capacity, since sickness absence is regarded as an important source of productivity loss, which largely accounts for the indirect costs of illness. The latest development is the appreciation that persons with a chronic disease who do go to work may experience a decreased productivity due to their health problems. The phenomenon where workers turn up at work despite health problems is sometimes referred to as sickness presenteeism, but in economic terms, it is better described as productivity loss at work [9]. It has been hypothesised that being less productive at work is an alternative choice to sickness absence for workers with chronic diseases, with both acting as alternative choices for a worker. However, several studies have shown that both measures of reduced productivity are strongly associated, clearly suggesting that productivity loss at work may precede or follow a spell of sickness absence [10].

Taking rheumatoid arthritis (RA) patients as an example, several studies have demonstrated the considerable impact of RA on all measures of work participation. In a systematic review, several participation categories were selected from the Comprehensive Core Set for RA, resulting in 30 studies on remunerative employment, 17 studies on recreation and leisure, and 3 studies with combined measures of participation. RA patients had an increased risk of being without paid employment (odds ratios varied from 1.2 to 3.4). Restrictions in employment occurred already within the early phase of RA, but varied greatly among studies. Two years after diagnosis, in some European cohort studies, up to 30 % of the RA patients had already enrolled in the disability benefit system while being without paid employment [11].

While many studies have focused on permanent work disability among patients with established RA, there is emerging evidence that RA will also contribute to temporary absence from work due to illness and a reduced performance while at work due to illness. However, there is scarce information on the work-related factors that prompt workers with RA to take sickness absence or to have reduced productivity at work. Recently, a systematic review was conducted on the occurrence and magnitude of workplace productivity loss and sick leave in patients with inflammatory arthritis (IA), which encompasses primarily patients with early RA as well as established RA. In total,

47 original studies were identified with 44 studies reporting on sickness absence and 20 studies describing productivity loss at work. The occurrence of sickness absence varied from 3.7 % in the past 4 days to 84 % in the past 2.5 years and the total duration of sickness absence ranged from 0.1 to 11 days in the past month. The large variation in sickness absence across studies was also observed for productivity loss at work. About 17–88 % of patients experienced any workplace productivity loss, and productivity was reduced by 4.9 % to over 35 % in the past weeks. In general, increased levels of pain and decreased functional abilities were consistently associated with sickness absence and productivity loss at work. The evidence on the particular role of working conditions that hampered or supported patients with RA to remain productive was poorly developed. There were some indications that heavy physical work, frequent manual material handling, high time pressure, low job control, and poor social support were work-related risk factors for sickness absence [12].

These studies on RA patients clearly demonstrate that RA will impact quantity and quality of work activities performed, frequency and duration of sickness absence, and exit from paid employment through work-related disability. Similar conclusions can be drawn for different patient groups, emphasising the need to study the influence of chronic diseases and all measures of work participation. The systematic reviews on RA and work performance also point at a clear lack of insight into the interplay between working conditions and chronic diseases, which will hamper the development of effective rehabilitation programmes.

3.4 Interplay Between Work Conditions and Chronic Diseases

In interviews with patients with a chronic disease about facilitators and barriers for an optimal performance at work, often, specific work-related factors are mentioned. Among patients with chronic musculoskeletal pain, adjustment latitude and job control were mentioned as success factors for staying at work [13]. In a study among patients with RA and patients with diabetes mellitus, the main factors at work that enabled employees to continue working were adequate working conditions and support from management and colleagues [14]. These qualitative studies strongly suggest that work-related factors modify the effect of ill health on sickness absence, but interestingly there is little quantitative evidence in the scientific literature on how work-related factors interfere with disease.

In order to better understand the effect of work on the influence of ill health on sickness absence, a longitudinal study was conducted among employed persons aged 46–64 years as part of the ongoing Study on Transitions in Employment, Ability, and Motivation ($n = 8{,}984$) [15]. The presence of common chronic health problems and work-related factors was determined at baseline and self-reported sickness absence at 1-year follow-up by questionnaire. Multinomial multivariate logistic regression analyses were conducted to assess associations between presence of a chronic health

Table 3.1 Interaction effects of work-related factors and health on sick leave over 10 days in the follow-up period of 1 year, after adjustment for age, education, and sex, among 6,534 workers aged 45–65 years in the Netherlands (Based on Ref. [15])

Health problem	Work-related factor	*N*	Odds ratio	95 % confidence interval	Relative excess risk due to interaction	95 % confidence interval
Psychological complaints	*Job demands*				3.51	0.67–6.34
Not present	Low	3,232	1			
Not present	High	3,061	1.27	1.13–1.43		
Present	Low	111	3.27	2.22–4.80		
Present	High	130	7.04	4.84–10.21		
Psychological complaints	*Autonomy*				2.94	0.17–5.70
Not present	Low	3,320	1			
Not present	High	2,973	1.38	1.23–1.55		
Present	Low	105	3.53	2.38–5.24		
Present	High	136	6.85	4.78–9.82		
Musculoskeletal complaints	*Autonomy*				0.57	0.05–1.08
Not present	Low	2,446	1			
Not present	High	2,069	1.37	1.18–1.59		
Present	Low	979	2.19	1.84–2.60		
Present	High	1,040	3.12	2.65–3.69		
Circulatory disorders	*Autonomy*				0.82	0.01–1.63
Not present	Low	3,102	1			
Not present	High	2,806	1.39	1.23–1.57		
Present	Low	323	1.76	1.36–2.28		
Present	High	303	2.97	2.32–3.79		
Severe headaches	*Job demands*				1.35	0.45–2.25
Not present	Low	3,121	1			
Not present	High	2,942	1.25	1.11–1.41		
Present	Low	222	1.52	1.12–2.06		
Present	High	249	3.12	2.39–4.07		

problem and sickness absence and the effect modification of these associations by work-related factors. The effect modification was expressed by the relative excess risk due to interaction (RERI), whereby values above 0 indicate that an additive interaction is present. In Table 3.1, the core findings are reported for high cumulative sickness absence of 10 days or more per year.

All common health problems were related to follow-up sickness absence, and several work-related factors in the absence of these health problems also predicted sickness absence. Several work-related factors modified the influence of chronic disease of sickness absence. For example, for workers with psychological complaints, a strong effect modification was found for job demands, as expressed by a

RERI of 3.51 (95 % CI 0.67–6.34). Workers with psychological complaints in jobs with lower demands had a probability on sickness absence of odds ratio = 3.27, relative to workers with chronic health problems. However, workers with psychological complaints in jobs with high demands had an increased risk of odds ratio = 7.04, relative to those without chronic health problems. Thus, among workers with psychological complaints, high job demands increased the likelihood of high cumulative sickness absence by 115 %. Consistently, the work-related factors of importance were job autonomy and job demands. Lower autonomy at baseline increased the likelihood of high sickness absence at follow-up among those with musculoskeletal (RERI 0.57), circulatory (RERI 0.82), and psychological health problems (RERI 2.94) at baseline. Higher job demands at baseline increased the likelihood of high sickness absence among those with severe headaches (RERI 1.35) and psychological complaints (RERI 3.51). For work-related physical load, no effect modifications were observed.

The key practical implications of this study are that higher job demands and lower autonomy increase the risk of sickness absence among persons with common chronic health problems and thus that focus on these work-related factors should be central in the promotion of sustainable employability. It may be hypothesised that psychosocial work-related factors are important because they allow an individual to exert control over how his or her work is conducted and inherently how adjustments therein can be made. These aspects are crucial components of the illness flexibility model, which addresses conditions influencing whether persons attend work or not when they experience an illness [16]. Health management at work should not only focus on return to work of persons on sickness absence but also on how working conditions should be modified to prevent onset of sickness absence.

Working conditions may modify the risk of sickness absence due to a chronic disease. Workers with psychological problems have a 115 % higher likelihood of sickness absence in jobs with high work demands compared to jobs with low work demands. For most chronic diseases, lower demands and higher autonomy in the job will buffer the risk of sickness absence.

3.5 Recommendations for Research, Policy, and Practice

The importance of health for entering and maintaining paid employment demands considerably more attention within health care organisations. Treatment regimes should support sustainable employability of persons with temporary or chronic health problems. For stakeholders the following important challenges can be identified:

- Research: Develop an evidence-based approach whereby treatment and rehabilitation programmes are properly evaluated for their cost-effectiveness from both health care and labour market perspectives. In most cost-effectiveness studies, the indirect costs due to productivity loss at work, sickness absence, and work-related disability will substantially exceed the direct medical costs. Thus, the ICF network should promote inclusion of remunerative employment in each comprehensive ICF core set, as was recently proposed as part of the development of a brief ICF core set for vocational rehabilitation of patients with subacute and chronic musculoskeletal pain [17]. In addition, further development of instruments that capture all relevant aspects of work participation is needed. In addition, randomised controlled trials on treatment should include work participation as a key outcome measure.
- Policy: Implement legislation and support schemes to make the workplace more 'disability friendly'. Legislation and specific arrangements should empower workers with chronic health problems to remain in paid employment, contributing as best as possible to a productive workforce. In the current shift towards self-management of disease, health care professionals and policymakers alike must not forget that remaining engaged in paid employment is most often not an individual choice, but the result of facilitators and barriers in the social and physical environment, including workplace adaptations, health care system orientation and support, entitlement programmes, and social stigma [18].
- Practice: In vocational rehabilitation for persons with chronic health problems, integrate labour market support with required medical treatment and guidance. Programmes must address important barriers for optimal work participation and work closely together with other stakeholders, such as employers and employment service providers.

Study Questions

1. Life expectancy has increased with approximately 1.5 years per 10 years in the past six decades. Consider the consequences for the proportion of persons in society who perform paid employment, relative to the same statutory retirement age in the next 20 years and relative to an increase in the statutory retirement age from 65 to 68 years.

   Answer: With unchanged retirement age, the proportion of persons in a society that work will decrease rapidly. With increase in retirement age of 3 years, the expected increase in life expectancy is balanced, and most likely the proportion will remain stable.

2. Ill health is an important reason for elderly workers to be forced out of paid employment. Mention the most important routes out of paid employment. Discuss whether ill health is of similar importance at the societal level in different routes out of paid employment.

Answer: Work-related disability and unemployment are the most important routes out of paid employment. Disability is primarily due to ill health. For unemployment ill health will explain certainly less. However, if many more persons become unemployed than disabled, in the total population, health-based unemployment may be more important than disability.

3. Which aspect of optimal participation at work is not covered well in the current ICF? Why would this aspect be a very useful addition?

   Answer: Productivity loss at work (presenteeism) is not covered in the current ICF. It is certainly an addition since presenteeism is very important for the indirect costs of disease, and as such will have a large impact on the cost-effectiveness of medical and nonmedical interventions.

4. Which factors may buffer the negative impact of chronic disease on sickness absence? Explain how these factors my support a worker with chronic disease to be a productive worker.

   Answer: Work-related factors such as autonomy at work and low job demands may prevent workers with chronic disease to take sickness absence. The illness flexibility model explains why these factors may act as a buffer: Workers who can plan or adjust their own work activities to their health needs will be less productive when their health really hampers their work and will compensate their productivity when they are in better health.

References

1. Huber M, Knottnerus A, Green L, et al. How should we define health. BMJ. 2011;343:d4163.
2. Hazes JMW, Geuskens GA, Burdorf A. Work limitations in the outcome assessment of rheumatoid arthritis. J Rheumatol. 2005;32:980–2.
3. Burdorf A. The importance of solid employment for health. Scand J Work Environ Health. 2008;34:81–2.
4. Van den Berg T, Schuring M, Avendano M, Mackenbach J, Burdorf A. The impact of ill health on exit from paid employment in Europe among older workers. Occup Environ Med. 2010;67:845–52.
5. Survey on Health and Ageing in Europe (SHARE). www.share-project.org (2013). Accessed Dec 2013.
6. Knudsen AK, Øverland S, Hotopf M, Mykletun A. Lost working years due to mental disorders: an analysis of the Norwegian disability pension registry. PLoS One. 2012;7:e42567.
7. Lacaille D, Hogg RS. The effect of arthritis on working life expectancy. J Rheumatol. 2001;28:2315–9.
8. Burdorf A, van den Berg T, Avendano M, Kunst A, Mackenbach J. The effects of ill health on displacement from the labour market and potential impact of prevention. In: Börsch-Supan A, editor. Health, ageing and retirement in Europe (2004–2007). Starting the longitudinal dimension. Mannheim: SHARE; 2008.
9. Koopmanschap M, Burdorf A, Jacob K, Meerding JW, Brouwer W, Severens H. Measuring productivity changes in economic evaluation; setting the research agenda. PharmacoEconomics. 2005;23:47–54.

10. Leineweber C, Westerlund H, Hagberg J, Svedberg P, Alexanderson K. Sickness presenteeism is more than an alternative to sickness absence: results from the population-based SLOSH study. Int Arch Occup Environ Health. 2012;85:905–14.
11. Geuskens GA, Burdorf A, Hazes JMW. Consequences of rheumatoid arthritis for performance of social roles – a literature review. J Rheumatol. 2007;34:1248–60.
12. Lenssinck MB, Burdorf A, Boonen A, Gignac MA, Hazes JMW, Luime JL. Consequences of inflammatory arthritis for workplace productivity loss and sick leave: a systematic review. Ann Rheum Dis. 2013;72:493–505.
13. de Vries HJ, Brouwer S, Groothoff JW, Geertzen JHB, Reneman MF. Staying at work with chronic nonspecific musculoskeletal pain: a qualitative study of workers' experiences. BMC Musculoskelet Disord. 2011;12:126.
14. Detaille SI, Haafkens JA, van Dijk FJ. What employees with rheumatoid arthritis, diabetes mellitus and hearing loss need to cope at work. Scand J Work Environ Health. 2003;29:134–42.
15. Leijten FRM, Van den Heuvel SG, Ybema JF, Robroek SJW, Burdorf A. Do work factors modify the association between chronic health problems and sickness absence among older employees? Scand J Work Environ Health. 2013;39:477–85.
16. Johansson G, Lundberg I. Components of the illness flexibility model as explanations of socioeconomic differences in sickness absence. Int J Health Serv. 2009;39:123–38.
17. Reneman MF, Beemster TT, Edelaar MJ, van Velzen JM, van Bennekom C, Escorpizo R. Towards an ICF- and IMMPACT-based pain vocational rehabilitation core set in the Netherlands. J Occup Rehabil. 2013;23:576–84.
18. Henry AD, Lucca AM. Facilitators and barriers to employment: the perspectives of people with psychiatric disabilities and employment service providers. Work. 2004;22:169–82.

Chapter 4
Workplace Integration Through Disability Management

Thomas Geisen

4.1 Introduction

Modern societies can be characterised as labour societies in which labour has become the main focus in human life [1]. This understanding of labour in modern societies contrasts with the premodern understanding of labour as a mere burden [2]. On the contrary, for individuals and for society, labour is no longer a mere means for livelihood but has become an end in itself. Work and labour are not only relevant in a functional dimension as a source of livelihood but also in a social-psychological sense, since social belonging, recognition, dignity and self-esteem of individuals, communities and societies are closely intertwined with the job a person does. Here, a further distinction is highly relevant for the understanding of labour in modern societies, the distinction of the private and public spheres, in which the different human activities are situated. According to Arendt [1], labour was in premodern times situated in the private sphere and included labour in the private household. This changed in modernity, when labour became the main focus in human life. The growing importance of labour went along with situating it more and more in the public sphere. For Arendt it is precisely here that the social realm gains new importance; by situating labour in-between the private and the public spheres, labour became an activity of public attention, stimulation, acknowledgement and recognition [3]. Only by transferring labour from privacy into public realm can the rise of the new meaning of labour in modernity be understood. Marx refers as well to this point when he argues that the national economy knows labour only as gainful employment and neglects all other forms of labour [2]. Only on the basis of that distinction, labour became a major focus in modern societies which is not only connected with the private existential needs of each individual for making a living

T. Geisen (✉)
School of Social Work, University of Applied Sciences and Arts Northwestern Switzerland, Riggenbachstrasse 16, 4600 Olten, Switzerland
e-mail: thomas.geisen@fhnw.ch

R. Escorpizo et al. (eds.), *Handbook of Vocational Rehabilitation and Disability Evaluation*, Handbooks in Health, Work, and Disability, DOI 10.1007/978-3-319-08825-9_4

but also a public activity imbued with the values of appreciation, acknowledgement and recognition. In other words, labour in modernity has an ambivalent character, it is a private activity and as such is neither appreciated nor acknowledged as much as it deserves. It is also perceived as a (semi)public activity in the context of gainful employment and as such is deemed a highly valued and accepted human activity. Even precarious and bad working conditions are often perceived as 'better' than not having a job at all. This shows that human well-being is often closely connected with labour and with the workplace. Akabas and Kurzman emphasise this high relevance of work and the workplace for individual and social life:

> On a manifest level, work is the principal way in which most individuals earn an income to support themselves and a family. In an economic system characterized by a free market, in which goods and services are produced for profit and labor is performed for wages, able-bodied adults are expected "to work for a living" or be a member of a family unit where such work is performed. To be outside this sphere implies marginality since a capitalist economic system depends upon the explicit exchange between the worker and employer to generate its products and services. [4]

This high level of relevance of work and labour for individual and social life is the starting point for the disability management approach, rendering it distinct from traditional rehabilitation, which primarily follows a medical model. The medical model emphasised restoration and was characterised largely by a mere functional perspective on workplace integration. This prevalence of the medical model, 'one of diagnosis and cure of pathology' [5], is also inscribed in the social security system: 'Without exception in the Western developed world the models of insurance and transfer payments depend on the medicalization of disability (. . .) Study after study (. . .) have shown, that the delays in recovery are associated with psychosocial issues that require psychological treatment. Yet we as a society are so fixated on the medical model that other forms of treatment are rarely provided' [5]. Workplace relations and social interactions in the lifeworld were especially neglected as relevant factors for a successful return to work by the dominant medical approach. Here return-to-work programmes were limited to the task of returning the injured or ill worker back to the workplace after successful medical treatment. One of the experiences in that largely medical approach was that little was done to analyse and change the working conditions and the workplace where employees experienced their injuries and illnesses. Consequently, many of the return-to-work cases later led again to a loss of ability to work and finally to a loss of health integration as well. Therefore, Harder and Scott argue, 'the goal of rehabilitation must shift from restoring function alone to also embrace the need to maintain working capacity and the connectedness with the workplace' [5]. This also includes the shift from 'the vocational model' of restorative rehabilitation to the 'competency model such that the object of rehabilitation was no longer vocational readiness but rather competency in independent daily living' [5]. From this perspective it becomes very clear: 'When the goal is to prevent the movement to unemployment and resulting dependency on transfer payments, the logical and expedient place to intervene is in the workplace' [5].

The emphasis on the great relevance of work and the workplace for individual and social well-being is the underlying principle and focus of disability management [6]. This chapter seeks to discuss this principle by focusing on the disability management concept. Initially it presents the fundamentals, history and principles of disability management. Second, the disability management concept is discussed by showing its strengths and pointing out the differences with other approaches for workplace integration. The final section looks at current challenges in disability management, followed by a conclusion touching likewise on possible further developments.

Modern societies can be characterised as labour societies. The emphasis on the great relevance of work and the workplace for individual and social well-being is the underlying principle and focus of disability management.

4.2 Fundamentals, History and Principles of Disability Management

In modern societies, not only do most adults of working age depend existentially on employment to make a living but a regular job is also important for successful participation in social and cultural lives. Consequently, the workplace and its social relations are very influential for individuals and their overall social well-being. Workplace integration in a comprehensive sense means first of all being able to have the competences and capacities to accomplish the tasks in a specific workplace, being part of and included in the social relations at the workplace and being integrated in terms of individual health. In the classic study on the unemployed from Marienthal first published in 1933 [7], the research showed the relevance of employment not only for the individuals but also for the social order itself. Employment in Marienthal meant hard industrial labour in the textile industry. However, before the company closed the plant, the village was well known for its social, political and cultural lives. But in quite a short time, the closing of the plant led to the destruction of social life in the village. People had more free time than ever before, but they did not know what to do with it. The example of Marienthal pointed out in classic fashion that work and social lives cannot be treated separately but are intrinsically interwoven with each other and positively interlinked. That means that even if work and labour are seen as a burden, exhaustive, dirty, difficult, exploitative and so on, there is something given to the individual by participating successfully in the labour market. This phenomenon is often understood and discussed by using terms and concepts like self-esteem, empowerment, dignity, emancipation, respect, independence and so on, which on the one hand describe a social relation and on the other hand indicate a highly emotional and affective dimension of social life at the workplace. Akabas and Kurzman emphasise: 'We derive status, self-sufficiency, sense of self-worth, social contacts, and organization of our day from our work' [4].

The affective dimension of work is even stronger by looking at the normative foundation of adulthood in modern societies. Here, the distinction between youth and adults is drawn by reaching the stage of employability and by successful integration into the labour market. Independence through employment in the sense of being able to care for yourself and for those depending on you, such as your family, is thus also the normative foundation of the Western models of the social welfare state. Only for those in need, those unable to work, does the state provide support [8, 9]. However, whatever the reason for unemployment, those who can work but do not, as well as those who can work but rely on social benefits, are not perceived as full members of the society. The normative foundations of the modern society degrade them as not being fully independent, and they thus face a loss of respect and dignity in society. Those in society who are not gainfully employed are outsiders at the bottom of the social order. In the past, vagabonds and scapegraces were seen this way, and Marx termed them a Lumpenproletariat [10]. Today, in the age of mass unemployment and given the recent transformation of the Western welfare states through austerity policies, those at the bottom of the society are a growing phenomenon, viewed by some as superfluous [11], i.e. of no use at all and worthless in a social sense. Therefore, being an adult and being dependent on others, for example, on the family or the welfare system, means living in a situation where people are not able to fulfil the normative standards of modern society for which successful labour market participation, including entrepreneurship and self-employment, is seen as the key for individuals to establish a basis of social belonging and participation. Therefore, non-participation in the labour market is regarded as negative for adults in modern societies, as long as there are no socially legitimised hindrances for labour market participation such as illness, family care work, lack of education or severe economic depression which can render large segments of the work force jobless.

Given this high degree of relevance of employment for individual and social well-being in modern societies, modern welfare states established return-to-work activities, especially after severe illnesses or accidents, which are accompanied by a loss of employability or a loss of efficiency on the job. However, return-to-work strategies had a strong emphasis mainly on medical care; they tended to neglect the relevance of work and employment itself for individuals as important basic conditions in the lifeworld and the social conditions within and beyond the workplace, as a crucial element in successful workplace integration. This situation changed in the 1980s, when the concept of disability management emerged, practitioners arguing that continual and ongoing workplace integration was crucial for social integration, well-being and health [5, 6]. Especially under conditions of severe illness or injuries, retaining close connections with the workplace is important for maintaining workplace integration and social life in the company and the private sphere. This helps to alleviate the loss of self-esteem and the fragmentation of identifications, which constitute some of the most severe psychological effects of illness and injuries along with its physical impact on the worker. It serves to help maintain existing social ties with colleagues, the workplace and the work activity itself. In such a situation of individual crisis due to severe health problems, it is important for workers to obtain support from their place of employment, for example, by developing professional strategies to assist a return to work as soon as possible through initial part-time arrangements. The latter can be increased step by step until full recovery is reached. This approach follows a different concept of illness or injury. Whereas traditional concepts say that illness and injury need to be cured before being able to return to work, the 'salutogenic model' is based on a gradualist concept of health and illness; it avoids the dichotomising classification of workers as either healthy or ill. Instead, this approach places individuals on a multidimensional 'health-ease versus disease continuum' [12]. The perspective is thus shifted from an either-or to a more variable dimension of 'as well as'. Viewed from such a perspective, in the case of illness or injury, the question is not if someone is either able to continue to work or ill. Rather, it focuses on determining what someone is still able to do under the current conditions of partial disablement, which can include a severe illness. In regard to employment, the question here is: under what perspectives and conditions can the person continue to work? Work and social relations in the workplace can be seen as crucial for maintaining and improving health conditions because they also provide the individual with a sense of self-esteem, of belonging and meaning and of playing a valuable part in the community and broader society.

Disability management foregrounds this orientation towards work and the workplace as highly valuable spaces of individual and social life and significant factors for maintaining health and well-being. For Harder and Scott:

> Disability management, unabashedly embracing the belief that society values work, has continued to focus on finding solutions to disability issues within the context of the workplace. Initially the focus was on temporary disabilities resulting from injury or illness, usually as a result of employment. However, this quickly expanded to include all acquired disabilities regardless of aetiology and is now expanding to include all issues of disability that impact on a person's ability. [5]

Through application of disability management, the conditions of work at the personal and organisational levels are kept in central focus. The core question is: what can be done for a person with disabilities to bring or keep her/him in the workplace? In an early definition of disability management, Akabas et al. describe disability management as:

> A workplace prevention and remediation strategy that seeks to prevent disability from occurring or, lacking that, to intervene early following the onset of disability, using coordinated, cost-conscious, quality rehabilitation service that reflects an organizational commitment to continued employment of those experiencing functional work limitations. The remediation goal of disability management is successful job maintenance, or optimum timing for return to work, for persons with disability. [13]

Disability here is understood as 'any condition, which results in functional limitations that interfere with an individual's ability to perform his or her customary work' [13]. In the pioneering work by Jarvikoski and Lahelma from 1980 on, quoted by Harder and Scott, disability management is defined as:

A coordinated activity which:

- Is directed toward an individual with a chronic or permanent functional limitation or disability, or an individual with symptoms indicating a risk of chronic functional limitations or disability
- Is intended to restore an individual's working or functional capacity, or prevent its lowering
- Includes measures aimed at developing an individual's own resources or removing obstacles imposed by the environment. [5]

From its beginnings in the 1980s, disability management has undergone significant development and spread as a company activity since the 1990s, first in Canada, the USA and Australia, and since 2000 likewise in European countries and more recently elsewhere worldwide. Several institutions and organisations are promoting disability management: most important and influential since 1994 has been the National Institute of Disability Management and Research (NIDMAR) in Canada. Since 2002, disability management has been further promoted worldwide by the biannual International Forum on Disability Management (IFDM), and the International Labour Organization (ILO) approved in 2002 a 'code of practice' for 'Managing Disability in the Workplace' [14].

Further influences on the development of the disability management approach can be traced back to the World Health Organization's (WHO) Ottawa Charter, ratified in 1986 [15], according to which individuals should be enabled 'to learn, throughout life, to prepare themselves to all of its stages and to cope with chronic illness and injuries is essential. This has to be facilitated in school, home, work and community settings' [15]. Here, the workplace and the company are considered as a focus of health promotion, which also includes comprehensive prevention measures, for example, on primary, secondary and tertiary levels. A recent incentive by the WHO is proposed in the 'World Report on Disability' [16]. The Report adopted the ICF as its 'conceptual framework' and understands

> functioning and disability as a dynamic interaction between health conditions and contextual factors, both personal and environmental (...). Promoted as a 'bio-psycho-social model', it represents a workable compromise between medical and social models. Disability is the umbrella term for impairments, activity limitations and participation restrictions, referring to the negative aspect of the interaction between an individual's contextual factors (environmental and personal factors). [16]

In the 'work and employment' chapter of the report, disability management is proposed as a measure to address the barriers to work and employment. Here, disability management refers:

> To interventions applied to individuals in employment who develop a health condition or disability. The main elements of disability management are generally effective case management, education of supervisors, workplace accommodation, and an early return to work with appropriate supports. [16]

From the beginning, accident insurance, which has traditionally a very close relation with the workplace because of labour protection laws, was a key factor in the disability management movement, followed by many other social and private social insurance schemes, such as pension funds, public and private and statutory health insurances and life insurance. Whereas insurance arrangements seek to support workers in companies by supplying external disability management as a professional service, companies implemented internal disability management to provide their employees with their own professional disability management services. There is no coherent and standardised concept for disability management services; moreover, there are many different concepts of disability management in use, often labelled health or case management. From an organisational perspective, the following strategies in disability management can be identified according to the position the person with a disability or changed work capacities has in the company: the integration model, separation model, flexibility model and the outsourcing-insourcing model [17].

Disability management is not a profession or a discipline but a concept that is multi-professional and multidisciplinary. Important contributions to disability management are made by work and health psychology, rehabilitation medicine and social work. Professional knowledge needed in disability management is manifold and includes social law and labour legislation, occupational therapy, work protection and related fields. In recent years the ICF has gained attention in disability management as a tool for disability management practitioners to improve knowledge about workers' abilities and change in functions.

> Disability management foregrounds the orientation towards work and the workplace as highly valuable spaces of individual and social life and significant factors for maintaining health and well-being. Through application of disability management, the conditions of work at the personal and organisational levels are kept in central focus. The core question is: what can be done for a person with disabilities to bring or keep her/him in the workplace?

4.3 The Disability Management Concept

Those seeking employment and the employees are the focus of disability management. Therefore, employment and the workplace are conditions for disability management as well as aims to which disability management is directed. Due to this fact, disability management is either dealing with company workers, looking for solutions to retain them, or dealing with unemployed workers who are encountering difficulties with successful labour market integration. For many of those workers, disability management comes into play due to severe health issues. However, aetiology does not play a significant role for disability management practice, i.e. regardless of the reasons for a lack of labour market participation or the danger of loss of workplace integration, disability management can be seen as a general and comprehensive concept for workplace integration. Before the concept of disability management is discussed, let us look at the types of disability management. In private and public companies, two types of disability management can be distinguished:

- *Internal disability management:* the firm implements internal structures for conducting disability management by its own team of qualified disability management practitioners. The recognised advantages of internal disability management are a high level of commitment in the firm to disability management, the availability of detailed knowledge in the firm regarding disability management practice and a better available opportunity to influence organisational development for improving workplace conditions and preventing disabilities.
- *External disability management:* firms can also use disability management services delivered by external service providers. The recognised advantages of external disability management are its position as an external service provider, which is not involved, in company policies and internal conflicts; in this case, mediation in the interest of workers with disabilities is often easier to achieve. Another advantage for companies involves flexibility and cost efficiency, because the external service will only be used for identified disability management cases. Critics of external disability management argue that there is a limitation in early identification of disability management cases and in co-operation with the different actors in private or public companies. Here it is argued that professional disability management practitioners involved in the firm's identification process know much better the working conditions, key actors and much more about possible internal solutions for continuing employment with disabilities. One important internal solution is working especially with supervisors on finding solutions for workplace adaptation or in finding a new workplace for the employee in the company that is in keeping with his/her work capabilities. Another difficulty is also the transfer of knowledge from case management to the organisation.

For internal and external disability management, the firm itself is the place where disability management services take place. Another profile involves disability management in social institutions and organisations or in social firms, a new type of integration company:

- *Disability management in social organisations:* The primary task of social institutions and organisations is not the production of goods and services for the market but to train people and support them in the process of labour market integration. In this case, disability management is an approach directed towards the primary integration in the labour market for those with disabilities. This includes the labor market integration of people with health conditions and impairments as well as reintegration into the labour market for those unemployed who have difficulties with successful reintegration.

The discussion of the different types of disability management shows that disability management, as a professional task, is not limited to a certain place, e.g. the firm, or to certain health problems, e.g. illness and injuries. Moreover, disability management is a professional practice, which focuses on difficulties of employees in employment due to individual crises because of illness or accident, resulting in difficult trajectories in the workplace, or labour market integration and fragmentations in the context of employment biographies, and can be applied in different organisational contexts. However, the common focus for disability management is to secure and to newly establish labour market participation by gainful employment. This includes the preservation of existing employment in companies, which is endangered by occurring disabilities or recurrent limitations in employability, the support of a person to be employed by a company other than his original company, assisting a person into self-employment and helping an unemployed person return into labour market participation. These different strategies in disability management are seen as adequate solutions and results of the disability management process because disability management is employee focussed and not focussed on the employer or workplace. Consequently the interest of the employer and workplace requirements are not of highest priority in disability management, but finding good solutions by an employee-driven disability management also contribute in different ways, for example, social, cultural and economic, to the interest of the employer and workplace.

Disability management, as a professional task, is not limited to a certain place, e.g. the firm, or to certain health problems, e.g. illness and injuries. Moreover, disability management is a professional practice, which focuses on difficulties of employees in employment due to individual crises because of illness or accident, resulting in difficult trajectories in workplace, or labour market integration and fragmentations in the context of employment biographies, and can be applied to in different organisational contexts. However, the common focus for disability management is to secure and to newly establish labour market participation by gainful employment.

From a methodological perspective, this comprehensive approach of disability management can be classified as a concept, which is oriented towards the principle of labour market participation. A concept is a coherent model for action, which brings aims, contents, methods and procedures in a meaningful relationship that is reasonable and justified [18]. For disability management, important elements include techniques, procedures, methods and instruments, which are applied to reach successful labour market integration. The ICF can be seen as a basic instrument in disability management, which contributes to a better understanding of the employee's functioning on the basis of a bio-psycho-social model. As a concept, disability management is distinct from other approaches for labour market integration such as techniques, for example, case management, or procedures, for example, supported employment, company health management, supported education and vocational rehabilitation. Techniques and procedures can be applied within the disability management concept for utilising the different principles underlying the various techniques and procedures in the field of labour market integration. The principles of supported employment, for instance, are ‘first place, then train’ and job coaching; and the principles of company health management are workplace integration and health integration. In contrast to these techniques and procedures, the disability management concept is a comprehensive approach, which encompasses a wide range of activities focussing on labour market integration by deploying them within a structured and guided disability management process. Such comprehensive disability management has interfaces with other approaches to workplace integration, e.g. supported employment, and company health promotion.

Based on the disability management concept, we can identify core elements and distinct tasks depending on the location of disability management:

- Disability management in a company: (1) systematic recording and judgement of absenteeism; (2) counselling and support of workers with disabilities; (3) coordination of activities and benefits for reintegration; (4) prevention in the framework of workplace health promotion.
- Disability management in a social organisation: (1) systematic recording and judgement of an employee’s working ability; (2) measures and activities to improve employability; (3) counselling and support of clients and human resource managers; (4) coordination of activities and benefits for reintegration.

The differences in the tasks to fulfil in disability management depending on the location where disability management takes place arise because of the specific demands in a company and in a social organisation, which focus on workplace integration activities. By contrast for private or public companies, disability management is not a major focus but only a distinct process for a minority of employees and to case-related actors. For social organisations in the field of disability management, workplace integration activities are at the centre of the organisational activities. However, counselling and the coordination of activities and benefits can be seen as crucial tasks in disability management. The available resources should be used in a timely manner and within the legal framework to achieve workplace integration. While engaging in disability management, practitioners act on different levels: on the individual level, they focus on health integration; on the organisational and institutional level, they focus on workplace integration; with reference to the society, the focus is social integration.

By looking at the procedures applied in disability management, the focus here is on a systematic structuring of the disability management procedures. A basic technique for structuring the disability management process is case management [19]. Case management combines the case level with the system and organisational level. On the case level, case management deals with the needs of the client in a systematic way by activating individual resources available and coordinating all activities needed to achieve health and workplace integration. On the systems level, case management deals on the one hand with different internal and external actors involved in the disability management processes in order to acquire resources needed to work with the clients. On the other hand, case management deals on the organisational level with questions of organisational and workplace improvements and prevention on the basis of individual case work. Harder emphasised the high relevance of case management for disability management:

> Case management is an important component of disability management (DM) programme. Case management provides the on-going connection between all parties, thereby becoming the communication link between the disabled employee, the workplace and the healthcare providers during absence and recovery. [5]

Case management is a systematic technique to structure the support process and is based on a closed loop, which includes the following steps: outreach, intake, assessment, planning, monitoring, evaluation and accountability [20–23]. Case management is applied in complex cases with a high density of actors. We can distinguish between internal and external actors. Internal actors in a company, an organisation or institution are employer, colleagues, team members, disability management practitioners or trainers. Relevant actors external to an institution or organisation are general practitioners, family and family members, disability management practitioners of social insurances and lawyers. Coordination and network management are the professional tasks, which a disability management practitioner needs in order to work successfully with those actors. Further instruments needed in case management for casework and organisational development are on the level of methods, counselling and coaching, empowerment and evaluation, and additionally, also on the level of instruments, genogram, sociogram, time axis, network map and supporters' conference. Applying the methods and using the instruments should direct the orientation of disability management towards emancipation, participation, autonomy and representation.

Due to the complexity of disability management, the profile of qualifications needed is quite broad. Consequently, disability management entails a multiplicity of professional functions. In a systematic way, the functions needed in disability management include the function to define the problem, to develop a concept, to structure the support process and to implement an adequate internal structure oriented to resources, to multiplication and to policy [24] (Fig. 4.1).

> The comprehensive approach of disability management can be classified as a concept, which is oriented towards the principle of labour market participation. A concept is a coherent model for action, which brings aims, contents, methods and procedures in a meaningful relationship that is reasonable and justified. For disability management, important elements include techniques, procedures, methods and instruments, which are applied to reach successful labour market integration. The ICF can be seen as a basic instrument in disability management, which contributes to a better understanding of the employee's functioning on the basis of a bio-psycho-social model.

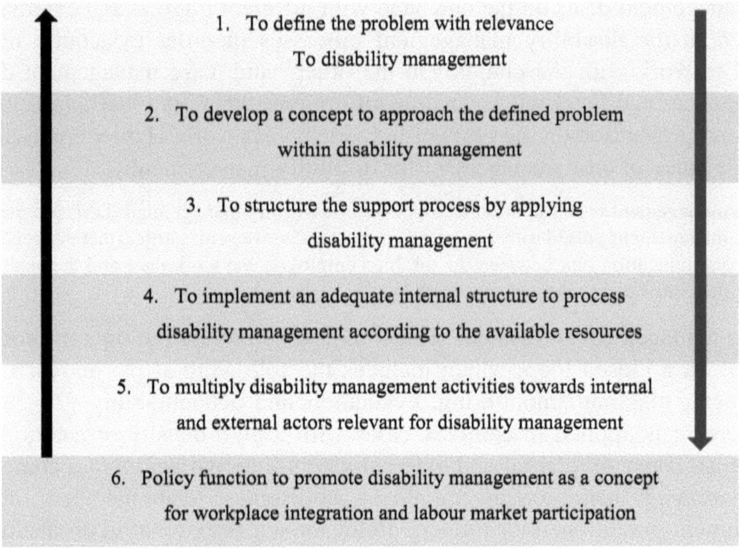

Fig. 4.1 Profile of professional functions in disability management

4.4 Challenges in Disability Management

Disability management is a concept in labour market integration based on the assumption that workplace integration can only be secured or restored by focusing equally on social, work and health integration. Therefore, challenges in disability management can be identified on different levels: (1) target groups, (2) organisations/institutions and (3) disability management practitioners.

A look at the challenges on the level of target groups shows that workers with mental health problems dominate in the debate, followed by migrant workers and the group of older workers. All three pose new challenges for disability management, because these new target groups challenge the assumption that health is only a medical issue. Here it becomes obvious that health problems within the three groups significantly involve aspects of the social conditions and relations individuals live in and work under. Approaches to find solutions for health problems and to solve problems in the workplace focus to a great extent on the individual and his/her social relations, geared towards better understanding the specific situation an individual is dealing with, and the person's positioning and interactions within the community and broader society.

Organisations and institutions are challenged by these recent developments as well. Management in particular has a responsibility to protect and support workers. For management and workers as well, further education programmes help to deal with the new challenges that organisations and institutions face, for example, with an ageing workforce. However, there is also a need to focus on the new challenges not only within human resource management (HR) but also by identifying the need for organisational change and development, e.g. by a change and redefinition of work processes.

Disability management can give support here and contribute to organisational development by the transfer of knowledge gained in casework to an organisational level. However, disability management can only contribute successfully to organisational learning and development if disability management and disability management practitioners have sufficient professional knowledge and competence, experience and concrete knowledge regarding methods, especially in the case of documentation and evaluation, and in organisational development itself as well.

Given these challenges, the orientation of disability management is directed towards the promotion of individual learning processes on the level of casework, of organisational learning processes on the organisational/institutional level and of professional learning processes on the level of the disability management practitioners.

Disability management is a concept in labour market integration based on the assumption that workplace integration can only be secured or restored by focusing equally on social, work and health integration. Therefore, challenges in disability management can be identified on different levels: (1) target groups, (2) organisations/institutions and (3) disability management practitioners.

4.5 Conclusion

Disability management is a complex and comprehensive approach to help enhance workplace integration. The worker and the workplace are the focus of disability management. On the one hand, disability management as a professional practice seeks to prevent workers from incurring disabilities, to support workers in workplace integration after severe illness or accident and to improve health integration in the company through organisational change. On the other, disability management endeavours to support people with disability and the unemployed in their attempts to return to the labour market. Labour market integration and gainful employment are important factors in modern societies for full social participation and for healthful well-being. Therefore, processes to keep workers with disabilities at work or to bring those unemployed back to work are important not only for individual well-being but for the society as well. The success of disability management is highly dependent on the knowledge and abilities of a disability management practitioner, not only in connection with case management but for contributing to organisational development as well.

Disability management is a complex and comprehensive approach to help enhance workplace integration. The worker and the workplace are the focus of disability management.

Study Questions

1. Labour market participation is seen as highly important in modern societies; what arguments can be found for that position?

   Answer:

   – Modern societies are labor societies in which labor is in the centre of human activities.
   – Social and individual well-being is highly depending on participating in gainful employment.
   – Work and social lives cannot be treated separately but are intrinsically interwoven with each other and positively interlinked.
   – Successful participation in the labour market contributes to self-esteem, empowerment, dignity, emancipation, respect, independence and so on.
   – Social life at the workplace has a highly emotional and affective dimension which does influence individual well-being.
   – Those in society who are not gainfull employed are outsiders at the bottom of the social order.
   – Non-participation in the labour market is regarded as negative for adults in modern societies, as long as there are no socially legitimised hindrances for labour market participation such as illness, family care, work, lack of education or severe economic depression.
   – Especially under conditions of severe illness and injuries, retaining close connections with the workplace is important for maintaining workplace integration and social life in the company and the private sphere. This helps to alleviate the loss of self-esteem and the fragmentation of identifications, which constitute some of the most severe psychological effects of illness and injuries along with its physical impact on the worker.

2. Disability management does contribute to health and workplace integration; what arguments can be found for the importance of that professional activity?

   Answer:

   – Disability management serves to help maintain existing social ties with the colleagues, the workplace and the work activity itself.
   – Disability management, unabashedly embracing the belief that society values work, has continued to focus on finding solutions to disability issues within the context of the workplace.
   – The remediation goal of disability management is successfull job maintainance, or optimum timing for return to work, for persons with disability.

3. What are core principles of a comprehensive disability management approach?

   Answer:

   – The common focus for disability management is to secure and to newly establish labor market participation by gainful employment. This includes the preservation of existing employment, the support of a person to be

employed by a company other than his original company, assisting a person into self-employment and helping an unemployed person return into labour market participation.
- Disability management is employee focussed and not focussed on the employer or workplace. Consequently the interest of the employer and workplace requirements are not the highest priority in disability management, but finding good solutions by an employee-driven disability management also contribute in different ways to the interest of the employer's and workplace.

4. What is disability management as a concept, and what procedures, instruments, techniques and methods are employed in disability management?

   Answer:

   - Disability management is a concept, which is oriented towards the principle of labour market participation. A concept is a coherent model for action, which brings aims, contents, methods and procedures in a meaningful relationship that is reasonable and justified.
   - Methods: counselling and coaching, empowerment, evaluation
   - Technique: case management
   - Instruments: genogram, sociogram, time axis, network map, supporters' conference, ICF
   - Procedures: supported employment, company health management, supported education, vocational rehabilitation

5. What relevance has ICF for disability management?

   Answer:

   - The ICF can be seen as a basic instrument in disability management, which contributes to a better understanding of the employee's functionning on the basis of a bio-psycho-social model.

6. There are more recent challenges in disability management; what are these challenges and how can disability management deal with these challenges?

   Answer:

   - More recent challenges in disability mangement are on the level of target groups (mental health, migrant workers, older workers), organisation/institutions (responsibility to protect and support workers, identifying the need for organisational change and development) and disability management practitioners (professional knowledge and competencies).
   - Disability management can deal with these challenges by promotion of individual learning processes on the level of casework, of organisational learning processes on the organisational/institutional level and of professional learning processes on the level of the disability management practitioners.

7. Disability management requires a complex profile of functions for disability management practitioners; what are the functions and what systematic elements can be identified?

   Answer:

   – Disability management entails a multiplicity of professional functions. In a systematic way, the functions needed in disability management include the function to define the problem, to develop a concept, to structure the support process and to implement an adequate internal structure oriented to resources, to multiplication and to policy.

References

1. Arendt H. Vita activa. Oder vom tätigen Leben. München: Piper; 1996.
2. Geisen T. Arbeit in der Moderne. Ein dialogue imaginaire zwischen Karl Marx and Hannah Arendt. Wiesbaden: VS Verlag; 2012.
3. Arendt H. Über die revolution. München: Piper; 1994.
4. Akabas SH, Kurzman PA. Work and workplace. A resource for innovative policy and practice. New York: Columbia University Press; 2005.
5. Harder HG, Scott LR. Comprehensive disability management. Toronto: Elsevier; 2005.
6. Geisen T, Harder HG, editors. Disability management and workplace integration. New perspectives. Fanham: Gower Publishing; 2011.
7. Jahoda M, Lazarsfeld PF, Zeisel H. Die Arbeitslosen von Marienthal. Ein soziographischer Versuch. Frankfurt am Main: Suhrkamp; 1975.
8. Geisen T. Sozialstaat in der Moderne. Zur Entstehung sozialer Sicherungssysteme in Europa. In: Kraus K, Geisen T, editors. Sozialstaat in Europa Geschichte, Entwicklung, Perspektiven. Wiesbaden: Westdeutscher Verlag; 2001. p. 21–42.
9. Kraus K, Geisen T, editors. Sozialstaat in Europa: Geschichte, Entwicklung, Perspektiven. Wiesbaden: Westdeutscher Verlag; 2001.
10. Marx K. Das Kapital. Berlin: Dietz Verlag; 1989.
11. Castel R. Die Metamorphosen der sozialen Frage. Konstanz: UVK Universitätsverlag Konstanz; 2000.
12. Antonovsky A. Salutogenese. Zur Entmystifizierung der Gesundheit. Tübingen: dgvt Verlag; 1997.
13. Akabas SH, Gates LB, Galvin DE. Disability management. A complete system to reduce costs, increase productivity, meet employee needs, and ensure legal compliance. New York: American Management Association; 1992.
14. ILO. Managing disability in the workplace. ILO code of practice. Geneva: International Labour Office; 2002.
15. WHO. Ottawa Charta for Health Promotion. Charter adopted at an international conference on health promotion. The move towards a new public health. 17–21 Nov 1986; Ottawa, 1986 Aug 19; 2010:[8 p.].
16. World Health Organization (WHO). World report on disability. Geneva: World Health Organization/The World Bank; 2011.
17. Ulich E, Wülser M, editors. Gesundheitsmanagement in Unternehmen. Arbetspsychologische Perspektiven. Wiesbaden: Gabler; 2009.
18. Hochuli Freund U, Stotz W. Kooperative Prozessgestaltung in der Sozialen Arbeit. Stuttgart: Kohlhammer; 2011.
19. Gursansky D, Harvey J, Kennedy R. Case management. Policy, practice and professional business. New York: Columbia University Press; 2003.

20. Löcherbach P, Klug W, Remmel-Faßbender R, Wendt WR, editors. Case management. Fall- und Systemsteuerung in der Sozialen Arbeit. München/Basel: Ernst Reinhardt Verlag; 2005.
21. Neuffer M. Case management. Soziale Arbeit mit Einzelnen und Familien. Weinheim/ München: Juventa; 2007.
22. Wendt WR. Case management im Sozial- und Gesundheitswesen. Freiburg im Breisgau: Lambertus; 2001.
23. Wendt WR, Löcherbach P, editors. Case management in der Entwicklung. Stand und Perspektiven in der Praxis. Heidelberg: Economica/MedizinRecht.de; 2006.
24. Becker A, Hamburger F, Lenninger PF. Anforderungsprofile und Qualifikationsmerkmale in der Sozialen Arbeit der Caritas mit MigrantInnen. Freiburg im Breisgau: Lambertus; 1998.

Chapter 5
Vocational Rehabilitation

Sven-Uno Marnetoft

5.1 Introduction

Vocational rehabilitation (VR) is a complex concept. There are many definitions of VR, and many organisations and specialised professions are involved in VR. It is also difficult to make comparisons from one country to another because of differences in the social insurance systems and vocational rehabilitation settings. The purpose of this chapter is to provide a picture of the growth of VR and the various social contexts in which VR exists and affects individuals and organisations working in VR. The aim is also to provide a picture of the importance of VR in providing individuals who – due to illness, injury or unemployment – are about to lose their foothold on the labour market with an opportunity to keep their job or to offer them another job that they can manage. The VR process is also described, along with the importance of implementing the International Classification of Functioning, Disability and Health (ICF) in VR. The International Classification of Functioning, Disability and Health (ICF) is a conceptual framework and classification system by the World Health Organisation (WHO) to provide a language and framework for the description of health and health-related states that can be used consistently across different countries and settings. The ICF seeks to encompass what a person does or can do, covering not just physical functions and structures but also activities and participation together with environmental and other contextual factors. Return to work (RTW) is described both as a process and as an outcome, and important components of the RTW process are emphasised and highlighted. A number of important VR interventions are described, with the focus being on workplace interventions. The text ends with a section on how to move forward from an ICF perspective, highlighting among other things the benefits of implementing the ICF concept.

S.-U. Marnetoft (✉)
Caseman Rehabilitering AB, Östersund, Sweden
e-mail: su.marnetoft@gmail.com

R. Escorpizo et al. (eds.), *Handbook of Vocational Rehabilitation and Disability Evaluation*, Handbooks in Health, Work, and Disability, DOI 10.1007/978-3-319-08825-9_5

5.2 How Vocational Rehabilitation Is Organised in Some Countries

Different countries have a history of the development of activities that have come to be collectively known as 'rehabilitation'. These rehabilitation activities bear a certain resemblance to what we now recognise as VR, although much of the rehabilitation that was carried out previously would nowadays be classified as 'sheltered employment'. The term VR came about in part on the basis of which clients were to be rehabilitated and for what reason. In the United States and the United Kingdom, the term VR came into being to denote the rehabilitation of soldiers returning from war. In Sweden, it was the growing cost to the social insurance system that increased the need to develop VR in line with that of many other countries. In the United States, VR was designed to help 'functionally impaired' veterans of World War I to return to work (RTW) [1]. Parallel with the development of VR in the United States, the concept of case management was also developed within the human services. In the United States, the concepts of RTW and case management are closely linked to each other. In the United Kingdom, the Disabled Persons Act of 1944 had the same purpose as VR in the United States: to help injured soldiers returning from World War II to get back to work. As a result of this legislation, industrial rehabilitation units and sheltered workshops were created, among other things. However, no further legislation with the focus on rehabilitation for an RTW was introduced in the United Kingdom between 1944 and 1995 [2]. Now, the United Kingdom has seen a large growth in private agencies in the field of VR, focusing on vocational activities such as retraining, job counselling and assistance with job seeking [3]. In Sweden, the word 'rehabilitation' in connection with people with illness and injury first came into use during the 1940s. It was also established that the Swedish language had no adequate equivalent of the word 'rehabilitation'. The term VR was therefore translated as 'arbetsvård' (in English 'work care') and used to describe all nonmedical measures within the context of the labour market. In January 1963, the General Insurance Act came into force. This allowed the general social insurance offices to take the initiative and to organise the measures to prevent and minimise the consequences of sickness and disability, in order to create the conditions for people to support themselves permanently through gainful employment. The concept of 'work care' was in use until 1982, when it was changed to VR. In 1992, a new rehabilitation reform was introduced in Sweden, which gave employers the responsibility for VR of their employees. The responsibility for VR of the unemployed was assigned to the employment office. The social insurance offices were tasked with the overall supervision of all kinds of rehabilitation. The role of the coordinators at the social insurance offices was also growing. The rehabilitation reform intended to minimise sickness absence and exclusion from working life and through this stop the rising cost of social insurance while also carrying out early and active rehabilitation efforts [4].

In order to gain an understanding of the complex social context in which VR is practised, a brief description follows of how responsibility for VR is assigned at the individual and organisational level in a number of countries. The countries described in brief are: Denmark, the United Kingdom, Finland, Germany, the Netherlands and Sweden. The source of the brief description is taken from a governmental investigation in Sweden [5].

5.2.1 Individual Level

In Denmark, there are clear requirements for the individual to take an active part in the process of rehabilitation in order to facilitate a rapid RTW. Frequently, regular personal meetings take place during the period of sickness absence. Job security is weak, and there is therefore a powerful incentive to RTW. After 120 days of sickness absence within the last 12 months, the employer has the right to dismiss the employee.

In Finland, the individual faces increasing incentives to RTW once payment of the contractual wage or salary ends after a few months of sickness absence and a lower rate of sickness benefit becomes payable.

In Germany, the financial payment to those on sickness absence provides no motivation to accelerate an RTW. One reason for this is that the level of the tax-free sickness benefit is 70 % of the gross income but a maximum of 90 % of the net income after tax. In the Netherlands, employees are under obligation to cooperate actively on their rehabilitation. Salary and wage payments may be stopped if the employee refuses redeployment. In such cases, the employer is also entitled to terminate the person's employment. There is little financial motivation to the employee, as full payment is made during the first year of sickness absence.

Individuals in the United Kingdom have a financial motivation to RTW, as the statutory payment is low. The low payment can make it difficult to manage financially on a day-to-day basis.

In Sweden, those on sickness absence are obliged to provide any information necessary to the investigation into the need for rehabilitation and to cooperate in their rehabilitation to the best of their ability. Sickness benefit provides a weak incentive for an RTW since the amount of sickness compensation is relatively high. A 1-year limit on sickness benefit has been introduced.

5.2.2 Organisational Level

In Denmark, employers have limited responsibility for employees on sickness absence. The employer has no statutory responsibility to carry out rehabilitation measures. The employer is entitled to terminate the employee's employment following a lengthy period of sickness absence.

In Finland, employers have an obligation to maintain the employee's working capacity. Employees may apply for group rehabilitation or individual rehabilitation. The financial motivation lends a high priority to the maintenance of the employee's working capacity. The occupational health care service has a central role in the sickness absence process. It is responsible, among other things, for ensuring that employers tailor the work according to the circumstances of the employee.

In Germany, the employer provides sick pay and compensates for the entire loss of earnings at the start of the period of sickness absence. The provision of sick pay provides a financial incentive for efforts to reduce sickness absence in the workplace. There are relatively strong financial incentives for employers to ensure that employees retain their working capacity. One of the tasks of the occupational health care service is to prevent work-related ill health and to maintain employees' working capacity. Rehabilitation has priority over a disability pension. Work-oriented rehabilitation offers help to people in returning to their normal job or in finding alternative employment.

In the Netherlands, employers have extensive responsibilities and incentives for ensuring that employees RTW. Employers are also responsible for financing occupational health care measures. The employer has a duty to draw up a plan for an RTW and to maintain close contact with the employee. If an RTW at the employer's place of work is not possible, the employer has a duty to try to arrange alternative work with a different employer. Employers have strong financial incentives to play an active part in the rehabilitation of their employees.

In the United Kingdom, the employer has a duty to arrange for a safe and healthy working environment and to monitor health in the workplace, which includes making modifications to the workplace. However, there is no requirement for the employer to provide rehabilitation to employees on sickness absence. There is no statutory occupational health care service. With the help of the social insurance administration service and employment offices, something called 'Jobcentre Plus' has been created. Its task is to focus on getting people on sickness absence back to work. Employment and Support Allowance (ESA) offers personal advice and work training to allow people to work despite a reduced working capacity. As well as the above, the 'Access to Work' programme is also available, offering help to people with a reduced working capacity.

In Sweden, the main responsibility for VR of those in employment lies with the employer. The employment offices are responsible for VR of those who are unemployed. The Swedish Social Insurance Agency has supervisory responsibility for rehabilitation. This applies both to VR and to medical rehabilitation. In July 2008, a Rehabilitation Chain with fixed limits for testing working capacity was introduced. During the first 90 days of sickness absence, efforts are made to enable a return to the person's existing job or a different job with the same employer. If the person is unable to return to their existing job, they have to look for a new job. After 180 days, sickness benefit can be retained only in special circumstances. For example, this may be ongoing care/treatment or VR with a focus on RTW. When sickness absence exceeds 1 year, the Social Insurance Agency is obliged to make a decision in terms of a disability pension, RTW or unemployment for the individual.

Table 5.1 Incentive of vocational rehabilitation at individual and organisational level

Countries	Individual	Organisational
Denmark	Strong	Weak
Finland	Strong	Strong
Germany	Weak	Strong
Netherlands	Strong	Strong
United Kingdom	Weak[a]	Weak
Sweden	Weak[b]	Weak

[a]The low sickness benefit can be an incentive to go back to work
[b]The incentive increases after 1 year's sickness absence

A disability pension can only be granted in the case of a permanent reduction in the person's working capacity and where VR is not expected to increase the working capacity [6].

In summary, it can be stated that occupation health care is mandatory in Finland and the Netherlands. In these countries, the task of the occupational health care service is to suggest measures to support an RTW and to monitor the efforts of the employer. In Denmark, the United Kingdom, Germany and Sweden, the responsibility of employers to take measures to help employees' RTW is limited. In Finland and, in particular, the Netherlands, employers have strong financial motives to accelerate the employees' RTW. There was a dramatic reduction in sickness absence in the Netherlands in the 2000s as a result of employers incurring increased liability for the cost of sickness absences and disability pension. The weak job security in Denmark puts pressure on individuals to cooperate with rehabilitation measures that lead to an RTW (Table 5.1). Note that the source of the description is dated 2010. There may have been changes made to the different countries' social insurance systems after that time which have not been taken into account in the description.

5.3 Employment Versus Unemployment and Health

Employment rates for people with disabilities are just above 40 %, compared with 75 % for people without disabilities. Employment opportunities for people with health problems or disabilities are limited. Only about one in four people who report mental health problems are in employment. Unemployment is twice as high for people with a disability as for those without. In 2007, an average of about 6 % of the Organisation for Economic Co-operation and Development (OECD) working-age population received a disability benefit. In some European countries, as many as 10–12 % of the population have a disability pension; in Sweden, the figure is almost 9 %. Rates of RTW after being granted a disability pension are less than 2 % per annum in the OECD countries [7].

VR, and how it can be reformed and improved, has been the subject of debate in several countries for a number of years. The OECD has also shown an interest in enhancing VR and provided examples of how it can be improved. There are several reasons why VR has been in focus. One of the reasons could be demographic. In order to sustain their welfare systems, many countries are obliged to have enough people working to safeguard the necessary tax revenues [8]. Another reason is the exceptionally high cost of sickness benefit and disability pensions. A third reason is the increasing number of unemployed people. Work has a central place in Western societies and is highly valued in people's lives. It is described as providing an important meaning to life, as well as providing structure to the various life domains that make up a person's social context. Having a job is also crucial to social inclusion. Having a job can also promote personal needs, such as enhanced self-efficacy and an ability to move away from a feeling of being lost and hopeless to one of feeling that you are making a contribution to society.

Health problems among unemployed people are common, as shown in many studies [9–12]. Unemployment was associated with an increased mortality risk for those in their early and middle careers. The risk of death was highest during the first 10 years of follow-up [11]. Paid employment improves quality of life and self-rated health. Labour force participation should be considered as an important measure to improve the health of unemployed people and to reduce socioeconomic inequalities in health [12]. Many countries have been affected by high rates of unemployment in the wake of the financial crisis. On the one hand, unemployment affects the young, who find it difficult to gain a foothold on the labour market; on the other, however, even those established on the labour market have been greatly affected by unemployment. Given the negative effects of unemployment on health that the latest research has shown in those in the early or middle stages of their careers, these results emphasise how important it is to offer VR as a way of supporting people in returning to work or obtaining a job before they are affected by ill health. However, more research is needed into why those unemployed when young or in middle age are affected by a higher mortality risk.

5.4 The Concept and Definition of Vocational Rehabilitation

VR plays an important role in people's lives when it comes to returning to work following a period of illness or injury. There is, however, no standard definition of VR. This is probably because so many different professional areas and organisations are involved in VR. In certain cases, it has been easier to describe the components of VR than to define the term [3]. VR forms a significant part of the efforts and measures undertaken to help people with a work disability to RTW. Despite the difficulties in defining the concept, many definitions have been proposed for VR, though it has been difficult to find agreement on a uniform definition that would be acceptable globally at individual, organisational and social levels. The one that seems to be most complete is the one that defines VR as: 'Medical, psychological, social and occupational activities aiming to re-establish among sick or injured people with previous work history their working capacity and prerequisites for returning to the labour market, i.e. to a job or availability for a job' [13]. However, this definition omits those who have never worked. Many young people today find it extremely difficult to enter the labour market and those with disabilities find it even harder. The words 'with previous work history' should therefore be erased from the definition. The suggestion is that the definition of VR should be: 'Medical, psychological, social and occupational activities aiming to re-establish among sick or injured people their working capacity and prerequisites for returning or entering the labour market, i.e. to a job or availability for a job' [6]. In 2011, the ICF devised a broad definition of VR, and this conceptual definition of VR contains the main component of the various definitions given above, e.g. 'optimising work participation' [14]. VR is a wide range of vocational and educational services that are offered to people who are working, as well as those out of work or who have never worked. Disabled people participate less in the labour market than do nondisabled people [7].

Some of the definitions that exist either build around some accreditation or qualifications, skills or legislative framework or around the main activity, which means helping people back to work. At an organisational level, some definitions emphasise the word 'facilitation', while those that start out from the main activity define VR as activities that help someone with health problems to obtain employment or to return to and remain at work. It is an idea and an approach as much as an intervention or a service [15]. The word 'facilitate' usually originates from case management activities. The definition by Wadell et al. [15] is more in line with the clinician's point of view and could refer to almost any activity that supports a person in returning to employment. This is a very broad definition and is not solely confined to measures to facilitate an RTW, such as medical treatment and medical rehabilitation alongside VR. It also includes efforts to prevent sickness absence and even covers measures to promote a sustainable working capacity. According to Langman [3], these two definitions can be regarded as two main threads in terms of understanding 'vocational rehabilitation'. The first definition may be regarded as a case management process, where the aim is to facilitate the client through a series of various rehabilitation activities that promote RTW [16].

There is also the debate as to what medical rehabilitation is and what VR is. Ekberg [17] takes the view that medical rehabilitation primarily aims to restore functional capacity, while VR is about the relationship between an individual's capacity for working and the requirements of the job. The measures taken need to focus on creating the right conditions to allow individuals to support themselves through employment. It can be difficult or impossible to distinguish between medical rehabilitation and VR, and one simple way of making the distinction depends on what is being focused on in terms of the individuals and their goals. If the aim is for the person to regain their working capacity and create the conditions whereby they can support themselves through employment, then this may be regarded as VR. This is entirely in line with the definition given and is based on that of the ICF [14]: 'Vocational Rehabilitation is a multi-professional, evidence-based approach that is provided in different settings, services and activities to working-age individuals with health-related impairments, limitations or restrictions with work functioning, and whose primary aim is to optimise work participation'. Looking at this definition, it seems to cover a broad spectrum of services and set of clients. One of the key expressions is 'optimising work participation'. Understanding this expression is not a problem; it can be shared and is an accepted view among different countries, settings, practitioners and clients as to what constitutes VR. If this definition can be accepted worldwide, then the obstacles relating to what constitutes medical rehabilitation and what constitutes VR can be avoided. We can then always have in mind that the objective of VR is work participation for the individual, regardless of whether we operate in a clinical setting or in various environmental settings in society at large – for example, Social Insurance Agencies, employment agencies or various kinds of private agencies. In the United States, VR is generally looked upon more as a social services intervention, whereas in Sweden and pretty much the rest of Europe, it is considered to be more a form of medical treatment [1]. With the definition proposed by the ICF, we can move more towards interventions that can be embedded in social services, where the individual will be the key person in the rehabilitation process. This would not only help cooperation among stakeholders and minimise the debate as to what are medical and what are vocational activities, it would also certainly help the worker-centred rehabilitation process. VR will then move away from being mostly rehabilitation for the organisations to being rehabilitation for the clients. Germundsson and Danermark conclude in their study [18] that the recognition of other people's knowledge and respectfulness towards other professions facilitates the process of VR and the collaboration process. The agencies' lack of flexibility increased the risk of conflicts as attempts were made to integrate the new working methods. The authors identified a number of obstacles, such as lack of collaborative competence, ignorance about collaborative partners, lack of support from management and lack of resources.

'Vocational Rehabilitation is a multi-professional, evidence-based approach that is provided in different settings, services and activities to working-age individuals with health-related impairments, limitations or restrictions with work functioning, and whose primary aim is to optimise work participation [14]'.

5.5 The Vocational Rehabilitation Process

The process of VR is discussed in the literature as a process in its own right but is also discussed as a process under the overarching disability management or as identical with the RTW process. Some also put forward the argument that disability

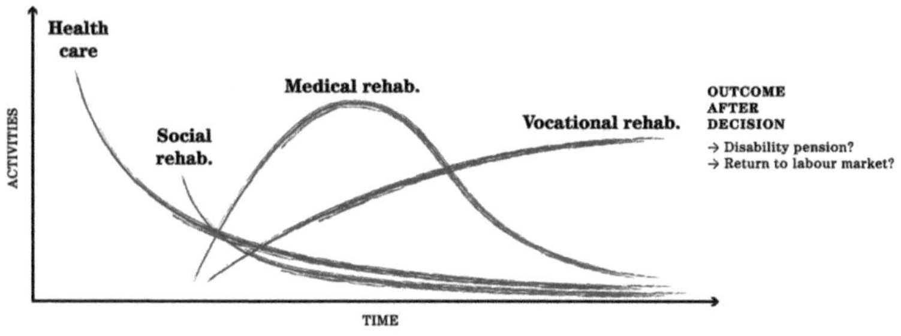

Fig. 5.1 An individual's progress from disease or injury towards a return to the labour market or disability pension [4]

management has to be looked upon as a broad term that encompasses all sorts of disabilities, including work disability [14]. However, there is no consensus among the stakeholders as to what is included in the VR process. VR can be seen both from an organisational level and from the level of the client involved in a rehabilitation activity aimed at facilitating an RTW. When describing the process of VR, we usually think of the term 'RTW' and all the necessary activities and efforts required to achieve the ultimate aim of gainful employment. How extensive the process will be depends on the definition of VR among the various stakeholders and in the different settings within the field of VR. Which activities or interventions are included in the VR process depends on the stakeholders involved and the rehabilitation programme offered.

A simple illustration (Fig. 5.1) can be used to demonstrate the VR process. The figure illustrates how a person affected by a work disability first arrives in the health care service, which treats the acute phase of the illness. If the illness subsides following conventional treatment, the individual returns to their job. If the illness process should become more prolonged and a number of measures are required, such as social rehabilitation in the form of various social measures, these can be initiated at an early stage in the course of the illness, in parallel with the medical treatment. During the person's medical treatment, the doctor may perhaps consider that the person needs to be examined and that they should contact the stakeholders in the field of VR or medical rehabilitation for a comprehensive assessment of any actions necessary for RTW. All of these measures can take place in parallel to avoid unnecessary waiting times. Once an individual has become the subject of various measures from different stakeholders, the RTW process ends with an outcome that results either in an RTW or a disability pension (see Fig. 5.1).

The assessment stage of the process is vital. It provides the foundation on which to establish goals and to develop and implement appropriate strategies to assist the individual in realising those goals. Reviews of the literature have found a huge number of assessment tools, none of which could be used to measure a worker's ability to perform real and relevant work tasks [19]. Across different disciplines and rehabilitation settings, assessment of functions for work has different meanings and a large number of definitions exist. Assessment is more than just assessing the individual's problems or limitations. It also involves identifying the strengths of the individual, and identifying the strengths within the environment in which the individual operates, which can be done if VR is based on the biopsychosocial model of the ICF. This is in accordance with the strengths perspective of social work [16].

5.5.1 Vocational Rehabilitation Core Sets

The WHO has developed both a comprehensive and a brief Core Set for VR based on the ICF. Twenty-three international experts in the field of vocational rehabilitation attended a consensus conference organised by the ICF Research Branch in Nottwil, Switzerland. Through a comprehensive voting process, the experts decided to include 90 ICF categories in the comprehensive Core Set. Forty categories from activities and participation, 33 from environmental factors and 17 from body functions comprised the final Core Set. The brief Core Set included 13 second-level categories from activities and participation, six environmental factors and four body function factors [20]. The aim of the Core Sets is to be a framework for practical tools to classify and describe an individual's functioning more efficiently. The core sets can help professionals to make more stringent evaluations of individuals' functioning and needs when participating in various vocational rehabilitation settings. The benefit of having core sets in the assessment phase is that it can also provide a standard and common language in the field of VR [3]. Finger et al. [20] concluded that the development of the ICF Core Sets in VR is the first step towards an internationally accepted and standardised framework in the field and practice of VR.

5.5.2 The ICF in VR practice

Saltychev et al. [21] found that the ICF codes extracted from the patients' records in their study showed a strong focus on body structures and functions, while only a few environmental factors were noted. They conclude that these findings show that the unstandardised clinical evaluation carried out represented a biomedical approach to defining disability, leaving important psychosocial factors unexplored. Therefore, the results of their study justify the use of the ICF for the purposes of VR because of its biopsychosocial focus. In their study, Ptyushkin et al. [22] identified both advantages and disadvantages to the use of the ICF among professionals involved in VR. The advantages are that it provides a holistic view of the person, comprehensively assesses functions and consequences, and provides a unified language. The disadvantages identified were that it contains complicated terminology, an assessor may perform rating of the coding subjectively, and it might be impractical because of the bulk of information; and various users may perceive the purpose of the ICF differently. Glässel et al. [23] found in their study that almost a fifth of the ICF factors identified were personal factors such as motivation, interest, autonomy, coping, beliefs, education and ability, which could be of use in a resource mobilisation phase in the VR process. For the rehabilitation counsellor, it is of great value to have a more comprehensive knowledge of the client's psychosocial factors in order to make the planning of interventions more effective. However, personal factors are not yet coded in the ICF [20, 23]. This stresses the importance of including an individual or personal context in VR [23, 24].

Glässel et al. [23] conducted a multicentre study with a focus group designed to explore by discussion how people who had been through the experience of VR ranked the importance of the respective ICF components. This was done from six open-ended questions relating to the ICF components. Glässel et al. conclude that VR of clients should not only focus on anatomical and pathophysiological changes but also include the client's demands, strategies and resources in and around the individual, as well as focusing on their working situation.

The study by Finger et al. [25] was focused towards clinical settings. Data were collected, documented and rated by health care professionals and additional data were obtained from the Extended ICF Checklist. The checklist is available at http://www.who.int/classifications/icf/training/icfchecklist.pdf.

The authors stated that the study has contributed to knowledge as to which factors to look at in the evaluation of individuals in VR from a clinical perspective. The study provided a comprehensive list of variables to address VR and functioning. However, components such as work status, work productivity, work ability and job type were not linked to ICF. To increase the utility of the ICF in clinical settings, specific VR indicators such as work status or job type and personal factors should be included.

Which activities or interventions are included in the vocational rehabilitation process depend on the stakeholders involved and the programme offered.

The assessment stage of the process is vital.

It is important to identify the strengths of the individual and the environment.

The ICF can help to make more stringent evaluations of individuals' functions and of consequences and can help to provide a common language in the process.

There should be a focus on the client's demands, strategies and resources in and around the individual and their working situation.

5.6 Return to Work: Both a Process and an Outcome

In a multimodal cohort study, Anema et al. [26] found cross-country differences in RTW rates following chronic occupational back pain. The study population was recruited from Denmark, Germany, Israel, the Netherlands, Sweden and the United States. The Netherlands had the highest reported RTW rate (62 %), while Germany had the lowest rate (22 %) after 2 years of follow-up. These differences could not be explained by differences in individual treatments between the countries. In the Netherlands, where there are strong incentives to RTW, modifications of work were significantly more common. The results show, among other things, that differences in the countries' social insurance systems and employer responsibilities may explain part of the difference in RTW rates reported in some studies. The study highlights the problems of studying the effects of various activities, such as rehabilitation counselling, RTW plans and job retention in the field of VR.

RTW is seen both as a process and an outcome, although according to some researchers, it is poorly defined and lacks a standardised definition [27–29]. The study by Leyshon and Shaw [29] focused on the stakeholder's perspective on concepts that need to be considered when understanding successful RTW and future research towards the development of outcome measurement. The stakeholders identified six new concepts, and these were, firstly, the concept of worker performance, worker job satisfaction and worker well-being. These three concepts focus on workers' ability to engage in activities related to work and life outside work and are also in line with the activities and participation dimension of the ICF. The other three concepts reflect the RTW process, and those are: human rights, seamless RTW through collaborative communication and the satisfaction of stakeholders. The authors concluded that the findings of the study indicate a definite need for a change in RTW outcome measurement.

Here, the RTW process will be described and discussed as both a process and an outcome. Among medical assessors, the view is sometimes taken that the diagnosis and diagnosis-related variables are of decisive importance in determining whether or not a person can RTW. However, not all share this view. Hunt et al. [30] concluded in their study that workers' subjective interpretation and appraisal might be more powerful predictors of the course of post-injury recovery than medical assessment alone. It is likely that the doctor, when seeing a patient with no objective signs of disease, will share the patient's negative views of the working capacity and sickness absence [31].

Laisne et al. [32] conclude that psychosocial variables were the most significant ones in predicting involvement in the RTW process. Hilborg et al. [33] stated that a holistic view that included both social and psychological aspects of individuals was considered crucial in the VR process. Hees et al. [34] conclude that successful RTW is not necessarily disease specific. They stress that consensus between supervisor and worker about important subjective criteria is more important for successful RTW.

Fig. 5.2 The return to work process – a working framework

Tjulin et al. [35] found in an RTW programme that key stakeholders in the programme expressed a more biomedical individual view of working capacity, while the programme was based on a more holistic and biopsychosocial view. Applied to the system in Sweden, the employment service can be taken as an example. They tend to focus on people who are already considered employable [36]. It appears that the biomechanical perspective remains deeply rooted among key stakeholders in the VR field. This may be due to the fact that many countries have enhanced the possibilities of obtaining sickness benefit or a disability pension, which favours the biomedical approach. The Core Sets developed by the ICF for assessment in VR have an important role to play in changing the perspective among some of the key stakeholders towards a more holistic view that includes all aspects of the RTW process.

Although the strategies of an RTW process may differ, there is usually some consensus as to which core factors are to be included in the process. The initial step in the RTW process often starts with an interview, followed by a needs assessment, the development of the rehabilitation plan including the activities to be carried out and the implementation of the plan. Although the strategies of the RTW process may differ, the process then has to be monitored and finally evaluated. By dividing the RTW process into these steps, it is also possible to gain an overall view of which stakeholders are involved in the process and which measures need to be initiated. How successful the RTW will be in terms of resulting in an RTW outcome will depend on how successful each component of the process is (Fig. 5.2).

Irrespective of where the assessment takes place, whether performed in a clinical setting, an outpatient vocational setting with various competences involved or in a single case management environment or facility, the assessment must be carried out thoroughly and the focus must be on enabling the individual to RTW. The professionals involved in the assessment must be skilled in different areas of promoting the RTW process. During the assessment stage, the professionals must have the skills to carry out a comprehensive interview covering all aspects of the individual, medical, social and work-based issues. Comprehensive interview instruments have been developed for use in clinical settings and can be helpful in the medical assessment phase [37]. Mcfadden et al. [38] suggest that other assessment tools should be used in combination with other tools when testing functions such as those that assess psychosocial, behavioural and environmental factors; this was also stressed by Sandqvist and Henriksson [39]. They have developed a comprehensive conceptual framework for the assessment of working capacity, focusing on the social perspective in work assessment. They also point out the importance of seeking out the clients' opinion. However, the conceptual framework proposed has to be validated in randomised control trials in order to test its evidence.

Some studies have identified communication as a key factor influencing outcomes in the RTW process. Effective communication is seen as an effective facilitator for an RTW [40]. Open, honest communication is one of the best ways to build a successful relationship between VR professionals and the client [41]. The level of caring or concern demonstrated by the counsellor has the greatest effect on participant satisfaction with the entire VR process [42].

Four prevailing models of disability management are described in the literature as emphasising different aspects of important factors that influence the outcome of the RTW process. The models are: 'medical model', 'physical rehabilitation model', 'job-match model' and 'managed care model'. Pransky et al. [43] stated that communication is often authoritative and unidirectional in these models, with workers and employers in a passive role. They suggest more communication-based interventions, which have been associated with improved satisfaction and outcomes among stakeholders. The common opinion that disability outcomes are unaffected by individual and contextual factors has to be changed. This can be done if all stakeholders involved around the person in need of rehabilitation activities duly inform all involved parties about the actions they have taken.

There is a shift towards greater self-direction in the RTW process, which is manifested in workers taking a leading role in making decisions, setting goals and managing the steps in the services process [44]. Encouraging the individual's participation in the establishment of goals is important as it enables them to be in the centre of the process. This will encourage their commitment and motivation towards attaining the goals. Playford et al. [45] state that the goal setting in rehabilitation is a core component of the rehabilitation process, and it should be specific, ambitious, relevant and time limited. Involvement of the individual in goal setting, goal planning and self-management in the rehabilitation process is emphasised in several studies [45–47]. Intervention plans may vary in content but there is general agreement that the structure of the plan should determine who does what and when and that the individual has to be in the centre.

The implementation stage and monitoring of the RTW process are crucial for understanding how well the components fit the outcome for RTW. Van Beurden et al. [48] conclude that it is essential to pay more attention to the implementation of the RTW process among other stakeholders involved in the process. Implementation is seen as a key stage in the design and evaluation of complex interventions. Martin et al. [49] state that thoroughly investigating the target population characteristics, contextual constraints and the needs and expectations of stakeholders will help the implementation of the RTW interventions. Egan et al. [50] included four systematic reviews in their study and looked at how well the implementation was described in the studies included in the various reviews. Many of the studies referred to implementation, but the reporting of factors important for the study design – such as intervention settings, resources, planning and collaboration – was generally poor and anecdotal in nature. They conclude that the evaluation of complex interventions should include more detailed reporting of the implementation and consider how to measure the quality of implementation. Finger et al. [25] conclude that research is needed to study the outcomes of VR.

5.6.1 Coordination and Monitoring the Process

The OECD [7] stated that better cooperation among stakeholders could lead to more people with disabilities being able to work if they were given the right support at the right time and if there was a more systematic, tailored engagement with clients.

Interventions that provide injured workers with social support in the early recovery stages facilitate RTW [51]. Social function appears to be an important factor in recovery from injury, and case managers or other coordinators could provide social support to increase the rate of RTW.

Schandelmaier et al. [52] found in a meta-analysis of randomised controlled trials moderate quality-level evidence that RTW coordination interventions result in small relative increases in the RTW. There was also a small improvement in function and pain. There was no evidence that one type of RTW coordination programme was superior to another.

Capella and Andrew [53] found in their study that job satisfaction among rehabilitation counsellors was significantly related to consumers' satisfaction. Vocational rehabilitation professionals stated in a study by Dekkers-Sánchez et al. [41] that the use of combined interventions in a holistic approach involving the worker and the environment is considered the best way to maximise the RTW. Shaw et al. [54] carried out a literature study with the objective of describing the activities of RTW coordinators, since they found that the role was poorly described in the literature. They identified six preliminary competence domains. These were ergonomic and workplace assessment, clinical interviewing, social problem solving, workplace mediation, knowledge of business and legal aspects and knowledge of medical conditions. They concluded that successful coordination may depend more on competences in terms of job accommodation, communication and knowledge about conflict resolution than training in medical issues. RTW coordinators and case managers are key players in the RTW process in terms of facilitating how well the process will succeed. This is despite little research into the competences required to manage the role of coordinator. Pransky et al. [55] conducted an Internet-based survey among 75 RTW coordinators from three countries about the competences needed in the field of RTW. Eighteen competences were selected as being necessary for success for RTW coordinators by a majority of the respondents. Some of the rated key competences were: maintaining confidentiality, ethical practices, responding in a timely manner and demonstrating good organisational and planning skills. Other important skills in the RTW context include listening, communication and problem-solving talents. Building a working alliance with the client is also important for better employment outcomes, especially among people with psychiatric disabilities [56].

Return to work is seen both as a process and as an outcome.

Psychosocial variables are important in predicting involvement in the return to work process.

Consensus between supervisor and worker about subjective criteria is important for successful return to work.

The steps in the return to work process often include the following: an interview needs assessment, rehabilitation plan, implementation, monitoring and evaluation.

Communication is a key factor and is seen as an effective facilitator for a return to work.

Stakeholders involved in the process should be informed of the actions taken by all parties as appropriate.

There is a shift towards greater self-direction in the return to work process. Social support in the early recovery stages facilitates return to work.

Satisfaction among rehabilitation counsellors was significantly related to consumers' satisfaction.

Some of the rated key competences for return to work coordinators were: maintaining confidentiality, ethical practices, responding in a timely manner and demonstrating good organisational and planning skills.

5.6.2 *Vocational Rehabilitation Interventions*

The ICF has identified the influence of personal and workplace factors and states that they affect activity and participation levels such as those in the RTW process [57]. Hence, there is a need for well-conducted studies focusing on the workplace. From an ICF perspective, it is important to continue to develop environmental factors to be included in the ICF classification system, since they are important factors in the assessment stage of the RTW process and in designing interventions. In RTW research, there is a need for more environmental factors to be tested in well-conducted studies.

There is a lack of knowledge as to which characteristics of intervention are generally effective and can be included in RTW interventions for multiple target populations [58]. In a systematic literature review Hoefsmit et al. found that early and multidisciplinary intervention and time-contingent mobilising interventions were effective in supporting an RTW in multiple target groups with back pain and adjustment disorders. The effectiveness of early rehabilitation has also been shown in other studies [59–62].

Carroll et al. [61] showed in a systematic review that interventions that implemented work modifications and where employees, health practitioners and employers worked together were more consistently effective than other interventions. They also found that interventions with a workplace component are more likely to be more cost-effective than those without. These results are also supported by an earlier systematic review by Franche et al. [63]. It appears that an RTW and resolution of symptoms are not equivalent. Workplace interventions focus on the work disability problem and not on the underlying medical problem. van Oostrom et al. [64] state that this is in line with the ICF model of the World Health Organisation (WHO) [65], in which the WHO stated that the restoration of (work) participation should be a major treatment goal. The Cochrane review of workplace interventions [64] defined a successful RTW as an interconnected period of 4 weeks without recurrence of sickness absence. The review supports the use of workplace interventions that focus on changes to the equipment in the workplace, how the work or workplace is organised, the working conditions and environment and cooperation between the person on sickness absence and the workplace to improve the rate of RTW following a long period of sickness absence. The authors found only six RCTs to include in the review, however. The lack of studies made it impossible to investigate the effectiveness of workplace interventions among workers with mental problems or other health conditions. In another Cochrane systematic review, Nieuwenhuijsen et al. [66] found no workplace interventions for depression. Neither did they find any effect on improved occupational health in people with depression participating in interventions consisting of medication, enhanced primary care, psychological interventions or a combination of these interventions. van Oostrom et al. [64] conclude that workplace interventions are also lacking for other health conditions, taking cancer as an example. In a systematic review of interventions to enhance RTW for cancer patients, de Boer et al. [67] found a positive effect of multidisciplinary interventions consisting of physical, psychological and vocational components of RTW compared with conventional care. However, they state that none of the interventions they included in their review showed high-quality evidence that any type of intervention was effective in reducing sickness absence or the time to RTW. They conclude that different types of work-related outcome measures, such as work functioning and work productivity, should be used besides sickness absence days and time to RTW.

Lambeck et al. [68] performed a randomised controlled study of individuals with chronic back problems. The results showed that integrated measures had a positive effect on the RTW. 'RTW' was defined as a return to a job of the same scope, either to the person's old job or to another job without loss of salary or wage and with no recurrence of sickness absence. The measures taken were a structured rehabilitation programme coordinated by the occupational health care service. Participants in the programme returned to work significantly earlier than those in the control group.

In a Cochrane review of interventions to facilitate an RTW in adults with adjustment disorder, Arends et al. [69] found nine relevant studies to include in their review. The treatment in the studies consisted of cognitive behavioural therapy (CBT) and problem-solving therapy (PST). The authors conclude that there is moderate-quality evidence that time until a partial RTW at 1-year follow-up was similar for workers receiving CBT as for those receiving no treatment. There was low-quality evidence indicating that CBT was not significantly effective in reducing the time to a full RTW at 1-year follow-up compared with no treatment. Results showed that there was moderate-quality evidence that PST significantly enhanced a partial RTW at 1-year follow-up compared with non-guideline-based care. However, the PTS did not significantly enhance the time taken for a full RTW at 1-year follow-up. In summary, it can be stated that there was insufficient evidence that PST or CBT are effective in restoring individuals back to their full duties. Aas et al. [70] conclude in their Cochrane review about workplace interventions for neck pain in workers that it is still not known whether a specific workplace intervention is likely to reduce pain or not. There is low-quality evidence that there is little or no difference in pain relief for workers with neck pain between those who do and those who do not receive workplace interventions. The authors recommend that researchers use the ICF terminology to ensure that all relevant dimensions of health and functioning are addressed in further trials. In addition, they state that the two main outcomes – pain relief and reduced sickness absence/ RTW – would benefit from standardisation. Another randomised controlled study examined active measures in the local environment and workplace as a means to reduce sickness absence and to promote an RTW in employees with musculoskeletal-related problems [71]. The results show that most measures had a small yet positive effect on the RTW. Modifications to the workplace and support in and around the workplace were somewhat more beneficial than individual measures such as physical training and stress management.

There is a lack of knowledge as to which characteristics of intervention are generally effective and can be included in return to work interventions.

There is a need for well-conducted studies focusing on the workplace.

However, a systematic review showed that interventions that implemented work modifications and where employees, health practitioners and employers worked together were more effective than other interventions.

There is a need for the use of workplace interventions that focus on changes to the equipment in the workplace, how the work or workplace is organised, the working conditions and environment and cooperation.

Other important types of work-related outcome measures to be used in well-conducted studies, besides sickness absence days and time to return to work, are: work functioning and work productivity.

5.7 How to Move Forward in Vocational Rehabilitation from an ICF Perspective

It is important to keep in mind that VR is not a panacea for everyone with a work disability. Many people who have some form of disability that is temporarily preventing them from working will return to some form of work without any special measures being taken. It is important to take note of this so that the measures are aimed at people who really need them in order to RTW. This avoids any problems of selection, i.e. the people who need VR the most are the ones who get it.

The OECD [7] has noticed the shortage of reliable instruments for the assessment of working capacity and stresses in its report the importance of developing reliable instruments for the assessment of working capacity that focus on the individual's opportunities rather than their limitations. The significant increase that has occurred in many countries in recent decades in the number of disabled benefit claimants with some form of work disability has forced a reassessment of the strategy for handling these people. An important reason why people with certain health problems, though with some remaining working capacity, were in practice pensioned off by the systems was that no reliable instruments existed with which to determine the reduction in working capacity.

In terms of assessing working capacity, there is still too much emphasis on a medical diagnosis and the loss of physical or mental functions, particularly when such an examination is performed by a physician with limited knowledge of workplace-related factors, or VR. Edlund and Dahlgren [72] found in their study that doctors have insufficient knowledge about the labour market and social insurance legislation.

This medically focused assessment may either lead directly to the granting of a disability pension or at least may become an important factor in the continued work of assessing how working capacity develops over time [7]. Another problem, which is related to this, is that there is sometimes a perception within the social insurance system that an individual's working capacity cannot be improved, leading to permanent exclusion from the labour market. This assumption is wrong, as nowadays many with some of the most common conditions get better. A third factor that promotes exclusion from the labour market is that individuals, in order to avoid a cut in, or termination of, their benefits, not only have to maintain that they cannot work but also cannot take part in any form of activity that could significantly increase their working capacity, even though financially they are living close to the poverty line. Finally, they need to avoid reporting to the doctor any improvements in their working capacity. In exchange they are given a lifelong disability pension based on the medical certificate.

Patients' demands to be signed off on sickness absence when they visit their doctor also play a role in getting a sickness certificate issued [73, 74]. Among those who, when visiting their doctor, demand to be signed off on sickness absence, there are a number of individuals with some working capacity remaining. From a VR perspective, relying solely on a medical assessment as the foundation for a decision to determine a person's options for returning to work is directly counterproductive. The OECD [7] states that a number of countries have recently made strenuous efforts to move away from assessing a person's illness, instead examining the person's remaining working capacity. This is also in line with the efforts to use the ICF in VR [14]. Such a change in attitude switches the focus to the options for rehabilitating people back into full-time or part-time work, instead of granting them a disability pension.

Denmark is the country that has most clearly changed its emphasis onto a broader approach to examining an individual's remaining working capacity and the possible jobs the person can still perform. A comprehensive individual resource profile covering a range of health and social issues and labour-market experience is also carried out [7]. The Netherlands, with its job-matching assessments, has also shifted its focus. The individual's working capacity is now examined against a hypothetical job on the job market and takes no account of whether or not the job exists. Several other countries have also enhanced their assessment towards a more vocational and RTW approach, which has put the return to the labour market at the centre of the assessment process. A shift is also taking place towards the case management field, where the individual is supported through the RTW process and where the person's abilities and aspirations are in focus.

5.7.1 Case Management

The process can be supported by a single case manager, as in Strengths Model case management, or by a team of professionals, as in the Assertive Community Treatment (ACT) model. In some countries such as the United States, Australia and New Zealand, case managers play an important role in the field of VR. Even in Europe, the case management approach is of growing interest in many countries. The OECD [7] states that case management approaches are important in countries that used to rely heavily on assessments by general practitioners. The trend seems to be towards a greater focus on working capacity, whether partial or full. These changes will put activities focusing on employment and active rehabilitation to the fore. This change in focus towards greater emphasis on relevant factors in individuals and their environment can accelerate an RTW. We should not, however, forget the other relevant factors involved in an RTW process. Naturally, factors relating to the person's physical and mental health status need to be examined and treated in a satisfactory manner. However, this aspect of a person's road towards an RTW should not be allowed to become the predominant phase in the rehabilitation process. Too much emphasis on deficiencies and limitations within the person can mean that the person becomes trapped in a process of examining various physical and mental health factors. The risk then is that the rehabilitation process becomes one that promotes the organisation, not the individual. The individual's strengths, abilities, talents and interests are what need to be mobilised in the RTW process. The Strengths Model-based approach concentrates on mobilising the strengths of the individual, social network, organisations and society in the rehabilitation process. These strengths are used to enable a recovery-oriented attitude to become the predominant approach in VR. This challenges the usual focus on clients' deficiencies to a focus on possibilities and solutions [16, 75]. Strengths-based approaches can work on a number of different levels, including individuals, associations and organisations right through to communities.

5.7.2 The Strengths Model

The strengths perspective is well known in the case management field through Strengths Model case management [16]. Strengths Model case management has different tools to promote a person's full integration into society. One tool is the Strengths-based assessment document, which focuses on the individual's strengths. It offers a holistic view of the individual. The primary focus is not on problems or deficiencies; instead, the individual is given support to recognise the inherent strengths and resources that exist within a person and which ones they can use in their rehabilitation process. The Strengths-based resources they have at their disposal operate in seven life domains. In brief, these are: day-to-day living, finance and insurance, employment and education, social networks, health, leisure, spirituality and culture. Within each domain, a comprehensive assessment is performed that looks at the strengths of the individual, focusing on those strengths previously employed by the individual and those which remain, as well as looking at which of these strengths can be mobilised to move the rehabilitation process forward [16].

5.7.3 The ICF Concept

The ICF is both a theoretical model and a classification system. Within the ICF, personal factors have not been coded, while environmental factors require further development and possibly specification of those factors that are important in VR. The discussion as to how the ICF system can be implemented and form an important instrument in VR and as such help to facilitate the VR process for people with a work disability needs to be based on both these perspectives. Is the ICF applicable as a theoretical model in VR, and can the classification instruments within the ICF developed for the assessment of a person's body structures, activities, participation and environmental factors, as well as personal factors, accelerate an RTW for a person with a work disability? In order to be able to reply to this question, we need to return to how the limitations that are currently associated with the use of the ICF may be resolved. Despite the limitations of the ICF, there are numerous advantages to implementing the ICF within VR (Fig. 5.3).

The importance of the need to be able to code personal factors has been emphasised in a number of studies [23, 25, 76]. One reason why they have not

Fig. 5.3 A visualisation of the present ICF concept with its benefits and limitations

been coded is the variety of cultural contexts in which people find themselves. How to perform the coding needs to be the subject of discussion, as it may be done both from a problem-oriented viewpoint and on the basis of the person's own strengths and abilities. The latter viewpoint would make it easier to code personal factors, as these are usually not dependent on the cultural context in which people find themselves. Everyone has abilities, talents, personal skills and strengths in various areas, though illness may have contributed to these being no longer in focus. For those people working in VR, it is a question of mobilising them. In order to do this, they need to be made visible. This can be achieved by coding the personal factors from a Strengths perspective. The Strengths assessment tool can be used for support in coding the personal factors. In this way, we are able to move away from terms such as 'losses' and 'deviations' during the assessment stage. This can be vital in determining whether or not rehabilitation later succeeds. It is also important when dealing with people to mention strengths and abilities, not weaknesses and problems. Building up a trusting relationship between the rehabilitator and the individual is regarded as fundamental to the success of the rehabilitation process [16]. Several studies have reported promising results when using the Strengths Model case management in the RTW process [77–80].

The ICF is complex and time-consuming [81]. A major challenge is to make the ICF a global classification system within a variety of rehabilitation settings. Time is often an item that is commonly constrained for people working in the health care area, including those who work in rehabilitation in clinical settings or outside clinical settings in case management agencies, social insurance administration and employment offices. In order for the implementation of the ICF to succeed in all these areas, it is, of course, necessary for the ICF to be implemented at both the society and organisational levels and made intelligible at the individual level. If support at the society level is available, the task remains to train those who will use the ICF. This can be done in a variety of ways. Training courses must be comprehensive enough to reach the stage where the advantages of using the ICF outweigh the disadvantages. They also need to be recurrent and to become a natural part of working with VR. With regard to this, it is important to examine whether or not the level of training is sufficiently high in those who work in the field of VR and who will be working on the ICF classification system to enable them to profit from the training.

In order to facilitate the classification of the various constituent factors of the ICF, a comprehensive and a brief Core Set have been developed. These Core Sets will make cooperation easier among the various stakeholders during the VR process. Core Sets have also to be developed in different settings and adjusted to the different environments. A core set for functional assessments in disability benefit claims has been developed to be used by medical doctors. It is intended for evaluation of rights to long-term benefits [82]. A VR-Pain Core Set has also been developed with content that covers relevant domains for pain and VR [83]. The social insurance agencies, job offices and case managers working in different settings, whether alone or in teams, may need other Core Sets developed by social workers – not only those that focus on medical assessment. Environmental factors such as important work factors have to be developed within the ICF as they are particularly important in job placement [25]. Core Sets are not the only tool to be used, but they can be a complement to, or used alongside, other assessment tools.

If the ICF is to be accepted in the area of VR, there will also need to be evidence of the ICF's classification instrument. In the day-to-day rehabilitation work in the field of VR, it will be important to know that the ICF classification is living up to its intended purpose, i.e. to facilitate rehabilitation work so that people with injury or a health condition can return to the labour market. It is also important to know that the ICF classification instrument is practical for use at individual, organisational and society levels in terms of VR. The common language must also facilitate communication between the various stakeholders, including the individual. It must also be possible for the ICF classification system to allow comparisons between countries, service operations and health and nursing care services. Suitable indicators need to be developed in order to validate the ICF and its aims, showing how well the ICF is working; it may be possible to validate these indicators in randomised controlled studies. Validation can also be performed via ongoing evaluations of how well the categories work in terms of describing what they are designed to describe. The search for evidence supporting the view that the ICF classification works must be pursued. Besides evaluation of the categories, tools and measuring instruments are used within the ICF, e.g. VR Core Sets and the ICF checklist; this can be done using various sources such as scientific journals, books and recurrent rehabilitation congresses, as well as via colleagues working actively with the ICF within their respective professional areas.

There is a need to develop reliable instruments for assessment of working capacity that focus on opportunities rather than limitations.

More focus must be placed on the individual's strengths, abilities, talents and interests in the return to work process.

The recovery-oriented attitude has to be the predominant approach in vocational rehabilitation.

The Strengths-based assessment document could be used in parallel with the ICF Core Sets or be incorporated into the ICF Core Sets.

ICF environmental factors, as well as important work factors, have to be developed, and personal factors have to be coded.

The ICF classification instrument has to be evaluated in well-conducted studies.

5.8 Conclusion

Helping people with injuries or health conditions that prevent them from working to return to the labour market and once again to be productive members of society can be regarded as one of the most important tasks of VR. This is also emphasised in the definition of VR that the ICF has drawn up, where some of the key words are 'optimising work participation'. VR is a complicated activity, partly because of the background of being practised in varied organisational bodies with the involvement of various specialised professionals. VR is also carried out under the social insurance systems of various countries, which can affect who becomes a subject for VR, how the VR process is performed, and what the outcome is. However, by using the definition drawn up by the ICF, a foundation has been established to allow constructive discussions to begin on what should be included in VR and what the concept stands for. It is hoped that the discussion about what is VR and what is medical rehabilitation will gradually subside, which will result in better cooperation between medical and vocational rehabilitation players. ICF Core Sets could facilitate the understanding of what VR is and what its aims are. VR can be regarded both as an overall process in its own right and also as being identical to the RTW process. The RTW process can be seen as both a process and an outcome in the VR process. Some researchers stress that the RTW process is poorly defined. There are, however, some components in the RTW process that are important to emphasise. This applies in particular to the assessment stage. There are a great many tools for assessment but these need to be validated in scientific studies. The VR ICF Core Sets, together with other assessment tools, can play an important role in the future in streamlining the RTW process. As far as VR interventions are concerned, there is some support for the idea that workplace interventions have a certain effect on the RTW. However, there are a limited number of well-conducted studies that focus on the RTW process from a workplace perspective. It is important to make use of individuals' remaining working capacity, something that is entirely in line with the ICF and its biopsychosocial approach. In this way, the focus is switched to rehabilitating people back to work instead of just providing disability pension without just cause or fair process. During the assessment phase, it is also important to mobilise the person's strengths and abilities rather than focusing on their limitations and weaknesses. This is where the Strengths assessment tools can help, and these can be applied in parallel with the VR Core Sets assessment. The visualisation of the present ICF concept on the basis of benefits and limitations shows a number of important benefits. The ICF concept has a comprehensive and integrative approach: it addresses the fragmentation of the rehabilitation services, such as the various inpatient and outpatient settings that exist today, and there is a common language as well as the VR Core Sets. What is important now is for the ICF Core Sets to be applied to various settings, for environmental factors to be developed and for personal factors to be coded. The ICF concept also needs to be evaluated in well-conducted studies. All efforts have to be taken into account in order to emphasise the importance of VR. This has to be done at all levels, i.e. at society, organisational and individual levels.

Study Questions It is well established in research that work is important for a person's health and well-being.

1. How can society promote this among staff working with vocational rehabilitation?

   Answer: Work has a central place in societies and is highly valued in people's lives. It provides an important meaning to life, as well as providing structure to the various life domains that make up a person's social context. Having a job is crucial to inclusion and it can also promote personal needs, such as enhanced self-efficacy, as well as giving a feeling of making a contribution to society. Health problems among unemployed people are common, as shown in many studies; it is therefore important that those working in the rehabilitation field are well educated and get the training and skills to work for the inclusion of sick and injured people in society. It is important for society to support the universities and other educational institutions so they can offer programmes in vocational rehabilitation to meet the needs of well-educated staff in the rehabilitation field.

2. When looking at the differences in the organisation of vocational rehabilitation in different countries, what conclusions can you draw regarding the differences of outcomes in vocational rehabilitation research?

   Answer: One conclusion that can be drawn is that the design of the social insurance systems in the different countries varies and makes comparing the outcome from different vocational rehabilitation systems difficult. In some countries vocational rehabilitation can start early, and in some countries it can start late, meaning that the conditions for rehabilitation are different, which can influence the outcome. How long-term sickness absence is defined can also make a difference. How return to work is defined can also play a role when looking at the outcome of vocational rehabilitation. Is the person going back to their normal work or to another job, and is it on a full-time or part-time basis? All these questions have to be taken into account when discussing outcomes from vocational rehabilitation research in the different countries. You also have to look at how the labour market in different countries is organised.

3. Now that you have read about the different definitions of vocational rehabilitation described in this chapter, what is your opinion on the definition given by the ICF? Is it comprehensive enough to support the person's aspirations to return to work?

   Answer: Sometimes it can be difficult to distinguish between medical rehabilitation and vocational rehabilitation. Some researchers stress that medical rehabilitation primarily aims to restore functional capacity, while vocational rehabilitation is about the relationship between an individual's capacity for working and the requirements of the job. If the aim is for the person to regain their working capacity and create conditions whereby they can support themselves through employment, then this may be regarded as vocational rehabilitation. This is in line with the definition proposed by the ICF, which covers a broad spectrum of services and set of clients and which includes the key expression "optimising work participation".

4. What evidence can you provide that good assessment is vital to the vocational rehabilitation process?

   Answer: Assessment is more than just assessing the individual's problems or limitations. It also involves identifying the strengths of the individual, and identifying the strengths within the environment in which the individual operates. Without knowing the individual's strengths, abilities and talents, the vocational rehabilitation process may be delayed or unsuccessful.

5. Do you agree that good communication skills are essential to provide effective support to a person's return to work process? If yes, what are they, and why are they important?

   Answer: Studies have identified communication as a key factor influencing outcomes in the RTW process. Open, honest communication is one of the best ways to build a successful relationship between VR professionals and the client. Research has shown that the level of caring or concern demonstrated by the counsellor has the greatest effect on participant satisfaction with the entire VR process. Communication at the first meeting with the physician is also probably crucial to how well the next steps in the VR process will succeed.

6. There is a shift towards greater self-direction in the return to work process. How can the person take a more active part in the return to work process?

Answer: Encouraging the individual's participation in the establishment of goals is important as it enables them to be in the centre of the process. This will encourage their commitment and motivation towards attaining the goals. Involvement of the individual in goal setting, goal planning and self-management in the rehabilitation process is emphasised in several studies.

7. Cooperation between the different stakeholders involved in the vocational rehabilitation process is seen as important. How can cooperation between different stakeholders be achieved in a more systematic way?

   Answer: To achieve a more systematic way to cooperate, the stakeholders can work in accordance with a coordinated interdisciplinary approach, which means that the team of stakeholders set mutual goals for the VR process and then work from each profession to reach the goals they have set.

8. Successful cooperation often depends on skills among people working in the rehabilitation field. Which skills do you rate as most important in bringing about effective cooperation among different stakeholders?

   Answer: Successful cooperation can be achieved if the coordinators have similar competences. Some rated key competences are: maintaining confidentiality, ethical practices, responding in a timely manner and demonstrating good organisational and planning skills. Other important skills are listening and communication and problem-solving talents and respect for each other's work.

9. When assessing the working capacity, it seems that much focus is put on weakness and limitations. How can this be changed to focus more on the strengths and abilities of the person?

   Answer: This can be done if rehabilitation counsellors and others working in the rehabilitation field use assessment tools that focus on the individual's strengths, abilities and talents instead of tools focusing on weakness, problems and deficits. In the Strengths Model case management, they use an assessment tool that focuses on the individual's strengths.

10. How can the ICF classification instrument be of practical use at individual, organisational and society levels in vocational rehabilitation?

    Answer: The different stakeholders can use a common language that will facilitate the understanding of the rehabilitation process at both individual, organisational and society levels.

11. In what way can PMR conferences and rehabilitation congresses highlight vocational rehabilitation and its importance at individual, organisational and society level?

    Answer: This can be done if PMR conferences and rehabilitation congresses highlight the importance of vocational rehabilitation by encouraging researchers in the vocational rehabilitation field to participate with papers at the conferences and congresses.

References

1. Stubbs J, Deaner G. When considering vocational rehabilitation: describing and comparing the Swedish and American systems and professions. Work. 2005;24(3):239–49.
2. Holmes J. Vocational rehabilitation. Oxford: Blackwell; 2007.
3. Langman C. Introduction to vocational rehabilitation: policies, practices and skills. London/New York: Routledge/Taylor and Francis; 2012.
4. Marnetoft S. Vocational rehabilitation of unemployed sick-listed people in a Swedish rural area: an individual-level study based on social insurance data. Stockholm: Diss. Stockholm: Karolinska institutet; 2000.
5. S 2010:04. Arbetslivsinriktad rehabilitering. Underlagsrapport nr 7 till den parlamentariska socialförsäkringsutredningen. Statens Offentliga Utredningar. S 2010:04. Available at: http://www.psfu.se/uploads/files/7_arbetslivsinriktad_rehabilitering.pdf. Accessed 4 Feb 2014.
6. Marnetoft S. The challenges of vocational rehabilitation in Sweden. Kuntoutus Fin J Rehabil. 2009;4:5–10.
7. Organisation for Economic Co-Operation and Development. Sickness, disability and work: breaking the barriers; a synthesis of findings across OECD countries. Paris: OECD; 2010.
8. Wikström J. Management of early retirement by improvement of wellbeing at work and by vocational rehabilitation in disability. 7th Mediterranean Congress of PRM. Book of abstracts Portorož, Slovenia; 2008. p. 55.
9. Reine I, Novo M, Hammarstrom A. Does the association between ill health and unemployment differ between young people and adults? Results from a 14-year follow-up study with a focus on psychological health and smoking. Public Health. 2004;118(5):337–45.
10. Stankunas M, Kalediene R, Starkuviene S, Kapustinskiene V. Duration of unemployment and depression: a cross-sectional survey in Lithuania. BMC Public Health. 2006;6:174.
11. Roelfs DJ, Shor E, Davidson KW, Schwartz JE. Losing life and livelihood: a systematic review and meta-analysis of unemployment and all-cause mortality. Soc Sci Med. 2011;72(6):840–54.
12. Carlier BE, Schuring M, Lotters FJB, Bakker B, Borgers N, Burdorf A. The influence of re-employment on quality of life and self-rated health, a longitudinal study among unemployed persons in the Netherlands. BMC Public Health. 2013;13:503.
13. Selander J. Unemployed sick-leavers and vocational rehabilitation: a person-level study based on a national social insurance material [thesis]. Stockholm: Karolinska institutet; 1999.
14. Escorpizo R, Reneman MF, Ekholm J, Fritz J, Krupa T, Marnetoft S, et al. A conceptual definition of vocational rehabilitation based on the ICF: building a shared global model. J Occup Rehabil. 2011;21(2):126–33.
15. Waddell G, Burton AK, Kendall NA. Vocational rehabilitation–what works, for whom, and when? (Report for the Vocational Rehabilitation Task Group); 2008.
16. Rapp CA, Goscha RJ. The strengths model: a recovery oriented approach to mental health services. 3rd ed. New York: Oxford University Press; 2012.
17. Ekberg K. Arbetslivsinriktad rehabilitering. In: Edling C, editor. Arbets- och miljömedicin: en lärobok om hälsa och miljö. Lund: Studentlitteratur; 2010.
18. Germundsson P, Danermark B. Vocational rehabilitation, interagency collaboration and social representations. Work. 2012;42(4):507–17.
19. Matheson L. Measuring work performance from an occupational performance perspective. In: Law MC, Baum CM, Dunn W, editors. Measuring occupational performance: supporting best practice in occupational therapy. Thorofare: Slack; 2001. p. 103–20.
20. Finger ME, Escorpizo R, Glassel A, Gmunder HP, Luckenkemper M, Chan C, et al. ICF Core Set for vocational rehabilitation: results of an international consensus conference. Disabil Rehabil. 2012;34(5):429–38.
21. Saltychev M, Kinnunen A, Laimi K. Vocational rehabilitation evaluation and the International Classification of Functioning, Disability, and Health (ICF). J Occup Rehabil. 2013;23(1):106–14.

22. Ptyushkin P, Vidmar G, Burger H, Marincek C, Escorpizo R. The International Classification of Functioning, Disability and Health (ICF) in vocational rehabilitation and disability assessment in Slovenia: state of law and users' perspective. Disabil Rehabil. 2011;33(2):130–6.
23. Glassel A, Finger ME, Cieza A, Treitler C, Coenen M, Escorpizo R. Vocational rehabilitation from the client's perspective using the International Classification of Functioning, Disability and Health (ICF) as a reference. J Occup Rehabil. 2011;21(2):167–78.
24. Dekkers-Sanchez PM, Wind H, Sluiter JK, Frings-Dresen MHW. A qualitative study of perpetuating factors for long term sick leave and promoting factors for return to work: chronic work disabled patients in their own words. J Rehabil Med. 2010;42(6):544–52.
25. Finger ME, Glassel A, Erhart P, Gradinger F, Klipstein A, Rivier G, et al. Identification of relevant ICF categories in vocational rehabilitation: a cross sectional study evaluating the clinical perspective. J Occup Rehabil. 2011;21(2):156–66.
26. Anema JR, Schellart AJM, Cassidy JD, Loisel P, Veerman TJ, van der Beek AJ. Can cross country differences in return-to-work after chronic occupational back pain be explained? An exploratory analysis on disability policies in a six country cohort study. J Occup Rehabil. 2009;19(4):419–26.
27. Pransky G, Gatchel R, Linton SJ, Loisel P. Improving return to work research. J Occup Rehabil. 2005;15(4):453–7.
28. Young AE, Roessler RT, Wasiak R, McPherson KM, van Poppel MNM, Anema JR. A developmental conceptualization of return to work. J Occup Rehabil. 2005;15(4):557–68.
29. Leyshon R, Shaw L. Using multiple stakeholders to define a successful return to work: a concept mapping approach. Work. 2012;41(4):397–408.
30. Hunt DG, Zuberbier OA, Kozlowski AJ, Berkowitz J, Schultz IZ, Milner RA, et al. Are components of a comprehensive medical assessment predictive of work disability after an episode of occupational low back trouble? Spine. 2002;27(23):2715–9.
31. Norrmen G, Svardsudd K, Andersson DKG. How primary health care physicians make sick listing decisions: the impact of medical factors and functioning. BMC Fam Pract. 2008;9:3.
32. Laisne F, Lecomte C, Corbiere M. Biopsychosocial determinants of work outcomes of workers with occupational injuries receiving compensation: a prospective study. Work. 2013;44(2): 117–32.
33. Hillborg H, Danermark B, Svensson T. Professionals' perceptions of and views about vocational rehabilitation for people with psychiatric disabilities. Work. 2013;44(4):471–80.
34. Hees HL, Nieuwenhuijsen K, Koeter MWJ, Bultmann U, Schene AH. Towards a new definition of return-to-work outcomes in common mental disorders from a multi-stakeholder perspective. PLoS One. 2012;7(6):e39947.
35. Tjulin A, Edvardsson Stiwne E, Ekberg K. Experience of the implementation of a multi-stakeholder return-to-work programme. J Occup Rehabil. 2009;19(4):409–18.
36. Stahl C, Svensson T, Petersson G, Ekberg K. A matter of trust? A study of coordination of Swedish stakeholders in return-to-work. J Occup Rehabil. 2010;20(3):299–310.
37. Durand M, Loisel P, Hong QN, Charpentier N. Helping clinicians in work disability prevention: the work disability diagnosis interview. J Occup Rehabil. 2002;12(3):191–204.
38. McFadden S, MacDonald A, Fogarty A, Le S, Merritt BK. Vocational assessment: a review of the literature from an occupation-based perspective. Scand J Occup Ther. 2010;17(1):43–8.
39. Sandqvist JL, Henriksson CM. Work functioning: a conceptual framework. Work. 2004;23(2): 147–57.
40. Friesen MN, Yassi A, Cooper J. Return-to-work: the importance of human interactions and organizational structures. Work. 2001;17(1):11–22.
41. Dekkers-Sanchez PM, Wind H, Sluiter JK, Hw Frings-Dresen MHW. What promotes sustained return to work of employees on long-term sick leave? Perspectives of vocational rehabilitation professionals. Scand J Work Environ Health. 2011;37(6):481–93.
42. Scovotti C, Peltier JW. Participant satisfaction with the vocational rehabilitation process: a micro perspective of relationship dimensions. Health Mark Q. 2005;22(4):3–26.

43. Pransky G, Shaw W, Franche R, Clarke A. Disability prevention and communication among workers, physicians, employers, and insurers–current models and opportunities for improvement. Disabil Rehabil. 2004;26(11):625–34.
44. Hatchard K, Henderson J, Stanton S. Workers' perspectives on self-directing mainstream return to work following acute mental illness: reflections on partnerships. Work. 2012;43(1): 43–52.
45. Playford ED, Siegert R, Levack W, Freeman J. Areas of consensus and controversy about goal setting in rehabilitation: a conference report. Clin Rehabil. 2009;23(4):334–44.
46. Jones F, Livingstone E, Hawkes L. "Getting the balance between encouragement and taking over" – reflections on using a new stroke self-management programme. Physiother Res Int. 2013;18(2):91–9.
47. Johnston V, Jull G, Sheppard DM, Ellis N. Applying principles of self-management to facilitate workers to return to or remain at work with a chronic musculoskeletal condition. Man Ther. 2013;18(4):274–80.
48. van Beurden KM, Vermeulen SJ, Anema JR, van der Beek AJ. A participatory return-to-work program for temporary agency workers and unemployed workers sick-listed due to musculoskeletal disorders: a process evaluation alongside a randomized controlled trial. J Occup Rehabil. 2012;22(1):127–40.
49. Martin MHT, Nielsen MBD, Petersen SMA, Jakobsen LM, Rugulies R. Implementation of a coordinated and tailored return-to-work intervention for employees with mental health problems. J Occup Rehabil. 2012;22(3):427–36.
50. Egan M, Bambra C, Petticrew M, Whitehead M. Reviewing evidence on complex social interventions: appraising implementation in systematic reviews of the health effects of organisational-level workplace interventions. J Epidemiol Community Health. 2009;63(1): 4–11.
51. Clay FJ, Fitzharris M, Kerr E, McClure RJ, Watson WL. The association of social functioning, social relationships and the receipt of compensation with time to return to work following unintentional injuries to Victorian workers. J Occup Rehabil. 2012;22(3):363–75.
52. Schandelmaier S, Ebrahim S, Burkhardt SCA, de Boer WEL, Zumbrunn T, Guyatt GH, et al. Return to work coordination programmes for work disability: a meta-analysis of randomised controlled trials. PLoS One. 2012;7(11):e49760.
53. Capella ME, Andrew JD. The relationship between counselor job satisfaction and consumer satisfaction in vocational rehabilitation. Rehabil Couns Bull. 2004;47(4):205–14.
54. Shaw W, Hong Q, Pransky G, Loisel P. A literature review describing the role of return-to-work coordinators in trial programs and interventions designed to prevent workplace disability. J Occup Rehabil. 2008;18(1):2–15.
55. Pransky G, Shaw WS, Loisel P, Hong QN, Desorcy B. Development and validation of competencies for return to work coordinators. J Occup Rehabil. 2010;20(1):41–8.
56. Donnell CM, Lustig DC, Strauser DR. The working alliance: rehabilitation outcomes for persons with severe mental illness. J Rehabil. 2004;70(2):12–8.
57. Wasiak R, Young AE, Roessler RT, McPherson KM, van Poppel MNM, Anema JR. Measuring return to work. J Occup Rehabil. 2007;17(4):766–81.
58. Hoefsmit N, Houkes I, Nijhuis FJN. Intervention characteristics that facilitate return to work after sickness absence: a systematic literature review. J Occup Rehabil. 2012;22(4):462–77.
59. Marnetoft SU, Selander J, Bergroth A, Ekholm J. Factors associated with successful vocational rehabilitation in a Swedish rural area. J Rehabil Med. 2001;33(2):71–8.
60. Kuoppala J, Lamminpaa A. Rehabilitation and work ability: a systematic literature review. J Rehabil Med. 2008;40(10):796–804.
61. Carroll C, Rick J, Pilgrim H, Cameron J, Hillage J. Workplace involvement improves return to work rates among employees with back pain on long-term sick leave: a systematic review of the effectiveness and cost-effectiveness of interventions. Disabil Rehabil. 2010;32(8):607–21.
62. Dekkers-Sanchez PM, Wind H, Sluiter JK, Frings-Dresen MHW. What factors are most relevant to the assessment of work ability of employees on long-term sick leave?

The physicians' perspective. Int Arch Occup Environ Health. 2012. Published online 2012/05/24. doi:10.1007/s00420-012-0783-3
63. Franche R, Cullen K, Clarke J, Irvin E, Sinclair S, Frank J, et al. Workplace-based return-to-work interventions: a systematic review of the quantitative literature. J Occup Rehabil. 2005;15(4):607–31.
64. van Oostrom SH, Driessen MT, de Vet HCW, Franche R, Schonstein E, Loisel P, et al. Workplace interventions for preventing work disability. Cochrane Database Syst Rev. 2009;(2):D006955.
65. World Health Organization. International classification of functioning, disability and health: ICF. Geneva: WHO; 2001.
66. Nieuwenhuijsen K, Bultmann U, Neumeyer-Gromen A, Verhoeven AC, Verbeek JHAM, van der Feltz-Cornelis CM. Interventions to improve occupational health in depressed people. Cochrane Database Syst Rev. 2008;(2):D006237.
67. de Boer AG, Taskila T, Tamminga SJ, Frings-Dresen MH, Feuerstein M, Verbeek JH. Interventions to enhance return-to-work for cancer patients. Cochrane Database Syst Rev. 2011;(2):D007569.
68. Lambeek LC, van Mechelen W, Knol DL, Loisel P, Anema JR. Randomised controlled trial of integrated care to reduce disability from chronic low back pain in working and private life. BMJ. 2010;340:1035.
69. Arends I, Bruinvels DJ, Rebergen DS, Nieuwenhuijsen K, Madan I, Neumeyer-Gromen A, et al. Interventions to facilitate return to work in adults with adjustment disorders. Cochrane Database Syst Rev. 2012;12, D006389.
70. Aas RW, Tuntland H, Holte KA, Roe C, Lund T, Marklund S, et al. Workplace interventions for neck pain in workers. Cochrane Database Syst Rev. 2011(4):D008160.
71. Palmer KT, Harris EC, Linaker C, Barker M, Lawrence W, Cooper C, et al. Effectiveness of community- and workplace-based interventions to manage musculoskeletal-related sickness absence and job loss: a systematic review. Rheumatol. 2012;51(2):230–42.
72. Edlund C, Dahlgren L. The physician's role in the vocational rehabilitation process. Disabil Rehabil. 2002;24(14):727–33.
73. Campbell A, Ogden J. Why do doctors issue sick notes? An experimental questionnaire study in primary care. Fam Pract. 2006;23(1):125–30.
74. Wrapson W, Mewse AJ. Does the doctor or the patient control sick leave certification? A qualitative study interpreting patients' interview dialogue. Fam Pract. 2011;28(2):202–9.
75. Saleebey D. Strengths perspective in social work practice, 4/e. New York: Allyn & Bacon; 2006.
76. Pless M, Adolfsson M. Handbok i att använda ICF och ICF-CY. Stockholm: Studentlitteratur; 2011.
77. Marnetoft S, Selander J. Multidisciplinary vocational rehabilitation focusing on work training and case management for unemployed sick-listed people. Int J Rehabil Res. 2000;23(4):271–9.
78. Selander J, Marnetoft S. Case management in vocational rehabilitation: a case study with promising results. Work. 2005;24(3):297–304.
79. Latimer E, Rabouin D. Case management for moderate-need patients and recovery: what can we learn from experimental and quasi-experimental studies? Sante Ment Que. 2011;36(1): 13–34.
80. Fukui S, Goscha R, Rapp CA, Mabry A, Liddy P, Marty D. Strengths model case management fidelity scores and client outcomes. Psychiatr Serv. 2012;63(7):708–10.
81. Helander E. A critical review of the International Classification of Functioning, Disability and Health (ICF). Available at: http://www.einarhelander.com/critical-review-ICF.pdf. Accessed 4 Feb 2014.
82. Brage S, Donceel P, Falez F, Working Group of the European Union of Medicine in Assurance and Social Security. Development of ICF core set for disability evaluation in social security. Disabil Rehabil. 2008;30(18):1392–6.
83. Reneman MF, Beemster TT, Edelaar MJA, van Velzen JM, van Bennekom C, Escorpizo R. Towards an ICF- and IMMPACT-based pain vocational rehabilitation core set in the Netherlands. J Occup Rehabil. 2013;23(4):576–84.

Part II
State of the Field: Vocational Rehabilitation and Disability Evaluation

Chapter 6
Work Disability Evaluation

Sören Brage, Ása Dóra Konráðsdóttir, and Gert Lindenger

6.1 Introduction

The International Classification of Functioning, Disability, and Health (ICF) was published in 2001 and was met with considerable interest in the field of social security [1]. Social insurance institutions and private insurance need to measure and assess the functioning of claimants, but there has been a lack of a universally accepted terminology, definitions, and classification. Physicians in social insurance medicine envision that the ICF could help provide guidance in their work [2].

Several attempts to make use of the ICF have been made in research, practice, and policy making in social insurance [3–5]. In this chapter, we aim to describe and discuss some of these attempts. Our focus will be on the European experience. We are aware of recent and important advances made in US Social Security [6] and expect that knowledge from other parts of the world will come as well.

This chapter describes and discusses the ICF in the perspective of social insurance and, in particular, in the evaluation of work disability. In many social insurance institutions, disability evaluation is also performed outside of the work context, for example, in determining the right to assistive aids or devices, or accident assurance, but that is not our scope here. It is also important to stress that disability is a relational term, meaning that a person cannot be disabled in general but has disability in relation to something external, in our case work [7]. We aim to describe the process of disability evaluation, how work ability is assessed,

S. Brage (✉)
Research Unit, Directorate for Labour and Welfare, Oslo, Norway
e-mail: soren.brage@medisin.uio.no

Á.D. Konráðsdóttir
VIRK Rehabilitation Fund, Reykjavik, Iceland

G. Lindenger
Main Office, Swedish Social Insurance Agency, Stockholm, Sweden

R. Escorpizo et al. (eds.), *Handbook of Vocational Rehabilitation and Disability Evaluation*, Handbooks in Health, Work, and Disability, DOI 10.1007/978-3-319-08825-9_6

the experience with a core set for social security, and examples from Scandinavian countries of the use of the ICF in social insurance institutions. We will also discuss the link between vocational rehabilitation and disability evaluation.

There is a need for commonly accepted terminology and definitions regarding work disability evaluations in social security.

6.2 Disability Benefit Rates Are Increasing

Over he last 20 years, there has been a growth in Europe in the number of persons who are dependent on disability benefits for their living [8]. From the midst of the 1990s up to 2008, only a few countries in the Organisation for Economic Co-operation and Development (OECD) (namely, Finland, Hungary, Luxembourg, the Netherlands, Poland, Portugal, and the Slovak Republic) had a decline in disability beneficiary rates, while the majority showed flat rates or increase, which were in some cases substantial. Around 6 % of the OECD working-age population received a disability benefit in 2007. The increase has been a major concern, since it is costly for the individual and society.

In addition, the social and economic situation for persons with disabilities has shown signs of deterioration in the last decades. Disabled persons are less employed than others, and they live more frequently in poverty. The situation is particularly grave for persons with disability due to mental health problems. This group is now the largest single group and includes many young persons, who will stay on disability benefit for a long time, with little hope for better social and economic integration. It is an important effort to make the labor market truly inclusive for persons with mental and physical disabilities [8].

In a series of reports, the OECD has suggested a shift in policy. Instead of granting passive, sometimes lifelong, benefits, they suggest a stronger focus on reintegration into employment if the persons can and wish to work. Such a shift has already taken place in many OECD countries with a search for a new balance between the two conflicting goals of disability policy, on one hand to provide an adequate and secure income for those who cannot work and on the other hand to provide good incentives and support to work for those who can. In some countries, a broad range of employment and rehabilitation services has been introduced.

To achieve higher work participation, the OECD recommends assessment of work capacity, not work disability. In the view of OECD, one should start "with an assessment of the remaining work capacity of a person applying for a benefit and provide adequate employment supports to try to maintain the claimant in contact with the labor market. The assessment and corresponding support should be done quickly so as to avoid claimants being inactive for too long and losing contact with the labor market" [8].

Some of the policy changes suggested by the OECD would have as a consequence a stronger and closer cooperation between the rehabilitation part of the health sector and the social insurance institutions. Vocational rehabilitation as a mandatory step before disability benefits is one example of such cooperation, but also later attempts to continue to rehabilitate persons already on benefits.

Disability benefit rates have increased in the larger part of OECD. It is better to reintegrate employees with reduced work ability and reform the labor market rather than to continue granting disability benefits.

6.3 Evaluation of Work Disability Is a Process in Several Steps

The disability evaluations in European social security are carried out in several steps, and the characteristics of these steps depend on type of benefit. In the present context, we only address benefits that are given to provide income substitution in case of ill health. For shorter time periods, sick leave (sickness absence) benefits are usually given. For longer periods, disability benefits are granted. In some countries, there is an intermediate period where medical or vocational rehabilitation can elicit other types of cash benefits, for example, rehabilitation allowance. We will describe and discuss disability evaluation in these different situations.

Our aim is to describe the various settings and methods for processing and deciding on claims for benefits, when the employee is unable to work due to ill health. We first describe the entire, institutionalized process of *evaluation* of work ability. Such evaluations are carried out to decide on the rights to various social or welfare benefits and encompass many steps and involve many actors and many professional areas. Later in this chapter, we will examine more closely the part of the evaluation process where the claimant's work ability is described and linked to his or her work demands and medical condition. This is named the *assessment* of work ability. A single-person assessor frequently does the assessment.

The terminology in this field is confusing. Different terms like work ability, work capacity, job capacity, and work capability, however, basically denote the same phenomenon. We prefer and try to be consistent in using "work ability" (and "disability" for the opposite). Occasionally we use other terms than work ability when we refer to specific national programs that use other terms.

In the European setting, employees are usually covered by insurance systems in case of absence from work due to illness or injury. For historical, political, cultural, and economic reasons, each country has constructed its own and unique insurance arrangements. The variation can at first be seemingly overwhelming, but many traits are shared between countries [9–11]. It is therefore possible to make some generalizations and describe some common traits.

There is, in general, national legislation on the rights to benefits, including both short-term and long-term benefits and, in addition, administrative rules that describe more in detail how claims for benefits are to be handled. The claims are sent to and processed in a Social Insurance Institution that either can be a public agency (typically in northern and eastern Europe) or large corporate agencies. An administrative officer at the Social Insurance Institution usually makes the decision on the claim. For the decision, however, the officer commonly relies on medical information from health professionals and on professional advice from social insurance physicians. Frequently, the social insurance physicians are employed or assigned by the Social Insurance Institution.

6.3.1 Short-Term Absence: Sick Leave

Most evaluations of work disability take place in the sick leave period. They are simpler than the evaluations for long-term benefits. There is an impressive variation in sick leave schemes in Europe but also some common traits. The sick leave schemes frequently cover a period of 26–52 weeks from the start of an illness period. In most countries, a sickness certification is needed from a physician, often a general practitioner or the family physician (with a notable exception in the Netherlands where the occupational health physician has the key role). The physician certifies that the employee is unable to work because of illness [11].

The work ability assessments that are done for such certifications are not comprehensive. The physician normally relates the work ability of the patient to his or her normal work tasks. Some countries have published guidelines to aid physicians in their sickness certification work [11].

In a few countries, physicians no longer issue a certification of sickness and reduced work ability. Instead, they issue a statement of fitness for work ("fit note") describing what the ill worker can do, in spite of illness. The fit note is given to the employer. Examples are the UK and Norway. These changes are in accordance with the recommendation from OECD to focus on ability rather than disability and resources rather than deficits [8].

6.3.2 Intermediate Phase of Rehabilitation

In most countries, an intermediate phase of rehabilitation is necessary after the sick leave period and before long-term benefits can be given. Many employees have the potential for some work activity, particularly if this is strengthened either by medical or vocational rehabilitation measures. This will then perhaps make a disability pension unnecessary, or at least postpone it. There has been an increasing interest for such rehabilitation, and several countries like Germany, the Netherlands, Switzerland, and Scandinavia have made them mandatory before an evaluation for disability benefits can take place. Rehabilitation is also started early. The rehabilitation is often provided by the health sector, but in many instances the agencies themselves or the employers provide such service. The rehabilitation phase may include medical rehabilitation, vocational rehabilitation, workplace adjustments, or combinations of them.

6.3.3 Long-Term Absence: Disability Benefits

If the person is unsuccessful in returning to work during or after the sick leave period, including the rehabilitation phase, he or she can claim for a long-term benefit. In most cases, this is a comprehensive process.[1] After the social insurance officer has checked the formal requirements for the claim, such as being of proper age, nationality, and work situation, one (sometimes several) physician in, or working for, the Social Insurance Institution (called insurance physician) assesses the claimant's work ability. This assessment can either be done in a personal encounter with the claimant including a medical examination or be done only by going through the files of the claimant and forming the advice based on existing information provided by other medical experts. This latter procedure is common in Scandinavian countries, and to some extent also in Germany and Belgium.

At this stage, the insurance physician assesses if sufficient and necessary medical information has been provided. If not, additional information from, e.g., the treating physician or the hospital can be requested. Providing the Social Insurance Institution with medical information on claimants is an important task for health professionals.

Based on existing information and possibly on own interview/examination of the claimant, the insurance physician gives his or her advice on whether the medical condition is sufficiently severe to elicit a benefit [12]. The advice is frequently given in form of a report. These reports vary in length, from only briefly presenting the advice to a more structured report, including presentation of evidence, argumentation, and linkage to relevant legislation. The medical reports of disability assessments share essential characteristics by reporting about the current functional disability, diagnoses, sociomedical history, need for vocational rehabilitation, and prognosis of disability [13]. While the medical assessors in some European countries use free text to describe functional disability, they make additional use of functional scales in others. In the UK, the Work Capability Assessment has been used for almost 20 years, and in the Netherlands, the Functional Ability List has been used for a similar length of time to describe the claimant's work ability. Research on the evidence base for these lists has started in the last years [14, 15].

In most countries, administrative officers, not physicians, take the legal decision on the benefit. There are exceptions such as Belgium and Russia, where physicians take the decision on the right to benefits. In some countries, long-term benefits

[1] Severely ill claimants often can be granted long-term benefits without comprehensive evaluation, for example, permanently hospitalized, terminally ill, or severely injured patients. The claimants are granted benefits solely on the basis of the severity and prognosis of their illness.

cannot be granted on a permanent basis, and a reevaluation needs to take place after varying lengths of time. The procedure in the reevaluation phase is basically similar to first-time evaluations, although usually less thorough.

The legal criteria for long-term benefits are given in social insurance and welfare legislation. These laws have similarities across Europe and contain similar elements. To be eligible for a long-term benefit, the person's work ability must be reduced to a substantial degree. This degree varies, but in many countries work ability must be reduced by at least 50 %. In addition, it is required that the person has undergone proper treatment and rehabilitation and that the reduction in work ability is caused by an illness or injury [16]. This one-way model is not harmonized with a reciprocal, medical model that understands function as a relational concept and causes tensions in the social insurance institutions and in policy making [17].

6.3.4 The Systems for Work Disability Evaluation Are Challenged

Many countries struggle with high disability rates in spite of carefully elaborated evaluation procedures [8]. This challenge has been met by reforms. One such is the introduction of rehabilitation, but there have also been attempts to modernize the evaluation procedures. These reforms often include a stronger emphasis on functional assessments in the evaluation [18]. A more systematic approach to handling claims and clients has also been advocated [8]. Attempts have been made to simplify and standardize the procedures [15]. The disability evaluations have also been subject to criticism for other reasons. They are not transparent, reproducible, and reliable. Their validity has not been tested, and they are not standardized [16, 19].

> Work disability is evaluated before sick leave, rehabilitation, and disability benefits are given by a social insurance institution. The evaluation is a stepwise process. One essential step is the functioning assessment done by health professionals, usually physicians.

6.4 Work Ability Assessments: The Potential Role of the ICF

In this section, we will look at the assessments of work ability, as done by the physicians in practice. Three different situations, sick leave, rehabilitation, and disability pension, will be described in separate parts.

6.4.1 Sick Leave

In the sick leave period, the physician who certifies the sickness regularly assesses work disability. The focus is on restoration of health and work ability and on supporting the return-to-work process. Work resumption should be addressed continuously, since it has been shown that prolonged sick leave period in itself is an independent risk factor for disability [20].

The most frequent reason for sick leave is that the employee's work ability has been lowered as a consequence of ill health and functional limitations and where work ability is too low for the work demands. This resulting gap can be addressed by improving his or her functional abilities through treatment and rehabilitation or by lowering the demands at the work place. Both individual restoration of health and work adjustments might be necessary.

To gain an understanding of what actually prevents the employee from going back to work, the physician should both describe the employee's functional abilities (a functional description) and assess the abilities in relation to work demands (a functional assessment). It is important to assess residual work capacity and, if it is permitted by the system, to consider partial work resumption [21].

The OECD has pointed out the need for controlling sickness certification practice among physicians [8]. One way of doing this is to introduce more systematic and standardized assessment methods in addition to clear guidelines for sickness certification practice [22]. Guidelines have been successfully introduced in Sweden [23]. It is also possible to use tools that assist physicians in understanding the activity limitations and participation restrictions that their patients have in relation to work. Probably such instruments are most useful in more long-standing and complicated cases [24]. Later in this chapter, we describe the instrument used in Sweden and the Norwegian Functional Assessment Scale that has been tested in Norway.

In the development of guidelines for sickness certification practice and in tools, the ICF as a framework could be useful to understand the dynamic relationship between functional abilities and the work requirements. Instruments that use ICF definitions and vocabulary to aid sick-listing physicians have been developed, but to our knowledge they have not made progress in practice [24]. The situation is, however, quite different if the sick-listed employee undergoes medical or vocational rehabilitation.

6.4.2 Rehabilitation

Rehabilitation interventions can be requested, supported, and financed by social insurance institutions. During rehabilitation, the employee can be covered by sickness absence benefits, disability benefits, or rehabilitation allowance.

The assessment of work ability in this phase is usually the task for specialists in medical or vocational rehabilitation. In some countries, these specialists work in close cooperation with the Social Insurance Institution, and they are frequently requested to provide information on (a) the effect of the rehabilitation intervention on the work ability of the employee and (b) the functional status of the employee when the rehabilitation program has ended. It is therefore necessary to assess functional ability before and after the rehabilitation program.

It is common to let the rehabilitation specialist decide what type of assessments that should be used. One frequent challenge, however, is to get the information on activity restrictions and possible resources in a format and language that is comprehensible for the Social Insurance Institution.

Rehabilitation medicine should focus on the health of the individual, but, at the same time, other important life areas, like work life, should not be neglected [25]. The strengthening of vocational rehabilitation in many European countries has therefore been greeted with much enthusiasm [26]. Vocational rehabilitation clinics include job training, work adaption, and labor market guidance as important parts of their programs.

The development of the ICF Core Sets for vocational rehabilitation is an important step in the same direction [27, 28]. A characteristic of this core set is that it is situation specific (not disease specific) and as such usable for many different health conditions of vocational rehabilitation clients. From the viewpoint of social insurance, many clients have unclear, poorly defined, and complex illness [29]. In such cases, medical diagnoses give little guidance to treatment, rehabilitation, and work reintegration. It is better not to choose a disease-specific core set but rather a situation-specific to gain information on the client's functional status.

In the rehabilitation phase, gathering structured information is important. There is a need for standardized instruments to measure the effect of the rehabilitation intervention and the functional status of the individual to be reintegrated into working life. Particularly important in this process of gathering information is to get a picture of the employee's total resources that further reintegration measures can be based upon. This is possible to achieve by applying existing instruments for functional assessments, such as the Icelandic Special Assessment [30], or developing new instruments on the basis of the ICF Core Sets for vocational rehabilitation.

The ICF is a necessary framework for vocational rehabilitation, and common ICF-based definitions of terms used by both rehabilitation medicine and social insurance institutions would be a distinct advantage. In practice, the ICF framework is used increasingly in vocational rehabilitation.

6.4.3 Disability Benefits

Insurance physicians usually do the assessment of work ability for disability benefits. The information they use for the assessment is to a large extent provided from the health sector. In the assessment, they shall relate the person's restrictions in activity and participation and his or her health problems to the rules for disability pension that exist in the country. It is usually not relevant for the insurance physician to assess all the possible functional limitations the claimant has, but only those that are mentioned or can be inferred from national legislation and administrative rules. This makes the assessment requirements in disability benefits quite different from the assessment in view of rehabilitation, where the assessor has to consider a wider spectrum of abilities and resources of the person.

The disability benefit assessments differ also from rehabilitation assessments in another way. While the focus in rehabilitation assessments is mainly on positive abilities and resources, it is more on the lack of ability, as described in national administrative routines or legislation in disability assessments.

In the Netherlands since 1976, a Functional Ability List is used as standard in work disability assessment [31]. The list contains around 70 items under six headings: personal functioning, social functioning, adjusting to physical environment, dynamic movement, static movements, and working hours. The list specifies both abilities and inabilities.

In the UK, standardized assessment in disability evaluation was introduced with the Personal Capability Assessment in 1995 [32]. In 2008, it was replaced by a modified version, the Work Capability Assessment (WCA) [15]. The present assessment form covers 17 physical, mental, cognitive, and intellectual activities. The intention is to assess if a claimant has limited capability for work or work-related activities.

These standards have not been subject to scientific testing, but both have proven to be robust in practice. The WCA has, since 2010, undergone a series of independent reviews [33]. Amendments have been made in both systems to adjust for changes in legislation and in morbidity of the populations. In particular, much effort has been made to adjust for increasing numbers of claimants with mental health problems and disability.

The ICF has been an important model and framework for the attempts to improve quality in medical assessments for long-term benefits. The ICF also provides a dictionary and definitions of impairments, activity limitations, and participation restrictions for use in social insurance.

The ICF Core Sets for specific conditions have been studied in disability evaluation for long-term benefits. In a study based in Switzerland, Schwegler et al. [19] examined if combinations of ICF Core Sets could capture the relevant content in disability evaluations on chronic widespread pain and low-back pain. Their analysis showed that important information on the claimants' functional abilities was covered by brief and disease-specific core sets on chronic widespread pain, low-back pain, and depression or obesity, but certain frequently reported aspects related to functioning, such as personal factors and individual experience, were not covered. To improve content validity, a combination of the abovementioned disease-specific core sets could be used but could result in a decline in efficiency (defined as being manageable and containing only as few categories as necessary). It is essential to consider this trade-off when assessment protocols or instruments are developed.

In another study in Germany, the interaction between work performance, motivational factors, and incapacity/activity limitation was studied [34]. To measure the latter, the authors used Mini-ICF-Rating for Mental Disorders (Mini-ICF-APP), which is a 13-item instrument for assessment of activities and participation. The authors found that work performance was related to activity limitations and incapacities, and to a much lesser degree to motivational factors.

Table 6.1 Characteristics of assessments in vocational rehabilitation and disability evaluation

Assessment	Vocational rehabilitation	Disability evaluation
Actors	A multidisciplinary and multi-stakeholder process	A few professions: medical, psychological, social worker, administrative
Placement	Health sector and social insurance institution	Social insurance institution
Purpose	Assess effects of clinical interventions and reintegration potential	Decisions on rights for benefits
Legal bindings	Few	Strong
Scope	Comprehensive	Limited
Dimension	Focus on ability	Focus on disability

6.4.4 *Comparing Assessment in Disability Evaluation and in Rehabilitation*

The assessment for disability benefits in social insurance is usually not an isolated procedure but is linked to requirements for rehabilitation and reintegration attempts. Therefore, the assessments for rehabilitation and for disability benefits are interwoven in practice. We can talk about a double function for assessments in social insurance, although they sometimes overlap. In the overview presented below, characteristics of these two types of assessment are given (Table 6.1).

While the assessment in vocational rehabilitation typically involves a multi-professional team, the disability evaluation process in social insurance only involves few actors. In many countries, only insurance physicians and social insurance officers cooperate, but others can also be involved, such as labor experts, social workers, and psychologists. The legal bindings are many and strong in disability claims, and the focus is mainly on the lack of functions. In vocational rehabilitation, there are less legal limitations, and focus is strongly on what the person can do and what possibilities he has.

> The ICF can be helpful for writing guidelines and constructing assessment tools in work disability evaluations.

6.5 The Need for Common Language

Although most European social security systems were initiated from the same principles, they have been elaborated more or less independently in each country. As a result, the definitions, criteria, and procedures that are used in determining eligibility for a disability benefit substantially differ among European countries. Development of common definitions and a generally accepted data set is therefore needed before comparative analyses and data exchange between different national schemes can be achieved. One of the aims of the ICF is to create a common language that is also useful and applicable in the field of social security and disability evaluation [1].

The ICF offers a worldwide consensus on key concepts describing human functioning and the consequences of health problems on activities and participation. This is also important for the common understanding of functioning within each country, where there are large differences in the interpretation of "functioning," "work disability," and other terms due to diverse context and political dynamics. For the social insurance institutions, it is absolutely essential that all professional groups working with claimants for assistance or benefits have the same understanding of concepts. It also is of great help if the policy makers, the health sector, and the general public understand the concepts in the same way.

6.5.1 Statistics

In general, the social insurance institutions in Europe have well-developed statistics about benefits, payments, and quality. With the strengthening of a more functional approach to benefits, there will probably be a need for statistics looking at the functional abilities of claimants in the future, not only of their medical diagnoses. Such accumulation of statistical information necessitates a coding system for functional status, and that could be a potential use for the ICF.

To our knowledge, no such coding of functional abilities has occurred yet. However, in the USA, the Washington Group on Disability Statistics has developed a short set of questions that internationally can be used for census purposes. The idea is that the questions can be linked to statistics on school attendance or employment. The purpose is to describe how disability in various countries can hamper participation in important life arenas. The questions are based on the ICF, and one question recognizes its basic model [35].

> The ICF meets the needs for common and consistent terminology in functioning assessments, and is an appropriate classification for statistical purposes.

6.6 The EUMASS Core Set for Disability Evaluation in Social Security

At the European level, physicians in social and private insurance are organized through the European Union of Medicine in Assurance and Social Security (EUMASS). In 2004, the EUMASS council created a working group on ICF in recognition of the potential usefulness of the ICF in social security [2]. One important task was to develop a core set for functional assessment in disability claims for use in European social security systems.[2]

It was evident from the beginning that a selection of ICF categories that encompasses every possible aspect of disability evaluation in all European countries would result in a very large and unpractical list. Therefore, the core set for disability evaluation should represent an acceptable minimal set of items. The core set should be useful but not necessarily sufficient for the disability evaluation in the social systems of European countries. It should go beyond differences related to legislation or organization. From the start, it was stressed that it was important to validate the proposed core set in different settings and to examine the need for additional items in national social security systems. The core set should offer a good and practical starting point for a harmonization of disability evaluation in different social insurance systems in Europe.

The aim of the core set was to aid medical advisors in social security to take decisions; to improve quality of decisions, interprofessional communication, and national and international comparisons; and to establish a firm basis for research. The core set for disability evaluation should be situation specific for disability evaluation and generic, i.e., applicable to all cases, regardless of diagnosis. A definition was accepted (Box 6.1).

Box 6.1: Definition of the Core Set for Disability Evaluation
ICF Core Sets in disability evaluation are necessary elements for the disability-evaluating physician in the evaluation of disability for work, including mainly the activity component, and environmental factors of the ICF

6.6.1 A Formal Process for the Decision on the Core Set

The development of the core set was carried out in a formal decision-making process. In a first step, the members of the working group organized eight national expert meetings to discuss and suggest relevant ICF categories. The working groups could suggest ICF categories but also other functional categories not included in the ICF.

In a second step, the core set was decided upon by voting in two rounds among 20 members of the EUMASS working group on the ICF. All participants were leading experts in social security, vocational rehabilitation, and disability

[2] The members of the EUMASS working group for ICF collaborated in the development of the core set: Wout de Boer, Ljiljana Bojičová, Søren Brage, Herina Brandtzæg, Peter Donceel, Freddy Falez, Maarit Gockel, Martine Gouello, Brigitte Heuls-Bernin, André Ingenbleek, Radomir Kučera, Jiři Kutina, Clement Leech, Gert Lindenger, Ferenc Moricz, Elisabeth Nüchtern, Christian Puppinck, Paul Stidolph, Hana Trnkócy, Annette de Wind.

evaluation. The definition and use of qualifiers was not a subject in this primary stage of the core set. The first voting round was finished during a 1-day meeting. A second voting round was completed by email.

6.7 The Core Set

In all, 191 suggestions for ICF categories were submitted to the working group from the national meetings (Table 6.2). Forty of them were on the third level of the ICF and were moved to the appropriate second level, as decided beforehand. Of the 362 ICF second-level categories, 151 (42 %) were suggested from at least one national meeting. Body structures had received the fewest votes (11 %).

When two or more related categories had been suggested from the national meetings, a consensus was reached to include only the most relevant one based on a careful explanation of the exact wording of the ICF. Thus, 96 of 151 items were excluded in the first voting. Of the remaining categories, 13 were included in the first voting and an additional 7 in the second. In total, 20 categories were selected for the core set, five from body functions and 15 from activities and participation. No category from environmental factors was included (Table 6.3).

The national meetings had also suggested categories outside the ICF that covered areas such as specific work restrictions, other health-related restrictions, dimensions of time, and personal factors. These categories were discussed at the meeting, and their importance in some countries was recognized. None of them, however, gained sufficient support to be included in the core set (Box 6.2).

Box 6.2: Suggested Categories Outside the ICF (Not Included in the Core Set)

Specific work restrictions

Tolerance of special work conditions; tolerance of distraction, disturbances, deadlines, and production peaks; tolerance of safety risk; work flexibility; speed of action and handling; need for intensive coaching; need for protection devices; and sensitive to draught

Temporal dimensions

Quantitative capacity for work (hours per day/week), distribution of workload within 24 h, intermittent change in activity, changes in functional level over time, earlier rehabilitation efforts and factor change

Personality factors

Job motivation

Other health-related restrictions

Allergy, vulnerability to infections, localisation of restrictions, left/right dominant

Other considerations

Caretaking for family and others

Table 6.2 Result of the selection procedure of EUMASS Core Set. Number and percentage of selected ICF second-level categories in each component

	Component				
ICF second-level categories	Body function	Body structure	Activities/ participation	Environmental factors	Total
In total	**114**	**56**	**118**	**74**	**362**
Suggested in national meetings	50 (44 %)	6 (11 %)	68 (58 %)	27 (36 %)	151 (42 %)
Final core set	5 (4 %)	0 (0 %)	15 (13 %)	0 (0 %)	20 (6 %)

Table 6.3 EUMASS Core Set for disability evaluation in social security

Code	Chapter	Title
b164	Mental functions	*Higher-level cognitive functions*
b280	Sensory functions and pain	*Sensation of pain*
b455	Functions of the cardiovascular, hematological, immunological, and respiratory systems	*Exercise tolerance functions*
b710	Neuromusculoskeletal and movement-related functions	*Mobility of joint functions*
b730	Neuromusculoskeletal and movement-related functions	*Muscle power functions*
d110	Learning and applying knowledge	*Watching*
d115	Learning and applying knowledge	*Listening*
d155	Learning and applying knowledge	*Acquiring skills*
d177	Learning and applying knowledge	*Making decisions*
d220	General tasks and demands	*Undertaking multiple tasks*
d240	General tasks and demands	*Handling stress and other psychological demands*
d399	Communication	*Communication, unspecified*
d410	Mobility	*Changing basic body position*
d415	Mobility	*Maintaining a body position*
d430	Mobility	*Lifting and carrying objects*
d440	Mobility	*Fine hand use*
d445	Mobility	*Hand and arm use*
d450	Mobility	*Walking*
d470	Mobility	*Using transportation*
d720	Interpersonal interactions and relationship	*Complex interpersonal interactions*

6.7.1 No Environmental Factors Included

The EUMASS Core Set is generic and contains categories that always, and irrespective of diagnosis, should be assessed and reported about by physicians in social insurance medicine. It is intended for the evaluation of rights to benefits or eligibility determination. Insurance physicians might also do assessments for sickness absence, rehabilitation, and return to work. When this is the case, the person's resources and possibilities must be addressed comprehensively.

The core set contains only 20 categories, a smaller number than the brief core sets for chronic conditions [36]. Important categories might be missing for some countries, and national administrations might add categories according to national standards and legislation if they use the EUMASS Core Set. This has occurred in Iceland and Sweden. A low number of categories will probably increase the feasibility of the core set. In the core set, there is a fair balance between categories pertaining to physical and mental functioning.

In the selection process, body structures categories were replaced by corresponding body functions categories. This probably reflects the fact that evaluation of incapacity for work in European social insurance is related to functional disability. Body structures would probably have been preferred in an impairment-oriented assessment system, such as the *Guides to the Evaluation of Permanent Impairment* of the American Medical Association [37].

The majority of the selected categories pertain to the activities and participation component. They include sensory functions, basic mental functions, mobility functions, and more complex functions such as d720 complex interpersonal interactions. The selection reflects the large variations in demands for functional abilities in working life and also the complexity of disability evaluation.

Contrary to expectation (see definition in Box 6.1), no environmental factor was included in the core set. To medical experts in social security, work environment evidently is a necessary element in the disability evaluation process. There might be several explanations to this paradox. There is a large difference between European countries' procedures in how they address work issues. In addition, the environmental factors in the ICF are probably not specific enough for a useful classification of working situations. It is also possible that disability evaluation in most countries is essentially medically defined with an emphasis on the medical consequences of illness and accidents. Social insurance physicians traditionally may accentuate the medical aspects of work incapacity. Moreover, participation categories also include the impact of environmental factors on the performance of the claimant [38]. It is possible that medical advisors integrate environmental factors in a more implicit, rather than explicit, way, when they assess work ability.

Although qualifiers were not included at this primary stage of the core set, their importance was recognized. Since there were no empirical data as to which level of functioning is making work participation impossible, it was stated that the level of functioning has to be related to common work demands within the framework of the national social insurance legislation of a country. However, an attempt to use qualifiers was done in a validation study.

6.7.2 Validation Study

To investigate the strength and weakness of the EUMASS Core Set, an international study of content validation was initiated [3]. The aim was to establish if the EUMASS Core Set captures the functional abilities of claimants for disability benefits, irrespective of the underlying medical condition and national social security system. The objective was to explore if the ICF categories of the core set were relevant, useful, and sufficient to express functional ability in claimants applying for long-term disability benefits in social insurance.

The validity was tested in an exploratory, cross-sectional multicenter study. Two different instruments (one for person-encounter disability evaluation and one for paper-file disability evaluation) were constructed by adding qualifiers to each of the 20 categories of the EUMASS Core Set. The qualifiers and definitions were taken from the ICF Checklist [39]. They ranged from no impairment/no limitation to complete impairment/limitation on a 5-item ordinal scale. The participating social insurance physicians could document categories that were missing, but only when they were necessary to express the functional ability of a particular claimant. They were also asked to what extent the core set was useful and sufficient to describe a claimant's functional capacities on a 5-item ordinal scale ranging from "totally agree" to "totally disagree."

EUMASS members of the participating countries translated the validation forms into their own languages using the ICF. They recruited 5–10 social insurance physicians that were experienced in evaluating claims for long-term work disability. Each physician applied the validation form to a maximum of ten consecutive claimants for disability evaluation.

In total, 48 physicians from six countries evaluated 446 claimants for long-term work disability benefits. The physicians from Belgium, France, Iceland, and Romania performed the evaluation in personal encounters. In Norway, the physicians exclusively did file-based disability evaluations, while Germany did both. The majority of claimants were women, and many were in unskilled occupations such as cleaning work. Musculoskeletal and mental disorders were the most frequently reported health conditions. These characteristics indicated that the sample was fairly representative of claimants for disability benefits in Europe.

The physicians used all 20 ICF categories of the core set to describe functional ability in their reports. The most frequently listed limitations of claimants were sensation of pain (66 %), lifting and carrying objects (64 %), and handling stress and other psychological demands (63 %). Subgroup analysis showed that the physicians of all six countries applied each of the 20 ICF categories of the core set at least once to express limitations, and each of the 20 ICF categories was represented at least once as a limitation in the main disease groups.

The physicians mentioned 42 different categories as missing to describe the claimants' functional abilities: 27 categories of body functions (17 of which were mental), 11 of activities and participation, 3 of environmental factors, and 1 of personal factors. Sixteen categories were mentioned more than once. Categories were missed most frequently for claimants with mental disorders.

In 68 % of the cases, the physicians rated the core set as useful to express functional ability (27 % "totally agree," 41 % "partly agree"). Physicians from Norway and Belgium found the core set significantly less useful compared to physicians from Germany, Romania, France, and Iceland. No difference in usefulness was found among the main disease groups.

The physicians also rated the core set as sufficient to express functional ability in 63 % of the cases (23 % "totally agree," 40 % "partly agree"). The physicians from Norway, Belgium, and Romania perceived the core set as significantly less sufficient, compared to physicians from Germany, France, and Iceland. They were significantly less satisfied with the sufficiency of the core set when they rated persons with circulatory disorders such chronic heart failure.

The validation study showed that the core set includes relevant categories, but it is not completely comprehensive since 42 additional categories were suggested. The physicians perceived the core set as useful and sufficient to express functional disability in the context of working life, but the judgments varied among countries and diagnostic groups. The findings suggest that the EUMASS Core Set can provide support in evaluating long-term work disability. The study demonstrated that it is possible to use an instrument to evaluate functional ability despite different national or local processes in disability evaluation. Such an instrument could promote transparency, reliability, homogenous presentation in practice, and data exchange in research. With adding more categories of mental functions such as temperament and personality functions or psychic stability, the EUMASS Core Set could also be more comprehensive.

6.7.3 The EUMASS Core Set in Other Studies

The EUMASS Core Set has been used and studied in other countries, notably in Germany, Sweden, and Iceland. In a German study, Timner found that insurance physicians frequently rated limitations in the category "handling stress and other psychological demands" [4]. The category "pain" was used less frequently compared with the validation study [3]. In Sweden, insurance physicians have tested an instrument with 18 categories based on the EUMASS Core Set in long-term work disability claimants. The physicians also evaluated the degree of the limitation, if the recorded limitations are a consequence of disease, e.g., reduced physical endurance caused by heart failure, and if they are based on observed findings, e.g., spirometric testing [22]. Preliminary results of the Swedish instrument testing show that "handling stress and other psychological demands" was the category most frequently reported as a limitation and as a consequence of disease [40]. In a study in Iceland, the insurance physicians found that the core set did not capture mental illness well enough [30].

The current evidence calls it necessary to conduct more validation studies. They should include more European countries, particularly the Netherlands and the UK, where there is a tradition of reporting functional ability systematically. Moreover, studies should report findings according to disease groups to look at disease-specific burden and more information of where in the process of disability evaluation medical examiners specify functional disability. A larger sample would allow sensitivity analyses to explore the best cutoff for relevant thresholds in activity limitations.

Another important consideration is to also explore if social insurance officers handling disability pension claims are able to integrate information from the core set in the decision-making process. It should also be investigated if claimants find the core set appropriate to express their functional disability. It is also a frequent observation in countries which use instruments in work disability evaluation, such as the UK, the Netherlands, Sweden, and Iceland, that detailed instructions are needed to support the use of the instruments [12].

The EUMASS Core Set for disability evaluation in social security contains 20 items, is simple to use and has been validated. Its primary target is the assessment for disability benefits.

6.8 Applications of the ICF in Social Insurance: Examples from Scandinavian Countries

6.8.1 Sweden: Methods to Assess Job Capacity Using the ICF

The ICF was translated to Swedish and published in 2003 by the National Board of Health and Safety. The introduction was well timed with respect for the need of reforms in Sweden, since the number of days paid for sickness allowance had doubled in the preceding 5-year period. Research showed that half of the increase was caused by an increased number of claims and the other half by prolonged periods of disability [41].

The forms for medical certification of sick leave were changed in 2003 to ensure more precise information of work "inability," using the ICF concepts of function and activity limitations. In the same year, a more elaborate method for assessing job capacity (SLU) was developed, and a number of physicians were trained to qualify for using this method.

In 2008, a new law was introduced that stipulated that a sick-listed person had to be assessed in relation to any job in the labor market after 6 months. The Swedish Social Insurance Agency appointed in 2009 a working group that should update the

SLU method of assessing job capacity, in order to better meet the new requirements of legislation. This resulted in a new method for the team-based job capacity assessment (TMU). Since this method involved several professions, it was relatively costly. In practice, TMU was mainly used for claims of longer duration than 6 months, and 3 % of the still sick listed were assessed at the 6-month time limit.

In 2010, the government gave the Social Insurance Agency the task to develop a new method for assessing job capacity. The new method had to be developed within the legal framework of the changed regulations from 2008, and it should primarily be used for assessments at day 180 at which point the claimant's original work is no longer the reference but any work that is theoretically available in the labor market. The goal was to achieve a fairer and uniform assessment and to increase the claimant's acceptance, commitment, and understanding of the assessment result. The method was named AFU (in English: activity ability assessment) and was introduced in 2013. Under this system, the aim is to increase the number of claims to 10–15 % of the still sick listed at the 6 months time limit of sick leave.

6.8.2 The ICF in the SLU/TMU Methods

A single physician carries out the job capacity assessment in SLU in case of a simple claim. In more complicated cases, the TMU assessment is done by a team with physician, physiotherapist, occupational therapist, and psychologist.

The assessment is based on:

- Medical information from treating physician
- Data from the insured called "A story of a regular day"
- Medical examination (in TMU this also includes examinations by all other involved professionals)
- Activity assessment with an ICF Core Set

The basis for the development of the activity assessment in SLU/TMU was the EUMASS Core Set [2]. The EUMASS Core Set includes five categories from the body functions component. These were all substituted by categories from the component of activities and participation, so that only scoring of activities was made possible. A few more categories from this component were replaced in order to create a better balance between mental and physical activities. The final result contained 18 described ICF activities (7 mental, 8 physical, and 3 combined activities). Two lines in the form were left open, so that the assessor could fill in two other relevant activity limitations, if that was needed.

The mere presentation of the EUMASS Core Set of what activities should be assessed was not sufficient. The activities had to be made operational by using fixed levels of descriptors for different levels of limitations. Fixed levels were considered needed to improve reliability in the evaluation process. Since the qualifiers used from the ICF for this purpose lacks strictly defined steps, new firmly defined descriptors had to be created.

Neither the descriptors from the personal capability assessment in the UK nor the functional ability list in the Netherlands were totally corresponding to the described activities for use in the EUMASS Core Set or for the Swedish version. Therefore, adjustments had to be made, and new descriptors were constructed to fit a five-graded scale.

In this construction of descriptors, the zero level was denominated to depict adequate level of activity, defined as the ability to cope with a job at the regular open labor market. The zero level is therefore set by the policy in the insurance system, referring to what should be considered to correspond to the lowest job demands. The other descriptor levels were chosen according to given examples to illustrate higher levels of limitations.

The assessor shall only indicate activity limitations that can be logically derived from the diagnosed medical conditions as such and that are consistent with the medical findings. Other activity limitations that are solely based on the claimants' statements shall not be depicted in the activity core set list but can be mentioned separately.

At the end, the assessor makes a statement of the evidence-based prognosis for each activity limitation, as well as any evidence-based serious medical risk of performing work tasks. The final job capacity is legally decided by the social insurance officer, as expressed in the decision of the claim. In the Swedish insurance, the law stipulates that this final step should be based on an individual and well-founded assessment.

6.8.3 The ICF in the AFU Method

A basic idea of the new AFU method is that the individual's medical conditions for work should be assessed and described with the same categories of abilities as described in the demands of the majority of jobs at the labor market. This makes it possible to relate the individual's ability to the demands of various professional requirements.

This is achieved by the development of descriptions of demands for a number of different jobs. At present, the numerically largest types of jobs in the 40 most common groups of occupations are described. This material has been developed in collaboration with the Swedish Public Employments Service and is now being used as a reference of demands in the open labor market. The efforts to evaluate the professional groups' demands are based on the US occupational information system (O*NET), a system to categorize and describe occupations based on extensive research (www.onetonline.org).

In the AFU method, the requirements for each occupational category are described in the same eight O*NET categories of activities as the claimant's ability profile. Each O*NET category for these ability profiles is fitted with a new type of five-graded descriptors. These are constructed by groups of ICF activities, for the reason that for most medical conditions, many activity limitations tend to occur in clusters.

The number of ICF activities within each O*NET category is:

- Physical strength and mobility, seven ICF activities (d4102, d4104, d4105, d4300, d4301, d4452, d450)
- Physical endurance, six ICF activities (d410, d4104, d4105, d4300, d4301, d450)
- Abilities related to sensory functions as well as vision and speech functions, three ICF activities (d110, d115, d330)
- Abilities related to balance, coordination, and fine motor quality, three ICF activities (b2351 as reflected in either of d410, d415, d450, or d455; b760 as reflected in either of d415, d450, d455, or d440)
- Cognitive functions related to memory, learning, and concentration, three ICF activities (b144 as reflected in d199, any of d130-159, and d160)
- Executive functions, five ICF activities (d175, d177, d179, d220, d230)
- Affective functioning, five ICF activities (d7100, d7104, d7200, d7202, d740)
- Abilities related to mental endurance, three ICF activities (d160, d220, d230)

In a medical job capacity assessment, a trained physician depicts the claimant's scores for each given activity.

In brief, the assessment consists of the medical information provided by treating physician and a self-assessment form on abilities, limitations, and the claimant's own opinion on the chances for returning to the present work. This information constitutes a basis for an extensive interview with the claimant. Then a standardized examination follows, performed by the trained physician, who at the time of examination conducts a minor standardized physical and, if required, a structured mental examination. If this would not be considered to be sufficient, the claimant will be referred to either a special physical assessment or special mental assessment. These are conducted by other professionals such as a physiotherapist, a occupational therapist, or a psychologist (performing neuropsychological testing).

The assessing physician then compiles the findings of the assessment and depicts the justified descriptor limitation level of the clustered ICF activities for each of the eight O*NET categories. If limitation degrees are chosen at level 3 or more (indicating more severe limitations), then each of the three most significant ICF activity limitations is specifically reported. This is to clarify which of the ICF activities that constitutes most of the claimant's disability, since each of O*NET category consists of a number of ICF activities that could have influenced the descriptor score.

There are two different outcome targets with the AFU. The first is to enable a comparison with the demands of the labor market. Here, the clustered ICF activities are just tools to construct descriptors for that purpose. The second outcome is, as clear as possible, to show what actually constitutes the claimant's disability, as shown by each specified activity limitation.

The AFU assessment will focus on the information from the preexisting medical documentation, self-assessment form, and any examination findings by the assessing physician. The findings are specified and evaluated in a written report and sent to the social insurance officer who then makes the legally binding decision of the claim.

6.8.4 Sweden: Using the ICF to Classify Information in Sickness Certificates for Research

In Sweden, medical certificates issued by physicians provide the basis for decisions on sickness benefits and vocational rehabilitation. An important part of the certificate is a description of the person's functional limitations. This information is given in narrative form (free text). In earlier studies, it has been reported that one of the most difficult parts of the physician's work is the assessment of the person's functional ability and work ability [42].

The quality and feasibility of the information on functional abilities has been subject to several studies. Morgell et al. found that the ICF could readily be used as a classification tool for information on function in 433 sick leave certificates [5]. They concluded that the ICF "could provide a better understanding of the consequences of diseases and how individual patients can cope with their health problems" and that the ICF is a useful complement to ICD-10 by adding information on functioning and disabilities.

In another study, Nilsing and coworkers found that the ICF could be used to structure information given in sickness certificates and clarify the assessment of functioning and work ability [43]. They used content analysis in 475 sickness certificates. The ICF was applicable to classify statements regarding functioning in 65 % of the certificates. Of the certificates where functioning was described, 92 % contained statements on body structures and body function, 35 % contained activities statements, and 12 % participation statements. A multiple regression analysis showed that use of activities statements was more frequent in certificates for mental disorders and among physicians working in primary care.

The same authors also found that sick leave guidelines that were introduced in Sweden in 2008 improved the quality of the sickness certificates as measured by increased amount of information on activity limitations among the sick-listed persons [23]. Based on analysis of 976 new certificates in 2007 and 2009, they found an increase in information linkable to the ICF from 65 % to 78 % in the years 2007–2009, and an increased use of activity limitations when the physicians described the patients' functioning.

6.8.5 Iceland: New Work Ability Assessment and Use of the ICF

Iceland has had a steady growth in disability benefits. As a consequence, evaluation procedures and the use of partial disability benefits have come under reconsideration [44]. A report from the Prime Minister's Office in 2007 stated the need for reassessing disability and strengthening vocational rehabilitation services. This marked the beginning of VIRK, the Vocational Rehabilitation Fund (VR Fund) that was established in 2008. The goal of the VR Fund is to systematically decrease the probability of employees leaving their jobs due to work disability.

As an important element in the change of the evaluation procedures, a new work ability assessment has been introduced. This is a comprehensive assessment of the individual's ability to participate actively in the labor market from a physical, mental, and social perspective. It is a continuous process of assessment/evaluation of abilities on one hand and activation measures/vocational rehabilitation and treatment on the other. Therefore, the focus of the work ability assessment is on what the individual is capable of doing, and his or her resources play a central role in supporting return to work [30].

The aim of the evaluation process is to increase the individual's work ability by exploring and trying all opportunities from a comprehensive view. This means that not only the physical and mental health of the individual is assessed but also his or her social situation and position in the labor market. As a consequence, less than optimal health in one area does not necessarily mean that the individual is not capable of working. Strength in other areas may balance out those weaknesses and reveal that the individual is capable of working with appropriate adaptations. At the same time, the assessment is intended to enhance available opportunities so that it enables and motivates the individual to be as active as possible in the labor market. The interaction of many different factors is therefore relevant in this context.

6.8.6 Main Features of the Work Ability Assessment

The work ability assessment can be divided into three phases (Fig. 6.1):

- *Basic assessment*
- *Special assessment*
- *Reassessment*

The purpose of the *basic assessment* is to promote health, improve social conditions, and motivate to early return to work. In the basic assessment, the emphasis is on early intervention, activation, and removal of barriers to work. The assessment is based on questionnaires and interviews, carried out by a vocational rehabilitation consultant who also empowers, motivates, and activates the individual in relation to his or her work and social environment. The conclusion of the basic assessment is based on this information.

Special assessment is a detailed assessment, analysis, and evaluation of possibilities in vocational rehabilitation and return to work done by external experts. External experts are, for example, physicians, physical therapists, occupational therapists, psychologists, and social workers. The individual's options are explored and evaluated in a more specialized manner than in the basic assessment. On the basis of the special assessment, a decision is made on whether and how work ability can be further promoted. A comprehensive vocational rehabilitation plan follows. Experts in the special assessment have to report the function loss of the individual

Fig. 6.1 The work ability assessment in Iceland

from 30 ICF categories, 20 of them come from the EUMASS Core Set [2]. It is recommended to use the special assessment when more than 6 months have passed after the basic assessment without acceptable success or when the activation plan or return-to-work plan is not working as expected. Special assessment is also recommended when the individual has complicating life circumstances, and detailed analyses and a comprehensive rehabilitation plan are required.

Reassessment is needed when the vocational rehabilitation plan has been carried out, and the individual has not returned to work. It is also used when it is necessary to decide on the residual work ability of the individual, i.e., when partial disability benefits are considered. The reassessment may indicate that vocational rehabilitation should be repeated because the best possible performance or maximum work ability has not yet been reached. If maximum work ability has been achieved, it is also stated how much work ability the individual has.

6.8.7 The Development of the Work Ability Assessment

When the work ability assessment and its tools were developed, one main goal was to secure early intervention. Such early intervention is essential in vocational rehabilitation as it can be the most effective measure against long-term benefit dependence. Early intervention is a simple, effective, and cost-effective way to prevent people with common health problems to go on long-term sickness absence [29]. In that respect, the basic assessment plays a key role in the work ability assessment and is intended to be used in early intervention. At the same time, it is important to recognize that individuals absent from work for many months can still be rehabilitated successfully through a comprehensive rehabilitation program [45]

Although diagnoses can define the causality of illness and prognosis of the individual, they are not sufficient in an assessment. The identification of functional limitations often provides the necessary information for planning an intervention in rehabilitation. This is in-line with the aims of the special assessment.

In both special assessment and reassessment, the experts are requested to assess 30 functional categories from the ICF. Twenty of them were extracted from the EUMASS Core Set [2]. The other ten were extracted from the basic assessment to investigate more closely social and environmental factors that were not included the EUMASS Core Set. The idea behind the use of the EUMASS Core Set early in the rehabilitation process was to improve the chances to influence important functions in the rehabilitation process.

The purpose of using the ICF categories in the special assessment and the reassessment is to give the experts the opportunity to assess them systematically during the rehabilitation period. In this way, transparency of the final decision on work disability is secured, efficiency in the work with the individual is enhanced, and attempts to improve his or her work ability have been carried out. The special assessment and the reassessment relate the individual's function to his or her work and detect how the barriers experienced by the individual can be avoided or decreased. At the same time, personal resources are utilized to achieve maximum activity. Therefore, the aim of the special assessment and the reassessment is to assess function loss and if adaptations to the function loss need to take place.

The ICF categories (impairments, activity limitations, or participation restrictions) are qualified from 0 (no problem), 1 (mild problem), 2 (moderate problem), 3 (severe problem) to 4 (complete problem) [1]. It has been shown that qualifiers support the understanding of function in a multidisciplinary team and enable all team members to quantify the extent of functional deficits [46]. Qualifiers can also be used to describe the effectiveness of treatment. A decrease in a qualifier score can be interpreted as an increase in functional ability. Such information can be important in the reassessment. It was decided to specifically target those functional categories that were given the qualifier 2 or higher. The decision was in conjunction with the WHO recommendations indicating that the cutoff qualifier used should be 2.

The experts that perform the special assessment and the reassessment are requested to take into account all relevant information from the basic assessment, the special assessment, interviews, and examinations before rating the disability with the use of qualifiers. They are also asked about the reasons for choosing the qualifier.

In a research study, Konráðsdóttir found that the development of the assessment methods was done in accordance with modern definitions and understanding of work ability [30]. The development was inspired by established methods from other countries that have been shown to be useful. The following development of instruments in the work ability assessment was done in collaboration with international experts and through an international development project.

Since the validation study of the EUMASS Core Set indicated a lack of mental health factors, the VF Fund established an expert group with psychiatrists and psychologists. The group examined the factors in the special assessment, the factors in the ICF Core Sets for depression and bipolar disorders, and the existing research on the most common functional losses in anxiety disorders. The group also compared the mental health problems and the functional loss in 70 individual cases. The group suggested a stronger emphasis on "b130 energy and drive functions" and to add two ICF categories: "b126 temperament and personality functions" and "d230 carrying out daily routine" to the special assessment and the reassessment.

6.8.8 Norway: The Work Ability Method

The Directorate for Health and Social Affairs published the Norwegian version of the ICF in 2003. The Labor and Welfare Agency has participated in a national group for the dissemination of the ICF in the health-care and welfare sectors. The ICF has been taken into use in education and research in social insurance medicine. In the period 2001–2006, the Norwegian welfare system was thoroughly reformed, with changes in the sickness benefit scheme, return-to-work programs, and disability benefit scheme. The aim was to modernize benefits and follow-up routines. This should include a much clearer emphasis on function rather than disease and on resources and capacities instead of limitations and disability. As a consequence, there was a change of interest to functional evaluation of claimants. The growing support for a functional approach became evident both on a structural level and on a practical level with piloting and testing of new instruments and routines for disability assessments.

At a structural level, all social insurance agency officers in all cases where reduced working capacity is established or suspected use a new work methodology (the work ability method) from 2009 onward. The method strongly resembles the Danish work ability method from 2003 and has also adopted elements from the ICF. The method is based on a biopsychosocial understanding of health and functioning, and there is a strong emphasis on the activity component of the ICF with correspondingly less focus on impairments. An analysis of the new method of assessing work ability, its historical roots, and comparisons with other assessment models has been published [18].

In 2002, the National Insurance Administration started to work on instruments that could be used for disability assessments in short-term sick leave and in disability pension claims. The Norwegian Functional Assessment Scale (NFAS) was developed as a 40-item functional scale to be completed by persons with reduced work ability [47]. The scale was based on the ICF categories from the activity component and was field tested on sick-listed persons. Factor analysis confirmed four physical domains of functioning (walking/standing, holding/handling, lifting/carrying, and sitting) and three mental domains (coping, communicating, and sensing). The NFAS showed considerably reduced functioning in sick-listed persons and was found to be valid.

In the later stages, the NFAS has been revised. The NFAS now contains 39 items [48]. The new, five-point scale version provides better data quality, better end effects, and higher levels of internal consistency than the earlier version. Construct validity, data quality, and test-retest reliability of the NFAS are acceptable. Population-based normative data on functional ability has also been published [49].

The NFAS has not been accepted as a standard instrument in the social insurance system but has attracted attention from vocational rehabilitation and in general practice [24, 50]. The advancement of the ICF in research in social insurance medicine in Norway has been encouraging, but the use in practical work in social security in general is still limited.

ICF-based methods are used in Swedish social insurance to assess the need for rehabilitation and the eligibility for long term benefits. The most recent method integrates functioning assessments and job demands. In Iceland, the process of rehabilitation is governed by ICF-based instruments that were developed on the basis of EUMASS Core Set.

6.9 Further Developments of the ICF in Social Security

The basic ideas of the ICF have been taken up in European social security. The relational concepts of illness and functioning and the emphasis on personal and environmental factors are in concordance with the recent progress made in social security. The biopsychosocial model has become more prevalent in social insurance institutions in Europe over the last decades.

With the use of qualifiers, it is possible to describe and analyze resources in functioning. Social insurance institutions have been strongly influenced by the recommendations from OECD to focus on ability and capacity instead of disability and incapacity. The ICF provides an understanding of positive and negative aspects of functioning and positive and negative influence of personal and environmental factors that could be used easily in social security systems.

The experience of Scandinavian countries on the use of the ICF in social security is valuable. It appears to be a fairly straightforward process to adopt ICF-based methods, protocols, and instruments in the rehabilitation phase in social security. In these cases, the reduction of health has lasted for a fairly long period, and there is a potential for reintegration into working life.

When disability is evaluated for long-term and permanent benefits, there is far less experience with using the ICF. It is probable that the social insurance institutions have found less need for the ICF in these evaluations. When disability is evaluated for short-term, sick leave benefits, there have been attempts to implement ICF-based instruments, e.g., the Norwegian Functional Assessment Scale. These attempts have not been successful, possibly because they are viewed as too time-consuming.

So far, the ICF has been most extensively used in relation to the phase of medical and vocational rehabilitation for persons with reduced work ability; that said, there are also problems. The full classification of the ICF is too large to use in social insurance. It needs to be discussed, and tested, in national social insurance institutions if disease-specific or generic core sets should be used. Some European countries have had a strong medical influence on the decision process, with a corresponding emphasis on diagnosis. In these countries, disease-specific core sets might be useful. However, such core sets need to be modified because the purpose of assessments in social insurance partly differs from the purpose in clinical medicine. In addition, to assess possibilities for return to work, there is, in social insurance, also a need to decide whether the person should be given welfare benefits or not.

There are shortcomings of disease-specific core set, and perhaps the most important in social insurance is the high prevalence of comorbidity in benefit claimants. In many cases, there is a combination of somatic and mental conditions that together limits activity. In such cases, there would be a need for several core sets, and that is undoubtedly a complex and cumbersome task to do. Generic core sets would be more cost-effective when several comorbidities exist.

In an increasing number of countries, a purely medical orientation of the disability evaluation processes has been abandoned. In these countries, a return to disease-specific core set would appear to be a backward move and away from a multi-professional approach. In these countries, situation-specific or setting-specific core sets need to be further developed and tested.

Whatever type of core sets is used, it should be kept in mind that instruments and protocols based on ICF Core Sets will have a dual purpose in social security. Guiding the individual back to work is the primary objective and, if that is not successful, to evaluate the need for financial support. The instruments will be different in scope, scaling, and content depending on situation.

The ICF is used in vocational rehabilitation and to assess the need for rehabilitation in European countries. In some situations, generic core sets will be useful, while disease-specific core sets can be better in others.

6.10 The Limits for the ICF in Social Security

The ICF has, so far, only been used to a limited extent in social security, mainly to support and clarify the assessment of the individual's functional ability and disability. Here, the work is in progress. On the other hand, in work disability evaluations, the description of environmental factors is at present less obvious, since the richness of modern working life factors is not represented in the ICF.

Anner et al. have addressed the limitations of the ICF in relation to disability evaluation [13]. They stress that the ICF is suitable for definitions and classification of the functional abilities of a claimant but also state that other important aspects of the disability evaluation cannot be described within the ICF, such as the health condition, the development of disability, the prognosis, and the causality.

The lack of classification for personal factors is a limit for the use of the ICF. Other inventories or instruments are necessary if one wants to describe personal factors, like motivation or sense of coherence, in a standardized way in disability evaluations in social insurance.

A conflict in this area relates to the inherent difficulty in finding a balance in social insurance between the concern for an individual's uniqueness and the need for general policy on disability. The adoption of ICF-based instruments and integrative thinking would undoubtedly strengthen the latter, making it easier to standardize questionnaires and protocols. In this situation, it is tempting, and natural, to overlook the unique experience of the individual. It is important, as has been done in the Swedish AFU test, to include open lines in forms where pertinent categories for that unique individual can be entered.

The use of standardized instruments must not interfere with the general principle that social insurance clients are individuals with unique background, unique possibilities, and equal rights.

6.11 Conclusions

In social security, the ICF can support the efforts to reach greater transparency and fairness of decisions. The framework and taxonomy, as well as recent developments in core sets, have been taken into use in social insurance institutions. The ICF meets the need for a stronger emphasis on return-to-work processes and on the individual functional and work ability in disability claims.

Study Questions

1. What is a "fit note?"

   Answer: Instead of issuing a certification of sickness and reduced work ability, physicians in the UK issue a statement of fitness for work ("fit note") describing what the ill worker can do, in spite of illness. This fit note is given to the employer.

2. How do European insurance physicians assess functioning and work ability in claims for disability?

   Answer: In most of Europe, the assessment is done in a personal encounter with the claimant including a medical examination. In some countries (Scandinavia, Germany, Belgium), the assessment is done by going through files of the claimant, and forming the advice based on existing information provided by other medical experts.

3. How can the ICF assist in sickness certification?

   Answer: ICF could be used to develop systematic and standardized assessment methods, guidelines for sickness certification practice, and tools that assist physicians in understanding the activity limitations and participation restrictions that their patients have in relation to work. The ICF as a framework could be useful to understand the dynamic relationship between functional abilities and the work requirements.

4. Why might situation-specific core sets be more practical than disease-specific core sets in social security?

   Answer: Many social security benefit claimants have a combination of somatic and mental conditions that together limits activity. In such cases, several disease-specific core sets would be needed. Situation-specific core sets are more effective when several comorbidities exist. Many countries have also already abandoned a purely medical orientation of the disability evaluation processes. A return to disease-specific core sets would be a backwards move, and away from a multi-professional approach.

5. What are the differences between assessments in vocational rehabilitation and in disability evaluations?

   Answer: Assessment in vocational rehabilitation (VR) is a multidisciplinary and multi-stakeholder process, while in disability evaluation (DE) it only involves a few professions like medical, psychological, social worker, and administrative. DE is only done in social insurance institutions, but VR can also be placed in the health sector. DE is done to decide on rights to benefits with strong legal requirements, but VR assesses the effect of clinical interventions and reintegration potential with few legal demands. The assessment in DE has a focus on disability and is limited in scope, while in VR the focus is on ability (resources) and is comprehensive.

6. What are the limits for ICF in social security?

   Answer: The ICF is suitable for definitions and classification of the functional abilities of a claimant, but some important aspects of the disability evaluation cannot be described within the ICF, such as the health condition, the development of disability, the prognosis, and causality. The lack of a classification for personal factors also limits the use of the ICF in social security. Other inventories or instruments must be used if one wants to describe personal factors, like motivation or sense of coherence, in a standardized manner.

References

1. World Health Organization. ICF-international classification of functioning, disability, and health. Genève: World Health Organization; 2001.
2. Brage S, Donceel P, Falez F. Development of ICF core set for disability evaluation in social security. Disabil Rehabil. 2008;30:1392–6.
3. Anner J, Brage S, Donceel P, Falez F, Freudenstein R, Oancea C, de Boer WEL. Validation of the EUMASS Core Set for medical evaluation of work disability. Disabil Rehabil. 2013;35: 2147–56.

4. Timner K. Die Bedeutung der ICF für die sozialmedizinische Beurteilung in der gesetzlichen Rentenversicherung. Der Medizinische Sachverständiger. 2008;104:15–7.
5. Morgell R, Backlund LG, Arrelöv B, Strender L-E, Nilson GH. Health problems and disability in long-term sickness absence: ICF coding of medical certificates. BMC Public Health. 2011; 11:860.
6. Escorpizo R, Stucki G. Disability evaluation, social security, and the international classification of functioning, disability, and health. J Occup Environ Med. 2013;55:644–51.
7. Nordenfelt L. The concept of work ability. Brussels: P.I.E. Peter Lang; 2008.
8. OECD. Sickness, disability and work: breaking the barriers. A synthesis of findings across OECD countries. Paris: OECD; 2010.
9. Mabbet D, Bolderson H, Hvinden B. Definitions of disability in Europe: a comparative analysis. Uxbridge: Brunel University; 2002.
10. de Boer WEL, Besseling JJM, Willems JHBM. Organisation of disability evaluation in 15 countries. Pratiques et organisation des soins. 2007;38:205–17.
11. EUMASS. Social security medicine in Europe: professional sick leave: the role and functions of professionals in managing sick leave in different European countries. 2011. At: www.eumass.com
12. Brage S. Legers oppgaver ved søknad om uførepensjon i fem europeiske land [Physician work tasks in applications for disability benefits in five European countries] (in Norwegian). Arbeid og Velferd. 2010;4:70–80.
13. Anner J, Schwegler U, Kunz R, Trezzini B, de Boer WEL. Evaluation of work disability and the international classification of functioning, disability and health: what to expect and what not. BMC Public Health. 2012;12:470.
14. Harrington M. An independent review of the work capability assessment – year two. London: The Stationery Office; 2011.
15. Medical Services. Training & development revised WCA handbook. ESA (LCW/LCWRA) Amendment Regulations; 2011.
16. Boer de WEL. Quality of evaluation of work disability. Ph.D. thesis, University of Amsterdam; 2010.
17. Ptyushkin P, Vidmar G, Burger H, Marinček C, Escorpizo R. The International Classification of Functioning, Disability and Health (ICF) in vocational rehabilitation and disability assessment in Slovenia: state of law and users' perspective. Disabil Rehabil. 2011;33(2):130–6.
18. Solli HM. Justice, objectivity and disability assessment within social insurance medicine. An ethical and scientific-philosophical analysis of three disability models, seen in a historical perspective (in Norwegian). Ph.D. thesis, Michael. 2007;4(3):195–520.
19. Schwegler U, Anner J, Boldt C, Glässel A, Lay V, de Boer WEL, Stucki G, Trezzini B. Aspects of functioning and environmental factors in medical work capacity evaluations of persons with chronic widespread pain and low back pain can be represented by a combination of applicable ICF Core Sets. BMC Public Health. 2012;12:1088.
20. Gjesdal S, Bratberg E. Diagnosis and duration of sickness absence as predictors for disability pension: results from a three-year, multi-register based and prospective study. Scand J Public Health. 2003;31:246–54.
21. Krohne K, Brage S. New rules meet established sickness certification practice: a focus-group study on the introduction of functional assessments in Norwegian primary care. Scand J Prim Health Care. 2007;25:172–7.
22. Larson J. Metoder för bedömning av arbetsförmåga inom sjukförsäkringen – slutrapport [Methods for assessment of job capacity in social insurance – a final report (in Swedish)]. Stockholm: Försäkringskassan; 2013.
23. Nilsing E, Söderberg E, Öberg B. Sickness certificates in Sweden: did the new guidelines improve their quality? BMC Public Health. 2012;12:907.
24. Østerås N, Gulbrandsen P, Benth JS, Hofoss D, Brage S. Implementing structured functional assessments in general practice for persons with long-term sick leave: a cluster randomised controlled trial. BMC Fam Pract. 2009;10:31.
25. Frank AO, Sawney P. Vocational rehabilitation. J R Soc Med. 2003;96:522–4.

26. Chamberlain MA, Moser VF, Ekholm KS, O'Connor RJ, Herceg M, Ekholm J. Vocational rehabilitation: an educational review. J Rehabil Med. 2009;41:856–69.
27. Escorpizo R, Finger ME, Glässel A, Cieza A. An international expert survey on functioning in vocational rehabilitation using the international classification of functioning, disability and health. J Occup Rehabil. 2010;20:502–11.
28. Finger ME, Escorpizo R, Glässel A, Gmünder HP, Lückenkemper M, Chan C, Fritz J, Studer U, Ekholm J, Kostanjsek N, Stucki G, Cieza A. ICF Core Set for vocational rehabilitation: results of an international consensus conference. Disabil Rehabil. 2012;34(5):429–38.
29. Waddell G, Burton AK, Kendall NAS. Vocational rehabilitation – what works, for whom, and when? Report for the Vocational Rehabilitation Task Group. London: TSO; 2008.
30. Konráðsdóttir ÁD. Work ability assessment – description and evaluation of a new tool in vocational rehabilitation and in disability claims. Master thesis, University of Bifröst; 2011.
31. Spanjer J. The disability assessment structured interview. Its reliability and validity in work disability assessment. Ph.D. thesis, University of Groningen; 2010.
32. Department of Work and Pensions. Transformation of the personal capability assessment. Report. London: DWP; 2006.
33. Litchfield P. An independent review of the work capability assessment – year four. London: The Stationery Office; 2013.
34. Linden M, Baron S, Muschalla B. Relationship between work-related attitudes, performance and capacities according to the ICF in patients with mental disorders. Psychopathology. 2010;43(4):262–7.
35. Madans JH, Loeb ME, Altman BM. Measuring disability and monitoring the UN convention on the rights of persons with disabilities: the work of the Washington Group on Disability Statistics. BMC Public Health. 2011;11 Suppl 4:54.
36. Cieza A, Ewert T, Üstün B, Chatterji S, Kostanjsek N, Stucki G. Development of ICF core sets for patients with chronic conditions. J Rehabil Med Suppl. 2004;44:9–11.
37. Rondinelli RD, editor. Guides to the evaluation of permanent impairment. 6th ed. Chicago: AMA Press; 2008.
38. Nordenfelt L. On health, disability and activity: comments on some basic notions in the ICF. Disabil Rehabil. 2006;28:1461–5.
39. World Health Organization. ICF-checklist. 2007. Available at: http://www3.who.int/icf/checklist/icf-checklist.pdf
40. Lindenger G. "Medical Conditions for Work" – how to assess work capacity using the international classification of functioning in Sweden. 15 Mar 2012. Available from: http://www.swiss-insurance-medicine.ch
41. SOU. Gränslandet mellan sjukdom och arbete [The borderland between sickness and work (in Swedish)]. SOU 2009:89. Stockholm; 2009.
42. Löfgren A, Hagberg J, Arrelöv B, Ponzer S. Frequency and nature of problems associated with sickness certification tasks: a cross sectional questionnaire study of 5455 physicians. Scand J Prim Health Care. 2007;25:178–85.
43. Nilsing E, Söderberg E, Normelli H, Öberg B. Description of functioning in sickness certificates. Scand J Public Health. 2011;39:508–16.
44. OECD. Transforming disability into ability. Policies to promote work and income security for disabled people. Paris: OECD; 2003.
45. Dekkers-Sánchez PM, Wind H, Sluiter JK, Frings-Dresen MHW. What promotes sustained return to work of employees on long-term sick leave? Perspectives of vocational rehabilitation professionals. Scand J Work Environ Health. 2011;37(6):481–93.
46. Rauch A, Cieza A, Stucki G. How to apply the International Classification of Functioning Disability and Health (ICF) for rehabilitation management in clinical practice. Eur J Phys Rehabil Med. 2008;44:329–42.
47. Brage S, Fleten N, Knudsrød OG, Reiso H, Ryen A. Norsk Funksjonsskjema – et nytt instrument ved sykmelding og uførhetsvurdering. Tidsskr Nor Laegeforen. 2004;124:2472–4.

48. Østerås N, Gulbrandsen P, Garratt A, Benth JS, Natvig B, Brage S. A randomised comparison of a four- and a five-point scale version of the Norwegian Function Assessment Scale. Health Qual Life Outcomes. 2008;6:14.
49. Østerås N, Brage S, Garratt A, Benth JS, Natvig B, Gulbrandsen P. Functional ability in a population: normative survey data and reliability for the ICF based Norwegian Function Assessment Scale. BMC Public Health. 2007;7:278.
50. Strupstad J, Ihlebaek C, Øyeflaten I, Espnes GA. Arbeidsrettet rehabilitering i Norge [Vocational rehabilitation in Norway (in Norwegian)]. Utposten. 2011;3:26–32.

Chapter 7
Legal Dimensions of Disability Evaluation: Work Disability and Human Rights

Jerome Bickenbach

7.1 Introduction

7.1.1 Disability and "the Worthy Poor"

Legally speaking, there is an unbroken historical link between modern laws of disability evaluation – used to evaluate work disability or determine eligibility for social security, disability pensions, and workers' compensation – and the English *Poor Law of 1531*. It was in that year that the Parliament tried to eliminate "idleness and vagabondry" by directing justices of the peace to authorize public begging for those physically or mentally unable to work and to send the fraudulent "able-bodied beggars" to workhouses. The *Law* was clear that only the blind, deaf, and feeble-minded, those who lacked limbs or were incurably diseased or mad, were the "worthy poor" who could be legally allowed to beg [1, 2]. Although the distant ancestor of modern welfare legislation, the *Poor Law* entrenched the view that without evidence of substantial and permanent impairment or disease, no one, because of unemployment alone, deserves the state's largesse (even the privilege to be a beggar). Since it was widely believed that vagabonds and the idle would deceive and cheat to avoid honest labor, the only legal safeguard was hard evidence of infirmity. This view has continued as the unspoken rationale for relying on medical evidence of disability, and medical professionals as gatekeepers to disability benefits [3–6].

We may have left behind the crude dichotomy between worthy and unworthy beggars, but the medical approach to disability determination still holds sway for social security, workers' compensation, and age- and disability-relevant pensions. Since the great nineteenth-century reformers Otto von Bismarck in Germany and

J. Bickenbach (✉)
Department of Health Sciences and Health Policy, University of Lucerne and Swiss Paraplegic Research, Guido-Zäch-Strasse 4, 6207 Nottwil, Switzerland
e-mail: jerome.bickenbach@paraplegie.ch

R. Escorpizo et al. (eds.), *Handbook of Vocational Rehabilitation and Disability Evaluation*, Handbooks in Health, Work, and Disability, DOI 10.1007/978-3-319-08825-9_7

Lord Beveridge in England, we have adopted the more altruistic aim of providing a "safety net" against abject poverty for people who are not able to work. But it is still commonly felt that since there are many reasons why a person cannot get and keep a job or support themselves and their families, disability programming must in fairness require proof that the person is unemployed *because of* an underlying medical condition directly responsible for the work disability.

The medical approach to work disability sits well with lawyers, who want legal rules that are authoritative, *prima facie* relevant, reliable, and administratively convenient. Lawyers and program administrators become uncomfortable with eligibility decisions that are highly discretionary or arbitrary or when rules are inconsistently applied, lack transparency, and are costly to administer. Law in general, and administrative law in particular, is governed by the principles of natural justice – otherwise known as "rules of procedural fairness" or "the duties of adjudicators to act fairly" [7].

In the criminal law, the right to a fair trial or hearing, the opportunity to be heard and defend oneself, and the right to a reasonable decision, free of actual or apparent bias, are familiar principles of fairness that have been at the heart of the Anglo-American common-law tradition for more than a millennium. They are also universally found in other legal regimes, from the Napoleonic Code to Sharia law. Social program eligibility determination may not be as consequential a legal matter as a criminal trial, but similar rules apply. Relying on an apparently neutral, knowledgeable, and transparent authority, such as a medical practitioner applying objective, evidence-based medical criteria, with demonstrable inter-rater reliability, is arguably as close to the legal ideal of fair procedure as one can get.

7.1.2 The Rise of Vocational Rehabilitation

The other thread that links present practice in disability law and policy to the sixteenth century is the evolution from the urge to restrict benefits to the truly needy to the early twentieth century belief that professional services, and especially vocational rehabilitation, can effectively remove the need for public charity. Although a worldwide phenomenon, at least in high-resource countries, the evolving role of vocational rehabilitation in the development of policy for persons with disabilities was clearest in the United States, most likely because it was one of the last high-resource countries to develop social welfare programming.

The legal and policy response to disability in the United States from the late nineteenth century onward was shaped by the evolving role of vocational rehabilitation [5, 8, 9].

The center of gravity for disability law and policy after World War I was overwhelmingly economic: the political justification for funding vocational rehabilitation services was the expected economic return of the policy. This meant that disability policy was grounded in the legal category of "employability" [4].

Following the underlying impulse of the *Poor Laws*, it was thought that only those who had the potential for gainful employment should be beneficiaries of rehabilitation services, vocational training, job placement, and counseling – and those who lacked this potential should be warehoused in institutions. It was only after the Great Depression that social security and assistance programs came on line, and access to these services was broadened. Yet, even then, the underlying political principle was not social solidarity or human rights as it was in Europe, but economic cost-effectiveness and social engineering. Professional experts, financed by federal or state governments, were tasked to change the person to fit the demands of the workplace. Much later these services became a matter of legal entitlement, effectively a matter of right rather than public charity. It was only then that individuals with disabilities played a more active role in designing rehabilitation programs that fit their needs, rather those of the experts providing them.

7.1.3 Modern Policy on "Disability Evaluation"

The first major piece of disability legislation in the United States was the *Vocational Rehabilitation Act of 1920*, which reached relatively few people with physical disabilities and none with mental problems or intellectual impairments. Although the incidence of people developing severe physical impairment was roughly 250,000 per year, from 1920 until the passage of the amended act in 1943, only 12,000 people per year benefited [10]. The New Deal changed little about how the program was run, although by 1938 its administration had shifted to the Federal Security Agency (FSA), under the Social Security Administration (SSA) that also administered the Social Security Act. Vocational rehabilitation stayed with the FSA until 1949, when the FSA was abolished and its functions transferred to the newly formed Department of Health, Education, and Welfare. There vocational rehabilitation found a champion in Mary Switzer, who, as head of the Office of Vocational Rehabilitation took the lead during World War II in expanding the conception of vocational rehabilitation from job education and counseling to the medical and other rehabilitation interventions designed to restore "the whole man" to employability [10].

The legal jurisprudence that developed around this time, and reached its apex in the 1954 *Vocational Rehabilitation Act,* reflected the developing view that it was good common sense to provide rehabilitation to a disabled person who could be made fit for employment since then he or she could become a tax producer rather than a tax consumer. Federal funds could be used to "prime the pumps" for private initiatives and to fund state vocational rehabilitation programs, the argument went, as long as the program did not unduly interfere with how the states used the funding. The Act made it clear that it was definitely not the job of the federal government to guarantee rights for persons with disabilities or to remove external barriers in the labor market; the policy was in place exclusively to provide extra assistance to disabled people to develop their potential [10].

The process of "disability evaluation" came onto the scene as the primary legal tool for determining eligibility for all social assistance, social protection, or social welfare programs designed to benefit people with disabilities and other vulnerable groups. Building on the original *Social Security Act of 1935*, two large and expensive programs came into existence in the United States, first in 1956 with Social Security Disability Insurance (SSDI), and then in 1970 with Supplemental Security Income (SSI). SSDI provided payments for those already covered by the Social Security program, while SSI was, and remains, a means-tested income assistance program for disabled, blind, and aged persons who have limited income, whether or not they were previously employed. Given the aim of income replacement for those unable to work because of disability, legal eligibility for both programs required a definition of disability that focused on the appropriate population in need, that is, the unemployable.

Thus, it was that from the mid-1930s onward an individual was considered disabled if he or she was unable "to engage in any substantial gainful activity by reason of any medically determinable physical or mental impairment which can be expected to result in death or which has lasted or can be expected to last for a continuous period of not less than 12 months" (42 U.S.C. 7 § 410). By the late 1970s, the SSA added the requirement that an applicant would only be deemed to have a disability "if his physical or mental impairment or impairments are of such severity that he is not only unable to do his previous work but cannot, considering his age, education, and work experience, engage in *any other kind of substantial gainful work* which exists in the national economy" (emphasis added). This provision is still in place.

To meet the challenge of operationalizing this definition, the SSA relied on the tried-and-true method of recruiting medical professionals as gatekeepers and a medicolegal procedure based on the so-called listings of impairments as a screening step in the disability evaluation process. The listings consist of medical signs, symptoms, and laboratory findings that purport to describe the level of severity required for each impairment to meet the administrative threshold for work disability. In response to a series of legal cases and political pressure in the 1980s.

The disability evaluation procedures for SSDI and SSI became a more complex mix of clinical evaluation on the basis of the listings; a rough assessment of the work-related functional limitations attributable to the impairment;

(continued)

a detailed vocational analysis of the individual's work history and acquired work skills, educational background, and age; and lastly an analysis of the individual's current vocational prospects.

All of which were described in great detail in what was informally called *The Blue Book*. Since SSA did not have the resources to perform the full five-stage assessment for each of the nearly three million new or returning applicants per year, and since negative decisions were reversed on appeal at an exceptionally high rate, the result was a politically unacceptably high level of successful applications.

In 1996 SSA came to the conclusion that the disability determination process needed to be refurbished and sought ideas for a fundamental revision. After a decade of study and several reports (see [11]), the prestigious Institute of Medicine expert committee in 2007 issued a report reluctantly conceding at the outset that it could find no compelling reason to abandon the purely medical determination by impairment listings and focused all its attention on improving their sensitivity [12]. In a modest attempt to move some distance away from a purely medical approach, the committee recommended research that would link the qualifying impairments in the listings to actual decreases in a person's functional capacity to perform standard or basic employment tasks, in the hope of making the listings a more relevant and realistic guide to the inability to work.

The American experience has been played out in similar ways in nearly all high-resource settings; from an initial position of relying entirely on a purely medical foundation for the legal determination of work disability, modifications have been suggested that widen the range of indicators, but in the end, the medical basis, both in legal criteria and the professional qualifications of the evaluators, remains authoritative.

7.1.4 Next Steps

Having briefly described its historical roots, this chapter develops the legal perspective of disability evaluation. It does this, first, by reviewing a typology of common patterns of disability evaluation used for determining work disability and other purposes within disability policy. Secondly, the chapter focuses on what has become the dominant approach, the Baremas or impairment-focused assessment method, and in particular the highly influential *American Medical Association Guides for the Assessment of Permanent Impairment* (henceforth, *AMA Guides*) [13]. Although, legally speaking, the *Guides* rarely cause much concern, there have always been academic and professional objections to them on the grounds that they fundamentally distort the notion of "work disability." Some have argued, for example, that the conceptualization of disability found in the World Health

Organization's *International Classification of Functioning, Disability and Health* or ICF [14] would cure the ills of the current methods.

When viewing disability evaluation in isolation and purely as a medicolegal tool for determining eligibility for benefits, the argument that the ICF would make a difference is weak. Since, legally speaking, the ICF would not make much difference, and as its implementation would require substantial changes in administration, it would be a difficult sell from a purely legal and administrative perspective. Nonetheless, when the social context is broadened to disability law and policy in general, and in particular when the role of disability determination is viewed from the perspective of the human right to work as enunciated in the United Nations *Convention on the Rights of Persons with Disabilities* [15], then the considerable legal significance of the ICF conception of disability becomes apparent.

7.2 Disability Evaluation Methods

7.2.1 The Typology of Methods

There are four medicolegal methodologies used, either alone or in combination, for assessing disability to determine eligibility for disability programs, and in particular those programs based on the notion of work disability:

1. **Baremas method**: A listing of impairments of bodily function or structure, ordinally ranked by severity, to which are arbitrarily attached values of "percentage of whole person disability." The claimant's impairments are compared to those listed and disability percentages combined to determine compensation level.
2. **Assessing care needs**: An assessment of overall care requirements linked to health conditions is made, usually in terms of the amount of time during the day or night in which a claimant needs help from another person coupled with an evaluation of the cost of providing that level of care. This calculation is then used to determine compensation level.
3. **Functional capacity method**: A medical assessor or other health professional is provided with a listing of disability descriptors for each level of disability, or with a profile of level of residual ability, and the claimant's assessed level is determined by a judgement as to which descriptor is closest to the claimant's actual situation.
4. **Economic loss method**: The loss of income of the claimant due to disability is calculated, either directly from the claimant's income or tax returns or by some calculation that models what the claimant could have earned if not disabled or what he or she is currently capable of earning, given the disability.

In many high-resource countries, a range of other considerations is considered, such as the age, educational level, and past work experience of the claimant or the extent of medical improvement that has already occurred. Although part of the evaluation, strictly speaking these factors are not relevant to the level of disability, but rather to the extent to which the claimant, with some assessed level of disability, can nonetheless engage in, to use the SSA's legal test, "substantial gainful activity."

These four methods are found around the globe, although in most low-resource settings, the procedures are extremely informal and highly discretionary (the International Labour Organization maintains a very useful website called NATLEX in which all relevant legislation around the globe is included for comparison [16]).

Another typology is possible, at least for European countries, in which a two-dimensional matrix further analyzes these four methods: the extent to which medical evidence is used and the extent to which discretion is sanctioned or allowed [17]. On this analysis, the four medicolegal methods, singly or in combination, can be arranged in a typology of high, medium, and low use of evidence and high, medium, and low reliance on discretion. Although this typology will not be pursued here, it should be noted that it does have the benefit of highlighting the considerable extent, in any of the disability evaluation arrangements currently in use, to which professional discretion supersedes medical evidence. From a legal perspective, this is understandable: it is legally more important for administrative decisions to be determinative and reliable than for them to be valid.

At the end of the day, however, all disability evaluation methods have to overcome a salient conceptual obstacle, created by the fact that aspects of a person's health – impairments of function and structure, levels of functional capacity, and degree of disability – are continuous rather than dichotomous phenomena.

Individuals have impairments in, for example, respiratory function to one degree or another, from very severe to very slight. Disability evaluation, however, is strictly a matter of whether an administrative category "disabled" applies or does not. This means that the legal or administrative category can only be applied if a threshold point, along the relevant continuum, is provided, or a high level of discretion is allowed to evaluators to set the threshold wherever they wish. As we shall see, the *AMA Guides* "solve" this conceptual problem by ignoring it and directly translating impairments' severity levels into whole-person disability percentages, leaving it to others to determine what percentage level qualifies as an eligible level for benefits.

7.2.2 *The Baremas Method and Its Problems*

Of the four methods of disability evaluation, the Baremas is by far the oldest. It is named after the seventeenth-century French mathematician Francois Barème who first proposed it as an academic exercise a chart of percentage values for each form of bodily damage. This approach was taken over in 1883 by the Bismarck government to be used in its emerging social insurance system. Although the method seems ancient and almost comically prescientific, it remains the most common assessment method, especially for workers' compensation benefit determination. Consider the following provision of the current US Code of Federal Regulations Employees' Benefits [18],

Section 8114(d)

Section 8106 compensation schedule if the disability is partial:

(1) Arm lost, 312 weeks' compensation.
(2) Leg lost, 288 weeks' compensation.
(3) Hand lost, 244 weeks' compensation.
(4) Foot lost, 205 weeks' compensation.
(5) Eye lost, 160 weeks' compensation.
(6) Thumb lost, 75 weeks' compensation.
(7) First finger lost, 46 weeks' compensation.
(8) Great toe lost, 38 weeks' compensation.
(9) Second finger lost, 30 weeks' compensation.
(10) Third finger lost, 25 weeks' compensation.
(11) Toe other than great toe lost, 16 weeks' compensation.
(12) Fourth finger lost, 15 weeks' compensation.

– or the following from the Ontario (Canada) *Workers Safety and Insurance Board* Rating Schedule [19]:

Metacarpals

The diagram which accompanies Chart 1 also provides disability rating values for metacarpals. The values shown do not include the thumb. The medical consultant uses the values shown as a minimum guide only, and assesses the function of the whole hand when establishing a disability rating. When calculating these, remember to apply the multiple only to those phalanges which are amputated or seriously impaired in common.

Percentage rating calculation To determine the percentage rating of the disability when more than one finger is injured, the decision-maker or WSIB medical consultant applies the following formulae:

- 2 Finger Disability = Sum of single digit value x 1.5
- 3 Finger Disability = Sum of single digit value x 2
- 4 Finger Disability = Sum of single digit value x 2.5

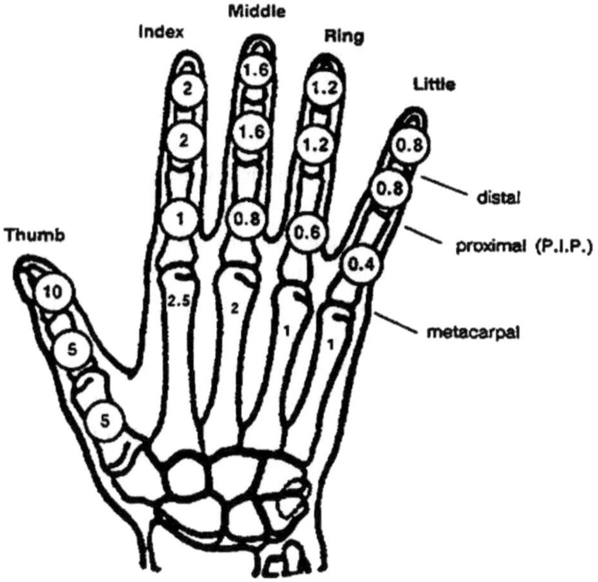

The *AMA Guides* are a highly sophisticated version of a Baremas method. First published in 1958, the *AMA Guides* are now in their 6th edition [13] and are used in 40 of 51 jurisdictions in the United States, Canada, Australia, New Zealand, South Africa, and many European countries, and informally and nonsystematically in countless low-resource countries. The intended purpose of the *Guides* is for workers' compensation, but they are the primary medicolegal tools for determining tort-based personal injury damage and disability claims management as well. Addressing academic objections to their use, the editors of the 6th edition argue that determination of the level of severity or class of impairment is not equivalent to a determination of work disability: "the Guides are not intended to be used for direct estimates of work participation restrictions. Impairment percentages derived according to the Guides' criteria do not directly measure work participation restrictions" [13, p. 6]. Problems of inter-rater reliability frequently raised in the literature (e.g., [20–22]) are acknowledged by the editors, as is the fact that the impairment percentages are based on professional consensus rather than evidence [23]. Although repeatedly raised over the years, the editors of the *AMA Guides* do not address the considerably more damning objection that the evaluation percentages embody retrograde gender and disability stereotypes (cf. [24]).

None of the scientific or political concerns about validity and reliability have had much impact on the extent to which the *Guides* are relied on, worldwide. The reason for this is very simple to understand: from a legal and administrative perspective, the *AMA Guides* adequately, and indeed admirably, fulfil the prerequisites of being presumptively authoritative, consistent, and objective. In many jurisdictions, the *AMA Guides* are used as a preliminary screening protocol for applications for disability benefits – so that only clear or severe instances of work disability are tagged – and once the claimant has jumped that hurdle, more subtle and relevant criteria are applied to determine both eligibility and *quantum* of benefit. The *AMA Guides*, in short, do the job asked of them.

And for many in the field, it is not clear that there is an alternative. Although assessing care needs and economic loss are relevant to the determination of the impact of impairments on a person's economic situation, they are at best indirect proxy measures of work disability. The same is not true of the more recently identified indicator of functional capacity. Indeed, occupational and vocational rehabilitation therapists have identified job-related functional capacity evaluation as the most intrinsically relevant indicator of work disability and therefore the most appropriate test of disability evaluation (see, e.g., [25, 26]). Nonetheless, practitioners have also argued that the relationship between impairments and work performance is simply not clear or predictable, especially when mental disorders or chronic pain is involved [27, 28], so why not stick with the standard already in place: the *AMA Guides*?

7.3 The Case for the ICF

Recent objections to the standard method of disability evaluation have been motivated by the belief that the closed world of disability evaluation needs to be exposed to more current and viable conceptions of disability in general, and work disability in particular. In no small part has this been the result of the increased acceptance by rehabilitation practitioners and researchers of the *International Classification of Functioning, Disability and Health* and its conceptualization of disability (see [29–32]).

Even the 6th edition of the *AMA Guides* announces its wholehearted adherence to the ICF approach to disability, although as it firmly maintains its long tradition of using impairment evaluation as a proxy for disability assessment, it is not clear what difference the adoption of the ICF has actually made.

As is well known, and certainly has been informally accepted theory within rehabilitation professionals for decades (see [33, 34]), disability is a complex notion that should be conceptualized, not as a feature of a person's body, but rather as an outcome of complex and not always well-understood interactions between health conditions and their associated impairments of body function and structure, simple and complex, and features of the individual's physical, human-built, social, and attitudinal environment.

This is the model of disability that is embodied in the ICF and is the basis for the classifications it contains.

Building on this understanding of disability, the more specific concept of work disability needs to take account of both the mental and physical demands of the job itself (sometimes called "work capacity," e.g., [35]), but also all features and dimensions of the job environment: the physical, psychological, social, and administrative features of the environment in which the worker performs the job. To take simple examples, a worker in a wheelchair needs an elevator to get to her office on the second floor; a worker who has severe pain when standing or sitting for long periods may nonetheless be fully able to perform the job if the requirements of the job are altered and he or she is allowed frequent rest breaks; or a worker with intellectual impairments may require helpful coworkers to carry out her job tasks. Since many aspects of the job environment are mutable by means of accommodations – both physical changes to the work site and alterations to the job tasks – impairments are not the only relevant determinants of work disability.

The difficulty, however, has been taking on board the ICF person-environment model of disability in the context of work disability evaluation. Even researchers and practitioners who deal closely with the notion of work disability hold inconsistent views about the concept. In a recent handbook on work disability, it is claimed that "work disability occurs when a worker is unable to remain at or resume work because of a health problem" [36, p. ix] – that is, work disability is directly and immediately caused by impairments. In the next sentence, though, the authors assert that "evidence indicates that work disability results from complex interplays involving several partners (workplace, insurer, healthcare providers) interacting with the patient/worker in the disability process. Addressing this systemic and multidimensional disability problem requires adopting a transdisciplinary perspective" (Ibid.). This implies that the prevention of work disability – the overall objective of the transdisciplinary endeavor – might have nothing to do with impairments at all but rather with environmental features of the workplace itself.

The Institute of Medicine studies of the Social Security Administration's disability evaluation already mentioned [11, 12] concluded that the ICF interactive model of work disability was both conceptually and empirically more realistic than the impairment-based model implicit in the SSA's disability evaluation determination of the claimant's ability "to engage in any substantial gainful activity." Nonetheless, they concluded, "SSA does not have the resources to perform such an extensive assessment for each of the approximately 2.6 million disability applicants who will come through its doors each year" [12, p. 53]. If this task cannot be feasibly accomplished in this high-resource country, it is unlikely that it is feasible in other countries with far fewer resources.

It is at this point that the far less commonly used "functional capacity" method described above is argued to be the second best option for reform. Although the literature on this slippery notion is vast and inconsistent, it appears that functional capacity serves two possible roles. First, it can be used as a screening criterion for a level of impairment that, as the IOM put it, is "strongly correlated" to a person's inability to work – that is, the person's inability regardless of any reasonable accommodations that might be made [12]. Although this role would seem to require some evidence that the level of an individual's capacity is so low that neither assistive technology nor job environmental changes would make a difference, it is not apparent whether this evidence is required, sought, or available.

Secondly, a person's functional capacity serves as a kind of proxy of the interaction between impairments and work environment. A purely impairment-based, medical assessment would hold the work environment constant and assess level of impairment. But a functional capacity assessment might be able to factor in the potential changes that could be made to the work environment to reach a more accurate assessment. Several authors suggested this use of functional capacity assessment [37–40]. One recent analysis links this role for functional capacity back to the ICF by suggesting that the "whole-person" perspective of the ICF dimension of activity limitations, rather than merely the body-level perspective of impairments, is at the core of functional assessment and as such provides a more comprehensive representation of a person's ability to work [32].

This is not the place to assess the plausibility of this role of "functional work capacity," let alone the interpretation of the ICF upon which it is based. Our focus here is the legal perspective on work disability evaluation. And from that perspective, the case for using the ICF, either directly or by means of the functional capacity method (suitably developed) remains weak. Put briefly, although much can be said in favor of using ICF for disability assessment, none of this matters much from the legal perspective.

Proponents of the ICF argue that as a well-crafted, conceptually clear, and international standard, the ICF would ensure transparency, terminological consistency, and (optimally) inter-rater reliability for disability evaluation [31, 41–45]. Yet these virtues are what legal practictioners already see in the AMA Guides, and why they believe that the Guides already provide an authoritative, international standard. Shifting existing administrative evaluation superstructures from the Guides to some operational ICF-based instrument would be, in a country like the United States, an enormous expense and so would require a powerful political and administrative argument about the long-term cost-effectiveness of this move. But there is no available evidence that savings would actually result, and the risk seems too great to take, when, legally speaking, the Guides do all that the law requires of them.

Arguably we are looking in the wrong place for an argument to move to the ICF conception of disability for work disability determination. In the narrow context of disability evaluation practice, administrative inertia and the weight of the long history of medical gatekeeping sketched out at the outset will continue to favor existing practice. There are potential legal objections to an impairment-based conception of work disability that reflect a very different historical and legal tradition that can be brought to bear at this juncture. This tradition is reflected in national and international antidiscrimination and human rights law as it applies to persons with disabilities. In effect, armed with the ICF, one might very well make a strong, legal argument that standard practices in work disability evaluation are discriminatory and violate human rights. And that is a legally very strong argument indeed.

7.4 Disability Evaluation from the Perspective of Equality and Human Rights Law

Legal definitions of disability used in equality and antidiscrimination law clearly reflect the ICF characterization of disability, or more specifically in ICF terminology, the dimension of participation. Consider the legal characterization of disability in the *Americans with Disabilities Act, 1990* (now the *ADA Amendments Act of 2008* Public Law 110–325), the first and seminal disability antidiscrimination law that has been the model for parallel legislation around the world:

Sec. 12102. Definition of disability

(1) Disability

The term "disability" means, with respect to an individual

(A) a physical or mental impairment that substantially limits one or more major life activities of such individual;
(B) a record of such an impairment; or
(C) being regarded as having such an impairment (as described in paragraph (3)).

(2) Major Life Activities

(A) In general

For purposes of paragraph (1), major life activities include, but are not limited to, caring for oneself, performing manual tasks, seeing, hearing, eating, sleeping, walking, standing, lifting, bending, speaking, breathing, learning, reading, concentrating, thinking, communicating, and working.

(B) Major bodily functions

For purposes of paragraph (1), a major life activity also includes the operation of a major bodily function, including but not limited to, functions of the immune system, normal cell growth, digestive, bowel, bladder, neurological, brain, respiratory, circulatory, endocrine, and reproductive functions.

(3) Regarded as having such an impairment

For purposes of paragraph (1)(C):

(A) An individual meets the requirement of "being regarded as having such an impairment" if the individual establishes that he or she has been subjected to an action prohibited under this chapter because of an actual or perceived physical or mental impairment whether or not the impairment limits or is perceived to limit a major life activity.
(B) Paragraph (1)(C) shall not apply to impairments that are transitory and minor. A transitory impairment is an impairment with an actual or expected duration of 6 months or less.

(4) (E) (i) The determination of whether an impairment substantially limits a major life activity shall be made without regard to the ameliorative effects of mitigating measures such as

(I) medication, medical supplies, equipment, or appliances, low-vision devices (which do not include ordinary eyeglasses or contact lenses), prosthetics including limbs and devices, hearing aids and cochlear implants or other implantable hearing devices, mobility devices, or oxygen therapy equipment and supplies;

(II) use of assistive technology;
(III) reasonable accommodations or auxiliary aids or services; or
(IV) learned behavioral or adaptive neurological modifications.

It does not take a lawyer to notice that this complex legal definition refers to, but goes far beyond, both impairments and functional capacities. We can be quite certain about this since the 2008 amendment to the original 1990 Act added, inter alia, clause (4)(E) (i) because a series of US Supreme Court decisions had misinterpreted the primary definition from the 1990 version as being limited to functional capacity. It is also important to notice that the mere fact that a person can be disabled by virtue of subsection (3) alone – namely, that the individual is "regarded as having an impairment" – makes it obvious that, as in the ICF definition, a disability can be wholly created by the effect of a person's environment – in this instance, the attitudes and beliefs of others – without an underlying impairment.

To put the point more generally, the legal significance of laws that protect against discrimination on the basis of disability address violation of individuals' right to participate in major life activities, such as employment, on an equal basis with others. But in the tradition of antidiscrimination law, the determination of when discrimination occurs presupposes an understanding of disability that is fully contextualized by the person's environment. In short, it is the environment – people's attitudes and beliefs, hiring practices, and the failure to provide accommodation – that creates discrimination, not the impairment or functional capacity.

There is another reason to be confident that disability antidiscrimination laws presume an ICF-like conceptualization of disability. These laws mandate a duty on the part of employers to provide "reasonable accommodation" for their disabled workers, up to the point of "undue hardship" in the form of excessive costs, health, and safety risks to other workers. Thus, to defend against a claim of discrimination by a disabled worker, an employer must assure the adjudicator that attempts to accommodate the disabled worker have been made, up to the point where making such accommodations would create undue hardship [46].

Accommodations are, in ICF terms, environmental factors that act as facilitators, either directly or indirectly as the removal of an environmental barrier. Legal doctrine in the area of antidiscrimination requires a notion of work disability understood as ICF participation, rather than merely as impairment or a problem of functional capacity.

Significantly, it is legally arguable that a failure to take the environment into account when determining work disability is itself a form of discrimination.

If we move from national antidiscrimination laws to the realm of human rights, the essential role of the ICF in work disability conceptualization is even clearer. The right to work and to enjoy the associated sense of living a life of meaning, self-worth, and dignity has been a central component of international human rights treaties since the original *Universal Declaration of Human Rights* in 1948 [47] Article 23: "...the right to work, to free employment, to just and favourable conditions of work and to protection against unemployment." Article 6 of the United Nations' *International Covenant on Economic, Social and Cultural Rights* not only recognizes a right to work, but also the obligation of states to provide "technical and vocational guidance and training programmes, policies and techniques" required to achieve the full realization of that right [48]. *The European Social Charter* that entered into force in 1965 begins in Article 1 by expressing the obligation of each state to ensure that "there is work for all who are available for and seeking work" [49], and Article 15 of the *Charter of Fundamental Rights of the European Union* states that "everyone has the right to engage in work and to pursue a freely chosen or accepted occupation ... and has the freedom to seek employment, to work, to exercise the right of establishment and to provide services in any Member State" [50].

These general statements of the human right to work have legal force, but it is necessary often to drill down to the comments and technical guidelines to disclose some of their conceptual presumptions and normative content. In the case of *ICESCR*, one of these technical comments explicitly links the right to work to the right to a physically accessible workplace ([51]; and see 52). The International Labor Office has, in all of its disability-related pronouncements and conventions, made accessibility – both in terms of the physical space of a worksite, but also its psychological and informational accessibility – a precondition of the right to work [53]. The 1983 ILO *Recommendation on Vocational Rehabilitation and Employment (Disabled Persons)*, for example, states that to ensure the right to a job, states must take "appropriate measures to create job opportunities on the open labour market, including financial incentives to employers to encourage them to provide training and subsequent employment for disabled persons, as well as to make reasonable adaptations to workplaces, job design, tools, machinery and work organisation to facilitate such training and employment" [53].

For persons with disabilities, the culmination of this long tradition of international law on the human right to work is Article 26 of the *United Nations Convention on the Rights of Persons with Disabilities* [15]. In Article 26, three legal assertions are made that, although implicit in previous treaties and legal instruments, are only in this document made explicit:

1. Disability, as in the ICF, is interactional between health conditions and the environment:

    Article 1 Purpose

    Persons with disabilities include those who have long-term physical, mental, intellectual or sensory impairments, which in interaction with various barriers may hinder their full and effective participation in society on an equal basis with others.

2. The right to work includes the right that the workplace be accessible to persons with disabilities:

Article 9 Accessibility

1. To enable persons with disabilities to live independently and participate fully in all aspects of life, States Parties shall take appropriate measures to ensure to persons with disabilities access, on an equal basis with others, to the physical environment, to transportation, to information and communications, including information and communications technologies and systems, and to other facilities and services open or provided to the public, both in urban and in rural areas. These measures, which shall include the identification and elimination of obstacles and barriers to accessibility.

3. The right to work entails the obligation on the part of the state to ensure access to impairment-related services such as vocational rehabilitation, but also to work environment modifications by way of reasonable accommodation:

Article 27 Work and Employment

1. States Parties recognize the right of persons with disabilities to work, on an equal basis with others ... by taking appropriate steps, including through legislation, to

(a) Prohibit discrimination on the basis of disability with regard to all matters concerning all forms of employment...
(d) Enable persons with disabilities to have effective access to general technical and vocational guidance programmes, placement services and vocational and continuing training; ...
(i) Ensure that reasonable accommodation is provided to persons with disabilities in the workplace;

Article 2

"Reasonable accommodation" means necessary and appropriate modification and adjustments not imposing a disproportionate or undue burden, where needed in a particular case, to ensure to persons with disabilities the enjoyment or exercise on an equal with others of all human rights and fundamental freedoms;

The CRPD is a relatively new law and its provisions are still to be tested and legally explained. The consequences of the full implementation of its provisions are yet to be fully known. Again, we rely on interpretative documents to fully appreciate the social significance of disability human rights. Because of the long tradition in international human rights law to emphasize the significance of work and employment on people's lives, the United Nations' Office of the High Commissioner on Human Rights produced its first thematic study on the potential impact of the CRPD in this area [54]. Emphasizing the environmental perspective, this study reviewed the extent of the obligation to accessible workplaces, to reasonable accommodation, and, in lieu of employment, to full access to social protection programs. Of particular significance is the Office's assessment that "disability classification systems" that categorize people with disabilities in terms of impairments and severity of functional capacity and use these systems for conditions of eligibility for disability-related compensation, or services are implicitly in violation of their CRPD human rights obligations.

The legal perspective captured in these antidiscrimination and human rights documents is very different from that found in the context of disability evaluation for work disability and other disability benefits and services. Disability evaluation, as its history has made clear, is built on a vision of disability as a severe and substantial decrement in the ability to work.

As a consequence, from the English *Poor Law* onward, disability evaluation has principally been a way to distinguish people who legitimately are unable to work from those who had no good reason not to work. The grounding in impairment and medical evidence, the administrative and legal apparatus that test applicants against the standard of infirmity and incapacity, and even the modern trend to assess disability in terms of the extent to which rehabilitation and other services could "fix" the individual, all reflect this tradition.

The human rights tradition, philosophically and legally, is entirely different. It is grounded in a conception of equality and universal humanity, recognizing implicitly the diversity of human capability and need. As a result, the ICF conception of disability has a more natural fit in this tradition, as it reflects the universalistic perspective on disability that impairments are permanent, unavoidable, and utterly natural features of the lived experience of human beings. Like all universal features of humanity, the impact of impairments can only be understood in interaction with the full environmental context in which people live and act. In the human rights tradition, similarly, people with disabilities are not deserving of special treatment – treatment that "fixes" them or compensates them for undeserved suffering and marginalization. Instead, people with disabilities, like all human beings, deserve equal opportunities that often require a balancing of the person-environment interaction to fully participate in basic human endeavors, such as work and employment.

7.5 Conclusion

At first glance, the legal dimensions of disability evaluation involve the simple, but pervasive legal demand for certainty and administrative convenience. As beginning law students are taught, there is no eternal or naturally "right" direction to drive on streets; you can drive on the right or the left. The law only demands that it is certain which direction to drive and that everyone is aware of it. From this somewhat cynical stance, the various methods and schemes of disability evaluation found in the world can only be assessed in terms of their reliability, consistent application, transparency, and administrative cost – characterized in this chapter as the principles of natural justice in application. As such, there is no legal issue of validity, no legal demand for a scientifically correct model of work disability. The survival of existing regimes is a matter of their authoritativeness, their rough reliability and intuitive relevance, and, typically the political support that undergirds their continuity. Therefore, the case for using the ICF is quite weak. The lawyer will ask whether the disruption in current practice would be worth the improvement that the

ICF would bring about. The expert committee of the Institute of Medicine, after years of study, came to the conclusion that fundamental change could not be justified, and they were likely correct.

Yet, there is a very strong case to be made that outside of the restricted borders of disability evaluation, and in light of national antidiscrimination law and the broader, international legal context of human rights obligations, the ICF conceptualization of disability has profound legal resonance. In this broader context, with its entirely different historical antecedents, there is indeed a "correct" conception of disability: it is that which captures the universal lived experience of people, their needs, and the contexts in which they live and act. Arguably, it would be a violation of basic principles of human rights, and the underlying values of equal dignity and respect, to ignore the evidence that people with disabilities are limited in their participation in major life activities, such as employment, not because of their health condition, their impairments, or their functional limitations but because of the barriers created by features of their physical, human-built, attitudinal, social, and political environment.

The role of the environment in restricting participation is at the heart of the ICF model of disability and as such is of deep legal significance.

References

1. Rushton P. Lunatics and idiots: mental disability, the community, and the poor law in north-east England, 1600–1800. Med Hist. 1988;32:34–50.
2. Stiker H. A history of disability. W. Sayers, Trans. Ann Arbor: University of Michigan Press; 1999.
3. Stone DA. Physicians as gatekeepers: illness certification as a rationing device. Public Policy. 1979;27(2):227–54.
4. Stone DA. The disabled state. Philadelphia: Temple University Press; 1984.
5. Drimmer JC. Cripples, overcomers, and civil rights: tracing the evolution of federal legislation and social policy for people with disabilities. UCLA Law Rev. 1993;40(5):1341–410.
6. Rummery K, Glendinning C. Access to services as a civil and social rights issue: the role of welfare professionals in regulating access to and commissioning services for disabled and older people under New Labour. Soc Policy Adm. 2000;34(5):529–50.
7. Lord W, Jowell J, de Smith A. De Smith's judicial review. 7th ed. London: Sweet & Maxwell; 2013.
8. Scotch RK. From good will to civil rights: transforming federal disability policy. 2nd ed. Philadelphia: Temple University Press; 2001.
9. Bickenbach JE. Ethics, law, and policy, SAGE reference series on disability: key issues and future directions, vol. 4. Thousand Oaks: Sage; 2012.
10. O'Brien R. Crippled justice: the history of modern disability policy in the workplace. Chicago: The University of Chicago Press; 2001.
11. Institute of Medicine, Wunderlich GS, Rice DP, Amado NL, editors. The dynamics of disability: measuring and monitoring disability for social security programs. Washington, DC: National Academy Press; 2002.

12. Institute of Medicine, Stobo JD, McGeary M, Barnes DK, editors. Improving the social security disability decision process. Washington, DC: National Academy Press; 2007.
13. Rondinelli RD, Genovese E, Kat RT, et al., editors. Guides to the evaluation of permanent impairment. 6th ed. Chicago: American Medical Association; 2008.
14. WHO. International classification of functioning, disability and health. Geneva: WHO; 2001.
15. UN. Convention on the rights of persons with disabilities. G.A. Res. 61/106. http://www.un.org/esa/socdev/enable/rights/contexte.htm (2007). Accessed 30 Dec 2013.
16. NATLEX. http://www.oit.org/dyn/natlex/natlex_browse.home
17. European Commission, DG Employment and Social Affairs. Definitions of disability in Europe: a comparative analysis. http://ec.europa.eu/social/BlobServlet?docId=2088&langId=en (2002). Accessed 30 Dec 2013.
18. US. Federal Employees' Compensation Act (FECA). Title 20, code of federal regulations employees' benefits. http://www.workerscompensation.com/regulations/statedepartment.php?ID=2064&state=federal&Parent=2064 (2012). Accessed 30 Dec 2013.
19. Ontario, Canada, 2012 workers safety and insurance board rating schedule. http://www.wsib.on.ca/en/community/WSIB/230/OPMDetail/24347?vgnextoid=d77dc0d9ca3d7210VgnVCM100000449c710aRCRD&vgnextchannel=e5ab8588e7a4e110VgnVCM1000000e18120aRCRD (2012). Accessed 30 Dec 2013.
20. McCarthy ML, McAndrew MP, MacKenzie EJ, et al. Correlation between the measures of impairment, according to the modified system of the American Medical Association, and function. J Bone Jt Surg Am Vol. 1998;80:1034–42.
21. Spieler EA, Barth PS, Burton Jr JF, Himmelstein J, Rudolph L. Recommendations to guide revision of the guides to the evaluation of permanent impairment. American Medical Association. JAMA. 2000;283:519–23.
22. Forst L, Friedman L, Chukwu A. Reliability of the AMA Guides to the evaluation of permanent impairment. J Occup Environ Med. 2010;52(12):1021–3.
23. Colledge A, Hunter B, Bundall LD, Holmes EB. Impairment rating ambiguity in the United States: the Utah Impairment Guides for calculating workers' compensation impairments. J Korean Med Sci. 2009;24 Suppl 2:S232–41.
24. Pryor ES. Flawed promises: a critical evaluation of the AMA's Guides to the evaluation of permanent impairment. Harv Law Rev. 1990;103(4):964–76.
25. Jette AM, Badley E. Conceptual issues in the measurement of work disability. In: Mathiowetz N, Wunderlich GS, editors. Survey measurement of work disability: summary of a workshop. Washington, DC: National Academy Press; 2002. p. 4–27.
26. Reneman MF, Dijkstra SJ. Introduction to the special issue on functional capacity evaluation: from expert based to evidence base. J Occup Rehabil. 2003;13:203–6.
27. Okpaku SO, Sibulkin AE, Schenzler C. Disability determinations for adults with mental disorders: Social Security Administration vs independent judgments. Am J Public Health. 1998;84:1791–5.
28. Wideman TH, Sullivan MJ. Differential predictors of the long-term levels of pain intensity, work disability, healthcare use, and medication use in a sample of workers' compensation claimants. Pain. 2011;152:376–83.
29. Bufka LF, Stewart D, Stark S. The International Classification of Functioning, Disability and Health (ICF) is emerging as the principal framework for the description of health and health related status. Can J Occup Ther. 2008;75(3):134.
30. Giannangelo K, Bowman S, Dougherty M, Fenton S. ICF: representing the patient beyond a medical classification of diagnoses. Perspect Health Inf Manag. 2005;5(2):1–9.
31. Escorpizo R, Stucki G. Disability evaluation, social security, and the international classification of functioning, disability and health: the time is now. J Occup Environ Med. 2013;55(6): 645–51.
32. Marfeo EE, Haley SM, Jette AM, Eisen SV, Ni P, Bogusz K, Meterko M, McDonough CM, Chan L, Brandt DE, Rasch EK. Conceptual foundation for measures of physical function and behavioral health function for social security work disability evaluation. Arch Phys Med Rehabil. 2013;94(9):1645–52.
33. Wright B. Physical disability – a psychosocial approach. New York: Harper & Row; 1960.

34. Safilios-Rothschild C. The sociology and social psychology of disability and rehabilitation. New York: Random House; 1970.
35. Soer R, van der Schans CP, Geertzen JH, Groothoff JW, Brouwer S, Dijkstra PU, Reneman MF. Normative values for a functional capacity evaluation. Arch Phys Med Rehabil. 2009;90(1): 785–94.
36. Loisel P, Anema JR, editors. Handbook of work disability prevention and management. New York: Springer; 2013.
37. Harten JA. Functional capacity evaluation. Occup Med. 1998;13(1):209–12.
38. Truchon M, Fillion L. Biopsychosocial determinants of chronic disability and low-back pain: a review. J Occup Rehabil. 2000;10:117–42.
39. Wind H, Gouttebarge V, Kuijer PP, Sluiter JK, Frings-Dresen MH. The utility of functional capacity evaluation: the opinion of physicians and other experts in the field of return to work and disability claims. Int Arch Occup Environ Health. 2006;79(6):528–34.
40. Wind H, Gouttebarge V, Kuijer PP, Sluiter JK, Frings-Dresen MH. Effect of functional capacity evaluation information on the judgment of physicians about physical work ability in the context of disability claims. Int Arch Occup Environ Health. 2009;82(9):1087–96.
41. Slebus FG, Sluiter JK, Kuijer PFM, Willems JHBM, Frings-Dresen MHW. Work-ability evaluation: a piece of cake or a hard nut to crack? Disabil Rehabil. 2007;29(16):1295–300.
42. de Boer W, Donceel P, Brage S, Rus M, Willems JHBM. Medico-legal reasoning in disability assessment: a focus group and validation study. BMC Public Health. 2008;8:335–44.
43. Schwegler U, Anner JB, Boldt C, et al. Aspects of functioning and environmental factors in medical work capacity evaluations of persons with chronic widespread pain and low back pain can be represented by a combination of applicable ICF Core Sets. BMC Public Health. 2012; 12:1088–103.
44. Anner J, Schwegler U, Kunz R, Trezzini B, de Boer W. Evaluation of work disability and the international classification of functioning, disability and health: what to expect and what not. BMC Public Health. 2012;12:470–8.
45. Saltychev M, Kinnunen A, Laimi K. Vocational rehabilitation evaluation and the International Classification of Functioning, Disability, and Health (ICF). J Occup Rehabil. 2013;23(1): 106–14.
46. ILO. Managing disability in the workplace: ILO code of practice. Geneva: ILO. http://www.ilo.org/wcmsp5/groups/public/@ed_emp/documents/publication/wcms_103324.pdf (2002). Accessed 30 Dec 2013.
47. UN. Universal Declaration of Human Rights. http://www.un.org/en/documents/udhr/ (1948). Accessed 30 Dec 2013.
48. UN. International Covenant on Economic, Social and Cultural Rights entry into force 3 January 1976, in accordance with article 27. http://www.ohchr.org/EN/ProfessionalInterest/Pages/CESCR.aspx. Accessed 30 Dec 2013.
49. EU. European Social Charter, 529 UNTS 89, entered into force 26 Feb. http://conventions.coe.int/Treaty/Commun/QueVoulezVous.asp?NT=035&CL=ENG (1965). Accessed 30 Dec 2013.
50. EU. Charter of Fundamental Rights of the European Union. http://eur-lex.europa.eu/en/treaties/dat/32007X1214/htm/C2007303EN.01000101.htm(2000). Accessed 30 Dec 2013.
51. UN. The Right to Work – General comment No. 18, Article 6 of the International Covenant on Economic, Social and Cultural Rights. E/C.12/GC/18. http://www.nesri.org/sites/default/files/CESCR_General_Comment_18.pdf (2006). Accessed 30 Dec 2013.
52. O'Connell R. The right to work in the European Convention on Human Rights. Eur Hum Rights Law Rev. 2012;2:176–90.
53. ILO. Vocational Rehabilitation and Employment (Disabled Persons) Convention (No. 159) and Recommendation (No. 168): United Nations Convention on the Rights of Persons with Disabilities. Geneva: ILO. http://www.ilo.org/wcmsp5/groups/public/—ed_emp/—ifp_skills/documents/publication/wcms_103529.pdf (2008). Accessed 30 Dec 2013.
54. OHCHR. Thematic study on work and employment of persons with disabilities. Report of the Office of the United Nations High Commissioner for Human Rights. http://www.ohchr.org/EN/Issues/Disability/Pages/WorkAndEmployment.aspx (2012). Accessed 30 Dec 2013.

Chapter 8
Vocational Assessment and Job Placement

Debra Homa and David DeLambo

8.1 Introduction

Although the vocational assessment and job placement processes occur at opposite ends of the rehabilitation spectrum, with vocational assessment in the initial stage and job placement as the culmination of vocational rehabilitation (VR) services, they work in tandem. For both processes, a holistic understanding of the client's functional capacities and barriers is essential to providing effective VR services. This chapter describes the applications of the International Classification of Functioning, Disability, and Health (ICF) [1] in vocational assessment and job placement and discusses their potential for improving the effectiveness of VR services. In addition, the chapter reviews empirical studies that have investigated predictors of successful employment outcomes in VR and links this research to the ICF conceptual framework. The ICF presents a dynamic model for understanding health and functioning and includes the following components: body functions (physiological changes in body functions, such as mental, sensory, and neuromusculoskeletal), body structures (anatomical changes, such as structures of the nervous system, cardiovascular and respiratory systems), activities and participation (e.g., learning and applying knowledge, communication, self-care, and employment), and contextual factors (environmental factors and personal factors). Within its classification system, the ICF presents precisely defined codes for all of the components, with the exception of personal factors, which have not yet been classified. Personal factors include demographic variables such as age, gender, race/ethnicity, coping styles, educational background, and lifestyle [1].

Previous studies have been supportive of using the ICF categories for assessing VR outcomes and identifying interventions [2]. The ICF categories appear to be

D. Homa (✉) • D. DeLambo
Department of Rehabilitation and Counseling, University of Wisconsin-Stout, Menomonie, WI 54751, USA
e-mail: homad@uwstout.edu

R. Escorpizo et al. (eds.), *Handbook of Vocational Rehabilitation and Disability Evaluation*, Handbooks in Health, Work, and Disability, DOI 10.1007/978-3-319-08825-9_8

sufficiently exhaustive and comprehensive in addressing the most important factors needed to understand an individual's abilities in relation to work participation as well as environmental factors that may act as barriers or facilitators [3, 4]. Interestingly, studies reviewing the ICF model in relation to clinical data in rehabilitation have noted that only a limited number of environmental factors are often identified in patients' records. However, this observation does not indicate that these factors are unimportant; rather, this suggests that environmental factors often are not addressed during the rehabilitation process. This highlights an important advantage of using the ICF framework in VR; that is, it ensures that rehabilitation practitioners assume a more holistic perspective by taking into account all factors that may have an impact on the individual's ability to be successful in a vocational rehabilitation program.

8.2 Person-Environment Interaction and VR

Parsons recognized the importance of person and environmental factors in vocational choice over 100 years ago in 1909 in his groundbreaking book, *Choosing a Vocation* [5, 6]. Both vocational assessment and job placement help optimize the "fit" between characteristics of the person and those of the work environment, including job requirements. Thus, an important goal is to maximize job satisfaction and job performance by helping individuals obtain jobs that match their interests, values, and abilities. According to the 14th Institute on Rehabilitation Issues [7], the vocational assessment process must include not only assessment of the individual, but also cultural, social, and physical aspects of the environment. Rehabilitation professionals must understand the environmental factors that have an impact on the individual's behavior and functioning, that is, the behaviors resulting from the interaction between the person and his or her environmental context. Accordingly, effective rehabilitation planning assesses the environment and the person, as well as the interaction between them [8].

Several key theories of career development form the underpinnings of both vocational assessment and job placement, especially trait-factor theory. The underlying principle of trait-factor theory is that it is possible to match individuals' aptitudes and interest, to job requirements and worker characteristics of jobs or job factors. When traits and factors "fit", the individual is more likely to experience job success. The Minnesota Theory of Work Adjustment is an extension of trait-factor theory and posits that worker satisfaction and job satisfactoriness predict work adjustment and job tenure. More recently, trait-factor theory has been replaced by the more contemporary Person X Environment (*P X E*) Fit approach, which recognizes the dynamic nature of the interaction of individuals with their environments. This process is reciprocal, as people influence their environments and vice versa. *P X E* fit takes from trait-factor theory the idea that the better the fit or congruence between characteristics of the person (such as skills and abilities) and requirements and reinforcers of the job (i.e., job characteristics that align with interests and values), the more likely the person will be successful [9, 10].

Since occupational success is contingent on the *P X E* interaction [11], effective VR strategies require practitioners to appreciate multiple issues that are interdependent and unique for each person on both a micro (individual) and macro (cultural/societal) level. In this light, the ICF can identify numerous factors that interact to promote or impede successful employment by taking into account the impact of multiple personal and environmental variables [12]. Research suggests that it is possible to classify disability according to the *P X E* interaction using the ICF conceptual framework. Moreover, the ICF framework can identify whether interactions are facilitative or problematic [13]. Research has confirmed the value of the ICF environmental factors for identifying both facilitators and barriers as well as indicating the potential of the environmental factors to act as mediators in helping individuals return to work [14]. *P X E* is a dynamic process that occurs on multiple levels and changes over time. By helping practitioners more accurately recognize strengths in a person's environment, the ICF can direct attention to aspects of a person's environment that could be further developed and which would, in turn, foster personal growth and improved capacities that are important for ultimate vocational success [15].

With vocational evaluation's emphasis on using work as the focal point of assessment, *P X E* fit is especially relevant, as the vocational evaluation considers the environmental context and allows individuals to have various work-related experiences during the evaluation. The vocational evaluator also develops recommendations to improve the *P X E* correspondence by recommending appropriate interventions or services, such as assistive technology or job accommodations.

> The ICF can identify numerous factors that interact to promote or impede successful employment by taking into account the impact of multiple personal and environmental variables.

8.3 Vocational Assessment

Vocational assessment is the initial stage of any well-planned VR program and sets the foundation for all other services and activities. In fact, Power [16] asserted, "many of the mistakes made in job placement can be avoided if an appropriate and accurate evaluation is performed" (p. 1). A number of studies have demonstrated that vocational assessment contributes to successful outcomes by promoting more effective VR planning [17]. For example, clients who have received vocational assessment have higher successful placement rates, especially when rehabilitation practitioners implement the recommendations from the evaluation report [18].

Although the terms vocational assessment and vocational evaluation are often used interchangeably, the two actually have distinct definitions. Vocational assessment is a generic overarching term for an information gathering process used for the purposes of rehabilitation planning and identification of vocational goals [19]. The Glossary of the Vocational Assessment, Evaluation, and Work Adjustment defines vocational assessment as:

> A comprehensive process conducted over a period of time, usually involving a multi-disciplinary team... with the purpose of identifying individual characteristics, education, training, and placement needs, serving as the basis for planning an individual's educational program and which provides the individual with insight into vocational potential. [20, p. 29]

Vocational assessment provides the foundation for future decisions regarding training, education, employment, and services individuals need to achieve a successful employment outcome [7]. As such, it describes and predicts work performance and behavior and identifies feasible vocational goals. To be effective, the vocational assessment must be holistic and must include social, psychological, medical, and other factors that have an impact on work functioning and vocational development [18, 21].

Depending on an individual's level of need, various levels of vocational assessment may be appropriate. The Level I vocational assessment is basically a screening process to gather information needed for service provision and typically includes interviewing, limited psychometric testing, and gathering of demographic information. For some individuals, such a short screening type of assessment may be sufficient for the purposes of identifying an employment goal and developing a rehabilitation plan. For example, this may be appropriate for someone with an established work history and clearly defined interests and skills that can be linked to a specific goal. However, this limited assessment is often not sufficient for many individuals receiving VR services, in which case the Level II or clinical vocational assessment would be needed. The Level II vocational assessment involves gathering more in-depth information for the purposes of diagnosis and prediction and to assess current functioning levels [17]. This level of assessment may involve reviewing and interpreting information from multiple disciplines, such as clinical psychologists, social workers, physicians, and physical therapists. It may include a transferable skills analysis and psychometric testing that is clinically interpreted. Although this level of assessment is in depth, it still may not provide sufficient information needed to determine a plan of action. If such is the case, a more comprehensive Level III vocational assessment is recommended. The Level III vocational assessment is also known as a comprehensive vocational evaluation. In a seminal research project investigating the field of vocational assessment, the Vocational Evaluation and Work Adjustment Association [VEWAA] defined vocational evaluation as:

> A comprehensive process that systematically uses either real or simulated work as the focal point for assessment and vocational exploration; the purpose [of which] is to assist individuals in vocational development. The vocational evaluation process incorporates medical, psychological, social, vocational, educational, cultural, and economic data. [22, pp. 17–18]

As reflected in the above definition, vocational evaluation should involve using a systematic approach that takes into account the key variables identified in career development theories, including individual characteristics, contextual factors (current as well as previous situations), cultural and societal attitudes, environmental factors, and a good fit between the person and the environment [18].

8.3.1 Usefulness the ICF in Vocational Assessment

Although the ICF is not in itself an assessment instrument, it provides a comprehensive and holistic framework for organizing a wealth of information within the vocational assessment process, and a variety of already existing instruments can be linked to the classification structure of the ICF [23, 24]. The ICF helps ensure a more comprehensive case conceptualization that is needed for VR planning. By applying the ICF's conceptual framework, vocational evaluators could systematically gather, organize, synthesize, and interpret this vast amount of assessment information. As noted, practitioners gather information from multiple sources, including medical and psychological reports, as well as data generated during the vocational assessment itself, such as interview and psychometric test results. The key to effectively organizing this information is to be able to integrate it in a way that is comprehensive and includes an understanding of the interaction of individuals with their environments and lived experiences [24]. The ICF conceptual model helps the evaluator take into account the dynamic interplay of the multiple biopsychosocial factors that are involved and thus counteract a linear viewpoint that focuses solely on characteristics of the individual, without taking into account the person's environmental context.

The ICF model could also be useful in helping the evaluator to organize information according to assets and barriers, which is a recommended way to synthesize vocational assessment information [25]. The ICF provides a comprehensive taxonomy of areas important for assessment planning that could be particularly helpful for less experienced practitioners; that is, it helps ensure that important areas will not be overlooked [26, 27]. In addition, the coding structure of the ICF could be linked to existing databases, such as the Job Accommodation Network (JAN), and crosswalk systems could be developed that link ICF components to the Abilities (Worker Characteristics) and Basic Skills (Worker Requirements) domains in the Occupational Information Network (O*NET), the occupational information system used in the United States [24]. In the process of analyzing and synthesizing vocational assessment results, the vocational evaluator could use linkages with these databases to formulate comprehensive and clearly defined recommendations. Ultimately, the resulting data could be gathered and used for the purposes of program evaluation to examine the effectiveness of the assessment program.

> The ICF helps ensure a more comprehensive case conceptualization that is needed for VR planning.

The ICF is highly comprehensive in addressing almost all aspects of functioning and disability, including environmental factors, and also illustrates the multi-dimensional, interactive nature of health and functioning, which is not necessarily linear [28] but one that is dynamic and evolving. For example, in a case study using an ICF-based assessment profile for rehabilitation planning, Glässel et al. [29] noted that the profile enabled the rehabilitation team to identify relationships between the patient's personal factors (e.g., coping skills) as assets that affected the patient's response to stress. Likewise, a study examining the ICF as a tool for organizing patient data found the ICF to be a useful format for assessing the effectiveness of interventions of persons with traumatic brain injury and particularly highlighted the importance of environmental factors that were helpful in identifying appropriate treatment [30].

In addition to rehabilitation planning, a key purpose of vocational assessment is to identify barriers and recommend services to overcome or minimize them [22]. The environmental factors of the ICF help ensure consideration of environmental factors when identifying barriers or strengths so that recommendations are most appropriately targeted to the person, environment, or both [24]. These environmental factors include not only physical aspects of an individual's home or workplace but also social factors, attitudes, and cultural factors that may act as either barriers or facilitators to a successful vocational outcome. Despite the importance of environmental factors in assessment, however, they are often overlooked, as a number of studies have noted inadequate attention to environmental factors in reviews of clinical data (e.g., [30]). A study examining the Comprehensive Core Set for VR [3] was supportive of the ICF as useful tool in VR, especially for the purposes of assessment and rehabilitation planning. However, similar to the finding of other studies, the researchers noted that VR assessments tended to focus primarily on biomedical concepts of disability and did not sufficiently address environmental factors. Implications are that using the Comprehensive Core Set during the evaluation process would help counteract the tendency to focus on biomedical factors and ensure that the vocational evaluator adopts a more holistic approach that incorporates the *P X E* interaction (i.e., the biopsychosocial model). Including consideration of ICF environmental factors in the assessment process can also help prevent a common error in clinical judgment, the fundamental attribution error, in which situational factors are not considered in explanations of behavior [31]. Using the ICF conceptual framework would help the evaluator take into account situational factors that could have an impact on behavior [24].

The fact that the ICF provides a universal, standardized language for describing functioning and health-related states [32] is an important advantage because vocational assessment is interdisciplinary in nature and may include a wide range of professional and health-related disciplines, including psychologists, occupational therapists, speech therapists, and physical therapists [22, 33]. In a vocational assessment program, communication is often bidirectional, with VR professionals receiving referral data from various disciplines as well as providing information of the assessment results to other health professionals [24]. The final outcome of vocational assessment is usually a set of recommendations that often include services that will be provided by others. Thus, the universal language of the ICF can help ensure seamless delivery of services and avoid miscommunications that could impede a client's progress.

A core principle of vocational assessment is that it should provide an empowering experience for the client. By providing clients with information about their capacities and information about how their skills and interests relate to the world of work, vocational assessment promotes empowerment, an important factor in rehabilitation success [17, 18]. The ICF provides an important advantage in this empowerment process because it can be used in a strengths-based way. That is, it can help specifically identify an individual's strengths in terms of capacities and environmental strengths, which can then be put together to identify where best to direct interventions [34]. Moreover, the ICF can be used in a collaborative manner with clients for communicating assessment results, which promotes empowerment [24].

For individuals with severe disabilities, an ecological approach to vocational assessment, that is, one that takes place within the actual work setting, is generally more appropriate for many individuals with severe disabilities. An ecologically based vocational evaluation involves assessing the individual, the environment, and the correspondence between the two [16]. Where there are discrepancies between the requirements of the work setting and the abilities of the individual, the evaluator must determine what types of interventions can be made that would resolve the discrepancies and produce a good "fit" between the worker and the job. The ICF has strong applicability for ecological assessment due to its clearly defined environmental factors and framework allowing the evaluator to distinguish between the individual's capacity and performance. That is, the ICF framework enables the evaluator to identify gaps between capacity and performance to determine what type of interventions are needed (including environmental interventions) to help the individual be successful in an actual job situation (i.e., performance), such as assistive technology or job modifications in the form of changes to the physical environment or adjustments in job duties and/or schedules [24].

8.4 Job Placement

Although job placement has been an essential component of VR since its inception, there has been a lack of consensus regarding its definition, that is, whether job placement is an outcome or a process in VR [35]. According to the Encyclopedia of Disability and Rehabilitation [36], job placement in VR "refers to the employment of persons with disabilities in suitable jobs" (p. 413). Placement is an essential outcome of VR services and key to the overarching goal of maximizing independence and enhancing quality of life for individuals with disabilities. As a commonly used term in VR, Vandergoot et al. [37] provided a more comprehensive definition of job placement as "the constellation of rehabilitation services that relate to employment and integration into the workplace" (pp. 305–307); this definition refers to job placement as an outcome, while including the concept of process, that is, employment-related activities and services.

The ICF is applicable to job placement services in a number of ways that are similar to vocational assessment, though with some differences. As with vocational assessment, ICF-based tools could help placement professionals organize client information and enhance their case conceptualization and problem-solving skills, and the ICF can promote a holistic understanding of the client, especially when serving individuals with severe disabilities who need multiple, integrative services. The ICF's focus on functioning, rather than diagnosis, can help the practitioner identify more effective and creative employment strategies, such as job modifications. Similar to its usefulness in vocational assessment, the ICF could facilitate collaboration among various disciplines and stakeholders by providing a common language, provide a framework for systematic assessment of job accommodations, and identify environmental factors that are barriers or facilitators. Using an ICF-based framework when developing a placement plan could help counteract the tendency to focus on the client as the target of change, when modification of the environment may be more effective [38]. Due to the coding structure of the ICF with its clearly defined classifications, data generated by the ICF could ultimately be used in program evaluation to identify what strategies targeted toward a certain aspect of the individual's functioning are most effective in the placement process.

One of the first steps in job placement is to identify an appropriate *P X E* fit. In most instances, this means identifying an appropriate job and work setting that match the individual's abilities and interests. More specifically, though, the placement professional could use the ICF model to identify gaps or discrepancies between the worker and the job and identify solutions. That is, when the fit between the person and job setting is less than optimal, an ICF-based profile of the individual and the work setting could be helpful in improving the correspondence between them by considering specific job requirements and job accommodation needs. A sound understanding of the environmental context is essential to job placement services, as the employment specialist often needs to provide interventions within the work environment and with the employer, in some cases more often than interventions that are targeted to the individual. The ICF's environmental factors are comprehensive and include factors such as employer attitudes, as well as services, systems, and policies related to finding employment. The placement practitioner could use the ICF as a basis for assessing potential work settings, such as the work culture and other variables that are important to employment success [38].

Using an ICF-based framework when developing a placement plan could help counteract the tendency to focus on the client as the target of change, when modification of the environment may be more effective.

8.5 The ICF and Evidence-Based Practices in Job Placement

To date, several studies have specifically examined the ICF framework in relation to employment outcomes in VR [39–41]. Minis et al. [39] conducted a systematic review of empirical studies that explored ICF factors associated with employment status (i.e., work participation) of individuals with neuromuscular diseases. Based on an expanded ICF format that includes work-related personal factors such as motivation and work experience [42], they found ten factors associated with work participation: disease-related factors (three types of neuromuscular disease), factors related to body functions (reduced physical functions and muscle power), general personal factors (age, gender, level of education), and work-related personal factors (type of occupation and expressed interest in work). The authors also noted that the studies identified personal factors of the ICF more often than other components (e.g., body functions and structures, activities/participation, and environmental factors). (A summary of this research is provided in Table 8.1.)

Wang and Lin [40] used a large sample size of almost 3,000 individuals receiving disability services in Taiwan (where the ICF framework is required in gathering survey data of persons with disabilities) to examine ICF factors in predicting employment outcomes. They found that the most important predictors of employment outcomes were marital status and education level, which are personal factors in the ICF. Other ICF codes that were associated with employment outcome were those pertaining to body function/structure (combined according to types of disabilities, such as vision, hearing, and intellectual disability), activities/participation (e.g., transportation and mobility factors, such as driving), and environmental factors (e.g., living arrangements). Overall, however, the study suggested the importance of personal factors and categories within the activity/participation domain, such as transportation and mobility.

The study by Young [41] sought to identify factors that help injured workers maintain successful employment and used the ICF conceptual model for coding, when possible. This study conducted phone interviews with 146 people who had experienced work-related injury and later returned to work in a different job after receiving vocational services. Results indicated many factors related to ICF components that were associated with the ability to stay at work, such as supportive relationships at work (coworkers), flexible working conditions, receiving a paycheck, having job duties consistent with physical capacities, positive relationships with other stakeholders (e.g., family, healthcare providers), workplace equipment, and coping styles (a personal factor in the ICF). Significantly, results highlighted the powerful impact of environmental facilitators in helping injured workers successfully maintain employment, suggesting that VR professionals can employ strategies that help prevent problems before they occur, a step beyond identifying and eliminating barriers [41].

Table 8.1 Summary of research investigating variables related to employment outcomes

Study	Population	Conclusions
Minis et al. [39]	Neuromuscular diseases	Based on the ICF model, Minis et al. found ten factors associated with work participation: disease-related factors (types of neuromuscular disease), body functions (reduced physical functions and muscle power), personal factors (age, gender, level of education), and work-related personal factors (type of occupation and expressed interest in work)
Wang and Lin [40]	Multiple disabilities (recipients of disability services)	Using the ICF model, Wang and Lin identified the following predictors of employment outcomes: marital status, education level, body function/structure, activities/participation (e.g., transportation and mobility), and environmental factors
Young [41]	Injured workers	Using the ICF model, Young identified many factors associated with the ability to maintain employment: supportive relationships at work, flexible working conditions, receiving a paycheck, job duties consistent with physical capacities, positive relationships with other stakeholders, workplace equipment, and coping styles
Li-Tsang et al. [49]	Musculoskeletal injuries (MSI)	Job-seeking skills training and vocational counseling were associated with successful job placement, as was having a good match between the person and occupation
Fleming et al. [48]	Multiple disabilities (reviewed 25 years of empirical research)	Fleming et al. identified seven categories associated with successful VR outcomes: collaboration among agencies, rehabilitation counselor education, interventions toward a targeted population, evidenced-based practice and supported employment, consumer self-concept and empowerment, critical service delivery components, and VR miscellaneous interventions and outcomes
Pack and Szirony [46]	Sensory and physical disabilities	VR clients who received the following services were more likely to achieve employment: job placement, on-the-job support, maintenance payments, vocational training, rehabilitation technology, VR counseling, restoration
Test and Cease-Cook [50]	Transition students	Successful outcomes associated with the following strategies: instruction to develop career awareness, training in job-seeking skills, inclusion in general education courses, integrating community experiences in the educational program, paid work experiences, vocational education/work study, and interagency collaboration

(continued)

Table 8.1 (continued)

Study	Population	Conclusions
Tyerman [51]	Traumatic brain injuries (TBI)	Direct comparisons of VR models were not feasible due to lack of consistent methodologies used; recommended conducting more controlled studies
Grauwmeijer et al. [53]	Moderate to severe TBI	Early identification of factors associated with poorer outcomes (e.g., psychiatric symptoms, cognitive limitations) could help treatment programs develop interventions targeted to individualized needs
Trexler et al. [54]	TBI	Participation in a structured program that includes case management, consumer education, referral for services, and coordination of services improved employment outcomes for individuals with TBI
Nightingale et al. [55]	TBI	Nightingale et al. reviewed almost 2,000 studies to identify variables that predict employment, concluded that the studies used too many variables to identify significant predictors, and recommended that future studies use measures of cognitive, physical, and behavioral functioning, as well as consistent key domains
Franceschini et al. [56]	Spinal cord injury	Individuals who were younger, had more education, lived alone, had prior work history, and were able to drive were more likely to be employed
Krause et al. [57]	Spinal cord injury	Education and injury severity predicted employment; individuals who completed a college degree post-injury were more likely to obtain employment
Michon et al. [58]	Mental illness	Assessed levels of social and work functioning during psychiatric vocational rehabilitation were stronger predictors of employment outcomes than variables such as diagnosis, symptom severity, and employment history
Tsang et al. [59]	Mental illness (schizophrenia)	Significant predictors of employment outcomes included age, prior work history, education, receipt of benefits, negative symptoms, and cognitive functioning
Gilbert and Marwaha [60]	Mental illness (bipolar disorder)	Cognitive limitations and education level predicted employment outcome
Bond et al. [63]	Mental illness	At 12–18-month follow-up, individuals in the Individual Placement and Support (IPS) model had a mean employment rate of 61 %, compared to 23 % for groups that received traditional VR services

(continued)

Table 8.1 (continued)

Study	Population	Conclusions
Campbell et al. [62]	Mental illness	Individuals in the IPS model were more likely to obtain and maintain employment over a period of time. Higher success rates were independent of demographic variables, such as age, race/ethnicity, education levels, work history, diagnoses, and symptoms
Campbell et al. [64]	Mental illness	Campbell at al. examined relationships between client characteristics (age, gender, race/ethnicity, education, marital status, hospitalization within last year, diagnosis, symptoms, work history, and receipt of disability benefits) and competitive supported employment outcomes. Prior work history was the only significant predictor of employment outcome
Melvin et al. [65]	Substance abuse	Employed individuals were more likely to successfully complete substance abuse treatment than those who were unemployed
Darensbourg [68]	Vision impairment	Darensbourg examined 25 demographic variables (e.g., age, gender, race/ethnicity, referral source, education level, weekly wages, and receipt of government-funded disability and medical benefits); six variables were strong predictors of competitive employment: age, gender, degree of vision loss, referral source, weekly wages at the time of application, and receipt of medical benefits

8.6 Evidence-Based Practices in Job Placement

Considerable research over the years has strongly supported the value of job placement in promoting successful employment outcomes for persons with disabilities [43]. A landmark longitudinal study that tracked the progress of over 8,500 clients in the US public VR services program over a 3-year period found that clients who received job placement services were significantly more likely to have a successful employment outcome [44]. In addition, a study by Rogers et al. [45] found that recipients of disability benefits who had job placement services were three times more likely to become successfully employed. Thus, job placement as a service is, in effect, an evidence-based practice (EBP). While many studies have examined personal factors, such as age, marital status, and receipt of benefits in relation to outcome, few included environmental factors. One notable exception was the longitudinal study of the VR services program, which included environmental factors (e.g., community resources) and organizational culture as variables in its research designed to explore factors associated with employment outcomes [44].

Surprisingly, despite its strong association with successful outcomes, many clients within the public VR program in the United States do not receive job placement assistance. For example, using a large national database of clients with sensory and physical disabilities whose cases were closed after receiving VR services, Pack and Szirony [46] reported that only about 17 % actually received job placement assistance. Similarly, Chan et al. [47] found that only 25 % of VR clients with orthopedic disabilities received job placement services. Thus, research suggests that a majority of clients (at least 75 %) do not receive this important service.

Although job placement services have demonstrated effectiveness in helping individuals achieve employment, much more research is needed to clarify which components of job placement services and job placement models are most successful and with which individuals, as studies suggest that there is no "one-size-fits-all" approach that is beneficial to all clients of VR services. That is, individuals with specific types of disabilities may benefit from a more targeted approach [48].

The rest of this section will focus on research examining VR-related services and job placement models in relation to successful employment, as well as those that appear to be most effective for specific consumer populations. This literature review is not intended to be exhaustive; rather, the focus is on more recent research that purports to be evidence based. Table 8.1 presents a summary of this research.

Many studies have examined various aspects of job placement strategies and services and their impact on employment outcomes. For example, in a randomized clinical trial (RCT) involving individuals with musculoskeletal injuries (MSI), Li-Tsang et al. [49] found that job-seeking skills training and vocational counseling were associated with more successful job placement. Consistent with *P X E* fit, the study also noted that a good match between the person and the occupation was an important factor in job success. In addition, the study highlighted the benefits of attending to psychosocial aspects such as coping with stress, not just physical factors, when working with individuals with MSI.

Fleming et al. [48] reviewed 25 years of empirical research in order to create a best practices model for VR, synthesizing their findings into seven key categories that were associated with successful VR outcomes: collaboration among agencies, rehabilitation counselor education, interventions toward a targeted population (i.e., disability type, race/ethnicity, age), evidenced-based practice and supported employment, consumer self-concept and empowerment, critical service delivery components, and VR miscellaneous interventions and outcomes (e.g., working alliance, services directed to families). Overall, their review suggests a number of strategies and interventions that, when combined, contribute to successful employment and can be incorporated within the ICF framework. For example, while personal factors in the ICF model, self-concept and empowerment, are associated with positive outcomes, Fleming et al. [48] noted that other studies have shown that VR clients who have received empowerment training were more likely to be successful. Thus, this is a personal factor that could be enhanced through appropriate VR intervention in the form of specific training. In addition, certain types of VR services and interventions (which in the ICF model can be seen as environmental facilitators) are related to successful outcomes for specific groups. For example, services such as on-the-job training and counseling and guidance were more powerful predictors of employment for clients with traumatic brain injury (TBI) than psychological and demographic variables (i.e., personal factors in the ICF) that are commonly included in prediction models. This is an important finding, as it supports the ICF model of functioning and highlights the importance of including environmental variables in studies of best practices. In the category of essential service components, Fleming et al. [48] noted that successful placements are enhanced when VR agencies utilize a team approach to providing services and direct interventions to improving clients' skills in key areas of independent functioning, such as self-care. In the area of miscellaneous interventions and outcomes, the authors identified the working alliance between the VR counselor and client as an essential best practice, as VR clients who had a stronger working relationship with their counselors were more likely to obtain employment than unemployed clients. Within the ICF model, this finding corresponds with the environmental factor of *support and relationships* (e.g., *e*360, other professionals).

Pack and Szirony [46] investigated employment predictors for clients with sensory and physical disabilities; after identifying predictors based on a series of statistical analyses, they described an evidence-based model of VR service predictors for this group of clients. As noted earlier, provision of job placement services was a strong predictor of successful outcomes, as clients who received this service were almost four times more likely to achieve competitive employment. Likewise, clients receiving on-the-job support increased their likelihood of competitive employment by 232 %. Those with a college education were 215 % more likely to obtain competitive employment. Providing clients with maintenance payments increased the chances of obtaining competitive employment by 186 %. In addition, those receiving vocational training were 186 % more likely to obtain competitive employment and those provided with rehabilitation technology were 182 % more apt to secure competitive employment. VR counseling increased the chances of competitive employment by 155 %. Surprisingly, although guidance and counseling can be provided throughout the VR process, Pack and Szirony noted that only 54 % of their sample received these services. In addition, those clients employed during the application process were almost four times more likely to secure competitive employment. This is consistent with results of other studies (e.g., [44]) and is not surprising, since individuals who are currently working are more likely to have the skills and experiences that employers seek, thus making them more competitive in the labor market. Clients who received restoration services (e.g., medical or psychological treatment for the disability) were 143 % more likely to have a successful outcome [46].

In combining these predictors into an evidence-based model, Pack and Szirony [46] proposed a flowchart of VR services for individuals with sensory and physical disabilities to increase the likelihood of competitive employment. In this model of VR services, every client should have a career assessment that includes assessment of assistive technology needs and a vocational evaluation that includes assessment of work-related values, skills, interests, and aptitudes. From this, the consumer and counselor can develop an individualized plan for employment, which may include the identified predictors of training (college/university, vocational, on-the-job), job-seeking assistance, and job placement services. Throughout the process, the VR counselor provides ongoing counseling and guidance, as well as maintenance payments, when appropriate. This proposed model is consistent with the ICF framework in that it includes potential environmental variables, such as rehabilitation technology, education and training, and employment services.

Test and Cease-Cook [50] reviewed an array of studies in the field of transition to highlight evidence-based strategies for students with disabilities who are making the transition from school to work. For example, students who had strong career awareness skills as a result of instruction were more likely to be successfully employed after leaving school, as were students who had been trained in traditional interview and job search skills. Students also benefitted from being included in general education courses such as math, reading, and science. In addition, integrating community experiences (e.g., transportation, mobility, recreation) within the educational program was an important predictor of post-school success, as were independent living skills and having strong social support systems that include teachers, family, and friends. In addition, students who participated in transition programs that included paid work experiences as well as those who received vocational education and opportunities for work study had a higher likelihood of success after leaving school. Social skills were another important predictor associated with employment, as was interagency collaboration involving parents, special education teachers, rehabilitation counselors, regular teachers, and other professionals. In addition, students who had stronger skills in the areas of decision-making, self-awareness, and self-advocacy had greater likelihood of employment. Many of these variables could be cross-linked to ICF codes in the domains of activities/participation and environmental factors (e.g., in areas related to independent living skills, transportation, education and training, and support and relationships).

As previously noted, research suggests that individuals with specific types of disabilities benefit from a targeted approach to job placement [48]. A number of studies that have examined evidence-based practices in relation to various disabilities, such as TBI, mental illness, spinal cord injury, substance abuse, and vision impairment, are reviewed in the following section.

8.7 Employment Outcomes and Specific Disabilities: Case Examples

Brain Injury. Tyerman [51] systematically reviewed empirical research spanning a 45-year period (1967–2012) to examine VR models for individuals who have sustained brain injuries (TBI). The models reviewed included VR models with TBI adaptations (e.g., supported employment), brain injury programs with VR components (e.g., work trials), consumer-directed (where participants are involved in running their own programs), and case coordination-resource facilitation models (case management involving coordination of multiple services). While noting the effectiveness of these models, Tyerman pointed out that direct comparisons between models were not feasible due to a lack of consistent methodologies and recommended conducting more controlled studies. These findings suggest an important role for the specificity and universality of the ICF, as ICF-based research could help provide consistency needed for comparisons among studies and different disciplines. Depending on the location and severity of damage, individuals with TBI can experience a broad range of effects in many areas of function, including communication, cognition, emotional responses, perception, and coordination, among others [52]. These disparate variables complicate research to identify evidence-based practices with this population; instruments based on the ICF, or cross-linked to it, could provide more consistency in identifying and classifying patient characteristics that would then allow for more productive cross-comparisons across studies.

Grauwmeijer et al. [53] investigated employment outcomes 3 years post-injury for individuals with moderate to severe TBI. They found that clients with psychiatric symptoms (e.g., depression and anxiety) as well as cognitive functioning limitations at hospital discharge were more likely to be unemployed at 3-year follow-up. This study investigated demographic variables, as well as scores on measures used to assess functioning during hospitalization. When compared to patients who were unemployed, those who were employed 3 years later were more likely to be younger, had shorter hospitalization periods, and were less likely to have psychiatric symptoms. At the time of hospital discharge, the employed patients had higher scores on the Glasgow Coma Scale, Barthel Index, Functional Independence Measure, and Functional Assessment Measure (FAM, which includes assessment of communication and cognitive functioning). Based on further analysis, Grauwmeijer et al. also found that FAM scores at 65 or under predicted unemployment and should be noted by rehabilitation professionals, as it underscores the need for adopting a holistic approach with this population that addresses both mental health problems (particularly depression and anxiety) and cognitive limitations. Early identification of factors associated with poorer outcomes would enable TBI treatment programs to develop more effective interventions that are targeted to individualized needs. Future studies could utilize existing measures, such as the FAM, which could be mapped onto the ICF categories [26] and used to identify evidence-based practices for individuals with TBI for a holistic approach to job placement.

Trexler et al. [54] conducted a randomized controlled trial (RCT) of an innovative approach to working with individuals with brain injury called Resource Facilitation (RF). Created by the Brain Injury Association, RF involves determining individuals' needs and resources; identifying appropriate community resources, goals, and services based on consumer input and matched to their needs; promoting access through education and advocacy; and active contact with clients by a Resource Facilitator (i.e., case manager) at least every 2 weeks to monitor progress. In addition, individuals in the RF group were encouraged to use VR services provided by the state-federal VR agency. Specifically, this study examined the impact of RF on employment and community participation for clients with brain injury. Results of the study indicated that at follow-up, individuals in the RF group were significantly more likely to be employed; this group had a 64 % employment rate, compared to 36 % for the control group. In addition, individuals in the RF group were more likely to be involved in community and home activities and to be clients of VR services, since this was promoted in the RF group. These results suggest that a structured program that includes regular contact through case management provided by the Resource Facilitator, combined with consumer education, referral for services targeted to individual needs, and coordination of services, can help improve employment outcomes for individuals with TBI.

Nightingale et al. [55] systematically investigated variables predicting employment for individuals with TBI. The impact of these variables was examined at pre-injury, injury, and post-injury. The review initially produced a total of 1,948 articles, but only 55 were ultimately included based on predetermined inclusion and exclusion criteria. From the resulting data set, the authors identified 240 plausible predictor variables. Subsequently, 27 of the 55 noted studies fit within the inclusion criteria. Based on further analysis, the authors found that only five of these studies met the methodological requirements. Of these, only two variables, age and education, emerged as significant predictors, though with somewhat limited support. Nightingale et al. concluded that the various studies used too many variables to identify significant predictors for employment and recommended that studies include measures of cognitive, physical, and behavioral functioning. In addition, they advised, "Future research in this area would benefit from an agreed set of core domains to be examined" [55, p. 138]. These findings underscore the potential value of utilizing ICF-based tools in research, as the ICF categories have precise definitions and provide a universal language to describe functioning. In addition, more precise identification of variables is needed in order to conduct evidence-based research in job placement.

Spinal Cord Injury. Franceschini et al. [56] investigated the incidence and predictors of employment for individuals with spinal cord injury (SCI) who were part of an epidemiological study of spinal cord injuries in Italy. Predictors of unemployment included age (older individuals were less likely to be employed), tetraplegia, being married, medical problems and/or re-hospitalization within past 6 months, welfare subsidy, and architectural barriers, such as inaccessible housing. Individuals who were younger, had more education, lived alone, had prior work history, and were able to drive were more likely to be employed. Although some of the predictors were demographic variables, such as age and education level, these findings also highlight the importance of environmental variables, such as architectural barriers that impact employment for persons with SCI and which could be addressed during VR services and job placement.

Krause et al. [57] investigated employment outcomes for persons with SCI, based on data gathered from three hospitals in the United States. Consistent with the findings of Franceschini et al. [56], they found that education and injury severity predicted employment. Education (4-year college or graduate degree) was associated with a longer duration of time spent working post-injury. In contrast, injury severity had more impact on obtaining employment rather than duration of employment after the SCI. The most important finding, according to the researchers, was the extent to which obtaining a college degree predicted employment. That is, individuals who completed a college degree post-injury were more likely to obtain employment, suggesting the benefits of providing further education as part of the VR plan for clients with SCI.

Individuals in the study who worked after the injury and who had completed a college degree before the injury had a longer duration of employment post injury, possibly because they were able to return to work more quickly.

Mental Illness. Research investigating predictors of employment for individuals with mental illness has yielded somewhat contradictory results. For example, Michon et al. [58] systematically investigated employment predictors for individuals in psychiatric vocational rehabilitation (PVR) programs and found that client social functioning and work functioning as assessed during their participation in the PVR program were stronger predictors of employment outcomes than variables such as diagnosis, symptom severity, and employment history. In contrast, in a meta-analysis investigating predictors of vocational success for individuals with schizophrenia, Tsang et al. [59] identified the following variables as significant vocational outcome predictors: age, prior work history, education, receipt of benefits (associated with poorer outcomes), negative symptoms, and cognitive functioning (i.e., general intelligence and executive functioning). While demographic variables, such as age, cannot be changed, the authors noted that some variables were modifiable. Thus, treatment programs could address aspects of functioning that have a significant impact on employment outcomes, such as negative symptoms and executive functioning. Gilbert and Marwaha [60] reviewed published research to investigate predictors of vocational outcome for individuals with bipolar disorder. Their analysis found that cognitive limitations and education level predicted employment outcome. Both executive functioning and verbal memory were significant predictors, and levels of social functioning, including relationship functioning, predicted work adjustment. In addition, as depression symptoms became more severe, absenteeism increased and the prospect of successful employment decreased. The authors were unable to conduct meta-analyses due to the varying types of measures used to assess work functioning in the studies they reviewed.

Research investigating placement models of employment has confirmed the supported employment model as an evidence-based practice for individuals with severe mental illness (SMI). The supported employment model is often described as "place-train," rather than the traditional VR approach ("train-place") of preparing individuals for employment through a process of training and preparation, often in a step-by-step manner as the client demonstrates improved work skills and behaviors. The supported employment model flips the traditional VR approach around by placing the individual into a job and providing supports, such as a job coach, to provide training and assistance within the job setting [61]. The most extensively studied model of supported employment is Individual Placement and Support (IPS), which was specifically developed to meet the needs of individuals with SMI [62]. The IPS model involves placing clients directly into competitive employment, taking into account their interests and preferences. Clients receive ongoing supports on the job, with emphasis on meeting individualized needs. Placement specialists work in coordination with the client's treatment team to ensure continuity of care, and clients receive benefits counseling.

Research has provided strong validation of the IPS model's effectiveness in helping individuals with SMI achieve successful employment. Bond et al. [63] reviewed randomized controlled trials of IPS programs. At 12–18 month follow-up, individuals receiving the IPS model had a mean competitive employment rate of

61 %, compared to an employment rate of 23 % for groups that received traditional VR services. IPS clients also obtained competitive employment approximately 10 weeks sooner than the control groups. Campbell et al. [62] conducted a meta-analysis of studies using randomized controlled trials to investigate which subgroup of clients with severe mental illness (SMI) benefited from IPS supported employment strategies when compared to clients in VR programs using the "train-place" model in which clients proceed, step-by-step from preparation (e.g., work adjustment training in a sheltered setting) to job placement services. Clients who received the IPS intervention fared better in regard to competitive employment as compared to the other strategies used with the control groups. That is, those receiving IPS were more likely to obtain and maintain employment over a period of time. In addition, when compared to the control groups, they had higher success rates that were independent of demographic variables, such as age, race/ethnicity, education levels, work history, diagnoses, and symptoms. These findings are consistent with ICF model by illustrating the importance of environmental factors on subsequent work functioning. That is, the combination of IPS interventions, which are individualized to meet the needs of the client and provided within the work setting, may have mitigated the impact of disability-related limitations in functioning.

In an effort to resolve contradictory findings of prior studies investigating the relationship of client variables on employment outcomes, Campbell et al. [64] examined relationships between clients' baseline characteristics and competitive supported employment outcomes (both for obtaining and maintaining a job). Their analysis pooled data from four randomly controlled trials for clients receiving IPS. Client characteristics included age, gender, race/ethnicity, education, marital status, hospitalization within last year, diagnosis, symptoms, work history, and receipt of disability benefits. Clients' prior work history (i.e., paid work within the last 5 years) was the only significant predictor of employment outcome in terms of obtaining employment but did not predict employment retention at 18-month follow-up. In addition, those receiving disability benefits worked fewer total weeks when measured at follow-up, suggesting that benefits created a disincentive to accumulate work hours, which could reduce their benefits.

Substance Abuse. Employment has been shown to be an important predictor for completion of substance abuse treatment. For example, in a study involving 232 participants with methamphetamine dependence in a treatment program, Melvin et al. [65] found that individuals who were employed were over two and one-half times more likely to successfully complete the substance abuse treatment program than those who were unemployed.

Melvin et al. concluded that it is important to integrate VR services within a traditional substance abuse treatment protocol. That is, helping individuals obtain employment as part of the treatment program could, in turn, enhance treatment success. At the same time, however, the VR professional should help individuals identify appropriate work settings that support sobriety, as individuals who return to a "wet" work environment are likely to experience relapse. A "wet" environment is one where drug use is promoted or tolerated (e.g., drinking with coworkers during lunch breaks) [66, 67].

Vision Impairment. Darensbourg [68] investigated the demographic predictors of competitive employment for 3,610 VR clients with visual impairments, using national data from the US public VR services program. Twenty-five demographic variables (e.g., age, gender, race/ethnicity, referral source, education level, weekly wages, and receipt of government-funded disability and medical benefits) were analyzed. Out of the 25 variables, six variables emerged as strongly predicting competitive employment: age, gender, degree of vision loss, referral source, weekly wages at the time of application, and receipt of medical benefits (Medicaid). In summary, clients who were male, 36 years of age or younger, self-referred, had less severe visual impairments, and did not receive Medicaid were at least two times more likely to obtain competitive employment. Darensbourg also noted that almost half of the clients in the data sample were between the ages of 55 and 65, and the lower employment rate for older clients suggested that VR counselors may need to adopt strategies that would be more effective in helping them achieve an employment outcome. In addition, the lower success rate for clients with more severe vision loss suggests they could benefit from assistive technology or related services needed for success in competitive employment. Since the study only addressed demographic factors, it is not known which VR services these clients received that also may have been associated with employment outcomes.

8.8 Conclusions and Future Directions

The ICF framework is consistent with VR's goals of maximizing independence and quality of life for individuals with disabilities. The ICF describes function independently of diagnosis, and considerable research has demonstrated the limitations of diagnosis in predicting employment outcomes. Many factors are involved, other than an individual's health condition, in determining whether or not an individual successfully returns to work [69, 70]. The ICF conceptual model is highly applicable to both vocational assessment and job placement in that it promotes a more holistic understanding of the dynamic interplay of multiple factors related to disability and health conditions [38]. These interacting variables are nonlinear and interact at multiple levels. Research suggests that even in the case of significant disabilities, such as SMI, a number of VR interventions can either eliminate functional barriers to employment or mitigate their impact. The ICF framework can help practitioners provide individualized services and assess the effectiveness of various interventions with different client populations. The ICF model can help vocational evaluators use a systematic approach to assessment that is biopsychosocial in nature; such an approach should result in recommendations for rehabilitation planning that promote employment and enhanced quality of life. Although the ICF provides useful information about what to evaluate, it is not in itself an assessment instrument. The key is to identify existing instruments that can be mapped onto the ICF codes [4, 26, 71].

The ICF framework can help VR practitioners provide individualized services and assess the effectiveness of various interventions with different client populations.

Effective service delivery requires VR professionals to fully understand their clients' functional limitations and how they compare to occupational requirements, with or without reasonable accommodations. This understanding includes knowing how to effectively utilize assistive technology (AT) and job accommodations and provides the foundation for individualized rehabilitation planning that maximizes independence and successful employment.

However, research indicates that clients in the public VR system are more likely to obtain positions in relatively unskilled types of jobs (e.g., stock clerk) that do not provide career advancement opportunities [72]. These results suggest that VR counselors do not have an accurate understanding of clients' functional limitations and how they relate to occupations that are stepping stones for career advancement. ICF-based tools could provide VR counselors with more precise definitions of clients' functional capacities and limitations, which could be cross-walked to occupational information databases [24].

Initial research suggests that the VR Comprehensive Core Set is suitable for VR purposes [3]. The public VR service program in the United States uses electronic case management systems for entering consumer data and could incorporate the Comprehensive ICF Core Set for VR [12] in the case management process, for example, for eligibility determination and assessment needed to develop the rehabilitation plan. Since these case management systems are electronic, it should be possible to ease data entry of the ICF data by using software that creates decision trees (e.g., requiring a yes/no answer) or computerized adaptive testing techniques that predict scores based on prior responses, which could make using ICF-tools more efficient, thus saving time [73].

Although the ICF has much to offer to the field of VR, some limitations exist. A major issue preventing its adoption in VR programs has been its length and complexity. However, the development of the Comprehensive ICF Core Set for VR should help encourage its use in broader VR settings [34]. Nevertheless, there is a need for more distinct codes that are applicable to the VR context, especially additional environmental codes [27, 38]. Further research is also needed to examine the reliability and validity of the code qualifiers (e.g., 0–4 indicating the degree of difficulty) [26, 29]. Although personal factors are part of the ICF model, they are not yet defined as are the other components, though this may be an area of future development. Personal factors such as demographic data, interests and values, coping styles, education level, and motivation have long been recognized as being important factors to assess in VR. Their importance is also recognized within the ICF's conceptual framework as having an impact on functioning [24].

VR research involves great diversity in types of disabilities, their functional impacts, VR settings, and client needs. This diversity highlights the importance of a holistic perspective and a framework that is comprehensive, yet specific enough to inform VR approaches that are individualized and provide targeted services. Lack of consistent methodology hampers an evidence-based approach to research in VR and makes results difficult to generalize to other contexts. Evidence-based practice requires a sound empirical foundation; by providing a comprehensive and systematic coding structure, the ICF could provide the framework needed for evidence-based research in VR [71]. To date, the preponderance of VR research suggests that while demographic factors such as age and race/ethnicity are common predictors of employment outcomes, variables involving diagnoses and severity are not necessarily predictive. In addition, many studies primarily focus on demographic variables and tend to ignore environmental factors. More research is needed to investigate the types of interventions that are associated with employment outcomes and to identify those that are most effective and with which populations. Of the studies that have included VR interventions in their analyses, results suggest that such interventions may help offset disability-related barriers to employment. Research informed by the ICF model could more specifically examine the impact of VR interventions and the environmental context on employment outcomes.

Study Questions

1. What is vocational assessment?

   Answer: Vocational assessment is a generic term for an information gathering process used for the purposes of rehabilitation planning and identification of vocational goals.

2. What is vocational evaluation and what is its relationship to vocational assessment?

   Answer: Vocational evaluation is an in-depth, comprehensive type of vocational assessment that uses either real or simulated work as the focal point for assessment and vocational exploration and which incorporates medical, psychological, social, vocational, educational, cultural, and economic data.

3. Describe some of the ways that the ICF could be useful in the vocational assessment process.

   Answer: It provides a comprehensive and holistic framework that can help practitioners systematically gather, organize, synthesize, and interpret extensive information, including environmental variables; help identify vocational strengths and barriers; recommend strategies for overcoming barriers to employment; provide a universal language for communicating with other professional and health-related disciplines; and provide an effective framework for ecological assessment.

4. Explain how the ICF could be applied during job placement services.

   Answer: ICF-based tools help placement professionals organize client information in a way that promotes a more holistic understanding of individuals' needs. The ICF's focus on functioning, rather than diagnosis, can help the practitioner identify more effective and creative employment strategies, such as job modifications. The ICF provides a framework for systematic assessment to help identify an appropriate job and work setting that match the individual's abilities and interests, as well as environmental factors that are barriers or facilitators.

5. What does current VR research tell us about predictors of employment outcomes, and how could the ICF be useful in future evidence-based research?

   Answer: Most VR research suggests that demographic factors such as age and race/ethnicity are often predictors of employment outcomes, but diagnoses and severity are not necessarily predictive. By providing a comprehensive and systematic coding structure, the ICF could provide the framework needed for evidence-based research in VR, which more specifically examines the impact of VR interventions and the environmental context on employment outcomes.

References

1. World Health Organization. International classification of functioning, disability and health. Geneva: World Health Organization; 2001.
2. Escorpizo R, Finger ME, Glässel A, Gradinger F, Lückenkemper M, Cieza A. A systematic review of functioning in vocational rehabilitation using the International Classification of Functioning, Disability and Health. J Occup Rehabil. 2011;21(2):134–46.
3. Saltychev M, Kinnunen A, Laimi K. Vocational rehabilitation evaluation and the International Classification of Functioning, Disability, and Health (ICF). J Occup Rehabil. 2013;23(1): 106–14.
4. Schwegler U, et al. Aspects of functioning and environmental factors in medical work capacity evaluations of persons with chronic widespread pain and low back pain can be represented by a combination of applicable ICF Core Sets. BMC Public Health. 2012;12:1088.
5. Ahmad KZ, Veerapandian K. The mediating effect of person-environment fit on the relationship between organisational culture and job satisfaction. Int J Psychol Stud. 2012;4(1):91–102.
6. Parsons F. Choosing a vocation. Broken Arrow: National Career Development Association; 1909.
7. Fourteenth Institute on Rehabilitation Issues. The use of vocational evaluation in VR. Menomonie: University of Wisconsin-Stout, Research and Training Center; 1987.
8. McCarthy H. A modest festschrift and insider perspective on Beatrice Wright's contributions to rehabilitation theory and practice. Rehabil Couns Bull. 2011;54(2):67–81.
9. Dawis RV. The theory of work adjustment and person-environment-correspondence counseling. In: Brown DB, Brooks L, editors. Career choice and development. 3rd ed. San Francisco: Jossey-Bass; 1996. p. 75–120.
10. Kosciulek JF, DeVinney DJ. The trait-factor approach. In: Chan F, Berven NL, Thomas KR, editors. Counseling theories and techniques for rehabilitation health professionals. New York: Springer; 2004. p. 211–23.
11. Strong S, Gruhl KR. Person-environment-occupation model. In: Brown C, Stoffel VC, editors. Occupational therapy in mental health: a vision for participation. Philadelphia: F. A. Davis; 2011. p. 31–46.

12. Escorpizo R, Ekholm J, Gmünder H, Cieza A, Kostanjsek N, Stucki G. Developing a core set to describe functioning in vocational rehabilitation using the International Classification of Functioning, Disability, and Health (ICF). J Occup Rehabil. 2010;20(4):502–11.
13. Francescutti C, Gongolo F, Simoncello A, Frattura L. Description of the person-environment interaction: methodological issues and empirical results of an Italian large-scale disability assessment study using an ICF-based protocol. BMC Public Health. 2011;11 Suppl 4:S11.
14. Finger ME, Glässel A, Erhart P, Gradinger F, Klipstein A, Rivier G, et al. Identification of relevant ICF categories in vocational rehabilitation: a cross sectional study evaluating the clinical perspective. J Occup Rehabil. 2011;21(2):156–66.
15. Neufeld JE, Rasmussen HN, Lopez SJ, Ryder JA, Magyar-Moe JL, Ford AI, et al. The engagement model of person-environment interaction. Couns Psychol. 2006;34(2):245–59.
16. Power PW. A guide to vocational assessment. 5th ed. Austin: Pro-Ed; 2013.
17. Thirtieth Institute on Rehabilitation Issues. A new paradigm for vocational evaluation. Hot Springs: University of Arkansas CURRENTS; 2003.
18. Breeding RR. The utility of proactive vocational assessment in advancing consumer empowerment. Vocat Eval Career Assess Prof J. 2005;2(2):39–56.
19. Power PW. A guide to vocational assessment. 4th ed. Austin: Pro-Ed; 2006.
20. Dowd LR, editor. Glossary of terminology for vocational assessment, evaluation and work adjustment: a project of the Vocational Evaluation and Work Adjustment Association. Menomonie: Materials Development Center, University of Wisconsin-Stout; 1993.
21. Larkin VM, Tew-Washburn S. Assessment of vocational and work adjustment. In: Mpofu E, Oakland T, editors. Assessment in rehabilitation and health. New York: Springer; 2010. p. 324–44.
22. Vocational Evaluation and Work Adjustment Association (VEWAA). Vocational evaluation project final report. Vocat Eval Work Adjust Bull. 1975;8.
23. Chan F, Keegan J, Sung C, Drout M, Pai C, Anderson E, et al. The World Health Organization ICF model as a framework for assessing vocational rehabilitation outcomes. J Rehabil Adm. 2009;33(2):91–112.
24. Homa D, Peterson D. Using the International Classification of Functioning, Disability and Health (ICF) in teaching rehabilitation client assessment. Rehabil Educ. 2005;19(2/3):81–94.
25. Berven NL. Assessment. In: Riggar TF, Maki DR, editors. Handbook of rehabilitation counseling. New York: Springer; 2004. p. 199–217.
26. Rauch A, Cieza A, Stucki G. How to apply the International Classification of Functioning, Disability and Health (ICF) for rehabilitation management in clinical practice. Eur J Phys Rehabil Med. 2008;44:329–42.
27. Stergiou-Kita M, Dawson D, Rappolt S. Inter-professional clinical practice guideline for vocational evaluation following traumatic brain injury: a systematic and evidence-based approach. J Occup Rehabil. 2012;22(2):166–81.
28. Cieza A, Stucki G. The International Classification of Functioning Disability and Health: its development process and content validity. Eur J Phys Rehabil Med. 2008;44(3):303–13.
29. Glässel A, Rauch A, Selb M, Emmenegger K, Lückenkemper M, Escorpizo R. A case study on the application of International Classification of Functioning, Disability and Health (ICF)-based tools for vocational rehabilitation in spinal cord injury. Work. 2012;41(4):465–74.
30. Ptyushkin P, Vidmar G, Burger H, Marincek C. Use of the International Classification of Functioning, Disability and Health (ICF) in patients with traumatic brain injury. Brain Inj. 2010;24(13–14):1519–27.
31. Lustig D. Clinical judgment in vocational assessment. Vocat Eval Work Adjust Bull. 1996;29: 59–63.
32. Stucki G, Kostanjsek N, Ustün B, Cieza A. ICF-based classification and measurement of functioning. Eur J Phys Rehabil Med. 2008;44(3):315–28.
33. Leconte P. Vocational appraisal services: evolution from multidisciplinary origins and applications to interdisciplinary practices. Vocat Eval Work Adjust Bull. 1994;27:119.

34. Escorpizo R, Reneman MF, Ekholm J, Fritz J, Krupa T, Marnetoft S, et al. A conceptual definition of vocational rehabilitation based on the ICF: building a shared global model. J Occup Rehabil. 2011;21(2):126–33.
35. Vandergoot D. Placement practices in vocational rehabilitation. J Appl Rehabil Couns. 1984; 15(3):24–8.
36. Orto AED, Marinelli RP. Encyclopedia of disability and rehabilitation. New York: Macmillan Library Reference USA; 1995.
37. Vandergoot D, Staniszewski S, Merlo A. Placement in rehabilitation counseling. In: Parker RM, Szymanski EM, editors. Rehabilitation counseling: basics and beyond. 2nd ed. Austin: Pro-Ed; 1992. p. 305–32.
38. Homa DB. Using the International Classification of Functioning, Disability and Health (ICF) in job placement. Work. 2007;29(4):277–86.
39. Minis M, Heerkens Y, Engels J, Oostendorp R, van Engelen B. Classification of employment factors according to the International Classification of Functioning, Disability and Health in patients with neuromuscular diseases: a systematic review. Disabil Rehabil. 2009;31(26): 2150–63.
40. Wang Y-T, Lin Y-J. Employment outcome predictors for people with disabilities in Taiwan – a preliminary study using ICF conceptual frameworks. J Rehabil. 2013;79(2):3–14.
41. Young AE. Return to work following disabling occupational injury-facilitators of employment continuation. Scand J Work Environ Health. 2010;36:473–83.
42. Heerkens Y, Engels J, Kuiper C, Van Der Gulden J, Oostendorp R. The use of the ICF to describe work related factors influencing the health of employees. Disabil Rehabil. 2004; 26(17):1060–6.
43. Vandergroot D. Review of placement research literature: implications for research and practice. Rehabil Couns Bull. 1987;30:243–72.
44. Hayward BJ, Schmidt-Davis H. Longitudinal Study of the Vocational Rehabilitation (VR) Services Program, third final report: the context of VR services. Washington, DC: U.S. Department of Education, Office of Special Education and Rehabilitative Services, Rehabilitation Services Administration; 2005.
45. Rogers JB, Bishop M, Crystal RM. Predicting rehabilitation outcome for supplemental security income and social security disability income recipients: implications for consideration with the Ticket to Work program. J Rehabil. 2005;71(3):5–10.
46. Pack TG, Szirony GM. Predictors of competitive employment among persons with physical and sensory disabilities: an evidence-based model. Work. 2009;33:67–79.
47. Chan F, Cheing G, Chan JYC, Rosenthal DA, Chronister J. Predicting employment outcomes of rehabilitation clients with orthopedic disabilities: a CHAID analysis. Disabil Rehabil. 2006; 28(5):257–70.
48. Fleming AR, Del Valle R, Muwoong K, Leahy MJ. Best practice models of effective vocational rehabilitation service delivery in the public rehabilitation program: a review and synthesis of the empirical literature. Rehabil Couns Bull. 2012;56:146–59.
49. Li-Tsang CW, Li EJ, Lam CS, Hui KY, et al. The effect of a job placement and support program for workers with musculoskeletal injuries: a randomized control trial (RCT) study. J Occup Rehabil. 2008;18(3):299–306.
50. Test DW, Cease-Cook J. Evidence-based secondary transition practices for rehabilitation counselors. J Rehabil. 2012;78:30–8.
51. Tyerman A. Vocational models after traumatic brain injury: models and services. NeuroRehabilitation. 2012;31:51–62.
52. Falvo D. Medical and psychosocial aspects of chronic illness and disability. 3rd ed. Sudbury: Jones and Bartlett; 2005.
53. Grauwmeijer E, Heijenbrok-Kal MH, Haitsma IK, Ribbers GM. A prospective study on employment outcome 3 years after moderate to severe traumatic brain injury. Arch Phys Med Rehabil. 2012;93:993–9.

54. Trexler LE, Trexler LC, Malec JF, Klyce D, Parrott D. Prospective randomized controlled trial of resource facilitation on community participation and vocational outcome following brain injury. J Head Trauma Rehabil. 2010;25:440–6.
55. Nightingale EJ, Soo CA, Tate RL. A systematic review for return to work after traumatic brain injury. Brain Impair. 2007;8:101–42.
56. Franceschini M, Pagliacci MC, Russo T, Felzani G, Aito S, Marini C. Occurrence and predictors of employment after traumatic spinal cord injury: the GISEM Study. Spinal Cord. 2011;50(3):238–42.
57. Krause JS, Terza JV, Erten M, Focht KL, Dismuke CE. Prediction of postinjury employment and percentage of time worked after spinal cord injury. Arch Phys Med Rehabil. 2012;93: 373–5.
58. Michon HW, Weeghel JV, Kroon H, Schene AH. Person-related predictors of employment outcomes after participation in psychiatric vocational rehabilitation programmes: a systematic review. Soc Psychiatry Psychiatr Epidemiol. 2005;40:408–16.
59. Tsang HWH, Leung AY, Chung RCK, Bell M, Cheung W-M. Review on vocational predictors: a systematic review of predictors of vocational outcomes among individuals with schizophrenia: an update since 1998. Aust N Z J Psychiatry. 2010;44:495–504.
60. Gilbert E, Marwaha S. Predictors of employment in bipolar disorder: a systematic review. J Affect Disord. 2013;145:156–64.
61. Rubin SE, Roessler RT. Foundations of the vocational rehabilitation process. 6th ed. Austin: Proed; 2008.
62. Campbell K, Bond GR, Drake RE. Who benefits from supported employment: a meta-analytic study. Schizophr Bull. 2011;37:370–80.
63. Bond GR, Drake RE, Becker DR. An update on randomized controlled trials of evidence-based supported employment. Psychiatry Rehabil J. 2008;31:280–90.
64. Campbell K, Bond GR, Drake RE, McHugo GJ, Xie H. Client predictors of employment outcomes in high-fidelity supported employment: a regression analysis. J Nerv Ment Dis. 2010;198(8):556–63.
65. Melvin AM, Davis S, Koch DS. Employment as a predictor of substance abuse treatment. J Rehabil. 2012;78(4):31–7.
66. Blankertz L, McKay C, Robinson S. Work as a rehabilitative tool for individual diagnoses. J Vocat Rehabil. 1998;11:113–23.
67. DeLambo DA, Chandras KV, Homa D, Chandras SV. Psychiatric disabilities and substance abuse: applications for rehabilitation professionals. In: Walz GR, Bleurer JC, Yep RK, editors. Compelling counseling interventions: celebrating VISTAS' fifth anniversary. Ann Arbor: Counseling Outfitters; 2008. p. 149–60.
68. Darensbourg BL. Predictors of competitive employment of VR consumers with blindness or visual impairments. J Vocat Rehabil. 2013;38:29–34.
69. Blank L, Peters J, Pickvance S, Wilford J, Macdonald E. A systematic review of the factors which predict return to work for people suffering episodes of poor mental health. J Occup Rehabil. 2008;18(1):27–34.
70. Pransky G, Loisel P, Anema J. Work disability prevention research: current and future prospects. J Occup Rehabil. 2011;21(3):287–92.
71. Chan F, Tarvydas V, Blalock K, Strauser D, Atkins BJ. Unifying and elevating rehabilitation counseling through model-driven, diversity-sensitive evidence-based practice. Rehabil Couns Bull. 2009;52:114–9.
72. Martin FH, Walls RT, Brodwin MG, Parker RM, Kurata E. Competitive employment outcomes of vocational rehabilitation. J Appl Rehabil Couns. 2012;43:3–10.
73. Jette AM, Haley SM. Contemporary measurement techniques for rehabilitation outcomes assessment. J Rehabil Med. 2005;37(6):339–45.

Chapter 9
State of Vocational Rehabilitation and Disability Evaluation in Chronic Musculoskeletal Pain Conditions

Michiel F. Reneman

9.1 Vocational Rehabilitation

9.1.1 Introduction

Vocational rehabilitation is defined as a multi-professional evidence-based approach that is provided in different settings, services, and activities to working age individuals with health-related impairments, limitations, or restrictions with work functioning and whose primary aim is to optimize work participation [1]. While this definition is comprehensive and fits within ICF, it is also quite complex. In simple language, vocational rehabilitation can also be defined as "anything that helps someone with a health problem to stay at, return to, and remain in work" [2].

One of the most comprehensive reviews of the scientific literature on vocational rehabilitation for workers with common health problems was published in 2008 by Waddell, Burton, and Kendell [2]. This review demonstrated that there is strong evidence that vocational rehabilitation interventions for workers with CMPC can be effective in terms of work outcomes. For many years the strongest evidence was on low back pain, but more recent evidence shows that the same principles apply to most people with the most common CMPCs such as complaints of pain in the neck, shoulders, and arms. It was also demonstrated that from a societal perspective, vocational rehabilitation in patients with CMPC has a good business case, indicating that society as a whole may benefit from investments in vocational rehabilitation. Although estimates vary, a ratio of 1:5 was mentioned: for every currency unit invested in vocational rehabilitation, the societal return will be fivefold [2].

M.F. Reneman (✉)
Center for Rehabilitation, Department of Rehabilitation Medicine, University Medical Center Groningen, University of Groningen, Groningen, The Netherlands
e-mail: m.f.reneman@umcg.nl

R. Escorpizo et al. (eds.), *Handbook of Vocational Rehabilitation and Disability Evaluation*, Handbooks in Health, Work, and Disability, DOI 10.1007/978-3-319-08825-9_9

Vocational rehabilitation principles and interventions are fundamentally the same for work-related and other comparable (non-work-related) health conditions, irrespective of whether they are classified as injury, condition, or disease. Healthcare has a key role, but vocational rehabilitation is not a matter of healthcare alone. Employers also have a key role – there is strong evidence that proactive company approaches to sickness, including temporary provision of modified work and accommodations, are effective and cost-effective [3], although there is less evidence on vocational rehabilitation interventions in small and medium enterprises. Overall, the evidence shows that effective vocational rehabilitation depends on work- and worker-focused healthcare and accommodating workplaces; both are necessary as they are interdependent and must be coordinated simultaneously [2].

9.1.2 Stepped-Care Approach and Differential Care

The concept of early intervention is central to vocational rehabilitation, because the longer a worker is off work, the greater the obstacle to return to work and the more challenging vocational rehabilitation becomes. It is simpler, more effective, and cost-effective to prevent people with a musculoskeletal condition from going on to a long-term sickness absence. A "stepped-care approach" starts with mono-disciplinary, low-intensity, and low-cost interventions, which will be adequate for most sick or injured workers (e.g., physical therapy, education, RTW coaching), and provides progressively more intensive and structured interventions for those who need additional help to return to work (from back schooling in a secondary care setting to multidisciplinary vocational rehabilitation in a tertiary care setting). This approach allocates resources most appropriately and efficiently to meet individual and payers' needs. Effective vocational rehabilitation depends on communication and coordination between the key players – particularly the individual, healthcare, and workplace.

Given that vocational rehabilitation is about helping people with health problems stay at, return to, and remain in work, the question is how to make sure that everyone of working age receives the help they require. This should start from the needs of people with health problems at various stages, build on the evidence about effective interventions, and consider potential resources and the practicalities of how these interventions might be delivered. From this perspective, there are three broad types of workers, who are differentiated mainly by the duration out of work and who have correspondingly different needs: workers who are absent short term (less than 6 weeks), intermediate (between 6 weeks and 12 months), and long term (more than 3 months) [3]. There is also a fourth type of worker that has recently started to gain attention: those workers who manage to stay at work despite a CMPC [4].

In the first few weeks, most people with CMPC can be helped to return to work by following a few basic principles of healthcare and workplace management. For the diagnosis of acute nonspecific low back pain, evidence-based European guidelines [5, 6] recommend to perform a case history and brief examination. If history taking indicates possible serious pathology or nerve root syndrome, more extensive physical examination including neurological screening when appropriate should be carried out. In this stage, it is also recommended to be aware of psychosocial factors and to review them in detail if there is no improvement. Diagnostic imaging tests (including X-rays, CT, and MRI) are not routinely indicated for nonspecific low back pain. Those patients who are not resolving within a few weeks after the first visit or those who are following a worsening course should be reassessed.

With regard to treatment, evidence-based guidelines recommend healthcare workers to [6]: give adequate information and reassurance; not prescribe bed rest as a treatment; advise patients to stay active and continue normal daily activities including work if possible; prescribe medication, if necessary for pain relief, preferably to be taken at regular intervals, being paracetamol and NSAIDs as the first choice and second choice, respectively; consider adding a short course of muscle relaxants on its own or added to NSAIDs, if paracetamol or NSAIDs have failed to reduce pain; and consider (referral for) spinal manipulation for patients who fail to return to normal activities. At the acute stage, workers may need to temporarily perform modified work or at reduced hours. Temporary refrain from work may be considered if modified work is not an option, but this should be followed by (gradual) re-engagement with work activities, whenever feasible.

> Within the stepped-care approach, the advice for (extensive) vocational rehabilitation will be a trade-off between prognosis, costs, and benefits.

For workers with subacute CMPC and sick leave for more than 4–8 weeks, multidisciplinary rehabilitation programs in occupational settings may be an option to offer to workers who need additional help to return to work. However, within the stepped-care approach, diagnostic triaging is needed to screen those who can benefit and to screen out those who will not benefit, for example, whose course of recovery may still be considered favorable without healthcare interventions. At this stage, the advice for vocational rehabilitation will be a trade-off between prognosis, costs, and benefits. Those with a prognosis that is unfavorable based on bio-, psycho-, or social factors, even though the time off work may be limited, may still be advised to follow vocational rehabilitation. The "risk" that the individual worker will regain normal work without healthcare interventions, because of the favorable prognosis based purely on limited time off work, should be weighed against the risk of not regaining work because of unfavorable other prognostic factors ("too much, too soon, and too costly" versus "too late"). At this point in time, however, validated instruments to assist with these decisions are unavailable.

9.1.3 Multidisciplinary Vocational Rehabilitation

For workers who are out of work more than about 6 months, multidisciplinary rehabilitation is recommended for workers with CMPC [2, 5]. There is strong evidence that multidisciplinary vocational rehabilitation is effective to facilitate work outcomes [2, 5]. However, there are also major challenges that accompany vocational rehabilitation. Even though its effectiveness has been established, the effect sizes are rather modest [2, 5]. This means that the average worker with CMPC will benefit somewhat from vocational rehabilitation, but there is a large variety of results: from no benefit at all to complete recovery of work outcomes. Theoretically, average effect sizes should increase when workers who will not benefit from these programs will not be offered such a program or should be offered a different program that will provide better results. This requires reliable and valid screening tools that would be able to differentiate between (groups of) workers, but these tools are presently not available.

Multidisciplinary vocational rehabilitation programs are delivered in many different shapes and forms. Literature describes a huge variety of content, disciplines, and dosage, and the optimum components for each individual worker are currently unknown. It is currently regarded as one of the main scientific challenges in this field. It requires a set of diagnostic instruments that can validly distinguish subgroups of workers in need of specific content ("what works for whom"). Perhaps because of the absence of these instruments, many vocational rehabilitation programs contain a more or less standard mix of content (mostly consisting of physical exercises, cognitive behavioral therapy or principles, education, graded activities) delivered by more or less standard disciplines (physical therapy, occupational therapy, psychology), with durations of vocational rehabilitation varying from a few hours/weeks to 100 h or more delivered over several months [7]. Theoretically, content, disciplines, and dosage that add nothing to the results can be removed from these programs, leading to similar effectiveness and improved cost-effectiveness. At this point, strong evidence-based recommendations for specific content [6] or dosage [7] cannot be given.

9.1.4 Effective Principles of Vocational Rehabilitation

Even though detailed recommendations about effective components of vocational rehabilitation cannot be given, effective principles of vocational rehabilitation can be derived from literature. Realizing that differences between jurisdictions with all its different barriers and facilitators do exist, these principles can be used to tailor vocational rehabilitation programs to the needs of the individual worker and within the context of work. An overarching principle is that it depends on work-focused healthcare and accommodating workplaces. To make a real and lasting difference, both need to be addressed and coordinated. The main principles are [8] the presence of a return to work (RTW) coordinator, the principle of graded activity and graded exposure to work including modified work, and a biopsychosocial orientation of the vocational rehabilitation team.

The main principles for successful vocational rehabilitation are:

- The presence of a return to work (RTW) coordinator
- The principle of graded activity and graded exposure to work, including modified work
- A biopsychosocial orientation of the vocational rehabilitation team

Many vocational rehabilitation programs may benefit from a separate discipline or the so-called RTW coordinator or case manager. This person may serve as liaison between the worker, work, healthcare, benefits office, and others. The effectiveness of communication between healthcare and the workplace has been established [3]. The role of RTW coordinator as key to the program's success and the competencies of the RTW coordinator may be more important than professional background. For this relatively new role in vocational rehabilitation for workers with CMPC, ten groups of essential competencies were established: individual traits/qualities, relevant knowledge base, RTW focus and attitude, organizational/administrative skills, assessment skills, communication skills, interpersonal relationship skills, conflict resolution skills, problem-solving skills, and RTW facilitation skills [9]. To facilitate work participation of the worker with CMPC, these competencies should be mustered to create and maintain one plan/goal for all stakeholders and keep all "aboard" along the process.

The second principle for vocational rehabilitation is that of graded activity and graded exposure to work, including modified work. During vocational rehabilitation, the worker should increase activities according to a schedule that the worker and the vocational rehabilitation team codevelop. This plan involves a gradual progressing of activities, regardless of daily fluctuations in pain intensity. "Activities" may involve exercise, physical activities, and sports activities but also work-related activities. Preferably, if jurisdictions allow for this, this should involve modified work [3]. Modifications can be duties, tasks, hours, days, etc., preferably based on shared decision by the worker and supervisor, guided by the RTW coordinator [10]. If modified work is not an option, vocational rehabilitation programs may involve simulated work activities performed at the rehabilitation clinic. These simulated work activities should follow the same principles of codevelopment and gradual increase of workload toward a predefined endpoint.

As a general principle, the vocational rehabilitation team and its members should embrace the biopsychosocial model to guide their functional diagnostic and treatment approach [2]. One of the key principles of vocational rehabilitation is to address dysfunctional beliefs and behavior. There is extensive clinical evidence that symptoms may originate from a health condition, but the development of chronic symptoms and disability also depends on psychosocial factors. There is now broad agreement that understanding and management of human illness and disability (particularly that associated with common health problems such as CMPC) must take account of biological, psychological, *and* social dimensions – a biopsychosocial model. It is an individual-centered model that considers the person, their health problem, *and* their social context: *biological* refers to the physical or mental health condition; *psychological* recognizes that personal/psychological factors also influence functioning; *social* recognizes the importance of the social context, pressures, and constraints on illness behavior and functioning. These elements are often described and dealt with separately. In reality, functioning depends on complex interactions between the individual, the health condition, and the environment in a dynamic social process over time [11].

The vocational rehabilitation team and its members should be regarded as one of the environmental factors that may positively influence the course of work disability. However, the opposite may also be the case. The attitude of healthcare professional may also be very relevant, as healthcare professionals can actually form a barrier for making progress in RTW. Workers are sick listed more often and longer when they have physicians who themselves hold fear-avoidant attitudes toward activities and work [12]. There is strong evidence that healthcare professionals who hold high fear-avoidance beliefs are associated with high fear-avoidance beliefs of their patients (suggesting a carry-over effect), and moderate-quality evidence that high fear-avoidant healthcare professionals more frequently advise to limit activities and work and increased sickness certification [13]. Additionally, healthcare professionals with a biomedical orientation (versus a biopsychosocial orientation) tend to nonadhere to clinical practice guidelines more often and to advise to limit activities and work more frequently [13]. It is of importance that healthcare professional should assess their fear-avoidance beliefs before exposing themselves to workers with CMPC [14].

9.2 Disability Evaluation

A consented definition of disability evaluation appears absent. Recent literature on disability evaluation is available [15–18]; however, definitions are not provided in any of those papers. This may be explained by the diversity of the settings and purposes of disability evaluation: it may be used in medical legal settings, social security settings, work rehabilitation settings, claim settings, and disability pension settings. However, within the scope of this chapter, the focus lies on the setting where disability is assessed as part of vocational rehabilitation. Within vocational rehabilitation, the purposes of disability evaluation may be to assess baseline functioning, to compare this baseline functional level to the target level of function, and to set vocational rehabilitation goals based on the difference between current functional level and target level.

Thus, disability evaluation will be considered as an assessment of work (dis) ability, which typically focuses on the activity level of functioning, defined within the International Classification of Functioning, Disability, and Health (ICF) as "the execution of a task or action by an individual." It includes complex interactions between the ICF components: body functions, body structures, and activities and participation. Related terms include activity (limitations), disability, functional capacity, and performance potential. Two qualifiers are used to define activities and participation: capacity and performance. Capacity is the environmentally adjusted inherent ability of the individual, or in other words, the highest probable functioning of a person in a given domain at a given point in time, in a standardized environment (what a person can do). Performance refers to what a person actually does in her or his current environment. It describes the person's functioning as observed or reported in the person's real-life environment with the existing facilitators and barriers (what a person does). In the remainder of this chapter, the capacity qualifier will be used. Within the vocational rehabilitation, there are three means to evaluate the capacity of a worker with CMPC to perform work activities in a "standardized" manner: self-report based, healthcare professional based, and capacity based.

9.2.1 Self-Report-Based Assessment

Self-report based means of evaluations are typically done via questionnaires. There are many questionnaires available that measure the activity level, and most of these are region specific, i.e., they ask for activities that are typically affected when the CMPC is located in the neck, back, or arms. Examples are the Neck Disability Index (NDI), the Neck Pain and Disability Scale (NPAD), the Roland–Morris Disability Questionnaire (RMDQ), the Oswestry Disability Index (ODI), and the Disabilities of the Arms, Shoulder, and Hands (DASH). An example of a non-region-specific questionnaire is the Pain Disability Index (PDI). These questionnaires have been translated in many languages, are freely available, and typically take only a few minutes to fill out. The measurement properties of these questionnaires have been studied extensively. Overall, these questionnaires are deemed reproducible, and for most questionnaires, an estimate for meaningful change has been established, typically about 15 % of the scale. This means that a change of 15 % is interpreted as clinically meaningful. This means that these questionnaires can be used to evaluate self-reported change at the level of activities due to vocational rehabilitation. When it comes to validity, it should be noted that these questionnaires are valid to measure self-reported capacity to perform activities, which may or may not be the same or similar as "objectifiable" capacity to perform activities. Additionally, these questionnaires cannot be used to determine abilities related to work. They rate the self-reported capacities, and these are typically compared to others with the same pain condition or to the worker himself or herself (i.e., before–after comparison). However, these self-reported capacities cannot be compared to the demands of work for reference, thus making them unusable as a tool to determine self-reported work disability.

9.2.2 Clinician-Based Assessment

Healthcare professionals typically assess work disability as part of their routine clinical vocational rehabilitation assessment procedures. This evaluation may range from implicit and nonstandardized manner that are typically applied in routine history to an explicit and "standardized" evaluation procedure. The measurement properties of these nonstandardized healthcare professional-based evaluations are questionable. The reliability is scarcely studied, but when studied in vivo, the reliability is poor [19–21]. Recent studies demonstrated some improvement [22, 23]; however, these studies were performed using a vignette, which limited the healthcare professional's task to data interpretation only, because the data collection phase was described in the vignette. Because the data collection phase of the study was fully standardized (the vignette), these results may not be as valid for real-life disability evaluations, because in these situations healthcare professionals are asked to collect data and interpret them. This involves many more variables, which will likely decrease its reliability. The validity for vocational rehabilitation has not been studied, but it has been stated that the outcomes of the healthcare professional's evaluation tend to resemble patients' preferences and tend to be inconsistent with evidence. As mentioned previously [13], it was hypothesized that the outcomes may be more consistent with the healthcare professional's own pain attitudes and cognitions than the "true" capacities of the worker [20].

9.2.3 Capacity Evaluation

The third means of evaluation is performance based. This means that the worker with a CMPC actually performs the activity according to a standardized procedure. These evaluations are typically referred to as functional capacity evaluations (FCEs), although numerous other terms are used to denote the same or similar: functional capacity assessment, physical capacity evaluation, physical performance analysis, work capacity evaluation, work tolerance screening, functional ability evaluation, and more. Based on the Delphi method, where it was consented to define and develop FCE with ICF as a framework, FCE was defined as an evaluation of the capacity of activities that is used to make recommendations for participation in work, while considering the person's body functions and structures, environmental factors, personal factors, and health status [24]. A theoretically and practically interesting aspect of FCE is that capacity is compared to the work demands, thereby creating meaningful outcomes for vocational rehabilitation. Typically, when deficits between capacities and demands are measured, the evaluation should also identify the reason for this deficit and determine whether and how this reason is modifiable. This may serve as meaningful input to guide the vocational rehabilitation program. There are many protocols available, some commercially, and others self-constructed or partially described in the peer-reviewed literature. When all relevant activities need to be tested, testing time may take multiple hours, making it costly and a burden for the worker and healthcare professional. Studies have demonstrated that substantially fewer tests may be as valid as comprehensive batteries [25–27].

Over the past decade, many studies have been performed to analyze the measurement properties of FCE in workers with CMPC. Reliability and safety have now been established in workers with chronic back pain, whiplash, osteoarthritis in the knees and hips, and healthy workers. Validity remains challenging to assess, because of the absence of a gold standard. There is evidence, however, that FCE in patients with CMPC should not be regarded as a physical measure but rather a measure that is composed of a person's body functions and structures, environmental factors, personal factors, and health status [28–32]. How these factors interact may differ between individual workers and between healthy workers and workers with CMPC [28]. While debatable, it has been suggested that FCE should be able to predict work ability and (future) work status. Indeed, studies have shown a moderate ability of FCE to predict (future) work status [33, 34]. However, it may be questioned whether FCEs by themselves will ever be found valid for the prediction of a safe and sustained RTW. The construct of "work ability" is widely regarded as multidimensional. Whether a patient successfully returns to work or not depends on more than just functional capacity. It is critical to understand that an instrument measuring a single dimension cannot be expected to assess a multidimensional construct. It is, therefore, by definition incorrect to suggest or to claim that the results of an FCE should be able to predict a person's work ability, or even more complex, a successful return to work. At best, one may expect an FCE to measure an individual's immediate functional ability to perform work-related activities. This should be seen as one of the prerequisites for a successful return to work [33].

9.2.4 Comparison

Each measure of disability (self-report based, clinician based, capacity based) has its positive and negative aspects; no single means of assessment can be regarded as perfect. Additionally, all studies comparing self-report-based, clinician-based, and performance-based disability evaluation strategies in workers with CMPC conclude that these measures are "related but different" [19, 31, 32, 35]. This means that each measure will have the ability to measure part of the construct of activity limitation, yet none of them should be regarded as comprehensive on its own. Consequently, leaving one of these measures out will lead to a suboptimal disability evaluation [34]. Thus, it is advised in disability evaluation with the setting of vocational rehabilitation to use all measurement strategies in order to as much a comprehensive picture of the capacity to perform activities as possible. Knowing that full batteries of tests may not be needed, this allows testing (the most time intensive of the three) to become an integral part of a comprehensive set of measures within vocational rehabilitation of workers with CMPC [36].

- Within vocational rehabilitation, there are three means to evaluate the capacity of a worker with CMPC to perform work activities in a "standardized" manner: self-report based, healthcare professional based, and capacity based.
- These measures are "related but different." None of them should be regarded as comprehensive on its own.
- It is advised to use all measurement strategies in order to obtain as much a comprehensive picture of the capacity to perform activities as possible.

Study Questions

Q1. What differentiates vocational rehabilitation from "normal" rehabilitation?
A1. Integrated work- and worker-focused healthcare and accommodating workplaces.

Q2. VR interventions can be classified based on the duration of absence from work. Which classes can be distinguished?
A2. Not absent; short term (less than 6 weeks); intermediate (between 6 weeks and 12 months); long term (more than 3 months).

Q3. Which strong evidence-based recommendations can be given regarding the content and dosage of VR for workers with CMPC?
A3. None.

Q4. What are the three main components of effective VR?
A4. The presence of a return to work coordinator; the principle of graded activity and graded exposure to work, including modified work; and the biopsychosocial orientation of the vocational rehabilitation team.

Q5. What VR team trade has shown to negatively influence work outcomes?
A5. Fear-avoidance beliefs of team members.

Q6. Name at least three settings in which disability evaluation is practiced.
A6. Medical legal settings, social security settings, work rehabilitation settings, claim settings, and disability pension settings.

Q7. What are the three most used means to evaluate the capacity of a worker with CMPC to perform work activities?
A7. Self-report based; healthcare professional based; and capacity based.

Q8. Name two disadvantages of healthcare professional-based and capacity-based disability evaluations.
A8. HCP: reliability unknown or substandard; associated with HCP's own pain attitudes. Capacity: time consuming; not comprehensive on its own.

References

1. Escorpizo R, Reneman MF, Ekholm J, Fritz J, Krupa T, Marnetoft SU, et al. A conceptual definition of vocational rehabilitation based on the ICF: building a shared global model. J Occup Rehabil. 2011;21(2):126–33.
2. Waddell G, Burton AK, Kendall NAS, editors. Vocational rehabilitation – what works, for whom, and when? Report for the vocational rehabilitation Task Group. London: TSO; 2008.
3. Franche RL, Cullen K, Clarke J, Irvin E, Sinclair S, Frank J, et al. Workplace-based return-to-work interventions: a systematic review of the quantitative literature. J Occup Rehabil. 2005;15(4):607–31.
4. de Vries HJ, Reneman MF, Groothoff JW, Geertzen JH, Brouwer S. Factors promoting staying at work in people with chronic nonspecific musculoskeletal pain: a systematic review. Disabil Rehabil. 2012;34(6):443–58.
5. Airaksinen O, Brox JI, Cedraschi C, Hildebrandt J, Klaber-Moffett J, Kovacs F, et al. Chapter 4. European guidelines for the management of chronic nonspecific low back pain. Eur Spine J. 2006;15 Suppl 2:S192–300.
6. van Tulder M, Becker A, Bekkering T, Breen A, del Real MT, Hutchinson A, et al. Chapter 3. European guidelines for the management of acute nonspecific low back pain in primary care. Eur Spine J. 2006;15 Suppl 2:S169–91.
7. Waterschoot FP, Dijkstra PU, Hollak N, de Vries HJ, Geertzen JH, Reneman MF. Dose or content? Effectiveness of pain rehabilitation programs for patients with chronic low back pain: a systematic review. Pain. 2014;155(1):179–89.
8. Main C, Sullivan MJL, Watson PJ, editors. Pain management; practical applications of the biopsychosocial perspective in clinical and occupational settings. 2nd ed. London: Elsevier Limited; 2008.
9. Gardner BT, Pransky G, Shaw WS, Nha Hong Q, Loisel P. Researcher perspectives on competencies of return-to-work coordinators. Disabil Rehabil. 2010;32(1):72–8.
10. Lambeek LC, Bosmans JE, Van Royen BJ, Van Tulder MW, Van Mechelen W, Anema JR. Effect of integrated care for sick listed patients with chronic low back pain: economic evaluation alongside a randomised controlled trial. BMJ. 2010;341:c6414.
11. Waddell G, Burton K, Aylward M. A biopsychosocial model of sickness and disability. Guides Newslett. American Medical Association; 2008.
12. Werner EL, Cote P, Fullen BM, Hayden JA. Physicians' determinants for sick-listing LBP patients: a systematic review. Clin J Pain. 2012;28(4):364–71.
13. Darlow B, Fullen BM, Dean S, Hurley DA, Baxter GD, Dowell A. The association between health care professional attitudes and beliefs and the attitudes and beliefs, clinical management, and outcomes of patients with low back pain: a systematic review. Eur J Pain. 2012;16 (1):3–17.
14. Nijs J, Roussel N, Paul van Wilgen C, Koke A, Smeets R. Thinking beyond muscles and joints: therapists' and patients' attitudes and beliefs regarding chronic musculoskeletal pain are key to applying effective treatment. Man Ther. 2013;18(2):96–102.
15. Anner J, Kunz R, Boer WD. Reporting about disability evaluation in European countries. Disabil Rehabil. 36(10):848–854.
16. Anner J, Schwegler U, Kunz R, Trezzini B, de Boer W. Evaluation of work disability and the international classification of functioning, disability and health: what to expect and what not. BMC Public Health. 2012;12:470-2458-12-470.
17. Escorpizo R, Stucki G. Disability evaluation, social security, and the international classification of functioning, disability and health: the time is now. J Occup Environ Med. 2013;55 (6):644–51.
18. Saltychev M, Kinnunen A, Laimi K. Vocational rehabilitation evaluation and the International Classification of Functioning, Disability, and Health (ICF). J Occup Rehabil. 2013;23(1):106–14.

19. Brouwer S, Dijkstra PU, Stewart RE, Goeken LN, Groothoff JW, Geertzen JH. Comparing self-report, clinical examination and functional testing in the assessment of work-related limitations in patients with chronic low back pain. Disabil Rehabil. 2005;27(17):999–1005.
20. Rainville J, Pransky G, Indahl A, Mayer EK. The physician as disability advisor for patients with musculoskeletal complaints. Spine (Phila Pa 1976). 2005;30(22):2579–84.
21. Brokaw JP, Walker WC, Cifu DX, Gardner M. Sitting and standing tolerance in patients with chronic back pain: comparison between physician prediction and covert observation. Arch Phys Med Rehabil. 2004;85(5):837–9.
22. Spanjer J, Krol B, Brouwer S, Groothoff JW. Inter-rater reliability in disability assessment based on a semi-structured interview report. Disabil Rehabil. 2008;30(24):1885–90.
23. Spanjer J, Krol B, Brouwer S, Popping R, Groothoff JW, van der Klink JJ. Reliability and validity of the Disability Assessment Structured Interview (DASI): a tool for assessing functional limitations in claimants. J Occup Rehabil. 2010;20(1):33–40.
24. Soer R, van der Schans CP, Groothoff JW, Geertzen JH, Reneman MF. Towards consensus in operational definitions in functional capacity evaluation: a Delphi Survey. J Occup Rehabil. 2008;18(4):389–400.
25. Gouttebarge V, Wind H, Kuijer PP, Sluiter JK, Frings-Dresen MH. How to assess physical work-ability with functional capacity evaluation methods in a more specific and efficient way? Work. 2010;37(1):111–5.
26. Gross DP, Battie MC, Asante AK. Evaluation of a short-form functional capacity evaluation: less may be best. J Occup Rehabil. 2007;17(3):422–35.
27. Reesink DD, Jorritsma W, Reneman MF. Basis for a functional capacity evaluation methodology for patients with work-related neck disorders. J Occup Rehabil. 2007;17(3):436–49.
28. Lakke SE, Soer R, Geertzen JH, Wittink H, Douma RK, van der Schans CP, et al. Construct validity of functional capacity tests in healthy workers. BMC Musculoskelet Disord. 2013;14:180-2474-14-180.
29. Lakke SE, Wittink H, Geertzen JH, van der Schans CP, Reneman MF. Factors that affect functional capacity in patients with musculoskeletal pain: a Delphi study among scientists, clinicians, and patients. Arch Phys Med Rehabil. 2012;93(3):446–57.
30. van Abbema R, Lakke SE, Reneman MF, van der Schans CP, van Haastert CJ, Geertzen JH, et al. Factors associated with functional capacity test results in patients with non-specific chronic low back pain: a systematic review. J Occup Rehabil. 2011;21(4):455–73.
31. van der Meer S, Reneman MF, Verhoeven J, van der Palen J. Relationship between self-reported disability and functional capacity in patients with Whiplash Associated Disorder. J Occup Rehabil. 2013;36(10):848–854.
32. Reneman MF, Jorritsma W, Schellekens JM, Goeken LN. Concurrent validity of questionnaire and performance-based disability measurements in patients with chronic nonspecific low back pain. J Occup Rehabil. 2002;12(3):119–29.
33. Kuijer PP, Gouttebarge V, Brouwer S, Reneman MF, Frings-Dresen MH. Are performance-based measures predictive of work participation in patients with musculoskeletal disorders? A systematic review. Int Arch Occup Environ Health. 2012;85(2):109–23.
34. Kuijer PP, Gouttebarge V, Wind H, van Duivenbooden C, Sluiter JK, Frings-Dresen MH. Prognostic value of self-reported work ability and performance-based lifting tests for sustainable return to work among construction workers. Scand J Work Environ Health. 2012;38(6):600–3.
35. Wittink H, Rogers W, Sukiennik A, Carr DB. Physical functioning: self-report and performance measures are related but distinct. Spine. 2003;28(20):2407–13.
36. Reneman MF, Beemster TT, Edelaar MJ, van Velzen JM, van Bennekom C, Escorpizo R. Towards an ICF- and IMMPACT-based pain vocational rehabilitation core set in the Netherlands. J Occup Rehabil. 2013;23(4):576–84.

Chapter 10
Functioning and Disability Evaluation as an Asset for Vocational Rehabilitation in Neurological Conditions

Matilde Leonardi, Davide Sattin, Rui Quintas, Ambra Mara Giovannetti, and Alberto Raggi

10.1 Introduction

Although there are different definitions of vocational rehabilitation (VR), this is a multidisciplinary intervention whose aim is to facilitate the return to work (RTW), or the maintenance of a work position, of a person with a disability [1–5]. The need for a multidisciplinary approach in VR is almost always highlighted, with special reference to medical, psychological, social and occupational aspects. Beginning with evaluation of the skills required for a specific work activity and the person's abilities, VR identifies a solution in which return to work (RTW) – or maintenance of a job – is the desired outcome [6]. Therefore, a comprehensive VR programme should include different kinds of interventions, such as clinical evaluation, vocational training, education, job counselling and placement.

Rehabilitation is a concept that opens to a broad range of interpretations. In the World Report on Disability, produced by the World Health Organization and the World Bank (2011), rehabilitation is defined as "a set of measures that assist individuals who experience, or are likely to experience, disability to achieve and maintain optimal functioning in interaction with their environments" (p. 96) [7]. Sometimes rehabilitation is also distinguished by "habilitation" whereby support services are meant for those who acquire disabilities congenitally or early in life, while "rehabilitation" would refer to those who have experienced a loss in function and therefore need support to regain maximal functioning. The overarch-

M. Leonardi • D. Sattin • R. Quintas • A.M. Giovannetti • A. Raggi (✉)
Neurology, Public Health and Disability Unit, Neurological Institute C. Besta IRCCS Foundation, Via Celoria 11, 20133 Milan, Italy
e-mail: araggi@istituto-besta.it

R. Escorpizo et al. (eds.), *Handbook of Vocational Rehabilitation and Disability Evaluation*, Handbooks in Health, Work, and Disability, DOI 10.1007/978-3-319-08825-9_10

ing objective of the rehabilitation process is the improvement in individual functioning: it occurs for a specific period of time, involving single or multiple interventions delivered by an individual or a team of rehabilitation workers, and can be needed from the acute or initial phase immediately following recognition of a health condition through to post-acute and maintenance phases [7].

Rehabilitation involves identification of persons' needs, relating them to relevant factors of the person and the environment, defining rehabilitation goals, planning and implementing interventions and assessing the effects. Rehabilitation covers a wide range of actions in the areas of health, employment, education and social services, which have the objective of allowing the full participation of persons with disabilities in their communities, and VR is one of the possible aspects of rehabilitation. A description of the process of VR is out of the scope of this chapter. We will instead focus on the description and evaluation of functioning and disability as a preliminary and essential step that anticipates VR interventions, and we will explore the connection between such evaluation and its outcome, with a specific focus on certain neurological conditions. We will specifically consider multiple sclerosis (MS), stroke and traumatic brain injury (TBI) as they share relevant components of cognitive and mental function impairment, as well as other impairments connected to neurological functions. We will present the International Classification of Functioning, Disability and Health (ICF) [8] as the necessary framework to understand this process, which has been recently identified as useful for describing the different aspects of VR [6, 9].

The focus of this chapter is on neurological conditions where – compared to mental and musculoskeletal conditions – there is less literature [6, 9]. However, neurological conditions are prevalent, associated with multiple difficulties in daily activities and costly. A recent study on the cost of disorders of the brain in Europe [10] reports that the prevalence of MS is approximately 105 per 100,000 persons, prevalence of stroke and its sequelae is approximately 1,603 per 100,000 and prevalence of TBI is approximately 729 per 100,000. The cost per patient associated with these disorders is approximately €27,000 per year for MS, €7,800 per year for stroke and €8,800 per year for TBI. Part of this cost is due to medical expenses, but a significant portion is due to indirect costs, namely, reduced productivity and work cessation. In the case of stroke, indirect costs represent approximately 8 % of total cost; for MS and TBI these figures are higher, being 32 % and 59 %, respectively. It is therefore clear that VR programmes should be considered to tailor comprehensive rehabilitation interventions for patients with these disorders.

Vocational Rehabilitation is a multidisciplinary intervention aimed to facilitate return to work in case of acute-onset diseases (e.g. stroke or TBI) or maintenance of a work position in case of progressive conditions (e.g. MS).

10.2 Functioning and Disability Evaluation in Selected Neurological Conditions

According to the biopsychosocial approach of the ICF, disability is a state of decreased functioning that arises out of the interaction between an individual with a health condition and his/her environment [8]. Practically, this means that disability involves difficulties at the body, person and societal levels, including activity limitations and participation restrictions, and environmental barriers [11]. However, to date, a disability assessment instrument that takes into account all these elements does not exist.

Among the existing disability assessment instruments, some measure part of the continuum of functioning related to the activities and participation domain. Examples of this are the WHO Disability Assessment Schedule, second version (WHODAS 2.0) [12], the screener part of the ICF Measure of Participation and ACTivities questionnaire (IMPACT-S) [13] and the Norwegian Function Assessment Scale (NFAS) [14]. A great number of instruments measure impairments of body functions; these are generally symptom-specific. Few instruments are available to assess the contribution of environmental factors as defined by the ICF; some of them measure the support persons receive from relevant others (e.g. the Medical Outcome Study Social Support Survey [15]) or features of the "physical" environment (e.g. the Housing Enabler [16] or the Walking and Biking Suitability Assessment [17]).

In general, disability evaluation is performed using disease-specific assessment instruments of known validity and reliability that measure core activities or chief symptoms. To our knowledge, there is only one instrument to screen for disability in neurological conditions that has been developed for use in resource-poor settings [18].

10.2.1 Disability Evaluation in Multiple Sclerosis

As a recent review acknowledged, many disability outcome measures used in MS research lack sensitivity to change [19], probably as a consequence of the features of the disease itself, which includes heterogeneous clinical manifestations, unpredictable relapse rates, severity and variability of recovery between relapses and the generally slow rate of progression. There are few assessment instruments aimed to measure disability in MS: the most frequently used are the Expanded Disability Status Scale (EDSS) [20] and the MS Functional Composite scale (MSFC) [21].

The EDSS is based on the standard neurological examination and takes into account a wide range of manifestations typical of MS (involving visual, brainstem, pyramidal, cerebellar, sensory, bowel/bladder and cerebral functions), such as walking distance, need for assistive devices and the ability to carry out daily living activities. MS specialists are familiar with the EDSS, and its scores are generally accepted by regulators. For these reasons it remains the most used MS-specific disability assessment measure, despite some of its shortcomings: poor reliability between and within raters, poor acknowledgment of cognitive impairments and the use of a non-linear ordinal scale [19].

The MSFC was developed to overcome some of the shortcomings of the EDSS. It is based on quantitative evaluation of three performance tests that measure walking ability, upper extremity functions and cognition. The MSFC is highly reliable and covers three major MS domains; its single score is on a continuum scale, and correlations with disease stage [22], magnetic resonance imaging (MRI) findings [23] and patient-reported outcome measures [24] have been demonstrated. However, it lacks a vision test and some concerns about the abstract and dimensionless nature of its summary score exist, thus making MSFC's score difficult to interpret clinically.

Other measures that have been used in MS research are composite end points, in particular disease-activity-free status [25]; global measures of activities of daily living, such as the Rankin Scale and the Barthel Index [26, 27]; and biomarkers such as MRI and optical coherence tomography. Some patient-reported measures are also available, including instruments such as the Symptom Inventory Disability-Specific Short Forms for Multiple Sclerosis [28] and the Multiple Sclerosis Impact Profile [29].

10.2.2 Disability Evaluation in Stroke

Like MS patients, stroke patients may experience a variety of symptoms depending on the nature of the acute event (broadly, ischemic or haemorrhagic), on the brain area damaged, and on the availability of prompt intervention. The result is that a great variety of outcome measures exists that assess disability in post-stroke patients. In 2001, a report on the outcome measures used for rehabilitation in Europe [30] showed that the most frequently used measures for stroke were the Functional Independence Measure (FIM) [31], the Barthel Index [27], the Scandinavian Stroke Scale [32] and the Katz ADL Index [33].

The FIM is composed of 18 items, each rated on a 7-point scale; summary scores range between 18 and 126, with higher scores indicating higher levels of functional independence. The items are divided into 13 motor tasks (eating, grooming, bathing, upper body dressing, lower body dressing, toileting, bladder management, bowel management, bed to chair transfer, toilet transfer, shower transfer, locomotion, ambulatory or wheelchair level, stairs climbing) and five cognitive tasks (cognitive comprehension, expression, social interaction, problem solving, memory). A cut-off score of 73 has been reported to predict the degree of functional gain after rehabilitation in survivors with a first-ever ischaemic stroke [34], and the FIM is deemed to have excellent internal consistency and adequate construct validity [35, 36]. The problem with the FIM is that its core content, i.e. independence, is strictly based on the old WHO International Classification of Impairment, Disabilities and Handicaps [37] and measures the level of disability based on how much assistance is needed by the patient to carry out daily activities. Such description of disability may be problematic in terms of goal setting when a wider approach to the patients' life is needed to identify the objectives of intervention.

10.2.3 Disability Evaluation in Traumatic Brain Injury

Disability of patients with TBI, similar to individuals with MS and stroke, cannot be easily described due to the variety of impairments caused by brain injury, which vary in terms of severity and location of damage. Moreover, TBI patients often suffer from polytrauma and thus have other body structures in addition to the head and brain that may be damaged; different injuries, different severity and different symptoms make the assessment of TBI-related disability difficult. According to the 2001 report on the outcome measures used for rehabilitation in Europe [30], the Glasgow Coma Scale [38] and the FIM [31] were the most used assessments in TBI patients. Other instruments commonly used are the Glasgow Outcome Scale [39], the Community Integration Questionnaire [40], the Rivermead Head Injury Follow-Up Questionnaire [41], the Disability Rating Scale [42], the Functional Assessment Measure [43] and the Rancho Los Amigos Scale of Cognitive Functioning [44].

The problem with some of these scales is that they are much too categorical to serve the scope of disability description. For example, the Glasgow Outcome Scale is a global scale for functional outcome that ranks and rates patients' status into one of five categories (dead, vegetative state, severe disability, moderate disability or good recovery). These categories are rated on the basis of presence of consciousness, level of independence and on ability to perform daily activities such as those connected to work and family activities. The Disability Rating Scale reports scores on a 0–30 scale and recognises ten different disability levels (none, mild, partial, moderate, moderately severe, severe, extremely severe, vegetative state, extreme vegetative state, dead). The items that lead to the definition of these scores are assigned to different domains: arousability, awareness and responsivity; cognitive ability for self-care activities; dependence on others; and psychosocial adaptability. Again, the ability to describe disability features with such a strict categorical approach is limited and does not meet the need for a full disability and functioning profile.

Disability assessments are mostly disease-specific or symptom specific. They are often too much categorical and do not fit well with the need for a broad disability description, or rely on concepts – such as independence – that reflect an out-dated disability classification description (i.e. based on the ICIDH-80) that is problematic to set intervention objectives.

10.3 Functioning and Disability in Multiple Sclerosis, Stroke and Traumatic Brain Injury: ICF-Based Approaches

Since its release, the ICF attracted the attention of clinicians and researchers, and as a 2011 literature review showed [45], almost 40 % of ICF-related literature is on the clinical application of the ICF or on the development of ICF-related instruments. Being a classification, its primary aim is not to assess disability, rather it is to describe the different components of functioning and disability, i.e. to describe which functions or domains are impaired or limited, and the positive or hindering role of relevant environmental factors. ICF-based data on functioning and disability, in fact, make it possible to address the complexity of an individual's daily lived experience of disability, irrespective of his or her health condition [46]. Such an approach should not preclude the use of validated and disability-specific assessment instruments; rather, it should complement and enrich information to describe functioning and disability derived from assessment instrument data.

What ICF-based data add is primarily a unified vision in which the different components of functioning (body impairments, activity limitations, participation restrictions and the role of environmental factors) are taken into account within a common framework. Second, it enables clinicians to address the needs of an individual, not only needs that can be identified as rehabilitation needs (e.g. achieving a goal in mobility or job activities) but also in terms of identifying facilitating environmental factors (e.g. an assistive device) or removal of barriers. These are advancements that the ICF enables VR professionals to systematically address, and its worth in the field of work disability description and vocational rehabilitation planning is of primary relevance [47].

After more than 10 years since its publication, there is considerable literature on functioning and disability in MS, stroke and TBI with an ICF-based approach. Although not fully exhaustive, we aim to provide some information on the main research findings on these topics. In the following sections, we will report a synthetic analysis of available data that describe functioning and disability in MS, stroke and TBI with an ICF-based approach. For each condition, the prevalence of use of ICF categories will be analysed, and a synthesis of these data – using a threshold for category retention of 33 % – will be presented. Such an approach has clear methodological limitations, since the use of ICF categories across different studies is subject to differences that are due to practical and theoretical reasons. However, it is a feasible approach to show how disability information can be collected with the ICF and the practical implications of these procedures. The 33 % threshold is strict enough to enable readers to focus on the most relevant condition-specific ICF items. A more conservative approach – i.e. a threshold of 10–20 % – would make cross condition comparison much more complex.

> ICF-based data make it possible to address the complexity of the lived experience of disability, irrespectively of underlying health conditions and clinical stages. This enables to set rehabilitation objectives in a broad perspective: from early acute stages, to post-acute and up to vocational settings.

10.3.1 ICF-Based Description of Disability in Persons with Multiple Sclerosis

The ICF Core Set for MS was released in 2011 [48]. It was developed through a formal and iterative decision-making and consensus process, in which 21 experts from 16 countries selected 138 ICF categories for the Comprehensive ICF Core Set for MS. These categories consisted of 40 body functions, 7 body structures, 53 activities and participation categories and 38 environmental factors. A Brief Core Set that includes 19 categories was also released. Future validation studies need to be undertaken; to date, two studies relying on the Delphi approach validated the Core Set from the perspectives of occupational therapists [49] and physical therapists [50].

To our knowledge, ICF-based data collected from MS patients have been published for three groups of MS patients. In 2007, Khan and Pallant reported data from 101 patients and reported that 170 different categories were identified; of these, 62 were reported for more than one-third of the participants and were included in the analysis [51]. In 2010, Holper and colleagues reported data from 205 patients in a rehabilitation setting and used a conservative approach that included all categories reported for more than 5 % of the patients. In total, 129 ICF categories were identified [52]. Again in 2010, Svestkova and colleagues reported data on 100 patients, using a threshold of 20 %, and selected 58 ICF categories [53]. Data reported in these three studies show differences related to prevalence of impairments, difficulties and environmental factors. This is due both to differences in sample composition, but also in the kind of instruments that have been used to address the dimensions of functioning and disability.

Based on our inclusion criterion of 33 % described earlier, 64 ICF categories are included in the analysis. The most common impairments in body functions and structures are shown in Table 10.1; there are 16 body functions and 7 body structures. The most common functional impairments refer to mobility and mental functions, with wide differences in the prevalence of those impairments. Similar differences are observed for body structures, where neurological and movement-related structures are the most impaired. The most common limitations in activities and participation are shown in Table 10.2; in total, 25 categories reached the inclusion threshold, with mobility-related and domestic life activities being the most commonly reported. Also in this case, relevant differences among samples exist. The most common facilitators and barriers in environmental factors are shown in Table 10.3; data have been aggregated and differences between facilitators and barriers are not shown. In total, 16 environmental factors have been reported, mostly related to personal support and attitudes from relevant others.

What emerges from these data is that there are more differences than similarities in the profiles of functioning collected by the three studies. These differences are likely to reflect the heterogeneous clinical manifestations of MS, with varying degrees of impairments in movement-related functions (e.g. muscle power was reported as impaired in 95 % of patients in the 2007 study by Khan and Pallant [51]

Table 10.1 Selection of ICF categories from body functions and structures reported as impaired in at least 33 % of cases across publications on functioning and disability in multiple sclerosis [51–53]

	Khan and Pallant [51] (*N* = 101)	Holper et al. [52] (*N* = 205)	Svestkova et al. [53] (*N* = 100)	All cases (*N* = 406)
Body functions				
b770 Gait pattern	98.0 %	89.8 %	54.0 %	83.0 %
b730 Muscle power	95.0 %	94.6 %	44.0 %	82.3 %
b620 Urination functions	93.1 %	81.5 %	70.0 %	81.5 %
b130 Energy and drive	97.0 %	71.2 %	52.0 %	72.9 %
b134 Sleep	83.2 %	68.3 %	60.0 %	70.0 %
b210 Seeing	46.5 %	75.1 %	65.0 %	65.5 %
b735 Muscle tone	93.1 %	63.4 %	41.0 %	65.3 %
b140 Attention	65.3 %	63.9 %	42.0 %	58.9 %
b280 Sensation of pain	75.2 %	55.1 %	–	54.2 %
b235 Vestibular	70.3 %	38.0 %	65.0 %	52.7 %
b152 Emotional functions	96.0 %	33.2 %	47.0 %	52.2 %
b640 Sexual functions	56.4 %	40.5 %	58.0 %	48.8 %
b710 Mobility of joint	–	82.9 %	–	48.5 %
b780 Sensation related to muscles	–	81.5 %	–	41.1 %
b525 Defecation	88.1 %	–	49.0 %	39.4 %
b144 Memory	61.4 %	–	41.0 %	37.9 %
Body structures				
s110 Brain	99.0 %	99.5 %	97.0 %	98.8 %
s120 Spinal cord	–	93.2 %	97.0 %	70.9 %
s750 Lower extremity	96.0 %	75.1 %	–	67.0 %
s610 Urinary system	92.1 %	80.0 %	–	63.3 %
s760 Trunk	84.2 %	47.3 %	–	44.8 %
s730 Upper extremity	43.6 %	59.0 %	–	40.6 %
S2 Eye, ear and related structures	–	73.2 %	–	36.9 %

Note: – Category below the 33 % threshold

Table 10.2 Selection of ICF categories from activities and participation reported as limited in at least 33 % of cases across publications on functioning and disability in multiple sclerosis [51–53]

	Khan and Pallant [51] ($N=101$)	Holper et al. [52] ($N=205$)	Svestkova et al. [53] ($N=100$)	All cases ($N=406$)
d450 Walking	100.0 %	90.7 %	63.0 %	86.2 %
d640 Doing housework	93.1 %	90.7 %	61.0 %	84.0 %
d620 Acquisition of goods and services	91.1 %	88.3 %	60.0 %	82.0 %
d920 Recreation and leisure	96.0 %	90.2 %	50.0 %	81.8 %
d850 Remunerative employment	89.1 %	74.6 %	63.0 %	75.4 %
d455 Moving around	98.0 %	88.3 %	–	74.4 %
d470 Using transportation	99.0 %	69.3 %	56.0 %	73.4 %
d650 Caring for household objects	83.2 %	69.8 %	58.0 %	70.2 %
d910 Community life	78.2 %	91.2 %	–	65.5 %
d475 Driving	98.0 %	67.3 %	–	63.8 %
d230 Carrying out daily routine	79.2 %	82.9 %	–	61.6 %
d465 Moving around using equipment	97.0 %	69.8 %	–	59.4 %
d870 Economic self-sufficiency	83.2 %	57.6 %	38.0 %	59.1 %
d460 Moving around in different locations	–	80.0 %	66.0 %	56.7 %
d440 Fine hand use	50.5 %	67.3 %	38.0 %	55.9 %
d660 Assisting others	86.1 %	63.4 %	–	53.4 %
d770 Intimate relationships	60.4 %	54.6 %	42.0 %	53.0 %
d430 Lifting and carrying objects	52.5 %	59.0 %	38.0 %	52.2 %
d630 Preparation of meals	88.1 %	55.1 %	–	49.8 %
d445 Hand and arm use	36.6 %	70.7 %	–	44.8 %
d220 Undertaking multiple tasks	87.1 %	41.0 %	–	42.4 %
d177 Making decisions	58.4 %	50.7 %	–	40.1 %
d510 Washing oneself	40.6 %	36.1 %	37.0 %	37.4 %
d166 Reading	–	69.8 %	–	35.2 %
d760 Family relationships	72.3 %	–	–	33.0 %

Note: – Category below the 33 % threshold

Table 10.3 Selection of ICF categories from environmental factors reported as barriers or facilitators in at least 33 % of cases across publications on functioning and disability in multiple sclerosis [51–53]

	Khan and Pallant [51] (*N* = 101)	Holper et al. [52] (*N* = 205)	Svestkova et al. [53] (*N* = 100)	All cases (*N* = 406)
e310 Immediate family	44.6 %	100.0 %	81.0 %	81.5 %
e110 Substances for personal consumption (food, medicines)	100.0 %	61.5 %	95.0 %	79.3 %
e120 Technologies for personal indoor and outdoor mobility and transportation	90.1 %	61.0 %	41.0 %	63.3 %
e320 Friends	–	96.6 %	50.0 %	61.1 %
e225 Climate	98.0 %	69.3 %	–	59.4 %
e315 Extended family	41.6 %	97.1 %	–	59.4 %
e410 Attitudes of family members	–	100.0 %	–	58.1 %
e580 Health SSP	78.2 %	64.9 %	–	52.2 %
e415 Attitudes of extended family	–	99.0 %	–	50.0 %
e420 Attitudes of friends	–	97.1 %	–	49.0 %
e150 Design, construction and building products and technology of buildings for public use	69.3 %	38.0 %	50.0 %	48.8 %
e325 Acquaintances, peers and colleagues	–	82.0 %	–	46.3 %
e355 Health professionals	–	69.8 %	30.0 %	42.6 %
e465 Social norms	–	46.3 %	64.0 %	39.2 %
e540 Transportation SSP	67.3 %	30.2 %	–	37.7 %
e450 Attitudes of health professionals	–	73.7 %	–	37.2 %

Notes: – Category below the 33 % threshold
SSP services, systems and policies

and in 44 % of patients in the 2010 study by Svestkova and colleagues [53]) as well as in mental functions (e.g. emotional functions were impaired in 95 % in the 2007 study by Khan and Pallant [51] and in 33.2 % in the 2010 study by Holper and colleagues [52]). In turn, this had an impact on the way in which patients were able to carry out daily life activities, as well as on the way in which assistive devices, or the support from relevant others, were needed. However, it is also correct to suppose that some of these differences are due to the way in which disease severity and disability were assessed in the three groups of MS patients, in terms of available instruments and domains taken into consideration in the settings in which the patients' data were collected. The issue of the differences related to assessment instruments and MS features was addressed in Sect. 10.2.1 of this chapter. By using a common framework to address functioning and disability, the ICF-based data add information on the consequences of these differences. The definition of functioning and disability shows the advantages for using the ICF in vocational rehabilitation practice with MS patients. ICF-based data, in fact, enable VR professionals to classify and collect data on problems at the personal or environmental level beyond those that are likely to be stipulated by the presence of MS symptoms or that are relevant to the disease's management. In fact, MS-related symptoms and problems in performing tasks and activities are difficult to capture with a limited set of assessment tools, which makes it critical to define VR goals. An ICF-based procedure of describing functioning and disability, on the contrary, enables VR professionals to collect information on a wide set of impairments and limitations, with a good balance between synthesis and comprehensiveness. Therefore, it can be used to create a profile of functioning that is strictly connected to the job tasks an individual is expected to perform. Moreover, it enables collection of data on environmental facilitators and barriers, including those connected to job-related activities. Thus, the ICF-based procedure achieves comprehensive and tailored planning for a person in the workplace.

The results of this synopsis on ICF-based data in MS show that there are wide differences across studies, reflecting differences in the clinical manifestation of MS and the variety of movement-related and mental functions impairments.

10.3.2 ICF-Based Description of Disability in Persons with Stroke

The ICF Core Set for stroke has been available since 2004 and is composed of 130 ICF categories, mostly from activities and participation (51 categories) and body functions (41 categories) [54]. A brief Core Set, composed of 18 categories, is also available. To our knowledge, ICF-derived data on samples of stroke patients have been reported in three studies [55–57].

In 2010, Algurén and colleagues collected data on body functions and activities and participation of the ICF Comprehensive Core Set for stroke on a sample of 89 stroke patients and selected as relevant those categories rated as impaired or limited in at least 10 % of the cases; 28 categories from body functions and 41 from activities and participation were considered relevant 3 months after stroke [55]. No data were collected from the components body structures and environmental factors. Using the ICF checklist, in 2010 Goljar and colleagues [56] collected data on a sample of 197 patients attending inpatient rehabilitation services and reported as relevant those categories in which at least 20 % of persons reported some problems (in the case of environmental factors, the threshold was based on the sum of barriers and facilitators). A total of 61 ICF categories reached the threshold, mostly from body functions and activities and participation. In 2012 Quintas and colleagues [57] collected data on a sample of 111 patients using the Brief ICF Core Set for stroke, reporting prevalence of problems only in those 18 categories included in this Core Set. Comparisons of these three studies indicate differences

Table 10.4 Selection of ICF categories from body functions and structures reported as impaired in at least 33 % of cases across publications on functioning and disability in stroke [55–57]

	Algurén et al. [55] (*N* = 89)	Goljar et al. [56] (*N* = 197)	Quintas et al. [57] (*N* = 111)	All cases (*N* = 397)
Body functions				
b770 Gait pattern functions	75.0 %	87.8 %	*nc*	83.8 %
b760 Control of voluntary movement functions	44.0 %	99.5 %	*nc*	82.2 %
b420 Blood pressure functions	76.0 %	79.7 %	*nc*	78.5 %
b144 Memory functions	61.0 %	94.9 %	62.7 %	78.3 %
b210 Seeing functions	96.0 %	67.5 %	*nc*	76.4 %
b455 Exercise tolerance functions	94.0 %	59.9 %	*nc*	70.5 %
b280 Sensation of pain	35.0 %	85.3 %	*nc*	69.6 %
b730 Muscle power functions	61.0 %	99.5 %	52.7 %	63.0 %
b265 Touch function	–	84.8 %	*nc*	61.5 %
b710 Mobility of joint functions	–	88.3 %	*nc*	60.8 %
b260 Proprioceptive function	–	68.5 %	*nc*	56.5 %
b735 Muscle tone functions	–	77.7 %	*nc*	53.5 %
b750 Motor reflex functions	–	54.8 %	*nc*	40.9 %
b152 Emotional functions	–	54.3 %	*nc*	37.4 %
b620 Urination functions	–	46.2 %	*nc*	36.8 %
b140 Attention functions	–	41.6 %	46.4 %	36.1 %
b410 Heart functions	42.0 %	33.0 %	*nc*	35.8 %
b130 Energy and drive functions	65.0 %	–	*nc*	34.2 %
Body structures				
s110 Structure of the brain	*nc*	96.4 %	100.0 %	97.7 %
s720 Structure of shoulder region	*nc*	35.5 %	*nc*	35.5 %

Note: – Category below the 33 % threshold
nc not considered in the original work

that are mostly due to the sets of ICF categories that were used to collect data. The amount of ICF categories ranged from only 18 (i.e. those of the Brief Core Set for stroke) to 128 (i.e. the ICF checklist). In addition, the fact that the protocol used by Algurén and colleagues did not include body structures and environmental factors limits analysis of data for these two domains.

Based on our inclusion criterion of 33 % described earlier, 44 ICF categories are included in the analysis. The most common impairments in body functions and

Table 10.5 Selection of ICF categories from activities and participation reported as limited in at least 33 % of cases across publications on functioning and disability in stroke [55–57]

	Algurén et al. [55] (*N* = 89)	Goljar et al. [56] (*N* = 197)	Quintas et al. [57] (*N* = 111)	All cases (*N* = 397)
d460 Moving around in different locations	67.0 %	93.3 %	*nc*	85.1 %
d440 Fine hand use	46.0 %	99.0 %	*nc*	82.5 %
d450 Walking	78.0 %	92.4 %	47.3 %	76.6 %
d410 Changing basic body position	37.0 %	86.3 %	*nc*	71.0 %
d520 Caring for body parts	33.0 %	85.7 %	*nc*	69.3 %
d175 Solving problems	–	84.8 %	*nc*	61.2 %
d510 Washing oneself	–	92.4 %	–	60.7 %
d540 Dressing	33.0 %	88.8 %	–	59.1 %
d415 Maintaining a body position	36.0 %	67.5 %	*nc*	57.7 %
d710 Basic interpersonal interactions	*nc*	80.7 %	*nc*	55.6 %
d550 Eating	–	90.6 %	–	53.9 %
d530 Toileting	–	78.6 %	–	48.4 %
d920 Recreation and leisure	39.0 %	48.2 %	*nc*	45.3 %
d465 Moving around using equipment	38.0 %	48.2 %	*nc*	45.0 %
d330 Speaking	–	62.4 %	–	42.5 %
d310 Communicating with – receiving – spoken messages	–	56.4 %	–	36.5 %
d166 Reading	34.0 %	37.6 %	*nc*	36.5 %

Note: – Category below the 33 % threshold
nc not considered in the original work

structures are shown in Table 10.4; there were 18 body functions and two body structures. The most common functional impairments were related to mobility functions, with very relevant differences in the prevalence of most of these impairments. Mental and sensory functions were also among the most frequently reported categories, again with noticeable differences between the samples. Table 10.5 shows the most common limitations in activities and participation; in total, 17 categories reached the inclusion threshold, with mobility-related and self-care activities being the most commonly reported. Also in this case, relevant differences between samples are observed. Table 10.6 shows the most common facilitators and barriers in environmental factors, where data have been aggregated without showing differences between facilitators and barriers. In total, seven environmental factors have been reported, mostly related to the domain of products and technologies.

Table 10.6 Selection of ICF categories from environmental factors reported as barriers or facilitators in at least 33 % of cases across publications on functioning and disability in stroke [55–57]

	Algurén et al. [55] (*N* = 89)	Goljar et al. [56] (*N* = 197)	Quintas et al. [57] (*N* = 111)	All cases (*N* = 397)
e110 Products or substances for personal consumption	*nc*	100.0 %	*nc*	100.0 %
e120 Products and technology for personal indoor and outdoor mobility and transportation	*nc*	85.3 %	*nc*	85.3 %
e310 Immediate family	*nc*	72.2 %	95.4 %	80.6 %
e125 Products and technology for communication	*nc*	58.4 %	*nc*	58.4 %
e115 Products and technology for personal use in daily living	*nc*	50.3 %	*nc*	50.3 %
e355 Health professionals	*nc*	–	83.6 %	47.0 %
e155 Design, construction and building products and technology of buildings for private use	*nc*	44.7 %	*nc*	44.7 %

Note: – Category below the 33 % threshold
nc not considered in the original work

ICF-based data that were herein reported show differences that are mostly due to the different kind of data set used to collect functioning and disability information. In addition, differences related to clinical and sociodemographic data also exist: for example, individuals in the study of Algurén and colleagues [55] were approximately 12–14 years older and had a higher prevalence of cerebral infarction (81 %). These differences have a clear impact on the kind and degree of impairments and limitations patients experience, as well as on the need for medical treatment, personal assistance and need for assistive devices. It is, however, problematic to define a "typical" situation of a person surviving a stroke, as the features of the stroke itself, patient's age and distance from the acute event play a fundamental role when rehabilitation programmes need to be planned. The issue of the differences related to assessment instruments and stroke features was addressed in Sect. 10.2.2 of this chapter. As noted earlier, ICF-based data highlight the consequences of these differences because they use a common framework to address functioning and disability. If the issues related to RTW are added to the complex situation of stroke outcomes, it is clear that VR professionals need to rely on a procedure for describing functioning and disability and of the tasks related to job activities. Such a procedure enables tailored goal planning, intervention procedures and criteria to evaluate goal achievements for each patient. Informed by the biopsychosocial model, ICF-based assessment procedures enable VR professionals to synthesise the various elements connected to the patient's health state and the requirements at both person and environmental levels needed for returning to work. Of course, it is also possible that the general health status of stroke survivors prevents them from returning to work; in this instance, the ICF provides an adequate framework that is crucial when RTW is not achievable and appropriate measures of social protection are needed.

The results of this synopsis on ICF-based data in stroke are indicative of differences that are partly connected to the settings in which the studies were carried out, but also to clinical and demographic features of participants. It is in fact problematic to define a "typical" functional status of a stroke survivor: the clinical features of stroke itself, patients' age and distance from event are fundamental issues to plan rehabilitative interventions.

10.3.3 ICF-Based Description of Disability in Persons with Traumatic Brain Injury

TBI may cause very different kinds of impairment, depending on the site of injury and presence of polytrauma. Therefore, defining a common set of ICF categories that should be used as a "minimum" set of functioning and disability information is challenging. The ICF Core Set for TBI was released in 2013 after some years of consultation and application of the ICF in clinical settings: the Comprehensive Core Set for TBI is composed of 139 categories, while the Brief Core Set is composed of 23 categories [58].

To our knowledge, ICF-derived data to describe functioning and disability in TBI patients have been reported in four studies [59–62]. Two studies used the WHO ICF checklist and two used the TBI Core Sets. In 2007 Koskinen and colleagues [59] evaluated medical records of a sample of 55 patients in a rehabilitation setting using the ICF checklist and judged the prevalence of impairments, limitations and environmental factors as relevant when these were reported in at least 30 % of patients by two different professionals. In total, 30 ICF categories – 12 body functions, one body structure, 11 activities and participation and six environmental factors – were judged as relevant to TBI patients in a post-acute setting. Aiachini and colleagues [60] reported the result of a cross-sectional study conducted in 24 Italian centres that collected data from 261 patients, of whom half were outpatients or day clinic patients. They used the ICF checklist to which other categories were added based on linking procedures with established assessment instruments. The resulting extended checklist was composed of 150 ICF categories, including 41 body functions, 16 body structures, 59 activities and participation and

34 environmental factors. They used a threshold of 5 % to report categories as relevant to TBI patients, and all the 150 categories reached the 5 % threshold. In 2010 Svestkova and colleagues [61] collected data on 100 outpatients with sequelae of TBI using the ICF checklist and selected categories as relevant if they occurred in at least 20 % of the cases. In total, 87 ICF categories were selected: 27 body functions and structures, 43 activities and participation and 17 environmental factors. Finally, Laxe and colleagues [62] collected data with the 150-item extended checklist used by Aiachini on a sample of 103 patients – mostly outpatients – and considered as relevant those reported by at least 10 %. In total, 130 categories were retained as relevant: 34 body functions, 7 body structures, 59 activities and participation and 30 environmental factors.

Data reported in these four papers show differences related to the prevalence of impairments, difficulties and environmental factors. These differences are likely to be due to the kind of impairments patients experienced – e.g. the not specified prevalence of polytrauma – as well as to the kinds of instruments that have been used to address the dimensions of functioning and disability and to the type of patients, as those in post-acute rehabilitation have different needs and difficulties compared to those of outpatients.

Based on our inclusion criterion of 33 % described earlier, 101 ICF categories are included in the analysis. Table 10.7 reports the most common impairments in body functions and structures; there were 22 body functions and three body structures. More than half of functional impairments are related to mental functions and five are related to mobility functions. Among body structures, in addition to the brain, lower and upper extremities were found to be impaired as a consequence of polytrauma. Table 10.8 reports the most common limitations and restrictions in activities and participation. In total, 54 categories were retained as relevant, and almost all ICF domains are widely represented in the list, with the most common difficulties related to the domains of mobility, interpersonal interactions and relationships. Table 10.9 reports the most commonly reported environmental factors: in total, 22 categories were reported as relevant, mostly related to support and relationships and to service, system and policy domains.

Such a list of categories for TBI patients is quite extensive (e.g. compared to those defined for MS and stroke; see Sects. 10.3.1 and 10.3.2). Moreover, it also seems that differences among studies are less extended. In general, the 2010 study from Svestkova and colleagues [61] reported a lower percentage of ICF categories, but it should also be taken into consideration that patients enrolled in that study were all outpatients. The ICF checklist was always used as the basis to plan and carry out data collection, so the effect of differences related to the sets of ICF categories is not relevant as it was for stroke (Sect. 10.3.2).

The use of an ICF-based procedure for the description of disability in TBI has potential advantages, mostly dealing with the variety of impairments and limitations that occur when the brain is traumatically injured. TBI outcome is, in fact, very difficult to predict, as several variables may determine its course,

Table 10.7 Selection of ICF categories from body functions and structures reported as impaired in at least 33 % of cases across publications on functioning and disability in traumatic brain injury [59–62]

	Koskinen et al. [59] ($N=55$)	Aiachini et al. [60] ($N=261$)	Svestkova et al. [61] ($N=100$)	Laxe et al. [62] ($N=103$)	All cases ($N=519$)
Body functions					
b152 Emotional functions	96.4 %	77.8 %	67.0 %	79.6 %	78.0 %
b164 Higher-level cognitive functions	100.0 %	77.7 %	49.0 %	90.3 %	77.0 %
b140 Attention functions	96.4 %	80.5 %	59.0 %	72.8 %	76.5 %
b144 Memory functions	100.0 %	78.9 %	53.0 %	80.6 %	76.5 %
b130 Energy and drive functions	85.5 %	70.0 %	70.0 %	84.5 %	74.5 %
b730 Muscle power functions	47.3 %	80.8 %	47.0 %	68.0 %	68.2 %
b710 Mobility of joint functions	–	75.0 %	38.0 %	56.3 %	56.2 %
b117 Intellectual	–	62.5 %	38.0 %	84.5 %	55.5 %
b126 Temperament and personality functions	–	77.4 %	–	83.5 %	55.5 %
b735 Muscle tone functions	–	65.1 %	38.0 %	57.3 %	51.4 %
b156 Perceptual functions	36.4 %	52.1 %	39.0 %	61.2 %	49.7 %
b167 Mental functions of language	76.4 %	52.7 %	–	50.5 %	49.0 %
b160 Thought functions	–	62.1 %	–	78.6 %	46.8 %
b760 Control of voluntary movement functions	–	58.8 %	–	51.5 %	45.6 %
b134 Sleep functions	72.7 %	44.0 %	39.0 %	–	42.7 %
b330 Fluency and rhythm of speech functions	–	61.9 %	–	53.4 %	41.7 %
b114 Orientation functions	–	53.7 %	33.0 %	38.8 %	41.1 %
b210 Seeing functions	45.5 %	41.3 %	51.0 %	–	41.0 %
b320 Articulation functions	–	50.1 %	–	48.5 %	40.8 %
b310 Voice functions	–	50.9 %	–	45.6 %	39.3 %

(continued)

Table 10.7 (continued)

	Koskinen et al. [59] (N=55)	Aiachini et al. [60] (N=261)	Svestkova et al. [61] (N=100)	Laxe et al. [62] (N=103)	All cases (N=519)
b280 Sensation of pain	69.1 %	45.0 %	–	–	38.6 %
b750 Motor reflex	–	54.4 %	–	56.3 %	38.5 %
Body structures					
s110 Structure of the brain	100.0 %	91.5 %	89.0 %	93.2 %	92.3 %
s750 Lower extremity	–	50.8 %	34.0 %	–	37.3 %
s730 Upper extremity	–	52.8 %	–	–	36.6 %

Note: – Category below the 33 % threshold

particularly age, trauma severity and location, neurological status and quality of care. In the last 20 years, the continuous improvement in TBI management and rehabilitation has been dramatic [63], but identification of patients' needs and descriptions of disability have not correspondingly improved. What is needed is a procedure and a set of instruments to track the information on functioning and disability at different stages, from the initial acute condition to the moment of RTW. As two previous studies have concluded [64, 65], an ICF-based procedure can help clinicians track the patients in their journey after TBI. In fact, literature findings estimate that RTW for individuals with TBI varies considerably, from 12 % to 70 %, according to the various parameters observed [66]. The ICF may help systematise information on RTW and to define areas needed for planning effective RTW programmes.

The results of this synopsis on ICF-based data in TBI show a greater variety – compared to MS and stroke – that is connected to several factors: type of setting, severity and type of traumatic event, presence of polytrauma, age of patients. The list of ICF categories is much more extended, as the aforementioned factors determine a great variety of outcomes: the potential advantage of ICF use in TBI, is to track the patient's journey from the acute event, up to the vocational intervention for returning to work.

Table 10.8 Selection of ICF categories from activities and participation reported as limited in at least 33 % of cases across publications on functioning and disability in traumatic brain injury [59–62]

	Koskinen et al. [59] (*N*=55)	Aiachini et al. [60] (*N*=261)	Svestkova et al. [61] (*N*=100)	Laxe et al. [62] (*N*=103)	All cases (*N*=519)
d220 Undertaking multiple tasks	58.2 %	79.9 %	55.0 %	81.6 %	73.1 %
d175 Solving problems	60.0 %	77.3 %	51.0 %	81.6 %	71.2 %
d720 Complex interpersonal interactions	69.1 %	75.3 %	45.0 %	84.5 %	70.6 %
d850 Remunerative employment	100.0 %	57.5 %	42.0 %	86.4 %	64.8 %
d475 Driving	34.5 %	69.1 %	38.0 %	79.6 %	61.5 %
d640 Doing housework	38.2 %	65.7 %	37.0 %	78.6 %	59.8 %
d620 Acquisition of goods and services	58.2 %	65.8 %	–	74.8 %	59.7 %
d440 Fine hand use	45.5 %	63.5 %	50.0 %	64.1 %	59.1 %
d730 Relating with strangers	–	65.3 %	43.0 %	86.4 %	58.3 %
d450 Walking	–	75.4 %	44.0 %	54.4 %	57.2 %
d660 Assisting others	–	73.5 %	–	79.6 %	56.8 %
d350 Conversation	89.1 %	64.6 %	33.0 %	42.7 %	56.8 %
d740 Formal relationships	–	63.1 %	40.0 %	83.5 %	56.0 %
d455 Moving around	–	80.4 %	–	52.4 %	55.7 %
d750 Informal social relationships	–	62.7 %	39.0 %	82.5 %	55.4 %
d920 Recreation and leisure	–	66.9 %	33.0 %	72.8 %	54.5 %
d430 Lifting and carrying objects	–	67.8 %	48.0 %	49.5 %	53.2 %
d870 Economic self-sufficiency	–	59.9 %	–	83.5 %	52.7 %
d770 Intimate relationships	–	62.7 %	40.0 %	66.0 %	52.3 %
d330 Speaking	81.8 %	60.7 %	–	37.9 %	52.3 %
d630 Preparing meals	–	64.6 %	–	77.7 %	52.1 %
d865 Complex economic transactions	–	65.6 %	–	89.3 %	50.7 %
d570 Looking after one's health	–	71.5 %	–	51.5 %	50.6 %
d710 Basic interpersonal interactions	–	58.8 %	40.0 %	66.0 %	50.4 %
d910 Community life	–	60.7 %	–	75.7 %	50.4 %
d760 Family relationships	–	59.6 %	37.0 %	64.1 %	49.8 %

(continued)

Table 10.8 (continued)

	Koskinen et al. [59] (*N* = 55)	Aiachini et al. [60] (*N* = 261)	Svestkova et al. [61] (*N* = 100)	Laxe et al. [62] (*N* = 103)	All cases (*N* = 519)
d230 Carrying out daily routine	–	74.7 %	–	61.2 %	49.7 %
d510 Washing oneself	–	66.8 %	–	48.5 %	49.0 %
d540 Dressing	–	66.3 %	–	51.5 %	48.8 %
d520 Caring for body parts	–	64.1 %	–	52.4 %	47.6 %
d210 Undertaking a single task	–	62.3 %	34.0 %	45.6 %	46.9 %
d410 Changing basic body position	–	64.0 %	–	41.7 %	46.6 %
d420 Transferring oneself	–	63.1 %	34.0 %	41.7 %	46.6 %
d845 Acquiring, keeping and terminating a job	–	57.5 %	–	84.5 %	45.7 %
d470 Using transportation	–	58.1 %	–	50.5 %	45.2 %
d465 Moving around using equipment	–	68.5 %	–	47.6 %	43.9 %
d840 Apprenticeship (work preparation)	–	54.1 %	–	83.5 %	43.8 %
d860 Basic economic transactions	–	54.6 %	–	80.6 %	43.5 %
d310 Communicating with – receiving – spoken messages	40.0 %	53.8 %	–	33.0 %	43.0 %
d345 Writing messages	–	64.7 %	–	50.5 %	42.6 %
d825 Vocational training	–	50.1 %	–	80.6 %	41.2 %
d166 Reading	–	60.9 %	–	50.5 %	40.6 %
d150 Learning to calculate	–	41.8 %	–	67.0 %	40.3 %
d145 Learning to write	–	43.6 %	–	59.2 %	39.8 %
d550 Eating	–	54.6 %	–	38.8 %	39.2 %
d830 Higher education	–	43.1 %	–	87.4 %	39.0 %
d530 Toileting	–	58.3 %	–	43.7 %	38.0 %
d810 Informal education	–	44.8 %	–	68.0 %	36.0 %
d820 School education	–	39.3 %	–	75.7 %	34.8 %
d950 Political life and citizenship	–	38.1 %	–	72.8 %	33.6 %
d335 Producing nonverbal messages	–	51.8 %	–	35.9 %	33.2 %
d140 Learning to read	–	37.5 %	–	40.8 %	33.1 %
d110 Watching	–	42.4 %	39.0 %	–	33.1 %
d560 Drinking	–	52.3 %	–	34.0 %	33.0 %

Note: – Category below the 33 % threshold

Table 10.9 Selection of ICF categories from environmental factors reported as barriers or facilitators in at least 33 % of cases across publications on functioning and disability in traumatic brain injury [59–62]

	Koskinen et al. [59] (N = 55)	Aiachini et al. [60] (N = 261)	Svestkova et al. [61] (N = 100)	Laxe et al. [62] (N = 103)	All cases (N = 519)
e310 Immediate family	81.8 %	86.6 %	68.0 %	91.2 %	83.4 %
e355 Health professionals	96.4 %	86.1 %	51.0 %	86.4 %	80.5 %
e110 Products for personal consumption	63.6 %	67.6 %	67.0 %	65.7 %	66.7 %
e580 Health SSP	100.0 %	78.0 %	–	81.6 %	66.0 %
e410 Individual attitudes of immediate family members	–	74.6 %	51.0 %	90.3 %	65.3 %
e570 Social security SSP	72.7 %	62.1 %	45.0 %	78.7 %	63.2 %
e320 Friends	–	61.2 %	60.0 %	67.9 %	55.8 %
e450 Individual attitudes of health professionals	–	68.0 %	–	82.8 %	55.4 %
e115 Products and technology for personal use in daily living	49.1 %	59.4 %	39.0 %	56.3 %	53.8 %
e120 Products and technology for personal indoor and out-door mobility and transportation	–	67.9 %	–	50.5 %	49.0 %
e420 Individual attitudes of friends	–	50.8 %	38.0 %	71.8 %	47.1 %
e360 Other professionals	–	62.3 %	–	74.8 %	46.2 %
e325 Acquaintances, peers, colleagues, neighbours and community members	–	43.9 %	50.0 %	66.6 %	44.9 %
e575 General social support SSP	–	44.4 %	–	71.9 %	41.6 %
e340 Personal care providers and personal assistants	–	40.8 %	–	81.6 %	36.7 %
e460 Societal attitudes	–	40.3 %	–	55.3 %	36.6 %
e440 Individual attitudes of personal care providers and personal assistants	–	40.8 %	–	77.4 %	35.9 %
e330 People in positions of authority	–	–	–	77.5 %	35.4 %
e150 Design, construction and building products and technology of buildings for public use	–	50.0 %	–	42.8 %	33.6 %
e590 Labour and employment SSP	–	–	35.0 %	57.2 %	33.6 %
e550 Legal SSP	–	40.3 %	–	66.9 %	33.5 %
e540 Transportation SSP	–	48.0 %	–	44.7 %	33.0 %

Note: – Category below the 33 % threshold
SSP services, systems and policies

10.4 The Right to Work and the UN Convention on the Rights of People with Disabilities: An Overview

In the past the approach to disability was mainly ruled by a medical model that was responsible for splitting society into two systems: one for persons with disabilities and the other for those without a disability. According to this model, people have a disability as a consequence of their health condition: healing the health condition would therefore mean to "solve" the disability problem. This mindset has been deeply rooted in society, in people's way of thinking about disability and on the way life was experienced for those with a disability. In concrete terms it led to the exclusion of individuals with disabilities from society; they were denied access to mainstream services and enjoyed fewer rights and opportunities. Only in the last 30 years has a shift of thinking about disability started to address societal barriers and led to the social model of disability. According to this model, it is not the person who is disabled; rather, it is the society that creates the conditions of a disability situation, in terms of hindrances to full inclusion. Therefore, to solve the disability problem, a societal change is needed.

The adoption of the Convention on the Rights of Persons with Disabilities (UN CRPD) in 2006 [67] indicates the consensus reached on this approach and paves the way for its further promotion in the world. The right to work is a fundamental right, recognised in several international legal instruments as the ILO Convention No. 159 (Vocational Rehabilitation and Employment – Disabled Persons – Convention, published in 2008), which is essential for realising other human rights and forms an inseparable and inherent part of human dignity, as it contributes to the survival of the individual and to that of his/her family and, insofar as work is freely chosen or accepted, to recognition within the community [68].

The right to work has been thoroughly elaborated by Articles 6, 7 and 8 of the International Covenant of Economic, Social and Cultural Rights (ICESCR, published in 1966) which deal, respectively, with the right to gain a living, the right to just and favourable conditions and the right to form trade unions [69]. Article 27 of the UN CRPD cross-references the prescriptions of the ICESCR, though not in an exhaustive way, as it intends by no means to replace the ICESCR, but to stress the importance of applying a disability lens to the right to work.

The UN CRPD applies human rights to a specific category of persons, namely, persons with disabilities. It reaffirms, reformulates, articulates and sometimes extends the rights of persons with disabilities. Along with this, the convention calls for a shift of paradigm in human rights from a biomedical and paternalistic approach to a social model of disability.

10.5 Issues Related to Employment in MS, Stroke and TBI

As previously noted (see Sect. 10.1) MS, stroke and TBI are burdensome neurological disorders and have relevant personal as well as societal costs, partly due to reduced employment rates or reduced ability to carry out work-related tasks.

The mean annual cost per case of MS in Europe is around €27,000; of this, approximately €8,700 are indirect costs. These costs are likely a consequence of the high unemployment rates of people with MS. As shown in a recent literature review, in which data from 32,507 patients (71.1 % of whom were women) were analysed, the mean unemployment rate was 59 % [70]. Data also show that there are differences among studies with regard to the employment status of MS patients: younger patients with a shorter disease duration had higher employment rates. The symptoms that more frequently were reported to reduce MS patients' ability to work were fatigue, mobility and cognitive impairments.

In contrast, research on workplace environment was almost lacking, and there was no study addressing the issue of work-related difficulties and of the factors promoting patients' ability to fulfil job requirements. A 2003 study from Roessler and Rumrill [71] concluded that there are several explanations for the high unemployment in patients with MS and that the most practical and effective approach to improve employment outcome is to improve organisational and physical workplace features. There are, in fact, several causes of workplace discrimination for people with MS; among those identified by the authors, employers' inability to provide support and reasonable accommodations, as well as hostile behaviours, such as harassment, intimidation, layoff and discharge, are among the most relevant [72, 73].

The mean annual cost per case of stroke in Europe is around €8,000; of this, approximately €600 are indirect costs. This is explained on the basis of the typical age of occurrence of the first stroke. However, a review from Daniel and colleagues showed that approximately one-fourth of strokes occur in persons less than 65 [74]. This review included 70 studies reporting post-stroke employment status and showed that an average of 44 % of patients returned to work after stroke. However, due to the differences in follow-up length and the lack of a uniform period to observe RTW, the authors concluded that an overall rate cannot be reliably estimated. Among the factors that predict RTW, stroke severity was the most robust one [75, 76], together with younger age [77, 78], reduced length of stay in the hospital and early admission to rehabilitation [79]. Other factors include provision of vocationally directed rehabilitation, flexibility, social benefits and support from relevant others [80–83].

The mean annual cost per case of TBI in Europe is around €8,800; of this, approximately €5,200 are indirect costs. These figures are influenced by the relatively young age of persons that survive a brain injury and by the low employability after injury. In fact, only about 40 % of persons returned to work within 2 years after the traumatic event [84]. However, studies indicate contrasting evidence. In 1999, a study of survivors from road traffic accidents found that 12 % of patients returned to their full premorbid level of work capacity and employment, and another 30 % had to switch to a lower-level position [85]. In another study (1990), it was instead found that approximately 66 % of TBI survivors were able to return to work [86]. Factors negatively influencing RTW were the invisibility of the injury, continuing symptoms affecting their ability to do the job, lack of advice and guidance on returning to work and any potential changes in life roles [87]. In contrast, studies identified the following factors associated with successful RTW: motivated individuals, flexible work, accommodating labour management and prolonged environmental support [88]. Other factors include severity of injury, pre-injury occupational or educational background and age at time of injury [89–93].

Mean unemployment rate of persons with MS is 59 % and 32 % of MS costs are due to reduced productiity/work cessation.

Fifty-six percent of previously stroke patients do not return to work, and 7.5 % of stroke costs are due to reduced productiity/work cessation.

Sixty percent of previously TBI patients do not return to work, and 59 % of TBI costs are due to reduced productiity/work cessation.

10.6 Issues Related to Vocational Rehabilitation in MS, Stroke and TBI

As stated earlier (Sect. 10.1), VR is a multidisciplinary intervention whose aim is to facilitate the RTW, or the maintenance of a work position, of a person with a disease or condition causing disability as defined by the biopsychosocial approach [1–5]. The process of decision-making therefore needs to take into account medical aspects as well as nonmedical ones related both to the person and to his/her environment; these include norms and regulations towards RTW or work cessation and the consequent eligibility for disability pensions. In this section of the chapter, we will report some experiences with VR specific to MS, stroke and TBI.

10.6.1 Vocational Rehabilitation for Persons with MS

A literature review evaluated the effectiveness of VR programmes compared to alternative programmes or usual care on return to work, workability and employment in patients with MS and showed inconclusive evidence to support VR for MS patients [94]. The review, however, highlighted some of the most relevant aspects that need to be taken into account in VR practice with MS patients, beginning with the need for clinicians to be aware of vocational issues and to understand and manage barriers for maintaining employment. These include the need to find practical solutions for workplace disability (i.e. solutions that are tailored to each specific person and workplace), to pursue the best possible and reasonable accommodation in the workplace, as well as the need to educate employers and colleagues about the importance of job maintenance.

Another systematic review published in 2012 gave a clear overview of the multidimensional level of health and disability involved when performing VR with MS patients. The authors included both quantitative and qualitative studies [95] and highlighted the importance of multidisciplinary team involvement in the VR of MS patients, in which accessibility and proximity of services provided are the gold standard; early intervention, open access, responsive and personal services are the pillars of the approach. Studies of MS patients highlight the need to improve work performance through intervention specifically focused to support work activities and not on reduction of impairments [96], as well as to increase self-belief and self-efficacy [97, 98]. In addition, MS patients may benefit from practical support, such as reducing work hours, working at home and making changes to the occupational environment [71, 99]. One of the most relevant variables for the positive outcome of the VR intervention was the patients' self-reported readiness about their ability to work [100].

A more recent study (2013) focussed on the impact of VR services on returning and maintaining employment [101]. The study showed that the employment success rate of MS participants was 48 % after receiving VR services; among these services, the most helpful were counselling and guidance, job placement, workplace support, assistive technology/job accommodation and maintenance services.

In addition, two studies highlighted the profile of individuals with MS who receive VR. The first is a 2003 study [102] that evidenced issues related to their financial profile, in addition to impairments or activity limitations. People with MS in the study were mid-career professionals who expected to perform well and be commeasurably compensated. When a full-time RTW was not possible, part-time work had to be considered, given existing social security subsidies. Parallel to this, home-based work options, often part-time, were developed within the context of the fatigue experienced by this population during a full work day, especially if work-related travel was required. The second study [103] was qualitative research based on four focus groups of persons with MS published in 2007. Topics of the focus groups included: barriers to working with MS, what people would like from vocational rehabilitation services and how this service should be delivered and promoted. Two themes emerged in this study. The first main theme corresponded to the need for support with managing performance in the workplace, and it dealt with the balance between the worker's performance and the social/personal expectations associated with employment. The second main theme was support with disclosure, managing anxiety and dealing with discrimination. The authors concluded that VR services should perform two distinct roles. The first role is for a professional who has expertise in managing the interactions among the impairments caused by MS, the physical environment and the demands imposed by the job. The second role is to provide expert knowledge about the working environment and the needs of employers, together with increasing awareness of relevant legislation and counselling in supporting people to adapt, adjust and resolve complex issues.

Experiences on VR for MS patients show contrasting results. Findings show that VR is effective for motivated persons (i.e. younger professionals that are expected to perform well and be commeasurably compensated for this), and in contexts that enable to move through different levels of performance and committment to work tasks. Practically, in contexts in which it is possible to move from full-time to part-time, or from office-based to home-based occupations (e.g. teleworking). In a study, a success rate of 48 % was reported.

10.6.2 Vocational Rehabilitation for Persons with Stroke

In 2011, a review of Baldwin and Brusco described the impact of VR on RTW after stroke [104]. The authors found that there were huge differences in studies with regard to the primary outcome, i.e. RTW, with definitions of work ranging from full-time to any form of activity regardless of reimbursement and voluntary work, which made comparison between rates of RTW difficult. They reported that RTW ranged between 12 % and 49 %, and, based on these figures, it is possible to estimate that approximately 31 % of stroke patients returned to work.

VR interventions followed different approaches, and it is difficult to extract commonalities between them. The most common intervention included job trial [105–107] and job placement [105, 107, 108], almost always preceded by an evaluation of skills, abilities and desired goals [105–108]. To our knowledge, no other studies have been published, and the authors of the present review conclude that although research indicates that VR has a positive impact on RTW, the quality of this research is not sufficient enough to make final recommendations. Compared to musculoskeletal conditions, rates of RTW are lower for this population, perhaps because patients and health professionals are not aware of the existence of VR programmes. What is particularly problematic within this field is the absence of studies comparing RTW rates between those participating in VR programmes and those receiving medical treatment only.

Few experiences on VR in stroke patients exist, due to the typical old-age of stroke onset. Job trial and job placement are the most common experiences, but no evidence of effectiveness exists.

10.6.3 Vocational Rehabilitation for Persons with TBI

A recent review presented different models of VR approaches for TBI patients, concluding that there is evidence supporting the usefulness of VR in TBI patients but that controlled studies are needed [109].

A first model integrates VR into rehabilitation programmes for individuals with brain injuries and adds other occupational interventions to rehabilitation procedures, such as guided voluntary occupational trials, assistance to find a tailored job, part-time work and supported job placement. Rates of success for this kind of intervention varied between 38 % and 84 % [110–113].

A second model is purely a VR one, which was mostly developed based on the experience derived from other conditions (e.g. persons with learning disabilities). These programmes usually consist of different phases that can be summarised into the following: evaluation of individuals' abilities and job requirements, a sort of "back-office" vocational training, job placement, on-site vocational trial phase and follow-up of the programme's effectiveness. Rates of success for this kind of intervention varied between 41 % and 78 % [114–117].

A third kind of approach is based on the professional role of a case coordinator, i.e. a person whose task is to develop a comprehensive RTW plan through counselling to the client and to the employer, performing regular calls and site visits and linking individuals to existing rehabilitation facilities and services. This kind of intervention has proven to be effective with a rate between 50 % and 80 % [118–121].

Some studies evaluated the effectiveness of VR approaches for TBI patients. Abrams and colleagues described a network of rehabilitation programmes developed to encourage placement and support of severely disabled people in the community that aimed to reduce the need for long-term nursing home placements. They showed that coordinated rehabilitation programming is consistent with managed care objectives in long-term care and is cost-effective [122]. Consistent results were reported by Kendall and colleagues, which collected data on 26 studies on RTW after TBI and showed that individuals with TBI returned to competitive employment and other productive activities earlier after receiving vocational intervention than without intervention [123].

Another review aimed to assess the effectiveness as well as the strengths and weaknesses of three approaches to VR in TBI [124]. The authors identified three broad models of VR: programme-based, supported employment and case coordination models. Programme-based models are aimed to maximise vocational outcomes and are organised in three phases: intensive individualised work skills rehabilitation, guided work trials and assisted placement with transitional job support. The strengths of the programme-based model are that it offers work skills training to build confidence and competence before entering a work environment, provides opportunities for independence in the workplace and offers transitional support. The weak elements include little follow-up regarding sustainability of employment and the fact that success of the intervention greatly depends on the individual staff involved and the availability and provision of services in each area. Supported employment models involve job placement, on-the-job training and long-term support and job skills reinforcement through on-the-job coaching. Key strengths of the model are the unlimited level and strength of support, which makes this approach particularly suitable for clients with significant disability, and the fact that support is highly individualised to the job and the worker. Weak aspects include the limit to personal independence due to the presence of a job coach and the fact that success is too much dependent on the skill and approach of the individual staff involved. Case coordination models are holistic approaches in which vocational rehabilitation is part of an overall rehabilitation programme that is individualised to suit specific needs and in which individuals are overseen by a case coordinator who assesses them for service needs. Strengths of this approach include the flexibility and coordination of rehabilitation services, which allow a smooth transition between rehabilitation services and the community, as well as the fact that this approach is focused on early intervention. Again, limitations of this model refer to the fact that success depends on the individual staff and on the availability of services.

A variety of experiences on VR in TBI exists, with some evidence of effectiveness. Three seem the most common approaches.

First, the integration of VR into rehabilitation programmes: rates of success 38–84 %.

Second, a purely VR intervention, carried out after clinical rehabilitation: rates of success 41–78 %.

Third, an approach based on a case-coordinator (active counseling between worker and employer): rate of success 50–80 %.

10.7 A Synopsis on VR in Neurological Conditions and a Step Forward

Despite differences in the VR approaches for patients with MS, stroke and TBI, several elements were commonly reported in the recent literature. First, almost all studies that attempted to compare or review results of research findings on VR in MS, stroke and TBI concluded that it is almost impossible to derive a general conclusion on the effectiveness of these approaches because the evidence is limited by inequalities in research designs and variables [94, 101, 104, 110, 123]. Controlled studies are lacking, and the outcomes are generally poorly defined. In the case of MS, this problem is determined also by the features of the disease itself and by the fact that there is no "acute" event. For this reason, maintaining a job or delaying job cessation, rather than returning to employment, is the outcome of VR. In the case of stroke and TBI, there is an acute event and there is a process aimed to enable RTW. However, what "work" means is not consistently defined.

Second, the duration of VR intervention is difficult to predict, especially when VR is included in the process of post-acute rehabilitation. This makes it difficult to address the issue of effectiveness and cost-effectiveness of VR interventions. Effectiveness of VR interventions for the selected conditions was very different: 48 % in MS (Sect. 10.6.1), 31 % for stroke (Sect. 10.6.2) and 38–84 % in TBI (Sect. 10.6.3). With regard to cost-effectiveness, there was no evidence for MS [94], no information was reported for stroke and for TBI there was one study showing that VR was cost-effective [121]. Therefore, the issue of reporting cost-effectiveness of VR is a relevant need for future research activities in the field.

Third, publications lack a comprehensive evaluation of functioning and disability like that provided by ICF-based evaluation procedures, although most of them recommend that the ICF be used to assess the effectiveness of VR interventions.

The issue of using the ICF and its biopsychosocial approach, in our opinion, should be welcomed as a relevant step forward, as it provides the necessary elements for assessing the impact of VR interventions on individuals' daily lives: a comprehensive, systematic and scientifically adequate definition of those variables that are needed to demonstrate the effectiveness of VR interventions. In fact, when researchers tried to define the main outcome – generally in terms of RTW – of VR, the result was a clear lack of consistency. If the outcome is RTW, researchers should define what work is. Narrow definitions (e.g. full-time employment, with at least 40 h of weekly paid work) may be difficult to apply in clinical practice, although they are more reliable; broad definitions (e.g. any kind of full-time or part-time paid activity) are less reliable for research but are easier to identify in clinical practice.

This consideration leads to the proposal to use the ICF in VR practice, a possibility that has been raised by several authors [6, 8, 66, 74, 84, 104, 123]. What would be the added value of using the ICF in VR? Based on our experience, we believe that at least two main advantages should be recognised.

First, in Sects. 10.3.1, 10.3.2 and 10.3.3 we presented summary findings of ICF-based descriptions of functioning and disability of persons with MS, stroke and TBI that can be used as a starting point for new data collection. A list of 87 ICF categories to be used in the VR context was proposed by Escorpizo and colleagues based on a review of the literature that identified the outcomes and the measures currently being used in VR [9]. Using ICF-based data sets enables comparison across interventions, settings and persons and allows researchers to longitudinally monitor the impact of VR interventions on a variety of domains of functioning, not only on RTW.

This leads to the second advantage of ICF use, i.e. the reliance on a taxonomy of human functioning that allows management of information at both the individual and group levels. At the individual level, it enables clinicians to identify activities in which individuals experience more difficulties, the factors connected to these difficulties, and which body functions and structures are most impaired. Being a classification of functioning, it also describes which aspects of functioning are not impaired or limited; longitudinally, it enables clinicians to address changes in a consistent way. At the group level, it enables researchers to collect and synthesise data about people not exclusively on the basis of their health condition. What research has shown is that it is difficult to address RTW because what "working" means is not clear at all. A job is made of specific actions and tasks; these constitute the skills that an individual should have in order to carry out an activity. In addition, a job also deals with roles, duties and expectations (e.g. relating to persons in positions of authority or subordinate persons, maintaining adequate behaviour), all of which can be described using the ICF.

The ICF makes it possible to profile individuals not only on the basis of their health condition, but on the basis of the kind of tasks and roles they need to fulfil in order to satisfy the requirements of a job. The ICF enables VR professionals to define the desired profile for a job position with scientific language and to verify if the requirements for this position are fulfilled by an individual after a VR intervention. The potential impact of this paradigm shift is huge; VR specialists could provide evidence that a person with a given profile of functioning – irrespective of a health condition – is able or not to carry out a specific activity. This also means that a specific activity requires a given profile of functioning which, in turn, is the outcome of the VR process. Thus, future research findings could provide information on which activities are more likely to be fulfilled by clients after a VR programme has been carried out, rather than providing information on the fact that 48 % of clients with MS return to work compared to 84 % of those with TBI. Understanding which job tasks are more likely to be fulfilled will be important if interventions aim to be cost-effective.

To our knowledge, only one published study has presented this ICF-based approach to organise data collection. The study by Conclave and colleagues [125] describes an experience of ICF use in the field of labour policies in Italy, in which the authors defined an *ICF-based worker checklist* that contains elements related to functioning with specific attention to tasks and requirements that are evaluated according to the Italian employment regulations. A 34-item schedule for evaluating persons' skills was developed and released by the Italian government [126] that focuses on several areas: relational abilities and mental functions (e.g. carrying out team work, facing difficulties due to work deadlines), communication abilities (e.g. understanding and remembering), mobility (e.g. staying seated, moving something using a movement device, lifting and carrying objects) and some information on the environment in which the person would work (e.g. tolerating noise or natural/artificial light). The aim of this evaluation process is a proper match between the worker and work activity that is based on the biopsychosocial approach.

Common elements of literature on VR in neurological condition show three main elements.

First: it is almost impossible to derive a general conclusion on the effectiveness of different approaches as the evidence is hampered by inequalities of research designs and variables, including the definition of work. Second: the duration of VR is difficult to predict (especially when VR is included in

(continued)

post-acute phases), making it difficult to address VR cost-effectiveness. Third: comprehensive evaluations of functioning and disability are lacking. Almost all studies recommend the use of ICF that, however, is not commonly used.

Two are the main advantages of ICF use. First, ICF-based data sets enable comparison across interventions, settings, and persons allowing clinicians to monitor longitudinal progresses. Second, the reliance on a taxonomy enables to manage informations on the single case and at group level, thus enabling analysis by disease, kind of impairment, tasks and roles.

10.7.1 Vocational Rehabilitation for Persons with Other Neurological Conditions?

As stated earlier (Sect. 10.1) we limited our analysis to MS, stroke and TBI as they share relevant components of cognitive and mental function impairments, as well as other impairments connected to neurological functions. These conditions highlight the connections between an ICF-based functioning and disability evaluation and the setting and objectives of VR programmes. However, all patients experiencing difficulties in returning to work after an acute event or in maintaining their positions as the disease worsens may benefit from VR interventions. Examples of this include individuals with brain cancer, epilepsy and headaches.

With regard to brain cancer, its annual cost per patient is estimated at €21,590; of this, approximately 38 % is due to reduced productivity or job cessation [10]. However, to our knowledge, there has been only one study referring to a VR programme for patients that survived brain cancer [127]. Results showed that a VR programme led to significant improvement over time, and the authors concluded that VR services should be available to patients with brain tumours and should focus on supporting patients wishing to return to or maintain their current work.

With regard to epilepsy, its annual cost per patient is estimated at €5,220; of this, approximately 41 % is due to reduced productivity or job cessation [10]. However, no published studies are available describing a VR approach with this population, and only two studies directly focused on employment issues in persons with epilepsy. The first study showed that patients with single seizures or early epilepsy had significantly lower employment rates than the general population and that unemployment was predicted by having fair/poor self-rated health and experiencing four or more seizures [128]. The authors concluded that those who have recently experienced a single seizure or who have early epilepsy are exposed to substantial employment disadvantage and that efforts are needed to help these people return to work or maintain their job. The second study evaluated employment outcomes after resective surgery [129]; it showed that 2 years after surgery there was a modest employment gain, which was higher for individuals with better seizure outcomes. The authors concluded that postsurgical VR is needed.

With regard to headaches, their annual cost per patient is estimated at €303 for tension-type headache, €1,222 for migraine and €3,561 for medication overuse headache, with 92–93 % of this amount due to reduced productivity or job cessation [130]. Although the issue of reduced productivity in patients with headaches is a well-known topic [131, 132], to our knowledge issues related to VR have never been taken into consideration for these individuals.

10.8 Conclusion

This chapter reviewed recent research findings on VR experiences for persons with MS, stroke and TBI that could be defined as paradigmatic for the majority of severe neurological conditions and connected ICF-based evaluation approaches with VR interventions that could increase access to the right to work as expressed in the UN CPRD articles 26 (Habilitation and Rehabilitation) and 27 (Work and Employment) [67]. Article 26 – dealing with issues concerning the "functioning" of the individual – renews the entitlement to habilitation and rehabilitation services, the latter having a connotation of a non-permanent treatment. Article 27 concerns the right to work, which should lead to the possibility of earning money and leading a life of dignity. In the framework of a holistic approach to persons with disabilities, where disability itself is not the focus of attention, but rather the individual and the enjoyment of his/her rights, it is essential to maintain balance in considering all aspects of a persons' life, including individuals' skills, personal choices, potential for further development and society's response [133].

Outcome evaluation is of primary relevance in rehabilitation and therefore also in VR. This discipline deals with the labour market, a field in which programmes – i.e. interventions aimed to facilitate RTW – differ one from the other according to several factors, including environmental features (i.e. the working conditions), payment schemes (including both salary and social security benefits), norms, practices and regulations. The results of our analysis show that available data are fragmented due to unequal duration of VR interventions, definitions of work and of RTW and varying rates of VR success. An ICF-based approach is deemed useful in defining the outcome of VR interventions. For example, it may promote a shift in the paradigm of research in the field of VR and could provide information on which activities clients are more likely to perform well after completing a VR programme. Understanding which job tasks are more likely to be fulfilled, on the basis of the person's profile of functioning, is important if VR interventions aim to be cost-effective. An ICF-based approach could define thresholds of cost-effectiveness on the basis of the duration of rehabilitation, gains in health and reduced indirect costs resulting from neurological diseases.

Within the field of neurological diseases, studies related to VR have been reported for TBI, MS and stroke but are lacking in other conditions. Given that the aim of VR is to promote RTW or the maintenance of a work position, there is no valid reason for the absence of interventions such as counselling, guidance and job placement for individuals with neurological disease. Future research in this field needs to be carried out, as well as expanding the scope of research to some less recognised conditions and settings. In our opinion, the most important aspects that future research needs to address involve three aspects: first, a clear definition of RTW or job maintenance; second, a systematic reporting on the duration of VR interventions; and third, a consistent evaluation of the balance between VR costs and the economic and health gains that VR interventions are likely to produce.

Study Questions

1. What are the limitations of common evaluations procedures in MS, stroke and TBI, when issues connected to VR are taken into account?

   Answer: Disability assessments are mostly disease-specific or symptom specific: on one side, this enable the precise tracking of information for longitudinal evaluations of change, thus impacting on clinical and research activities.

   However, some of these assessment are too much categorical (e.g. the GOS) and thus do not fit well with the need for a broad disability description. Other instruments rely on concepts – such as independence in the case of FIM – that reflect an out-dated disability classification description (i.e. based on the ICIDH-80): this is problematic to set intervention objectives for a broad approach like that of VR.

2. What is the most relevant benefit in the use of ICF, coupled with available calibrated assessment instruments?

   Answer: ICF-based data make it possible to address the complexity of the lived experience of disability, at the individual and at the group level, irrespectively of the underlying health condition and its clinical stage, as well as in consideration of comorbidities that might be present.

   This enables to set rehabilitation objectives for each single rehabilitant in a broad perspective: from early acute stages, to post-acute and up to vocational settings, relying on a comprehensive taxonomy. Such an approach enables to track "single individuals" as well as groups: for research this has the great added value to enable users to choose which variable are of interest to monitor the results of interventions.

3. VR is a multidisciplinary intervention whose aim is to facilitate the return to work (RTW), or the maintenance of a work position, of a person with a disability: what are the main differences in conditions such as the three – MS, stroke and TBI – herein considered with regard to VR aims?

   Answer: While for TBI and stroke a clear acute event can be detected – i.e. the cerebrovascular accident and the injury – MS is a progressive disease. Therefore, for stroke and TBI it is reasonable to define RTW as the objective of VR, that for MS will instead be the maintenance of the work position.

Parallel to this, a significant demographic difference is also to be considered, as stroke patients that are candidate to VR are expected to be generally older than those with MS and TBI.

4. The unemployment rates of the three conditions are somewhat similar (ranging between 56 % and 60 %): why are the portions of indirect cost so different?

   Answer: These differences are partly due to the kind of direct costs: for example, in MS the portion of direct cost is high, as the costs themselves are high. Other differences are due to the age of onset: for example, a minor part of stroke patients (approximately 25 %) are of working age and therefore the "average stroke patient" is likely to be already out of the job market.

5. Can VR be considered effective?

   Answer: The amount of evidence available up to now does not enable us to make an unambiguous statement on this. In the case of MS, VR seems to be effective in motivated, young persons, and in favourable contexts, i.e. where social security systems make it possible to move to part-time or to home-based work. Experiences on stroke patients are so limited that it makes little sense to address effectiveness issues. More experiences are available for TBI: different models exist and effectiveness has been found in a percentage of subjects varying between 40 % and 80 %.

6. What are the most important actions that should be undertaken to face the shortcomings connected to effectiveness and cost-effectiveness of VR in neurological conditions?

   Answer:

   First: improve the quality of research design and identify variables of interest (including the definition of "work") in a clear way. In particular, implement clinical trials, with a single-blind evaluation procedure, to prove the effectiveness of VR interventions compared to standard medical rehabilitation.

   Second: identify, among the outcomes, a reasonable duration of VR, so that cost-effectiveness issues can be appropriately accounted.

   Third: implement comprehensive evaluations of functioning and disability, such as those based on the ICF.

References

1. International Labor Organization. Vocational rehabilitation and employment of disabled persons. International labor conference, 86th session. Geneva: ILO; 1998.
2. British Society of Rehabilitation Medicine. Vocational rehabilitation: the way forward. London: BSRM; 2000.

3. Selander J. Unemployed sick leavers and vocational rehabilitation. A person level study based on a national social insurance material. Dissertation from the Department of Rehabilitation Medicine. Stockholm: Karolinska Institute; 1999.
4. Gobelet C, Franchignoni F. Vocational rehabilitation. Paris: Springer; 2006.
5. Ekholm J, Schüldt Ekholm K. Guest editorial: vocational rehabilitation. J Rehabil Med. 2009; 41:113–4.
6. Chamberlain MA, Fialka Moser V, Schüldt Ekholm K, O'Connor RJ, Herceg M, Ekholm J. Vocational rehabilitation: an educational review. J Rehabil Med. 2009;41:856–69.
7. World Health Organization. World report on disability. Geneva: WHO; 2011.
8. World Health Organization. International classification of functioning disability and health. Geneva: WHO; 2001.
9. Escorpizo R, Finger ME, Glässel A, Gradinger F, Lückenkemper M, Cieza A. A systematic review of functioning in vocational rehabilitation using the international classification of functioning, disability and health. J Occup Rehabil. 2011;21:134–46.
10. Gustavsson A, Svensson M, Jakobi F, Allgulander C, Alonso J, Beghi E, CDBE 2010 Study Group, et al. Cost of disorders of the brain in Europe 2010. Eur Neuropsychopharmacol. 2011;21:718–79.
11. Leonardi M, Bickenbach J, Ustun TB, Kostanjsek N, Chatterji S, MHADIE Consortium. The definition of disability: what is in a name? Lancet. 2006;368:1219–21.
12. Ustün TB, Chatterji S, Kostanjsek N, Rehm J, Kennedy C, Epping-Jordan J, Saxena S, von Korff M, Pull C, WHO/NIH Joint Project. Developing the World Health Organization Disability Assessment Schedule 2.0. Bull World Health Organ. 2010;88:815–23.
13. Post MW, de Witte LP, Reichrath E, Verdonschot MM, Wijlhuizen GJ, Perenboom RJ. Development and validation of IMPACT-S, an ICF-based questionnaire to measure activities and participation. J Rehabil Med. 2008;40:620–7.
14. Østerås N, Brage S, Garratt A, Benth JS, Natvig B, Gulbrandsen P. Functional ability in a population: normative survey data and reliability for the ICF based Norwegian Function Assessment Scale. BMC Public Health. 2007;7:278.
15. Sherbourne CD, Stewart AL. The MOS social support survey. Soc Sci Med. 1991;32:705–14.
16. Iwarsson S. The Housing Enabler: an objective tool for assessing accessibility. Br J Occup Ther. 1999;62:491–7.
17. Emery J, Crump C, Bors P. Reliability and validity of two instruments designed to assess the walking and bicycling suitability of sidewalks and roads. Am J Health Promot. 2003;18: 38–46.
18. Bower JH, Howlett W, Maro VP, Wangai H, Sirima N, Reyburn H. A screening instrument to measure the prevalence of neurological disability in resource-poor settings. Neuroepidemiology. 2009;32:313–20.
19. Cohen JA, Reingold SC, Polman CH, Wolinsky JS, International Advisory Committee on Clinical Trials in Multiple Sclerosis. Disability outcome measures in multiple sclerosis clinical trials: current status and future prospects. Lancet Neurol. 2012;11:467–76.
20. Kurtzke JF. Rating neurologic impairment in multiple sclerosis: an expanded disability status scale (EDSS). Neurology. 1983;33:1444–52.
21. Cutter GR, Baier ML, Rudick RA, Cookfair DL, Fischer JS, Petkau J, et al. Development of a multiple sclerosis functional composite as a clinical trial outcome measure. Brain. 1999;122: 871–82.
22. Ozakbas S, Ormeci B, Idiman E. Utilization of the multiple sclerosis functional composite in follow-up: relationship to disease phenotype, disability and treatment strategies. J Neurol Sci. 2005;232:65–9.
23. Kalkers NF, Bergers L, de Groot V, Lazeron RH, van Walderveen MA, Uitdehaag BM, et al. Concurrent validity of the MS functional composite using MRI as a biological disease marker. Neurology. 2001;56:215–9.
24. Miller DM, Rudick RA, Cutter G, Baier M, Fischer JS. Clinical significance of the multiple sclerosis functional composite. Relationship to patient-reported quality of life. Arch Neurol. 2000;57:1319–24.
25. Lublin FD. Disease free activity status. Mult Scler Relat Dis. 2012;1:6–7.

26. Rankin J. Cerebral vascular accidents in patients over the age of 60. II. Prognosis. Scott Med J. 1957;2:200–15.
27. Mahoney F, Barthel D. Functional evaluation: the Barthel index. Md State Med J. 1965;14: 61–5.
28. Schwartz CE, Bode RK, Quaranto BR, Vollmer T. The symptom inventory disability-specific short forms for multiple sclerosis: construct validity, responsiveness, and interpretation. Arch Phys Med Rehabil. 2012;93:1617–28.
29. Wynia K, Middel B, Van Dijk JP, De Ruiter H, De Keyser J, Reijneveld SA. The Multiple Sclerosis impact Profile (MSIP). Development and testing psychometric properties of an ICF-based health measure. Disabil Rehabil. 2008;30:261–74.
30. Haigh R, Tennant T, Biering-Sørensen F, Grimby G, Marincek C, Phillips S, et al. The use of outcome measures in physical medicine and rehabilitation within Europe. J Rehabil Med. 2001;33:273–8.
31. Keith RA, Granger CV, Hamilton BB, Sherwin FS. The functional independence measure: a new tool for rehabilitation. In: Eisenberg MG, Grzesiak RC, editors. Advances in clinical rehabilitation. New York: Springer; 1987. p. 6–18.
32. Scandinavian Stroke Study Group. Multicenter trial of hemodilution in ischemic stroke. Background and study protocol. Stroke. 1985;16:885–90.
33. Katz S, Ford AB, Moskowitz RW, Jackson BA, Jaffe MW. Studies of illness in the aged. Index of ADL: a standardized measure of biological and psychosocial function. JAMA. 1963; 185:914–9.
34. Inouye M, Hashimoto H, Mio T, Sumino K. Influence of admission functional status on functional change after stroke rehabilitation. Am J Phys Med Rehabil. 2001;80:121–5.
35. Hsueh IP, Lin JH, Jeng JS, Hsieh CL. Comparison of the psychometric characteristics of the functional independence measure, 5 item Barthel index, and 10 item Barthel index in patients with stroke. J Neurol Neurosurg Psychiatry. 2002;73:188–90.
36. Tur BS, Gursel YK, Yavuzer G, Kucukdeveci A, Arasil T. Rehabilitation outcome of Turkish stroke patients: in a team approach setting. Int J Rehabil Res. 2003;26:271–7.
37. World Health Organization. International classification of impairments, disabilities and handicaps. Geneva: WHO; 1980.
38. Teasdale G, Jennet B. Assessment of coma and impaired consciousness: a practical scale. Lancet. 1974;2:81–3.
39. Jennett B, Bond M. Assessment of outcome after severe brain damage. Lancet. 1975;1:480–4.
40. Willer B, Ottenbacher KJ, Coad ML. The community integration questionnaire. A comparative examination. Am J Phys Med Rehabil. 1994;73:103–11.
41. Crawford S, Wenden FJ, Wade DT. The Rivermead head injury follow up questionnaire: a study of a new rating scale and other measures to evaluate outcome after head injury. J Neurol Neurosurg Psychiatry. 1996;60:510–4.
42. Rappaport M, Hall KM, Hopkins K. Disability rating scale for severe head trauma: coma to community. Arch Phys Med Rehabil. 1982;63:118–23.
43. Hall KM, Mann N, High W, Wright J, Kreutzer J, Wood D. Functional measures after traumatic brain injury: ceiling effects of FIM, FIM1FAM, DRS and CIQ. J Head Trauma Rehabil. 1996;11:27–39.
44. Malkmus D. Cognitive assessment and goal setting. In: Hagan C, Malkmus D, Durham P, editors. Rehabilitation of the head injured adult: comprehensive physical management. Downey: Professional Staff Assoc Rancho Los Amigos Hospital; 1979.
45. Cerniauskaite M, Quintas R, Boldt C, Raggi A, Cieza A, Bickenbach J, Leonardi M. Systematic literature review on ICF from 2001 to 2009: its use, implementation and operationalisation. Disabil Rehabil. 2011;33:281–309.
46. Raggi A, Leonardi M, Cabello M, Bickenbach JE. Application of ICF in clinical contexts across Europe. Disabil Rehabil. 2010;32 Suppl 1:17–22.

47. Anner J, Schwegler U, Kunz R, Trezzini B, de Boer W. Evaluation of work disability and the international classification of functioning, disability and health: what to expect and what not. BMC Public Health. 2012;12:470.
48. Coenen M, Cieza A, Freeman J, Khan F, Miller D, Weise A, et al. The development of ICF Core Sets for multiple sclerosis: results of the international consensus conference. J Neurol. 2011;258:1477–88.
49. Conrad A, Coenen M, Schmalz H, Kesselring J, Cieza A. Validation of the comprehensive ICF core set for multiple sclerosis from the perspective of occupational therapists. Scand J Occup Ther. 2012;19:468–87.
50. Conrad A, Coenen M, Schmalz H, Kesselring J, Cieza A. Validation of the comprehensive ICF core set for multiple sclerosis from the perspective of physical therapists. Phys Ther. 2012;92:799–820.
51. Khan F, Pallant JF. Use of International Classification of Functioning, Disability and Health (ICF) to describe patient-reported disability in multiple sclerosis and identification of relevant environmental factors. J Rehabil Med. 2007;39:63–70.
52. Holper L, Coenen M, Weise A, Stucki G, Cieza A, Kesselring J. Characterization of functioning in multiple sclerosis using the ICF. J Neurol. 2010;257:103–13.
53. Svestkova O, Angerova Y, Sladkova P, Keclikova B, Bickenbach JE, Raggi A. Functioning and disability in multiple sclerosis. Disabil Rehabil. 2010;32 Suppl 1:59–67.
54. Geyh S, Cieza A, Schouten J, Dickson H, Frommelt P, Omar Z, et al. ICF Core Sets for stroke. J Rehabil Med. 2004;44(Suppl):135–41.
55. Algurén B, Lundgren-Nilsson A, Sunnerhagen KS. Functioning of stroke survivors–a validation of the ICF core set for stroke in Sweden. Disabil Rehabil. 2010;32:551–9.
56. Goljar N, Burger H, Vidmar G, Marincek C, Krizaj J, Chatterji S, et al. Functioning and disability in stroke. Disabil Rehabil. 2010;32 Suppl 1:50–8.
57. Quintas R, Cerniauskaite M, Ajovalasit D, Sattin D, Boncoraglio G, Parati EA, Leonardi M. Describing functioning, disability, and health with the International Classification of Functioning, Disability, and Health Brief Core Set for Stroke. Am J Phys Med Rehabil. 2012; 91 Suppl 1:14–21.
58. Laxe S, Zasler N, Selb M, Tate R, Tormos JM, Bernabeu M. Development of the International Classification of Functioning, Disability and Health core sets for traumatic brain injury: an international consensus process. Brain Inj. 2013;27:379–87.
59. Koskinen S, Hokkinen EM, Sarajuuri J, Alaranta H. Applicability of the ICF checklist to traumatically brain-injured patients in post-acute rehabilitation settings. J Rehabil Med. 2007;39:467–72.
60. Aiachini B, Pisoni C, Cieza A, Cazzulani B, Giustini A, Pistarini C. Developing ICF core set for subjects with traumatic brain injury: an Italian clinical perspective. Eur J Phys Rehabil Med. 2010;46:27–36.
61. Svestkova O, Angerova Y, Sladkova P, Bickenbach JE, Raggi A. Functioning and disability in traumatic brain injury. Disabil Rehabil. 2010;32 Suppl 1:68–77.
62. Laxe S, Zasler N, Tschiesner U, López-Blazquez R, Tormos JM, Bernabeu M. ICF use to identify common problems on a TBI neurorehabilitation unit in Spain. NeuroRehabilitation. 2011;29:99–110.
63. von Holst H. Traumatic brain injury: evidence-based management and epidemiology updates. Neuroepidemiology. 2009;33:314–5.
64. Rauch A, Cieza A, Stucki G. How to apply the International Classification of Functioning, Disability and Health (ICF) for rehabilitation management in clinical practice. Eur J Phys Rehabil Med. 2008;44:329–42.
65. Scarponi F, Sattin D, Leonardi M, Raggi A, Zampolini M. The description of severe traumatic brain injury in light of the ICF classification. Disabil Rehabil. 2009;31 Suppl 1: 134–43.
66. Shames J, Treger I, Ring H, Giaquinto S. Return to work following traumatic brain injury: trends and challenges. Disabil Rehabil. 2007;29:1387–95.
67. United Nations. UN Convention on the rights of persons with disabilities. New York: United Nations; 2006.

68. International Labour Organization. ILO vocational rehabilitation and employment (disabled persons) convention (no. 159) and recommendation (no. 168): United Nations convention on the rights of persons with disabilities/International Labour Office. Geneva: ILO; 2008.
69. UN General Assembly. International covenant on economic, social and cultural rights, 16 December 1966, United Nations, Treaty series, vol. 993, p. 3. Available at: http://www.refworld.org/docid/3ae6b36c0.html. Accessed 21 Jan 2014.
70. Schiavolin S, Leonardi M, Giovannetti AM, Antozzi C, Brambilla L, Confalonieri P, et al. Factors related to difficulties with employment in patients with multiple sclerosis: a review of 2002–2011 literature. Int J Rehabil Res. 2013;36:105–11.
71. Roessler RT, Rumrill PD. Multiple sclerosis and employment barriers: a systemic perspective on diagnosis and intervention. Work. 2003;21:17–23.
72. Neath J, Roessler RT, McMahon BT, Rumrill PD. Patterns in perceived employment discrimination for adults with multiple sclerosis. Work. 2007;29:255–74.
73. Rumrill PD, Roessler RT, McMahon BT, Hennessey ML, Neath J. Gender as a differential indicator of employment discrimination experiences of Americans with multiple sclerosis. Work. 2007;29:303–11.
74. Daniel K, Wolfe CD, Busch MA, McKevitt C. What are the social consequences of stroke for working-aged adults? A systematic review. Stroke. 2009;40:e431–40.
75. Wozniak MA, Kittner SJ. Return to work after ischemic stroke: a methodological review. Neuroepidemiology. 2002;21:159–66.
76. Treger I, Shames J, Giaquinto S, Ring H. Return to work in stroke patients. Disabil Rehabil. 2007;29:1397–403.
77. Howard G, Till JS, Toole JF, Matthews C, Truscott L. Factors influencing return to work following cerebral infarction. JAMA. 1985;253:226–32.
78. Wozniak MA, Kittner SJ, Price TR, Hebel JR, Sloan MA, Gardner JF. Stroke location is not associated with return to work after first ischemic stroke. Stroke. 1999;30:2568–73.
79. Black-Schaffer RM, Osberg JS. Return to work after stroke: development of a predictive model. Arch Phys Med Rehabil. 1990;71:285–90.
80. Corr S, Wilmer S. Returning to work after a stroke: an important but neglected area. Br J Occup Ther. 2003;66:186–92.
81. Medin J, Barajas J, Ekberg K. Stroke patients' experiences of return to work. Disabil Rehabil. 2006;28:1051–60.
82. Lock S, Jordan L, Bryan K, Maxim J. Work after stroke: focusing on barriers and enablers. Disabil Soc. 2005;20:33–47.
83. Alaszewski A, Alaszewski H, Potter J, Penhale B. Working after a stroke: survivors' experiences and perceptions of barriers to and facilitators of the return to paid employment. Disabil Rehabil. 2007;29:1858–69.
84. Van Velzen JM, van Bennekom CA, Edelaar MJ, Sluiter JK, Frings-Dresen MH. How many people return to work after acquired brain injury? A systematic review. Brain Inj. 2009;23: 473–88.
85. Ruffolo C, Freidland J, Dawson D, Colantonio A, Lindsay P. Mild TBI from motor vehicle accidents: factors associated with return to work. Arch Phys Med Rehabil. 1999;80:392–8.
86. Rao N, Rosenthal M, Cronin-Stubbs D, Lambert R, Barnes P, Swanson B. Return to work after rehabilitation following traumatic brain injury. Brain Inj. 1990;4:49–56.
87. Gilworth G, Eyres S, Carey A, Bhakta BB, Tennant A. Working with a brain injury: personal experiences of returning to work following a mild or moderate brain injury. J Rehabil Med. 2008;40:334–9.
88. Rubenson C, Svensson E, Linddahl I, Bjorklund A. Experiences of returning to work after acquired brain injury. Scand J Occup Ther. 2007;14:205–14.
89. Wehman P, Targett P, West M, Kregel J. Production work and employment for persons with traumatic brain injury: what have we learned? J Head Trauma Rehabil. 2005;20:115–27.
90. Klonoff PS, Watt LM, Dawson LK, Henderson SW, Gehrels JA, Wethe JV. Psychosocial outcomes 1–7 years after comprehensive milieu-oriented neurorehabilitation: the role of pre-injury status. Brain Inj. 2006;20:601–12.

91. Keren O, Cohen M, Lazar-Zwecker I, Gorswasser Z. Tracheotomy in severe TBI patients: sequelae and relation to vocational outcome. Brain Inj. 2001;15:531–6.
92. Keyser-Marcus L, Bricout J, Wehman P, Campbell L, Cifu D, Englander J, et al. Acute predictors of return to employment after traumatic brain injury: a longitudinal follow-up. Arch Phys Med Rehabil. 2002;83:635–41.
93. Walker WC, Marwitz J, Kreutzer J, Hart T, Novack T. Occupational categories and return to work after traumatic brain injury: a multicenter study. Arch Phys Med Rehabil. 2006;87: 1576–82.
94. Khan F, Ng L, Turner-Stokes L. Effectiveness of vocational rehabilitation intervention on the return to work and employment of persons with multiple sclerosis. Cochrane Database Syst Rev. 2009;21, CD007256.
95. Sweetland J, Howse E, Playford ED. A systematic review of research undertaken in vocational rehabilitation for people with multiple sclerosis. Disabil Rehabil. 2012;34:2031–8.
96. Yorkston KM, Johnson K, Klasner ER, Amtmann D, Kuehn CM, Dudgeon B. Getting the work done: a qualitative study of individuals with multiple sclerosis. Disabil Rehabil. 2003; 25:369–79.
97. Simmons RD, Tribe KL, McDonald EA. Living with multiple sclerosis: longitudinal changes in employment and the importance of symptom management. J Neurol. 2010;257:926–36.
98. Roessler R, Rumrill P. Strategies for enhancing career maintenance self-efficacy of people with multiple sclerosis. J Rehabil. 1994;60:54–9.
99. Crooks V, Stone S, Owen M. Multiple sclerosis and academic work: socio-spatial strategies adopted to maintain employment. J Occup Sci. 2009;16:25–31.
100. Pack TG, Szirony GM. Predicting readiness to return to work in a population with multiple sclerosis. J Vocat Rehabil. 2009;31:91–105.
101. Chiu CY, Chan F, Bishop M, Cardoso ED, O'Neill J. State vocational rehabilitation services and employment in multiple sclerosis. Mult Scler. 2013;19:1655–64.
102. Fraser RT, Johnson EK, Clemmons DC, Getter A, Johnson KL, Gibbons L. Vocational rehabilitation in multiple sclerosis (MS): a profile of clients seeking services. Work. 2003; 21:69–76.
103. Sweetland J, Riazi A, Cano SJ, Playford ED. Vocational rehabilitation services for people with multiple sclerosis: what patients want from clinicians and employers. Mult Scler. 2007;13:1183–9.
104. Baldwin C, Brusco NK. The effect of vocational rehabilitation on return-to-work rates post stroke: a systematic review. Top Stroke Rehabil. 2011;18:562–72.
105. McMahon R, Crown D. Return to work factors following a stroke. Top Stroke Rehabil. 1998; 5:54–60.
106. Kempers E. Preparing the young stroke survivor for return to work. Top Stroke Rehabil. 1994;1:65–73.
107. Leng CM. Description of a return-to-work occupational therapy programme for stroke rehabilitation in Singapore. Occup Ther Int. 2008;15:87–99.
108. Bisiker J, Millinchip K. Developing a work rehabilitation project: "equal pathways to work". Br J Occup Ther. 2007;70:259–63.
109. Tyerman A. Vocational rehabilitation after traumatic brain injury: models and services. NeuroRehabilitation. 2012;31:51–62.
110. Ben-Yishay T, Silver SM, Piasetsky E, Rattok J. Relationship between employability and vocational outcome after intensive holistic cognitive rehabilitation. J Head Trauma Rehabil. 1987;2:35–48.
111. Johnson RP. Return to work after severe head injury. Int Disabil Stud. 1987;9:49–54.
112. Tyerman A, Young K. Vocational rehabilitation after severe traumatic brain injury: II Specialist interventions and outcomes. J Appl Occup Psychol Employ Disabil. 2000;2:13–20.
113. Wehman PH, Kreutzer JS, West MD, Sherron PD, Zasler ND, Groah CH, Stonnington HH, Burns CT, Sale PR. Return to work for persons with traumatic brain injury: a supported employment approach. Arch Phys Med Rehabil. 1990;71:1047–52.

114. Wall JR, Rosenthal M, Niemczura JG. Community-based training after acquired brain injury: preliminary findings. Brain Inj. 1998;12:215–24.
115. Murphy L, Chamberlain E, Weir J, Berry A, Nathaniel-James D, Agnew R. Effectiveness of vocational rehabilitation following acquired brain injury: preliminary evaluation of a UK specialist rehabilitation programme. Brain Inj. 2006;20:1119–29.
116. O'Neill JH, Zuger RR, Fields A, Fraser R, Pruce T. The program without walls: innovative approach to state agency vocational rehabilitation of persons with traumatic brain injury. Arch Phys Med Rehabil. 2004;85 Suppl 2:68–72.
117. Curl RM, Fraser RT, Cook RG, Clemmons D. Traumatic brain injury vocational rehabilitation: preliminary findings for the coworker as trainer project. J Head Trauma Rehabil. 1996; 11:75–85.
118. Buffington ALH, Malec JF. The vocational rehabilitation continuum: maximising outcomes though bridging the gap from hospital to community based services. J Head Trauma Rehabil. 1997;12:1–13.
119. Malec JF, Moessner AM. Replicated positive results for the VCC model of vocational intervention after ABI within the social model of disability. Brain Inj. 2006;20:227–36.
120. O'Brien L. Achieving a successful and sustainable return to the workforce after ABI: a client-centred approach. Brain Inj. 2007;21:465–78.
121. Trexler LE, Trexler LC, Malec JF, Klyce D, Parrott D. Prospective randomized controlled trial of resource facilitation on community participation and vocational outcome following brain injury. J Head Trauma Rehabil. 2010;25:440–6.
122. Abrams D, Barker LT, Haffey W, Nelson H. The economics of return to work for survivors of traumatic brain injury. Vocational services are worth the investment. J Head Trauma Rehabil. 1993;8:59–76.
123. Kendall E, Muenchberger H, Gee T. Vocational rehabilitation following traumatic brain injury: a quantitative synthesis of outcome studies. J Vocat Rehabil. 2006;25:149–60.
124. Fadyl JK, McPherson KM. Approaches to vocational rehabilitation after traumatic brain injury: a review of the evidence. J Head Trauma Rehabil. 2009;24:195–212.
125. Conclave M, Fusaro G, Sala M, Martinuzzi A, Russo E, Frare M, et al. The ICF and Labour Policies Project: the first Italian nation-wide experience of ICF implementation in the labour sector. Disabil Rehabil. 2009;31 Suppl 1:16–21.
126. Decreto del Presidente del Consiglio dei Ministri 13 gennaio 2000. Atto di indirizzo e coordinamento in materia di collocamento obbligatorio dei disabili, a norma dell'art. 1, comma 4, della legge 12 marzo 1999, no. 68. http://www.handylex.org/stato/d130100.shtml. Accessed 21 Jan 2014.
127. Rusbridge SL, Walmsley NC, Griffiths SB, Wilford PA, Rees JH. Predicting outcomes of vocational rehabilitation in patients with brain tumours. Psychooncology. 2013;22:1907–11.
128. Holland P, Lane S, Whitehead M, Marson AG, Jacoby A. Labor market participation following onset of seizures and early epilepsy: findings from a UK cohort. Epilepsia. 2009; 50:1030–9.
129. Chin PS, Berg AT, Spencer SS, Sperling MR, Haut SR, Langfitt JT, et al. Employment outcomes following resective epilepsy surgery. Epilepsia. 2007;48:2253–7.
130. Linde M, Gustavsson A, Stovner LJ, Steiner TJ, Barré J, Katsarava Z, et al. The cost of headache disorders in Europe: the Eurolight project. Eur J Neurol. 2012;19:703–11.
131. Michel P, Dartigues JF, Duru G, Moreau J, Salamon R, Henry P. Incremental absenteeism due to headaches in migraine: results from the Mig-Access French national cohort. Cephalalgia. 1999;19:503–10.
132. Stewart WF, Wood GC, Manack A, Varon SF, Buse DC, Lipton RB. Employment and work impact of chronic migraine and episodic migraine. J Occup Environ Med. 2010;52:8–14.
133. Ferrarina S. Analysis of the legal meaning of Article 27 of the UN CRPD: key challenges for adapted work settings. Cornell University ILR, GLADNET Collection 3-14-2012. Available at: http://digitalcommons.ilr.cornell.edu/gladnetcollect/. Accessed 21 Jan 2014.

Chapter 11
Spinal Cord Injury: Vocational Rehabilitation and Disability Evaluation

Reuben Escorpizo, Logan M. Trenaman, and William C. Miller

11.1 Introduction

11.1.1 Burden of SCI

Spinal Cord Injury (SCI) is a familiar term that denotes insult or injury to the spinal cord. The injury may be caused by a non-traumatic event (e.g., progressive spinal disease) or traumatic event (e.g., fall, motor vehicular accident). SCI can be classified according to completeness of injury (complete vs. incomplete) or affected limbs (paraplegia vs. quadriplegia). There are many consequences of SCI including loss of sensation and muscle paralysis, which can contribute to difficulty with mobility, self-care, and participation in the community and society such as recreation, sport, and employment. SCI is also known to be associated with secondary

R. Escorpizo (✉)
Department of Rehabilitation and Movement Science, The University of Vermont, Burlington, VT 05405, USA

Swiss Paraplegic Research, Nottwil, Switzerland

ICF Research Branch, WHO CC FIC in Germany (DIMDI), Nottwil, Switzerland
e-mail: escorpizo.reuben@gmail.com

L.M. Trenaman
School of Population and Public Health, University of British Columbia, Vancouver, BC, Canada

GF Strong Rehabilitation Center, Vancouver, BC, Canada

W.C. Miller
GF Strong Rehabilitation Center, Vancouver, BC, Canada

Graduate Program in Rehabilitation Sciences, University of British Columbia, Vancouver, BC, Canada

Department of Occupational Sciences and Occupational Therapy, University of British Columbia, Vancouver, BC, Canada

R. Escorpizo et al. (eds.), *Handbook of Vocational Rehabilitation and Disability Evaluation*, Handbooks in Health, Work, and Disability, DOI 10.1007/978-3-319-08825-9_11

complications such as urinary tract infection, pressure sores, and other comorbidities and also low quality of life and sense of well-being.

SCI is one of the most devastating injuries that an individual can experience. It imposes a significant physical and psychological burden on the affected individual, in addition to a considerable financial burden associated with the high cost of medical and long-term care and lost of productivity. SCI not only affects the individual but also his or her family, caregivers, and the society. The incidence worldwide varies greatly by region, with estimates as low as three persons per million inhabitants per year, to as high as 246 persons per million per year [1]. The prevalence of SCI is also increasing, owing to improvements in SCI care, which has resulted in increased life expectancy. Prevalence estimates range from 50 to 906 cases per million populations worldwide [1].

SCI is a multifaceted disability that can influence all aspects of an individuals' functioning. Due to the complex impact of SCI on the individual, the disability associated with SCI can be examined using the comprehensive and integrative biopsychosocial perspective of the International Classification of Functioning, Disability and Health (ICF) [2]. In the ICF, different aspects of functioning are captured. The aspects that are particularly relevant to persons with SCI are embodied in the ICF Core Sets for SCI [3, 4]. ICF Core Sets refer to a short list of ICF categories out of the whole ICF classification system that is relevant to a particular health condition or setting. In summary, when using the ICF, the interaction between SCI, functioning and disability, and contextual factors can be elucidated. An illustration of the interaction between the different domains of functioning in SCI through the ICF Core Set for SCI is presented in Fig. 11.1.

A full list of the ICF Core Set for SCI can be found and downloaded for free on the ICF Research Branch website (http://www.icf-research-branch.org/index.php). Figure 11.1 only includes a sample of ICF categories and domains of functioning that are considered "core" to SCI. For work and employment specifically, the ICF Core Sets can be used as a disability evaluation for persons with SCI. A work disability evaluation can guide practitioners and case managers towards necessary intervention, referrals to other healthcare professionals, and proper return to work programs.

SCI is one of the most devastating injuries that can have a significant physical and psychological burden on the affected individual, in addition to a considerable financial burden associated with the high cost of medical and long-term care and lost of productivity.

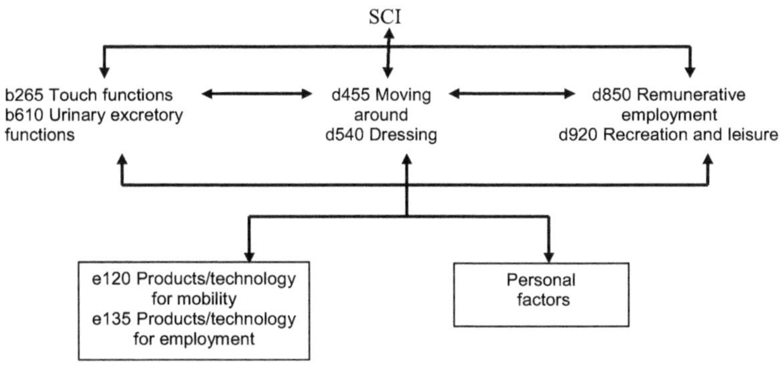

Fig. 11.1 International Classification of Functioning, Disability and Health (*ICF*) (From World Health Organization [2])

11.1.2 Work Disability Related to SCI

Employment following SCI is recognized as an important component of life and has been studied since the early 1950s [5]. Not only does gainful employment help individuals achieve economic self-sufficiency; it is considered a source of personal growth [6] and disability adjustment [7], and it is associated with social integration and life satisfaction [8]. Published studies demonstrate considerable variation in employment rates among individuals with SCI (2–80 %), largely due to variations in sample characteristics such as the participants' age, duration of injury, and work experience prior to injury, as well as differences in how the concept of "employment" is defined [9]. Despite this, evidence from systematic reviews [10] suggests that since the 1970s, the rate of employment for persons with SCI is between 30 % and 50 %. The most recent data from the US Model Systems suggests that 35 % of people with SCI are employed 20 years post-injury (https://www.nscisc.uab.edu) compared to an average unemployment rate of the US general population of 6.1 % for a 20-year period (1993–2013) [10].

There is a crucial need to explain why involvement in employment is significantly lower in individuals with SCI than the general population and this is despite the significant proportion of unemployed people with SCI judge themselves able to work and wish to work [11]. Over the past decades there have been significant advances in environmental features, including assistive devices (technology, robotics, environmental controls) and accessible design, in addition to the attenuation of disability-related prejudices. Despite this progress, it is astonishing that the employment rate has not improved sufficiently enough to promote full integration in terms of employment of those individuals with SCI.

This dilemma reveals the complexity of returning to work. An individual's employment state is also a result of a complex interaction between personal and environmental characteristics [12, 13]. Given the advancements described above, it is incorrect to state that people with SCI experience low employment rates only because of intrinsic or personal characteristics [12]. To ensure a higher likelihood of success in returning to work, interventions must target several factors, including work retraining, interventions geared towards the environment, and addressing other modifiable factors.

11.2 Disability Evaluation in SCI

Disability evaluation starts by identifying those functioning domains that must be assessed and evaluated from the perspective of the patient and healthcare professionals. A list of domains is provided by existing ICF Core Sets, namely, the ICF Core Set for SCI, which was developed to capture SCI-related functioning and disability depending on the temporal setting: early post-acute and long-term settings.

11.2.1 ICF Core Set: Early Post-Acute SCI

The ICF Core Set for early post-acute setting was developed and intended for use during the first comprehensive rehabilitation period after the acute onset of traumatic or non-traumatic SCI. A list of ICF categories under this Core Set is included in Table 11.1.

11.2.2 ICF Core Set: Long-Term Context SCI

The ICF Core Set for long-term setting was developed and intended for use after the first comprehensive rehabilitation period of the acute onset of traumatic or non-traumatic SCI. A list of ICF categories under this Core Set is included in Table 11.1.

11.2.3 ICF Core Sets for Vocational Rehabilitation and Social Security

Using the ICF Core Sets for SCI, the list of domains to capture disability and work disability can be complemented using other Core Sets, namely, the ICF Core Set for Social Security [14] and the ICF Core Set for Vocational Rehabilitation [15]. Essentially, these Core Sets can capture the disability of those individuals with SCI in relation to work and employment. The information gained from looking into the ICF categories consisting the Core Sets can be used to inform services and care

Table 11.1 Title and description of ICF categories [2] in the ICF Core Set for Vocational Rehabilitation [11] brief version ($n = 13$ categories) and the ICF Core Set for Disability Evaluation in Social Security [12] ($n = 20$ categories)

ICF code and title	Title and definition	ICF Core Set for SCI in early post-acute setting	ICF Core Set for SCI in long-term setting	ICF Core Set for Vocational Rehabilitation	ICF Core Set for Disability Evaluation in Social Security
b130 Energy and drive functions	General mental functions of physiological and psychological mechanisms that cause the individual to move towards satisfying specific needs and general goals in a persistent manner			√	
b152 Emotional functions	Specific mental functions related to the feeling and affective components of the processes of the mind	√	√		
b164 Higher-level cognitive functions	Specific mental functions especially dependent on the frontal lobes of the brain, including complex goal-directed behaviors such as decision-making, abstract thinking, planning and carrying out plans, mental flexibility, and deciding which behaviors are appropriate under what circumstances; often called executive functions			√	√
b280 Sensation of pain	Sensation of unpleasant feeling indicating potential or actual damage to some body structure	√	√		√

(continued)

Table 11.1 (continued)

ICF code and title	Title and definition	ICF Core Set for SCI in early post-acute setting	ICF Core Set for SCI in long-term setting	ICF Core Set for Vocational Rehabilitation	ICF Core Set for Disability Evaluation in Social Security
b440 Respiration functions		√			
b455 Exercise tolerance functions	Functions related to respiratory and cardiovascular capacity as required for enduring physical exertion			√	√
b525 Defecation functions		√	√		
b620 Urination functions		√	√		
b640 Sexual functions			√		
b710 Mobility of joint functions	Functions of the range and ease of movement of a joint		√		√
b730 Muscle power functions	Functions related to the force generated by the contraction of a muscle or muscle groups	√	√	[a]	√
b735 Muscle tone functions		√	√		
b810 Protective functions of the skin	Functions of the skin for protecting the body from physical, chemical, and biological threats	√	√		
d110 Watching	Using the sense of seeing intentionally to experience visual stimuli, such as watching a sporting event or children playing				√
d115 Listening	Using the sense of hearing intentionally to experience auditory stimuli,				√

(continued)

Table 11.1 (continued)

ICF code and title	Title and definition	ICF Core Set for SCI in early post-acute setting	ICF Core Set for SCI in long-term setting	ICF Core Set for Vocational Rehabilitation	ICF Core Set for Disability Evaluation in Social Security
	such as listening to a radio, music, or a lecture				
d155 Acquiring skills	Developing basic and complex competencies in integrated sets of actions or tasks so as to initiate and follow through with the acquisition of a skill, such as manipulating tools or playing games like chess			√ √	√
d177 Making decisions	Making a choice among options, implementing the choice, and evaluating the effects of the choice, such as selecting and purchasing a specific item or deciding to undertake and undertaking one task from among several tasks that need to be done			[a]	√ √
d220 Undertaking multiple tasks	Carrying out simple or complex and coordinated actions as components of multiple, integrated, and complex tasks in sequence or simultaneously			[a]	√ √
d230 Carrying out daily routine	Carrying out simple or complex and coordinated actions in order to plan, manage, and		√		

(continued)

Table 11.1 (continued)

ICF code and title	Title and definition	ICF Core Set for SCI in early post-acute setting	ICF Core Set for SCI in long-term setting	ICF Core Set for Vocational Rehabilitation	ICF Core Set for Disability Evaluation in Social Security
	complete the requirements of day-to-day procedures or duties, such as budgeting time and making plans for separate activities throughout the day				
d240 Handling stress and other psychological demands	Carrying out simple or complex and coordinated actions to manage and control the psychological demands required to carry out tasks demanding significant responsibilities and involving stress, distraction, or crises, such as driving a vehicle during heavy traffic or taking care of many children		√	√	√
d399 Communication, unspecified					√ √
d410 Changing basic body position	Getting into and out of a body position and moving from one location to another, such as getting up out of a chair to lie down on a bed, and getting into and out of positions of kneeling or squatting	√	√	[a]	√
d415 Maintaining a body position	Staying in the same body position as required, such as remaining seated or			[a]	√

(continued)

Table 11.1 (continued)

ICF code and title	Title and definition	ICF Core Set for SCI in early post-acute setting	ICF Core Set for SCI in long-term setting	ICF Core Set for Vocational Rehabilitation	ICF Core Set for Disability Evaluation in Social Security
	remaining standing for work or school				
d420 Transferring oneself		√	√		
d430 Lifting and carrying objects	Raising up an object or taking something from one place to another, such as when lifting a cup or carrying a child from one room to another			[a]	√ √
d440 Fine hand use	Performing the coordinated actions of handling objects, picking up, manipulating, and releasing them using one's hand, fingers, and thumb, such as required to lift coins off a table or turn a dial or knob			[a]	√ √
d445 Hand and arm use	Performing the coordinated actions required to move objects or to manipulate them by using hands and arms, such as when turning door handles or throwing or catching an object	√	√	[a]	√ √
d450 Walking	Moving along a surface on foot, step by step, so that one foot is always on the ground, such as when strolling, sauntering, and walking forwards, backwards, or sideways	√		[a]	√ √

(continued)

Table 11.1 (continued)

ICF code and title	Title and definition	ICF Core Set for SCI in early post-acute setting	ICF Core Set for SCI in long-term setting	ICF Core Set for Vocational Rehabilitation	ICF Core Set for Disability Evaluation in Social Security
d455 Moving around	Moving the whole body from one place to another by means other than walking, such as climbing over a rock or running down a street, skipping, scampering, jumping, somersaulting, or running around obstacles		√		
d465 Moving around using equipment	Walking and moving around in various places and situations, such as walking between rooms in a house, within a building, or down the street of a town		√		
d470 Using transportation	Using transportation to move around as a passenger, such as being driven in a car or on a bus, rickshaw, jitney, animal-powered vehicle, or private or public taxi, bus, train, tram, subway, boat, or aircraft		√	[a]	√ √
d510 Washing oneself		√			
d520 Caring for body parts			√		
d530 Toileting	Planning and carrying out the elimination of human waste (menstruation, urination, and defecation) and cleaning oneself afterwards	√	√		

(continued)

Table 11.1 (continued)

ICF code and title	Title and definition	ICF Core Set for SCI in early post-acute setting	ICF Core Set for SCI in long-term setting	ICF Core Set for Vocational Rehabilitation	ICF Core Set for Disability Evaluation in Social Security
d540 Dressing	Carrying out the coordinated actions and tasks of putting on and taking off clothes and footwear in sequence and in keeping with climatic and social conditions, such as by putting on, adjusting, and removing shirts, skirts, blouses, pants, undergarments, saris, kimono, tights, hats, gloves, coats, shoes, boots, sandals, and slippers	√			
d550 Eating		√	√		
d560 Drinking		√			
d720 Complex interpersonal interactions	Maintaining and managing interactions with other people, in a contextually and socially appropriate manner, such as by regulating emotions and impulses, controlling verbal and physical aggression, acting independently in social interactions, and acting in accordance with social rules and conventions			√	√ √

(continued)

Table 11.1 (continued)

ICF code and title	Title and definition	ICF Core Set for SCI in early post-acute setting	ICF Core Set for SCI in long-term setting	ICF Core Set for Vocational Rehabilitation	ICF Core Set for Disability Evaluation in Social Security
d845 Acquiring, keeping and terminating a job	Seeking, finding, and choosing employment; being hired and accepting employment; maintaining and advancing through a job, trade, occupation, or profession; and leaving a job in an appropriate manner			√	
d850 Remunerative employment	Engaging in all aspects of work, as an occupation, trade, profession, or other form of employment, for payment, as an employee, full or part time, or self-employed, such as seeking employment and getting a job, doing the required tasks of the job, attending work on time as required, supervising other workers or being supervised, and performing required tasks alone or in groups			√	
d855 Non-remunerative employment	Engaging in all aspects of work in which pay is not provided, full time or part time, including organized work activities, doing the required tasks of			√	

(continued)

Table 11.1 (continued)

ICF code and title	Title and definition	ICF Core Set for SCI in early post-acute setting	ICF Core Set for SCI in long-term setting	ICF Core Set for Vocational Rehabilitation	ICF Core Set for Disability Evaluation in Social Security
	the job, attending work on time as required, supervising other workers or being supervised, and performing required tasks alone or in groups, such as volunteer work, charity work, working for a community or religious group without remuneration, and working around the home without remuneration				
e110 Products and technology for personal consumption			√		
e115 Products and technology for personal use in daily living	Equipment, products, and technologies used by people in daily activities, including those adapted or specially designed, located in, on, or near the person using them	√	√		
e120 Products and technology for personal indoor and outdoor mobilities and transportation	Equipment, products, and technologies used by people in activities of moving inside and outside buildings, including those adapted or specially designed, located in, on, or near the person using them	√	√		

(continued)

Table 11.1 (continued)

ICF code and title	Title and definition	ICF Core Set for SCI in early post-acute setting	ICF Core Set for SCI in long-term setting	ICF Core Set for Vocational Rehabilitation	ICF Core Set for Disability Evaluation in Social Security
e150 Design, construction, and building products and technology for public use	Products and technology that constitute an individual's indoor and outdoor human-made environment that is planned, designed, and constructed for public use, including those adapted or specially designed		√		
e155 Design, construction, and building products and technology for private use	Products and technology that constitute an individual's indoor and outdoor human-made environments that is planned, designed, and constructed for private use, including those adapted or specially designed		√		
e310 Immediate family	Individuals related by birth, marriage, or other relationship recognized by the culture as immediate family, such as spouses, partners, parents, siblings, children, foster parents, adoptive parents, and grandparents	√	√	√	
e330 People in positions of authority	Individuals who have decision-making responsibilities for others and who have			√	

(continued)

Table 11.1 (continued)

ICF code and title	Title and definition	ICF Core Set for SCI in early post-acute setting	ICF Core Set for SCI in long-term setting	ICF Core Set for Vocational Rehabilitation	ICF Core Set for Disability Evaluation in Social Security
	socially defined influence or power based on their social, economic, cultural, or religious roles in society, such as teachers, employers, supervisors, religious leaders, substitute decision-makers, guardians, or trustees				
e340 Personal care providers and personal assistants	Individuals who provide services as required to support individuals in their daily activities and maintenance of performance at work, education, or other life situation, provided either through public or private funds or else on a voluntary basis, such as providers of support for homemaking and maintenance, personal assistants, transport assistants, paid help, nannies, and others who function as primary caregivers	√	√		
e355 Health professionals	All service providers working within the context of the health system, such as doctors, nurses, physiotherapists,	√	√		

(continued)

Table 11.1 (continued)

ICF code and title	Title and definition	ICF Core Set for SCI in early post-acute setting	ICF Core Set for SCI in long-term setting	ICF Core Set for Vocational Rehabilitation	ICF Core Set for Disability Evaluation in Social Security
	occupational therapists, speech therapists, audiologists, orthotist-prosthetists, and medical social workers				
e580 Health services, systems, and policies	Services, systems, and policies for preventing and treating health problems, providing medical rehabilitation, and promoting a healthy lifestyle		√	√	
e590 Labor and employment services, systems, and policies	Services, systems, and policies related to finding suitable work for persons who are unemployed or looking for different work or to support individuals already employed who are seeking promotion			√	
s120 Spinal cord and related structures		√	√		
s430 Structure of respiratory system		√	√		
s610 Structure of urinary system		√	√		
s810 Structure of areas of skin			√		

[a]Included in the comprehensive version (n = 90 ICF categories) of the ICF Core Set for Vocational Rehabilitation [11]

Table 11.2 ICF categories that overlap in at least three ICF Core Sets

Body functions
b280 Sensation of pain
b710 Mobility of joint functions
b730 Muscle power functions
Activities and participation
d240 Handling stress and other psychological demands
d410 Changing basic body position
d445 Hand and arm use
Environmental factors
e310 Immediate family
e580 Health services, systems, and policies
Additional
d850 Remunerative employment[a]

[a]Remunerative employment is included in the brief version of the ICF Core Set for Vocational Rehabilitation and in the comprehensive version of the ICF Core Sets for SCI

to mitigate the debilitating effects of SCI-related disability and guide return-to-work strategies.

The three Core Sets can be examined closely by looking at the differences and similarities in terms of the ICF categories (Table 11.1).

Based on Table 11.1, pooling all the categories that are common across at least three of the Core Sets can derive an "essential" list of domains (Table 11.2). Examining the list closely, a broad spectrum of functioning domains can be found, ranging from physical aspects such as joint mobility and muscle strength, activity-based upper extremity use and body positioning, mental aspects like handling stress, and environmental features that can influence work and employment such as family support and services by healthcare professionals. Gainful employment was found to be common in three Core Sets. This essential and broad-construct list of categories can be utilized as a basis for assessment of individuals with SCI in the context of work and employment and disability evaluation. Each ICF category can be operationalized using existing patient-reported instruments such as the Visual Analogue Scale (VAS) or Numerical Rating Scale (NRS) for pain, clinician-reported measure such as the manual muscle test or handgrip strength test to examine muscle power, or proxy measures on the level of activity and participation by asking the family members or caregivers of the person with SCI.

A list of domains is provided by existing ICF Core Sets, namely, the ICF Core Set for SCI, which was developed to capture functioning and disability in early post-acute and long-term settings. The ICF Core Sets for Vocational Rehabilitation and also that of Social Security can be used to supplement the ICF Core Sets for SCI.

11.3 Assessment of Contextual Factors in Work and SCI

Within the last decade, there has been growing interest in contextual factors that influence the employment status of individuals with SCI. In the ICF, contextual factors include both environmental and personal factors. These factors contextualize the "setting" or "situation" of an individual and aim to accurately characterize how disability can modify, confound, or mediate the effects of vocational rehabilitation. The Spinal Cord Injury Rehabilitation Evidence project (www.scireproject.com) has been instrumental in synthesizing evidence on contextual factors in relation to employment of persons with SCI. The most recent SCIRE review revealed a host of contextual factors that can positively or negatively impact vocational rehabilitation in SCI [16].

11.4 Personal Factors Associated with Employment Post-SCI

The ICF defines "personal factors" to be individual features such as "gender, age, race, other health conditions, fitness, lifestyle, habits, upbringing, coping styles, social background, education, profession, past and current experience, behavior, character and psychological assets" [2]. Several personal characteristics have been identified as factors that may either interfere with or promote return to the labor market [9, 17, 18]. Some of these characteristics cannot be modified (e.g., level of injury), while others such as level of education, health status, and work skills can be modified with appropriate interventions.

Based on the SCIRE work [16], several personal characteristics cannot be modified but must be taken into consideration in the assessment of potential (re) employment after SCI. Being Caucasian is a demographic factor that favors employment. Male gender has been a strong demographic predictor of employment, but a number of recent studies have shown no significant difference between males and females. The interaction between age, age at injury, and the duration of injury is complex, making it difficult to determine their individual and exact influence on employment. While the proportion of employed people tends to increase with age (up to about age 30 and maintained up to age 40), younger age at injury and longer duration of injury (up to 20 years post-injury) are better predictors of being employed. Due to a nonlinear effect of age on labor market participation, it is likely that work participation may decrease with increasing age at some point after 40. This effect has been observed, where individuals aged 45–54 were significantly more likely to be employed than those aged 55–64 [19]. A more severe injury tends to decrease the probability of employment. A higher level of education seems to be a factor in increasing the probability of employment. Factors related to pre-injury work such as being employed at injury, returning to pre-injury job, or holding a job that is less physically demanding tend to positively influence employment.

Several factors can be modified in the post-injury period to exert a positive influence on the likelihood of employment after SCI. Secondary health complications such as spasticity, pressure ulcers, severe urinary tract infections, and respiratory problems are likely to limit employment opportunities, but this finding should be considered in conjunction with the severity of injury. For example, having tetraplegia (or paralysis of both upper limbs and lower limbs) leads to a higher occurrence of secondary health complications due to the larger extent of impact than paraplegia (or paralysis of both lower limbs). The level of education or pursuit of training after SCI remains to be a key factor that can offset other factors such as the severity of injury. Specifically, a professional degree and work that is not physically demanding increase the likelihood of employment. Some psychological attributes, such as an internal locus of control and positive values and expectations regarding work, including internalization of positive work outcomes, are also likely to favor employment.

11.5 Environmental Factors Associated with Employment Post-SCI

Based on the ICF, the environment consists of several different dimensions, including products and technology (e.g., assistive device), natural environment and human-made changes to environment (e.g., geographic location), support and relationships from others (e.g., support from employer), attitudes (e.g., discrimination due to disability), and services, systems, and policies (e.g., healthcare provision) [2]. According to SCIRE [16], the most obvious barriers and facilitators are related to the physical environment. However, the social, attitudinal, and cultural environments can also create barriers. Being able to drive transportation independently was positively associated with returning to work post-injury. Reduced dependence on the inflexible, inaccessible, or unreliable options of public transportation was likely to be the main reason for this finding [20]. People with SCI who have computer skills tend to return to work faster after suffering their injury and also have higher earnings, than otherwise similar workers who lack computer skills [21]. Studies specific to persons who experience SCI reported that of those who return to work, the majority were able to do so, in part, because of modifications to the work including job adaptations and decreased work hours.

Financial disincentives are gaining empirical support as having a detrimental effect on return to work post-injury. For example, in British Columbia, Canada, social assistance deters recipients from returning to work because once more than $400/month is earned, benefits received while on social assistance, such as dental care and prescription medication, are lost [22]. This also appears to be the case in Australia, as the perceived disadvantages of losing social security benefits (which would lead to exclusion from accessing government funded equipment and medical supplies) seemed to deter people from seeking employment post-SCI [20]. Health insurance benefits that could be thought to be threatened for abolishment or reduction with an increase in work-related income could hinder people with SCI from going back to work.

Disability discrimination is due largely to negative or naïve employer perceptions about the potential productivity of individuals with SCI. Ravaud et al. [23] found that companies tend to discriminate against individuals with SCI by offering interviews less frequently when the injury was disclosed [23]. Similarly, 80 % of Canadians agreed with the statement "Canadians with disabilities are less likely to be hired for a job than those without disabilities, even if they are equally qualified" [24]. Not surprisingly, Jongbloed et al. [22] found that individuals with SCI viewed the negative attitudes of employers regarding people with disabilities as a barrier to employment [22]. The lack of physical accessibility to the workplace has also been found to hinder return to work.

11.6 Vocational Rehabilitation in SCI

Access to vocational counseling, education, or job training is a key component of enabling return to work after SCI [17, 22, 25]. Despite this, there is a lack of intervention studies such as randomized or controlled clinical trials looking at return-to-work as primary or secondary outcomes or looking into the effectiveness of job placement strategies and interventions to the worker (e.g., workplace accommodation, ergonomics, flexibility of scheduling). The preponderance of evidence is derived from cross-sectional, observational studies.

In total, there have been two randomized controlled studies evaluating employment outcomes in SCI populations. Allen et al. found that access to trained service dogs improved psychosocial status, including self-esteem, internal locus of control, and overall psychological well-being. This was associated with additional benefits, such as a decrease in assistance time by a professional assistant or family and friends, an increase in school attendance and part-time employment, and an increase in social participation and community [26].

The second randomized trial evaluated a supported employment intervention compared to conventional rehabilitation. Supported employment integrates members into the care continuum and promotes a more personalized experience by incorporating the preferences of the individual. Ottomanelli et al. found that a supported employment intervention was more effective at returning individuals to work than treatment as usual (TAU) [27]. Those receiving supported employment were 2.5 times more likely than those receiving TAU at the intervention sites (offering both supported employment and TAU) and 11.4 times more likely than those receiving TAU at the observation sites (offering only TAU) to achieve employment over the 12-month follow-up period.

Other than randomized trials, the influence of vocational rehabilitation on employment has been investigated through observational studies. Perhaps the most comprehensive observational study in this area is by Arango-Lasprilla et al. [28], who looked at individual program components, thus allowing a better understanding of what aspects of vocational rehabilitation programs provide the most benefits to individuals. With over 3,500 individuals in the study, on-the-job training demonstrated the greatest effect size, with an odds ratio (OR) of 2.97 (95 % CI, 1.55–5.69). This means that, on average, individuals who received on-the-job training had nearly three times the odds of gaining competitive employment compared to those that did not. Other components that increased an individual's odds of employment included job search assistance (OR = 1.35, 1.10–1.67), job placement assistance (OR = 1.81, 1.48–2.20), on-the-job support (OR = 1.65, 1.25–2.17), maintenance services (OR = 1.60, 1.32–1.94), and "other" services (OR = 1.51, 1.29–1.78). Conversely, receiving personal attendant services and miscellaneous training were associated with a decreased odds of gaining employment (OR = 0.56, 0.35–0.89) and (OR = 0.74, 0.60–0.92), respectively.

11.7 Summary

On average, individuals who go through vocational rehabilitation have a higher probability of returning to work. Effective work reintegration for individuals with SCI is essential because, despite their disability, many of these individuals possess the potential to remain or become productive members of the society while deriving positive psychosocial benefits at the same time. Many factors that could facilitate return to work are at a level that is beyond the realm of healthcare. These include changing employer and societal perceptions and attitudes and lobbying for social change that would include improved transportation [20]. Eliminating policies to reduce financial disincentives are key to eliminating barriers for those who return to work. Policy change requires a strong lobbying voice and a social will to overcome attitudes and arguments from opponents who may otherwise see provision of funding for personal care attendants and/or worksite modification as a poor investment of resources.

Study Questions

1. What ICF Core Sets can be used to be able to assess and report the disability of individuals with SCI?

   Answer: The ICF Core Set for SCI can be used which comes in two versions depending on the setting: early post-acute and long-term settings. The ICF Core Set for Vocational Rehabilitation and ICF Core Set for Social Security can also be used to supplement the SCI-specific Core Sets.

2. What are the modifiable personal factors in SCI?

   Answer: Secondary health complications such as spasticity, pressure ulcers, severe urinary tract infections and respiratory problems, level of education or pursuit of training after SCI, nature of job post-SCI, some psychological attributes such as an internal locus of control, and positive values and expectations regarding work, including internalization of positive work outcomes.

3. What are the non-modifiable personal factors in SCI?

   Answer: Race, gender, biological age, age at injury, duration of injury, severity of injury, level of education, being employed at injury, and nature of job prior to injury.

4. What are the different environmental factors that should be considered in SCI?

   Answer: Physical, social, attitudinal, and cultural environments can all create barriers or facilitators to functioning post-SCI: specifically, transportation independence, skills training provision, work accommodation, financial disincentives, social security benefits, health insurance benefits, employer perceptions and attitudes, and lack of physical accessibility to the workplace.

References

1. Furlan JC, Krassioukov A, Miller WC, Sakakibara B. Epidemiology of traumatic SCI. In: Eng J, Teasell R, Miller WC, Wolfe D, Townson A, Hsieh J, et al., editors. Spinal cord injury rehabilitation evidence, vol. 4.0. Vancouver: Spinal Cord Injury Rehabilitation Evidence; 2012. p. 1–16.
2. World Health Organization. International classification of functioning, disability and health. Geneva: World Health Organization; 2001.
3. Cieza A, Kirchberger I, Biering-Sorensen F, Baumberger M, Charlifue S, Post MW, et al. ICF core sets for individuals with spinal cord injury in the long-term context. Spinal Cord. 2010;48(4):305–12.
4. Kirchberger I, Cieza A, Biering-Sorensen F, Baumberger M, Charlifue S, Post MW, et al. ICF core sets for individuals with spinal cord injury in the early post-acute context. Spinal Cord. 2010;48(4):297–304.
5. Guttmann L. The place of our spinal paraplegic fellowman in society. Rehabilitation. 1959; 15–27.
6. Ville I, Ravaud JF. Work values: a comparison of non-disabled persons with paraplegia. Disabil Rehabil. 1998;20(4):127–37.
7. Krause JS. Longitudinal changes in adjustment after spinal cord injury: a 15-year study. Arch Phys Med Rehabil. 1992;73(6):564–8.
8. Vogel LC, Klaas SJ, Lubicky JP, Anderson CJ. Long-term outcomes and life satisfaction of adults who had pediatric spinal cord injuries. Arch Phys Med Rehabil. 1998;79(12):1496–503.
9. Ottomanelli L, Lind L. Review of critical factors related to employment after spinal cord injury: implications for research and vocational services. J Spinal Cord Med. 2009;32(5): 503–31.
10. Unemployment rate: Labor force statistics from the current population survey [Internet]. United States Department of Labor. Available from: http://data.bls.gov/pdq/SurveyOutputServlet (2014).
11. Tomassen PC, Post MW, van Asbeck FW. Return to work after spinal cord injury. Spinal Cord. 2000;38(1):51–5.

12. Fougeyrollas P, Noreau L, Boschen KA. Interaction of environment with individual characteristics and social participation: theoretical perspectives and applications in persons with spinal cord injury. Top Spinal Cord Inj Rehabil. 2002;7:1–16.
13. Chan SK, Man DW. Barriers to returning to work for people with spinal cord injuries: a focus group study. Work. 2005;25(4):325–32.
14. Brage S, Donceel P, Falez F. Development of ICF core set for disability evaluation in social security. Disabil Rehabil. 2008;30(18):1392–6.
15. Finger ME, Escorpizo R, Glassel A, Gmunder HP, Luckenkemper M, Chan C, et al. ICF core set for vocational rehabilitation: results of an international consensus conference. Disabil Rehabil. 2012;34(5):429–38.
16. Escorpizo R, Miller W, Trenaman L. Work and employment. In: Eng J, Teasell R, Miller W, Wolfe D, Townson A, Hsieh J, et al., editors. Spinal cord injury rehabilitation evidence, vol. 4.0. Vancouver: Spinal Cord Injury Rehabilitation Evidence; 2012. p. 1–22.
17. Lidal IB, Huynh TK, Biering-Sorensen F. Return to work following spinal cord injury: a review. Disabil Rehabil. 2007;29(17):1341–75.
18. Anderson D, Dumont S, Azzaria L, Le Bourdais M, Noreau L. Determinants of return to work among spinal cord injury patients: a literature review. J Vocat Rehabil. 2007;27:57–68.
19. Hirsh AT, Molton IR, Johnson KL, Bombardier CH, Jensen MP. The relationship of chronological age, age at injury, and duration of injury to employment status in individuals with spinal cord injury. Psychol Inj Law. 2009;2(3–4):263–75.
20. Conroy L, McKenna K. Vocational outcome following spinal cord injury. Spinal Cord. 1999; 37(9):624–33.
21. Kruse D, Krueger A, Drastal S. Computer use, computer training, and employment. outcomes among people with spinal cord injuries. Spine (Phila Pa 1976). 1996;21(7):891–6.
22. Jongbloed L, Backman C, Forwell SJ, Carpenter C. Employment after spinal cord injury: the impact of government policies in Canada. Work. 2007;29(2):145–54.
23. Ravaud JF, Madiot B, Ville I. Discrimination towards disabled people seeking employment. Soc Sci Med. 1992;35(8):951–8.
24. Social Development Canada. Canadian attitudes towards disability issues. Ottawa: Government of Canada; 2004.
25. Jang Y, Wang YH, Wang JD. Return to work after spinal cord injury in Taiwan: the contribution of functional independence. Arch Phys Med Rehabil. 2005;86(4):681–6.
26. Allen K, Blascovich J. The value of service dogs for people with severe ambulatory disabilities. A randomized controlled trial. JAMA. 1996;275(13):1001–6.
27. Ottomanelli L, Goetz L, McGeough C, Suris A, Sippel J, Sinnott P, et al. Methods of a multisite randomized clinical trial of supported employment among veterans with spinal cord injury. J Rehabil Res Dev. 2009;46(7):919–30.
28. Arango-Lasprilla JC, Cardoso EDS, Wilson LM, Romero MG, Chan F, Sung C. Vocational rehabilitation service patterns and employment outcomes for hispanics with spinal cord injuries. Rehabil Res Policy Educ. 2011;25(3–4):149–62.

Chapter 12
Traumatic Brain Injury

Robyn L. Tate, Grahame K. Simpson, and Philippa McRae

12.1 Vignette

'Peter' was a 24-year-old apprentice electrician when he sustained a very severe traumatic brain injury (TBI) in May 2009 after falling 3 m onto a concrete floor while at work. The duration of post-traumatic amnesia was 3 weeks, and his acute recovery was complicated by generalised tonic-clonic seizures. He was hospitalised for 4 weeks in the acute hospital, followed by 8 weeks in an inpatient brain injury rehabilitation unit. Although Peter did not have any physical impairment, he experienced marked cognitive impairments (severe expressive aphasia, reading and writing difficulties, mild reduction in visuospatial processing and difficulties with mental arithmetic). These deficits continued to improve after discharge, and during the next 3 months, he was engaged in a community-based rehabilitation programme, focusing on speech and language therapy, as well as a gym programme

R.L. Tate (✉)
John Walsh Centre for Rehabilitation Research, Sydney Medical School – Northern, Level 9, Kolling Institute of Medical Research, University of Sydney, Royal North Shore Hospital, St. Leonards, NSW 2065, Australia
e-mail: rtate@med.usyd.edu.au

G.K. Simpson
John Walsh Centre for Rehabilitation Research, Sydney Medical School – Northern, Level 9, Kolling Institute of Medical Research, University of Sydney, Royal North Shore Hospital, St. Leonards, NSW 2065, Australia

Liverpool Brain Injury Rehabilitation Unit, Liverpool Hospital, Sydney, Australia

Brain Injury Rehabilitation Research Group, Ingham Institute of Applied Medical Research, Sydney, Australia

P. McRae
Liverpool Brain Injury Rehabilitation Unit, Liverpool Hospital, Sydney, Australia

Brain Injury Rehabilitation Research Group, Ingham Institute of Applied Medical Research, Sydney, Australia

R. Escorpizo et al. (eds.), *Handbook of Vocational Rehabilitation and Disability Evaluation*, Handbooks in Health, Work, and Disability, DOI 10.1007/978-3-319-08825-9_12

to overcome physical deconditioning which had occurred while he was hospitalised.

Peter resumed work at 6 months post-trauma, initially 2 days per week. Over the next 6 months, he gradually upgraded to 4 days per week, but was limited by fatigue, restricted from working at heights and required assistance to interpret plans and perform calculations. A setback occurred at almost 2 years post-trauma with onset of a series of seizures, which adversely affected his work hours, ability to work at heights and driving. In spite of these difficulties, Peter persevered with the apprenticeship, which he completed at 3 years post-trauma. Long-term prospects for his trade were considered poor, however, due to the effects of his seizures, fatigue and residual cognitive disability. At this point, contact with the TBI vocational rehabilitation service was reinstated, and Peter participated in further vocational assessment. He elected to pursue a new career in youth work, initially through volunteer work, and was successful in obtaining employment. Peter is currently working 3 days per week as a youth worker and, with the exception of driving, is able to manage all other tasks within this position and is studying for a community service certificate.

12.2 Vocational Rehabilitation After Traumatic Brain Injury

Return to work is an important indicator of recovery after TBI and is often perceived as a key element of successful rehabilitation [1]. The case of Peter demonstrates the long-term vocational rehabilitation involvement that can be necessary for people with severe levels of TBI to maximise their vocational outcomes. In Peter's case, the vocational rehabilitation intervention occurred over a 3-year period and totalled 65 service hours. Peter's experience also highlights the need for flexibility, with the redirection of career requiring adaptation and creativity on the part of the client and vocational rehabilitation team.

At the personal level, reviews of the literature have found that people who return to work after TBI report higher levels of quality of life, social integration and enhanced self-esteem than those who do not return to work, as well as better physical health and lower usage of health services [2, 3]. In addition to earning an income, people with TBI, like other individuals without injury, value the intangible benefits such as social relationships, personal growth, happiness and success [4]. The lost productivity arising from young adults who sustain TBI and are unable to return to work constitutes a significant social cost [5]. Therefore, return to work also produces major benefits at the societal level.

This chapter is divided into four sections. In the first part, we set the scene by providing definitions and commonly used clinical classifications of TBI, as well as briefly describing its epidemiology and neuropathology. The effects of TBI are described in the second section, with particular reference to disability evaluation and the International Classification of Functioning, Disability and Health [6]. The third section focuses on empirical studies of return to work, along with evidence for the effectiveness of vocational interventions for people with TBI. The final section of the chapter provides information on the state of the field in terms of the practical application of vocational rehabilitation after TBI.

12.3 Setting the Scene

12.3.1 Traumatic Brain Injury Defined

TBI is defined as 'craniocerebral trauma, specifically, an occurrence of injury to the head (arising from blunt or penetrating trauma or from acceleration-deceleration forces) that is associated with any of these occurrences attributable to the injury: decreased level of consciousness, amnesia, other neurologic or neuropsychological abnormalities, skull fracture, diagnosed intracranial lesions, or death' [7, p. 603]. This definition highlights two key issues:

- First, the injury is caused by an *external* mechanical force to the head. This factor distinguishes TBI from other acquired neurological disorders where the cause is related to *internal* abnormality of brain function (e.g. stroke, multiple sclerosis, dementia, cerebral tumour). The most common causes of TBI in civilians are road traffic crash, fall and assault associated with violence [8]; blast injuries have replaced gunshot wounds as the signature cause of TBI in modern warfare [9].
- Second, the injury to the head needs to be of sufficient impact to cause damage to the brain which is encased inside the skull; such damage may be transient or permanent. The older literature used the term 'head injury' rather than 'brain injury', and although occasionally the two terms continue to be used synonymously, the use of the term 'head injury' is now discouraged if the health condition of relevance is actually brain injury. The term 'traumatic' is an important qualifier to 'brain injury', because nonprogressive neurological conditions, such as stroke, are often also referred to as a brain injury.

12.3.2 Epidemiology of Traumatic Brain Injury

TBI is important because (a) it is common and (b) it is the leading cause of acquired disability in previously healthy young adults [7]. In a systematic review of epidemiological studies conducted in European countries, Tagliaferri et al. [10] estimated an annual incidence of 235 per 100,000 population, which translates to 775,500 new cases of TBI each year in the European Community alone. This incidence figure is at the upper limit of those reported for other industrialised countries such as the United States [7, 11] and Australia [12]. The peak incidence occurs in young adults, and males outnumber females in the ratio of at least 2:1; in the Australian population study of Tate et al. [13], the peak incidence escalated from 100/100,000 population overall to 400/100,000 in 15–24-year-old males.

The prevalence of disability after TBI is high, even though the risk of death is two to three times higher than in the general population [14, 15]. Two main factors are responsible: (a) the highest incidence group is young adults [8, 13], and (b) a significant proportion of people sustaining severe degrees of injury have permanent functional disability [16]. The prevalence of impairment, disability and participation restriction from TBI in the European Community was conservatively estimated to be 6.2 million persons [10], this figure being extrapolated from the prevalence of 5.3 million for the United States [17]. Thus, worldwide, TBI is a health condition that has significant morbidity and major resource implications, in both health-care and community settings.

TBI is caused by an external force to the head that is of sufficient force to cause disruption of neurological function. It occurs across the lifespan, but is particularly common in young adult males.

12.3.3 Classification of Traumatic Brain Injury

It is important to emphasise that not all TBI results in permanent disability. The reason is that TBI has a wide range of severity. TBI refers equally to transient loss of consciousness sustained by a football player who falls to the ground after a blow to the head, then gets up and resumes the game, as it does to a car driver who sustains profound brain damage in a road traffic crash and lies in an unresponsive and vegetative state for many months. Accordingly, TBI is classified in relation to the severity of injury: mild, moderate or severe. The vast majority (in the order of 75 %) of injuries are mild, and 16 % are fairly evenly divided between moderate and severe degrees of injury, with the remainder being dead on arrival at hospital [7, 13]. With some qualifications (see below), many people with a TBI eventually make a complete recovery and are able to resume their premorbid lifestyles, including work.

Various methods are used to classify the initial injury severity, the most common being the depth of coma and duration of post-traumatic amnesia. Coma is a state of impaired consciousness in which the person lies with eyes closed and does not respond to external environmental stimulation. The Glasgow Coma Scale [18] is the most commonly used instrument to measure depth of coma. Following emergence from coma, there is usually a subsequent period of altered consciousness, referred to as post-traumatic amnesia, in which the patients are confused and show

Table 12.1 Conventional classifications of traumatic brain injury severity

	GCS score (at 6 h post-trauma)	PTA duration[a] Jennett and Teasdale [20]
Very mild	NA	Less than 5 min
Mild	13–15	5–60 min
Moderate	9–12	1–24 h
Severe	3–8	1–7 days
Very severe	NA	1–4 weeks
Extremely severe	NA	More than 4 weeks

Note: *GCS* Glasgow Coma Scale, *PTA* post-traumatic amnesia, *NA* not applicable
[a]The WHO Collaborating Task Force on Mild Traumatic Brain Injury, Carroll et al. [21] has revised the definition of mild TBI to include PTA durations up to 24 h, thereby subsuming the moderate injury classification

generalised disturbance of cognition (particularly orientation, memory, attention and the higher-level executive functions) and sometimes agitated behaviour, even though they may be quite capable of walking around and being able to talk. The duration of post-traumatic amnesia is one of the best predictors of recovery and outcome. A number of standard instruments to measure post-traumatic amnesia are available (see Ref. [19] for detailed description); Table 12.1 shows the conventions for different injury severity grading for coma depth and post-traumatic amnesia duration, drawn from Jennett and Teasdale [20] and Carroll and colleagues [21].

In considering the consequences of TBI, a distinction needs to be made between the severity of the initial injury (as measured by coma, post-traumatic amnesia or other method, e.g. time between the injury and the ability to follow commands, such as 'squeeze my hand') and the severity of outcome. Although there is an association between severity of the initial injury and outcome, it is not always the case that all mild injuries result in a good outcome, nor do all severe degrees of injury necessarily result in severe disability. For example, in the consecutive series of 466 patients with TBI reported by Dikmen et al. [22], almost 20 % of those with mild injury did *not* make a good recovery as measured by the Glasgow Outcome Scale [23], and conversely approximately 25 % of the patients with severe injury *did achieve* a good recovery.

> TBI ranges in severity from mild to extremely severe. Severity is measured by the duration of coma and post-traumatic amnesia. The distinction between the severity of the initial injury and severity of outcome is important: not all patients with mild injury have a good outcome and not all patients with severe injury have a poor outcome.

12.4 Effects of Traumatic Brain Injury, with Particular Reference to Disability Evaluation and the International Classification of Functioning, Disability and Health

12.4.1 Course of Recovery After Traumatic Brain Injury

At the moment of impact of the injury, the brain is subject to sudden onset of both acceleration-deceleration and rotational forces, which cause characteristic types of structural brain damage (contusions and diffuse axonal injury, respectively) and set in train a series of neurochemical reactions (for further detail on the medical aspects of the acute period, which are varied and complex, see Refs. [20, 24]). Other neurological events that can occur after TBI (e.g. skull fractures, hypoxic damage, intracranial haemorrhage, brain infection) can exacerbate brain dysfunction.

Areas of the brain that are the most vulnerable to structural damage from severe contusions are the frontal and temporal lobes (because of contact between the brain and the sharp sphenoidal ridges of the interior surface of the skull); the brain area most vulnerable to diffuse axonal injury is the subcortical white matter as a consequence of rotational forces at the moment of impact causing shearing and tearing of nerve fibres.

With the rare exception of some penetrating brain injuries, TBI initially results in coma. Following emergence from coma, most patients have a variable period of post-traumatic amnesia (ranging from mere minutes to many months), its duration being a function of the severity of the initial injury and any subsequent medical complications (e.g. brain infection). Post-traumatic amnesia is primarily characterised by confusion, disorientation and inability to lay down new memories. By convention, if a patient has not emerged from post-traumatic amnesia by 6 months post-trauma, it is likely that he or she is experiencing global and profound cognitive impairment, rather than the transient state of post-traumatic amnesia. In cases of the most extreme severity, a patient may transit from coma to vegetative/minimally conscious states before entering the phase of post-traumatic amnesia. A very small number of patients remain in the vegetative/minimally conscious state in the longer term [25].

Following emergence from post-traumatic amnesia, a period of active recovery of brain function ensues. For severe TBI, spontaneous recovery plateaus around 6–12 months post-trauma [26]. During this time, many patients undergo inpatient and/or community-based neurorehabilitation from a multidisciplinary team including the following disciplines: rehabilitation medicine, nursing, physiotherapy, occupational therapy, speech and language therapy, clinical and neuropsychology and social work. Continued recovery, along with functional adaptation, may continue to occur over the next year or so. The recovery trajectory for milder degrees of TBI is less protracted. Thus, unlike many other health conditions, the process of recovery from severe degrees of TBI is measured in terms of months or years, rather than weeks or days.

Recovery after severe TBI follows the same course for the majority of patients: coma, followed by post-traumatic amnesia, followed by a period of active recovery of brain function over 6-12 months. Functional adaptation over the longer-term can also enhance outcome.

12.4.2 Clinical Profile of Traumatic Brain Injury

The clinical profiles of mild versus the more severe degrees of TBI differ significantly. Post-concussion symptoms are common after mild TBI, comprising a mixture of somatic (most commonly headaches and dizziness), cognitive (forgetfulness and poor concentration) and behavioural (fatigue and irritability) symptoms. These symptoms can be debilitating but resolve within weeks or the first few months in the majority of cases [27].

With severe degrees of injury, the contusions and diffuse axonal injury in the brain, which were described earlier, bear a direct relationship to the patterns of impairments characterising TBI. Contusions in the frontal lobes have an impact on executive functions and the regulation of behaviour, contusions in the temporal lobes are responsible for impairments in memory and learning functions, and diffuse axonal injury in the subcortical white matter disrupts speed of information processing. These three areas of impairments fall within the neuropsychological domain, and indeed cognitive and behavioural impairments are more common than physical impairments after TBI. A state-wide multicentre cohort study of severe TBI [28] found that by 18 months post-trauma, a smaller proportion (15 % and 20 %) continued to have clinically significant problems with mobility and hand function, respectively, in comparison with the key cognitive domains of executive functioning (54 %) and memory (62 %). Consequently, while acknowledging that a small proportion of people certainly experience *physical* disability after TBI, the fact is that many people with clinically significant impairments do not present as typically disabled, and for this reason TBI has been described as the 'hidden disability'.

Clinical profiles of mild versus severe TBI differ. The majority of patients with mild TBI have a good outcome, but some may experience post-concussive symptomatology in the longer term. The profile of severe TBI is more variable. It ranges from residual neurocognitive impairment to profound physical, cognitive and/or behavioural disability. Clients suitable for vocational rehabilitation often have minimal physical disability but experience the common triad of neurocognitive impairments after TBI (impairments in memory, executive, and processing speed functions).

12.4.3 ICF Core Set for Traumatic Brain Injury

The introduction of ICF Core Sets both for TBI [29] and vocational rehabilitation [30, 31] are welcome developments. One advantage of core sets is the streamlining of the assessment process to ensure a comprehensive yet efficient evaluation of function. The Comprehensive Core Set for TBI contains 139 categories (37 for body functions, 2 for body structure, 61 for activities/participation and 39 for environmental factors), and the Brief Core Set contains 23 codes (see Table 12.2). These categories are the best ones to target in evaluating TBI.

There is a large, but not complete, overlap between the ICF Core Set for TBI and the ICF Core Set for vocational rehabilitation (see Table 12.2), the latter containing 90 categories in the Comprehensive Core Set and 13 in the Brief Core Set. Only 4 of the 17 body function categories from the Vocational Rehabilitation Comprehensive Core Set are not also represented in the TBI Comprehensive Core Set, 2 of the 40 activities/participation categories and 8 of the 33 environmental categories. This close correspondence between the TBI and Vocational Rehabilitation Core Sets is advantageous.

Outcome studies have repeatedly documented the wide variety of impairments that occur after TBI. For example, in a sample of 55 people with TBI of all severity levels drawn from a rehabilitation hospital, Koskinen et al. [32] found that 100 of the 123 ICF Checklist categories were problem areas, with 48 of the categories present in 30 % or more of the sample. These findings vindicate the large number of categories contained in the TBI Comprehensive Core Set. They also indicate that at the clinical level, there is wide individual variability – even though some areas of function are almost always compromised (e.g. neurocognitive) – other types of dysfunction (e.g. motor-sensory) may also occur.

> The ICF Core Set for TBI reflects the significance of neurocognitive impairments, along with the widespread effects of TBI on everyday activities and social participation, as well as the importance of environmental factors. There is considerable overlap between the core sets for TBI and vocational rehabilitation.

12.4.4 Disability Evaluation of the Client with Traumatic Brain Injury, with Particular Reference to Neuropsychological Function

The evaluation of function and disability after TBI is the vital first step to good clinical management. At the body function level, a thorough evaluation of *both* motor-sensory and neuropsychological performance is necessary to evaluate

Table 12.2 ICF Comprehensive Core Set for TBI [29]

Body functions (*n* = 37)	**Activities/participation** (*n* = 61)
b110 Consciousness functions[a]	d110 Watching
b114 Orientation functions	d115 Listening
b126 Temperament and personality functions[b]	d155 Acquiring skills[b]
b130 Energy and drive functions[a,b]	d160 Focusing attention[b]
b134 Sleep functions[b]	d163 Thinking[b]
b140 Attention functions[a,b]	d166 Reading[b]
b144 Memory functions[a,b]	d170 Writing[b]
b147 Psychomotor functions	d175 Solving problems[b]
b152 Emotional functions[a,b]	d177 Making decisions[b]
b156 Perceptual functions	d210 Undertaking a single task[b]
b160 Thought functions[b]	d220 Undertaking multiple tasks[b]
b164 Higher-level cognitive functions[a,b]	*d230 Carrying out daily routine*[a,b]
b167 Mental functions of language	d240 Handling stress and other psychological demands[b]
b210 Seeing functions[b]	d310 Communicating with – receiving – spoken messages[b]
b215 Functions of structures adjoining the eye	d315 Communicating with – receiving – nonverbal messages[b]
b235 Vestibular functions[b]	d330 Speaking
b240 Sensations associated with hearing and vestibular function	d335 Producing nonverbal messages
b255 Smell function	d345 Writing messages
b260 Proprioceptive function	*d350 Conversation*[a,b]
b280 Sensation of pain[a,b]	d360 Using communication devices and techniques[b]
b310 Voice functions	d410 Changing basic body position[b]
b320 Articulation functions	d415 Maintaining a body position[b]
b330 Fluency and rhythm of speech functions	d420 Transferring oneself
b420 Blood pressure functions	d430 Lifting and carrying objects[b]
b455 Exercise tolerance functions[b]	d440 Fine hand use[b]
b510 Ingestion functions	d445 Hand and arm use[b]
b525 Defecation functions	*d450 Walking*[a,b]
b555 Endocrine gland functions	d455 Moving around[b]
b620 Urination functions	d465 Moving around using equipment[b]
b640 Sexual functions	d470 Using transportation[b]
b710 Mobility of joint functions	d475 Driving[b]
b730 Muscle power functions[b]	d510 Washing oneself
b735 Muscle tone functions	d520 Caring for body parts
b755 Involuntary movement reaction functions	d530 Toileting[b]
b760 Control of voluntary movement functions[a]	d540 Dressing[b]
b765 Involuntary movement functions	d550 Eating
b770 Gait pattern functions	d560 Drinking

(continued)

Table 12.2 (continued)

Environmental factors (*n* = 39)	d570 Looking after one's health[b]
e1100 Food	d620 Acquisition of goods and services
e1101 Drugs[b]	d630 Preparing meals
e1108 Non-medicinal drugs and alcohol	d640 Doing housework
e115 Products and technology for personal use in daily living[a,b]	d660 Assisting others
e120 Products and technology for personal indoor and outdoor mobility and transportation[a,b]	d710 Basic interpersonal interactions[b]
e125 Products and technology for communication[b]	*d720 Complex interpersonal interactions*[a,b]
e135 Products and technology for employment[b]	d730 Relating with strangers
e150 Design, construction and building products and technology of buildings for public use[b]	d740 Formal relationships[b]
e155 Design, construction and building products and technology of buildings for private use[b]	d750 Informal social relationships
e160 products and technology of land development	*d760 Family relationships*[a]
e165 Assets	d770 Intimate relationships
e210 Physical geography	d825 Vocational training[b]
e250 Sound[b]	d830 Higher education[b]
e310 Immediate family[a,b]	d840 Apprenticeship (work preparation)[b]
e315 Extended family	*d845 Acquiring, keeping and terminating a job*[a,b]
e320 Friends[a,b]	d850 Remunerative employment[b]
e325 Acquaintances, peers, colleagues, neighbours and community members[b]	d855 Non-remunerative employment[b]
e330 People in positions of authority[b]	d860 Basic economic transactions
e340 Personal care providers and personal assistants[b]	d865 Complex economic transactions
e355 Health professionals[b]	d870 Economic self-sufficiency[b]
e360 Other professionals[b]	d910 Community life
e410 Individual attitudes of immediate family members	*d920 Recreation and leisure*[a]
e415 Individual attitudes of extended family members	d930 Religion and spirituality
e420 Individual attitudes of friends	*(+Brief Core Set only: d5 self-care)*[a]
e425 Individual attitudes of acquaintances, peers, colleagues, neighbours and community members	**Body structures (*n* = 2)**
e440 Individual attitudes of personal care providers and personal assistants	*s110 Structure of brain*[a]
e450 Individual attitudes of health professionals[b]	s710 Structure of head and neck region
e455 Individual attitudes of other professionals	
e460 Societal attitudes[b]	
e515 Architecture and construction services, systems and policies	
e525 Housing services, systems and policies[b]	

(continued)

Table 12.2 (continued)

e535 Communication services, systems and policies[b]	
e540 Transportation services, systems and policies[b]	
e550 Legal services, systems and policies[b]	
e570 Social security services, systems and policies[a,b]	
e575 General social support services, systems and policies	
e580 Health services, systems and policies[a,b]	
e585 Education and training services, systems and policies[b]	
e590 Labour and employment services, systems and policies[b]	

[a and italics]Also contained in the TBI Brief Core Set (Note: an additional code, d5 (covering all pertinent categories of self-care) is also included)
[b]Also contained in the Vocational Rehabilitation Comprehensive Core Set

functions that may impact the client's work capacity. The TBI and Vocational Rehabilitation ICF Core Sets provide helpful guidance in this respect. The components of a comprehensive vocational rehabilitation evaluation for TBI are described in detail in Sect. 12.6.1.

Neuropsychological assessment is necessary in order to understand the cognitive strengths and weaknesses of the individual client with TBI (which are not always apparent with formal interview), so that the goals and strategies used in the rehabilitation programme can be tailored appropriately. In this context, assessment takes several hours for the administration of performance-based cognitive tests conducted by a certified neuropsychologist. The reader is referred to Lezak et al. [33] which is one of the most commonly used texts in the field, and the systematic review of Tate et al. [34] details all instruments currently used in the TBI field ($n = 728$) which are linked to ICF categories. Because of the complexity of neuropsychological impairments, we elaborate below on the characteristic neurocognitive impairments after TBI (but keeping in mind that key motor-sensory impairments may also profoundly affect work performance, e.g. balance problems for a roof tiler).

As noted, the typical neurocognitive impairments after TBI are in the following body function (designated as code b in the ICF) areas, which will affect day-to-day activities (ICF code d) within those respective areas:

- Memory (b144, memory functions; d155, acquiring skills)
- Executive function (b164, higher-level cognitive functions; d175, solving problems; d177, making decisions)
- Processing speed (b147, psychomotor functions; d179, applying knowledge, other specified)

Neurocognitive impairments may also have an impact more broadly across multiple activity/participation domains, for example, work and employment (cf. d840-d859 – work and employment).

It is emphasised that these neurocognitive labels are umbrella terms covering a multitude of different types of component processes, which need to be evaluated. The 'memory' domain, for example, includes the following functional systems: autobiographical, episodic, implicit, procedural, prospective and semantic memory; working memory predominantly involves executive abilities (see Ref. [35]).[1] Episodic (i.e. memory for events) and prospective (i.e. remembering to remember) memory functions are commonly impaired after TBI. A distinction needs to be made between memories that were established prior to the injury (which will be largely intact) versus the acquisition of new information to be consolidated in memory and retrieved when required (which is the typical problem area after TBI). Knowing the stage at which the memory process is disrupted is also important – problems may occur at any of the initial encoding/acquisition (cf. ICF b1440 – short-term memory), consolidation (cf. ICF b1441 – long-term memory) and/or retrieval (cf. ICF b1442 – retrieval of memory) stages.

Similarly, 'executive function' is an umbrella term referring to 'specific mental functions especially dependent on the frontal lobes of the brain, including complex goal-directed behaviours such as decision-making, abstract thinking, planning and carrying out plans, mental flexibility, and deciding which behaviours are appropriate under what circumstances' [6, p. 57]. The factor that unites these superordinate and integrative functions is the capacity to *utilise* intellectual skills in a flexible and adaptive way to regulate behaviour. Although processing speed is a more unidimensional construct than memory or executive functions, a particular challenge in this area is to confirm that the underlying deficit is indeed processing speed, as opposed to other dysfunction which may masquerade and affect processing speed yet is not the underlying problem (e.g. inertia, depression and attentional problems can also affect processing speed).

Thus, it is not sufficient to say a client has a 'memory', 'executive' or 'processing speed' problem – rather, understanding the nature, stage of processing and severity of the impairment is crucial, along with the combined impact of other impairments and knowing about the way in which the client's 'memory' (or other) impairment will interfere with work tasks. Such information will also form the basis for providing the client with specific and targeted compensatory strategies to address his or her problem areas.

A detailed neuropsychological assessment is the first step in disability evaluation. Its purpose is to identify the client's cognitive strengths and weaknesses, which are not always readily apparent in interview. Disability evaluation should also involve motor-sensory impairments. A comprehensive vocational rehabilitation evaluation is also required (described in detail in section 12.6.1).

[1] It is noted that the ICF 3rd level categories for memory do not refer to these functional systems of memory; rather the focus is on the storage/retrieval processes (e.g. short-term/long-term memory).

12.5 Return to Work After Traumatic Brain Injury: A Literature Review

12.5.1 Rates of Return to Work

Outcomes in relation to return to work vary widely after TBI, particularly as a function of injury severity. Although a proportion of people are able to resume work at a similar level to their pre-injury employment, many people have reduced work hours compared to pre-injury, particularly after severe TBI [36]. Some also report that their work skills and performance are adversely affected [37]. For others with major disability resulting from the TBI, return to the workforce is not an option, and other avocational alternatives need to be considered. As a result of such changes, significant numbers experience decreased earnings from pre- to post-injury [38].

The Dikmen et al. [22] study referred to earlier in this chapter provided detailed examination of one of the largest, most representative and controlled outcome studies of TBI in civilians. The samples comprised a consecutive series of 466 patients with TBI admitted to a level 1 trauma hospital in Seattle, USA, along with two control groups (one with non-neurological trauma, $n = 124$, and the other consisted of 88 non-injured friends of the TBI patients, hence providing control for important demographic features). The TBI sample spanned the entire injury severity spectrum and was followed up at 12 months post-trauma.

A range of outcomes was reported, but in terms of work status, a significantly smaller percentage of the TBI group (49 %) was working at 12 months post-trauma compared to the trauma controls (63 %) or the 'friend controls' (82 %). Six TBI severity subgroups were compared, using a proxy measure of coma duration (time to follow commands), and a dose-response relationship was apparent within the TBI group. The least injury severity subgroup (time to follow commands less than 1 h post-injury) contained the largest proportion of those employed at 12 months (64 %), followed by 50 % and 51 % working for the next two severity subgroups (1–24 h and 1–6 days, respectively, post-injury), then 36 % working in the 1–2-week subgroup, 18 % in the 2–4-week subgroup and 6 % in the most severe subgroup (more than 1 month to follow commands).

The pattern of these results has been confirmed in other studies from different countries, using the duration of post-traumatic amnesia as the injury severity marker; return to work rates for mild TBI usually fall in the 75–80 % range (e.g. Refs. [37, 39]). Levels of returning to work after moderate injury may be lower, with van der Naalt and colleagues [39] reporting a 61 % return to work. In contrast, return to work rates for people with severe TBI usually fall within the 20–40 % range [40–42].

People who sustain a mild TBI and were employed at the time of their injury usually resume work rapidly, returning after an average of 9 working days, with 95 % back at work by 3 months post-injury [37]. By contrast, people with severe TBI generally take much longer and may not commence a vocational rehabilitation programme until 3–6 months post-injury. As a result of such differences, longitudinal studies documenting the trajectory of return to employment post-injury have found that the rates of people resuming mainstream competitive employment peak around the first or second year post-injury. The rate then remains stable or slowly declines over time [42–44].

Given that a large number of people, particularly those with severe TBI, are unable to return to mainstream competitive employment, other reported outcomes are relevant, including home duties, volunteer work and 'sheltered employment' (now referred to as disability segregated employment). Rates of people taking up these options range from 7 % to 18 % [37, 41]. Although these activities are important options in terms of meaningful occupation after TBI, they do not constitute mainstream competitive employment.

Belonging to an increasingly recognised subgroup are those adults who sustained their TBI as children; their vocational outcomes are also adversely impacted [45, 46]. Anderson et al. [47] studied outcomes for 124 young adults who sustained a mild, moderate or severe TBI between the ages of 0–16 years and were followed up at 13.7 years post-injury. Overall, young adults with a history of paediatric TBI were 1.7 times more likely to be unemployed or working in an unskilled capacity compared with the general population, 2.1 times less likely to be working in a skilled occupation and 1.6 times less likely to be working in a professional capacity.

Rates of return to work post TBI vary across studies and there are many factors influencing return to work outcomes. One important factor is the severity of injury. The return to work rate for mild TBI usually falls in the 75 % to 80 % range, moderate injury may be lower (61 % reported in the literature), whilst the return to work rate for severe TBI usually falls within the 20 % to 40 % range.

12.5.2 Prognostic Factors Associated with Return to Work

Identifying valid prognostic factors associated with return to work can assist in clinical decision making and setting rehabilitation goals with clients. In their systematic review, Nightingale et al. [48] highlighted the importance of predictive models for return to work, sampling variables from pre-injury, injury and post-injury domains in order to adequately identify key prognostic factors. Furthermore, the authors highlighted the importance of identifying prognostic factors from the *early* phase post-injury as being of maximum clinical value in assessing return to work potential.

Nightingale et al. [48] found that although concerns about the employability of people with TBI who were older or more poorly educated were commonly highlighted in the literature, these factors were rarely associated with lower rates of return to work in the methodologically strongest studies. However, there was evidence to suggest that pre-injury employment was positively associated with post-injury return to work. The second category, *injury severity*, can only really be tested in studies that include participants with more than one category of injury severity (e.g. mild vs. severe). In the only high-quality study in the review that investigated a broad range of injury severity among a large number of variables, Temkin et al. [49] found that injury severity was in fact the only predictor of return to work status. In terms of early *post-injury* predictors, Nightingale and colleagues [48] found limited evidence among good quality studies for any of the key domains of factors including cognitive (i.e. attention and processing speed, memory, executive functioning) or neurophysical impairment, functional status and community participation, highlighting the need for future research.

Van Velzen and colleagues [50] reviewed the evidence for return to work after TBI among prognostic variables grouped according to the ICF components (body function, activity, participation) and contextual (i.e. environmental, personal). The authors found limited evidence supporting any prognostic factors in any of the ICF domains and made an observation similar to Nightingale et al. [48] about the fragmented nature of the evidence base due to the large diversity of variables tested across studies. Further research is clearly required into prognostic factors.

In comparison to severe injuries, studies into prognostic factors after mild injuries have focused on persisting post-concussion symptoms or the presence of post-traumatic stress disorder [51–53]. Stulemeijer and colleagues [53] found that a combination of higher education (more than 11 years), absence of nausea and vomiting on admission to hospital, no additional extracranial injuries apart from the mild TBI and no severe pain soon after the injury was associated with a 95 % probability of full return to work at 6 months follow-up.

A large array of factors have been shown in various studies to predict return to work, including pre-injury factors (e.g., employment status, education history, type of employment), injury factors (e.g., severity), and post-injury factors (e.g., level of functioning, mental health status). Consensus has not yet been reached, however, regarding the most significant prognostic factors.

12.5.3 The Evidence Base for Vocational Rehabilitation After Traumatic Brain Injury

Vocational rehabilitation is the primary intervention for achieving return to work following TBI. Numerous vocational rehabilitation programmes are outlined in international studies [54], with the meta-analysis of Kendall et al. [55] finding

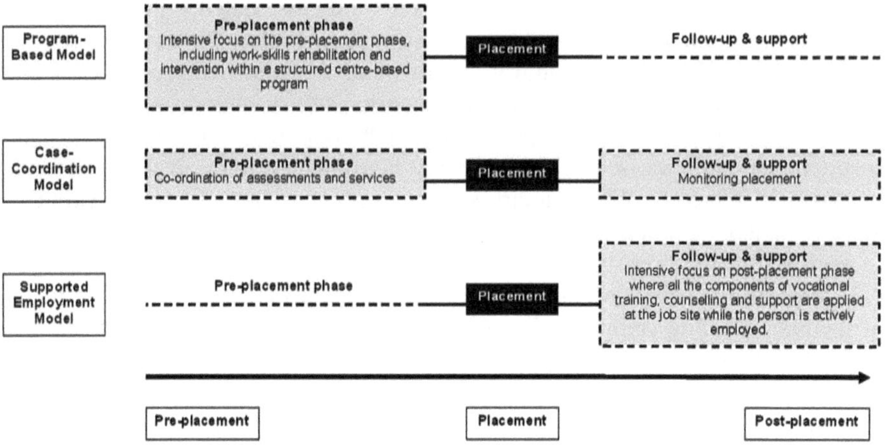

Fig. 12.1 Models of vocational rehabilitation

that the provision of vocational rehabilitation increased the likelihood of an earlier return to work. In a systematic review, Fadyl and McPherson [56] grouped vocational intervention programmes into three broad models, namely, supported employment, case coordination and programme based (see Fig. 12.1), and evaluated the evidence for each model type.

Programme-based models are centre-based programmes that focus mainly on the pre-placement phase including intensive work skills rehabilitation and intervention within a structured centre-based facility [56]. They are characterised as a *train and place* model. Most commonly, clients attend a structured outpatient programme for a number of weeks, participating in individual and/or group therapies with emphasis on cognitive, behavioural, psychosocial and/or metacognitive skills as well as education to families and employers, targeting return to work goals [57, 58]. Reporting on outcomes from this type of programme, Klonoff and colleagues [57] described 164 participants of whom 67 % achieved paid work or school, with 32 % resuming their 'pre-injury status'. Despite the positive outcomes from such individual studies, overall there was only *weak evidence* from the Fadyl and McPherson [56] review of improved outcomes for people with TBI completing programme-based vocational rehabilitation. Although programme-based models focus on addressing impairments, they provide only limited on-job support and long-term follow-up.

Case coordination is the most contemporary approach to vocational rehabilitation for clients with TBI. Rather than provide vocational rehabilitation sequentially after the medical rehabilitation phase has been completed, the case coordination approach involves the early commencement of vocational rehabilitation concurrently with medical rehabilitation, through the introduction of a vocational counsellor into the rehabilitation service. Programmes are designed to suit specific individual needs and provide opportunities to access other vocational rehabilitation elements, such as work trials or supported employment programmes through referral to external services [59]. In one study, Malec and Moessner [60] reported that 80 % of 138 participants in a case coordination approach remained in employment 1 year post-placement. Importantly, clients who were less than 12 months post-injury were placed significantly more quickly than clients more than 12 months post-injury (3.7 months vs. 6 months, respectively), highlighting the value of early intervention associated with this approach [59]. Fadyl and McPherson [56] concluded that there was a *moderate level* of evidence that the case coordination model improved employment outcomes for people with TBI.

Supported employment models were developed within the disability field in the late 1970s and then later trialled for applicability to acquired brain injury (e.g. [2, 61, 62]) (see Fig. 12.1). Supported employment takes a *place and train* approach in which individuals are first placed into a job and then all the components of vocational training, counselling and support are applied at the job site while the person is actively employed [63]. Components of place and train intervention include sourcing an appropriate work environment, job placement, job-site training and advocacy, ongoing assessment and retention/monitoring [64]. Wehman et al. [65] reported on a study of 87 clients who were all placed into a job using this model. These clients took 15 weeks, on average, to achieve stability in the placement and were working on average 31 h per week. In their review, Fadyl and McPherson [56] only found *weak evidence* for this model. Furthermore, despite early positive results, Wehman et al. [2] have found little implementation of the model with acquired brain injury populations outside the United States centre in which it was pioneered, either more broadly across the United States or internationally.

Hybrid approaches to vocational rehabilitation have also been developed, combining the three model elements in varying combinations, although these were not included in the Fadyl and MacPherson [56] review. Two United Kingdom examples of this approach have been published. The 'Rehab UK' programme [66] comprised three stages: centre-based cognitive training programme of 12 weeks duration, followed by work trial placement with job coaching and then job seeking for paid work and long-term monitoring. The 'working out' project, UK [67], comprises four phases: assessment, work preparation (individual and group settings), voluntary work trials and supported work placements (paid). Service-based outcomes of both programmes have reportedly been positive.

Vocational rehabilitation has been found to contribute significantly to positive outcomes for people with TBI. Three different models of service delivery have been identified in the literature: programme- based (focussing on preparing people for employment through centre-based activities or therapy), case co-ordination (organising services and steps to assist an individual achieve independent employment) and support employment (direct employment placement followed by intensive on-job support). Some vocational rehabilitation services offer a hybrid approach, combining elements of these three models.

12.6 Vocational Rehabilitation in Practice: The State of the Field in Traumatic Brain Injury

This section presents the practical application of vocational rehabilitation for clients with TBI, and a pathway flowchart is presented in Fig. 12.2.

12.6.1 Assessment

Accurate and thorough assessment is crucial for developing safe, appropriate and realistic vocational goals following TBI. A systematic assessment process is required, which is tailored to suit each client's goals and circumstances (see also Sect. 12.2 for general information on evaluating people with TBI). More specifically, Stergiou-Kita et al. [68] describe the process of vocational evaluation for people with TBI which comprises seven steps:

Step 1: Define the purpose of assessment. Assessments are requested for a variety of rehabilitation purposes, including assessing a client's readiness to commence employment, determining the suitability of returning to pre-injury employment, identifying restrictions in developing a return to work plan and providing a profile of abilities and deficits to formulate a new vocational goal.

Step 2: Intake information. Gathering background information from relevant sources, including both written reports and discussions with members of the treating team to compile a client file. In this step, any medical issues that complicate return to work, such as seizures, balance and other sensory deficits, are documented.

Step 3: Assessment of the person. Examining multiple performance components to develop a profile of the client's current functional status. Assessment protocols may be specific to the service, but should contain the methods of interview, observation and measurement. Assessment generally commences with interviewing the client to discuss his or her work history and perspective of the changes resulting from injury. Involving family member(s) in the interview process is important to gain details the client may be unable to recall, confirm the accuracy of the client's responses (or discrepancy in perspectives related to current functioning) and gain additional information not presented by the client.

Functional Capacity Evaluation. As described earlier in this chapter, TBI can result in multiple impairments within motor-sensory, cognitive and behavioural domains. Additional biomechanical restrictions can arise from multi-trauma incurred in the accident. There is no single tool that will address all performance domains. Instead activities are selected from a set of tools, depending on the client's presenting problems and the purpose of assessment, to create an individualised assessment process:

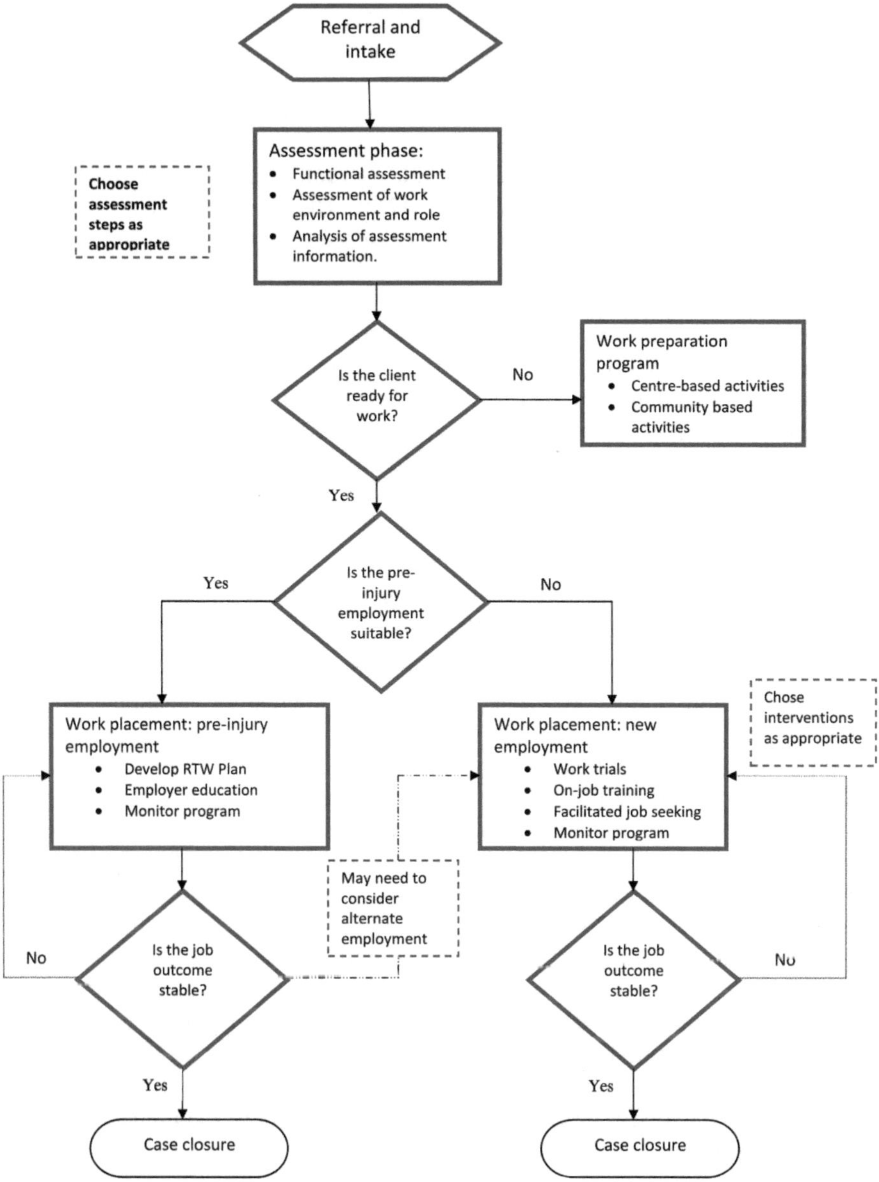

Fig. 12.2 Pathway flowchart

- Assessment tools addressing *biomechanical* aspects of function have been well developed for use in vocational rehabilitation (e.g. Valpar, Work Evaluation Systems Technology, Isernhagen work system, the Blankenship system, WorkHab), although they fall short of adequately assessing the domains affected by TBI. Such tools focus mostly on manual handling; additional tools are required to assess *sensory-motor* performance components, including balance and upper-limb coordination (see systematic review of Tate et al. [34], for instruments to assess sequelae of TBI).

- Specific and standardised instruments to assess *cognitive* functioning applied to a vocational context are lacking. Neuropsychological testing is commonly undertaken following TBI which provides a profile of cognitive impairments and preserved abilities (see also Sect. 12.2). The most helpful neuropsychological evaluations will also take into account the client's functioning in a work environment which may differ from the clinical setting, depending on the task familiarity, task demands and elements of the social and physical environment.

  Predictability power can be increased through observing performance in simulated tasks. Work tasks can either be tailored for each client, with observations measured using tools such as the Assessment of Work Performance [69] or Perceive Recall Plan Perform [70] or alternatively using prescribed tasks contained within a tool such as the Assessment of Motor and Process Skills [71]. With respect to those cognitive aspects that are most relevant to a return to work context, a literature review by Donovan et al. [72] identified six constructs for assessment: attention, memory, speed of processing, executive functioning, social communication and emotional management; these domains also represent a comprehensive sampling of neurocognitive functioning after TBI in general.

Vocational Profiling. Clients who are unable to resume their pre-injury employment will require further assessment to develop alternative vocational options. Commercial tools that rate a client's interests, preferences and skills are widely used in vocational rehabilitation (e.g. Career Assessment Inventory [73], Occupational Search Inventory [74]). Such tools have the advantage of generating job options the client may otherwise have not identified, though self-rated questionnaires need to be used cautiously with this population. Without the opportunity to test their abilities in a work setting post-injury, clients may complete the inventory based on their pre-injury skills, which are often not reflective of current abilities, thereby arriving at inappropriate and potentially unsafe vocational goals. Any impairment in insight and self-awareness will compound the valid completion of self-report instruments. Aptitude and achievement testing may also be required to both observe and measure aspects of literacy, numeracy and learning capacity (e.g. Wide Range Achievement Test [75]). The analysis of transferrable skills and labour market factors, as well as consideration of training requirements for the identified vocational goals, completes this assessment.

Step 4: Assessment of the environment. Workplace assessment examines the context in which the occupational performance occurs, encompassing both physical and social contexts. The primary physical elements of a work environment to consider for people with TBI who are returning to work include the following: light, noise, level of distractions, heat and potential safety hazards. The social context includes aspects such as the following: attitudes towards individuals with disabilities, capacity to provide accommodations, supervision structures, the social milieu and the injured worker's pre-injury relationships with management and co-workers. These aspects are observable at the workplace, and further details can be gained through discussions with the client and workplace management.

Step 5: Assessment of the work role. Specific assessment of the client's job requirements encompasses work hours, schedule of breaks, pace of work, task complexity, productivity targets, task variation and multitasking demands. Obtaining a job description from the employer will provide an overview of the responsibilities. Job roles containing manual operations can be assessed via observation, with either the client or co-worker demonstrating the task, allowing for observation of physical, cognitive and communication performance demands. Structuring of observations and rating of demands can be achieved using a tool such as the Toronto Behavioural/Cognitive Checklist [76], a 16-item checklist that rates demands on a 4-point scale. For jobs that are not possible to observe (e.g. management and professional roles), this same checklist can be used as an interview tool to identify the most demanding aspects of the client's role.

Step 6: Analysis of assessment information. The assessment process concludes when saturation of data is achieved. A comparison of the workplace demands and the client's current functional status will identify strengths as well as the impact of injury on work reintegration. Specific consideration of the client's level of insight into the changes caused by TBI and their stage of adjustment is required. In addition, the client's condition may continue to change over time, while further neurological recovery occurs, which makes for a complex and dynamic synthesis of assessment data. Throughout this process it is important to achieve a balance of the client's strengths as well as deficits. It is often the positive aspects that make a work option viable.

Step 7: Recommendations. The conclusion and recommendations will vary across cases, depending on the purpose of the assessment and the client's circumstances. Statements may include whether the client is ready to commence vocational activities or whether the client is able to return to their pre-injury workplace, in what capacity and with what specified compensatory strategies. Alternatively, it may be recommended that the client participate in a pre-vocational programme or he/she may be presented with alternative job roles and a plan for seeking new work.

> Assessment processes are tailored to each client, depending on their employment circumstances and presenting functional difficulties. Information will be gained from multiple assessment methods: interview (client, family, employer, clinicians) measurement (FCE components) and observation (task performance, workplace environment).

12.6.2 Work Preparation

An assessment may conclude that the client is not yet 'work ready', and further time and rehabilitation is required to upgrade physical and cognitive work abilities. This requires coordination with the treating team to incorporate work preparation activities into the therapy routine. Following TBI, clients are often deconditioned due to the period of hospitalisation and reduced activity levels post discharge. Furthermore, home life may under-challenge cognitive abilities, and upgrading of activities is required to simulate the demands of working. Activity options will need to be individualised to match the client's interests, vocational goal, the stage of rehabilitation and support needs. For people with severe TBI, the work preparation phase may extend for many months, with gradual upgrading of the programme over time, so that clients transit from one activity to the next in line with progressive improvements in their condition. By contrast, individuals with mild injury and/or good neurological recovery are often best placed directly into paid work for a graduated return to work programme.

There are two main approaches to work preparation:

Centre-based work preparation:
Group activities are usually discussion based or task based. Discussion groups include topics such as education about TBI and compensatory strategies to manage cognitive difficulties. Task groups require resources (such as a carpentry workshop) to upgrade physical work tolerances and information processing abilities through completing prescribed tasks, within a regular routine. In this environment, it is also possible to address independent transport, punctuality, attendance, workplace behaviour and communication. Individual vocational counselling is continued during this phase to refine the vocational goal and support the client in planning the transition back to work or into a new career area.

Community-based work preparation:
Where possible, clients also engage in mainstream community activities. Voluntary work provides a meaningful pre-vocational activity which can often be tailored to the client's work goals. Support will be required to source the placement and provide on-job training and monitoring (as appropriate). Undertaking a training course at a local college is another option, which may be acquiring a new skill (e.g. a computer course) or specific to the client's industry (e.g. revising laboratory techniques, completing a welding certificate, practising forklift driving).

12.6.3 Work Placement: Pre-injury Employment

Returning to the pre-injury employment provides the best chance of success following TBI, for a number of reasons. First, the loyalty and established relationship between employer and employee provides the basis for commitment and flexibility in accommodating altered working conditions. Second, the client feels comfortable and supported in returning to the familiar social networks in the workplace (thereby reducing anxiety); third, returning to familiar tasks and routine minimises the need for new learning (which may be complicated by memory impairments resulting from the TBI). A person with mild TBI may manage the return to work programme independently with their employer and treating doctor, although the input of a vocational rehabilitation provider will be required for more complex cases. The key aspects involved in facilitating a return to work programme are as follows:

Timeframe of return to work commencement – It is important to commence discussions with the pre-injury employer at an early stage post-injury to preserve the job opportunity and gather details regarding the client's job and workplace culture. However, the timing of work commencement requires more careful consideration. Commencing work too early can be just as problematic as delaying return to work, because the impact of cognitive and personality changes may take some time to become clear.

Graduated return to work programmes – Employers do not commonly encounter TBI and will therefore require guidance via a written plan that specifies the schedule of upgrading tasks and hours, specific restrictions and compensatory strategies.

- The routine commences with part-time hours to pre-empt fatigue, with gradual upgrading over time. This process may take months or years and may plateau for some periods before further upgrading is possible.
- Compensatory strategies allow the client to operate more independently. Kowalske, et al. [77] outlined general strategies for the return to work programme: doing more demanding tasks when alert, increasing the level of structure and reducing distractions, note taking throughout the day, double checking work and focussing on more routine and familiar work.
- Once the client has commenced work, regular monitoring of the programme proceeds. The employer provides direct supervision and/or support to the client and feedback to the vocational rehabilitation provider to adjust the programme and problem-solve any issues. Following TBI, people generally retain their procedural memory and therefore do not require task training to 'relearn' their job role. In many cases there are no observable deficits, and subtle changes take some time to emerge. Therefore, monitoring for the duration of the programme is important to allow for extended neurological recovery.

Providing information to the employer about the client's injury is an important aspect of developing the return to work programme and must be tailored to each case. This can be a delicate undertaking, particularly when the degree to which the assessed difficulties will impact on work is uncertain. Providing extensive information about TBI may be unnecessary and can overwhelm or alarm the employer; however, too little information may underprepare them.

A rehabilitation priority is to investigate the option for a client to return to their pre-injury employer as this pathway is likely to result in the best outcome. Early discussions are held with the employer to exchange information even if the client will not immediately commence work. A graduated return to work programme is recommended following TBI, to pace the upgrading of hours and duties over time.

12.6.4 Work Placement: New Employment

If a client is unable to resume work with their pre-injury employer, or indeed was unemployed at the time of injury, an alternative job placement programme is required. There are no 'typical jobs' that people with TBI seek. Given the diversity of each client's background, individual vocational goals are generated through the process of vocational assessment. Undoubtedly, the greatest challenge for a vocational rehabilitation provider is in assisting a client with considerable difficulties affecting their work capacity to obtain competitive employment. People with severe impairments can still perform meaningful work tasks, although they often lack the capacity to manage full-time hours and the full range of duties stated in a job description. They are therefore not competitive in applying for work in the mainstream market.

It is often necessary to train a client with TBI to acquire new skills to carry out work duties. Training techniques used widely in brain injury rehabilitation to overcome memory and executive impairments include chaining and errorless learning:

- *Chaining*: step-by-step instruction following a task analysis, via either forward or backward task instruction. With forward chaining, the client performs the first step of the task with gradual addition of further steps as each successive step is mastered. With backward chaining, the trainer provides substantial assistance with the initial steps and allows the client to independently complete the final steps of the task.
- *Errorless learning*: the trainer demonstrates a task to be performed in the correct way and closely observes the client, preventing him or her from straying from the instructed technique in order to prevent errors. This is useful for those with more severe cognitive impairments impacting memory and planning/problem-solving abilities on the grounds that it prevents the inadvertent consolidation of the incorrect response.

A variety of job placement methods have been reported internationally. Different employment legislation, funding models and service systems influence the approach taken at the local level. Irrespective of placement methods, achieving the right job match is crucial, that is, matching the client's skills (accounting for the complex interaction of injury-related deficits, premorbid work history and social factors) to fit an available job role. Outlined below are common job placement methods for people with TBI (see also Sect. 12.5.3 for an evidence-based review of their effectiveness):

- *Work trials* – A work trial is an unpaid work placement that provides opportunity for practical assessment, upgrading of work skills, updating work experience for the résumé and circumventing the formal recruitment process to achieve paid work. It is best if the client is an extra member of the team, so that he or she is not required to work full hours or achieve the same level of productivity as existing staff. The duration of placements will vary although a period of up to 6 months may be required to allow the client to adjust to the workplace and reach their full capacity. The vocational rehabilitation provider supports the placement through providing additional on-site training, insurance coverage (if required) and employer negotiation. Not all work trial placements will achieve a paid work outcome, and multiple placements may be required to fine-tune the job match and achieve paid work. In a survey of TBI vocational rehabilitation professionals in Australia [78], work trials were the intervention considered to be most effective, with traditional job seeking perceived as the least effective intervention.
- *The 'place and train' model* (see Sect. 12.5.3) allows for open disclosure of injury and therefore tends to most suit those people with severe disability, requiring ongoing support at the workplace. The drawbacks of this approach include the presence of the job coach possibly limiting the social inclusion of the client in the workplace; it is also very expensive to provide this level of one-to-one support, and there is a limit to the job roles in which the coach can provide training [79].
- *Facilitated job seeking* – some clients, particularly those with mild injury and no obvious deficits may apply for advertised positions, with background support from the vocational rehabilitation provider (e.g. prepare résumé, cover letters, assist with online applications, interview training). Disclosure of injury is an issue that arises for clients presenting to employers independently. There is no consistent approach to injury disclosure. Coaching through methods of injury disclosure and presenting information favourably is part of the facilitated job seeking process. Utilising the client's social contacts may be useful in sourcing a new work option and eases the injury disclosure issue. O'Brien [78] refers to this approach as 'accessing the hidden job market'.

Clients requiring a new job will often require a more intensive vocational rehabilitation program to achieve a job placement and learn new skills. Where possible, it is best to align the job goal closely to his/her previous work experience to utilise intact industry knowledge and minimise the need for new learning.

12.6.5 Post-Placement Support

In addition to the barriers encountered in achieving paid work, it is widely recognised that the TBI client group has difficulty in sustaining employment. For instance, Wehman and colleagues [80] found in their study that only 18 (44 %) of the 41 individuals with severe TBI placed into employment were able to sustain their positions. The remaining 23 were either placed into a second job ($n = 10$, 24 % of the total group) or remained unemployed ($n = 13$, 32 % of the total group). Therefore, interventions for both gaining and maintaining employment are essential components of vocational rehabilitation in TBI [81].

In terms of reasons for job separation, Macaden et al. [82] referred to studies by Wehman et al. [80] and Sale [83] in which poor behavioural regulation abilities were found to most commonly cause work failure. This included such issues as verbal outbursts, difficulties in interpreting and responding appropriately to social situations and disinhibited behaviour. Other factors found to relate to sustaining employment include the following: intrinsic motivation, coping skills and implementation of strategies, work that is closely linked to clients' interests, pre-injury personality traits, supportive employers, 'buddying' (working alongside an allocated co-worker), transportation demands, availability of suitable duties, flexibility in tailoring workload and the vocational rehabilitation provider's capacity for providing appropriate placements and follow-up [82].

There is also evidence that intensive support improves vocational outcomes for people with TBI. For instance, Catalano et al. [84] reported data on 7,366 cases that had completed a vocational rehabilitation programme. A positive relationship was found between case hours and outcomes, suggesting that greater investment in direct client support contributed to better outcomes.

Additional support will be required for those clients requiring more intensive training that the new employer is able to provide. Supervisors unfamiliar with brain injury will expect that the demonstration of a task on one occasion is sufficient for a new worker to retain the knowledge. However, people with TBI invariably require repetition to consolidate the new memory, as well as very gradual exposure to additional tasks over the initial orientation period. Additionally, episodic on-job training may be warranted to cope with changes in the job role that occur over the longer term, due to difficulty generalising learning to different situations [81].

Suggestions for providing post-placement support are as follows:

(i) *Tailor supports and intensity of intervention for each client*
People with TBI require varying degrees of workplace support. Certain characteristics of each client, their job and the workplace will determine the individual need for training support on site. Younger clients, with little or no prior work experience, will generally require more on-site support than older clients, because they need to establish the requisite workplace behaviours.

(ii) *Work and lifestyle balance*
Fatigue is a common problem following TBI that tends to persist for the longer term and impacts greatly on the ability to sustain a routine of multiple

activities. Work can be so taxing that little energy is left for other activities, which becomes an unsustainable lifestyle. In turn, fatigue will often cause headaches and irritability and lead to other issues in work performance. A permanent part-time work schedule is often the best solution, and clients may need regular short holidays from work to 'recharge'.

(iii) *Establishing natural supports*
When providing on-site training, the vocational rehabilitation provider involves other workplace personnel to establish natural supports and gradually withdraw the external support. Natural support is defined as 'a type of support that is provided for the worker by the employer, co-worker or mentor. These supports are more permanent and ingrained in the workplace than supports provided by the job coach from the outside supported employment program' [81].
The vocational rehabilitation provider continues to monitor the placement until it is considered stable. Job stability is achieved when a client is able to perform at an acceptable level for the employer and manage within the support systems available at the workplace. In some cases a client will have upgraded to full pre-injury status, although in many cases, the client will maintain a part-time work schedule, with permanent restrictions in place.

Commencing work post TBI is not the last step of the vocational rehabilitation programme. Continued monitoring post-placement is required to ensure that the programme is suiting the needs of both client and employer. Clients may require assistance to compensate for cognitive impairments, manage issues/incidents at work, co-ordinate their routine, learn new processes and adapt to change.

12.6.6 Alternatives to Mainstream, Competitive Employment

For many people with severe disability resulting from TBI, paid work is not an option available to them. Others whose attempts at return to work have been unsuccessful also find themselves seeking a replacement for the work role. Unfortunately, suitable activity options in the community that fulfil the nonmonetary benefits of working for young adults are scarce. Options that may exist include:

(i) *Volunteer work* can provide a more flexible routine and task structure with less pressure than competitive paid work.
(ii) *Disability segregated employment* (previously known as 'sheltered work') is offered by disability agencies, mostly operating in factory environments or via mobile work crews. The employees are generally paid a small wage to supplement welfare payments. In our experience, people with TBI have been reluctant to take up such employment when the service's predominant client group is people with intellectual disabilities.

12.7 Conclusions

Outcome after TBI spans the gamut of possibilities from death, the minimally conscious states, severe and moderate disability, through to good and even complete recovery. The evidence is overwhelming that those with milder degrees of injury have a very good chance of returning to the workforce. The involvement of a vocational rehabilitation professional can facilitate this process and is particularly important in situations where the client may have residual neurocognitive impairments that are not readily apparent yet which will interfere significantly with work performance. The more severe degrees of TBI can profoundly and permanently alter a person's life. Huge efforts are made by people with TBI, their families, health professionals and community services to maximise their recovery and community integration. Securing and maintaining work is one of the key milestones in a journey that, for many people, involves considerable challenges, multiple attempts and gradual redefinition of their work identity. Vocational rehabilitation plays a critical role in assisting people with TBI to maximise their opportunities for achieving employment. A service approach that provides multiple avenues for work placement, with elements of flexibility, advocacy and continuity, is required for this client group.

Study Questions

1. How long does it take to recover from a TBI?
2. What are the common neurocognitive impairments after TBI that are likely to impact return to work? In which domain of the ICF are they classified?
3. Describe the three main models of vocational rehabilitation interventions and the strength of the evidence for the effectiveness of each of the models.
4. Describe the elements in a case coordination model of vocational rehabilitation for people with TBI.
5. Outline the seven steps for systematic assessment in vocational rehabilitation.
6. What is meant by 'work preparation' in the context of vocational rehabilitation for TBI and what is involved?
7. What are the elements of a graduated return to work programme and why are they important?
8. When a person is *not* able to return to their pre-injury employment due to neurocognitive disability and needs to acquire new skills, what are two techniques used in brain injury rehabilitation to teach competency in new tasks?
9. Why is it important to provide post-placement support for people with TBI and how would you go about this?
10. Reflecting on the case study presented at the opening of this chapter, in what way did the TBI impact Peter's ability to return to work?

References

1. Wagner AK, Hammond FM, Sasser HC, Wiercisiewski D. Return to productive activity after traumatic brain injury: relationship with measures of disability, handicap, and community integration. Arch Phys Med Rehabil. 2002;83(1):107–14.
2. Wehman P, Targett P, West M, Kregel J. Productive work and employment for persons with traumatic brain injury: what have we learned after 20 years? J Head Trauma Rehabil. 2005; 20(2):115–27.
3. van Velzen JM, van Bennekom CAM, Edelaar MJA, Sluiter JK, Frings-Dresen MHW. How many people return to work after acquired brain injury? A systematic review. Brain Inj. 2009;23(6):473–88.
4. Lefrancois GR. The lifespan. 4th ed. Belmont: Wadsworth Publishing; 1993.
5. Access Economics. The economic cost of spinal cord injury and traumatic brain injury in Australia. Melbourne: Victorian Neurotrauma Institute; 2008.
6. World Health Organization. International classification of functioning, disability and health. Geneva: World Health Organization; 2001.
7. Thurman DJ, Alverson C, Dunn KA, Guerrero J, Snieze JE. Traumatic brain injury in the United States: a public health perspective. J Head Trauma Rehabil. 1999;14(6):602–15.
8. Kraus JF, Black MA, Hessol N, Ley P, Rokaw W, Sullivan C, Bowers S, Knowlton S, Marshall L. The incidence of acute brain injury and serious impairment in a defined population. Am J Epidemiol. 1984;119(2):186–201.
9. Galarneau MR, Woodruff SI, Dye JL, Mohrle CR, Wade AL. Traumatic brain injury during operation Iraqi freedom: findings from the United States navy-marine corps combat trauma registry. J Neurosurg. 2008;108:950–7.
10. Tagliaferri F, Compagnone C, Korsic M, Servadei F, Kraus J. A systematic review of brain injury epidemiology in Europe. Acta Neurochir (Wien). 2006;148:255–68.
11. Kraus JF, McArthur DL. Epidemiologic aspects of brain injury. Neurol Clin. 1996;14(2): 435–50.
12. Fortune N, Wen X. The definition, incidence and prevalence of acquired brain injury in Australia. Canberra: Australian Institute of Health and Welfare; 1999.
13. Tate RL, McDonald S, Lulham JM. Incidence of hospital-treated traumatic brain injury in an Australian community. Aust NZ J Public Health. 1998;22:419–23.
14. Baguley IJ, Nott MT, Howie AA, Simpson GK, Browne S, King AC, Cotter RE, Hodgkinson A. Late mortality after severe traumatic brain injury in New South Wales: a multicentre study. Med J Aust. 2012;196:40–5.
15. Ventura T, Harrison-Felix C, Carlson N, DiGuiseppi C, Gabella B, Brown A, DeVivo M, Whiteneck G. Mortality after discharge from acute care hospitalization with traumatic brain injury: a population-based study. Arch Phys Med Rehabil. 2010;91:20–9.
16. Tate RL, Broe GA, Cameron ID, Hodgkinson AE, Soo CA. Pre-injury, injury and early post-injury predictors of long-term functional and psychosocial recovery after severe traumatic brain injury. Brain Impair. 2005;6(2):75–89.
17. Langlois J, Rutland-Brown W, Thomas K. Traumatic brain injury in the United States: emergency department visits, hospitalizations, and deaths. Atlanta: Centers for Disease Control and Prevention, National Center for Injury Prevention and Control; 2004.
18. Teasdale G, Jennett B. Assessment of coma and impaired consciousness: a practical scale. Lancet. 1974;2(7873):81–4.
19. Tate RL. A compendium of tests, scales and questionnaires: the practitioner's guide to measuring outcomes after acquired brain impairment. Hove: Psychology Press; 2010.
20. Jennett B, Teasdale G. Management of head injuries. Philadelphia: F. A. Davis Company; 1981.
21. Carroll LJ, Cassidy JD, Holm L, Kraus J, Coronado VG. Methodological issues and research recommendations for mild traumatic brain injury: the WHO Collaborating Centre Task Force on mild traumatic brain injury. J Rehabil Med. 2004;43 (Suppl):113–25.

22. Dikmen SS, Ross BL, Machamer JE, Temkin NR. One year psychosocial outcome in head injury. J Int Neuropsychol Soc. 1995;1:67–77.
23. Jennett B, Bond M. Assessment of outcome after severe brain damage: a practical scale. Lancet. 1975;305(7905):480–4.
24. Whyte J, Hart T, Laborde A, Rosenthal M. Rehabilitation issues in traumatic brain injury. In: DeLisa JA, Gans MB, Walsh NE, et al., editors. Physical medicine and rehabilitation: principles and practice, vol. 2. 4th ed. Philadelphia: Lippincott Williams and Wilkins; 2005. p. 1677–713.
25. Lammi MH, Smith VH, Tate RL, Taylor CM. The minimally conscious state and recovery potential: a follow-up study 2–5 years after traumatic brain injury. Arch Phys Med Rehabil. 2005;86:746–54.
26. Stuss DT, Buckle L. Traumatic brain injury: neuropsychological deficits and evaluation at different stages of recovery and in different pathologic subtypes. J Head Trauma Rehabil. 1992;7(2):40–9.
27. Carroll LJ, Cassidy JD, Peloso PM, Borg J, von Holst H, Holm L, Paniak C, Pépin M. Prognosis for mild traumatic brain injury: results of the WHO Collaborating Centre Task Force on mild traumatic brain injury. J Rehabil Med. 2004;43 (Suppl):84–105.
28. Tate RL, Harris RD, Cameron ID, Myles BM, Winstanley JB, Hodgkinson AE, Baguley IJ, Harradine PG, On behalf of the Brain Injury Outcomes Study (BIOS) Group. Recovery of impairments after severe traumatic brain injury: findings from a prospective, multicentre study. Brain Impair. 2006;7(1):1–15.
29. Laxe S, Zasler N, Selb M, Tate R, Tormos JM, Bernabeu M. Development of the International Classification of Functioning, Disability and Health core sets for traumatic brain injury: an international consensus process. Brain Inj. 2013;27(4):379–87.
30. Escorpizo R, Ekholm J, Gmünder H-P, Cieza A, Kostanjsek N, Stucki G. Developing a core set to describe functioning in vocational rehabilitation using the International Classification of Functioning, Disability, and Health (ICF). J Occup Rehabil. 2010;20:502–11.
31. Finger ME, Escorpizo R, Glässel A, Gmünder HP, Lückenkemper M, Chan C, Fritz J, Studer U, Ekholm J, Kostanjsek N, Stucki G, Cieza A. ICF Core Set for vocational rehabilitation: results of an international consensus conference. Disabil Rehabil. 2012;34(5):429–38.
32. Koskinen S, Hokkinen E-M, Sarajuuri J, Alaranta H. Applicability of the ICF checklist to traumatically brain-injured patients in post-acute rehabilitation settings. J Rehabil Med. 2007;39:467–72.
33. Lezak MD, Howieson DB, Bigler ED, Tranel D. Neuropsychological assessment. 5th ed. New York: Oxford University Press; 2012.
34. Tate RL, Godbee K, Sigmundsdottir L. A systematic review of assessment tools for adults used in traumatic brain injury research. NeuroRehabilitation. 2013;32:729–50.
35. Baddeley AD, Kopelman MD, Wilson BA, editors. Handbook of memory disorders. 2nd ed. Hoboken: Wiley; 2002.
36. Agency for Clinical Innovation. Investigation of vocational programs and outcomes for people with traumatic brain injury in New South Wales. Sydney: Brain Injury Rehabilitation Directorate, Agency for Clinical Innovation; 2013.
37. Powell TJ, Collin C, Sutton K. A follow-up study of patients hospitalized after minor head injury. Disabil Rehabil. 1996;18(5):231–7.
38. Johnstone B, Vessell R, Bounds T, Hoskins S, Sherman A. Predictors of success for state vocational rehabilitation clients with traumatic brain injury. Arch Phys Med Rehabil. 2003; 84(2):161–7.
39. van der Naalt J, van Zomeren A, Sluiter W, Minderhoud J. One year outcome in mild to moderate head injury: the predictive value of acute injury characteristics related to complaints and return to work. J Neurol Neurosurg Psychiatry. 1999;66(2):207–13.
40. Harradine PG, Winstanley JB, Tate R, Cameron ID, Baguley IJ, Harris RD. Severe traumatic brain injury in New South Wales: comparable outcomes for rural and urban residents. Med J Aust. 2004;181(3):130–4.
41. Lippert-Grüner M, Lefering R, Svestkova O. Functional outcome at 1 vs. 2 years after severe traumatic brain injury. Brain Inj. 2007;21(10):1001–5.

42. Sander AM, Kreutzer JS, Rosenthal M, Delmonico R, Young ME. A multicenter longitudinal investigation of return to work and community integration following traumatic brain injury. J Head Trauma Rehabil. 1996;11(5):70–84.
43. Graumeijer E, Heijenbrok-Kal MH, Haitsma IK, Ribbers M. A prospective study on employment outcome 3 years after moderate to severe traumatic brain injury. Arch Phys Med Rehabil. 2012;93:993–9.
44. Olver JH, Ponsford JL, Curran CA. Outcome following traumatic brain injury: a comparison between 2 and 5 years after injury. Brain Inj. 1996;10(11):841–8.
45. Anderson V, Brown S, Newitt H, Hoile H. Long-term outcome from childhood traumatic brain injury: intellectual ability, personality, and quality of life. Neuropsychology. 2011;25(2):176–84.
46. Nybo T, Sianio M, Müller K. Stability of vocational outcome in adulthood after moderate to severe preschool brain injury. J Int Neuropsychol Soc. 2004;10:719–23.
47. Anderson V, Brown S, Newitt H, Hoile H. Educational, vocational, psychosocial, and quality of life outcomes for adult survivors of childhood traumatic brain injury. J Head Trauma Rehabil. 2009;24(5):303–12.
48. Nightingale EJ, Soo CA, Tate RL. A systematic review of early prognostic factors for return to work after traumatic brain injury. Brain Impair. 2007;8(2):101–42.
49. Temkin NR, Holubkov R, Machamer JE, Winn HR, Dikmen SS. Classification and regression trees (CART) for prediction of function at 1 year following head trauma. J Neurosurg. 1995;82:764–71.
50. van Velzen JM, van Bennekom CAM, Edelaar MJA, Sluiter JK, Frings-Dresen MHW. Prognostic factors of return to work after acquired brain injury: a systematic review. Brain Inj. 2009;23:385–95.
51. Fourtassi M, Hajjioui A, El Ouahabi A, Benmassaoud H, Hajjaj-Hassouni N, El Khamlichi A. Long term outcome following mild traumatic brain injury in Moroccan patients. Clin Neurol Neurosurg. 2011;113:716–20.
52. Friedland JF, Dawson DR. Function after motor vehicle accidents: a prospective study of mild head injury and posttraumatic stress. J Nerv Ment Dis. 2001;189:426–34.
53. Stulemeijer M, van der Werf S, Borm GF, Vos PE. Early prediction of favourable recovery 6 months after mild traumatic brain injury. J Neurol Neurosurg Psychiatry. 2008;79:936–42.
54. Tyerman A. Vocational rehabilitation after traumatic brain injury: models and services. NeuroRehabilitation. 2012;31(1):51–62.
55. Kendall E, Muenchberger H, Gee T. Vocational rehabilitation following traumatic brain injury: a quantitative synthesis of outcome studies. J Vocat Rehabil. 2006;25:149–60.
56. Fadyl JK, McPherson KM. Approaches to vocational rehabilitation after traumatic brain injury: a review of the evidence. J Head Trauma Rehabil. 2009;24(3):195–212.
57. Klonoff PS, Lamb DG, Henderson SW. Milieu-based neurorehabilitation in patients with traumatic brain injury: outcome at up to 11 years postdischarge. Arch Phys Med Rehabil. 2001;81(11):1535–7.
58. Ownsworth T. A metacognitive contextual approach for facilitating return to work following acquired brain injury: three descriptive case studies. Work. 2010;36(4):381–8.
59. Buffington AL, Malec JF. The vocational rehabilitation continuum: maximizing outcomes through bridging the gap from hospital to community-based services. J Head Trauma Rehabil. 1997;12(5):1–13.
60. Malec JF, Moessner AM. Replicated positive results for the VCC model of vocational intervention after ABI within the social model of disability. Brain Inj. 2006;20(3):227–36.
61. Gamble D, Moore CL. Supported employment: disparities in vocational rehabilitation outcomes, expenditures and service time for persons with traumatic brain injury. J Vocat Rehabil. 2003;19(1):47–57.
62. Wehman P, Kregel J, Keyser-Marcus L, Sherron-Targett P, Campbell L, West M, Cifu DX. Supported employment for persons with traumatic brain injury: a preliminary investigation of long-term follow-up costs and program efficiency. Arch Phys Med Rehabil. 2003;84(2):192–6.

63. Babineau JL. The value of early placement in a supported employment program for individuals with traumatic brain injury. Work. 1998;10(2):137–46.
64. Chestnut RM, Carney N, Maynard H, Patterson P, Mann NC, Helfand M. Rehabilitation for traumatic brain injury (Report No. 99-E006). Rockville: Agency for Health Care Policy and Research; 1999.
65. Wehman PH, West MD, Kregel J, Sherron P, Kreutzer JS. Return to work for persons with severe traumatic brain injury: a data-based approach to program development. J Head Trauma Rehabil. 1995;10(1):27–39.
66. Murphy L, Chamberlain E, Weir J, Berry A, Nathaniel-James D, Agnew R. Effectiveness of vocational rehabilitation following acquired brain injury: preliminary evaluation of a UK specialist rehabilitation programme. Brain Inj. 2006;20(11):1119–29.
67. Tyerman A, Young K. Vocational rehabilitation after severe traumatic brain injury: II-specialist interventions and outcomes. J Occup Psychol Employ Disabil. 2000;2(2):13–20.
68. Stergiou-Kita M, Dawson D, Rappolt S. An integrated review of the processes and factors relevant to vocational evaluation following traumatic brain injury. J Occup Rehabil. 2011; 21(3):374–94.
69. Sandqvist JL, Tornquist KB, Henriksson CM. Assessment of Work Performance (AWP) – development of an instrument. Work. 2006;26:379–87.
70. Bootes K, Chapparo CJ. Cognitive and behavioural assessment of people with traumatic brain injury in the workplace: occupational therapists' perceptions. Work. 2002;19:255–68.
71. Fisher AG. Assessment of motor and process skills. 3rd ed. Fort Collins: Three Star Press; 1997.
72. Donovan NJ, Heaton SC, Kimberg CI, Wen P, Waid-Ebbs JK, Coster W, Singletary F, Velozo CA. Conceptualizing functional cognition in traumatic brain injury rehabilitation. Brain Inj. 2011;25(4):348–64.
73. Johansson CB. Career Assessment Inventory: the advanced version. San Antonio: Pearson; 2003.
74. Pryer R. Occupational Search Inventory manual (Form 3). Sydney: Congruence; 2006.
75. Wilkinson GS. Wide range achievement test 3 manual. Wilmington: Psychological Assessment Resources; 1993.
76. Occupational Health, Safety and Workers' Compensation. Job demands analysis procedure manual: behavioural/cognitive job demands analysis. Toronto: City of Toronto; 2003.
77. Kowalske K, Plenger PM, Lusby B, Hayden ME. Vocational re-entry following TBI: an enablement model. J Head Trauma Rehabil. 2000;15(4):989–99.
78. O'Brien L. Achieving a successful and sustainable return to the workforce after ABI: a client-centred approach. Brain Inj. 2007;21(5):465–78.
79. Yasuda S, Wehman P, Targett P, Cifu D, West M. Return to work for persons with traumatic brain injury. Am J Phys Med Rehabil. 2001;80(11):852–64.
80. Wehman PH, Kreutzer JS, West MD, Sherron PD, Zasler ND, Groah CH, Stonnington HH, Burns CT, Sale PR. Return to work for persons with traumatic brain injury: a supported employment approach. Arch Phys Med Rehabil. 1990;71(13):1047–52.
81. Holzberg E. The best practice for gaining and maintaining employment for individuals with TBI. Work. 2001;16:245–58.
82. Macaden AS, Chandler BJ, Chandler C, Berry A. Sustaining employment after vocational rehabilitation in acquired brain injury. Disabil Rehabil. 2010;32(14):1140–7.
83. Sale P, West M, Sherron P, Wehman PH. Exploratory analysis of job separations from supported employment for persons with traumatic brain injury. J Head Trauma Rehabil. 1991;6:1–11.
84. Catalano D, Pereira AP, Wu M, Ho H, Chan F. Service patterns related to successful employment outcomes of persons with traumatic brain injury in vocational rehabilitation. NeuroRehabilitation. 2006;21(4):279–93.

Chapter 13
Mental Health Management in Vocational Rehabilitation and Disability Evaluation: Applying the International Classification of Functioning, Disability and Health (ICF) Conceptual Framework

David B. Peterson

This chapter reviews how the International Classification of Functioning, Disability and Health (ICF)'s conceptual framework and parts of the classification system apply to mental health management in vocational rehabilitation and related services. Mental health management in this chapter refers to all aspects of the scope of practice of rehabilitation counseling and related rehabilitation service provision to people who have psychiatric diagnoses and/or developing mental health needs. The ICF conceptual framework and classification system have been reviewed earlier in Chaps. 1 and 2 of this text, so this chapter assumes the reader has the knowledge presented there.

We begin this chapter with a review of the prevalence of psychiatric diagnoses and the related need for mental health management in vocational rehabilitation and related services. We then apply the ICF conceptual framework to mental health management issues. The ICF's biopsychosocial framework is considered for the case conceptualization of a specific disability scenario and later to psychiatric rehabilitation in general. We conclude with a brief discussion of a core set of ICF codes related to the most frequently encountered psychiatric diagnosis in mental health management, depression.

D.B. Peterson (✉)
Charter College of Education, Division of Special Education and Counseling, Rehabilitation Education Programs, California State University, Los Angeles, 5151 State University Dr, King Hall C1064, Los Angeles, CA 90032, USA
e-mail: dpeters3@exchange.calstatela.edu

R. Escorpizo et al. (eds.), *Handbook of Vocational Rehabilitation and Disability Evaluation*, Handbooks in Health, Work, and Disability, DOI 10.1007/978-3-319-08825-9_13

13.1 Growing Need for Mental Health Management

There is undoubtedly a need to give special consideration to ICF implementation in vocational rehabilitation and disability evaluation with respect to mental health management. Psychiatric diagnoses and related mental health needs have affected a significant portion of the United States and the world in recent history. At the end of the twentieth century, the Global Burden of Disease Study found that neuropsychiatric disorders were collectively the third leading cause of loss of healthy years of life and the leading cause of disability [1], and the Surgeon General's Report on Mental Health indicated that mental illness was the second leading cause of disability and premature mortality in established economies such as the United States [2]. Four of the ten leading causes of disability worldwide were mental disorders, the foremost of which was major depression [3].

The prevalence of psychiatric diagnoses has been increasing over time. As we entered the new millennium, according to the 2004 World Health Report of the World Health Organization, mental disorders were the leading cause of disability in the United States and Canada for ages 15–44 during the year 2002 [4]. The US Census Bureau's American Community Survey (ACS) of 2008 suggested that the prevalence of disability in general, for people age 5 and older in the United States, was over 36.1 million people, roughly 12.1 % of the then estimated civilian noninstitutionalized population (CNIP), and of this number, 13.4 million (37 % of those surveyed indicating disability or 4.8 % of the CNIP) lived with some cognitive difficulty associated with a mental or emotional condition [5]. This may suggest that over one-third of people with disabilities seeking services from rehabilitation counselors and related rehabilitation service providers may have had one or more psychiatric diagnoses affecting cognitive functioning as of 2008. The most recent iteration of the ACS for 2011 yielded similar results [6]. These data are based on reports from only those persons who responded to the particular surveys conducted, so they may significantly underrepresent persons living with chronic psychiatric diagnoses.

According to the National Comorbidity Survey Replication (NCS-R) conducted by Kessler and his associates, which surveyed the prevalence, severity, and comorbidity of 12-month duration DSM-IV disorders, prevalence rates for psychiatric diagnoses alone are much higher than ACS estimates for a much broader presentation of types of disability [7]. According to this survey, an estimated 26.2 % of Americans age 18 and older (not including children from age 5 to 17 as with the ACS) had a diagnosable mental disorder within a given year. Using 2004 US Census residential population estimates for this age range, 57.7 million adults had a psychiatric diagnosis at that time.

It is important to note when considering these numbers that nearly half (45 %) of those with any mental disorder met criteria for two or more disorders, with severity of the condition strongly associated with this comorbidity [7]. Results from the NCS-R further suggested that the lifetime prevalence of having any mental disorder during 2004 was a startling 46.4 %, nearly half of the population. Remarkably, the prevalence of psychiatric diagnoses is highlighted in the 2007 update of the National Institute of Mental Health (NIMH), where the lifetime prevalence percentage increased to 57.4 % [8].

According to Geoffrey Reed, a World Health Organization psychologist involved in the update to the International Classification of Diseases, 11th Revision (ICD-11) classification system, "Mental disorders contribute more to global disability and disease burden than any other category of non-communicable disease" [9]. Given the historical prevalence of psychiatric diagnoses, there is no doubt that mental health management concerns will be at the forefront of vocational rehabilitation and disability evaluation efforts.

People with psychiatric diagnoses are encountered often within vocational rehabilitation and disability evaluation.

13.2 The ICF Conceptual Framework and Mental Health Management

The ICF conceptual framework portrays health as a dynamic interaction between a person's functioning and disability within a given context and has its basis within the biopsychosocial model of disability and function [10]. The biopsychosocial model of disability integrates useful aspects of both the medical and social models of disability, addressing biological, individual, and societal perspectives on health [11, 12]. Planning treatments and documenting outcomes of mental health interventions from the body, individual, and societal perspectives can improve the quality of mental health management and related service provision and consequently the quality of life of people with disabilities, as well as increase the participation of individuals with disabilities in society [13]. The biopsychosocial perspective, and the ICF itself, has the potential to inform mental health services in the broadest sense, while providing specific benefit to people with psychiatric disabilities by using a universal, culturally sensitive, integrative, and interactive model of health and disability that is sensitive to social and environmental aspects of functioning [14].

The ICF conceptual framework is useful in informing case conceptualization within mental health management and also in the education of future mental health service providers [10]. All of this review of the conceptual framework of the ICF is referenced to the original source [14]. The conceptual framework of the ICF consists of two parts: *functioning and disability* and *contextual factors*. Each part contains two components.

13.2.1 The Body

Within the first part of the ICF conceptual framework, *functioning and disability*, the *body* component consists of two parallel classifications, *body functions* and *body structures*. The person is described physically with respect to *body structure*, which in the instance of psychiatric diagnoses would involve the brain and nervous system. At the same time *body function* describes a change in function as a result of a change in *body structure*. For example, a lack of a specific neurotransmitter in the brain, serotonin, could result in a change in the brain's neurochemistry, and the related change of function could be unremitting depressive symptoms.

The second component, *activities and participation*, covers domains of functioning from both an individual and societal perspective. This component involves one's potential to function, or *activity*, in comparison with one's actual functioning within a current context, or *participation*.

Conceptualizing mental health management within the context of the first part of the ICF first explores the biological bases of behavior (body functions and body structures). What role might biology play based on our current research [15]? What evidence-based practices in treatment are most effective under these circumstances, either psychotherapeutic or psychopharmacological [16]? Once biological factors are considered, psychological functioning is classified according to manifest symptoms and possible diagnoses. After the physical and mental health and functioning of an individual are clarified at the individual level, how that person functions in his or her environment can be explored with respect to demonstrated potential (activity) versus actual ability to participate within a social context (participation). The discrepancy between identified potential activity and actual participation can serve as the focus of clinical attention for intervention targeting in mental health management, as well as in related research. For example, if a person dealing with symptoms associated with schizophrenia was capable of focusing on detailed and complex work (potential activity) but his ability to do that within his context is compromised by his lack of compliance with medication (actual participation), the target of intervention would be to provide environmental supports (e.g., alarm system in a PDA, fieldwork team to visit with regular doses of medication) to encourage medication compliance so that his actual participation was consistent with his activity potential.

13.2.2 Contextual Factors

The second part of the ICF classification addresses *contextual factors* through two components. The first is *environmental factors*, or factors in the physical, social, or attitudinal world ranging from the immediate to more general environment. The biopsychosocial model has supported the utility of considering facilitators and barriers present in the environment when planning treatment interventions for people with disabilities. This component of the ICF's conceptual framework assists the healthcare professional in taking into account the physical, social, or attitudinal world, ranging from the immediate to more general environment, and its impact on the difference between an individual with a disability's potential functioning and actual functioning within a given context. Interventions implemented in a person's environment can be very effective in eliminating or ameliorating the impact of impairment on functioning. The solutions described previously for the person with schizophrenia included a PDA and a support staff member, both of which would be considered facilitators within that person's environment. Example of a barrier could be limited funding to provide such supports.

The second component of the second part of the ICF, *personal factors*, calls attention to the need to consider unique factors such as gender, race, age, fitness, religion, lifestyle, habits, upbringing, coping styles, social background, education, profession, past and current experience, overall behavior pattern and character, individual psychological assets, and other health conditions. Initially the ICF did not specifically code or classify this component due to the unique nature and diverse presentations of these factors worldwide. For example, while race is often reduced to a simplified list for medical records, establishing a worldwide nominal system for race in the ICF was an extremely complex task [13]. Disability advocates have since highlighted the need to invest in this component of the ICF's conceptual framework [10, 13]. Mental health management is obviously more effective if the stakeholders are sensitive to regional and cultural differences as they affect the complexity of a person's racial and ethnic identity and how they interact with factors in the mental healthcare environment. *Personal factors* call attention to the need for healthcare professionals to consider unique factors influencing an individual's health and functioning.

13.2.3 Qualifiers

Finally, the ICF conceptual framework is made practical through the application of qualifiers of functioning that describe the extent or magnitude of impairment in function (e.g., no impairment, mild, moderate, severe, or profound). Within mental health management, the data that informs qualifiers comes from clinical contact, structured interviews and assessments, and overall clinical decision-making and clinical judgment [17]. At the individual functioning and disability level, changes in body structure – in the case of mental health management, the central or peripheral nervous systems – are considered in light of related changes in psychological functioning. These changes are qualified by an individual's capacity (what a person can do in a standard, nonintrusive environment) and an individual's ability to perform (what someone does do in his or her current context). At the contextual level, qualifiers rate the degree to which environmental factors in the physical, social, and attitudinal world hinder or facilitate function. Further details on the use of qualifiers can be found in Chaps. 1 and 2 of this text [11, 14].

Table 13.1 Overview of the ICF and mental health functioning [14]

Two parts: (a dynamic interaction)	Part 1: functioning and disability		Part 2: contextual factors	
Each part has two components	Body functions and structures	Activities and participation	Environmental factors	Personal factors
Domains (Contain the categories or units of classification of the ICF)	Psychological functions	Life areas (tasks, actions)	External influences on functioning and disability	Internal influences on functioning and disability
	Body structures: central and peripheral nervous systems (CNS and PNS)	Learning and applying knowledge		
Constructs (Defined through use of qualifiers that modify the extent or magnitude of function or disability)	Change in psychological function	Capacity: executing tasks in a standard environment "can do"	Facilitating or hindering impact of features of the physical, social, and attitudinal world	Impact of attributes of the person
	Change in body structure: central and peripheral nervous systems	Performance: executing tasks in the current environment "does do"		

Note: Units of classification are situations, not people [14]

Ultimately the ICF conceptual framework is multidimensional in its scope, and the relationships that exist between its two parts and four components are reciprocal among all constructs. A change in any one of the two parts of health and function (body functions or structures), or the two parts of contextual factors (environmental or personal factor), affects the other parts of the conceptual framework. Understanding the dynamic interaction among ICF constructs can help a rehabilitation service provider anticipate the potential impact on someone's functional potential (activity) or his or her actual performance in his or her environment (participation) [13].

The ICF conceptual framework lends itself well to portraying the complex interactions between factors in mental health management. Table 13.1 provides a summary table of the ICF conceptual framework reflected in this discussion, with annotations relative to mental health functioning. The two major parts of the framework, functioning and disability and contextual factors, are useful in portraying the dynamic interaction between persons and their environmental contexts within any mental health management paradigm.

The ICF classifies functioning, disability, and health from biological, psychological, and social perspectives.

13.3 Application of the Biopsychosocial Framework

In the case of depression, a person's symptoms may include psychomotor slowing that would impact ability to keep pace in a work environment; the impairment produced by the depression, psychomotor slowing, affects the *activity* of keeping pace in the work environment. If within a specific context the person has access to effective medication in the form of antidepressants, in time the psychomotor slowing could improve. The provision of medication in this *context* can impact a person's ability to *participate* effectively, in this case to keep pace in the work environment. Interventions like medication or reasonable accommodations in a work setting target disparities between a person's potential (activity) and actual performance (participation) in a given context. Let us turn our focus from the general to a specific scenario.

The following scenario will help illustrate the utility of the biopsychosocial framework of the ICF for case conceptualization and research in mental health management. A similar presentation is included in a recent discussion of the ICF and its contributions to qualitative research in healthcare outcomes [13]. Our scenario involves a 19-year-old female who is gay, who due to a head trauma has a mild neurocognitive disorder and a co-occurring diagnosis of major depressive disorder, recurrent and severe, due to general medical condition (the head trauma). The ICF's conceptual framework would first encourage us to consider any changes in body structures (head trauma to brain structures and their sequelae, changes in brain neurotransmission that may be associated with depression) and related body functions (impaired neuropsychological functioning, including physical, cognitive, and emotional functioning, depressed mood, and all of its potential consequences). We may measure these changes through clinical interviews, psychological testing, and evaluations by other medical specialties such as neurology, physiatry, counseling, and psychotherapy, with both quantitative data and clinical observation.

During this assessment process, the ICF conceptual framework encourages us to note the differences between functioning potential (activity) and actual functioning within the person's environmental context (participation). With careful analysis of the person's context and sensitivity to personal differences (like being a gay woman), the complex relationships between the person's optimal and actual functioning in her environment can serve as starting points for interventions that will enhance overall functioning and inform research of associated healthcare outcomes.

With respect to contextual factors, if the head injury resulted in mobility impairment, it may be necessary to remove environmental barriers to functioning. If the sequelae of the head trauma or symptoms of depression are difficult for the patient's coworkers to understand, psychoeducational interventions for coworkers and supervisors may be very useful in creating a supportive environment that maximizes potential for success. Such activities have historically been the domain of job development and support personnel within the vocational rehabilitation system, and the rehabilitation counseling literature has a great deal to offer mental health management professionals in this regard [18].

The interaction between personal and environmental factors may provide targets for intervention. For our example, if the client was not "out" to her family as a gay woman prior to her injury and her family did not know any of her friends from that community and now due to the injury the family is in close contact with her network of friends, there may be a need for healthcare professionals to provide support to the client or, with permission, to family and friends, as relationships evolve in a new social context. This social support system could be critical to achieving optimal rehabilitation outcomes.

Mental health managers or researchers may encounter a variety of perspectives across and within allied healthcare agencies, and understanding differing perspectives of healthcare provision may facilitate future collaborations. If a therapist encounters a healthcare entity focused on the medical model of service provision, the therapist's advocacy efforts can focus on social and contextual factors to encourage a holistic program of healthcare. A hospital treating the young woman in our example may be focused on medical sequelae of her head trauma, as well as the degree of depressive symptomatology and related risks. The ICF's conceptual framework addresses these foci through body functions and body structures (which include the brain). In addition, the biopsychosocial approach embraced within the ICF's conceptual framework will take into careful account contextual issues such as the client's family system, social circles, and the greater community. Using an interdisciplinary approach across treating sources and with social system support, activities and participation (the client's potential based upon her functioning and impairments) can be compared with how her current context facilitates or hinders her functioning. In addition, as case conceptualization continues to develop, targeted interventions can proceed in the most comprehensive fashion across treating systems.

13.4 Integrating Functional Data into Mental Health Management

The ICF and its conceptual framework can meet a critical need in mental health management, to integrate more detailed information on functional status into health records. The National Committee of Vital and Health Statistics, an academic medical advisory board of the US Department of Health and Human Services, explained the state of the art in 2001, and we have made very modest progress since then:

> The point has already been made that administrative data generally do not include information on functional status. The significance of this fact is that information on this dimension of health – increasingly the sine qua non for understanding health – is not available to the healthcare system (e.g., insurers and health plans), nor to the researchers, public health workers, and policy makers who depend on administrative data. What is needed, therefore, is a standardized code set that will enable providers, with minimal burden, to include functional status information in administrative data. [19]

While insurance companies are demanding higher accountability in order to receive payment for services, the information collected is not standard or consistent across entities. Considering our discussion of the ICF conceptual framework as it applies to mental health management, the utility of using the ICF to enhance communication between providers and mental healthcare systems is abundantly clear. See Peterson [10] for a discussion of the international trend to integrate the ICF into national healthcare policies and structures.

A promising development from the American Psychiatric Association in their release of the DSM-5 [17] is the elimination of the Global Assessment of Functioning index, a single number designed to reflect a very complex global construct of overall functioning, and the suggestion to adopt the WHODAS 2.0 in its place, an ICF-based instrument that requires assessment of specific functioning across 36 functional domains. The APA also proposes a variety of crosscutting symptom measures, both within the DSM-5 and many more specific measures that are available on their website, to encourage more careful consideration and documentation of mental health functioning within our healthcare system. The World Health Organization and its ICF appear to have played an important role in this expansion in the consideration of functioning in mental health.

Data on functional status is the sine qua non for understanding health; the ICF provides a standardized code set to that end.

13.5 Confluence of the ICF Conceptual Framework and Psychiatric Rehabilitation

A powerful recovery model paradigm of practice in mental health management, also known as the Boston Model of Psychiatric Rehabilitation, complements the conceptual framework of the ICF and its application to the scenarios just presented. Here is the definition of psychiatric rehabilitation as approved by the United States Psychiatric Rehabilitation Association (USPRA):

> Psychiatric rehabilitation promotes recovery, full community integration and improved quality of life for persons who have been diagnosed with any mental health condition that seriously impairs their ability to lead meaningful lives. Psychiatric rehabilitation services are collaborative, person directed and individualized. These services are an essential element of the healthcare and human services spectrum, and must be evidence-based. They focus on helping individuals develop skills and access resources needed to increase their capacity to be successful and satisfied in the living, working, learning, and social environments of their choice. [20]

The recovery model has been advocated within public mental health management [21–23], and its origins lie within psychiatric rehabilitation. The Boston

Model of Psychiatric Rehabilitation is a comprehensive model with many elements, not all of which will be reviewed here. One important element of the model is to help the clients manage and live with their mental disorders, rather than expecting or waiting to be symptom-free before returning to full participation in society. The model emphasizes self-determination and input from clients and their family members in the recovery process and in the design and operation of the mental health service system [20].

The psychiatric rehabilitation process as defined by the Boston University Center for Psychiatric Rehabilitation is an evidence-based approach with specific job descriptions, record-keeping formats, and quality assurance mechanism that require intensive training and supervision over time to implement fully [20]. Essential services provided within a recovery-oriented system include treatment for symptom relief, crisis intervention for personal safety, case management for access to services, establishing rehabilitation goals, enrichment activities for self-development, rights protection for equal opportunity, and support for healthy lifestyle, empowerment, and basic support of essential needs. Based on the content of this chapter thus far, there is an obvious confluence of the recovery model and the ICF's conceptual framework. The individual and contextual foci of both paradigms of practice both promote the utility of a biopsychosocial approach to mental health management.

13.6 Managing Stigma

At the end of the twentieth century, the Surgeon General's Report on Mental Health [2] suggested that while public understanding of mental illness has improved in recent years, stigma continues to be a major social barrier for people with mental illness. Careful consideration of historical and even recent social discourse, as well as media portrayal of people with psychiatric diagnoses, suggest that the public tends to view people with severe mental illness more negatively than those with physical illnesses [24]. Over the years they have been considered by some to be undesirable as friends, coworkers, tenants, and employees. The mass media often misrepresents and demeans people with psychiatric diagnoses, portraying them as unreliable, erratic, irrational, and violent [25, 26].

In reality, while some people with serious psychiatric diagnoses may be violent, the majority of them are not. There is very little risk of harm to a stranger from casual contact with a person with mental illness, and overall, mental illness has historically made a very small contribution to the total level of violence in society [2]. These stereotypes are humiliating, embarrassing, and painful for people with psychiatric diagnoses [27]. Healthcare management that focuses on actual functioning of people with psychiatric diagnoses could go a long way toward educating the public and disputing long held myths and stereotypes of people dealing with mental illness. The ICF and its conceptual framework, and its etiological neutral approach to disability and function, may help to shift mental health management from the often inaccurate focus on illness onto what is meaningful, actual functioning in an individual's context [14].

Stigma affects people with mental illness in other ways [26]. It may discourage them from seeking help for their conditions [27]. It may affect their self-esteem and may cause additional stress on those in their social support system. Stigma may have an adverse impact on social relations and may reduce employment and housing opportunities. On the public policy level, stigma has negatively affected the public's willingness to provide resources for providing mental health treatment and for supporting excellent preparation of mental healthcare service providers.

Using the ICF conceptual framework for intervention targeting, there are things that rehabilitation professionals can do to help reduce stigma [28]. At the contextual level, rehabilitation professionals may address stigma in society by simply bringing psychiatric diagnoses out in the open, allowing people just to talk about it, in order to refute harmful stereotypes and reduce social stigma [27]. They may seek out opportunities to collaborate with other mental health professionals and client advocacy groups (e.g., the National Alliance on Mental Illness) to promote an accurate and sensitive image of people with psychiatric disabilities.

At the workplace environment, rehabilitation professionals may need to help employers and coworkers to dispel the myths surrounding psychiatric diagnoses. Some might fear that people with psychiatric disabilities could become disruptive or violent at work. Others might be concerned that if they accidentally say the "wrong thing," it will cause the person with a psychiatric disability to become unstable. While these concerns are relevant in some cases, they are overly generalized to encompass all individuals with mental disorders.

Those who have worked long enough in psychiatric rehabilitation realize the value of using counseling skills to help those close to the person with a psychiatric diagnosis to demystify the diagnosis, refute negative stereotypes, offer ideas for reasonable accommodation, and provide an opportunity to change the focus from disability to ability. Rehabilitation professionals providing job follow-up support may need to address ostracism by coworkers or occasional jokes or remarks by insensitive colleagues, whether intentional or unintentional. Finding supportive ways to meet with stakeholders and proactively address such concerns may help avoid the creation of a hostile and stressful work environment.

At the individual level, the client may or may not desire to disclose his or her disability to an employer, depending on the particular job setting, degree of recovery, and personal preferences. Counselors can advise clients about the appropriateness of disclosing or not disclosing psychiatric disability. The decision of whether or not to disclose and how much information to disclose is made on an individual basis and can be informed by good clinical judgment of the rehabilitation counselor. Ultimately, whether there needs to be disclosure depends on a client's desire to request reasonable accommodation. The consumer and counselor can weigh together the pros and cons of disclosure, so that the consumer can make an informed choice [28].

The ICF helps shift the focus from stigma-influenced diagnostic labels to meaningful, actual functioning in context.

13.7 ICF Core Set Development: Depression

To conclude this chapter, we will spend some time reviewing the ICF Core Sets developed for depression, the most commonly occurring psychiatric diagnosis in mental health management. ICF Core Sets are specific codes from the ICF related to a specific condition, assembled in order to increase the likelihood of adaption in healthcare settings. The ICF has over 1,400 codes, so developing user-friendly ICF Core Sets focused on specific conditions is a sensible endeavor. Developing an ICF Core Set for depression creates a list of ICF codes related to the most prevalent functional health limitations for depressive disorders.

13.7.1 Historical Context

ICF Core Sets development efforts for the ICF within the mental health realm have focused on those conditions most frequently encountered in clinical practice: psychiatry in general [29], addiction [30], bipolar disorder [31], depressive disorders [32–34], and anxiety depression and schizophrenia [35]. The ICF Core Sets typically were generated through consensus building processes involving experts in the area based upon their clinical expertise, specific instruments in wide use, and contextual factors as they relate to the ICF code structure. Generic ICF Core Sets were aspired to through the use of regression modeling, a complex statistical procedure [36]. Ultimately the consensus in ICF Core Set development is that there are a number of approaches necessary to construct them, including both quantitative and qualitative approaches. The ICF Core Set development protocol was eventually developed into a multistep empirical process. The preparatory phase involved four different methods: (1) an empirical multicenter study, (2) a systematic literature review, (3) a qualitative study, and (4) an expert survey [37, 38]. There are ongoing validation studies of these ICF Core Sets that involve patient focus groups.

In order to understand psychiatric diagnoses, the rehabilitation professional must be able to distinguish between normal life variations and transient responses to stress and serious symptomatology manifested as disturbances in behaviors, cognition, personality, physical signs, and syndrome combinations [17]. The functional aspect of the ICF codes, in combination with the diagnostic criteria of systems like the DSM-5 or the International Classification of Diseases [39], creates a fuller, more complete clinical picture for mental health management, which may increase diagnostic accuracy and contribute more effectively to an international database that continues to inform diagnostic research. Accurate diagnosis of psychiatric conditions by rehabilitation professionals leads to appropriate referrals, selection of the most appropriate evidence-based treatments, and ultimately amelioration or elimination of problematic symptoms that negatively impact health and functioning [10].

13.7.2 Two-Level Classification of Mental Health Functioning

To begin the core sets presentation, let us first take a look at the ICF two-level classification codes for mental functions. Table 13.2 provides us with a snapshot of

Table 13.2 Body functions, Chap. 1, mental functions: two-level classification of the ICF

Branch	ICF code	Two-level descriptor
Global mental functions (b110-b139)	b110	Consciousness functions
	b114	Orientation functions
	b117	Intellectual functions
	b122	Global psychosocial functions
	b126	Temperament and personality functions
	b130	Energy and drive functions
	b134	Sleep functions
	b139	Global mental functions, other specified and unspecified
Specific mental functions (b140-b189)	b140	Attention functions
	b144	Memory functions
	b147	Psychomotor functions
	b152	Emotional functions
	b156	Perceptual functions
	b160	Thought functions
	b164	Higher-level cognitive functions
	b167	Mental functions of language
	b172	Calculation functions
	b176	Mental functions of sequencing and complex movements
	b180	Experience of self and time functions
	b189	Specific mental functions, other specified and unspecified
	b198	Mental functions, other specified
	b199	Mental functions, unspecified

the scope of two-level classification of mental health-related functioning according to the ICF. This two-level classification applies to all mental health conditions, not just depression.

13.7.3 ICF Core Sets for Depression

Next, we present several tables related to the established ICF Core Set for depression. These ICF Core Sets are based upon the work of Cieza and associates [33] and also appear in a compendium of ICF Core Sets [37, 38]. Table 13.3 provides us with a presentation of ICF codes at a more detailed level of classification, coding related to depression from the body functions component of the ICF, a total of 45 specific codes. Table 13.4 presents codes associated with depression under the activities and participation component of the ICF, providing an additional 48 codes for this component of the ICF. Table 13.5 illustrates coding possible for depressive symptoms according to the environmental factors component of the ICF, 28 different codes in total. Finally, Table 13.6 provides a brief core set for depression, presented in rank order of importance according to the work of Cieza and associates [33]. The brief core set contains classification codes from all three of the body functions, activity and participation, and environmental factors combined.

Table 13.3 ICF categories for body functions in the comprehensive ICF Core Set for depression [33]

ICF code 2nd level	ICF code 3rd level	ICF category title
b117		Intellectual functions
b126		Temperament and personality functions
	b1260	Extraversion
	b1261	Agreeableness
	b1262	Conscientiousness
	b1263	Psychic stability
	b1265	Optimism
	b1266	Confidence
b130		Energy and drive functions
	b1300	Energy level
	b1301	Motivation
	b1302	Appetite
	b1304	Impulse control
b134		Sleep functions
	b1340	Amount of sleep
	b1341	Onset of sleep
	b1342	Maintenance of sleep
	b1343	Quality of sleep
	b1344	Functions involving the sleep cycle
b140		Attention functions
b144		Memory functions
b147		Psychomotor functions
b152		Emotional functions
	b1520	Appropriateness of emotion
	b1521	Regulation of emotion
	b1522	Range of emotion
b160		Thought functions
	b1600	Pace of thought
	b1601	Form of thought
	b1602	Content of thought
	b1603	Control of thought
b164		Higher-level cognitive functions
	b1641	Organization and planning
	b1642	Time management
	b1644	Insight
	b1645	Judgement
b180		Experience of self and time functions
	b1800	Experience of self
	b1801	Body image
b280		Sensation of pain

(continued)

Table 13.3 (continued)

ICF code 2nd level	ICF code 3rd level	ICF category title
b460		Sensations associated with cardiovascular and respiratory functions
b530		Weight maintenance functions
b535		Sensations associated with the digestive system
b640		Sexual functions
b780		Sensations related to muscles and movement functions

Table 13.4 ICF categories for activities and participation in the comprehensive ICF Core Set for depression [33]

ICF code 2nd level	ICF code 3rd level	ICF category title
d110		Watching
d115		Listening
d163		Thinking
d166		Reading
d175		Solving problems
d177		Making decisions
d210		Undertaking a single task
d220		Undertaking multiple tasks
d230		Carrying out daily routine
	d2301	Managing daily routine
	d2302	Completing the daily routine
	d2303	Managing one's own activity level
d240		Handling stress and other psychological demands
d310		Communicating with – receiving spoken messages
d315		Communicating with – receiving nonverbal messages
d330		Speaking
d335		Producing non-verbal messages
d350		Conversation
d355		Discussion
d470		Using transportation (car, bus, train, plane, etc.)
d475		Driving (riding bicycle and motorbike, driving car, riding animals, etc.)
d510		Washing oneself
d520		Caring for body parts
d540		Dressing
d550		Eating
d560		Drinking
d570		Looking after one's health

(continued)

Table 13.4 (continued)

ICF code 2nd level	ICF code 3rd level	ICF category title
d620		Acquisition of goods and services
d630		Preparing meals
d640		Doing housework
d650		Caring for household objects
d660		Assisting others
d710		Basic interpersonal interactions
d720		Complex interpersonal interactions
d730		Relating with strangers
d750		Informal social relationships
d760		Family relationships
d770		Intimate relationships
d830		Higher education
d845		Acquiring, keeping and terminating a job
d850		Remunerative employment
d860		Basic economic transactions
d865		Complex economic transactions
d870		Economic self-sufficiency
d910		Community life
d920		Recreation and leisure
d930		Religion and spirituality
d950		Political life and citizenship

Table 13.5 ICF categories for environmental factors in the comprehensive ICF Core Set for depression [33]

ICF code 2nd level	ICF code 3rd level	ICF category title
	e1101	Drugs
e165		Assets
e225		Climate
e240		Light
e245		Time-related changes
e250		Sound
e310		Immediate family
e320		Friends
e325		Acquaintances, peers, colleagues, neighbours and community members
e330		People in positions of authority
e340		Personal care providers and personal assistants
e355		Health professionals
e360		Health-related professionals
e410		Individual attitudes of immediate family members
e415		Individual attitudes of extended family members
e420		Individual attitudes of friends
e425		Individual attitudes of acquaintances, peers, colleagues, neighbours and community members
e430		Individual attitudes of people in positions of authority
e440		Individual attitudes of personal care providers and personal assistants
e450		Individual attitudes of health professionals
e455		Individual attitudes of health-related professionals
e460		Societal attitudes
e465		Social norms, practices and ideologies
e525		Housing services, systems and policies
e570		Social security services, systems and policies
e575		General social support services, systems and policies
e580		Health services, systems and policies
e590		Labour and employment services, systems and policies

Table 13.6 ICF categories: brief ICF Core Set for depression, rank order

ICF component	Rank order	ICF code	ICF category title
Body functions	1	b1263	Psychic stability
	2	b1300	Energy level
	3	b1301	Motivation
	4	b1522	Range of emotion
	5	b1265	Optimism
	6	b140	Attention functions
	7	b1521	Regulation of emotion
	8	b1302	Appetite
	9	b147	Psychomotor functions
Activities and participation	1	d2301	Managing daily routine
	2	d177	Making decisions
	3	d175	Solving problems
	4	d770	Intimate relationships
	5	d240	Handling stress and other psychological demands
	6	d760	Family relationships
	7	d350	Conversation
	8	d570	Looking after one's health
	8.5	d163	Thinking
	9	d510	Washing oneself
	10	d2303	Managing one's own activity level
	10	d845	Acquiring, keeping and terminating a job
Environmental factors	1	e310	Immediate family
	2	e320	Friends
	3	e355	Health professionals
	4	e1101	Drugs
	5	e410	Individual attitudes of immediate family members
	6	e325	Acquaintances, peers, colleagues, neighbours and community members
	7	e420	Individual attitudes of friends
	8	e580	Health services, systems and policies
	9	e450	Individual attitudes of health professionals
	10	e415	Individual attitudes of extended family members

13.8 Conclusion

This chapter focused specifically on the application of the ICF conceptual framework to mental health management within the vocational rehabilitation and disability evaluation enterprises. The implications for practice were many, including: the growing need to focus on mental health and disability; the utility of using a biopsychosocial framework as presented in the ICF to inform case conceptualization, intervention targeting, and related research in vocational rehabilitation and related services; the confluence of the recovery model and the ICF; and implications for managing stigma. We concluded with an overview of specific ICF Core Sets of ICF codes in mental health management, those dealing with the most commonly occurring psychiatric diagnosis, depression. We will continue this discussion into the next chapter by addressing current issues in mental health management in vocational rehabilitation, specifically, implementation of the DSM-5 with the WHODAS as the new paradigm in disability severity and the implementation of the ICD-10-CM in the United States.

Questions:

1. What portion of people with disabilities seeking services from rehabilitation counselors and related rehabilitation service providers are likely to have one or more psychiatric diagnoses?

   (a) One fourth
   (b) One third
   (c) One half
   (d) Three quarters

   Correct answer b.

2. Of those people with psychiatric diagnoses, what portion will have two or more diagnoses?

   (a) Very few
   (b) About one fourth
   (c) Nearly half
   (d) Almost all

   Correct answer c.

3. What model informs the conceptual framework of the ICF?

   (a) A medical model of disability
   (b) A social model of disability
   (c) An environmental model of disability
   (d) A biopsychosocial model

   Correct answer d.

4. What important change to the most recent iteration of U.S. system of psychiatric diagnoses (DSM-5) reflects the influence of the ICF on the classification of functioning, disability, and health?

   (a) The removal of the Global Assessment of Functioning
   (b) The inclusion of the WHODAS 2.0 in the Emerging Measures and Models section of the DSM-5
   (c) The use of the ICF to inform the revision of the WHO-DAS 2.0 to include 36 domains of functioning
   (d) All of the above

   Correct answer d.

References

1. Murray S. The global burden of disease: a comprehensive assessment of mortality and disability from diseases, injuries, and risk factors in 1990 and projected to 2020. In: Murray CJL, Lopez AD, editors. The global burden of disease and injury series. Cambridge: Harvard University Press; 1996. p. 247–93.
2. U. S. Department of Health and Human Services. Mental health: a report of the Surgeon General. Rockville: U. S. Department of Health and Human Services, Substance Abuse and Mental Health Services Administration; 1999.
3. Ustun TB, Chatterji S, Bickenbach J, Kostanjsek N, Schneider M. The International Classification of Functioning, Disability and Health: a new tool for understanding disability and health. Disabil Rehabil. 2003;25(11–12):565–71.
4. World Health Organization. The World Health report 2004: changing history, annex table 3: burden of disease in DALYs by cause, sex, and mortality stratum in WHO regions, estimates for 2002. Geneva: World Health Organization; 2004.
5. Brault MW. Review of changes to the measurement of disability in the 2008 American Community Survey. Washington, DC: U.S. Census Bureau; 2009.
6. U.S. Census Bureau. American community survey: 1-year estimates. Washington, DC: U.S. Department of Commerce; 2011.
7. Kessler RC, Chiu WT, Demler O, Merikangas KR, Walters EE. Prevalence, severity, and comorbidity of 12-month DSM-IV disorders in the National Comorbidity Survey Replication. Arch Gen Psychiatry. 2005;62(6):617–27.
8. National Institute of Mental Health. Life time prevalence of DSM-IV/WMH-CIDI disorders by sex and cohort. 2007. Available from: www.nimh.nih.gov. Accessed 8 Sept 2013.
9. Martin S. Improving diagnosis worldwide. Monit Psychol. 2009;40(9):62–5.
10. Peterson DB. Psychological aspects of functioning, disability and health. New York: Springer; 2011.
11. Peterson DB. International Classification of Functioning, Disability and Health (ICF): an introduction for rehabilitation psychologists. Rehabil Psychol. 2005;50:105–12.
12. Peterson DB, Elliott TR. Advances in conceptualizing and studying disability. In: Brown S, Lent RW, editors. Handbook of counseling psychology. 4th ed. Hoboken: Wiley; 2008. p. 212–30.
13. Peterson DB, Threats TT. Ethical and clinical implications of the international classification of functioning, disability and health (ICF) in rehabilitation education. Rehabil Educ. 2005;19:129–38.
14. World Health Organization. International classification of functioning disability and health (ICF). Geneva: World Health Organization; 2001.
15. Oltmanns TS, Emery RE. Abnormal psychology. Englewood Cliffs: Prentice Hall; 2012.
16. Preston J, O'Neil JH, Talaga M. Handbook of clinical psychopharmacology for therapists. Oakland: New Harbinger Publications; 2013.
17. American Psychiatric Association. Diagnostic and statistical manual of mental disorders. 5th ed. Arlington: American Psychiatric Publishing; 2013.
18. Homa D, Peterson DB. Using the international classification of functioning, disability and health (ICF) in teaching rehabilitation client assessment. Rehabil Educ. 2005;19:119–28.
19. National Committee on Vital Health Statistics. Classifying and reporting functional status. Washington, DC: U.S. Dept. of Health and Human Services; 2001.
20. Anthony WA, Farkas MD. A primer on the psychiatric rehabilitation process. Boston: Boston University Center for Psychiatric Rehabilitation; 2009.
21. Anthony WA. A recovery-oriented service system: setting down system level standards. Psychiatr Rehabil J. 2000;24(2):159–68.
22. Davidson L, O'Connell M, Tondora J, Styron T, Kangas K. The top ten concerns about recovery encountered in mental health system transformation. Psychiatr Serv. 2006;57(5):640–5.

23. Jacobson N, Greenley D. What is recovery? A conceptual model and explication. Psychiatr Serv. 2001;52(4):482–5.
24. Penn DL, Martin J. The stigma of severe mental illness: some potential solutions for a recalcitrant problem. Psychiatr Q. 1998;69(3):235–47.
25. Corrigan P. The impact of stigma on severe mental illness. Cognit Behav Pract. 1998;5:201–22.
26. Hinshaw SP, Cicchetti D. Stigma and mental disorder: conceptions of illness, public attitudes, personal disclosure, and social policy. Dev Psychopathol. 2000;12(4):555–98.
27. Carter R, Golant SK, Cade KE. Within our reach: ending the mental health crisis. New York: Rodale Inc.; 2010.
28. Peterson DB, Hong G. Psychiatric diagnoses. In: Brodwin MG, Siu FW, Howard J, Brodwin ER, Du AT editors. Medical, psychosocial, and vocational aspects of disability. 5th ed. Athens: Elliott & Fitzpatrick, Inc.; 2014.
29. Alvarezz AS. The application of the international classification of functioning, disability, and health in psychiatry: possible reasons for the lack of implementation. Am J Phys Med Rehabil. 2012;91(13 Suppl 1):S69–73.
30. Amann K, Stracke R, Veltrup C, Kufner R, Roeb-Rienas W. Towards a consent on developing the ICF-core set alcohol and drug dependence. Suchttherapie. 2011;12(1):20–8.
31. Avila CC, Cabello M, Cieza A, Vieta E, Ayuso-Mateos JL. Functioning and disability in bipolar disorders: a systematic review of literature using the ICF as a reference. Bipolar Disord. 2010;12(5):473–82.
32. Brockow T, Wohlfahrt K, Hillert A, Geyh S, Weigl M, Franke T, et al. Identifying the concepts contained in outcome measures of clinical trials on depressive disorders using the international classification of functioning, disability and health as a reference. J Rehabil Med. 2004;36 (44 Suppl):49–55.
33. Cieza A, Chatterji S, Andersen C, Cantista P, Herceg M, Melvin J, et al. ICF Core Sets for depression. J Rehabil Med. 2004;36(44 Suppl):128–34.
34. Ewert T, Fuessl M, Cieza A, Andersen C, Chatterji S, Kostanjsek N, et al. Identification of the most common patient problems in patients with chronic conditions using the ICF checklist. J Rehabil Med. 2004;36(44 Suppl):22–9.
35. Tenorio-Martinez R, del Carmen Lara-Munoz M, Medina-Mora ME. Measurement of problems in activities and participation in patients with anxiety, depression and schizophrenia using the ICF checklist. Soc Psychiatry Psychiatr Epidemiol. 2009;44(5):377–84.
36. Cieza A, Geyh S, Chatterji S, Kostanjsek N, Ustun BT, Stucki G. Identification of candidate categories of the International Classification of Functioning Disability and Health (ICF) for a Generic ICF Core Set based on regression modelling. BMC Med Res Methodol. 2006;6:36.
37. Bickenbach JCA, Rauch A, Stucki G, editors. ICF core sets: manual for clinical practice. Göttingen: Hogrefe; 2012.
38. Selb M, Escorpizo R, Kostanjsek N, Stucki G, Ustün B, Cieza A. A guide on how to develop an international classification of functioning, disability and health core set. Eur J Phys Rehabil Med. 2014 Apr 1. [Epub ahead of print]
39. World Health Organization. International Classification of Diseases, 10th revision, Clinical Modification (ICD-10-CM). Geneva: World Health Organization; 2014.

Chapter 14
Critical Issues for Mental Health Management in Vocational Rehabilitation: DSM-5, ICD-10-CM, and Implementing the WHODAS

David B. Peterson

14.1 Introduction

This chapter provides a review of critical issues for mental health management in vocational rehabilitation within the context of the implementation of the International Classification of Functioning, Disability and Health [1]. We begin with a discussion of the importance of competency in psychiatric diagnoses for vocational rehabilitation professionals working in mental health management. We follow with a review of the release of the Diagnostic and Statistical Manual of Mental Disorders (DSM), Fifth Edition [2], highlighting significant changes from the previous version. Of particular interest to the ICF, we introduce the inclusion of the World Health Organization Disability Assessment Schedule [3], an instrument closely linked to the ICF, within the DSM-5 as a replacement for the Global Assessment of Functioning (GAF) that was in previous versions of the DSM [4].

Following our discussion of the DSM, we focus on the ongoing development of a more ubiquitous classification of psychiatric diagnoses, the ICF's sister classification, the International Classification of Diseases (ICD) to its tenth and eleventh revisions [5, 6]. Vocational rehabilitation professionals working in mental health management will need to have facility with both the ICD and DSM systems to work effectively within the US clinical practice paradigm.

Within the context of the DSM and ICD systems, we turn our attention to the DSM's current definition of psychiatric diagnosis and the related conceptualization of psychiatric disability according to the ICF. Taken together, we discuss how the WHODAS [3] can be used to conceptualize severity of psychiatric disability, as currently employed within the DSM-5.

D.B. Peterson (✉)
Charter College of Education, Division of Special Education and Counseling, Rehabilitation Education Programs, California State University, Los Angeles, 5151 State University Dr, King Hall C1064, Los Angeles, CA 90032, USA
e-mail: dpeters3@exchange.calstatela.edu

R. Escorpizo et al. (eds.), *Handbook of Vocational Rehabilitation and Disability Evaluation*, Handbooks in Health, Work, and Disability, DOI 10.1007/978-3-319-08825-9_14

14.2 Competency in Psychiatric Diagnoses

One may ask the question, why do rehabilitation professionals involved in mental health management need to have a good understanding of psychiatric diagnoses, when they can refer consumers to appropriate sources for treatment? The most important answer to this question is that rehabilitation services professionals may be the first to have established any type of therapeutic relationship with their consumer, revealing information that previously had never been a focus of clinical attention. Rehabilitation counselors may be the first allied health professional to accurately identify a psychiatric diagnosis for a consumer and make appropriate referrals to psychiatric treatment and/or psychotherapy. After a consumer begins training or job placement in the rehabilitation process, he or she may encounter significant stressors and circumstances that lead to the development of psychiatric symptoms, which rehabilitation support personnel may need to identify and plan for in order to support maximum levels of functioning [7].

In order for vocational rehabilitation professionals to understand psychiatric diagnoses, the skilled clinician must be able to distinguish between normal life variations and transient responses to stress and serious symptomatology manifested as disturbances in behaviors, cognition, personality, physical signs, and syndrome combinations [2]. The accurate diagnosis of psychiatric conditions leads to appropriate referrals, selection of the most appropriate evidenced-based treatments, and ultimately amelioration or elimination of problematic symptoms that negatively impact health and functioning [8, pp. 5–6]. The DSM-5 is the most contemporary system available in the USA to help clinicians make these distinctions.

In light of this development and given the importance of the DSM system in the USA, we review next its key features, changes from the IV-TR to the 5th version, and discuss the WHODAS and its role in establishing severity of a psychiatric diagnosis.

> The DSM-5 is the most contemporary system available in the USA to inform psychiatric diagnoses.

14.3 DSM-5

The intent of the latest iteration of the DSM was to be useful to mental health professionals, consumers of mental health services and their families, and researchers, by providing clear and concise descriptions of psychiatric diagnoses. Using the DSM-5 effectively requires knowledge of factors that predispose one to mental disorders, events that may precipitate them, dynamics that perpetuate psychological impairment, as well as factors that protect and preserve mental health, all of which is informed by an individual's social and cultural context [2, p. 19].

The new DSM suggests that advances in science indicate that boundaries between psychiatric diagnoses are less clear than once thought and that most conditions can be placed on a spectrum with closely related diagnoses that share symptoms, genetic and environmental risk factors, and probable biological bases of behavior. The latest edition of the DSM is an attempt to include the latest knowledge in this regard but is admittedly a diagnostic system in ongoing development and refinement. Mental health management professionals have learned a great deal about psychiatric diagnoses in the last two decades. This new information will continue to grow exponentially with advances in science that should improve our understanding of psychiatric diagnoses, reduce social stigma associated with them, and ultimately improve treatment outcomes [2].

The DSM-5 is made up of three sections. Section I describes the history and developmental process of the latest revision of the DSM and presents a guide to the basics of DSM-5 clinical diagnosis. Section II contains the diagnostic criteria and codes, classifying psychiatric disorders into 22 major categories, an expansion of the DSM-IV-TR's 17 major categories. The primary purpose of Sect. II of the DSM-5 is "to assist trained clinicians in the diagnosis of their patient's mental disorders as part of a case formulation assessment that leads to a fully informed treatment plan" (p. 19). Each diagnosis provides explicit diagnostic criteria, dimensional measures that cut across diagnoses, and a concise overview of a given diagnosis, risk factors, associated features, related research, and possible manifestations of the diagnosis [2, p. 5].

Section III of the DSM-5, Emerging Measures and Models, provides new assessment measures, cultural formulations, an alternative model for disorders of personality, as well as conditions for further study. The contents of Sect. III are suggested to require further study before full implementation with Sect. II of the manual, but users are encouraged to use them to enhance clinical decision-making [2]. It is within this Sect. III that the WHODAS is presented as an alternative to the former GAF to describe severity of impairment or disability.

The DSM-5 has its share of critics and was revised almost exclusively by psychiatrists, to the exclusion of many other allied health professionals who contributed to previous iterations of the system [8]. However, the DSM-5 is an important diagnostic system in the USA and will continue to be so for some time to come.

> The DSM-5 is a diagnostic system that is in ongoing development and refinement.

14.3.1 Diagnostic Criteria

There are currently 22 diagnostic categories within the DSM-5 to which the aforementioned diagnostic principles need to be applied. Diagnostic matters are not always clear-cut; diagnostic criteria are complex, so familiarity with the information available and good clinical training and supervision are essential to good clinical decision-making and the most accurate diagnosis. Readers are referred to the DSM-5 itself for a thorough review of the updated diagnostic system [2]. The 22 diagnostic categories include:

1. Neurodevelopmental disorders
2. Schizophrenia spectrum and other psychotic disorders
3. Bipolar and related disorders
4. Depressive disorders
5. Anxiety disorders
6. Obsessive-compulsive and related disorders
7. Trauma- and stressor-related disorders
8. Dissociative disorders
9. Somatic-symptom and related disorders
10. Feeding and eating disorders
11. Elimination disorders
12. Sleep-wake disorders
13. Sexual dysfunctions
14. Gender dysphoria
15. Disruptive, impulse-control, and conduct disorders
16. Substance-related and addictive disorders
17. Neurocognitive disorders
18. Personality disorders
19. Paraphilic disorders
20. Other mental disorders
21. Medication-induced movement disorders and other adverse effects of medication
22. Other conditions that may be a focus of clinical attention

14.3.2 Changes from DSM-IV-TR to DSM-5

Changes highlighted here regarding changes in the new DSM-5 are most useful to those familiar with the DSM-IV-TR. The reader is referred to pages 809–816 of the DSM-5 for a more thorough discussion of these changes and to the DSM-IV-TR for further details [2, 4]. The reader will note the Roman numeral system has been abandoned from the DSM-IV-TR for a numeric system allowing updates not unlike the numeric systems used for software program revision (e.g., 5.1 as a potential future revision).

The organization of the diagnostic categories in the DSM-5 was changed to harmonize with the most recent version of the mental and behavioral disorders section of the ICD [5, 6]. This was done in order to minimize the impact of having two different diagnostic systems affecting collection of health statistics and future research replication. Advances in neuroscience are reflected in expanded diagnostic categories and subtypes of neurocognitive disorders [2].

The DSM-5 has transitioned away from the multiaxial system of diagnosis to a non-axial system. Axes I and II are combined, and Axis III physical conditions, if they affect psychological functioning, are to be noted along with the psychiatric diagnoses. Axis IV was eliminated, as the DSM-5 task force decided not to further develop its own psychosocial and environmental problems classification schema [2, p. 16], perhaps allowing room for more of the ICF and its conceptual framework, beyond the WHODAS 2.0, in future iterations of the DSM [8]. Finally, with the elimination of the axial system, the order of diagnoses presented in the DSM-5 reflects a developmental and lifespan perspective [2].

The frequently used "not otherwise specified" or "NOS" qualifier for DSM-IV-TR, which meant a diagnosis came close to but did not satisfy all of the diagnostic criteria required for the formal diagnosis, has been changed to one of two new options. *Other specified disorder* is used to highlight the specific reason why a set of symptoms does not meet diagnostic criteria. *Unspecified disorder* is the qualifier used if the clinician decides not to highlight the specific reason. Clinical judgment is used in determining whether there is sufficient evidence to use *other specified* versus *unspecified disorder* [2].

The DSM-5 also has online supplemental information, including more symptom and functional impairment severity measures that cut across diagnostic categories. Additionally, in an effort to enhance cultural sensitivity of DSM diagnoses, the *Cultural Formulation Interview* is provided with supplements (see www.psychiatry.org/dsm5). Pages 14 and 15 of the DSM-5 provide an excellent overview of the myriad cultural, as well as gender issues that affect the boundary between normality and pathology, and the systems in which healthcare is provided.

There are a number of diagnostic changes in the revised DSM, and some details will not be covered here; the reader is referred to pages 809–816 of the DSM-5 for all of the specifics. Some of the diagnostic changes in the DSM-5 most relevant to vocational rehabilitation include the pervasive developmental disorders combined into an *autism spectrum disorder*, and the term mental retardation has been replaced by *intellectual disability* (or intellectual developmental disorder). Severity of these conditions is estimated using measures of adaptive functioning rather than measures of IQ as in the DSM-IV-TR. The various learning disorders have been combined into one *specific learning disorder* diagnosis. Substance abuse and dependence are now described as *substance use disorders*, and the distinction between tolerance and withdrawal (formerly associated with dependence) and addiction is made clear. The subtypes of schizophrenia in the DSM-IV-TR (i.e., paranoid, disorganized, catatonic, undifferentiated) have been removed due to their lack of clinical utility. The commonly used cognitive disorder not otherwise specified is now a *neurocognitive disorder* [2].

14.3.3 Internalizing and Externalizing Factors Groups and the ICF

Published empirical research supports a framework that divides most psychiatric diagnoses into one of two categories [2]. The two-factor framework will inform future research and is already affecting psychological assessment of personality functioning [9]. This framework is presented here as it has already had an impact on the organization of the order of diagnoses as presented in the DSM-5.

The *internalizing factors* group represents disorders with prominent anxiety, depressive, and somatic symptoms; the experience of symptoms may be considered more internal in their manifestation. The second group, *externalizing factors*, represents disorders with prominent impulsive, disruptive conduct, antisocial behavior, and substance use symptoms, "acting out" that manifests more prominently in the external environment. There appear to be genetic and environmental risk factors in common within these two groups and high comorbidity of disorders within them as well. Combinations of internalizing and externalizing dysfunction may play a role in more complex psychiatric diagnoses such as posttraumatic stress disorder and borderline personality disorder [9].

14.3.4 Emerging Model of Personality Disorders

In Sect. III of the DSM-5, there is a newly proposed research model for further study of personality disorders. Many allied health professionals who attended prerelease DSM-5 training anticipated that this alternative approach would be the new method for diagnosing personality disorders, as the current system often results in overlapping diagnoses and often required the assignment of "not otherwise specified" due to multiple similarities across more specific diagnoses. The APA decided to maintain continuity with the DSM-IV-TR until more research was conducted on the new approach [2].

The proposed model considers first the level of personality functioning, defined as disturbances in self (identity and self-direction) and interpersonal functioning (empathy and intimacy). The proposed *Level of Personality Functioning Scale* [2, pp. 775–778] is used to determine where among a five-level continuum a person is functioning. Second, pathological personality traits are organized along five broad domains: negative affectivity, detachment, antagonism, disinhibition, and psychoticism. Measures of this model also suggest 25 specific trait facets that further define the personality disorder diagnosis. Pervasiveness and stability of personality pathology are also part of the assessment. Further explanation of this model is beyond the scope of this chapter, so the reader is referred to Sect. III of the DSM-5 for greater detail [2].

14.3.5 The WHO Disability Assessment Schedule 2.0 (WHODAS 2.0)

Axis V, the Global Assessment of Functioning or GAF score, has been eliminated. In its place, within Sect. III of the DSM-5, Emerging Measures and Models, and related to our prior ICF discussion, the World Health Organization Disability Assessment Schedule 2.0 [3, 10], closely linked to the ICF, provides a new standard method for assessing global disability levels for mental disorders [2, p. 16]. The WHODAS will be discussed in greater detail further on in this chapter.

Also included in Sect. III are crosscutting symptom measures for both adults and children. These measures address 13 symptom domains with dimensional measures of severity proposed for all DSM diagnostic groups. The domain names are clearly related to the 22 existing diagnostic categories of the DSM-5 and include: depression, anger, mania, anxiety, somatic symptoms, suicidal ideation, psychosis, sleep problems, memory, repetitive thoughts and behaviors, dissociation, personality functioning, and substance use. These domains relate to severity of symptoms and not to severity of functional impairment or disability, which is the domain of the WHODAS 2.0. These measures can be based upon responses from the patient, the treating professional, or an informant. Respondents are asked to rate behaviors over the last 2 weeks, as having occurred not at all (0), rarely or less than a day or 2 (slight or 1), several days (mild or 2), more than half the days (moderate or 3), or nearly every day (severe or 4). See pages 734–741 of the DSM-5 for specific details [2].

14.4 International Classification of Diseases (ICD)

International classification of population health began in the 1800s with a focus on the prevalence of medical diagnoses that were causes of death; once standing for the International Causes of Death (ICD), the acronym persists to this day. The International Classification of Diseases (ICD) evolved over time to include not only conditions that cause death but also illness. Subsequent iterations of the ICD have provided an etiological classification of health conditions (e.g., diseases, disorders, injuries) related to mortality (death) and morbidity (illness).

A growing body of literature suggests that diagnostic information alone is limited in its utility to target and plan interventions and evaluate effectiveness of treatment/healthcare outcomes [1, 8]. Medical documentation typically focuses on the use of systems like the ICD, but most lack the classification of associated functioning. These data are important because functional implications of a given diagnosis across individuals may be quite disparate. Diagnoses may manifest through a variety of impairments that range in their potential impact on functioning. Individual differences in coping styles may impact an individual's reaction to a given impairment, for example, coping with or succumbing to a given difficulty.

Diagnoses alone are limited without clear descriptions of associated functioning [1, 8].

The ICD provides an etiological classification of health conditions related to mortality and morbidity.

14.4.1 ICD-10-CM

On the international stage the DSM has not enjoyed the same success that it has in the USA. The system used more commonly throughout the world is the ICD, now in its Tenth Revision, Clinical Modification [5, 6]. The ICD systems have been available online for use free of charge, in contrast with the DSM-5 which approaches $200 for a hard copy in some marketplaces. As mentioned earlier, there have been efforts to "harmonize" the DSM-5 revision with the ICD-10-CM and the upcoming ICD-11 revision planned for completion in 2017 [2, p. xli, 6].

It bears mentioning here that the USA only recently adopted the ICD-9-CM [11], with plans for adopting the ICD-10-CM uncertain given institutional resistance to the cost of implementing the newer system. For this reason the DSM-5 lists the codes for both the ICD-9-CM and the ICD-10-CM. The ICD-9-CM will continue to be used within the USA through October 1, 2014, with plans to implement the ICD-10-CM thereafter in coordination with its scheduled adoption [2, pp. xiii, xli]. For the short term, vocational rehabilitation professionals in mental health management will need to be comfortable using the DSM-IV-TR, DSM-5 and the ICD-9-CM and 10-CM.

Vocational rehabilitation professionals in mental health management will need to be comfortable using the DSM-IV-TR, DSM-5, ICD-9-CM, and the ICD-10-CM.

14.4.2 ICD-11

Planned for completion in 2017, WHO's latest revision of the ICD promises to move toward more unified classification of psychiatric diagnoses through harmonization with the DSM-5 [2, p. xli]. WHO's webpage for the ICD-11 makes clear its intention to remain the world's standard tool to capture mortality and morbidity data for both physical and psychiatric conditions. The current revision process involves a Web-based platform inviting feedback from a wide range of stakeholders, as well as a peer-review process, in order to incorporate the most recent developments in health sciences and medical practice [6].

14.5 Clinical Significance of Psychiatric Diagnoses Versus Severity of Psychiatric Disability

The ICD has not historically relied on level of impairment or disability to establish the existence of a disease process or diagnosis. The ICD refers to its sister classification, the ICF, to address the concept of disability and its relative severity. The DSM-IV-TR [4] requires clinical thresholds of significant distress or impairment in functioning that rely heavily on clinical judgment in order to establish a diagnosis, addressing diagnosis and disability simultaneously.

The APA and WHO in their current revision efforts of the DSM and ICD agreed upon the importance of clarifying the role of functional impairment in the diagnosis of mental disorders [12]. Prior to this consensus the WHO's international efforts to classify psychiatric functioning, health, and disability were not consistent with the APA's efforts within the USA and those countries relying on the DSM to inform mental health management and practice.

It was agreed between the two organizations that for future revision efforts, in order to encourage international research consistency, that disability should be operationally defined through expert consensus, separate and apart from expert consensus on clinically significant disease processes associated with the diagnoses of mental disorders, for both the ICD and the DSM. One of the key features of the ICF conceptual framework is the acknowledgment that severity or clinical significance of a diagnosis is not reliably associated with the level of severity of functional impairment manifested in one's environment. The manifestation of disability is based upon the interaction of the person's impairment in functioning within a specific personal and environmental context. Because of this clinical reality, the clinical significance of a psychiatric diagnosis needs to be considered separate and apart from the severity of associated psychiatric disability [1]. What follows is a more detailed discussion of clinical significance of a psychiatric diagnosis, and establishing the severity of a psychiatric disability.

> Future ICD and DSM efforts will seek to separate the concepts of clinical significance of psychiatric diagnosis and severity of disability.

14.5.1 Clinical Significance of Psychiatric Diagnoses

In versions prior to the 5th edition of the DSM, diagnoses were based upon meeting certain diagnostic criteria (specific phenomenology, signs, and symptoms) that caused clinically significant psychological distress. The significance of psychological distress was left to considerable clinical judgment. The Global Assessment of Functioning (GAF) of the DSM was designed to provide gross estimates of the severity of a given diagnosis (distress experienced by the individual) and also its related impact on functioning (functional impairment), presented as two separate GAF scores. This paradigm acknowledged that specific diagnoses were not reliably associated with specific manifestations of disability.

The ICD operationalized psychiatric diagnoses similar to the DSM with respect to specific phenomenology, signs, and symptoms, but no clinical significance was required for the disease process to exist in order to establish a diagnosis. Difficulties in functioning were occasionally included in some ICD classifications, but the intention for the 11th revision of the ICD is to cleanly separate disability and disease constructs [12]. The ICD-11 will refer the classification of functioning and severity of impairment to its sister classification, the ICF, and its conceptualization of disability [1].

For the DSM-5 [2], the clinical significance of a psychiatric diagnosis is similarly established based upon updates in the health and science literature, but the GAF has been eliminated due to its lack of clinical utility and inconsistent implementation among healthcare professionals. In its place, the DSM-5 is recommending the use of the WHODAS 2.0, developed based upon the ICF, to operationalize disability [2]. Next, we turn to a discussion of historical perspectives on the severity of psychiatric disability within the DSM-IV-TR and the ICD.

14.5.2 Severity of Psychiatric Disability

There is a paucity of research on the form, frequency, and outcomes of disability in mental disorders [12]. Historically the definition of the severity of psychiatric disability has been poorly defined or not considered at all in the establishment of psychiatric diagnosis. Neither the ICD nor the DSM versions prior to the 5th edition formulated an operational definition of disability or the manifestation of functional impairment in an individual's context [1, 8, 12].

The DSM-IV-TR [4] addressed severity of disability in three different ways, the first being functional impairment as a clinical determination of symptoms surpassing a threshold of distress or disability in order to establish any given diagnosis. However, clear guidance is not given as to where that threshold exists for most specific diagnoses, with the exception of mood disorders providing relatively more explicit criteria than other diagnoses.

The second method uses a qualifier of the severity of the diagnosis once the diagnostic threshold is reached, consisting of three broadly defined levels of severity of a diagnosis, based upon both symptoms and related impairments in social or occupational functioning. Mild impairment implies few symptoms above the required number of symptoms for a diagnosis, with minor impairments in social or occupational functioning. Severe impairment implies the existence of many symptoms above the required number, with marked impairments in social or occupational functioning. No guidance is provided as to how few, many, minor, or marked impairments are operationalized in the DSM-IV-TR. To cloud the matter further, moderate was employed as a level of severity existing between the already vaguely defined mild and severe.

The third method of establishing severity of impairment in the DSM-IV-TR employs the Global Assessment of Functioning (GAF) to plan and track treatment progress, as well as predict treatment outcome [4]. We have already discussed this index and noted its elimination from the DSM-5. We have also noted that the ICD used the ICF to conceptualize severity of psychiatric diagnoses.

Given our comparison of the clinical significance of psychiatric diagnoses with the severity of psychiatric disability, we next turn our attention to the DSM-5 definition of psychiatric diagnosis (clinical significance) and the ICF's conceptualization of psychiatric disability. We end with an introduction of the WHODAS 2.0 as a measure of functional impairment (severity of disability) for people with psychiatric diagnoses.

14.5.3 DSM Definition of Psychiatric Diagnosis

Psychiatric diagnoses are *mental disorders* that manifest certain symptoms, or diagnostic criteria, that significantly impair psychological functioning. Based upon our most contemporary understanding of how psychiatric symptoms may manifest, psychiatric diagnoses can be recognized and identified by trained mental health professionals [2]. The American Psychiatric Association defines a *mental disorder* as:

> ...a syndrome characterized by clinically significant disturbance in an individual's cognition, emotion regulation, or behavior that reflects a dysfunction in the psychological, biological, or developmental processes underlying mental functioning. Mental disorders are usually associated with significant distress or disability in social, occupational, or other important activities. (p. 20)

It goes on to say that a mental disorder is NOT...

> ...an expectable or culturally approved response to a common stressor or loss, such as the death of a loved one... socially deviant behavior (e.g., political, religious, or sexual) and conflicts that are primarily between the individual and society... unless the deviance or conflict results from a dysfunction in the individual as described above. (p. 20)

In summary, the DSM has not historically provided clear operational definitions for clinical significance, dysfunction, nor distress or disability in social, occupational, or other important activities, but relied considerably upon clinical judgment to identify signs and symptoms of the disease process that create sufficient distress or disability to cross the threshold warranting a diagnosis. Assessment of symptoms leading to diagnosis was never done separate and apart from the assessment of functioning. However, Sect. III of the DSM-5 encourages the use of the WHODAS 2.0 to move in the direction of operationalizing what is significant clinical dysfunction and impairment in social and occupational functioning (disability). Next, we turn to the parent classification of the WHODAS 2.0, the ICF, and its conceptualization of psychiatric disability, after which we will discuss the WHODAS 2.0.

14.5.4 ICF Conceptualization of Psychiatric Disability

The most contemporary definition of disability to date can be found within the World Health Organization's conceptualization of health, the sister classification to the ICD, the ICF [1], fully described in Part 1 of this series and in Chap. 13 as a concise overview [8, 13–16]. Psychiatric disability, according to the WHO model of health, can be defined as a function of how a person's mental impairment manifests within a given context. Impairments may reduce psychological functioning (e.g., consciousness, orientation, energy, sleep, attention, memory, emotional regulation), which in turn may limit functional activity, and based upon contextual factors may also limit one's ability to participate in society [1, 12].

The clinical utility of noting the influence of context on mental health and function is how it informs intervention targeting. It allows a mental health management professional to target disparities between someone's potential and current functioning that result from contextual factors, identify remediation that is sensitive to context, ameliorate or eliminate psychological difficulties, maximize potential function, and minimize the impact of disability [8].

14.6 WHODAS 2.0 and Severity of Disability

One of the most significant contributions of the ICF to mental health management in recent times is its linking with an assessment tool developed specifically to reflect the ICF, the World Health Organization Disability Assessment Schedule 2.0 [3, 10], into Sect. III of the latest revision of the DSM-5. Included to "enhance the clinical decision-making process," the WHODAS 2.0 is intended to replace the Global Assessment of Functioning of the previous multiaxial version DSM-IV-TR [2, p. 731].

14.6.1 Development

The WHODAS 2.0 was developed on the basis of an extensive cross-cultural study involving 19 countries and used item-response theory to construct the 36-item scale. Psychometric analysis suggests excellent evidence for reliability. It is short and easy to use; the 12-item self-administered version takes about 5 min, or the 36-item interviewer-administered format (which requires some training) takes about 20 min. It measures day-to-day activities across a range of activity domains. The intent and clinical value of the WHODAS is that it helps to distinguish between measurement of symptoms, disability, and subjective appraisal [10]. The original version of the WHODAS [17] was developed to work with psychiatric inpatients. The WHODAS 2.0 is completely redeveloped to include all diseases, including mental, neurological, and addictive disorders, and can be used for adults (a child and youth version is in development) across cultures in both clinical and general population settings.

14.6.2 Measured Domains

The WHODAS 2.0 produces standardized disability levels and profiles that reflect a direct conceptual link to the ICF. The WHODAS 2.0 covers six domains of function, as reflected in Table 14.1.

Considering the WHODAS 2.0 domains alone, the relationship between it and the ICF's conceptual framework are clear. The ability to make the distinction between life activities and participation is consistent with the ICF conceptual framework, accounting for the relationship between the individual's functioning, disability, and health and his or her personal and environmental context. As mentioned in Chap. 13, gaps between someone's potential functioning (activity) and his or her actual participation in a given context provide a focus for intervention targeting.

Reviewing the descriptions of the WHODAS 2.0 domains, one can see how clinical interview data of the respondent's answers to questions would be extremely useful in clinical case conceptualization (e.g., one's ability to tend to personal hygiene, the ability to get along with others). Further, one can see how rehabilitation professional could associate a number of objective psychological test domains to inform the assessment of the domain descriptions, as noted in the third column of Table 14.1 (author's contribution).

Table 14.1 WHODAS 2.0 domains, descriptions, and psychological testing domains [3]

WHODAS 2.0 domain	WHODAS 2.0 domain description	Objective psychological test domains
Cognition	Understanding and communicating	Neuropsychological/intellectual functioning, aptitudes, and achievement
Mobility	Moving and getting around	Neuropsychological/adaptive functioning
Self-care	Hygiene, dressing, eating, and staying alone	Adaptive functioning
Getting along	Interacting with other people	Personality functioning, psychopathology
Life activities	Domestic responsibilities, leisure, work, and school	Aptitude testing, adaptive functioning, career development, interests, and values
Participation	Joining in community activities	Adaptive functioning, in vivo assessment (e.g., job tryout, supported employment)

14.6.3 Administration and Scoring

For the interviewer-administered 36-item version of the WHODAS 2.0, the interviewer elicits difficulties the respondent has because of health conditions. The respondent is asked to consider all conditions present: diseases, illnesses, or other health problems of any duration; injuries; mental or emotional problems; and problems with alcohol or drugs. The interviewer elicits whether over the past 30 days the respondent has had difficulty with a given activity as demonstrated by the need for increased effort, the experience of discomfort or pain, slowness, or changes in the way the interviewee does an activity. The respondent is encouraged to consider these difficulties for activities performed as he or she usually does the activity. These key foci are also presented on a flashcard so that the respondent can read the instructions as well as listen to the interviewer speak them. A second flash card is presented to the respondent, and the interviewer encourages the respondent to use the following scale when responding: none, mild, moderate, severe, extreme or cannot do. Both flashcards remain present throughout the interview so that the respondent can refer to them at will.

The WHODAS 2.0 scoring can occur through a simple summing and averaging of scores, which may be desirable in fast-paced clinical settings. There is also a computerized scoring option available that uses item-response theory to weight the 36 items based upon normative data in order to present a more precise summary score reflecting the level of disability [10].

14.6.4 Limitations

An obvious dilemma facing respondents using the five-point scale to describe how much difficulty they have experienced in the past 30 days is that the severity levels are not operationalized in any way to encourage consistency across respondents. The extreme or cannot do choices may be clear enough, but what are the finer distinctions between mild, moderate, and severe? This dilemma is reminiscent of our earlier discussion of DSM-IV-TR disability severity as it related to the Global Assessment of Functioning, which is no more. Added complexity arrives from asking the respondents to select these levels of difficulty without adequate distinctions between severity levels.

If the clinician is making the assessment, perhaps a metric can be developed that links to commonly administered objective psychological tests so that rating the domains is more consistent across evaluations. Or perhaps further clarification can be added to the second card to help respondents reply on a more consistent metric.

Employing the WHODAS 2.0 within the DSM-5 highlights another important limitation; notwithstanding the list of objective psychological testing domains in Table 14.1 that are available, current limitations in psychological measurement mean that many psychiatric diagnoses lack reliable measures of severity to inform the use of the WHODAS 2.0. Despite our best efforts, in many cases the clinical significance of a psychiatric diagnosis remains a matter of clinical judgment as to whether "the disturbance causes clinically significant distress or impairment in social, occupational, or other important areas of functioning" [2, p. 21].

14.7 Conclusion

As the APA and WHO work toward revising their seminal classifications of psychiatric diagnoses and related disability and functioning, efforts are underway to clarify the relationship between clinical significance of diagnosis and the severity of the related functional limitations and disability. The ICF-related literature has been instrumental in directing our scholarly discourse in this regard and has resulted in the inclusion of the WHODAS 2.0 as an instrument suggested for further study in the DSM-5. Further research and collaboration between APA and WHO will hopefully help rehabilitation professionals to make clearer distinctions between the clinical significance of psychiatric diagnoses and the related manifestations of psychiatric disability. Providing this clarity will serve to remind mental health professionals that diagnoses are not reliably associated with any specific functional profile. The focus on establishing functional estimates of psychiatric impairment will inform the selection of appropriate evidence-based treatments, and the outcomes of these interventions will serve to inform researchers and clinicians alike regarding the implementation of future interventions.

Questions:

1. What is the most contemporary system of psychiatric diagnosis available in the USA?

    (a) WHODAS 2.0
    (b) ICD-9-CM
    (c) DSM-5
    (d) ICF

    Correct answer c.

2. Vocational rehabilitation counselors need to be able to identify

    (a) The difference between normal life variations and transient responses to stress versus serious symptoms that suggest diagnosis
    (b) Disturbances in behaviors, cognitions, personality, physical signs, and syndrome combinations
    (c) Appropriate resources for effective treatment
    (d) All of the above

    Correct answer d.

3. Mental health professionals are encouraged to use the WHODAS 2.0 in place of the GAF to enhance clinical decision-making, and describe severity of impairment or disability.

    (a) True
    (b) False

    Correct answer b.

4. What is the WHODAS 2.0?

    (a) A new standard method for assessing global disability levels for mental disorders
    (b) A revision of the WHODAS influenced by the ICF
    (c) The suggested replacement for the GAF of DSM versions prior to the DSM-5
    (d) All of the above

    Correct answer d.

5. The diagnostic system used most commonly for psychiatric diagnoses throughout the world is

    (a) DSM-5
    (b) ICD-10-CM
    (c) ICF
    (d) ICD-9-CM

    Correct answer b.

6. Severity or clinical significance of a diagnosis is
   (a) Not reliably associated with the level of severity of functional impairment manifested in ones' environment
   (b) Reliably associated with the level of severity of functional impairment manifested in ones' environment
   (c) May or may not be reliably associated with the level of severity of functional impairment manifested in ones' environment
   (d) are hypothetical constructs that defy classification

   Correct answer a.

References

1. World Health Organization. International classification of functioning, disability and health (ICF). Geneva: World Health Organization; 2001.
2. American Psychiatric Association. Diagnostic and statistical manual of mental disorders. 5th ed. Arlington: American Psychiatric Publishing; 2013.
3. World Health Organization. Measuring health and disability: manual for WHO Disability Assessment Schedule (WHODAS 2.0). Geneva: World Health Organization; 2012.
4. American Psychiatric Association. Diagnostic and statistical manual of mental disorders, Text revision (DSM-IV-TR). 4th ed. Washington, DC: American Psychiatric Publishing; 2013.
5. World Health Organization. International classification of diseases, 10th revision, Clinical modification (ICD-10-CM). Geneva: World Health Organization; 2014.
6. World Health Organization. ICD-11.
7. Peterson DB, Hong G. Psychiatric diagnoses. In: Brodwin MG, Siu FW, Howard J, Brodwin ER, Du AT, editors. Medical, psychosocial, and vocational aspects of disability. 5th ed. Athens: Elliott & Fitzpatrick; 2014.
8. Peterson DB. Psychological aspects of functioning, disability and health. New York: Springer; 2011.
9. Ben-Porath YS. Interpreting the MMPI-2-RF. Minneapolis: University of Minnesota Press; 2012.
10. World Health Organization. WHODAS 2.0. 14 Sept 2013. Available from: http://www.who.int/classifications/icf/whodasii/en/
11. World Health Organization. International classification of diseases, 9th revision, Clinical modification (ICD-9-CM). Geneva: World Health Organization; 2011.
12. Ustun B, Kennedy C. What is "functional impairment"? Disentangling disability from clinical significance. World Psychiatry. 2009;8(2):82–5.
13. Peterson DB. An international conceptualization of disability: the International Classification of Functioning, Disability & Health (ICF). In: Marini I, Stebnicki M, editors. The psychological and social impact of illness and disability. 6th ed. New York: Springer; 2012. p. 405–22.
14. Peterson DB, Elliott TR. Advances in conceptualizing and studying disability. In: Brown S, Lent RW, editors. Handbook of counseling psychology. 4th ed. Hoboken: Wiley; 2008. p. 212–30.
15. Peterson DB, Paul H. Using the International Classification of Functioning, Disability and Health (ICF) to conceptualize disability functioning in psychological injury and law. Psychol Inj Law. 2009;2(3-4):205–14.
16. Peterson DB, Mpofu E, Oakland TD. Concepts and models in disability, functioning, and health. In: Mpofu E, Oakland TD, editors. Rehabilitation and health assessment: applying ICF guidelines. New York: Springer; 2010. p. 3–26.
17. World Health Organization. WHO psychiatric disability assessment schedule (WHO/DAS). Geneva: World Health Organization; 1988.

Chapter 15
Serious Mental Illness, Vocational Rehabilitation, and Employment

Terry Krupa, Shu-Ping Chen, and Glenda Carter

15.1 Introduction

The focus of this chapter is on employment support and vocational rehabilitation that assists people with serious mental illness to find, enjoy, and sustain meaningful employment in their communities. Work is considered to be fundamental both to recovery in mental illness and full citizenship, and subsequently designing effective employment services and approaches has received much attention within the field of psychiatric vocational rehabilitation.

The chapter begins by defining serious mental illness from an employment perspective and is followed by a review of key principles underlying vocational rehabilitation and employment support programs. The field has witnessed the development of a range of services and initiatives meant to create and support real work opportunities for people with serious mental illness. Three of these approaches are described. In addition, complementary interventions that have the potential to enhance vocational outcomes are presented, as well as a few of the ongoing challenges and debates that exist in the field. Finally, the chapter will discuss the relevance of the International Classification of Functioning, Disability and Health (ICF) [1] core set categories to psychiatric vocational rehabilitation and employment support services for people with serious mental illness. The potential application of the ICF core set categories for vocational rehabilitation is highlighted by its application to one vocational rehabilitation program that has a mission to

T. Krupa (✉)
School of Rehabilitation Therapy, Queen's University, Kingston, ON K7L 3N6, Canada
e-mail: terry.krupa@queensu.ca

S.-P. Chen
School of Rehabilitation Therapy, Queen's University, Kingston, ON, Canada

G. Carter
Frontenac Community Mental Health and Addictions Services, Kingston, ON, Canada

R. Escorpizo et al. (eds.), *Handbook of Vocational Rehabilitation and Disability Evaluation*, Handbooks in Health, Work, and Disability, DOI 10.1007/978-3-319-08825-9_15

enable successful and satisfying work experiences for people with serious mental illness.

15.2 Defining Serious Mental Illness and Employment

Rates of unemployment among people with mental illness are high, but understanding their actual employment status is complicated by the fact that people with serious mental illness are a diverse group, heterogeneous both with respect to their illness experiences and their participation in important life domains such as work. Definitions of serious mental illness typically include consideration of both mental ill health and evidence of problems in function. In this chapter, we suggest that consideration of serious mental illness in relation to employment should include reference to the high levels of marginalization and detachment from the community workforce experienced by the population.

15.2.1 Serious Mental Illness and Diagnosis

The concept of "serious mental illness" engenders assumptions about particular mental illness diagnoses. For example, serious mental illness is often equated with diagnoses of schizophrenia, bipolar disorder, and other major mood disorders that have a persistent quality, even when acute episodes are episodic. Although there has been much debate about the relationship between diagnosis and employment rates, research evidence has not supported that employment can be predicted by diagnosis [2]. Yet, schizophrenia and mental illnesses with psychotic components have long been regarded as serious mental illnesses with lower rates of employment than other mental illnesses. For example, analyzing US national health interview survey on disability distinguished between *serious mental illness* with employment rates of 37 % and *severe mental illness* (defined as including those with schizophrenia and related disorders), with employment rates at 22 % [3].

Estimating employment rates according to diagnosis is a complex undertaking and findings are not easily interpreted. For example, a broad review of literature reporting employment rates for people with schizophrenia demonstrated huge variations internationally [4]. It was highlighted that interpreting employment rates among this population is complicated by differences in how diagnosis is determined, what activities are actually included as employment in national statistics, and a host of social and cultural differences, including access to social welfare, expectations regarding employment, and labor market opportunities.

15.2.2 Serious Mental Illness and Functional Impact

Contemporary conceptualizations of serious mental illness go beyond diagnosis to consider the extent to which there are significant functional implications related to the mental health condition. In this way a broader range of diagnostic categories can be included under the label of serious mental illness if a consequence is significant functional impairment and disability [5].

Symptoms, impairments, and experiences associated with serious mental illness that have been associated with negative employment outcomes include the following:

- Impairments of psychological and emotional health related to persistent feelings of low volition and drive and disruptions in emotional connections to activities and people have been linked to poorer employment outcomes [6].
- A broad array of cognitive impairments are associated with serious mental illnesses, such as working memory, processing speed, sustained attention, and executive functioning, and have been associated with poorer employment outcomes and limited job tenure [7]. Disturbances in cognition can interfere with the ability to meet the demands of important job tasks and social relations on the job. In addition they can limit an individual's improvement within rehabilitation programs designed to improve work performance [8].
- Personal insight has been linked to employment outcomes. Insight refers to a range of mental processes, such as the ability to identify and accept particular experiences as disturbances of mental function, the capacity to identify that one is being impacted by these mental disturbances, and acceptance of the need for treatment, supports, or strategies to address these disturbances [9]. Insight is important in the context of employment, where the capacity to receive feedback, have self-awareness, understand personal strengths and weaknesses, self-monitor, and self-correct is fundamental to work performance and social relations [8, 10]. While insight is believed to be related to neurocognitive function, awareness and acceptance of illness has also been identified as an important task in the process of recovery in serious mental illness. Recovery is believed to be moderated by the meaning that people give to their illness experiences. For example, the extent to which the meanings given to the mental illness are self-stigmatizing (i.e., mental illness means incompetence, a grim future, low expectations, etc.), the less likely people are to engage in important social roles such as work [11].
- The capacity for self-management of the functional implications of mental illness has been linked to employment. Since serious mental illnesses involve a range of significant functional consequences, the individual's sense of agency and ability to effectively cope with these consequences will be instrumental in meeting work-related expectations [12].

  The age of onset of a serious mental illness has been linked to employment success. When experienced in adolescence and young adulthood, it can disrupt the many developmental activities associated with adult employment including:

educational achievement, work experience, basic life skills that support working, the development of social networks that can provide work connections and opportunities, the evolution of a work identity and career planning, and the financial autonomy to pursue work-related ambitions [13]. The growth of early intervention for psychosis services internationally has evolved largely from an interest in preventing disability, including unemployment, labor force detachment, and social dependence among young people [14].

15.2.3 Serious Mental Illness as Marginalization

Perhaps a defining work-related characteristic of people with serious mental illness is the extent to which their employment status can be characterized as marginalized, or at high risk for marginalization. This position of marginalization has been identified by scholars in the field for over 30 years as an explanation for their high levels of unemployment. For example, Warner [15] described how the employment status of people with a diagnosis of schizophrenia can be understood as a social-political response in the context of broader economic conditions. Warner demonstrated how attitudes related to employability of the population, and actual employment rates, improve in market-based economies during economic booms but recede during times of economic depression. Baron and Salzer [16] added to this by arguing that the social and economic circumstances of people with serious mental illness, such as low educational achievement and poverty, needed to be added to the "usual suspects" in explaining low employment rates.

Marginalization from the workforce suggests that people with serious mental illness have weak labor market attachments demonstrated in a variety of ways, including:

- The notion of "return to work" used in vocational rehabilitation does not apply, since they may have no employment situation awaiting or expecting their return.
- Their social networks are often exceptionally limited, providing few opportunities to develop employment or work-related connections. Indeed, their social networks may not be expecting them to engage in employment and may even see employment as harmful if it is perceived as potentially disrupting stability in community life or undermining the financial security of disability income benefits.
- They may have limited access to important material resources such as clothing, food, transportation, etc. that are basic to supporting employment.
- They may not have access to quality treatment or evidence-informed employment support services. Indeed, historically mental health services were not developed from a firm belief that employment is possible (or even positive) for this group of people. An often sited publication by Marrone and Galowka [17] highlighted that while the mental health field has concerned itself with the harmful impacts of work stress, there has historically been less concern about the

stress associated with chronic unemployment and ultimately the field projects an attitude of paternalism. Historically, vocational initiatives for people with serious mental illnesses were directed to creating work activities that were alternatives to the community labor force, such as sheltered workshops. These initiatives have been linked to the stigma of mental illness and in particular assumptions that providing work to people with a serious mental illness is a form of charity rather than a right of citizenship [18].

- It is common for people with a serious mental illness to be financially supported by government disability incomes. Compared to other populations, people who receive disability benefits in the context of mental illness are less likely to leave this public assistance [19]. Receipt of disability benefits can act as a disincentive to pursue and sustain employment in a number of ways. For example, it can promote an internalized view of the self as too disabled to work and leave individuals feeling financially insecure and even compromised should they pursue employment because of complicated administrative processes or taxation policies that impact earnings [20].
- Those who have current work experience are typically working in entry-level and part-time work, often with limited or no benefits. These types of employment conditions have been identified as a form of underemployment [16, 19] and marginalization *within* the workforce [21].

A closer look at the employment rates of people with mental illness suggests a high level of marginalization. Kozma and colleagues [22] analyzed the employment status of a population of individuals with a diagnosis of schizophrenia and found that among the many who were not employed, the majority were not even looking for work. Interestingly, research and personal accounts from people with serious mental illness suggest that they value employment and generally desire to be able to work [23]. It is this positive inclination to work that led the Mental Health Commission of Canada to use the label the "Aspiring Workforce" to describe the employment status of this population [24].

15.3 Principles Underlying Vocational Approaches

Contemporary vocational rehabilitation interventions and approaches are evolving from a set of principles. These principles address the employment marginalization experienced by this population by focusing on accessing, supporting, and creating *real work opportunities* as the foundation of best practice. They challenge the assumptions underlying traditional vocational rehabilitation approaches which focused primarily on understanding and addressing the work-related deficiencies (i.e., work attitudes, aptitudes, knowledge, skills, etc.) of individuals, or creating alternative work structures (such as sheltered workshops or day programs). The development of these principles was sparked by evidence indicating that traditional vocational rehabilitation approaches were not leading to employment [25].

These principles largely emerged during the development of supported employment as an evidence-based vocational rehabilitation approach [25, 26]. While the principles have largely been applied to a specific evidence-based model for practice, the individual placement and support (IPS) model, we argue here that they have broader relevance in the field, serve as a foundation for the development of a range of approaches, and contribute positively to a high-level debate within the field about the philosophy and nature of employment support and vocational rehabilitation. Kirsh and colleagues [27], for example, have examined how philosophies, principles, and practices related to vocational rehabilitation and employment support are cutting across different populations (those with brain injury, intellectual disability, or mental illness) that are vulnerable to high levels of marginalization.

What are these principles?

1. Creating and supporting real work opportunities is the focus of vocational rehabilitation.
2. Access to real work opportunities should be available to anyone who aspires to work.
3. Individuals with serious mental illness should be supported to consider employment as a real possibility.
4. Work opportunities should offer good work conditions, with health and safety, psychological well-being, and wage structures that are consistent with societal standards and expectations.
5. Work participation should be based on individual preferences and choice.
6. People with serious mental illness who engage in real work opportunities should have available to them ongoing, follow-along supports and access to a range of specific employment enabling interventions.
7. Treatments and services for mental illness should be delivered in an integrated fashion along with vocational rehabilitation.
8. Employment supports should attend to the material conditions of people's lives that impact employment, offering, for example, assistance related to finances, transportation, housing, personal safety, etc.
9. Employment supports and vocational rehabilitation approaches should act to improve the social and economic status of individuals with serious mental illness. This includes, for example, attention to social inclusion within work, evidence of improved material conditions in life, opportunities for advancement, work-life balance, and maintaining a career perspective.
10. Evaluation of vocational rehabilitation should include a range of individual-level outcomes (e.g., satisfaction and meaning in work, work abilities, quality of life), occupation-level outcomes (nature of accommodations offered, workplace social climate, etc.), and societal-level outcomes (cost-benefit, improved attitudes and actions toward marginalized groups, etc.).

15.4 Vocational Rehabilitation Approaches

In this paper we focus on three contemporary approaches to addressing the employment needs of people with serious mental illnesses, all having the potential in their implementation to be consistent with the principles outlined above.

15.4.1 Supported Employment

The most widely disseminated, well-defined, and standardized approach in the field is supported employment, particularly in the form of Individual Placement and Support (IPS). Standardization of IPS implementation is promoted by the application of fidelity scales with good psychometric properties [28]. In this approach "real work" is defined as employment in the existing community workforce. Clients of the IPS service receive counseling to identify personal strengths and possibilities and employment preferences to match conditions of work to individual needs. Rapid job entry is offered rather than prolonged vocational assessment and preparation. Clients are assisted with finding and securing their own jobs, or jobs may be secured by IPS providers; but regardless of how a job is secured ultimately, the individual is employed by the community work site. While clients served by IPS are generally expected to fit into existing work structures and expectations, employment support can include identifying and advocating for accommodations, and increasing employer awareness, providing the workplace with training and otherwise enlisting their support in the process. Ongoing follow-along supports are meant to enable job success and stability and can address symptoms, impairments, and other mental health issues, workplace task or social demands and experiences, or broader life issues impacting employment. The model includes counseling around financial benefits to ensure that clients are well informed about their benefit plans to support related decision-making [25, 28–32].

Supported employment in the form of IPS has been the subject of much research, and randomized controlled trials have demonstrated the capacity of the model to improve vocational outcomes compared to traditional forms of vocational support or mental health treatment [26]. These findings have been repeated across different mental health care contexts, with special populations (such as those with co-occurring substance use problems) and across several countries worldwide (see, e.g., [33–35]). To date, the majority of jobs found in supported employment are entry-level and part-time jobs [36]. There have been varying results with respect to the socioeconomic outcomes of supported employment, but there has been some indication that it can lead to reduced reliance on government disability benefits [32]. A comprehensive review of the literature by Kirsh [36] indicated several positive personal level changes through involvement with supported employment, including improvements in self-concept, expansion of social networks, improved quality of life, improved financial resources, and improvements in work skills and adaptation.

In recognition of the need to address educational achievement in order to improve career prospects and job status, the components of the supported employment model have been applied to develop supported education services. Supported education focuses on assisting individuals to make choices about their studies, securing entry into educational programs, and offering ongoing support to enable educational achievement while maintaining well-being. Program models can be located off campus or can be integrated within educational settings, for example, as distinct educational programs offered within the postsecondary setting or as support services located on campus [37, 38]. Recent adaptations of the model have been linked directly to supported employment as a means to facilitate the smooth transition to work [39].

15.4.2 Social Entrepreneurship

Social entrepreneurial approaches use market-based strategies to create employment opportunities for people with serious mental illnesses. Unlike supported employment approaches, which seek to secure jobs for people in the existing community workforce, these entrepreneurial initiatives aim to create new employment opportunities within business structures that sell goods and services in competition within the general marketplace.

Perhaps the most common approach is the creation of employment opportunities by the development of legally registered businesses that operate within the broader economy. These businesses are often referred to as "social businesses," "social firms," or work integration social enterprises (WISES [40–42]). They hold dual missions; a social mission, which in this case is creating employment for a disenfranchised population; and an economic mission focusing on promoting business sustainability. As legal workplaces they are expected to meet workplace standards for payment and health and safety. The work organization itself is structured to enable the work participation of individuals who experience disabilities and participation limitations. For example, workplace operations may be structured to accommodate for differences in the ability to manage complex tasks, or rates of production, and attention may be directed to ensuring that workers are provided with the material goods they require to work. Other businesses have been developed to capitalize on specific strengths of a population. For example, businesses designed for homeless youth have attempted to translate their street skills to develop income-generating activities [43]. Similarly, opportunities for advancement through the ranks to management can be intentionally structured. Some businesses offer a mix of stable job positions, with places reserved for those in training positions. Given the implications for financial sustainability, attention directed to structural issues is considered an imperative.

Social businesses/firms have proliferated internationally with variations in business structures and models across locations. In the mental health field, the business cooperatives that were developed in Italy in response to the national move to deinstitutionalization are a good example [42]. In some jurisdictions social firms are expected to have at least 1/3 of their workforce be people without mental illness and labor disadvantage (see, e.g., [44], while in others these businesses have been completely owned, operated, and staffed by people with mental illness [45, 46]. Interactions within the community economy are expected to take place through a variety of business transactions within the broader public and even through membership within community business organizations.

While guidelines for the development of social businesses/firms do exist, the lack of clearly defined and accepted models defining key features of the approach (or approaches) hampers development, dissemination, and evidence building in the field. A recent review of the scholarship related to this approach demonstrated that most of the knowledge building has been focused on business processes and outcomes related to issues such as sustainability [47]. Literature related to individual worker experience suggested that they largely use their incomes to supplement their disability pensions, although a significant minority do appear to reduce their use of social assistance [48], and experience the businesses as promoting their recovery [49, 50]; and a significant minority have aspirations to find jobs outside of the business in the open market [51]. Individuals working within these social businesses will typically continue to receive support from mental health professionals, although the extent to which the business itself is linked to the mental health system has both advantages and disadvantages. For example, the mental health system may create market opportunities for the sale of goods and services, but businesses that are located structurally within the mental health system can find their autonomy around business decisions compromised [40]. Indeed, the focus on development of a distinct *business* structure is inconsistent with the focus on development of *programs and services.*

A second entrepreneurial approach is the development of self-employment among people with mental illnesses. In this approach, individuals with an entrepreneurial spirit are supported to develop the feasibility of their business ideas and provided with supports that can be offered in the form of business advice and mentorship, shared business resources, and small low-interest business loans [41, 52]. An example of this approach is a partnership developed between the Rotman School of Business at the University of Toronto and Toronto's Centre for Addictions and Mental Health, which began as a local pilot and became a province-wide initiative to fund prospective entrepreneurs [53].

Conceptual foundations of the approach can be traced back to community economic aims to address the poverty and social conditions of disadvantaged groups using market rather than care strategies [54] and asset-based community development frameworks [55]. While these perspectives provide the vocational rehabilitation field access to a wide range of relevant and high profile international scholarship, they are largely outside of the health and mental health systems and subsequently have not been readily integrated into the field.

15.4.3 Employment Opportunities Within Health and Social Systems

A third approach to the creation of employment opportunities has been the development of jobs for people within the mental health system. This approach emerged primarily in recognition of the many benefits associated with integrating people with lived experience of mental illness actively in program development and implementation [56, 57]. The approach has disseminated rapidly, leading to transformations in hiring and employment structures across the system. The expansion of these job positions has included a variety of paid positions from peer-provider jobs, service developers and managers, research associates, and educators. The hiring of peer providers is now considered a best practice in many jurisdictions, and this suggests that a growing number of employment positions are being created. Most of the scholarship focusing on these affirmative employment positions has focused on the tasks and challenges associated with integrating new types of jobs into existing employment structures. For example, the literature includes discussions about challenges related to developing job descriptions, identifying and providing for training needs, ensuring inclusion and emotional well-being in the workplace, and the nature of the job responsibilities (see, e.g., [58–60]).

15.5 Complementary Interventions

Consistent with the idea of providing ongoing employment support to people with serious mental illnesses as required, several research studies have demonstrated that vocational outcomes can be improved by the implementation of specific interventions focused on improving work functioning. The studies primarily investigate these complementary interventions in the context of evidence-based supported employment, but, at least in theory, they should be applicable to the other employment approaches described above.

There is some evidence that work-focused social skills training integrated within supported employment leads to better employment outcomes [61, 62]. Cognitive remediation, when integrated with supported employment, has been shown to lead to better cognitive and employment outcomes than offering either approach alone [63]. While there appears to be some support for the integration of cognitive behavioral therapy with employment support programs for people with serious mental illnesses, research is still limited in this area [64]. Interestingly, given the high percentage of individuals with a serious mental illness who are not pursuing employment, there has been limited attention to the development and evaluation of focused motivational interventions.

15.6 Challenges in the Field: Tensions Related to Defining Work

In the midst of the rapid growth and development, the field of psychiatric vocational rehabilitation is facing multiple debates and challenges. The underlying differences between the employment approaches outlined in this paper are differences of philosophy with regard to what constitutes "*real work.*" When employment in the open, competitive workforce is considered the only real form of work, then supported employment models will be considered the ideal approach. That said, challenges to supported employment have included arguments that (1) the approach has lead largely to entry-level jobs with low pay, low skill, and few benefits; (2) the levels of job tenure within the supported employment has been troublesome; and (3) individuals receiving supported employment services remain "clients" of a service system, perhaps undermining their identity as worker [65]. Entrepreneurial approaches and jobs within the mental health system have been criticized as potentially perpetuating segregation and stigma, perceived as protected environments. Yet, they have also been viewed as important venues to develop leadership, social learning, and collective action among mental health service users [46] and to effect change in the broader employment structures within which they have historically been disenfranchised. As highlighted by Kirsh and colleagues [27], reconciling these conflicting philosophies will be important to further development in the field: "Advancing interventions that may improve work participation requires ongoing reflection on the conceptual underpinnings of selected approaches as they relate to the end goal of productive employment, in addition to consideration of the individual" (p. 400).

15.7 Applying the ICF Core Set Categories to Vocational Rehabilitation for People with Serious Mental Illness

Within the mental health system, psychiatric rehabilitation is the field that has directly focused on enabling the full, successful, and satisfying community lives of people with serious mental illness. Psychiatric rehabilitation has largely focused on addressing the activity and participation needs of people with a serious mental illness, given the extent to which, historically, the population has been socially and economically marginalized. Within psychiatric rehabilitation, the distinction between mental illness and disability has been clear. It is well known within psychiatric vocational rehabilitation, for example, that diagnosis does not predict participation in important life roles such as employment, that work participation is possible even while experiencing ongoing symptoms of mental illness, and that environmental factors play a large role in determining work participation. Indeed, the employment support and vocational rehabilitation models described previously in this chapter have all been designed to address the comprehensive range of illness, personal, occupational, and environmental factors that can contribute to well-being, satisfaction, and success at work. In this way, there are notable consistencies between the ICF classification system and the field of psychiatric rehabilitation (and specifically psychiatric vocational rehabilitation), with regard to how they view and conceptualize health, disability, and participation.

Applications of the ICF in psychiatric rehabilitation have included its use as a tool to frame rehabilitation education [66] and its potential in interpreting the differences in disability among individuals with serious mental illnesses across cultural contexts [67]. Another potentially useful approach is to implement the ICF, and specifically the ICF core categories that have been developed for vocational rehabilitation [68], as a means to describe the critical elements of vocational programs and employment support services. Table 15.1 summarizes the brief core set for vocational rehabilitation [68, p. 7] with a definition for each [1]. The rest of this chapter describes the application of the ICF categories for vocational rehabilitation to a specific employment support and vocational rehabilitation program.

The psychiatric vocational rehabilitation program is located in a small city center in southern Ontario, Canada. The vocational service is one service element within a multiservice community mental health agency that focuses on supporting recovery and community life for people with mental illnesses, particularly those with serious mental illnesses. The agency is committed to the philosophy and principles of psychosocial rehabilitation and implementing practices that are evidence based. The agency saw the value of applying the ICF core set categories for vocational rehabilitation to its vocational service as a means to develop clarity about the processes and nature of services offered, facilitate communication about services to a range of stakeholders and audiences, and facilitate evaluation of services and as a guide for training and education.

The employment support and vocational rehabilitation services are offered in a phased, but individualized manner, with multiple service components accessible at each phase (see Table 15.2). The core focus of the vocational program, or its central mission, is consistent with the ICF core categories for vocational rehabilitation, d845, acquiring, keeping and terminating a job, and d850, remunerative employment. This distinction is important for clearly communicating the goals of the program; it is solidly focused on connecting people to *paid work opportunities*. Given the large number of people with serious mental illnesses who are engaged in few or no work-related productivity activities, referrals to the program from other mental health or social service sectors often mistakenly expect that the program will address a broader range of productivity options, such as non-remunerative employment options (d855). Where the expectations of individuals who access the service and the goals of the service are not consistent, efforts are made to connect individuals to more appropriate services that focus on other vocational options. The initial phases of the program, including referral, intake/orientation, and even assessment, reflect a collaborative process to ensure that individuals are, in fact, oriented toward paid work and to begin developing an appreciation for the strengths, challenges, and preferences that individuals bring toward this goal.

Table 15.1 ICF core set for vocational rehabilitation – a guide with definitions

ICF code number and category	Definition of ICF core category
Activity and participation	Activity is the execution of a task or action by an individual. Participation is involvement in a life situation
d155 Acquiring skills	Developing basic and complex competencies in integrated sets of actions or tasks so as to initiate and follow through with the acquisition of a skill, such as manipulating tools or playing games like chess
d240 Handling stress and other psychological demands	Carrying out simple or complex and coordinated actions to manage and control the psychological demands required to carry out tasks demanding significant responsibilities and involving stress, distraction, or crises, such as driving a vehicle during heavy traffic or taking care of many children
d720 Complex interpersonal interactions	Maintaining and managing interactions with other people, in a contextually and socially appropriate manner, such as by regulating emotions and impulses, controlling verbal and physical aggression, acting independently in social interactions, and acting in accordance with social rules and conventions
d845 Acquiring, keeping and terminating a job	Seeking, finding, and choosing employment; being hired and accepting employment; maintaining and advancing through a job, trade, occupation or profession; and leaving a job in an appropriate manner. Includes seeking employment, preparing a resume or curriculum vitae, contacting employers and preparing interviews, maintaining a job, monitoring one's own work performance, giving notice, and terminating a job
d850 Remunerative employment	Engaging in all aspects of work, as an occupation, trade, profession, or other form of employment, for payment, as an employee, full or part time, or self-employed, such as seeking employment and getting a job, doing the required tasks of the job, attending work on time as required, supervising other workers or being supervised, and performing required tasks alone or in groups
d855 Non-remunerative employment	Engaging in all aspects of work in which pay is not provided, full time or part time, including organized work activities, doing the required tasks of the job, attending work on time as required, supervising other workers or being supervised, and performing required tasks alone or in groups, such as volunteer work, charity work, working for a community or religious group without remuneration, working around the home without remuneration
Environmental factors	Environmental factors make up the physical, social, and attitudinal environment in which people live and conduct their lives
e310 Immediate family	Individuals related by birth, marriage, or other relationship recognized by the culture as immediate family, such a spouses, partners, parents siblings, children, foster parents, adoptive parents, and grandparents

(continued)

Table 15.1 (continued)

ICF code number and category	Definition of ICF core category
e330 People in positions of authority	Individuals who have decision-making responsibilities for others and who have socially defined influence or power based on their social, economic, cultural, or religious roles in society, such as teachers, employers, supervisors, religious leaders, substitute decision-makers, guardians, or trustees
e580 Health services, systems and policies	Services, systems, and policies for preventing and treating health problems, providing medical rehabilitation and promoting a healthy lifestyle
e590 Labor and employment services	Services, systems, and policies related to finding suitable work for persons who are unemployed or looking for different work or to support individuals already employed who are seeking promotion
Body functions	Body functions are the physiological and psychological functions of body systems
b130 Energy and drive functions	General mental functions of physiological and psychological mechanisms that cause the individual to move toward satisfying specific needs and general goals in a persistent manner. Includes function of energy level, motivation, appetite, craving, and impulse control
b164 Higher-level cognitive functions	Specific mental functions especially dependent on the frontal lobes of the brain, including complex goal-directed behaviors such as decision-making, abstract thinking, planning and carrying out plans, mental flexibility, and deciding which behaviors are appropriate under what circumstances; often called executive functions
b455 Exercise tolerance functions	Functions related to respiratory and cardiovascular capacity as required for enduring physical exertion. Includes functions of physical endurance, aerobic capacity, stamina, and fatiguability

Job preparation is a time-limited phase, oriented to solidifying readiness for work. A central focus is building up the capacity for sustained motivation for employment, consistent with b130 energy and drive functions. Challenges related to energy and drive are prevalent among people with serious mental illnesses and can result from biomedical factors associated with the disease process (e.g., negative, avolitional symptoms), psychological processes (e.g., the loss of self-confidence, tentative goal structures), and social processes (e.g., the experience of stigma, poverty). Job preparation is also oriented to addressing the handling of stress and other psychological demands (d240). A particular focus at this point are stress and psychological demands related to: shifting activity patterns to accommodate employment; managing self-care including illness management; beginning to identify triggers for illness experiences, possible supports, and coping strategies; developing crisis plans; and determining eligibility for special government employment resources.

Table 15.2 Employment support and psychiatric vocational rehabilitation: a case example

Mission: providing people with the supports they require to enable employment. The service helps people in getting ready for work, finding work, and keeping work.	
Phase-specific approach	**Service elements**
Referral intake and orientation	The focus is on determining whether the vocational rehabilitation service is the most appropriate to meet an individual's needs and to link individuals to other services/supports when they are more appropriate
Assessment	The assessment process is focused on developing a clear picture of an individual's strengths, needs, and interests in relation to employment. Assessment is a *collaborative* process that includes: evaluation of current support needs across a wide range of daily living domains that influence employment; mental health stability and strengths; physical abilities; eligibility for government employment supports/resources (e.g., transportation support, wage subsidies); interest in employment, readiness for employment, and employment preferences
Job preparation: meeting intrinsic and external needs	This component of the service focuses on preparing people for employment. Service components can include a structured, group intervention focusing on developing sustained motivation for those who are unsure about their commitment to work, the development of self-care and wellness plans, vocational counseling, and obtaining needed employment supports and resources. Consistent with the philosophy of rapid entry to work, this "preparation" phase is intended to be completed within 3 months
Job development	In this service component job development activities facilitate the creation of employment opportunities and individual access to a range of employment opportunities, including work in the community workforce with support, employment in a social enterprise, job trials with wage subsidies, and access to micro-loans for small business creation. Some opportunities for supported education tied to employment are available. Supports focus on ensuring a good job match and meeting the task and social demands of the job and addressing cognitive issues that might compromise employment
Job retention	Service components are directed to providing ongoing support to ensure sustained commitment to and satisfaction with work, facilitate mental health and well-being, and develop further career plans
Graduation from service	Employment support and vocational services are no longer needed, but program reentry is possible as needed, as is access to other services offered by the agency

The job development phase of the service focuses on successfully transitioning individuals to one of a range of paid work opportunities. Creating job opportunities is a key activity of dedicated job development staff who engage with labor-related systems, policies, and services to secure employment possibilities (e590). Once in the job, the individual is supported in meeting work-related stress and psychological demands (d240) and acquiring the range of skills associated with the specific job (d150). For many participants, the lack of recent work experience has contributed to physical deconditioning, and individualized fitness programs are offered as an additional support (b455 exercise tolerance functions). Many people experience specific cognitive impairments (e.g., attention, memory) associated with their mental illnesses (b140-b189 specific mental functions), and for these individuals complementary neurocognitive enhancement training is offered in partnership with a local university psychology program.

As service recipients continue in their work situation, issues and challenges (as well as positive experiences) unfold and job retention activities focus on sustaining commitment to work, while promoting a good job match. In this phase, in addition to handling stress and psychological demands of work (d240), an important focus of support is on meeting the challenges associated with a range of complex interpersonal interactions (d720), such as relations with coworkers and customers; people in positions of authority (e330), such as immediate supervisors, and employers; and meeting expectations that require high-level cognitive functions (b164), such as organization and planning, problem solving, and time management. Consistent with evidence-informed principles of psychiatric vocational rehabilitation, the service pays close attention to ensuring the ongoing delivery of health services to ensure the mental health and well-being fundamental to sustained employment (e580) and to labor system policies and practices to sustain motivation for employment (e590).

The exercise of applying the ICF core set categories was a useful one for the vocational service. The process engaged them in clearly defining the objectives of their work and considering how they communicate these to their community partners, potential service recipients, and other stakeholders. It also helped them to further develop the rationale underlying the specific elements of their services. The resulting framework may be applied for training and evaluation purposes.

15.8 Summary

This chapter focuses on employment support and vocational rehabilitation applied to those with serious mental illnesses. Current approaches to enabling employment have largely been directed to reducing the profound levels of social and economic marginalization that have historically been experienced by this population and subsequently have been directed to creating and supporting real work opportunities. The ICF core set categories for vocational rehabilitation provide a potentially useful resource for developing a shared language and understanding about the critical features of these programs applied to people with serious mental illnesses. They also provide the opportunity for cross-cultural comparisons and international programs of evaluation and research.

- The employment status of the population of people with a serious mental illness can be described as "marginalized."
- Employment marginalization suggests that individuals have weak labor market attachments. This means that they have few work-related social networks and are often inactive with respect to pursuing or even expecting to work.
- Contemporary approaches to vocational rehabilitation for people with serious mental illnesses are oriented to developing real work opportunities and providing support to ensure individual success and satisfaction.
- Employment supports for people with a serious mental illness integrate attention to personal, illness, occupational, and environmental factors that influence work participation.
- The ICF core set categories for vocational rehabilitation can be applied to describe the critical elements of vocational programs and employment support services for people with serious mental illnesses.

Study Questions

1. Why do you think that diagnosis has not been a good predictor of employment among people with serious mental illnesses?
2. There is considerable controversy in the vocational rehabilitation field about what constitutes "real work." How would you define "real work"?
3. Explain why the term "unemployed" does not fully capture the employment status of people with serious mental illnesses?
4. Compare the three approaches to creating employment opportunities outlined in this chapter with regard to their potential to positively impact the inclusion of people with serious mental illnesses in broader society?
5. Describe why health service providers may not encourage or expect people with serious mental illnesses to consider working in paid jobs.

References

1. World Health Organization. International classification of functioning, disability and health. Geneva: World Health Organization; 2001.
2. Tsang H, Leung A, Chung R, Bell M, Cheung W. Review on vocational predictors: a systematic review of predictors of vocational outcomes among individuals with schizophrenia: an update since 1998. Aust N Z J Psychiatry. 2010;44:495–504.
3. Bilder D, Mechanic S, McAlpine DD. Employing persons with serious mental illness. Health Aff. 2002;21(5):242–53.
4. Marwaha S, Johnson S. Schizophrenia and employment – a review. Soc Psychiatry Psychiatr Epidemiol. 2004;39(5):337–49.

5. Wang PS, Demloer O, Kessler RC. Adequacy of treatment for serious mental illness in the United States. Am J Public Health. 2002;92:92–8.
6. Razzano L, Cook J, Burke-Miller J, Mueser K, Pickett-Schenk S, Grey D, et al. Clinical factors associated with employment among people with severe mental illness: findings from the employment intervention demonstration program. J Nerv Ment Dis. 2005;193:705–13.
7. McGurk SR, Mueser KT. Cognitive functioning, symptoms, and work in supported employment: a review and heuristic model. Schizophr Res. 2004;70:147–74.
8. Lysaker P, Bryson G, Davis L, Bell M. Relationship of impaired processing speed and flexibility of abstract thought to improvements in work performance over time in schizophrenia. Schizophr Res. 2005;75:211–8.
9. Giugiario M, Crivelli B, Mingrone C, Montemagni C, Scalese M, Sigaudo M, et al. Cognitive function and competitive employment in schizophrenia: relative contribution of insight and psychopathology. Soc Psychiatry Psychiatr Epidemiol. 2012;47:553–61.
10. Krupa T. Interventions to improve employment outcomes for workers who experience mental illness. Can J Psychiatry. 2007;52:339–45.
11. Yanos PT, Roe D, Lysacker PH. The impact of illness identity on recovery from severe mental illness. Am J Psychiatr Rehabil. 2010;13(2):73–93.
12. Michon HW, van Weeghel J, Kroon H, Schene AH. Illness self-management assessment in psychiatric vocational rehabilitation. Psychiatr Rehabil J. 2011;35(1):21–7.
13. Jonikas JA, Laris A, Cook J. The passage to adulthood: psychiatric rehabilitation service and transition-related needs of young adult women with emotional and psychiatric disorders. Psychiatr Rehabil J. 2003;27(2):114–20.
14. International First Episode Vocational Recovery (iFEVR) Group. Meaningful lives: supporting young people with psychosis in education, training and employment. Parkville: International First Episode Vocational Recovery; 2008.
15. Warner R. Recovery from schizophrenia: psychiatry and political economy. London: Routledge; 1985.
16. Baron RC, Salzer MS. Accounting for unemployment among people with serious mental illness. Behav Sci Law. 2002;20:585–99.
17. Marrone J, Golowka E. If work makes people with mental illness sick, what do unemployment, poverty, and social isolation cause? Psychiatr Rehabil J. 1999;23:187–93.
18. Krupa T, Kirsh B, Cockburn L, Gewurtz R. Understanding the stigma of mental illness in employment. Work. 2009;3:413–25.
19. Cook JA. Employment barriers for persons with psychiatric disabilities: update of a report for the President's Commission. Psychiatr Serv. 2006;57:1391–405.
20. Krupa T, Oyewumi K, Archie S, Lawson JS, Nandlal J, Conrad G. Early intervention services for psychosis and time until application for disability income support: a survival analysis. Community Ment Health J. 2012;48(5):535–46.
21. Hotchkiss JL. Growing part-time employment among workers with disabilities: marginalization or opportunity? Econ Rev Third Q. 2004;89(3):25–40.
22. Kozma C, Dirani R, Canuso C, Mao L. Change in employment status over 52 weeks in patients with schizophrenia: an observational study. Curr Med Res Opin. 2011;27:327–33.
23. Dunn EC, Wewiorski NJ, Rogers ES. The Meaning and importance of employment to people in recovery from serious mental illness: results of a qualitative study. Psychiatr Rehabil J. 2008;32(1):59–62.
24. Mental Health Commission of Canada. Aspiring workforce: employment and income for people with serious mental illness [Internet]. Calgary: Mental Health Commission of Canada; 2013 [cited 9 Oct 2013]. Available from: www.mentalhealthcommision.ca
25. Bond GR. Supported employment: evidence for an evidence-based practice. Psychiatr Rehabil J. 2004;27(4):345–59.
26. Bond GR, Drake RE, Becker DR. An update on randomized controlled trials of evidence-based supported employment. Psychiatr Rehabil J. 2008;31:280–90.

27. Kirsh B, Stergious-Kita M, Gewurtz R, Dawson D, Krupa T, Lysaght R, et al. From margins to mainstream: what do we know about work integration for persons with brain injury, mental illness and intellectual disability? Work. 2009;32:391–405.
28. Bond GR, Peterson AE, Becker DR, Drake RE. Validation of the Individual Placement and Support Fidelity Scale (IPS-25). Psychiatr Serv. 2012;63:758–63.
29. Lexén A, Hofgren C, Bejerholm U. Support and process in individual placement and support: a multiple case study. Work. 2013;44(4):435–48.
30. Areberg C, Bjorkman T, Bejerholm U. Experiences of the individual placement and support approach in persons with severe mental illness. Scand J Caring Sci. 2013;27:589–96.
31. McGuire AB, Bond GR, Clendenning DR, Kukla M. Service intensity as a predictor of competitive employment in an individual placement and support model. Psychiatr Serv. 2011;62:1066–72.
32. Bond GR, Xie HY, Drake RE. Can SSDI and SSI beneficiaries with mental illness benefit from evidence-based supported employment? Psychiatr Serv. 2007;58:1412–20.
33. Burns T, White SJ, Catty J. Individual placement and support in Europe: the EQOLISE trial. Int Rev Psychiatry. 2008;20:498–502.
34. Killackey E, Jackson H, McGorry PD. Vocational intervention in first-episode psychosis: individual placement and support v. treatment as usual. Br J Psychiatry. 2008;193:114–20.
35. Becker DR, Drake RE, Naughton WJ. Supported employment for people with co-occurring disorders. Psychiatr Rehabil J. 2005;28:323–8.
36. Kirsh B. Supported employment: a review of the literature and Canadian perspectives [Internet]. Calgary: Mental Health Commission of Canada. Aspiring Workforce: Employment and income for people with serious mental illness; 2013 [cited 9 Oct 2013]. Available from: www.mentalhealthcommision.ca
37. Hain R, Gioia D. Supported Education Enhancing Rehabilitation (SEER): a community mental health and community college partnership for access and retention. Am J Psychiatr Rehabil. 2004;7:315–28.
38. Collins ME, Bybee D, Mowbray CT. Effectiveness of supported education for individuals with psychiatric disabilities: results from an experimental study. Community Ment Health J. 1998; 34:595–613.
39. Rudnick A, Gover M. Combining supported education with supported employment. Psychiatr Serv. 2009;60:1690.
40. Krupa T, Lysaght R, Brown J, Vallée C. Environmental scan of social businesses [Internet]. Calgary: Mental Health Commission of Canada. Aspiring Workforce: Employment and income for people with serious mental illness; 2013 [cited 9 Oct 2013]. Available from: www.mentalhealthcommision.ca
41. Mandiberg J. The failure of social inclusion: an alternate approach through community development. Psychiatr Serv. 2012;63:458–60.
42. Warner R, Mandiberg J. An update on affirmative businesses or social firms for people with mental illness. Psychiatr Serv. 2006;57:1488–92.
43. Ferguson K. Implementing a social enterprise intervention with homeless, street-living youth in Los Angeles. Soc Work. 2007;52(2):103–12.
44. Social Firms Europe. Definition [Internet]. Surrey: Social Firms Europe; 2013 [cited 18 Oct 2013]. Available from: http://socialfirmseurope.org/social-firms/definition/
45. Allen JB, Granger B. Helping people with psychiatric disabilities start and develop consumer run businesses. In: Moxley DP, Finch JR, editors. Sourcebook of rehabilitation and mental health practice. New York: Kluwer Academic/Plenum; 2004. p. 319–31.
46. Church K, Fontan JM, Ng R, Shragge E. Social learning among people who are excluded from the labour market. Part one: context and cases [Internet]. Toronto: Centre for Study of Education and Work, Ontario Institute for Studies in Education of the University of Toronto; 2000 [cited 26 Oct 2013]. Available from: https://tspace.library.utoronto.ca/bitstream/1807/2725/2/11sociallearning.pdf
47. Krupa T, Chen S-P. Psychiatric/Psychosocial Rehabilitation (PSR) in relation to vocational and educational environments: work and learning. Curr Opin Psychiatry. 2013;9(3):195–206.

48. Krupa T, Lagarde M, Carmichael K. Transforming sheltered workshops into affirmative businesses: an evaluation of outcomes. Psychiatr Rehabil J. 2003;26:359–67.
49. Svanberg J, Gumley A, Wilson A. How do social firms contribute to recovery from mental illness? A qualitative study. Clin Psychol Psychother. 2010;17:482–96.
50. Williams A, Fossey E, Harvey C. Sustaining employment in a social firm: use of the Work Environment Impact Scale v2.0 to explore views of employees with psychiatric disabilities. Br J Occup Ther. 2010;73:531–9.
51. Zaniboni S, Fraccaroli F, Villotti P, Corbière M. Working plans of people with mental disorders employed in Italian social enterprises. Psychiatr Rehabil J. 2011;35:55–8.
52. Prince JD. Promoting consumer empowerment through entrepreneurship: a proposal. Psychiatr Rehabil J. 2007;30:223–5.
53. Boar C. Micro-loans unlock trap of mental illness [Internet]. Toronto: Thestar.com; 10 Jan 2012 [cited 26 Oct 2013]. Available from: http://www.thestar.com/opinion/editorialopinion/2012/01/10/goar_microloans_unlock_trap_of_mental_illness.html
54. The Canadian CED Network. What is CED? [Internet]. Victoriaville: CCEDNet; 2012 [cited 26 Oct 2012]. Available from: http://www.ccednet-rcdec.ca/en/what_is_ced
55. Kretzmann J, McKnight J. Building communities for the inside out: a path toward finding and mobilizing a community's assets. Evanston: The Asset-Based Community Development Institute, Institute for Policy Research, Northwestern University; 1993.
56. Carlson LS, Rapp CA, McDiarmid D. Hiring consumer-providers: barriers and alternative solutions. Community Ment Health J. 2001;37:199–213.
57. Chinman M, Young AS, Hassell J, Davidson L. Toward the implementation of mental health consumer provider services. J Behav Health Serv Res. 2006;33:176–94.
58. Moran GS, Russinova Z, Vasudha G, Gagne C. Challenges experienced by paid peer providers in mental health recovery: a qualitative study. Community Ment Health J. 2013;49(3):281–91.
59. Mancini MA, Lawson HA. Facilitating positive emotional labor in peer-providers of mental health services. Adm Soc Work. 2009;33:3–22.
60. Macias C, Aronson E, Barreira PJ, Rodican CF, Gold PB. Integrating peer providers into traditional service settings: the Jigsaw strategy in action. Adm Policy Ment Health. 2007; 34(5):494–6.
61. Mueser KT, Aalto S, Becker DR, Ogden JS, Wolfe RS, Schiavo D, et al. The effectiveness of skills training for improving outcomes in supported employment. Psychiatr Serv. 2005;56: 1254–60.
62. Tsang HW, Chan A, Wong A, Liberman RP. Vocational outcomes of an integrated supported employment program for individuals with persistent and severe mental illness. J Behav Ther Exp Psychiatry. 2009;40(2):292–305.
63. McGurk SR, Mueser KT, De Rosa TJ, Wolfe R. Work, recovery, and comorbidity in schizophrenia: a randomized controlled trial of cognitive remediation. Schizophr Bull. 2009;35: 319–35.
64. Binnie J. Cognitive behavioural therapy in vocational rehabilitation with the severely mentally ill: review, design and implementation. J Ment Health. 2008;17(1):105–17.
65. Drake RE, Bond G. The Future of supported employment for people with serious mental illness. Psychiatr Rehabil J. 2008;31(4):367–76.
66. McDonald-Wilson KL, Nemec PB. The International Classification of Functioning, Disability and Health (ICF) in psychiatric rehabilitation. Rehabil Educ. 2005;19:159–76.
67. Vrooman K, Arthanat S. ICF and mental functions: applied to cross cultural case studies of schizophrenia. Buffalo: International Encyclopedia of Rehabilitation; 2012 [cited 1 Oct 2013]. Available from: http://cirrie.buffalo.edu/encyclopedia/en/
68. Finger ME, Escorpizo R, Glässel A, Gmünder HP, Lückenkemper M, Chan C, et al. ICF core set for vocational rehabilitation: results of an international consensus conference. Disabil Rehabil. 2012;34(5):429–38.

Chapter 16
Using WHO's ICF Model on Service Needs of Patients with Pneumoconiosis

Chetwyn C.H. Chan, Eric W. Tsang, Andrew Siu, Henry Kwok, and Andy Cheng

16.1 Introduction

Pneumoconiosis is a chronic disease of the respiratory system [1, 2]. Patients with pneumoconiosis require long-term comprehensive rehabilitation services [3]. The International Classification of Functioning, Disability and Health (ICF) model of the World Health Organization can be applied to reveal the details of how pneumoconiosis influences as well as how participation in rehabilitation programs can improve the general physical and psychosocial well-beings of patients [4]. The ICF model conceptualizes health as successful participation in home, work, and social environments. Instead of impairment and disability, the ICF model stresses the importance of the extent to which the person participates in activities relevant to his or her roles in life. The ICF model can be utilized to identify distinctive domains of various aspects of physical and psychosocial functioning, resulting in a more thorough understanding of an individual's lived experience. In the context of rehabilitation, recent studies of the ICF revealed that the main obstacles to successful outcomes are related to activities and participation [5, 6]. Therefore, the ICF conceptualizes vocational rehabilitation within the context of patients' body structures and functions, activities and participation, and biopsychosocial factors within their environments [7].

Pneumoconiosis has been commonly classified as an occupational disease [1, 2]. Patients with pneumoconiosis are likely to be male, manual workers, and retired from their work due to impaired lung and bodily functions. These patients need

C.C.H. Chan (✉)
Department of Rehabilitation Sciences, Applied Cognitive Neuroscience Laboratory, The Hong Kong Polytechnic University, Hung Hom, Kowloon, Hong Kong
e-mail: Chetwyn.Chan@polyu.edu.hk

E.W. Tsang • A. Siu • H. Kwok • A. Cheng
Department of Rehabilitation Sciences, The Hong Kong Polytechnic University, Hung Hom, Kowloon, Hong Kong

R. Escorpizo et al. (eds.), *Handbook of Vocational Rehabilitation and Disability Evaluation*, Handbooks in Health, Work, and Disability, DOI 10.1007/978-3-319-08825-9_16

long-term rehabilitation to tackle the problems associated with the losses of their work and life roles. The ICF model contains over 1,400 categories that describe the full spectrum of functioning for many major health and social human experiences or issues [5, 6]. ICF Core Sets were developed to capture a short list of ICF categories that reveal relevant information about more specific health conditions [8]. The ICF Vocational Rehabilitation Core Set is a short list of ICF categories that are designed to be applied to many health conditions within different environmental settings. It can be applied to patients for the description of many aspects of disabilities and health-related issues within the context of their environment [9] and for describing the various aspects of their functioning during vocational rehabilitation processes [6]. Since the current project involved the evaluation of rehabilitation services for pneumoconiosis patients, the Core Set for Vocational Rehabilitation was suitable for this project. Examples of activities and participation factors in the Core Set for Vocational Rehabilitation deemed relevant to this study are acquiring skills (d155), handling stress and other psychological demands (d240), and complex interpersonal interactions (d720). Relevant factors related to body functions are energy and drive functions (b130), exercise tolerance functions (b455), and higher-level cognitive functions (b164). (The reader is referred to Chap. 2 of this volume for more detailed information about the ICF coding structure.)

This chapter uses a case study that explores the rehabilitation needs of patients with pneumoconiosis in Hong Kong to illustrate the usefulness of the ICF model for understanding how restrictions of activities and participation relate to the patients' impaired lung functions. The content is extracted from the report entitled "Independent Review: Current Rehabilitation Programs in Hong Kong Funded by the PCFB" [10].

16.2 Rehabilitation Service Provision for Chronic Pneumoconiosis Patients

Rehabilitation services for pneumoconiosis patients in Hong Kong have been administered by the Pneumoconiosis Compensation Fund Board (PCFB) since 1980. The PCFB manages compensation to patients and finances education, research, and other programs to prevent pneumoconiosis and conducts rehabilitation programs to promote health and quality of life for patients [11].

In addition, health service providers for pneumoconiosis care in Hong Kong have been adopting an integrated healthcare delivery system based on the framework of the Kaiser Permanente model [12, 13]. This model integrates various healthcare disciplines which share a unified budget to provide care to patients of chronic diseases based on their needs as indicated by three levels of disease severity. The bottom or the lowest level of the pyramid consists of services which aim to serve a vast majority of patients. In general, the aims of these services are to equip the patients and their caregivers with knowledge, skills, and confidence for dealing with problems associated with chronic diseases. Service provision at this level includes various disease management classes for patients and caregivers. Services delivered at this level are provided mainly by social workers in two nongovernmental organizations (NGOs) and in collaboration with medical and rehabilitation professionals in three designated hospitals within Hong Kong. The middle level consists of services designed for patients with relatively higher risk than those in the lower level. In addition to chronic diseases, these patients may have multiple diseases or have lower abilities for self-care. Services for these patients are more specialized and commonly delivered by a multidisciplinary team of specialists according to a disease-specific protocol. The top or highest level of the pyramid consists of services tailored to the needs of patients who suffer from highly complex conditions or are in a terminal phase of the disease. These patients require intensive case management by a multidisciplinary professional team. Specialized medical doctors who guide specialists of various disciplines, including senior nurses, physiotherapists, occupational therapists, and other medical professionals to provide more specialized and comprehensive treatment to these patients, generally manage patients in the second and third levels. Services such as counseling and home support are delivered by social workers. Similarly, the services are delivered and coordinated among the three hospitals and two nongovernmental organizations (NGOs). The division of labor among these service providers is mainly based on the geographic regions where the patients reside or the patients' preferences.

Although service provision has taken place for more than a decade by PCFB, the patients' needs and the degree of patients' satisfaction with their needs are uncertain. To better understand the patients' needs and their satisfaction, a survey was conducted to solicit feedback from patients who are currently utilizing or had previously utilized rehabilitation services funded under the PCFB. The content of the survey was partially based on the factors included in the ICF Core Set for Vocational Rehabilitation [6, 8]. The results of this survey would be useful for service providers to evaluate the relevance of their existing services as well as to identify potential gaps for future service development. The findings would also shed light on the meaningfulness and usefulness of the ICF factors for describing the service needs and for reflecting the needs satisfaction among patients with pneumoconiosis in Hong Kong.

16.3 Methods

16.3.1 Research Design

The survey was conducted using a face-to-face interview format. Sampling methods adopted convenience and snowball methods, where all subjects from the service providers who were available to participate in the survey were recruited.

The subject pool was further expanded as participants were asked to solicit their friends to participate in the survey. The responses solicited from the participants were cross-sectional and based on their needs and satisfaction of these needs according to factors selected from the ICF Core Set for Vocational Rehabilitation.

16.3.2 Participants

The targeted population was patients diagnosed with pneumoconiosis, who had registered with the PCFB and received PCFB funded rehabilitation services in Hong Kong. The staff of PCFB and the five service providers, i.e., three hospitals and two NGOs, assisted recruitment of the participating patients. A total of 158 male and four female patients completed the interviews ($N = 162$). The average age of the patients was 72.3 years (ranging from 52 to 87 years). The majority of the patients ($N = 152$, 93.8 %) were not employed. The degree of incapacity (DOI), which is an index to describe the patient's loss of lung function resulting from pneumoconiosis, ranged from 5 % to 70 %. Only a small fraction of the participants were smokers ($N = 23$, 14.2 %), while the majority were ex-smokers ($N = 87$, 53.7 %) or nonsmokers ($N = 52$, 32.1 %). The demographic profile of the participating patients was found to be similar to that of patients registered with the PCFB.

16.3.3 Survey Questionnaire

The questionnaire contained 15 categories of functions (Appendix 16.1). These items were developed primarily based on the following factors stipulated in the Core Set for Vocational Rehabilitation [4, 6]:

- Activities and participation functions: carrying out daily routines, undertaking multiple tasks, walking, looking after one's health, complex interpersonal interactions, recreation and leisure, non-remunerative employment, and remunerative employment.
- Body functions that inhibit participation: breathlessness from physical activity, feeling of pressure, energy and drive functions, emotional functions, exercise tolerance functions, and muscle endurance functions.
- Environmental factors: individual attitudes of health professionals and health services, systems, and policies) [4, 6, 8].
- Recreation and leisure, which is a general ICF factor in the activities and participation domain (d920), was included as it was deemed important for the patients with pneumoconiosis recruited in this study.

Within the survey, each category of function had five subitems, one of which was open-ended. The other four subitems were closed-ended in that they asked the participants to select a number on a rating scale. Examples of the five subitems are illustrated for the first category [Respiration Functions (Exchange of Gases)] in Appendix 16.1. The four closed-ended subitems addressed the following: (1) how important a function was in affecting the patient's well-being, (2) level of function impairment, (3) the need to restore/maintain a function to promote the patient's well-being, and (4) whether the need to restore/maintain a function had been satisfied. The participant was to assign a number based on a five-point Likert scale that best represented the judgment of each item. The rating of "1" in the scale represented "least/little/lowest/not at all," while "5" represented "most/mostly/highest" depending on the context of the item (see Appendix 16.1). The open-ended subitem required the participant to write down ideas regarding how their needs could be satisfied, whether any rehabilitation services would be useful for fulfilling these needs, and suggestions for the rehabilitation services deemed useful.

16.4 Results

For each category of function, the first question in the survey asked the participants to judge the importance of a category of function in affecting their well-being (see Appendix 16.1). A sample question in this category was, "How important is respiratory function in affecting your well-being?" The results of this question showed that the categories respiratory function (exchange of gas) and respiratory function (breathing, coughing, and sneezing) were regarded with the utmost importance by all participants among other categories of functions and received a maximum average rating of 5 (most important). Another three categories of functions that received high importance ratings were support and relationship with family (mean = 4.8); health services, systems, and policies (mean = 4.7); and emotional functions (mean = 4.7) (see Table 16.1). The three categories of functions that received the lowest importance ratings from the participants were remunerative employment (mean = <1.1); labor and employment services, systems, and policies (mean = 1.1); and voluntary work (mean = 1.3).

The second question for each category of function in the survey asked participants to judge the extent to which a function has been impaired. A sample question in this part of the questionnaire is, "At what level has respiratory function been impaired?" The five categories of functions that received the highest ratings from the participants were health services, systems, and policies (mean = 4.5), respiratory functions (exchange of gases) (mean = 4.2), other respiratory functions (breathing, coughing, and sneezing) (mean = 4.1), walking (mean = 4.1), and exercise tolerance (mean = 3.9) (Table 16.2). The three categories of functions that received the lowest ratings were remunerative employment (Mean = <1.1); labor and employment services, systems, and policies (mean = 1.1); and voluntary work (mean = 1.2).

The third question in the survey asked the participants to judge the importance of each category of function that they found necessary to restore or maintain for the

Table 16.1 Summary of importance of the categories of functions rated by participants listed in needs assessment ($N = 162$)

	Mean	Standard deviation (SD)
Respiratory function (exchange of gas)	5.0	0.0
Respiratory function (breathing, coughing, and sneezing)	5.0	0.0
Support and relationship with family	4.8	0.5
Health services, systems, and policies	4.7	0.7
Emotional functions	4.7	0.7
Walking function	4.6	0.7
Exercise tolerance	4.4	0.9
Recreation and leisure	4.2	0.9
Community life	4.2	0.9
Sensations associated with cardiovascular and other respiratory functions	3.3	1.3
Relationship with friends	3.3	1.2
Housework	2.7	1.2
Non-remunerative employment	1.3	0.9
Labor and employment services, systems, and policies	1.1	0.5
Remunerative employment	1.0	0.4

Table 16.2 Summary of level of impairment of categories of functions rated by participants listed in needs assessment ($N = 162$)

	Mean	SD
Health services, systems, and policies	4.5	0.9
Respiration functions (exchange of gases)	4.2	1.0
Respiratory functions (breathing, etc.)	4.1	1.0
Walking function	4.1	0.9
Exercise tolerance	3.9	0.9
Emotional functions	3.8	1.1
Community life	3.7	1.0
Recreation and leisure	3.3	1.1
Support and relationship with family	3.0	1.2
Relationship with friends	2.9	1.3
Sensations associated with cardiovascular and other respiratory functions	2.4	1.5
Housework	2.3	1.3
Non-remunerative employment	1.2	0.7
Labor and employment services, systems, and policies	1.1	0.5
Remunerative employment	1.0	0.4

promotion of their well-being. For example, participants were asked, "What are your needs for restoring/maintaining respiratory functions for promoting your well-being?" The five categories of functions that received the highest ratings from the participants as needs for restoring/maintaining the functions for promoting well-

Table 16.3 Summary of the needs for restoring/maintaining the functions for promoting well-being of the participants listed in the needs assessment ($N = 162$)

	Mean	SD
Respiration functions (exchange of gases)	4.0	1.1
Respiratory functions (breathing, etc.)	4.0	1.1
Health services, systems and policies	3.9	1.3
Walking function	3.8	1.1
Exercise tolerance	3.8	1.3
Emotional functions	3.6	1.2
Community life	3.5	1.0
Recreation and leisure	3.2	1.0
Support and relationship with family	2.9	1.2
Relationship with friends	2.7	1.2
Sensations associated with cardiovascular and other respiratory functions	2.4	1.5
Housework	2.2	1.2
Non-remunerative employment	1.2	0.5
Labor and employment services, systems, and policies	1.1	0.4
Remunerative employment	1.0	0.3

being were respiratory function (exchange of gases) (mean = 4.0); respiratory functions (breathing, coughing, and sneezing) (mean = 4.0); health services, systems, and policies (mean = 3.9); walking function (mean = 3.8); and exercise tolerance (mean = 3.8) (Table 16.3). The three categories of functions that received the lowest ratings were remunerative employment (mean = <1.1); labor and employment services, systems, and policies (mean = 1.1); and voluntary work (mean = 1.2).

The fourth question in the survey asked participants to judge their degree of satisfaction that each category of function had been restored/maintained. For example, participants were asked, "To what extent have the needs for restoring/maintaining respiratory functions been satisfied?" The five categories of functions that received the highest ratings for needs satisfaction were: support and relationship with family (mean = 4.5); health services, systems, and policies (mean = 4.4); recreation and leisure (mean = 3.9); respiratory functions (breathing) (mean = 3.8); and exercise tolerance (mean = 3.8) (see Table 16.4). The three categories of functions that received the lowest ratings were remunerative employment (mean = <1.1); labor and employment services, systems, and policies (mean = 1.1); and voluntary work (mean = 1.3).

Table 16.4 Summary of the extent to which needs for restoring/maintaining the categories of functions have been satisfied in participants listed in the needs assessment ($N = 162$)

	Mean	SD
Support and relationship with family	4.5	0.8
Health services, systems, and policies	4.4	0.9
Recreation and leisure	3.9	1.0
Respiratory functions (breathing, etc.)	3.8	0.8
Exercise tolerance	3.8	0.9
Respiration functions (exchange of gases)	3.8	1.0
Community life	3.8	1.0
Walking function	3.7	0.9
Emotional function	3.7	1.0
Relationship with friends	3.0	1.3
Housework	2.8	1.6
Sensations associated with cardiovascular and respiratory functions	2.7	1.7
Non-remunerative employment	1.3	1.0
Labor and employment services, systems, and policies	1.1	0.6
Remunerative employment	1.0	0.3

16.5 Discussion

The results of the study indicate that the participants regarded *respiratory functions* as the most important factors affecting their well-being. Also, they reported that their respiratory functions had been mostly affected by the pneumoconiosis. The participants appeared to express the strongest needs for restoring and maintaining these respiratory functions. Nevertheless, according to the participants, these needs had been somewhat satisfied. The category of *health services, systems, and policies* was revealed as the second most important issue to the participants. The common knowledge of this aspect, as shared by the participants, included the current policies of the PCFB, the rehabilitation services funded by PCFB, and the public hospitals and health services. Health services, systems, and policies were also regarded by the participants as one of the most important factors affecting their well-being (average = 3.9 out of 5). Moreover, the participants regarded this factor as crucial for influencing the outcomes of their pneumoconiosis treatments. The participants expressed strong needs for the current level of services, systems, and policies to be maintained in order to sustain their current well-being status. In addition, the participants in general were satisfied with their needs for the existing health services, systems, and policies.

The respiratory functions of patients with pneumoconiosis and the health services, systems, and policies (in this study, provided by the PCFB, the three hospitals and the two NGOs) are obviously closely interconnected. The reasons for these findings may be due to the deterioration of respiratory functions among these patients, which would consume the health and rehabilitation services available [14, 15]. Provision of these services would help maintain or at least slow down such deterioration [16]. Our results are similar to those of research that explored the rehabilitation needs of chronic obstructive pulmonary disorders (COPD). For instance, recent advancements in rehabilitation care for patients with COPD in Europe and the United States have taken steps to develop more advanced rehabilitation programs to fulfill both physical and emotional needs of patients [17–19]. These recent studies indicate that only focusing on symptomatic management is not an ideal rehabilitation approach for COPD patients. An optimal rehabilitation program should consider patients' functioning both physically and emotionally in their environment. The results of the current study indicate that the use of the ICF Vocational Rehabilitation Core Set was useful for capturing the participants' views on this important causal relationship, i.e., between the body functions and environmental factors [8]. The results also suggest that the participants were able to understand their needs (e.g., respiratory functions), including how and to what extent these needs could be satisfied. This information is important for service providers to further improve rehabilitation interventions designed to meet the needs of these patients.

The participants in general viewed *support and relationships with family* as very important. In fact, it received the highest importance rating (4.8 out of 5) next to the respiratory functions. It is noteworthy that the patients did not perceive support and relationships with their family members as being affected by pneumoconiosis. Hence the needs for restoring and maintaining such functions were not strong. More importantly, they felt that the support and relationships with their family members had been very satisfactory. Our findings are somewhat consistent with other studies on the influence caregivers have on patients with COPD. For instance, patients with COPD displayed better adherence to medical treatments when they were cared for by their spouses than those who received care from non-spouses [20]. Another study found that COPD patients who had stronger family supports demonstrated greater self-care behaviors [21]. The support gained from the positive relationships with family appeared to be a strong asset for the patients. This again illustrates the usefulness of using the ICF model to address the factors that can influence the potential activity limitations and participation restrictions of individuals with disabilities. The survey questionnaire constructed using the ICF categories can reveal the importance of factors that influence the patient's functioning in his or her environment [22, 23]. For example, support and relationships with family became assets for enhancing the activities and participation for our group of patients. Future development of rehabilitation services for pneumoconiosis patients may put emphasis on strengthening this environmental factor.

The patients regarded *recreation and leisure* as a relatively important factor to their well-being (4.2 out of 5). The rehabilitation services provided by PCFB serve a function of satisfying the recreation and leisure needs of the patients. There are two main reasons for providing recreation and leisure activities in the PCFB's rehabilitation services. First, the ages of the patients under the registry are largely beyond retirement age (which is 60 years old). In 2012, the average age of pneumoconiosis patients who were funded by the PCFB was 65 [11]. Second, the patients were under an occupational disease compensation scheme and had retired from their jobs. The more the patients participate in the PCFB's services, the more their needs for recreation and leisure can be satisfied. In contrast, the patients did not regard the role of productivity as an important factor that affected their well-being. The role of productivity includes remunerated and non-remunerated employment; labor and employment services, systems, and policies; and housework. In fact, this cluster of functions was given the lowest rating among other factors. Similar trends were observed in the needs for restoring this cluster of functions. It suggests that employment was not the patients' main concern. Instead, their main concerns were their respiratory functions and physical and emotion functions, which are more personal and the driving forces of their satisfaction. Our findings are somewhat inconsistent with those revealed in other studies. The role of engaging in productivity has been shown to enhance the quality of life of patients with COPD, although their respiratory functions were not improved by employment or other voluntary work [24]. In the context of pneumoconiosis and the local culture of Hong Kong, non-remunerated activities may be more appropriate for consideration by the patients. Examples of such activities include community volunteer services, childcare for family members, and volunteer services at the NGOs, which are appropriate for patients who are relatively young and with less severe respiratory/physical dysfunction. These results could be useful for service providers to further strengthen the productivity role of these patients if deemed appropriate. These findings demonstrate the usefulness of using the ICF model to address the areas of activity and participation of patients who may or may not have formal employment, or who are beyond the working age.

Last but not least, the cluster of walking functions, exercise tolerance, and emotional functions received somewhat comparable ratings. In general, the patients regarded this cluster of functions as important factors affecting their well-being (3.4–3.7 out of 5.0). These functions were regarded as moderately affected by pneumoconiosis; hence the needs for restoring and maintaining these functions were in general quite high. Similar to respiratory functions, the patients' needs for these functions had been somewhat satisfied. The ICF model's inclusion of body function suggests that it is one of the major factors influencing activity and participation. In the current study, results suggest that the environmental factors outweighed the influence of body function factors on the activity and participation of patients with pneumoconiosis.

16.6 Conclusion

This book chapter sets out to describe the results of a satisfaction of needs survey of a group of pneumoconiosis patients who had had experience with utilizing the rehabilitation services funded under the Pneumoconiosis Compensation Fund Board of Hong Kong. These results can, in turn, illustrate how the ICF model can be meaningful and useful for describing the service needs and reflecting the needs satisfaction among these patients. In general, the results of the study indicate that the current health management and rehabilitation services provided under the Pneumoconiosis Compensation Fund Board in Hong Kong are leading to satisfaction among these patients. The findings are useful for guiding future service development of the Fund Board. For the ICF model, the findings suggest the close relationships among the activity and participation, body functions, and environmental factors. The patients regarded respiratory function as their most important needs, which would be the case for those suffering from chronic lung disease such as pneumoconiosis. More importantly, the patients fully recognized that the most influential factors affecting their respiratory functions were the environmental factors, such as health systems, services, and policies and support and relationships with family. Further research should validate the causal relationships among these factors and explore wider application of the ICF model to the needs assessment of different groups of patients.

Acknowledgment The authors would like to thank the Pneumoconiosis Compensation Fund Board of Hong Kong for providing the funding and assistance for completing the satisfaction of needs survey of pneumoconiosis patients in Hong Kong. Thanks should also go to the patients who participated in this survey and Ms Elsie Ong who implemented the study.

Appendix 16.1

Needs Assessment for Patients of Pneumoconiosis

Data Base

Name:
Age:
Education:
Breadwinner (Yes/No):
Smoking Status:

Previous Occupation:
Duration of Occupation Related to Pneumoconiosis:
Year of Diagnosis of Pneumoconiosis:
Presence of Concomitant Disease (comorbidity):
Date / Year of Start of Compensation:
Level of Severity (at diagnosis):
Level of Severity (at recent assessment (and when)):

Length of Employment After Diagnosis of Occupational Disease:
End of Employment (which year)

Needs Assessment Questionnaire

Below is a list of functions which you may find important to your well-being. For each function, you will be asked to indicate its importance and whether it has been impaired. You will then be asked the needs to restore/maintain the function, and suggest ways to fulfill the needs.
Please answer to the best of your knowledge. [Note: The same set of closed-ended questions (a to d) and two open-ended questions are applied to each of the 15 categories of functions.]

1. Respiration Functions (Exchange of Gases)
Functions of inhaling air into the respiratory system, the exchange of gases between air and blood, and exhaling air.

a) How important is respiratory function in affecting your well-being?

Least				Mostly
1	2	3	4	5

b) At what level has respiratory function been impaired?

Little				Mostly
1	2	3	4	5

c) What are your needs for restoring/maintaining respiratory functions for promoting your well-being?

Lowest					Highest
1	2	3	4	5	

d) To what extent have the needs for restoring/maintaining respiratory functions been satisfied?

Not At All				Mostly
1	2	3	4	5

Please suggest how the needs can be satisfied.

____

____

Please indicate if any which program(s) in the rehabilitation services is useful for fulfilling your respiratory function needs.

____

____

2. Respiratory Functions (Breathing, Coughing and Sneezing)
These functions related to breathing, coughing, sneezing and yawning.

3. Exercise Tolerance Functions
Functions related to the duration of the body withstand continuous physical exercise including upper limb, lower limbs and/or truck movements.

4. Sensations Associated with Cardiovascular and Respiratory Functions
Sensations such as missing a heartbeat, palpitation and shortness of breath.

5. Walking Function
Moving along a surface on foot, step by step, so that one foot is always on the ground, such as when strolling, sauntering, walking forwards, backwards, or sideways

6. Doing Housework
Managing a household by cleaning the house, washing clothes, using household appliances, storing food and disposing of garbage, such as by sweeping, mopping, washing counters, walls and other surfaces; collecting and disposing of household garbage; tidying rooms, closets and drawers; collecting, washing, drying, folding and ironing clothes; cleaning footwear; using brooms, brushes and vacuum cleaners; using washing machines, driers and irons.

7. Emotional Functions
Specific mental functions related to the feeling and affective components of the processes of the mind.

8. Community Life
Engaging in all aspects of community life, such as engaging in charitable organizations, service clubs or professional social organizations

9. Recreation and Leisure
Engaging in any form of play, recreational or leisure activity, such as informal or organized play and sports, programmes of physical fitness, relaxation, amusement or diversion, going to art galleries, museums, cinemas or theatres; engaging in crafts or hobbies, reading for enjoyment, playing musical instruments; sightseeing, tourism and travelling for pleasure.

10. Support and Relationship with Family
Individuals related by birth, marriage or other relationship recognized by the culture such as spouses, partners, parents, siblings, children, foster parents, adoptive parents and grandparents.

11. Support and Relationship with Friends
Individuals who are close and ongoing participants in relationships characterized by trust and mutual support.

12. Remunerative Employment
Engaging in all aspects of work, as an occupation, trade, profession or other form of employment, for payment, as an employee, full or part time, or self-employed, such as seeking employment and getting a job, doing the required tasks of the job, attending work on time as required, supervising other workers or being supervised, and performing required tasks alone or in groups.

13. Non-remunerative Employment
Engaging in all aspects of work in which pay is not provided, full-time or part-time, including organized work activities, doing the required tasks of the job, attending work on time as required, supervising other workers or being supervised, and performing required tasks alone or in groups, such as charity work, working for a community or religious group without remuneration, working around the home without remuneration.

14. Health Services, Systems and Policies
Services, systems and policies for preventing and treating health problems, providing health and rehabilitation services, and policies for promoting healthy lifestyle.

15. Labour and Employment Services, Systems and Policies
Services, systems and policies related to finding suitable work for persons who are unemployed or looking for different work, or to support individuals already employed who are seeking promotion.

References

1. Laney AS, Weissman DN. The classic pneumoconioses: new epidemiological and laboratory observations. Clin Chest Med. 2012;33(4):745–58.
2. Wagner GR. Asbestosis and silicosis. Lancet. 1997;349(9061):1311–5.
3. Ochmann U, Kotschy-Lang N, Raab W, Kellberger J, Nowak D, Jorres RA. Long-term efficacy of pulmonary rehabilitation in patients with occupational respiratory diseases. Respiration. 2012;84(5):396–405.
4. World Health Organization. International classification of functioning, disability and health: ICF. Report. Geneva: World Health Organization; 2001.
5. ICF Research Branch. ICF core sets for vocational rehabilitation [homepage on the internet] [updated 3 May 2010]; cited Available from: http://www.icf-research-branch.org/icf-core-sets-projects/diverse-situations/icf-core-setsfor-vocational-rehabilitation.html
6. Escorpizo R, Ekholm J, Gmunder HP, Cieza A, Kostanjsek N, Stucki G. Developing a Core Set to describe functioning in vocational rehabilitation using the international classification of functioning, disability, and health (ICF). J Occup Rehabil. 2010;20(4):502–11.
7. Escorpizo R, Reneman MF, Ekholm J, Fritz J, Krupa T, Marnetoft SU, et al. A conceptual definition of vocational rehabilitation based on the ICF: building a shared global model. J Occup Rehabil. 2011;21(2):126–33.
8. Stucki G, Ewert T, Cieza A. Value and application of the ICF in rehabilitation medicine. Disabil Rehabil. 2002;24(17):932–8.
9. Cieza A, Ewert T, Ustun TB, Chatterji S, Kostanjsek N, Stucki G. Development of ICF Core Sets for patients with chronic conditions. J Rehabil Med. 2004;36(44 Suppl):9–11.
10. Chan CC, Tsang EW, Siu A, Kwok H, Cheng A. Independent review: current rehabilitation programs in Hong Kong funded by the PCFB. Report. Hong Kong: Pneumoconiosis Compensation Fund Board; 2013.
11. Pneumoconiosis Compensation Fund Board 2012 Annual Report. Report. Hong Kong: Pneumoconiosis Compensation Fund Board; 2013.

12. Food and Health Bureau. Primary care development in Hong Kong strategy document. Report. Hong Kong: Government of Hong Kong; 2010.
13. Wallace PJ. Physician involvement in disease management as part of the CCM. Health Care Financ Rev. 2005;27(1):19–31.
14. Spieth PM, Guldner A, de Abreu MG. Chronic obstructive pulmonary disease. Curr Opin Anaesthesiol. 2012;25(1):24–9.
15. Macintyre NR. Chronic critical illness: the growing challenge to health care. Respir Care. 2012;57(6):1021–7.
16. Corhay JL, Dang DN, Van Cauwenberge H, Louis R. Pulmonary rehabilitation and COPD: providing patients a good environment for optimizing therapy. Int J Chronic Obstr Pulm Dis. 2014;9:27–39.
17. Norweg A, Collins EG. Evidence for cognitive-behavioral strategies improving dyspnea and related distress in COPD. Int J Chronic Obstr Pulm Dis. 2013;8:439–51.
18. Troosters T, van der Molen T, Polkey M, Rabinovich RA, Vogiatzis I, Weisman I, et al. Improving physical activity in COPD: towards a new paradigm. Respir Res. 2013;14:115.
19. Almeida P, Rodrigues F. Exercise training modalities and strategies to improve exercise performance in patients with respiratory disease. Rev Port Pneumol. 2014;20(1):36–41.
20. Trivedi RB, Bryson CL, Udris E, Au DH. The influence of informal caregivers on adherence in COPD patients. Ann Behav Med. 2012;44(1):66–72.
21. Kara KM, Alberto J. Family support, perceived self-efficacy and self-care behaviour of Turkish patients with chronic obstructive pulmonary disease. J Clin Nurs. 2007;16(8):1468–78.
22. Simeonsson RJ, McMillen JS, Huntington GS. Secondary conditions in children with disabilities: spina bifida as a case example. Ment Retard Dev Disabil Res Rev. 2002;8(3):198–205.
23. Heinemann AW, Magasi S, Hammel J, Carlozzi NE, Garcia SF, Hahn EA, et al. Environmental factors item development for persons with stroke, traumatic brain injury and spinal cord injury. Arch Phys Med Rehabil. 2013;13:1308-7.
24. Orbon KH, Schermer TR, van der Gulden JW, Chavannes NH, Akkermans RP, Schayck OP, et al. Employment status and quality of life in patients with chronic obstructive pulmonary disease. Int Arch Occup Environ Health. 2005;78(6):467–74.

Chapter 17
ICF-Based Process Management in Vocational Rehabilitation for People with Spinal Cord Injury

Stefan Staubli, Urban Schwegler, Klaus Schmitt, and Bruno Trezzini

17.1 Introduction

The biopsychosocial understanding of health and disability represented by the *International Classification of Functioning, Disability and Health* (ICF) of the World Health Organization (WHO) has enjoyed particular popularity within rehabilitation. It is, however, not always clear whether the implementation of the ICF in clinical practice is conceptually overstated or indeed refer to concrete implementations [1]. The ICF provides a framework as well as a standard for the classification of a person's health and health-related functioning. However, the ICF does not offer a theory nor concrete instructions for vocational rehabilitation (VR) [2]. Nevertheless, its compatibility with an ecological, system-based understanding of VR as applied in job placement has been emphasized [3].

The broad applicability and generic nature of the ICF has been highlighted as an advantage for elaborating a generally applicable definition of VR. Escorpizo et al., for example, suggest the following ICF-based definition of VR [4]:

> VR is a multi-professional evidence-based approach that is provided in different settings, services, and activities to working age individuals with health-related impairments, limitations, or restrictions with work functioning, and whose primary aim is to optimize work participation. (p. 130)

S. Staubli (✉) • K. Schmitt
Swiss Paraplegic Center, Nottwil, Switzerland
e-mail: stefan.staubli@paraplegie.ch

U. Schwegler
Swiss Paraplegic Research, Nottwil, Switzerland

Department of Health Sciences and Health Policy, University of Lucerne, Lucerne, Switzerland

B. Trezzini
Swiss Paraplegic Research, Nottwil, Switzerland

R. Escorpizo et al. (eds.), *Handbook of Vocational Rehabilitation and Disability Evaluation*, Handbooks in Health, Work, and Disability, DOI 10.1007/978-3-319-08825-9_17

However, as the authors of the definition added, this definition requires additional specification depending on the particular context of VR. VR for persons with spinal cord injury (SCI), for example, involves different challenges than VR for persons with traumatic brain injury or mental disorders. Moreover, in clinical practice more specific return to work models are used [5] such as the supported employment approach with its "place first, train later" strategy.

According to Gobelet and Franchignoni, and formulated in a less abstract way than the abovementioned definition, the process of VR can be characterized as follows [6]:

> Vocational rehabilitation deals largely with vocational assessment, work re-training, education and counseling, work guidance and ergonomic modifications, and psycho-social interventions (including vocational orientation and all other forms of preparation for returning to work). (p. 6)

Furthermore, according to Langman [7], the VR process aimed at competitive employment in an integrated setting can be subdivided into four main stages: (1) initial evaluations, inclusion, and rehabilitation planning; (2) assessment and evaluation; (3) preplacement support and job development; and (4) placement, job retention, and case closure.

There is limited literature on the type and amount of VR services utilized or preferred by persons with SCI in general and for those living in Switzerland in particular. In a study on a U.S. sample of 445 with SCI, one third of the respondents reported having received work-related support [8]. The service most frequently utilized was counseling on job opportunities or on how to get a job (19.8 % of the respondents), followed by an assessment of work ability in different types of jobs (15.5 %). Interestingly, only 9 % of the respondents received modifications to equipment. However, only 13.9 % stated they were in need of such modifications. A more substantial need was found regarding assistance with developing new job skills (24.2 %) and assistance with finding a job (21.3 %). The results of this U.S. study, however, are likely to be applicable only to a limited extent in other countries.

The objective of this chapter, then, is to illustrate first experience with the practical application of an ICF-based rehabilitation management in the Swiss Paraplegic Centre (SPZ) in Switzerland, a specialized rehabilitation clinic for persons with SCI. To do so, we have chosen to focus on VR in particular.

> Vocational rehabilitation is a multi-professional evidence-based approach that is provided in different settings, services, and activities to working age individuals with health-related impairments, limitations, or restrictions with work functioning, and whose primary aim is to optimize work participation.

17.2 Organizational and Legal Context

17.2.1 The Swiss Paraplegic Centre

The Swiss Paraplegic Centre (SPZ) is the largest specialized rehabilitation clinic for people with SCI in Switzerland. In 2012, the clinic was equipped with 140 beds; and 924 hospitalizations and 49,446 patient days were registered [9]. Forty-four out of 100 initial rehabiliations were completed by persons with paraplegia and 56 by persons with tetraplegia. While in the years 2010 and 2011, the SCI was about equally often caused by accidents and illnesses, in 2012 66 % of the SCIs were due to accidents.

The SPZ is part of a comprehensive service network for individuals with para- and tetraplegia which is supported by the Swiss Paraplegic Foundation (SPS) and aims to enable persons to live as autonomously as possible. The clinic itself covers both acute care and inpatient rehabilitation. The outpatient clinic, which is also part of the SPZ, plays an important role in the long-term care of persons with SCI. In addition to this "vertical integration" across different organizational units, the SPZ follows a "horizontal integration" of the different specialist disciplines involved in the rehabilitation process [10]. This latter form of integration is based on weekly ICF team meetings, i.e., interdisciplinary case discussions attended by medical doctors, physiotherapists, and occupational therapists, as well as by social counselors and VR specialists.

In 2011 and 2012, the SPZ undertook an extensive analysis of management and treatment processes, resulting in the development of a detailed rehabilitation concept and process organization structure compulsory for all sectors in the clinic [10]. The basis for this rehabilitation concept were so-called patient pathways that structure the complex rehabilitation processes from admission to discharge of a patient. While the general rehabilitation philosophy is still holistic and refers to a lifelong process, the rehabilitation process is now increasingly based on goal-oriented patient management. By applying participation-focused discharge goals, the SPZ subscribes to a rehabilitation concept that reflects a top-down approach [11]. The use of discharge goal categories allows for planning and selecting clearly defined interventions. In light of the interdisciplinary rehabilitation process, a structured and goal-oriented strategy is required for successful treatment. The different disciplines involved in the process provide their services primarily based on jointly defined goals and ensure in regularly scheduled meetings that all relevant areas are considered and redundancies avoided. The ICF model, with its participation-oriented focus, serves as an overarching framework with regard to the definition of the various discharge goal categories [10, 11].

The Swiss Paraplegic Center (SPZ) is the largest specialized rehabilitation clinic for people with SCI in Switzerland. The SPZ follows a rehabilitation concept that is based on patient pathways and participation-focused discharge goals. The ICF serves as an overarching framework with regard to the definition of the discharge goal categories.

17.2.2 The Institute of Vocational Counseling at the Swiss Paraplegic Centre

The Institute of Vocational Counseling (IBF) supports persons with SCI in returning to the labor market. Its services are utilized when work-related goals are defined in consultation with the patient. In 2012, 50 SCI patients passed through a work-related assessment on behalf of the Swiss Invalidity Insurance (SII). The IBF team consists of ten employees. Three vocational counselors collect the social and occupational case history of the patient, carry out tests based on standardized assessment tools, and provide vocational counseling. During the initial rehabilitation, the patients also receive professional support from specialist vocational teachers.

The IBF provides all patients with the opportunity for work-related training, regardless of whether the goal is to achieve competitive employment in an integrated setting (i.e., "pension-relevant" employment) or to work in sheltered employment after discharge from initial rehabilitation. Motivation programs regarding specific work activities are offered as well.

17.2.3 Collaboration with Swiss Invalidity Insurance

Swiss Invalidity Insurance (SII) aims to integrate, keep, and/or reintegrate people with disabilities in the primary labor market. To achieve this goal, SII can assign people with disabilities to work-related assessments and work reintegration programs such as vocational counseling, retraining, or job coaching. SII may provide such services itself or delegate them to third parties. For this purpose, SII concluded service-level agreements with different service providers such as the Institute of Vocational Counseling (IBF). These agreements determine the type, quality, compensation, and coordination of services and are intended to ensure their proper, cost-effective, and goal-oriented implementation. Different federal laws, regulations, and administrative ordinances form the legal basis for these agreements.

From SII's point of view, the main goal of a systematic individual VR program is to train an insured person for the primary labor market or to ensure that he or she successfully graduates from vocational training or retraining and is prepared for integration into the labor market. The four main general outcome dimensions of a VR program are:

1. Pension reduction
2. Successful graduation from educational training
3. Competitive employment in the primary labor market
4. Cost-effective implementation

More specific goals can be negotiated on a case-by-case basis and upon contracting one of the four services the IBF provides on behalf of the SII and for which it is compensated by the SII at a fixed rate. These four services are:

1. *Basic vocational assessment:* Basic work-related abilities are assessed and work-related potentials identified during a period of 80 hours and by means of an interdisciplinary standardized assessment instrument.
2. *Comprehensive vocational assessment:* Based on the information obtained from the basic assessment, clients are assigned to a specific work-related assessment program. During the assessment process, clients are accompanied and supported in their job-related decision making by vocational counselors.
3. *Job training:* Based on the results of the basic and/or comprehensive vocational assessment, clients receive training in specific work-related skills and abilities. Continuous support from the specialist teachers (i.e., vocational and adult educators) facilitates an optimal and gradual return to work.
4. *Job coaching:* The client and his or her employer receive close professional support through a vocational specialist at the time of or shortly before returning to competitive employment or attending vocational training in the primary labor market. This significantly enhances the chances of a sustainable return to work outcome.

The Institute of Vocational Counseling (IBF) at the SPZ works in close collaboration with the Swiss Invalidity Insurance (SII). The IBF provides four services for persons with spinal cord injury on behalf of the SIII: Basic vocational assessments, comprehensive vocational assessments, job training and job coaching.

17.3 ICF-Based Rehabilitation Management at the Swiss Paraplegic Centre

17.3.1 Goal Setting, Goal Categories, and the ICF

For goal-oriented rehabilitation management, it is crucial to not only consider medical diagnoses but also the various dimensions of health integrity and disability. Rehabilitation is defined as the individual-related, multi-, and interdisciplinary management of impairments and limitations in functional health [12]. The ultimate goal is to achieve the best possible level of functioning to ensure the person's optimal reintegration into society. The ICF can facilitate the implementation of this definition since it considers not only health conditions but also the dimensions of body functions and structures, activities and participation, and the influence of environmental and personal factors. These dimensions can be systematically addressed by using the common language of the ICF.

Intervention goals and programs in rehabilitation can only partly be derived from medical diagnoses. A young patient with SCI, for example, who is unable to perform his or her former job following an accident, needs vocational retraining and, thus, a different rehabilitation program as compared to an elderly patient with SCI, with limited physical resources who is faced with the decision to live independently or be admitted to a nursing home. Hence, two identical diagnoses may require completely different intervention goals and rehabilitation programs.

By contrast, a structured integration of ICF categories allows for elaborating precise treatment pathways and for implementing the ensuing treatment measures. The development and standardization of participation goals, also taking into account other ICF components such as personal factors, facilitates the practical implementation of diagnosis- and functioning-based treatment pathways. A standardized approach using ICF-based assessments and treatments allows for a course of action that fits the individual much better than approaches focusing primarily on the medical diagnosis. An ICF-based assessment promotes transparent and comprehensible evaluation of functioning and could thus improve vocational evaluations in particular.

An assessment and treatment process that aims at measuring and enhancing a person's participation requires an interdisciplinary approach to ensure joint intervention planning, multilateral communication, and goal setting supported by the entire rehabilitation team. Such an approach reduces the length of a patient's stay at the hospital and promotes employee satisfaction as well as effective teamwork in rehabilitation [13, 14]. The ICF offers a road map for goal setting and team communication [15] and enhances the quality of teamwork in an interdisciplinary rehabilitation process [16].

A standardized approach using ICF-based assessments and treatments allows for a course of action that fits the individual much better than approaches focusing primarily on the medical diagnosis. The ICF offers a road map for goal setting and team communication and enhances the quality of teamwork in an interdisciplinary rehabilitation process.

17.3.2 Applying Goal Categories at the Swiss Paraplegic Center

To select appropriate interventions, a patient-centered goal setting process should focus on participation goals such as work reintegration or independent living. Goal categories are a suitable means for such a process because they are usually defined on the participation level.

The SPZ applies 20 goal categories for participation, covering the domains "living" (seven categories), "social activities" (five categories), and "work" (eight categories). Each goal category is based on criteria referring to the ICF components "activities and participation", "body functions and structures", and "environmental factors". Table 17.1 shows the goal categories of the domain "work" and the criteria to be met on the different ICF components for achieving the respective goals. The goal category to be achieved by the time of discharge should be determined within the first days after admission. The criteria referring to the three ICF components facilitate the goal setting process by illustrating those factors that generally need to be met as a prerequisite for achieving the corresponding goal category (see Table 17.1).

Personal factors, which are not classified in the ICF taxonomy so far, refer to aspects inherent to the individual and represent essential parts of a person's life and living that influence the impact of a health condition on functioning. Aspects such as age, occupational and educational background, as well as work attitudes are strongly related to work participation and return to work [17, 18] and should be considered in the goal setting process of VR. The same is true for work motivation, job satisfaction, and expectations regarding return to work [19, 20]. Finally, personality and coping strategies should also be considered as important aspects of vocational assessments [21, 22].

A patient-centred goal setting process should focus on participation goals such as work reintegration, social activities or independent living.

Table 17.1 Goal categories and criteria for the participation domain "work" as applied at the SPZ

Goal categories	Activities and participation	Body functions and structures	Environmental factors
C1 - Meaningful work for day structuring	Basic social and communication skills	Mental and physical capacity for day structuring of at least 4 hours per day	Availability of a day-structuring service
	Ability to deal with simple challenges	Socially acceptable bladder and bowel control	Full pension and financing ensured
	Sufficient mobility		Accommodation of the environment (architectural, organizational, assistive devices)
	Ability for interpersonal relationships		
C2 - Sheltered employment	Ability to acquire skills	Mental and physical capacity of at least 4 hours per day	Involvement of a vocational counselor from the SII
	Ability to focus attention on work activities	Socially acceptable bladder and bowel control	A vocational assessment should be carried out
	Ability to perform simple tasks with support		Access to accompanying therapeutic intervention
	Ability to perform tasks on a regular basis		Accommodation of the environment (architectural, organizational, assistive devices)
	Sufficient communication skills		Willingness of the environment regarding work in sheltered employment
	Sufficient mobility		Financing ensured
	Ability for interpersonal relationships		
C3 - Preparation for educational or occupational measures in the following inpatient, semi-inpatient, or outpatient rehabilitation	Ability to acquire skills	Mental and physical capacity of at least 4 hours per day	Involvement of a vocational counselor from the SII and the accident insurance
	Ability to focus attention on work activities	Socially acceptable bladder and bowel control	A vocational assessment should be carried out
	Ability to perform simple tasks with support		Access to accompanying therapeutic intervention
	Ability to perform tasks on a regular basis		Accommodation of the environment

(continued)

Table 17.1 (continued)

Goal categories	Activities and participation	Body functions and structures	Environmental factors
			(architectural, organizational, assistive devices)
	Sufficient communication skills		Financing ensured
	Sufficient mobility		
	Ability for interpersonal relationships		
C4 - Vocational adjustment/vocational reorientation at the former job	Ability to perform adapted work tasks after vocational reorientation and according to the current functioning profile	Work capacity of at least 4–8 hours per day	Involvement of a vocational counselor from the SII and the accident insurance
	Ability to learn and acquire skills	Stable work-related motor and mental functions	A vocational assessment should be carried out
	Ability to apply knowledge	Socially acceptable bladder and bowel control	Adequate conditions provided by the employer
	Ability to perform general work tasks and demands		Access to accompanying therapeutic intervention
	Communication skills		Accommodation of the (work) environment (architectural, organizational, assistive devices)
	Sufficient mobility		Financing ensured
	Ability for interpersonal relationships		
C5 - Vocational adjustment at a new job	Ability to perform adapted work tasks according to the current functioning profile	Work capacity of at least 4–8 hours per day	Involvement of a vocational counselor from the SII, accident insurance, and placement service
	Ability to learn and acquire skills	Stable work-related motor and mental functions	A vocational assessment should be carried out
	Ability to apply knowledge	Socially acceptable bladder and bowel control	Adequate conditions provided by the employer
	Ability to perform general work tasks and demands	Adequate motivation	Access to accompanying therapeutic intervention
	Communication skills		Accommodation of the (work)

(continued)

Table 17.1 (continued)

Goal categories	Activities and participation	Body functions and structures	Environmental factors
			environment (architectural, organizational, assistive devices)
	Sufficient mobility		Financing ensured
	Ability for interpersonal relationships		
C6 - Vocational retraining after inpatient rehabilitation	Ability to perform a vocational retraining according to the current functioning profile	Work capacity of at least 4–8 hours per day	Involvement of a vocational counselor from the SII and the accident insurance
	Ability to learn and acquire skills	Stable work-related motor and mental functions	A vocational assessment should be carried out
	Ability to apply knowledge	Socially acceptable bladder and bowel control	Educational institution ensures care and living
	Ability to perform general work tasks and demands	Adequate learning potential and motivation	Access to accompanying therapeutic intervention
	Communication skills		Accommodation of the (work) environment (architectural, organizational, assistive devices)
	Sufficient mobility		Financing ensured
	Ability for interpersonal relationships		
C7 - Part-time work in former job (including housework) *or education*	Ability to perform part-time work in the former job according to the current functioning profile	Work capacity of at least 4–8 hours per day	Involvement of a vocational counselor from the SII and the accident insurance
	Ability to learn and acquire skills	Stable work-related motor and mental functions	A vocational assessment should be carried out
	Ability to apply knowledge	Socially acceptable bladder and bowel control	Adequate conditions provided by the employer
	Ability to perform general work tasks and demands		Access to accompanying therapeutic intervention
	Communication skills		Accommodation of the (work) environment (architectural, organizational, assistive devices)
	Sufficient mobility		Financing ensured

(continued)

Table 17.1 (continued)

Goal categories	Activities and participation	Body functions and structures	Environmental factors
	Ability for interpersonal relationships		
C8 - Full-time work in former job (including housework) *or education*	No significant limitations in the activities and participation domains regarding the demands of the former job or the education	Work capacity of at least 4–8 hours per day	Involvement of a vocational counselor from the SII and the accident insurance
		Stable work-related motor and mental functions	A vocational assessment should be carried out
		Socially acceptable bladder and bowel control	Adequate conditions provided by the employer
			Financing of alterations ensured by the SII
			Access to accompanying therapeutic intervention
			Accommodation of the (work) environment (architectural, organizational, assistive devices)
			Financing ensured

17.3.3 Modern Management Techniques in a Rehabilitation Center

A growing number of rehabilitation centers in Europe structure their patient rehabilitation program along "critical pathways" (also known as "patient pathways" or "clinical pathways") and use process management techniques to improve the quality and outcome of rehabilitation efforts in the most efficient way possible. Business processes are defined as a sequence of activities necessary to complete an operational task, such as the rehabilitation of patients with a certain diagnosis and specific participation goals. Therefore, the treatment program of a patient with SCI would be different from the one for a patient with an orthopedic problem. This means that a program is organized according to its key processes (e.g., rehabilitation of SCI patients) and not primarily based on its functional structure (e.g., OT department, PT department). Overall a process organization can be understood as the permanent structuring and continuous optimization of processes. *Patient pathways* (or *clinical pathways*) describe the key business processes or the workflow of a rehabilitation clinic.

By developing the concept "Rehabilitation at the SPZ" in 2012, the SPZ initiated a process-based organizational structure. The concept refers to a fundamental reorganization in which employees are brought together in ways that enable them to fully focus on the patient and thereby improve the effectiveness and efficiency of the rehabilitation process. Studies show that structured patient management with coordinated processes improves goal attainment and patient satisfaction, reduces the length of patients' stay at the hospital, and prevents organizational bottlenecks as well as resource underutilization [14].

The implementation of patient-centered treatment procedures holds great promise for achieving significant improvements in patient outcomes [23]. Patient pathways have proved a useful concept for the management of various health conditions [24]. However, a uniform definition for clinical pathways or patient pathways is not yet available. Definitions vary depending on the main focus of a particular rehabilitation context [25]. For the purpose of this chapter, we refer to Roeder and Küttner who understand patient pathways as a multidisciplinary plan that defines the treatment stages between admission to and discharge from a rehabilitation clinic [24].

> Patient pathways describe the key business processes or the workflow of a rehabilitation clinic. They refer to a multidisciplinary plan that defines the treatment stages between admission to and discharge from a rehabilitation clinic.

The patient pathways at the SPZ (see Fig. 17.1) rely on a comprehensive and integrative ICF-based rehabilitation concept that includes the criteria of effectiveness, sustainability, practicability, and economic efficiency. The pathways encompass the entire range of inpatient and outpatient services and define the processes from admission to discharge. The regulation of interdisciplinary measures and processes is essential to ensure an optimal treatment process with an efficient

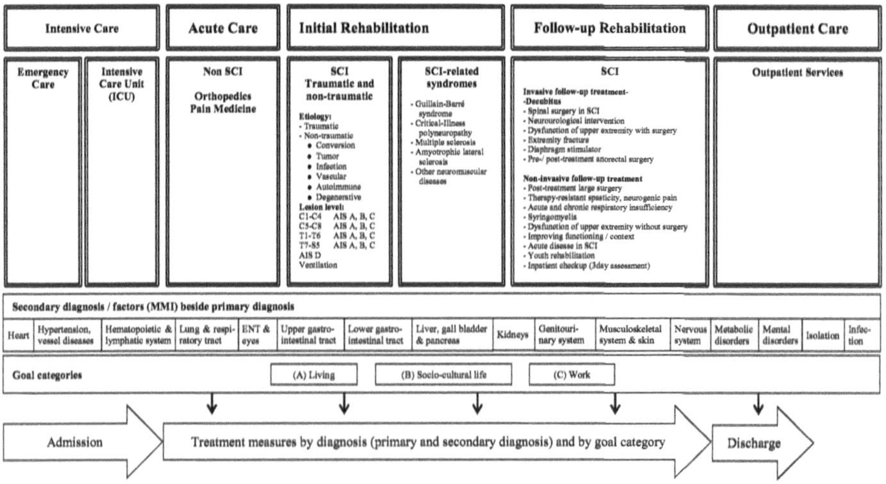

Fig. 17.1 Overview of the five major patient pathways at the SPZ

allocation of resources. The pathways are incorporated into a process management system with indicators and defined responsibilities and are structured into key processes, processes (i.e., paths), subprocesses, and sub-subprocesses. Each process includes process goals, definitions of possible key goals, inputs, outputs, and performance metrics. This structure provides the basis for a transparent quality management system. Patient pathways represent key elements for control and documentation in a clinical information system and allow for structured and patient-centered transdisciplinary communication. Moreover, they facilitate standardized rehabilitation services and serve as a basis for quality improvement and financial control with a process cost analysis.

Figure 17.1 illustrates the five patient pathways at the SPZ and their three "subprocesses":

1. Admission
2. Treatment measures by diagnosis (primary and secondary diagnosis) and by goal category
3. Discharge

These subprocesses are further divided into "sub-subprocesses" such as "housing assessment", "ergonomic counseling", or "vocational measures". For each sub-subprocess, a specific "patient management cockpit" is available defining the different stages of the goal attainment process, appropriate assessments and interventions for the different stages, and the disciplines in charge.

Interdisciplinary communication plays a key role in the rehabilitation process at the SPZ. In this regard the current coexistence of various information technology (IT) application systems, which work perfectly for their original particular purpose, represents a big challenge for the members of the rehabilitation team. Currently, team members have to seek essential information in unconnected IT application systems, which is extremely time consuming. In addition, these unconnected systems reduce the team's ability to share interdisciplinary knowledge of specific interventions, and a common thread is not always apparent. Documenting specific treatment measures and their progress is important for an interdisciplinary team approach, as it facilitates the structuring of work processes and the clarification of interfaces between the various professional disciplines involved in the rehabilitation process.

The patient management cockpit provides the basis for an overarching clinic information system and visualizes the workflow in all medical, nursing, and therapeutic measures. It consists of a basic module which works up and digitally illustrates the structure of the work processes in a set of rules. The tool fulfills the function of a parent layer with access to all applications. It serves as a navigation tool as well as a working tool in clinical practice. Furthermore, the tool provides users with immediate access to all information defined in the workflow and allows for bidirectional documentation of treatment results.

A survey of the different disciplines involved in the rehabilitation process at the SPZ showed that the team members expect the patient management cockpit to provide information on the current status of the patients in their own as well as in other disciplines. This information includes current findings (e.g., consultation reports), medical prescriptions (e.g., pre- or postoperative), courses of treatment (e.g., general or discipline specific), and patient status (e.g., treatment status or insurance status). In addition, the respective intermediate goals and their status should be made available.

> The patient pathways at the SPZ rely on a comprehensive and integrative ICF-based rehabilitation concept and are incorporated into a process management system with indicators and defined responsibilities. The patient management cockpit serves as a clinical navigation tool and provides the basis for an overarching clinical information system that visualizes the workflow in all medical, nursing, and therapeutic measures.

17.3.4 Vocational Measures at the Institute of Vocational Counseling (IBF)

In this section, we briefly describe the nature of the patient management cockpits as they are being applied in the SPZ, using the treatment process "vocational measures" as a specific example. Figure 17.2 presents a flowchart that provides a detailed overview of the treatment process "vocational measures" as it currently takes place at the IBF of the SPZ. The horizontal axis represents the time course, whereas the vertical axis illustrates the different actors involved in the VR process. The process starts with the decision by the medical doctors and the persons involved in the interdisciplinary ICF meetings that vocational measures are needed.

The optimal coordination of treatment processes prevents redundancies in the rehabilitation process overall. For example, it clearly defines how the treatment processes "vocational measures" and "workplace assessment" are dependent on each other. Furthermore, regular alignment of goal categories and intermediate goals in an interdisciplinary setting is necessary and helpful.

The ICF-based treatment process "vocational measures" is subdivided into the following stages (see textbox):

1. Initial phase
2. Assessment phase
3. Evaluation and decision phase
4. Interdisciplinary coordination of goals and measures
5. Intervention phase
6. Goal evaluation
7. Discharge phase

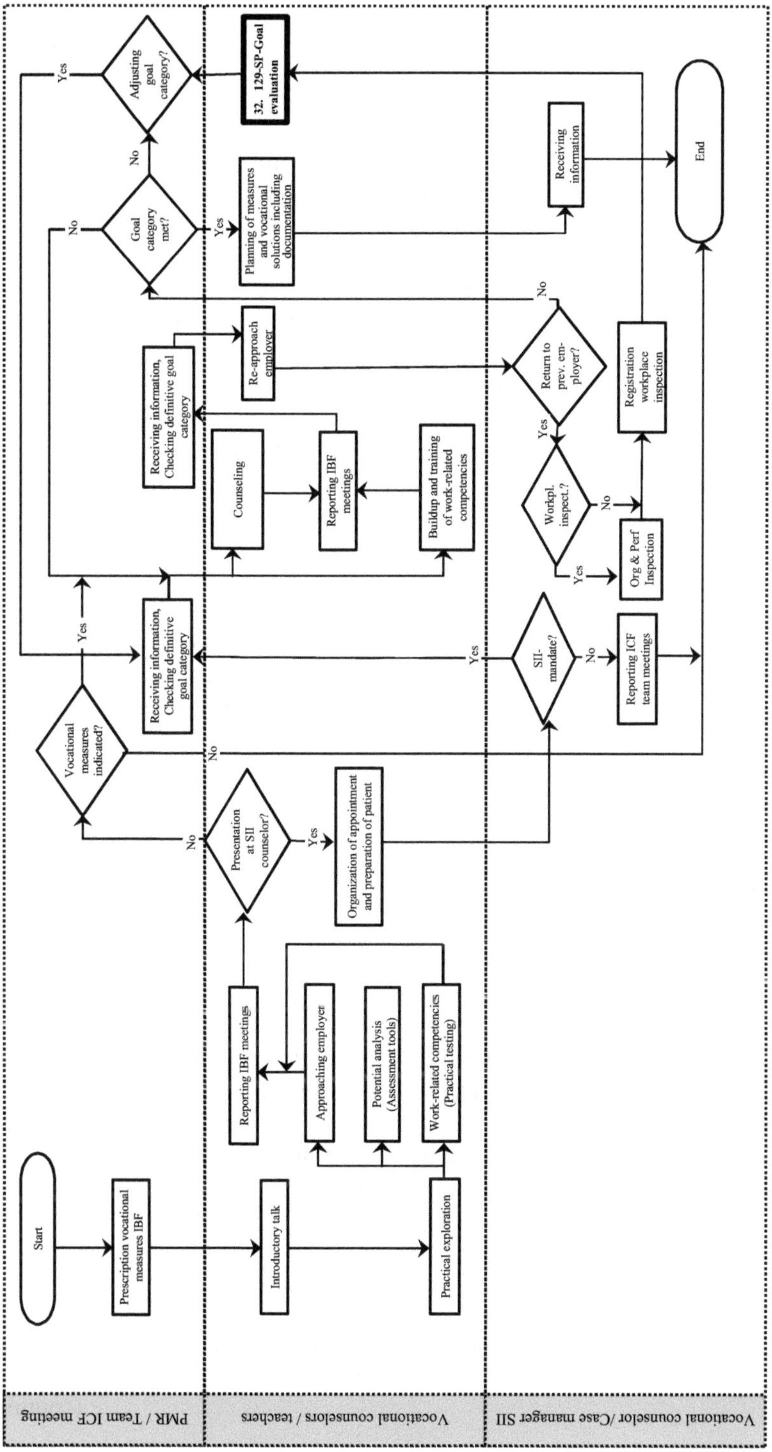

Fig. 17.2 Flowchart of the patient management "cockpit" for the treatment process vocational measures at the IBF

▪

1. Initial phase
   This stage focuses on motivational aspects and confidence building. It includes an introductory talk among the IBF team members. In this initial meeting, patients introduce themselves to the IBF team. The recording of the occupational case history is one of the key aspects of the initial phase. Based on this information, the team formulates a vocational hypothesis (e.g., a trained bricklayer is manually skilled and may therefore be retrained as a draftsman). This hypothesis determines the type of tests and assessments that will be conducted in the assessment phase. The initial phase also includes a practical exploration by the specialist vocational teachers to detect patients' interests for particular work activities, to study their work attitude, and to generate their motivation for participation in the VR programs.
2. Assessment phase
   This phase represents the vocational assessment process, which includes work-related abilities, skills, and potential. Additionally, the employer is contacted, and information regarding environmental factors at the former workplace and insurance-related aspects are collected. The potential analysis provides insights into the patient's work-related abilities and involves the application of assessment tools such as performance tests, work-related intelligence tests, interest tests, aptitude tests, or personality tests. The monitoring of the patient's behavior and personal factors plays a crucial role for the assessments as well. Moreover, work-related competencies are also rated through practical testing by the specialist vocational teachers. The principal goal of the assessment phase is to define a first hypothetical job goal that ensures the best possible match between the patient's work-related skills and interests and the demands of the job. For this purpose, a matching tool is developed by the IBF.
3. Evaluation and decision phase
   This stage deals with the determination of the specific work-related discharge goal, which is intended to be attainable within 12 weeks after discharge from the clinic. A first important decision at the beginning of this phase concerns the question of whether the case should be presented to the vocational counselor of the SII to receive an official mandate for further assessment. If this is the case, the specific goal category to be attained is then defined (e.g., vocational retraining).
4. Interdisciplinary coordination of goals and measures
   This phase includes the determination of measures and specific intermediate goals needed to achieve the primary job goal. The measures and the

(continued)

specific steps to achieve the intermediate goals are assigned to the corresponding disciplines involved in the rehabilitation process.

5. Intervention phase
   During the intervention phase, the patient is supported by the vocational counselor and receives work-related training of the specialist vocational teachers in one or more out of four areas, i.e., crafts, informatics, commercial occupations, and foreign languages.
6. Goal evaluation
   The status of goal attainment is examined by using the abovementioned matching tool and checked to determine how close the work-related skills and abilities of the patient have come to the demands of the defined goal (job or school), whether the goal is already met, or whether it needs to be adjusted. The former or future employer or the headmaster of a school is approached regarding limiting or facilitating environmental factors. In addition, inspections of the planned workplace or school and ergonomic counseling are conducted by occupational therapists.
7. Discharge phase
   This last inpatient phase focuses on discharge procedures. Additional measures for after discharge are planned and the vocational follow-up solution firmed up. In an ideal situation, the inpatient VR process ends with the attainment of the original defined goal category, the planning and initiating of a concrete vocational follow-up solution, and a final report to the SII. Since May 2013, the SII can also assign patients to the IBF for follow-up counseling such as by means of job coaching.

17.4 Case Study Using ICF-Based VR at the Institute of Vocational Counseling

The following case example refers to the treatment process "vocational measures" and is arranged according to the different phases of the VR process at the IBF.

Mr. A was 36 years old when he had SCI (tetraplegia) as a consequence of a mountain bike accident. According to the treatment process "vocational measures", the attending senior physician instructed the IBF to conduct a screening of the occupational situation of Mr. A. Due to the young age of Mr. A and his previous professional career, the IBF recommended a participation-oriented VR goal.

17.4.1 Initial Phase

The first meeting of the patient with the vocational counselor involved the presentation of the IBF team members and the services provided by the IBF. In the next session, the occupational case history was recorded.

Mr. A. attended 6 years of primary and 3 years of middle school. He then completed a 4-year apprenticeship as a carpenter where he mainly acquired skills in building wood element houses and roof construction. Afterwards, he continued working for 12 years as a carpenter and assembler in his training company and took over the position as deputy team leader. In addition, he acted as an operator of cutting machines, was responsible for maintaining plants and machines, and performed carpentry and assembly of doors. During this time, he also attended a computer course and completed a forklift course. Three years ago, he changed jobs and joined a company that manufactures saunas. There, he produced and installed wellness facilities and was responsible for their service and maintenance. In addition, he completed a sauna construction course.

Mr. A. was married and had three sons aged 3, 5, and 6 years. He described his family environment as good. Mr. A was also actively involved in associations and community life at his place of residence. His work attitude was very positive and achievement oriented.

17.4.2 Assessment Phase

17.4.2.1 Potential Analysis: Vocational Counselors

A number of meetings with the vocational counselor took place as part of the assessment phase, and different assessments focusing on functional performance as well as on personal and environmental factors were conducted.

The following assessment tools were applied:

- *Multicheck:* computer-based competence analysis in terms of a vocational aptitude test, including a personality test regarding achievement motivation and social competence
- *KV-interest test:* assesses interests for further education in the commercial field
- *Worker role interview:* a structured interview for assessing psychosocial and environmental factors influencing labor market integration
- *Standard Progressive Matrices (SPM, Raven):* a test which assesses nonverbal intelligence and the ability for clear and structured thinking

From the beginning of the rehabilitation process, Mr. A was a highly motivated, independent, and optimistic person with good resources and coping strategies. Already at the first meeting, he expressed that he wanted to return to work after completing rehabilitation.

In consultation with Mr. A, his employer was approached to clarify the environmental factors at the former workplace. The employer expressed the willingness of the company to actively contribute to Mr. A's work reintegration.

Table 17.2 Work-related abilities and potential of Mr. A based on the matching tool

Category definitions	Assessment					Comments
	0					= Nonexistent (none, 0–4 %)
		1				= Poor (insufficient, 5–24 %)
			2			= Medium (sufficient, 25–49 %)
				3		= High (good, 50–95 %)
					4	= Complete, total (very good, 96–100 %)
Team behavior/social skills					x	Agreeable and very cooperative collaboration
Manual skills/ dexterity					x	High dexterity in working with machines and materials
Fine motor skills					x	High accuracy in assembly work
Technical understanding				x		Very good ability to connect ideas
Visual and spatial perception				x		No problems in understanding and interpreting drawings and graphics
Concentration				x		Is able to work concentrated up to 2 hours
Learning ability/ retentiveness				x		Is able to quickly acquire new practical and manual functions
Creativity/design					x	Develops successfully his own solutions

17.4.2.2 Assessment of Work-Related Competencies: Specialist Vocational Teachers

By means of different practical work tests (computer-based tasks), the specialist vocational teacher in charge compiled a profile regarding Mr. A's work-related abilities and potential based on the previously mentioned matching tool (see Table 17.2).

17.4.3 Evaluation and Decision Phase

Based on the collected information, the work-related goal setting was evaluated, and a suggestion was made to the interdisciplinary rehabilitation team accordingly. The recommended goal category was *C6 Vocational retraining after inpatient rehabilitation* (see Table 17.1).

17.4.4 Interdisciplinary Coordination of Goals and Measures

The suggested work-related goal category was approved at the interdisciplinary ICF team meeting. Based on the intended goal category, measures for attaining the goal were formulated and assigned to the rehabilitation disciplines in charge.

Upon request by the IBF and based on the interdisciplinary evaluation, the SII mandated the IBF to conduct a basic vocational assessment to specifically examine the work-related resources of Mr. A and to identify and evaluate occupations adapted to his disability.

17.4.5 Intervention Phase

17.4.5.1 Skills Training

Before his accident Mr. A had only limited experience in working with computers. He learned some basics in computer classes during school but rarely used the computer at work or at home.

In a first step of VR, Mr. A worked with the Auto CAD 2013 which is a software for construction, planning, graphical design, and modeling in the field of architecture. This was done in anticipation of a return to his former employer where Mr. A could perform planning and administrative tasks. These tasks involved no additional challenges for Mr. A, since he already knew the basics of technical drawing from his education as a carpenter.

Using Auto CAD 2013, Mr. A learned to compare different construction methods as well as to create standard plans and different plot layouts. Mr. A was able to learn the functionality of Auto CAD 2013 quickly. He was quick-witted, capable of learning, and worked thoughtfully. He worked independently according to instructions and tried to solve problems at first on his own, but asked for help when needed. Despite his physical limitations, Mr. A worked in a concentrated and efficient manner.

During the entire rehabilitation, Mr. A never missed a training course. He was motivated and enjoyed the technical drawing. He usually was friendly, kind, and cheerful, and his interpersonal dealings with the IBF team members and the other patients were always commendable.

Mr. A needed a tetra mouse with side click and scroll wheel to optimally handle the computer and the different functions of the CAD. If he pursued further education a speech recognition system would be recommended to optimize his writing speed.

17.4.5.2 Additional Skills Training

In view of the new work areas and additional office work, Mr. A was trained in commercial fields focusing on computer classes. The following goals were pursued:

- Activation and generating motivation for new working areas
- Assessment of existing knowledge
- Assessment of ability for computer work (focusing on hand functions)
- Assessment of work performance and ability to concentrate
- Assessment of reliability and independence
- Instruction and training in working with the computer

Three to four times per week, in lessons of 45 min, Mr. A was trained in using Microsoft Office programs, working in the Internet, and writing e-mails and correspondence in High German. In addition, he was supported in preparing an up-to-date résumé.

17.4.6 Goal Evaluation

Due to his limited hand functions, Mr. A received a touchpad (instead of a mouse) and two sticks for handling the keyboard. His shoulder and arm mobility was within normal active range of motion. After some time, Mr. A started working without the touchpad and the sticks. Instead, he used a tetra mouse and used the pressure of his hands to handle the keyboard with his forefinger, middle finger, and thumb. Mr. A nevertheless achieved good working speed.

In a relatively short time, Mr. A was able to acquire basic knowledge for working with Microsoft Word, Excel, and Outlook. Because he tested and applied new applications on his own, he progressed well and developed additional knowledge.

The most significant difficulties he faced were related to corresponding in High German. He reported being dyslexic, which could be observed in the correspondence exercises he performed (e.g., writing and correcting letters and texts), in which he made quite a few mistakes. However, he was open to suggested corrections and could avoid similar mistakes in subsequent exercises because of his quick-wittedness. In case Mr. A would often have to write letters in his new job, it was felt that he should attend further courses in orthography and correspondence to gain more confidence.

Mr. A was reliable and always on time for the lessons. He was active and highly motivated to learn new knowledge, performed well at all times, and was able to concentrate on his work. Finally, Mr. A showed high personal responsibility and independence.

Naturally, due to Mr. A's limited hand functions, he required more time to perform work activities. However, he worked efficiently and achieved a good working speed.

17.4.7 Discharge Phase

17.4.7.1 Contacts with Employers and Schools

In the course of the rehabilitation, it became apparent that a return to the previous employer, a company for sauna constructions, was not realistic. A major barrier proved to be the fact that it was a small company with strongly fluctuating order volumes. In addition, a workplace inspection revealed that the necessary architectural accommodations would have caused high costs.

As suggested by Mr. A, a meeting could be scheduled with his former employer where he had worked as a carpenter. As a result of the meeting, Mr. A was offered to participate in a "job-shadowing" day to learn more about the work of a project manager. The day also served as a trial day to get an impression about the amount of time Mr. A is currently able to work per day and potential barriers to work. Mr. A was also given the opportunity to become familiar with planning activities and to observe the work of other project managers. The experience was positive for Mr. A, and he was eventually offered an internship as a drafter and project manager at another company.

17.4.7.2 Suggestions for Vocational Reintegration

Because of his physical limitations, and since returning to the former job was not possible for Mr. A, he had to reorient himself with regard to his vocational situation. Initial efforts to find an adapted job at his previous employer turned out to be unrealistic and thus the company dismissed Mr. A.

During several counseling sessions, different potential vocational scenarios were discussed. His affinity for the construction sector was ultimately a major factor in Mr. A's decision to return to work in this vocational area.

Further trial work will show how Mr. A can be employed and what activities of his previous job he is still able to perform. The trial will also determine Mr. A's functional capacity.

17.4.7.3 Vocational Reintegration Plan

Mr. A reached his vocational discharge goal. The IBF suggested a reintegration plan that included several stages:

- In 2 months Mr. A will start working as a drafter, for a therapeutic purpose only 3 hours per day.
- In 3 months a meeting with the IBF is planned to review the vocational solution and to make adjustments if necessary.
- A gradual increase of his working hours during the following months may be possible, depending on Mr. A's capacity.
- Mr. A will attend additional work-related courses in accordance with the demands of his workplace and in consultation with the vocational counselor of the SII.

17.5 Conclusion

An ICF-based VR process using concrete participation-based goal categories promises to be beneficial for reintegrating persons with SCI in the labor market. The ICF comprehensively illustrates the key aspects and determinants of the goal attainment process in VR, such as the individual's ability to perform job tasks, his or her biological health, and the impact of influencing contextual factors. A transparent documentation of functioning and its determinants allows for comparing individuals' abilities with specific job demands, as well as for identifying mismatches and, thus, starting points for VR interventions. VR programs such as job placement or job matching can benefit from such documentation because interventions can be planned and conducted in a more goal-oriented way. An ICF-based matching tool allows for evaluating the status of individuals' goal attainment. However, specific ICF categories as such do not play a prominent role in this matching process because they currently do not allow for addressing specific job demands. Therefore, the goal categories and matching criteria should be selected from occupational information systems such as the *Occupational Information Network* (O*NET).

Additionally, the ICF does not classify personal factors that are particularly essential in VR. Aspects such as educational and occupational background, work attitudes and motivation, self-efficacy, and personality characteristics determine a successful VR and, ultimately, a sustainable and permanent return to work. Personal factors should, therefore, always be considered in the VR of persons with SCI, and a proper classification of personal factors in the ICF could be important in this particular context.

The interdisciplinary approach to process management applied in the SPZ offers a transparent, well-coordinated, and efficient rehabilitation process. In order to follow and track the overall process of rehabilitation, the SPZ devised a rehabilitation management tool that serves as a kind of "patient management cockpit". This tool improves communication among team members and leads to effective interdisciplinary teamwork which, in turn, promotes successful rehabilitation. The ICF serves as a structuring device for a top-down rehabilitation process and goal-oriented intervention planning; its ultimate goal is to promote participation and reintegration in work and social life, providing the optimal basis for patients to live as independently as possible after rehabilitation.

Study Questions

1. Provide an ICF-based definition of vocational rehabilitation.

   Answer: VR is a multi-professional evidence-based approach that is provided in different settings, services, and activities to working age individuals with health-related impairments, limitations, or restrictions with work functioning, and whose primary aim is to optimize work participation.

2. How can the rehabilitation concept of the Swiss Paraplegic Center be characterized and what role does the ICF play?

   Answer: The Swiss Paraplegic Center follows a rehabilitation concept that applies a top-down approach and is based on patient pathways and participation-focused discharge goals. The ICF model with its participation-oriented focus serves as an overarching framework with regard to the definition of the discharge goal categories.

3. What are patient pathways?

   Answer: Patient pathways describe the key business processes or the workflow of a rehabilitation clinic. They refer to a multidisciplinary plan that defines the treatment stages between admission to and discharge from a rehabilitation clinic.

4. Describe the seven stages of the process vocational measures at the SPZ and their most important elements.

   Answer:

   1. Initial phase

      - Introductory talk
      - Recording of the occupational case history
      - Formulation of vocational hypothesis
      - Practical exploration by specialist vocational teacher

   2. Assessment phase

      - Contact previous employer
      - Collection of information on former workplace and environment, including insurance-related aspects
      - Vocational assessment: (a) Potential analysis (work-related abilities, interests and aptitudes); (b) Practical testing (work-related competencies)
      - Definition of first hypothetical job goal (based on match between person and job)

3. Evaluation and decision phase
   - Definition of work-related discharge goal
   - Decision on whether case will be presented to SII
4. Interdisciplinary coordination of goals and measure
   - Determination of measures to achieve primary job goal
   - Assignment of measures to corresponding rehabilitation disciplines
5. Intervention phase
   - Vocational counseling
   - Work-related training by specialist vocational teacher
6. Goal evaluation
   - Examination of goal attainment by using matching tool
   - Approaching future employer regarding environmental facilitators or barriers
   - Workplace inspections
   - Ergonomic counseling
7. Discharge phase
   - Planning of measures after discharge
   - Firming up of a vocational follow-up solution
   - Planning follow-up job coaching

5. What is the main benefit of the patient management cockpit at the Swiss Paraplegic Center?

   Answer: The patient management cockpit serves as a clinical navigation tool and provides the basis for an overarching clinical information system that visualizes the workflow in all medical, nursing, and therapeutic measures. It improves communication among team members and leads to effective interdisciplinary teamwork which, in turn, promotes successful rehabilitation.

References

1. Wiegand NM, Belting J, Fekete C, Gutenbrunner C, Reinhardt JD. All talk, no action?: the global diffusion and clinical implementation of the international classification of functioning, disability, and health. Am J Phys Med Rehabil. 2012;91(7):550–60.
2. Schultz I, Stowell A, Feuerstein M, Gatchel R. Models of return to work for musculoskeletal disorders. J Occup Rehabil. 2007;17(2):327–52.
3. Homa DB. Using the International Classification of Functioning, Disability and Health (ICF) in job placement. Work. 2007;29(4):277–86.

4. Escorpizo R, Reneman MF, Ekholm J, Fritz J, Krupa T, Marnetoft S-U, et al. A conceptual definition of vocational rehabilitation based on the ICF: building a shared global model. J Occup Rehabil. 2011;21(2):126–33.
5. Ross J. Occupational therapy and vocational rehabilitation. Chichester: Wiley; 2007.
6. Gobelet C, Franchignoni F. Vocational rehabilitation. In: Gobelet C, Franchignoni F, editors. Vocational rehabilitation. Paris: Springer; 2006. p. 3–16.
7. Langman C. Introduction to vocational rehabilitation. London: Routledge; 2012.
8. Meade MA, Armstrong AJ, Barrett K, Ellenbogen PS, Jackson MN. Vocational rehabilitation services for individuals with spinal cord injury. J Vocat Rehabil. 2006;25(1):3–11.
9. SPG. Annual report 2012 of the Swiss Paraplegic Group. Nottwil: Swiss Paraplegic Foundation; 2013.
10. SPZ. Concept "rehabilitation in the SPZ". Nottwil: Swiss Paraplegic Center; 2012.
11. Fries W. Rehabilitation for participation: current state. In: Fries W, Lössl H, Wagenhäuser S, editors. Participating! New concepts of neurorehabilitation – for a successful return to work and everyday life. Stuttgart: Thieme; 2007. p. 1–6.
12. Stucki G, Müller K, Bochdansky T, Schwarz H, Smolenski U. Is the ICIDH checklist suitable for classification of functional health in rehabilitation practice? – results of a workshop of the consensus conference of the three societies for physical medicine and rehabilitation of Germany, Austria and Switzerland. Phys Rehabil Kur Med. 2000;10(3):78–85.
13. Adler SL, Bryk E, Cesta TG, McEachen I. Collaboration: the solution to multidisciplinary care planning. Orthop Nurs. 1995;14(2):21–9.
14. Bakheit AM. Effective teamwork in rehabilitation. Int J Rehabil Res. 1996;19(4):301–6.
15. Martinuzzi A, Salghetti A, Betto S, Russo E, Leonardi M, Raggi A, et al. The International Classification of Functioning Disability and Health, version for children and youth as a roadmap for projecting and programming rehabilitation in a neuropaediatric hospital unit. J Rehabil Med. 2010;42(1):49–55.
16. Salghetti AM, Betto S, Russo E, Petacchi E, Pradal M, Martinuzzi A. Projecting and programming rehabilitation based on ICF-CY format in a neuropediatric hospital unit. Disabil Rehabil. 2009;31 Suppl 1:S55–60.
17. Slebus FG, Sluiter JK, Kuijer PP, Willems JH, Frings-Dresen MH. Work-ability evaluation: a piece of cake or a hard nut to crack? Disabil Rehabil. 2007;29(16):1295–300.
18. Brouwer S, Reneman MF, Bultmann U, van der Klink JJ, Groothoff JW. A prospective study of return to work across health conditions: perceived work attitude, self-efficacy and perceived social support. J Occup Rehabil. 2010;20(1):104–12.
19. Sjöberg L. Risk and willingness to work. Int J Risk Assess Manag. 2007;7(2):224–36.
20. Finger ME, Escorpizo R, Glässel A, Gmünder HP, Lückenkemper M, Chan C, et al. ICF Core Set for vocational rehabilitation: results of an international consensus conference. Disabil Rehabil. 2012;34(5):429–38.
21. Sjögren-Rönkä T, Ojanen MT, Leskinen EK, Tmustalampi S, Mälkiä EA. Physical and psychosocial prerequisites of functioning in relation to work ability and general subjective well-being among office workers. Scand J Work Environ Health. 2002;28(3):184–90.
22. Schwegler U, Peter C, Trezzini B, Anner J, Geyh S. Toward transparent documentation in medical work capacity evaluations: identifying personal factors in medical reports on Swiss disability claimants with chronic widespread pain. Int J Rehabil Res. 2013;36(4):298–307.
23. Salfeld R, Hehner S, Wichels R. Modern clinic management: concepts and solutions. Second, updated and extended edition. Berlin/Heidelberg: Springer; 2009.
24. Roeder N, Küttner T. Clinical pathways in the light of cost effects in the context of the DRG system. Internist. 2006;7:684–9.
25. Bartz M. Patient pathways – a tool for process optimization in the hospital. 1st ed. Saarbrücken: VDM-Verlag Dr. Müller; 2006.

Chapter 18
Applying the ICF in Disability Evaluation: A Report Based on Clinical Experience

Jörg Jeger, Bruno Trezzini, and Urban Schwegler

18.1 The Significance of Disability Evaluation in Determining Eligibility for Benefits

With the introduction of various social insurance schemes towards the end of the nineteenth century, medical doctors were handed a new task. Before this, employment contracts were solely regulated by agreements between the employee and employer. When a worker became sick, the decision of how to take care of him or her was left to the owner of the company. While private organizations and the church provided a certain amount of social security, the state did not play a significant role. This changed fundamentally with the introduction of comprehensive social insurance schemes. Now national legislation specifies which health problems entitle employees to insurance benefits and what such benefits should look like. Furthermore, insurers require claimants to provide proof of their reported health condition and its consequences. Subjective complaints about the symptoms of a health condition (e.g., pain) are usually not sufficient. Rather, an objective assessment and evaluation of the severity of the health problems (i.e., impairments and functioning limitations due to illness or an accident) is needed for a proper decision regarding a claimant's eligibility for both social and private insurance benefits. However, the employer, the insurance case worker, and the claimant are

J. Jeger (✉)
MEDAS Zentralschweiz, Hirschengraben 33, 6003 Lucerne, Switzerland
e-mail: Joerg.Jeger@medaslu.ch

B. Trezzini
Swiss Paraplegic Research, Nottwil, Switzerland

U. Schwegler
Swiss Paraplegic Research, Nottwil, Switzerland

Department of Health Sciences and Health Policy, University of Lucerne, Lucerne, Switzerland

R. Escorpizo et al. (eds.), *Handbook of Vocational Rehabilitation and Disability Evaluation*, Handbooks in Health, Work, and Disability, DOI 10.1007/978-3-319-08825-9_18

usually not able to settle the case on their own; to do so they need medical expertise. In this case, the physician acts no longer just as a diagnostician or therapist, but takes on the additional task of a medical expert.

This new role definition often leads to role conflicts [1, 2]. While a therapist is primarily committed to the interests and the well-being of his or her patients, a medical expert has to approach and examine the claimant's situation in an objective and neutral manner. Research and jurisprudence are in agreement that the longer the disease persists and the higher the potential insurance benefits are, the more important it is to clearly distinguish between the "therapist" and "medical expert" functions. In the case of an acute disease lasting a few days, the attending physician can undoubtedly attest to a temporary work disability. But when it comes to long-term benefits, especially to decisions about a disability pension, it is vital that the claimant's situation be assessed and evaluated by an outside medical expert who is not involved in the treatment process. In many countries, therefore, the evaluation of pension entitlements requires an independent medical examination [3].

The legal system expects the medical expert to assess the claimant's situation neutrally and objectively, independent of the claimant's personal interests, and unaffected by the client's (i.e., insurers, courts) interests. Equal treatment of the claimants before the law is a legally protected right. The legal system also expects medical experts to arrive at comparable assessments when dealing with comparable circumstances (i.e., high interrater reliability). This applies to both the diagnoses made and the assessment of functional capacity. The fact that different experts evaluate similar situations very differently contravenes the requirement of equal treatment before the law. Low interrater reliability is less of a problem in assessments of somatic disorders, where symptoms can be measured objectively by medical instrumentation. For instance, after a myocardial infarction, the extent of structural damage can be detected echocardiographically, and cardiovascular capacity can be measured by ergometry. In this case, the appraisal of the claimant's functional capacity for a specific occupation appears transparent and well justified to the disability claims adjudicator and legal practitioner and hardly provides a target for criticism.

By contrast, disability evaluations involving claimants with mental disorders are more challenging. Mental disorders appear among the most common health conditions in disability evaluations worldwide [4–6]. However, they manifest themselves almost exclusively through symptoms and show few objective signs of illness that could be quantified.

This represents a huge challenge for both the medical expert and the disability claims adjudicator. How can the health state of claimants with mental disorders be described objectively and how can their functional capacity be assessed transparently if there are no parameters that can be measured by objective means? While the diagnosis can be operationalized using the *International Classification of Diseases*

(ICD-10) or the *Diagnostic and Statistical Manual of Mental Disorders* (DSM-5), the diagnosis in and of itself allows only very limited inferences as to the claimant's functioning status. This is true for both somatic and mental disorders. The *International Classification of Functioning, Disability and Health* (ICF), on the other hand, provides a holistic biopsychosocial approach for describing functioning and health that could facilitate the illustration of functional limitations resulting from a health condition. Therefore, the ICF has been suggested for application in disability evaluation in general [7, 8] and for the documentation of functioning in psychiatric evaluation in particular [9, 10].

18.2 Current State of the Disability Evaluation Procedure in Switzerland: Advantages and Problems

Internationally, existing social insurance systems can be traced back to two fundamentally different underlying models. First, there is the insurance model introduced in the 1880s in Germany by Otto von Bismarck, which is characterized by a statutorily regulated insurance and benefits catalogue, funded by contributions from insured citizens. Second, there is the insurance model based on recommendations by William H. Beveridge, which was implemented in England after the Second World War and is characterized by a National Health Service funded by taxes. Switzerland's social security system follows the Bismarckian model and currently comprises ten different insurance schemes addressing different risks of income loss [11, 12]. The discussion that follows focuses mainly on the Swiss Invalidity Insurance (IV) system, which is responsible for returning persons with disabilities to work and for determining their eligibility for disability pensions.

The IV system and the Swiss Accident Insurance Fund (SUVA) each has its own sociomedical service that insurance case managers can draw upon when reviewing disability claims. When necessary, they can order medical reports from independent medical experts, clinics, or specialized medical assessment centers. MEDAS Zentralschweiz is a private institute located in Lucerne, Switzerland and maintained by an independent foundation. The institute produces multidisciplinary evaluations commissioned by social or private insurance providers and courts. The business is governed by a service contract with the Swiss Federal Office of Social Security, which stipulates the neutrality and objectivity of the evaluations.

> Recently, there has been increasing criticism in the legal and medical literature as well as the lay press regarding the quality of consultative functional capacity evaluations, especially when they involve mental disorders. It has been suggested that these evaluations are not transparent, hardly understandable, and often more dependent on the particular expert doing the evaluation than on the claimant's situation [2, 13, 14].

Therefore, MEDAS Zentralschweiz started to look for tools that allow for more transparent and reliable evaluations of claimants with mental disorders that are also easier to understand for disability claims adjudicators and legal practitioners.

18.3 Experiences with the Mini-ICF-APP in Disability Evaluations of Claimants with Mental Disorders

18.3.1 The Mini-ICF-APP by Linden and Baron

The ICF shifts the focus from the diagnosis (structural impairment) to the functional health state. Thus, the following key questions should be answered by a disability evaluation:

- Which body or mental functions are impaired?
- Which abilities are limited?
- Which abilities are not significantly limited?
- How do the limited abilities affect the claimant's participation?
- What is the influence of contextual factors?

Answering these questions is particularly important in the case of mental disorders because the psychiatric diagnosis alone provides almost no information about these points. The social participation of persons with disabilities, however, is strongly dependent on their functional limitations, for example, problems in focusing attention. Therefore, it appears sensible to apply the ICF framework in psychiatric assessments as part of disability evaluations [15, 16].

Applying the ICF taxonomy in its entirety would be too cumbersome and time consuming in the context of disability evaluation and would fail in clinical practice because of its lack of practicability. In recent years, ICF Core Sets have been developed in order to make the ICF suitable for application in clinical practice [7, 17–22]. ICF Core Sets are short lists of ICF categories relevant for a specific health condition [23] or in a specific health or health-related setting [24]. These categories describe aspects of functioning and environmental factors that are particularly important to consider in a specific health condition. However, none of the published ICF Core Sets currently provide any guidance for how to properly operationalize the included categories.

The "Mini-ICF rating for limitations of activities and participation in psychological disorders" (Mini-ICF-APP), developed by Linden and Baron [25], represents a ICF-based tool that offers clear instructions on how to analyze and rate specific ability limitations. The Mini-ICF-APP has been derived from the activities and participation component of the ICF and is partly based on the "Groningen Social Disabilities Schedule II" [26]. The tool has been validated by the authors

[27], and recently additional studies on the reliability and validity of the Mini-ICF-APP have been published based on data from the UK and Italy [28, 29].

By using the Mini-ICF-APP, the following specific ability limitations and activities can be assessed and rated on a scale from 0 to 4 (0 = no limitation, 1 = mild limitation, 2 = moderate limitation, 3 = severe limitation, 4 = total limitation):

1. Adherence to regulations
2. Planning and structuring of tasks
3. Flexibility
4. Professional competency
5. Competence to judge and decide
6. Endurance
7. Assertiveness
8. Contact with others
9. Group integration
10. Intimate relationships
11. Nonwork activities
12. Self-care
13. Mobility

The authors of the Mini-ICF-APP provide detailed anchor definitions to clarify the exact meaning of the five rating levels. Furthermore, the Mini-ICF-APP manual, which was published in 2009 [27], also includes general rating instructions as well as specific descriptions for each of the 13 ability limitations. This should ensure that different users understand the ratings in the same manner and thus should contribute to a higher interrater reliability of the ratings.

18.3.2 Applying the Mini-ICF-APP to a Case at MEDAS Zentralschweiz

The following case study describes how the Mini-ICF-APP rating is applied in a psychiatric assessment as part of a disability evaluation.

The claimant is a 50-year-old woman and the youngest of five siblings. She lost her father in a car accident when she was 7 years old. After primary school, she started training for work as a saleswoman in a butchery, which she was not able to complete because of test anxiety. She then worked for various companies as a data typist. Twenty-four years ago, she started working as a clerk in a company for prints and reprographic products. Over the years, she was given more and more responsibilities and finally became head of the company's technical service department. She was the only woman in the department and was appreciated and respected for her professional and social competence by the men subordinate to her. Eventually, she even became a member of the company management. The marriage she entered into at the age of 25 remained childless and ended in divorce after 28 years. Her health problems started 5 years ago, about 1 year after her divorce. Within a short period of time, several somatic diseases emerged that required extensive treatments. Five years before the current evaluation, a pituitary adenoma had been detected and operated on. The postsurgical hormonal substitution therapy proved difficult and unsettled the claimant. Two years later, a falx meningioma had to be surgically removed. One and a half years before the current evaluation, a spinal fusion was performed due to an advanced segment degeneration with secondary spinal stenosis at L5-S1. From a purely technical point of view, all surgeries have been successful, but the accumulation of all these diseases within such a short period of time debilitated this very achievement-oriented woman. After several lengthy absences from work, she had to give up her executive position and reduce her workload to only 50 %. As a consequence, she was assigned to another position within the company. Finally, the claimant became completely unable to work. For more than a year, she was not working anymore and applied, therefore, for a pension with the IV system. During the medical evaluation, she mainly complained of a lack of power and energy, increased irritability, tension, and thought blocking as well as forgetfulness. In her own words, she felt as if she was "burned out." Regarding the back complaints, there were only minor residual symptoms. Taking into consideration her somatic diseases, her former job was considered to be still reasonably manageable for her. The psychiatric assessment resulted in the diagnosis of a severe neurasthenia (ICD-10 F48.0), combined with an atypical mild depressive disorder (ICD-10 F33.8).

When applying the Mini-ICF-APP, the psychiatrist transforms the information gathered from the exploration into a profile of functioning. One of the benefits of using the Mini-ICF-APP is that medical experts design their explorations differently. That is, it enables experts to interrelate psychiatric symptoms with limitations or restrictions in activities and participation in a more targeted way, which broadens the scope of the exploration. The functioning profile for the above-described claimant looked as follows (see also Fig. 18.1):

- Not limited in the ability for family and intimate relationships (item 10) and the ability for self-care (item 12).
- Mildly limited in the ability for contact with others (item 8), the ability for group integration (item 9), and mobility (item 13).
- Moderately limited in the ability for adherence to regulations (item 1), the ability for planning and structuring tasks (item 2), assertiveness (item 7), and the ability for performing nonwork activities (item 11).
- Severely limited in flexibility (item 3), professional competency (item 4), competence to judge and decide (item 5), and endurance (item 6).
- None of the assessed abilities is completely limited.

Based on the established functioning profile, the psychiatrist concluded that the claimant is no longer able to work in her former job as an executive leader. For a leadership position, assertiveness and the ability to make flexible decisions depending on the situation are particularly important. It is also crucial that a leader

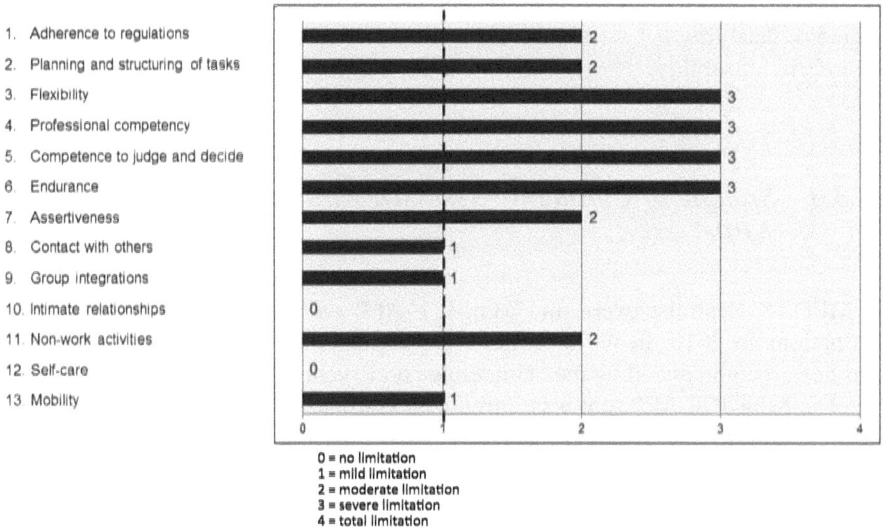

Fig. 18.1 The functioning profile of the evaluated claimant. The *dashed line* indicates that, based on the underlying anchor definitions, ability limitations with a rating of "*1*" are considered to entail no significant negative consequences to date

shows a high degree of endurance and is able to apply his or her professional competencies in stressful situations. In the claimant's case, these abilities are limited to a degree that does not allow her to resume her former job. In an adapted job which takes into account the established limitations and does not involve extraordinary demands on the claimant's psychological resilience, the psychiatrist considered the claimant's reasonably manageable work capacity to be 40 % of a normal workload.

The legal framework of Switzerland requires medical experts to provide at the end of their reports an assessment regarding the percentage of a normal workload that is still reasonable for the claimant to perform in light of his or her health condition and functional limitations. From the medical expert's point of view, it has to be emphasized that this percentage represents a judgment rather than a formal determination of the claimant's work capacity. This judgment is strongly dependent on the expert's clinical experience and cannot be derived directly from the Mini-ICF-APP rating. It remains part of the "medical art" and is, therefore, a subject of constant criticism [30]. However, the functioning profile of the Mini-ICF-APP provides useful information and could enhance the transparency and understandability of the expert's judgment regarding the claimant's work capacity. Disability claims adjudicators, for instance, need the exact percentage of a claimant's residual work capacity in an adapted job so as to be able to determine the final degree of disability, which determines the amount of benefits the claimant is entitled to. The degree of disability is then calculated based on a comparison of two types of income. More specifically, the (potential) income of the claimant in an adapted job (AJ) is compared to the income received in his or her former job (FJ), i.e., degree of disability = 1 − (AJ/FJ). Thus, the lower the ratio of AJ to FJ, the higher the inferred disability.

18.3.3 Sample of Claimants Assessed with the Mini-ICF-APP

In MEDAS Zentralschweiz, the Mini-ICF-APP was introduced for psychiatric evaluations in 2010. In the meantime, the application of the Mini-ICF-APP has also been recommended by the "Guidelines on Psychiatric Evaluations for the IV" [9]. The Mini-ICF-APP tool was introduced gradually. Initially, only one psychiatric expert used it; from February 2011 onwards, four out of five psychiatrists working for MEDAS Zentralschweiz have been using it. In tandem with the introduction of the Mini-ICF-APP tool, MEDAS Zentralschweiz has embarked on a research study that recorded all reports that included a diagnosis of a work-related mental disorder in a database. Between February 2010 and May 2013, a total number of 1,148 multidisciplinary reports were prepared at the institute. Of these, 1,102 involved a psychiatric evaluation. However, the Mini-ICF-APP was only applied in those cases where a mental disorder could be diagnosed and where the impact of the disorder on activities and participation was to be assessed. In 446 out of the 1,102 psychiatric reports, this was not the case as the mental disorder was not deemed severe enough. Another 209 reports did indeed involve a mental disorder, but the respective medical expert had not yet applied the Mini-ICF-APP for the psychiatric assessment. In the end, a total of 447 claimants were assessed using the Mini-ICF-APP rating during the stated period of time. All of these assessments were included in the present data analysis.

18.3.4 Results of the Research Study

Of the 447 claimants assessed with the Mini-ICF-APP, 52.9 % were male and 47.1 % were female. The average age was 47.4 years for the women and 50.1 years for the men. The majority of the claimants suffered from an affective or a somatoform disorder. In fact, in most of these cases, there was a combination of several diagnoses. On the other hand, our sample only included eight reports with psychotic disorders. This is probably due to the fact that severely disabling forms of psychotic disorders are usually evaluated solely through psychiatric evaluation and do not require multidisciplinary evaluations like those provided by MEDAS Zentralschweiz.

The 13 abilities were assessed using the published anchor definitions [27]. The means of the assessments were calculated for the 447 psychiatric reports which

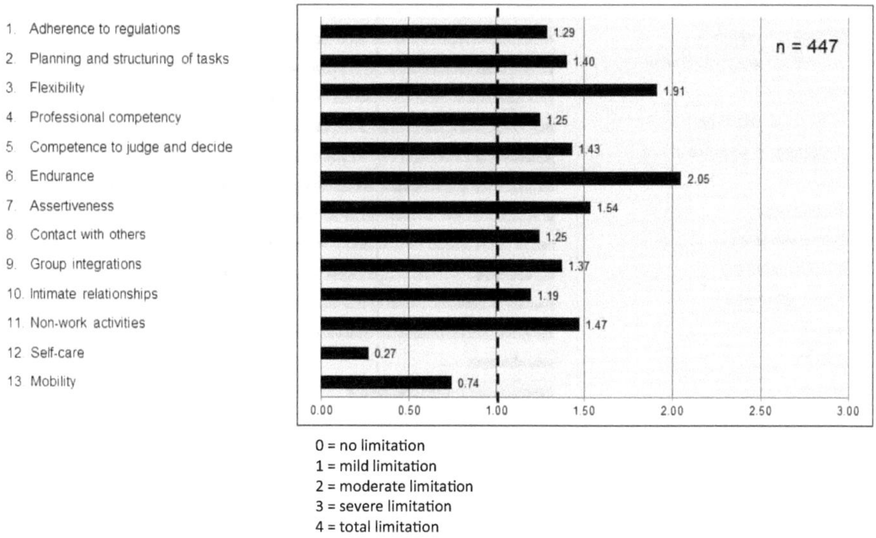

Fig. 18.2 Average functioning profile using the Mini-ICF-APP over all mental assessments

included an evaluation with the Mini-ICF-APP. Figure 18.2 shows the average functioning profile over all assessments.

Overall, flexibility (item 3) and endurance (item 6) turned out to be the most limited abilities. Yet they prove particularly important in modern service industries. Limited flexibility and endurance can easily lead to situations where people with mental disorders are unable to achieve the required level of work performance. In addition, the following abilities are affected in descending order: assertiveness (item 7), ability for nonwork activities (item 11), competence to judge and decide (item 5), ability for planning and structuring tasks (item 2), ability for group integration (item 9), ability for adherence to regulations (item 1), ability to apply professional competencies (item 4), ability for contact with others (item 8), and ability for family and intimate relationships (item 10). Ability for self-care (item 12) and mobility (item 13) were rarely limited to a significant degree, except in severely depressed claimants who are affected by high doses of psychotropic drugs.

In Switzerland, medical experts are required to provide an appraisal of a claimant's work capacity expressed as a percentage of a normal workload. As mentioned the IV system needs this information for calculating the degree of disability and determining the amount of disability pension benefits the claimant is entitled to.

An assumed work capacity of 70 % indicates that the medical expert considers it reasonable for the claimant to be expected to perform at 70 % of a normal workload in an adapted job. However, any such estimate as a percentage of the norm, and

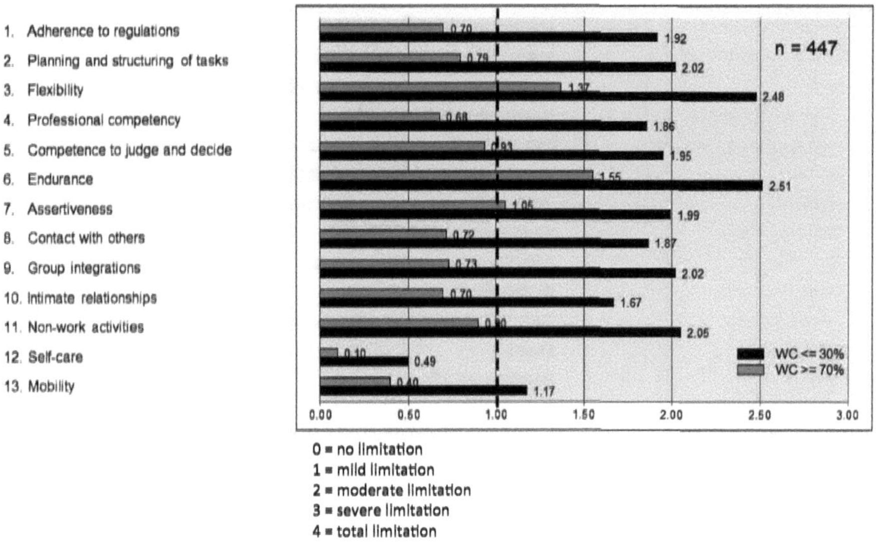

Fig. 18.3 Differences in Mini-ICF-APP functioning profiles between claimants with high (≥70 %) and low (≤30 %) attested work capacity in an adapted job. *WC* work capacity

without specification of a confidence interval, is fraught with many uncertainties and has long been part of the criticism leveled against medical evaluations [30].

Therefore, we examined whether the functioning profiles of claimants with high attested work capacity significantly do indeed differ from the ones of claimants with low work capacity when using the Mini-ICF-APP. Figure 18.3 provides a comparison of the functioning profiles for these two groups.

Figure 18.3 indicates clear differences between the two comparison groups. This suggests that the medical experts applied the Mini-ICF-APP tool in a consistent manner. The question, however, remains open as to how valid the work capacity ratings are that the medical experts derived from the functioning profiles, since no authoritative gold standard for these ratings currently exists.

18.3.5 Comparison with the Data of Linden and Baron

Linden et al. analyzed data from 213 patients who took part in a psychosomatic rehabilitation program [27]. In their study, they distinguished between patients who were able to work and patients who were unable to work at the time of admission to the clinic. Figure 18.4 illustrates the differences they found between the two groups with regard to their average Mini-ICF-APP functioning profiles.

Item 5 (competence to judge and decide) was included in the Mini-ICF-APP only at a later stage by the authors. It was, therefore, not yet part of their study. Regarding the most limited abilities and activities, our results in Fig. 18.3 are very much in line with the findings of Linden et al. reproduced in Fig. 18.4. However,

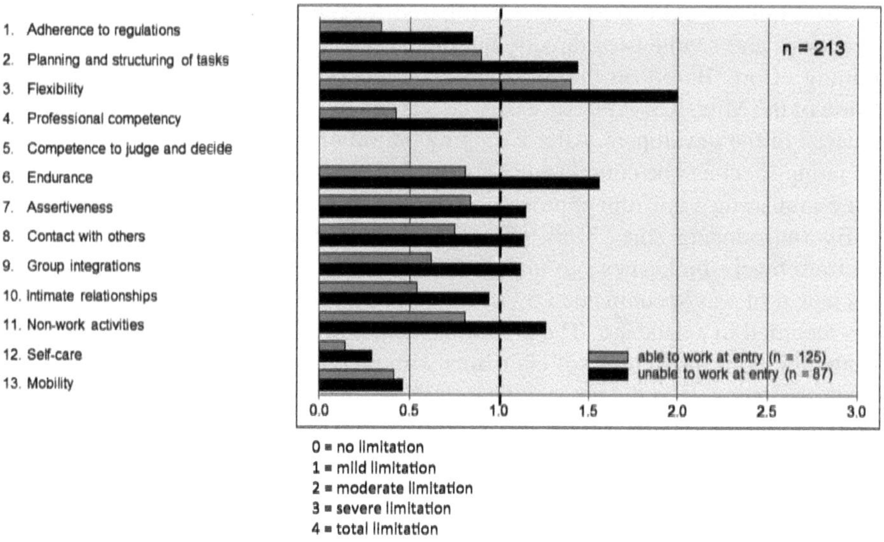

Fig. 18.4 Differences in Mini-ICF-APP functioning profiles between patients who are able to work and patients who are unable to work at the time of admission to the clinic according to Linden et al. [27]

overall our group of claimants appears to be more limited in their functioning; i.e., the average item ratings tend to be higher. This may be the case because most of the claimants who were assessed at MEDAS Zentralschweiz had not been working for several months. Another reason for the differences could be that the psychiatrists of MEDAS Zentralschweiz interpret the anchor definitions differently from Linden et al.

18.4 Discussion

For many years, the research literature and social policy debates have noted that functioning assessments as part of disability evaluations tend to be low in transparency and high on arbitrariness. Moreover, it has been argued that the evaluations are subject to chance and hardly reproducible. Against this backdrop, the use of the ICF framework provides significant advantages for disability evaluation.

> The ICF builds a bridge between the diagnosis and the assessment of work capacity and enhances the transparency of disability evaluations by making it easier for disability claims adjudicators to understand how the medical expert determines a certain level of work capacity.

The Mini-ICF-APP is a robust ICF-based tool that provides validated anchor definitions and can be used directly in clinical practice with a comparatively small training effort. Based on the experiences at MEDAS Zentralschweiz, the application of the Mini-ICF-APP can easily be learned by self-study, using the published material of the developers. After a training period of approximately 20–30 reports, the rating sheet can be completed in about 15–20 min. For exchanging experiences and establishing a uniform approach, a peer supervision group proved to be useful.

By introducing the Mini-ICF-APP for disability evaluations, MEDAS Zentralschweiz broke new ground in Switzerland. Therefore, the application of this new tool was accompanied by a research study where every psychiatric report was recorded in a database. The preliminary findings after roughly 450 reports and using a random distribution of claimants with mental disorders show that the four psychiatrists involved did not significantly differ in their ratings regarding 10 out of 13 items included in the Mini-ICF-APP. This can be interpreted as an indication of high interrater reliability. The exceptions are the items "ability for contact with others," "ability for family and intimate relationships," and "mobility," where the variance of the average ratings across the different psychiatrists is considerably higher than in the other ten items (e.g., $SD = 0.32$ in the case of "ability for family and intimate relationships" as compared to, e.g., $SD = 0.12$ in the case of "endurance"). It might be that the anchor definitions of these three items are not yet precise enough, so that they allow different interpretations.

The Mini-ICF-APP forces the medical expert to relate the work capacity assessment to the requirements of the claimant's former job and to reflect on how an adapted job should be designed so that it accommodates the claimant with his or her health condition in an optimal manner. Moreover, in psychiatric evaluations, it should be possible, in principle, to define an adapted job where a higher work capacity can be attained than in the former occupation. Until now, most psychiatric evaluations only provided a statement that the claimant should be able to work x% based on his or her diagnoses, often without any reference to a specific occupation to be performed. The introduction of the Mini-ICF-APP for psychiatric evaluations in MEDAS Zentralschweiz urged medical experts to differentiate between the claimant's former job and an occupation that is optimally adapted to the claimant's medical condition. This, however, requires that the client (i.e., insurers, courts) provides the medical expert with an objective workplace description of the former job, which preferably does not only address the physical job demands but also the mental abilities required for performing the job. Unfortunately, such comprehensive descriptions are still the exception rather than the rule.

18.5 Conclusion

The diagnosis taken by itself allows few, if any, conclusions regarding the impact of the disease on the claimant's functioning at the workplace [31]. This is true for both somatic and mental health conditions. By contrast, the ICF does not focus on the diagnosis but on the description of limitations in functioning. In this respect, the application of the ICF provides crucial benefits for disability evaluations compared to a merely diagnosis-oriented assessment. However, the ICF as a documentation tool does not solve all issues in disability evaluations. The ICF neither describes the course of a disease nor explains causal relationships between activity limitations and impairments or contextual factors. Moreover, it does not provide a direct way to assess work capacity. Work capacity assessment remains the judgment of the medical expert and is thus subjective and dependent on the expert. The Mini-ICF-APP instructs the medical expert as to which ability limitations should be particularly focused on in the assessment and illustrates how they should be assessed. Applying the ICF in disability evaluation by means of an operationalized tool such as the Mini-ICF-APP may enhance the interrater reliability of work capacity assessments. This, however, is only an assumption, and it remains an issue for future research to empirically test the value of the ICF in disability evaluation.

References

1. Strasburger LH, Gutheil TG, Brodsky A. On wearing two hats: role conflict in serving as both psychotherapist and expert witness. Am J Psychiatry. 1997;154(4):448–56. Epub 1997/04/01.
2. Jeger J, Murer E. Medizinische Begutachtung: Vorschläge zur Lösung des Unabhängigkeitsproblems und zur Qualitätssteigerung [Socio-medical assessment – suggestions for resolving the issue of independency and improving quality]. In: Murer E, editor. Möglichkeiten und Grenzen der medizinischen Begutachtung [Opportunities and limitations of socio-medical assessments]. Bern: Stämpfli; 2010. p. 247–74.
3. de Boer WEL, Besseling JJM, Willems JHBM. Organisation of disability evaluation in 15 countries. Prat et Organ des Soins. 2007;38(3):205–17.
4. World Health Organization. The global burden of disease: 2004 update. Geneva: WHO Press; 2008.
5. World Health Organization. Global health risks: mortality and burden of disease attributable to selected major risks. Geneva: WHO Press; 2009.
6. Schmid B, Buri M. Statistiken zur sozialen Sicherheit: IV-Statistik 2011 [Social security statistics – SII-Statistic 2011]. Bern: Bundesamt für Sozialversicherungen (BSV); 2012.
7. Brage S, Donceel P, Falez F. Development of ICF core set for disability evaluation in social security. Disabil Rehabil. 2008;30(18):1392–6.
8. Deutsche Rentenversicherung Bund, editor. Sozialmedizinische Begutachtung für die gesetzliche Rentenversicherung [Socio-medical assessment for the statutory pension insurance]. Berlin: Springer; 2011.
9. Schweizerische Gesellschaft für Psychiatrie und Psychotherapie, editor. Qualitätsleitlinien für psychiatrische Gutachten in der Eidgenössischen Invalidenversicherung [Quality guidelines for psychiatric evaluations in the Swiss Invalidity Insurance]. Bern; 2012.
10. Schwegler U, Peter C, Trezzini B. Toward standardized documentation in psychiatric evaluation of medical work capacity: identifying aspects of functioning and contextual factors in psychiatric reports on Swiss disability claimants with CWP. BMC Public Health. Under review.
11. Portwich P. The Swiss social insurance system: social security and grass-roots democracy. Int Soc Secur Rev. 2011;64(1):95–110.
12. SSA, ISSA. Social security programs throughout the world: Europe, 2012. Washington, DC/Geneva: Social Security Administration; International Social Security Association; 2012.

13. Dickmann JRM, Broocks A. Das psychiatrische Gutachten im Rentenverfahren – wie reliabel? [Psychiatric expert opinion in case of early retirement – how reliable?]. Fortschr Neurol Psychiatr. 2007;75(7):397–401. Epub 10.10.2006.
14. Pizala H. Evaluation psychiatrischer Gutachten [Evaluation of psychiatric expertises]. [PhD thesis]. University of Basel; 2011.
15. Sanderson K, Nicholson J, Graves N, Tilse E, Oldenburg B. Mental health in the workplace: using the ICF to model the prospective associations between symptoms, activities, participation and environmental factors. Disabil Rehabil. 2008;30(17):1289–97. Epub 2008/07/09.
16. Baron S, Linden M. The role of the "International Classification of Functioning, Disability and Health, ICF" in the description and classification of mental disorders. Eur Arch Psychiatry Clin Neurosci. 2008;258 Suppl 5:81–5.
17. Cieza A, Chatterji S, Andersen C, Cantista P, Herceg M, Melvin J, et al. ICF Core Sets for depression. J Rehabil Med. 2004;36(44 Suppl):128–34. Epub 2004/09/17.
18. Stucki G, Cieza A, Geyh S, Battistella L, Lloyd J, Symmons D, et al. ICF Core Sets for rheumatoid arthritis. J Rehabil Med. 2004;36(44 Suppl):87–93.
19. Cieza A, Stucki G, Weigl M, Kullmann L, Stoll T, Kamen L, et al. ICF Core Sets for chronic widespread pain. J Rehabil Med. 2004;36(44 Suppl):63–8.
20. Stucki A, Daansen P, Fuessl M, Cieza A, Huber E, Atkinson R, et al. ICF Core Sets for obesity. J Rehabil Med. 2004;36(44 Suppl):107–13. Epub 2004/09/17.
21. Schwarzkopf SR, Ewert T, Dreinhofer KE, Cieza A, Stucki G. Towards an ICF Core Set for chronic musculoskeletal conditions: commonalities across ICF Core Sets for osteoarthritis, rheumatoid arthritis, osteoporosis, low back pain and chronic widespread pain. Clin Rheumatol. 2008;27(11):1355–61. Epub 2008/06/04.
22. Finger ME, Escorpizo R, Glässel A, Gmünder HP, Lückenkemper M, Chan C, et al. ICF Core Set for vocational rehabilitation: results of an international consensus conference. Disabil Rehabil. 2012;34(5):429–38.
23. Biering-Sorensen F, Scheuringer M, Baumberger M, Charlifue SW, Post MW, Montero F, et al. Developing core sets for persons with spinal cord injuries based on the International Classification of Functioning, Disability and Health as a way to specify functioning. Spinal Cord. 2006;44(9):541–6. Epub 2006/09/07.
24. Grill E, Ewert T, Chatterji S, Kostanjsek N, Stucki G. ICF Core Sets development for the acute hospital and early post-acute rehabilitation facilities. Disabil Rehabil. 2005;27(7–8):361–6. Epub 2005/07/26.
25. Linden M, Baron S. Das 'Mini-ICF-Rating für psychische Störungen (Mini-ICF-P)'. Ein Kurzinstrument zur Beurteilung von Fähigkeitsstörungen bei psychischen Erkrankungen [The 'Mini-ICF-Rating for Mental Disorders (Mini-ICF-P)' – a short instrument for the assessment of disabilities in mental disorders]. Rehabilitation. 2005;44(3):144–51.
26. Wiersma D, DeJong A, Ormel J. The Groningen Social Disabilities Schedule: development, relationship with I.C.I.D.H., and psychometric properties. Int J Rehabil Res. 1988;11(3): 213–24.
27. Linden M, Baron S, Muschalla B. Mini-ICF-APP: Mini-ICF-Rating für Aktivitäts- und Partizipationsstörungen bei psychischen Erkrankungen [The Mini-ICF-APP: Mini-ICF-Rating for activity and participation disorders in mental disorders]. Bern: Huber; 2009.
28. Molodynski A, Linden M, Juckel G, Yeeles K, Anderson C, Vazquez-Montes M, et al. The reliability, validity, and applicability of an English language version of the Mini-ICF-APP. Soc Psychiatry Psychiatr Epidemiol. 2013;48(8):1347–54.
29. Balestrieri M, Isola M, Bonn R, Tam T, Vio A, Linden M, et al. Validation of the Italian version of Mini-ICF-APP, a short instrument for rating activity and participation restrictions in psychiatric disorders. Epidemiol Psychiatr Sci. 2013;22(01):81–91.
30. Jeger J. Sicherheit und Unsicherheit in medizinischen Gutachten [Certainty and uncertainty in socio-medical reports]. In: Riemer-Kafka G, Rumo-Jungo A, editors. Soziale Sicherheit – Soziale Unsicherheit [Social security – social insecurity]. Bern: Stämpfli Verlag; 2010. p. 319–48.
31. Waddell G. Preventing incapacity in people with musculoskeletal disorders. Br Med Bull. 2006;77–78:55–69.

Part III
ICF-Based Functioning Measurement

Chapter 19
Selection of ICF Core Sets for Functioning Assessment in Disability Evaluation Toward the Assignment to Return to Work Programs and/or Disability Benefits

Urban Schwegler, Melissa Selb, Reuben Escorpizo, and Gerold Stucki

Abbreviations

AS	Ankylosing spondylitis
CWP	Chronic widespread pain
EUMASS	European Union of Medicine in Assurance and Social Security
GHS	German National Health Interview and Examination Survey
ICF	International Classification of Functioning, Disability and Health
ICF-CS	ICF Core Set

U. Schwegler (✉)
Swiss Paraplegic Research, Nottwil, Switzerland

Department of Health Sciences and Health Policy, University of Lucerne, Lucerne, Switzerland
e-mail: urban.schwegler@paraplegie.ch

M. Selb
Swiss Paraplegic Research, Nottwil, Switzerland

ICF Research Branch, WHO CC FIC in Germany (DIMDI), Nottwil, Switzerland

R. Escorpizo
Swiss Paraplegic Research, Nottwil, Switzerland

ICF Research Branch, WHO CC FIC in Germany (DIMDI), Nottwil, Switzerland

Department of Physical Therapy, Louisiana State University Health Sciences Center, 1900 Gravier St, New Orleans, LA 70112, USA

G. Stucki
Swiss Paraplegic Research, Nottwil, Switzerland

Department of Health Sciences and Health Policy, University of Lucerne, Lucerne, Switzerland

ICF Research Branch, WHO CC FIC in Germany (DIMDI), Nottwil, Switzerland

R. Escorpizo et al. (eds.), *Handbook of Vocational Rehabilitation and Disability Evaluation*, Handbooks in Health, Work, and Disability, DOI 10.1007/978-3-319-08825-9_19

LBP	Low back pain
NHANES	United States National Health and Nutrition Examination Survey
RTW	Return to work
SCI	Spinal cord injury
VR	Vocational rehabilitation

19.1 Introduction

19.1.1 Challenges in Disability Evaluation

Disability evaluation is crucial for deciding on the benefits eligibility of persons with disabilities (henceforth *claimants*) or on their assignment to appropriate return to work (RTW) programs. To provide a fair eligibility determination process, disability evaluation should be comparable in terms of content validity and inter-rater reliability between the medical experts who perform the assessments [1]. Furthermore, the evaluations should also be documented in a transparent way [2] and comprehensibly describe whether and how functional limitations at work are affected by a claimant's health condition and/or by contextual factors.

Recently emerging criticism, however, points to low transparency and poor comparability of disability evaluation [1, 3, 4]. Current evaluations are often reported in a poorly standardized way and focus on the determination of a claimant's health condition rather than on the documentation of his or her functioning at work [5]. By contrast, modern medical thinking defines disability as the consequence of complex biopsychosocial interactions and not as the result of a health condition alone [6]. Moreover, the key information in disability evaluation usually refers to functioning and disability. Functioning assessments represent core elements and provide useful information for evaluating work disability [7]. The reporting in disability evaluation should, therefore, follow a comprehensive biopsychosocial framework and include a proper assessment of the claimant's functioning as a basis for transparent and comprehensible eligibility decisions. To ensure comparable evaluations, such a functioning assessment should be documented in a standardized way.

Current disability evaluation is being criticized for low transparency and poor standardization.

19.1.2 The ICF: A Standard for Disability Evaluation

The International Classification of Functioning, Disability and Health (ICF) [6] is the international standard for reporting on functioning and disability. The biopsychosocial *framework* of the ICF conceptualizes functioning as the interplay between body functions and structures, activities and participation, as well as environmental and personal factors. It allows illustrating how work disability is affected by impairments or contextual factors [8] and thus facilitates transparent reporting of functioning assessments in disability evaluation. Moreover, the ICF *taxonomy* provides a comprehensive spectrum of categories and a common language for standardized documentation of functioning assessments and could ensure comparability of disability evaluations in terms of high inter-rater reliability [9].

The ICF may facilitate transparent and standardized reporting of functioning assessments in disability evaluation.

19.1.3 ICF Core Sets: Practical Lists for Disability Evaluation

The ICF taxonomy with its 1,424 ICF categories is cumbersome to use in daily practice. Therefore, *ICF Core Sets* (henceforth ICF-CS) have been introduced. ICF-CS are shortlists of ICF categories developed by means of an established scientific process [10] and reflect the most relevant categories for describing the lived experience of a person with a specific health condition [11] or in a specific health or health-related setting [12]. Whereas Comprehensive ICF-CS cover the wide spectrum of typical problems a claimant may experience, Brief ICF-CS contain the minimum number of categories to capture a person's lived experience related to functioning and disability. Thirty-four ICF-CS have been developed so far [13], including the context-specific ICF-CS for vocational rehabilitation (VR) [10]. The brief version of this ICF-CS includes 13, whereas the comprehensive version contains 90 ICF categories.

Additional sets of ICF categories have been developed using different methodologies. Both the Minimal Generic Set and the Disability Set are based on a psychometric study using data from the ICF-CS studies conducted between 2004 and 2010, the German National Health Interview and Examination Survey 1998 (GHS) and the United States National Health and Nutrition Examination Survey 2007/2008 (NHANES). The Minimal Generic Set includes the 7 ICF categories that were considered relevant in both the clinical (ICF-CS studies) and general population (GHS and/or NHANES surveys) and should always be addressed as a minimum standard when using any of the ICF-CS [13, 14]. The Minimal Generic Set is included in a larger set called Disability Set. The Disability Set contains 32 categories, i.e., the seven categories of the Minimal Generic Set and 25 categories that were found to be relevant solely in the clinical population (ICF-CS studies) [14]. The categories of the Disability Set should be routinely applied for ICF-based reporting in clinical settings.

Finally, the *European Union of Medicine in Assurance and Social Security* (EUMASS) developed a generic ICF-CS for social security evaluation [15] based on a formal voting procedure. This set includes 20 ICF categories.

As ICF-CS describe a person's lived experience in a comprehensive and systematic way, they could be applied as practical standards for *what* should be documented in functioning assessments in disability evaluation. This is important because disability evaluation should be efficient and practical considering the limited time resources of medical experts and high costs associated with the evaluations [16].

So far there have only been a few attempts to examine the applicability of ICF-CS in disability evaluation [9, 17, 18]. A recently conducted study in Switzerland showed that the ICF-CS for chronic widespread pain (CWP), low back pain (LBP), and major comorbidities (i.e., depression and obesity) are able to capture the relevant aspects of functioning and environmental factors in medical reports on disability claimants with CWP and LBP [9]. Thus, the ICF-CS showed a potential for guiding and structuring multidisciplinary functioning assessments in disability evaluation and for enhancing their transparency and standardization in terms of *what* should be documented.

While the Minimal Generic Set includes the most important categories in both the clinical and general population, the Disability Set addresses the most relevant categories solely in the clinical population. The ICF Core Sets for VR and the EUMASS as context-specific sets of ICF categories are geared towards functioning assessments in the context of return to work and social security evaluation.

ICF Core Sets may serve as practical standards for what should be documented in functioning assessments in disability evaluation.

19.1.4 Challenges When Using the ICF in Disability Evaluation

Applying the ICF in the context of disability evaluation seems to be promising. However, some challenges have to be addressed when applying the ICF *in* functioning assessments as part of a disability evaluation. Context-specific additions to the ICF taxonomy are needed if one aims for a precise description of functioning-related aspects. For disability evaluation involving CWP and LBP, for instance, the ICF taxonomy was found to lack precision in addressing specific aspects of pain assessment and work activities [19]. In addition, the ICF does not yet offer a taxonomy for personal factors although they are a part of the ICF conceptual model and are deemed to be an important aspect in transparent disability evaluation and a predictor for return to work [20, 21].

In addition, there are important procedural and decision-making challenges in disability evaluation *beyond* functioning assessments and thus outside of the scope of the ICF taxonomy [7]. In current disability evaluation systems, medical experts are generally encouraged to first draw a comprehensive picture of the claimant's functioning and functional limitations, but then are required to make the overall judgment of work disability based on the limitations exclusively caused by the impairment without considering the influence of contextual factors. Functioning assessments do not allow defining causal relationships between impairments, contextual factors, and limitations in functioning. Furthermore, the dynamic development of disability over time, which is necessary to explore a claimant's sociomedical history and prognosis, cannot be addressed with only a single functioning assessment. This would require a lineup of several functioning assessments at different points in time [6]. Finally, the consistency between the impairments, activity limitations, and work restrictions can only partly be captured with functioning assessments.

Despite the abovementioned challenges, the ICF seems to echo the modern view of medical experts that sees functioning as a biopsychosocial concept. Thus, employing ICF in functioning assessments as part of disability evaluation facilitates a comprehensive description of work disability and supports a systematic and standardized reporting of functional capacity [7, 9].

When deciding on what to describe in functioning assessments for disability evaluation using the ICF and ICF-CS, some guidance is needed to select suitable ICF-CS or sets of ICF categories and to use them in combination with other ICF-CS, if appropriate. Although a handbook is available that proposes one strategy for selecting individual and combinations of ICF-CS for clinical and rehabilitation settings [13], there is still a need for a focused strategy to select the most suitable combinations of sets of ICF categories for functioning assessments particularly in disability evaluation.

Although some procedural and decision-making challenges in disability evaluation are outside of the scope of the ICF, the ICF facilitates a comprehensive and standardized description of work disability and functional capacity.

19.1.5 Objective

The objective of this chapter is to illustrate the selection of sets of ICF categories for functioning assessments in the context of disability evaluation toward the assignment to RTW programs and/or eligibility determination for disability benefits.

19.1.6 Specific Aims

The specific aims are (1) to present three scenarios of functioning assessments in which the ICF can be used in disability evaluation, (2) to describe and compare suitable sets of ICF categories for each scenario and provide arguments for their selection, and (3) to demonstrate the process of selecting and combining different sets of ICF categories in these scenarios using case examples.

19.2 Scenarios for Functioning Assessments in Disability Evaluation

19.2.1 Scenario A: Assignment to RTW Programs

This scenario is geared toward a specific kind of outcome. The claimant has applied for participation in an RTW program and/or his or her functioning has reached a level at which return to work appears to be feasible [22]. The functioning assessment intends to clarify the type of RTW program the claimant should be assigned to.

19.2.2 Scenario B: Eligibility Determination for Disability Benefits

Scenario B also aims at a specific kind of outcome. The claimant has applied for disability benefits. The diagnosis and/or the results of a functional capacity assessment (i.e., the assessment of a claimant's functioning under standardized conditions with environmental influences held constant) form the basis for the appraisal of the claimant's work disability which, in turn, is the (legal) basis for the decision on his or her eligibility for disability benefits. Functioning assessments should provide a comprehensible picture of the claimant's work disability and its influencing factors to ensure transparent eligibility decisions [9].

19.2.3 Scenario C: Interactive Decision-Making Process

In this scenario the kind of outcome of the disability evaluation is not predefined. Scenario C represents an interactive decision-making process in which either RTW programs or disability benefits or a combination of both is considered. There are two sub-scenarios which require further clarification regarding the claimant's work situation: (1) it is unclear whether the claimant should be assigned to an RTW program or directly receive disability benefits, or (2) it is unclear whether the claimant should first be assigned to an RTW program before deciding on his or her benefits eligibility [23, 24].

Disability evaluation may be geared towards different kinds of scenarios: the assignment to appropriate return to work programs, eligibility determination for disability benefits or an interactive decision-making process between both of them.

19.3 Selection of ICF Sets for the Scenarios

In the following sections, we will describe and compare suitable sets of ICF categories for the three scenarios described before by providing an overview of the ICF categories contained in the Brief ICF-CS for VR, the Disability Set, and the EUMASS Set and by analyzing the overlap between the categories of these ICF sets. We will then provide arguments for the selection of one or more of these sets as the default for a scenario and advocate their combination with condition-specific ICF-CS.

19.3.1 Description and Comparison of the ICF Sets

Table 19.1 presents the number of categories included in the ICF sets analyzed and their distribution among the different ICF components body functions, body structures, activities and participation, and environmental factors. The Brief ICF-CS for VR includes 13, the Disability Set 32 and the EUMASS Set 20 ICF categories (see Table 19.1).

Table 19.2 provides an overview on the ICF categories included in the three ICF sets analyzed, while. Figure 19.1 illustrates the overlap between the three sets. The comparison of the three sets indicates that only two categories (*b455 Exercise tolerance functions* and *d240 Handling stress and other psychological demands*) are included in all of them, denoting that these ICF sets focus on different aspects of (work) disability.

The Brief ICF-CS for VR, the Disability Set and the EUMASS Set focus on different aspects of (work) disability.

Table 19.1 Number of ICF categories included in different ICF sets analyzed

	Brief ICF-CS for VR	Disability Set	EUMASS Set
Body functions	3	8	5
Activities and participation	6	14	15
Environmental factors	4	10	–
Total	*13*	*32*	*20*

Table 19.2 Overview of the ICF categories included in the Brief ICF Core Set for VR, the Disability Set, and the EUMASS Set. *(G)* = categories of the Minimal Generic Set

		Brief ICF Core Set for VR	Disability Set	EUMASS Set
b130	*Energy and drive functions (G)*	*X*	*X*	
b134	Sleep functions		X	
b152	*Emotional functions (G)*		*X*	
b164	Higher-level cognitive functions	X		X
b280	*Sensation of pain (G)*		*X*	*X*
b455	Exercise tolerance functions	X	X	X
b640	Sexual functions		X	
b710	Mobility of joint functions		X	X
b730	Muscle power functions		X	X
d110	Watching			X
d115	Listening			X
d155	Acquiring skills	X		X
d177	Making decisions			X
d220	Undertaking multiple tasks			X
d230	*Carrying out daily routine (G)*		*X*	
d240	Handling stress and other psychological demands	X	X	X
d399	Communication, unspecified			X
d410	Changing basic body position			X
d415	Maintaining a body position			X
d430	Lifting and carrying objects			X
d440	Fine hand use			X
d445	Hand and arm use			X
d450	*Walking (G)*		*X*	*X*
d455	*Moving around (G)*		*X*	
d470	Using transportation		X	X
d510	Washing oneself		X	
d540	Dressing		X	
d570	Looking after one's health		X	
d640	Doing housework		X	
d660	Assisting others		X	
d710	Basic interpersonal interactions		X	
d720	Complex interpersonal interactions	X		X
d770	Intimate relationships		X	
d845	Acquiring, keeping and terminating a job	X		
d850	*Remunerative employment (G)*	*X*	*X*	
d855	Non-remunerative employment	X		

(continued)

Table 19.2 (continued)

		Brief ICF Core Set for VR	Disability Set	EUMASS Set
d920	Recreation and leisure		X	
e110	Products or substances for personal consumption		X	
e120	Products and technology for personal indoor and outdoor mobility and transportation		X	
e135	Products and technology for employment		X	
e150	Design, construction and building products and technology of buildings for public use		X	
e155	Design, construction and building products and technology of buildings for private use		X	
e225	Climate		X	
e310	Immediate family	X	X	
e320	Friends		X	
e330	People in positions of authority	X		
e450	Individual attitudes of health professionals		X	
e580	Health services, systems and policies	X	X	
e590	Labour and employment services, systems and policies	X		

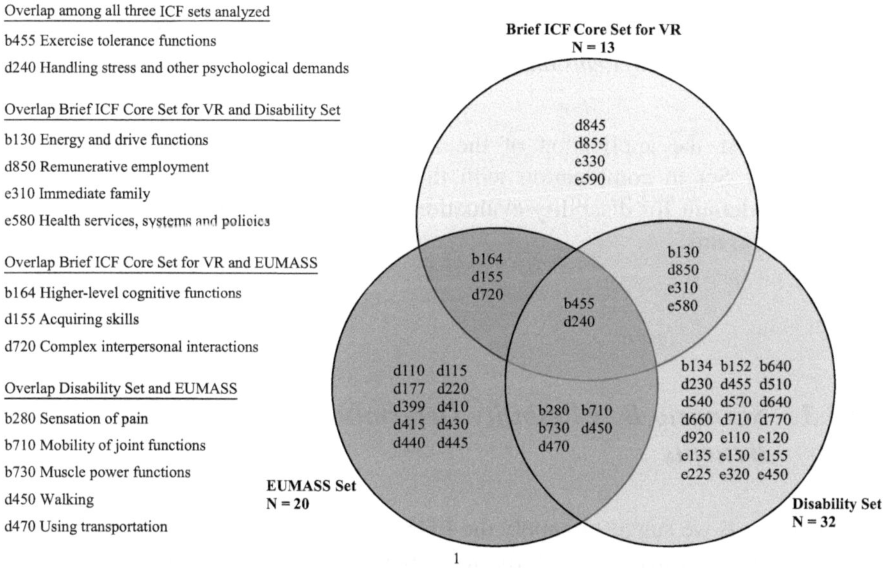

Note: For the description of the category codes that are only included in one of the three sets analyzed see Table 21.2

Fig. 19.1 Overlap among the sets of ICF categories analyzed

19.3.2 Scenario A: Assignment to RTW Programs

The ICF-CS for VR provide a framework to describe the functioning of individuals who are in or propose to enter an RTW program as well as to address RTW outcomes and the multiple factors associated with return to work [10]. Therefore, we suggest using the Brief ICF-CS for VR as a default for functioning assessment in this scenario. In addition, we also propose the use of the Disability Set as a default because its categories represent a standard to be reported in clinical settings. Included in the Disability Set are the 7 ICF categories of the Minimal Generic Set which should always be used as a minimal standard when using any of the ICF-CS [13, 14].

To address the influence of the claimant's health condition on work disability, we recommend to add the categories of the brief version of the condition-specific ICF-CS. Optional and depending on the claimant's specific problems, categories from the Comprehensive ICF-CS for VR, the comprehensive version of the condition-specific ICF-CS, or also ICF categories not included in the ICF-CS can be added to complete the claimant's functioning profile.

Developed for determining eligibility for benefits rather than for the RTW context [15, 25], the EUMASS Set was not selected for scenario A. Furthermore, it contains no environmental factors that would be relevant for intervention planning and assigning claimants to appropriate RTW programs that are directly influenced by the "environment" such as labor or health policy and services provided by the state. In contrast to the EUMASS set, the Brief ICF-CS for VR includes the environmental factors *e310 Immediate family*; *e330 People in positions of authority*; *e580 Health services, systems and policies*; and *e590 Labour and employment services, systems and policies.*

> We suggest the application of the Brief ICF Core Set for VR and the Disability Set in combination with the Brief condition-specific ICF Core Set as a default for disability evaluation toward the assignment to return to work programs.

19.3.3 Scenario B: Eligibility Determination for Disability Benefits

For Scenario B we suggest to apply the EUMASS Set as a default because it offers categories specifically selected for a proper evaluation of rights to long-term benefits [15]. In addition, we propose to use the Disability Set which can be applied across a variety of clinical settings, including eligibility determination for benefits. The overlap between the EUMASS Set and the Disability Set is only moderate (seven categories of the EUMASS Set are included in the Disability Set as well). When analyzing the categories from the EUMASS Set missing in the Disability Set such as *d430 Lifting and carrying objects* or *d440 Fine hand use*, it becomes apparent that the EUMASS Set has a stronger focus on work- and mobility-related aspects. However, using the EUMASS Set alone would be insufficient for transparent documentation of work disability due to again the absence of environmental factors. Guidelines for disability evaluation recommend to the medical experts to first present a holistic picture of the claimant's functioning including environmental influences before discarding their influence from the overall judgment of work disability [7]. For transparent reporting in this scenario, it is, therefore, crucial to also address environmental factors although functional limitations caused by environmental influences do not usually entitle an individual to disability benefits.

The brief version of the condition-specific ICF-CS is recommended for use in scenario B as well. Likewise, categories from the corresponding comprehensive ICF-CS or ICF categories not included in the ICF-CS can be added optionally depending on the specific case.

The Brief ICF-CS for VR was not selected for scenario B since it focuses on RTW programs rather than on eligibility determination for benefits. This is reflected in the fact that only five categories of the Brief ICF-CS for VR overlap with the EUMASS Set.

> We suggest the application of the EUMASS Set and the Disability Set in combination with the Brief condition-specific ICF Core Set as a default for disability evaluation toward eligibility determination for disability benefits.

19.3.4 Scenario C: Interactive Decision-Making Process

For scenario C we suggest the Brief ICF-CS for VR, the Disability Set, and the EUMASS Set jointly as default sets. Although the EUMASS Set is neither comprehensive nor geared toward functioning assessments in the RTW context, we still propose using it for this scenario as well, because it has been specifically developed for functioning assessments toward eligibility determination for disability benefits. Also in scenario C, the brief condition-specific ICF-CS should be considered, and categories from the Comprehensive ICF-CS for VR and the comprehensive condition-specific ICF-CS may be selected if appropriate to provide a proper description of the claimant's functioning. The joint use of the Brief ICF-CS for VR and the two other ICF sets promises a more comprehensive evaluation for this scenario that deals with two decision-making directions. The latter argument is in agreement with Escorpizo and Stucki [25] who argue that a combined use of the ICF-CS for VR and the EUMASS Set could be beneficial given that in many cases

Table 19.3 Suggested combination of ICF sets for the different scenarios of functioning assessments in disability evaluation

	Minimum number of categories to be assessed*	Default	Recommendation	Option 1 (single categories to be added from)	Option 2 (single categories to be added from)	Option 3 (single categories to be added from)
(A) Assignment to return to work programs	39	Brief ICF Core Set for VR Disability Set (including Minimal Generic Set)	Brief condition-specific ICF Core Set	Comprehensive ICF Core Set for VR	Comprehensive condition-specific ICF Core Set	Whole ICF taxonomy
(B) Eligibility determination for benefits	45	EUMASS Set Disability Set (including Minimal Generic Set)	Brief condition-specific ICF Core Set	–	Comprehensive condition-specific ICF Core Set	Whole ICF taxonomy
(C) Interactive process	49	Brief ICF Core Set for VR EUMASS Set Disability Set (including Minimal Generic Set)	Brief condition-specific ICF Core Set	Comprehensive ICF Core Set for VR	Comprehensive condition-specific ICF Core Set	Whole ICF taxonomy

Note: * = Overlap between the default ICF sets considered

disability evaluation related to return to work and eligibility determination for disability benefits lies on a continuum.

Table 19.3 gives an overview on the suggested combinations of ICF sets for the different scenarios of functioning assessments in disability evaluation.

We suggest the joint use of the Brief ICF Core Set for VR, the Disability Set and the EUMASS Set in combination with the Brief condition-specific ICF Core Set as a default for disability evaluation toward eligibility determination for disability benefits.

19.4 Illustrating the Scenarios with Case Studies

The following case examples demonstrate a way to select and combine the different sets of ICF categories for each of the above-described scenarios. The ICF categories applied in the case examples are specified. Explanations in square brackets indicate whether a category is part of the default sets [DS], of the brief condition-specific ICF-CS [BCS], or whether the category is an optional choice [OC] from the comprehensive ICF-CS or the whole ICF taxonomy. The case examples refer to three persons either with spinal cord injury (SCI), chronic widespread pain (CWP), or ankylosing spondylitis (AS). CWP and AS were chosen because they represent a major burden for the affected persons and cause high costs for disability insurance schemes [26, 27]. Since the impact of pain, a prevalent symptom in both CWP and AS, on work functioning is difficult to objectify and dependent on complex biopsychosocial interactions [28], a proper functioning assessment based on a biopsychosocial approach is particularly crucial for transparent disability evaluation involving CWP and AS. SCI was selected as a case in point for a biopsychosocial assessment in the RTW context to underline the relevance of environmental factors in vocational rehabilitation. In addition, SCI often severely impacts a claimant's social activities and employment leading to significant lifelong social and economic cost [29].

19.4.1 Scenario A: Assignment of a Claimant with SCI to an RTW Program

J. Meyer, a 35-year-old male and information technology (IT) specialist, suffered a complete SCI that affected his motor and sensory function below the waist. He is currently participating in a multidisciplinary inpatient rehabilitation program. Mr. Meyer is able to move around in his wheelchair (*d465 Moving around using equipment [BCS], e120 Products and technology for personal indoor and outdoor mobility and transportation [DS, BCS]*), has full control of his upper body, and has regained independence in activities of daily living such as washing (*d510 Washing oneself [DS]*) and dressing (*d540 [DS]*). Bladder management (*d530 Toileting [BCS]*) is regulated by emptying his catheter (*e115 Products and technology for personal use in daily living [BCS]*) 4–5 times per day for approximately 15 min each time, and Mr. Meyer takes medication (*e110 Products or substances for personal consumption [BCS]*) that facilitates bowel movements (*b525 Defecation functions [BCS]*) every other day in the morning. The clinic's vocational rehabilitation department initiated discussions with Mr. Meyer about return to work possibilities 2 weeks after admission. Mr. Meyer and the vocational rehabilitation specialist agreed that Mr. Meyer should pursue returning to work to his pre-injury employer – a mid-size biomedical company – where he worked at the IT help desk. He mostly sat at his desk (*d415 Maintaining a body position [OC]*) finding solutions to IT problems (*d175 Solving problems [OC]*) experienced by the company's employees over the phone and working on his computer (*d350 Conversation [OC]; d360 Using communication devices and techniques [OC]*). He periodically went to other offices within the company to install computers and other small devices (*d430 Lifting and carrying objects [OC]*). His workplace was wheelchair accessible with elevators and doors that were easy to open and close (*e150 Design, construction and building products and technology of buildings for public use [DS, BCS]*).

To get a complete picture of Mr. Meyer's RTW situation and for optimal assignment to an RTW program, a categorical profile [30] based on the 39 categories from the Brief ICF-CS for VR and the Disability Set (accounting for the six overlapping categories) and the 33 categories of the Brief ICF-CS for SCI in the long-term context [31] was compiled. Each of the 57 categories (15 categories overlapped between the Brief ICF-CS for VR, the Disability Set, and the Brief ICF-CS for SCI) included in the profile was assigned to the corresponding discipline of the multidisciplinary rehabilitation team made up of a physician, occupational therapist, physical therapist, and vocational rehabilitation specialist. Some categories were assessed by more than one discipline. Mr. Meyer was also asked to describe his functioning related to activities and participation and selected categories of environmental factors. The completed categorical profile was first discussed within the rehabilitation team, with the vocational rehabilitation specialist leading the discussion on RTW recommendations. The vocational rehabilitation specialist then discussed the recommendations with Mr. Meyer, resulting in a 6-month RTW program that included getting Mr. Meyer's employer involved in the RTW process (*e330 People in positions of authority [DS]*), a workplace evaluation by the occupational therapist, on-the-job coaching by the vocational rehabilitation specialist (*e355 Health professionals [BCS]*), and providing an adaptive accessory to Mr. Meyer's wheelchair that would allow him to bring laptops and small devices to offices (*e135 Products and technology for employment [DS]*). Involving Mr. Meyer's employer would entail rearranging Mr. Meyer's work schedule to allow breaks necessary for bladder management and modifying Mr. Meyer's job so that he would only be required to install laptops rather than PCs.

19.4.2 Scenario B: Determining Eligibility for Disability Benefits for a Claimant with CWP

K. Smith, a 45-year-old female and marketing executive, started to feel muscle pain (*b280 Sensation of pain)* and stiffness (*b780 Sensations related to muscles and movement functions [OC]*) first in her neck and shoulder and later in several other parts of her body. After a few months, Mrs. Smith started to experience extreme fatigue (*b130 Energy and drive functions [DS, BCS], b455 Exercise tolerance functions [DS, BCS]*) during the day. Despite worsening symptoms, she continued to work until her symptoms were so severe that she sought medical advice from her family doctor who then referred her to a rheumatologist (*e355 Health professionals [BCS]*). The rheumatologist diagnosed her with fibromyalgia and prescribed medications (*e1101 Drugs [BCS]*) aimed at reducing pain and daytime fatigue as well as provided her with an information sheet describing a trigger point self-treatment, i.e., a treatment that involves pressing points on the body to relieve some pain. After another week of sick leave and complying with the prescribed treatment (*d570 Looking after one's health [DS]*), Mrs. Smith was able to return to work. However after 2 months, the symptoms relapsed and worsened. Despite various treatments, Mrs. Smith continued to experience symptoms so that she was forced to stay at home often. Consequently, her job performance suffered accompanied by increasing criticism from her supervisor (*e430 Individual attitudes of people in positions of authority [OC]*), who insinuated that her symptoms were malingering. As a result, Mrs. Smith began to get depressed, further intensifying her fatigue. Luckily Mrs. Smith's husband and sister provided moral support (*e310 Immediate family [DS, BCS]*) as well as help in the household (*d640 Doing housework [DS, BCS]*). However, after a long sick leave that included 4 weeks of unsuccessful therapy at an outpatient pain clinic, Mrs. Smith decided to apply for disability benefits. She felt unable to continue working in her current job or any other job.

The regional social security office recently implemented a standardized ICF-based system for evaluating disability to determine a claimant's eligibility for benefits that balances the impairment orientation of disability assessments by moving toward a functioning-based assessment. This system implements a functioning profile that combines the Disability Set and the EUMASS Set resulting in 45 categories (accounting for the seven overlapping categories). To consider the claimant's health condition, the Brief ICF-CS for CWP was also consulted. In Mrs. Smith's case, 9 of the 24 categories of the Brief ICF-CS for CWP that were not yet part of the functioning profile were added, leading to a total of 54 categories to be assessed. This functioning profile was then sent to a rheumatologist trained to conduct disability evaluations using this functioning assessment system. He concluded that Mrs. Smith is able to work 100 % finding no structural impairment that clarified her symptoms and considered her functional limitations resulting from contextual factors such as issues with co-workers and supervisors and difficulties in coping with the imbalance between her job demands and health problems. However, the medical expert recommended a psychiatric assessment to clarify Mrs. Smith's mental health status before making a final decision on her eligibility for disability benefits.

19.4.3 Scenario C: An Interactive Decision-Making Process for a Claimant with AS

B. Jones, a 29-year-old male carpenter, was diagnosed with AS after years of misdiagnosis. Mr. Jones' health problems include gradual and progressively worsening pain (*b280 Sensation of pain*) and stiffness in the lower back and upper buttock area (*b780 Sensations related to muscles and movement functions [BCS]*), fatigue (*b130 Energy and drive functions [DS, BCS], b455 Exercise tolerance functions [DS, BCS]*), sensitivity to light resulting in redness of the eyes (*b210 Seeing functions [OC]*) and eye pain (*b280 Sensation of pain [DS, BCS]*), as well as difficulty with breathing (*b460 Sensations associated with cardiovascular and respiratory functions [OC]*). Mr. Jones was prescribed a 3-week intensive inpatient rehabilitation program. For 2 years before diagnosis, Mr. Jones had been on and off sick leave from his family's furniture manufacturing business. In the first week of rehabilitation, Mr. Jones consulted with the rehabilitation program doctor and the social worker about the possibilities for exploring another career as well as the possibility for receiving disability payment even if partial or for a designated period. Mr. Jones did not want to further burden his family's business with his illness-related absenteeism. Mr. Jones had been taking continuing education classes in web design and Photoshop with the goal of developing a more professional website and brochure for his family's business. He enjoyed the classes and discovered he had some talent in this area. However, with the exacerbation of symptoms, he stopped participating in the classes.

Since the rehabilitation facility also conducts disability evaluations for the local social security office, the social worker was able to coordinate an evaluation of Mr. Jones' vocational potential and disability status using a standardized form. The form consists of 49 ICF categories that resulted from combining the categories of the Brief ICF-CS for VR, the Disability Set, and the EUMASS Set (overlapping categories were only counted once). In addition, the six categories of the Brief ICF-CS for AS that were not included in the three default ICF sets were added, making a total of 55 ICF categories to be assessed. The physical therapist, the rehabilitation doctor, and the social worker, who also served as the vocational specialist, were each assigned specific categories to assess and completed the form. In some cases, more than one team member assessed the same categories. Mr. Jones was also asked to describe his functioning. A challenge in this process was to properly quantify the various categories because the ICF currently does not provide a suitable operationalization for measuring its categories. Finally, the social worker compiled the results and sent them to the social security-designated medical expert. The expert considered the results from the rehabilitation program but also conducted additional assessments that led to assigning Mr. Jones to a job training program on web and graphic design and vocational counseling. Mr. Jones was determined eligible for partial disability benefits during his participation in the RTW program.

19.5 Discussion

We illustrated the selection and combination of sets of ICF categories for functioning assessments in different scenarios of disability evaluation. If disability evaluation is geared toward the assignment to an RTW program, functioning assessments should be documented using the Brief ICF-CS for VR, the Disability Set, and the Brief ICF-CS corresponding to the claimant's health condition. These categories may be augmented by categories from the Comprehensive ICF-CS for VR, the Comprehensive ICF-CS for the claimant's health condition, or by additional ICF categories particularly relevant for the specific case. The combination of these ICF sets provides a comprehensive picture of the claimant's work-related functioning and influencing environmental factors that allows for assigning him or her to an appropriate RTW program. Furthermore, the information of the functioning assessment facilitates the planning of vocational rehabilitation interventions focusing on the claimant's work environment such as job placement or work place accommodation.

In the context of eligibility determination for disability benefits, functioning assessments should be based on the joint use of the EUMASS Set and the Disability Set. As the EUMASS Set only includes a limited number of categories and no environmental factors, it should be combined with the Disability Set which can be applied across all clinical settings. Together with the condition-specific ICF-CS, these two sets allow for a comprehensive assessment of functional capacity. Such a comprehensive assessment as well as a proper documentation of environmental factors influencing a claimant's work functioning is crucial for transparent and understandable eligibility decisions [32]. Guidelines for disability evaluation toward eligibility determination for benefits encourage medical experts to first draft a holistic picture of the claimant's functioning and then to discard the influence of environmental factors from their overall judgment of work disability [7].

When part of an interactive decision-making process, where it is unclear whether claimants should be assigned to an RTW program or receive disability benefits, functioning assessments should address the categories from the Brief ICF-CS for VR as well as from the Disability Set and the EUMASS Set and also consider the appropriate categories from the Comprehensive ICF-CS for VR and the one for the claimant's health condition. The assessments should comprehensively describe the claimant's functional limitations and abilities as well as contextual factors influencing his or her work-related functioning. A proper documentation of whether or not and how environmental factors relate to the claimant's functional limitations makes eligibility decisions on disability benefits more understandable. In case the limitations result from the environment rather than from the health condition, the same documentation facilitates the selection of appropriate RTW programs such as workplace accommodation or job placement.

Since disability evaluations incur high costs and time resources are limited, functioning assessments in the context of disability evaluation should be practical [16]. Therefore, it appears reasonable to use ICF sets with a limited number of categories such as the Disability Set, the Brief ICF-CS for VR, and/or the EUMASS Set as a minimum standard and default in each scenario. As suggested in a recent study, the assessment then may be augmented by ICF categories relevant to a particular case or context [9].

Disability claimants with chronic conditions do not usually suffer from one single health condition but often present comorbid disorders as well. It has, for instance, been shown that CWP often goes along with affective disorders such as depression [33]. In such cases, the Brief ICF-CS for the main condition can be combined with the Brief ICF-CS for the comorbidities, if available, so as to also address aspects relevant to the comorbid disorders. Escorpizo and Stucki argue that combining appropriate ICF sets facilitates data collection and evaluation efficiency in complex situations involving multiple health conditions [25]. Additionally, the importance of taking into account ICF-CS for comorbidities in disability evaluation was illustrated by a study that suggested the joint use of the ICF-CS for CWP, LBP, and depression for claimants with CWP and of the ICF-CS for LBP, CWP, and obesity for claimants with LBP [9]. Additionally, it was shown how to properly combine ICF-CS for main conditions and comorbidities in the rehabilitation setting [13].

For functioning assessments that need to be precise, the ICF taxonomy might not offer categories that are accurate enough to describe specific issues related to a particular health condition. In such cases, there might be a need for case- or context-specific specifications of ICF categories as explained and introduced in previous studies [19, 34]. In the first instance, it may help to select a category referring to a more precise ICF level, i.e., a third or fourth level category. If this is not sufficient, a category specification can be introduced for describing specific aspects of functioning or contextual factors in a more accurate manner. Aspects that do not directly relate to functioning and are, thus, not covered by the ICF such as genetic aspects could be illustrated by introducing specification categories as well [19].

The fact that the ICF taxonomy does not provide categories for addressing personal factors, although they are part of the ICF framework, has been discussed and criticized in the literature [35, 36]. Personal factors are crucial for disability evaluation and return to work because aspects such as educational and professional background, work motivation, or expectations regarding return to work strongly influence work participation [10, 20, 37]. In disability evaluation toward eligibility determination for benefits, a standardized documentation of personal factors could enhance transparency in illustrating whether functional limitations are likely to be caused by a health condition (e.g., depressive symptoms) or by personal factors (e.g., a lack of work motivation) [21]. Although authors argue that it is an ethical issue to address personal aspects such as a claimant's nationality in disability evaluation [38], personal factors are still relevant for transparent eligibility decisions. Their explicit documentation in functioning assessments would allow claimants for formally objecting against unwarranted decisions. Despite of the lack of personal factor categories within the ICF, personal factor categorizations specifically developed for the context of disability evaluation [39] and/or tested regarding their applicability to address personal factors in this particular context could be used for functioning assessments [21, 40].

For practicability reasons it appears useful to apply ICF Core Sets with a limited number of categories in disability evaluation.

The reporting of personal factors such as professional background and work motivation is crucial for transparent disability evaluation. Although not classified by the ICF taxonomy these aspects should be explicitly documented in the evaluations.

19.5.1 Practical Implication

This chapter proposes selections of ICF sets for functioning assessments in different scenarios in disability evaluation. The sets can be used in the suggested combination to provide a comprehensive picture on the claimant's functioning as the basis for appropriate recommendations for RTW programs and decisions on disability benefits. Using the ICF in disability evaluation promises transparent, fair, and comparable assessments and eligibility decisions comprehensible to the different parties involved in the evaluation process. A comprehensive ICF-based documentation of functioning assessments can highlight starting points for interventions toward return to work and facilitate the planning of specific interventions in vocational rehabilitation.

However, although comprehensive functioning assessments appear important for transparency reasons, it may be not feasible for medical experts to assess and document a long list of ICF categories, especially in *eligibility determination for disability benefits* and *interactive decision making*. To ensure feasible assessments, the suggested categories should, therefore, be subdivided and allocated to the most pertinent health disciplines involved in the disability evaluation process [19].

The suggested approach to use ICF-CS for functioning assessment in disability evaluation provides guidance regarding which ICF categories to assess as a minimum standard (Brief and context-specific ICF-CS) and which ICF categories to take from a pool (Comprehensive ICF-CS, case-specific ICF categories). It facilitates the standardization of functioning assessments in terms of *what* to report. However, the ICF does not provide a proper operationalization for its categories, and the ICF-CS do not offer information of *how* ICF categories should be measured. This issue should be addressed in future research and may be approached by assigning already existing measurement tools to ICF categories.

Our suggestions of how to select and combine sets of ICF categories in disability evaluation are conceptual. Although the ICF-CS for VR have already been tested in the RTW context [41] and the EUMASS Set in the context of disability evaluation toward eligibility for benefits [18], empirical studies would be needed to practically test and validate our findings.

Finally, the unique individual experience of the claimant cannot be addressed with a standard alone. Therefore, in addition to the suggested standardized approach of using predetermined ICF categories, the claimant's individual experience should always be considered to properly assess his or her functioning and capacity at work.

The suggested approach of selecting ICF Core Sets for different scenarios in disability evaluation facilitates the standardization of functioning assessments in terms of what to report. However, as the ICF Core Sets do currently not offer a proper operationalization and measurement for its categories existing validated measurement tools should be linked to ICF categories.

19.5.2 Conclusion

In this chapter we illustrated the selection and combination of sets of ICF categories for functioning assessments in different scenarios in disability evaluation. In the right combination, the ICF sets can facilitate standardized and transparent reporting of functioning assessments as well as contribute to enhanced planning of vocational rehabilitation interventions and fair decisions on eligibility for disability benefits. However, in addition to such a standardized documentation, the unique lived experience of the claimant has to be considered to address his or her work disability comprehensively.

Study Questions

1. What are the main challenges in current disability evaluation?

   Answer: Low transparency and poor comparability in terms of insufficient standardization.

2. What are the procedural and decision-making challenges in disability evaluation that are beyond functioning assessments and thus beyond the scope of the ICF?

   Answer: – The description of causal relationships between impairments, contextual factors and limitations in fucntioning; – The documentation of the dynamic development of disability over time; – The reporting of the consistency between impairments, activity limitations and work. restrictions.

3. What are the three main scenarios disability evaluation may be geared to?

   Answer: – Assignment to appropriate return to work programs; – Eligibility determination for benefits; – Interactive decision-making process between return to work programs and disability benefits.

4. Which ICF Core Sets should be used as a default and recommendation in the different scenarios of disability evaluation?

   Answer: – Scenario "Assignment to return to work programs": Brief ICF Core Set for VR, Disability Set, condition-specific ICF Core Set; – Scenario "Eligibility determination for disability benefits": EUMASS Set, Disability Set, condition-specific ICF Core Set; – Scenario "Interactive decision-making": Brief ICF Core Set for VR, Disability Set, EUMASS Set, Brief condition-specific ICF Core Set.

5. What are the main advantages of using ICF Core Sets for functioning assessments in disability evaluation?

   Answer: – Transparent and comprehensible reporting of functioning assessments; – Standardized reporting of functioning assessments to ensure the comparability of disability evaluation; – Ensuring practicability of functioning assessments in disability evaluation; – Basis for fair decisions on eligibility for disability benefits and return to work programs.

References

1. Rudbeck M, Fonager K. Agreement between medical expert assessments in social medicine. Scand J Public Health. 2011;39(7):766–72.
2. Meershoek A, Krumeich A, Vos R. Judging without criteria? Sickness certification in Dutch disability schemes. Sociol Health Illn. 2007;29(4):497–514.

3. Horan TA, Daniels SM, Feldman SS. The prospective role of personal health records in streamlining and accelerating the disability determination process. Disabil Health J. 2009;2(3):153–7.
4. de Boer WE, Rijkenberg AM, Donceel P. Guidelines for assessment of work disability: an international survey. Gesundheitswesen. 2011;73(6):e103–10.
5. APPLICA, CESEP, European Centre. Study of compilation of disability: statistical data from the administrative registers of the member states. Brussels: APPLICA, CESEP, European Centre; 2007.
6. World Health Organization. International classification of functioning, disability and health (ICF). Geneva: World Health Organization; 2001.
7. Anner J, Schwegler U, Kunz R, Trezzini B, de Boer W. Evaluation of work disability and the international classification of functioning, disability and health: what to expect and what not. BMC Public Health. 2012;12:470.
8. Sanderson K, Nicholson J, Graves N, Tilse E, Oldenburg B. Mental health in the workplace: using the ICF to model the prospective associations between symptoms, activities, participation and environmental factors. Disabil Rehabil. 2008;30(17):1289–97.
9. Schwegler U, Anner J, Boldt C, Glässel A, Lay V, De Boer WEL, et al. Aspects of functioning and environmental factors in medical work capacity evaluations of persons with chronic widespread pain and low back pain can be represented by a combination of applicable ICF Core Sets. BMC Public Health. 2012;12(1):1088.
10. Finger ME, Escorpizo R, Glässel A, Gmünder HP, Lückenkemper M, Chan C, et al. ICF Core Set for vocational rehabilitation: results of an international consensus conference. Disabil Rehabil. 2012;34(5):429–38.
11. Biering-Sörensen F, Scheuringer M, Baumberger M, Charlifue SW, Post MW, Montero F, et al. Developing core sets for persons with spinal cord injuries based on the International Classification of Functioning, Disability and Health as a way to specify functioning. Spinal Cord. 2006;44(9):541–6.
12. Grill E, Ewert T, Chatterji S, Kostanjsek N, Stucki G. ICF Core Sets development for the acute hospital and early post-acute rehabilitation facilities. Disabil Rehabil. 2005;27(7–8):361–6.
13. Bickenbach J, Cieza A, Rauch A, Stucki G, editors. ICF Core Sets: manual for clinical practice. Göttingen: Hogrefe; 2012.
14. Cieza A, Oberhauser C, Bickenbach J, Chatterji S, Stucki G. Towards a Minimal Generic Set of domains of functioning and health. BMC Public Health. 2014;14:218.
15. Brage S, Donceel P, Falez F. Development of ICF core set for disability evaluation in social security. Disabil Rehabil. 2008;30(18):1392–6.
16. Gouttebarge V, Wind H, Kuijer PP, Sluiter JK, Frings-Dresen MH. How to assess physical work-ability with functional capacity evaluation methods in a more specific and efficient way? Work. 2010;37(1):111–5.
17. Schult ML, Ekholm J. Agreement of a work-capacity assessment with the World Health Organisation International Classification of Functioning, Disability and Health pain sets and back-to-work predictors. Int J Rehabil Res. 2006;29(3):183–93.
18. Anner J, Brage S, Donceel P, Falez F, Freudenstein R, Oancea C, et al. Validation of the EUMASS Core Set for medical evaluation of work disability. Disabil Rehabil. 2013;35(25):2147–56.
19. Schwegler U, Anner J, Glässel A, Brach M, de Boer WE, Cieza A, et al. Towards comprehensive and transparent reporting: context-specific additions to the ICF taxonomy for medical evaluations of work capacity involving claimants with chronic widespread pain and low back pain. In revision. BMC Health Serv Res. 2014.
20. Slebus FG, Sluiter JK, Kuijer PP, Willems JH, Frings-Dresen MH. Work-ability evaluation: a piece of cake or a hard nut to crack? Disabil Rehabil. 2007;29(16):1295–300.
21. Schwegler U, Peter C, Trezzini B, Anner J, Geyh S. Towards transparent documentation in medical work capacity evaluations: identifying personal factors in medical reports on Swiss disability claimants with chronic widespread pain. Int J Rehabil Res. 2013;36(4):298–307.

22. Chamberlain MA, Fialka Moser V, Schüldt Ekholm K, O'Connor RJ, Herceg M, Ekholm J. Vocational rehabilitation: an educational review. J Rehabil Med. 2009;41(11):856–69.
23. Stover M, Pape K, Johnsen R, Fleten N, Sund ER, Claussen B, et al. Rehabilitation time before disability pension. BMC Health Serv Res. 2012;12:375.
24. Gensby U, Labriola M, Irvin E, Amick 3rd BC, Lund T. A classification of components of workplace disability management programs: results from a systematic review. J Occup Rehabil. 2014;24(2):220–41.
25. Escorpizo R, Stucki G. Disability evaluation, social security, and the international classification of functioning, disability and health: the time is now. J Occup Environ Med. 2013;55 (6):644–51.
26. Boonen A. Socioeconomic consequences of ankylosing spondylitis. Clin Exp Rheumatol. 2002;20(6 Suppl 28):S23–6.
27. Schmidt J, Schwebach RG. Preliminary trial on the effectiveness of early intervention manual therapy in reducing costs of presenteeism due to musculoskeletal pain. J Health Prod. 2007;2 (1):26–32.
28. Gatchel RJ, Peng YB, Peters ML, Fuchs PN, Turk DC. The biopsychosocial approach to chronic pain: scientific advances and future directions. Psychol Bull. 2007;133(4):581–624.
29. Franceschini M, Pagliacci MC, Russo T, Felzani G, Aito S, Marini C. Occurrence and predictors of employment after traumatic spinal cord injury: the GISEM Study. Spinal Cord. 2012;50:238–42.
30. Rauch A, Cieza A, Stucki G. How to apply the International Classification of Functioning, Disability and Health (ICF) for rehabilitation management in clinical practice. Eur J Phys Rehabil Med. 2008;44(3):329–42.
31. Cieza A, Kirchberger I, Biering-Sörensen F, Baumberger M, Charlifue S, Post MW, et al. ICF Core Sets for individuals with spinal cord injury in the long-term context. Spinal Cord. 2010;48(4):305–12.
32. Jahiel RI, Scherer MJ. Initial steps towards a theory and praxis of person-environment interaction in disability. Disabil Rehabil. 2010;32(17):1467–74.
33. Bair MJ, Robinson RL, Katon W, Kroenke K. Depression and pain comorbidity: a literature review. Arch Intern Med. 2003;163(20):2433–45.
34. Cieza A, Boldt C, Ballert CS, Eriks-Hoogland I, Bickenbach JE, Stucki G. Setting up a cohort study on functioning: deciding what to measure. Am J Phys Med Rehabil. 2011;90(11 Suppl 2):S17–28.
35. Duchan JF. Where is the person in the ICF? Adv Speech-Lang Pathol. 2004;6(1):63–5.
36. Geyh S, Peter C, Müller R, Bickenbach JE, Kostanjsek N, Üstün BT, et al. The personal factors of the international classification of functioning, disability and health in the literature: a systematic review and content analysis. Disabil Rehabil. 2011;33(13–14):1089–102.
37. Sjöberg L. Risk and willingness to work. Int J Risk Assess Manag. 2007;7(2):224–36.
38. Bickenbach JE, Chatterji S, Badley EM, Üstün TB. Models of disablement, universalism and the international classification of impairments, disabilities and handicaps. Soc Sci Med. 1999;48(9):1173–87.
39. Grotkamp SL, Cibis WM, Nüchtern EAM, von Mittelstaedt G, Seger WKF. Personal factors in the international classification of functioning, disability and health: prospective evidence. Aust J Rehabil Couns. 2012;18(1):1–24.
40. Geyh S, Cieza A, Bickenbach JE, Stucki G. ICF personal factors preparatory outline. [Internal manuscript]. In press; 2009.
41. Saltychev M, Kinnunen A, Laimi K. Vocational rehabilitation evaluation and the International Classification of Functioning, Disability, and Health (ICF). J Occup Rehabil. 2013;23(1):106–14.

Chapter 20
Survey of Patient-Reported Questionnaires Using the ICF as a Reference: An Illustration Using the ICF Core Set for Vocational Rehabilitation

Sabrina Kohler, Miriam Lückenkemper, Monika E. Finger, and Reuben Escorpizo

20.1 Introduction

Work disability is an important and growing public health burden. Over the past decades, employment rates have fluctuated, while rates of disability claims have remained high or even increased in many countries of the Organisation for Economic Co-operation and Development (OECD) [1]. It is estimated that on average, OECD countries spend 1.2 % of gross domestic product on disability benefits alone. Furthermore, around 6 % of the OECD-wide working-age population collected disability benefits in 2007 [2]. Work disability is a problem largely faced by developed and developing nations and is expected to increase with the ageing workforce and the increasing prevalence of chronic health conditions.

Working industries experience lost productivity, and financial impacts on work stakeholders and the healthcare system can be significant. For example, in the United States, the national cost of lost work productivity resulting from chronic conditions has been estimated at $234 billion annually [3]. Work disability also has

S. Kohler (✉)
School of Medicine, University of Western Sydney, Sydney, Australia
e-mail: sabrina.christa@gmail.com

M. Lückenkemper
ICF Unit, Swiss Paraplegic Research, Nottwil, Switzerland

M.E. Finger
ICF Unit, Swiss Paraplegic Research, Nottwil, Switzerland

ICF Research Branch of the WHO CC FIC in Germany (DIMDI), Nottwil, Switzerland

R. Escorpizo
ICF Unit, Swiss Paraplegic Research, Nottwil, Switzerland

ICF Research Branch of the WHO CC FIC in Germany (DIMDI), Nottwil, Switzerland

Department of Rehabilitation and Movement Science, The University of Vermont, Burlington VT 05405 USA

R. Escorpizo et al. (eds.), *Handbook of Vocational Rehabilitation and Disability Evaluation*, Handbooks in Health, Work, and Disability, DOI 10.1007/978-3-319-08825-9_20

an effect on caregivers, in particular financial, employment and psychological stress. Finally, for the worker, there are higher rates of reported depression, loss of confidence, inability to cope, loss of income and loss of satisfaction in all aspects of life. For those with work disability, working is a "normalising" experience, allowing individuals to participate in society, promoting self-esteem and quality of life, as well as financial remuneration [4].

One key process to address work disability is vocational rehabilitation (VR), which has been used interchangeably with work or occupational rehabilitation [5]. Return-to-work strategies have been found to be helpful in mitigating the burden of chronic health conditions and the associated work disability [6]. For these reasons, the importance of VR and the desire to improve quality of care in the context of VR are vital in facilitating early and sustained return to work of individuals with work disability.

VR can be briefly defined as an approach provided to participants to optimise work participation [7]. It applies to patients with various health conditions, which can include mental, musculoskeletal and neurological health conditions and settings [8–10]. The broad variety of conditions and settings presents a challenge in choosing measurement tools or questionnaires which can be used. At the same time, there is a growing need to improve healthcare measurement in VR as part of assessment and quality reporting, and the shift in paradigm from traditional biomedical to biopsychosocial understanding of functioning has been significantly emerging in the last decade. Given these conditions, we need a common conceptual model and reference framework that can provide us with a platform to examine patient outcomes.

The International Classification of Functioning, Disability and Health (ICF) [11] by the World Health Organization (WHO) is a unifying framework to describe the functioning of individuals in VR [5, 7]. VR is a multifaceted specialty in rehabilitation and occupational medicine, and the ICF possesses the ability to encompass many of those facets using the ICF's comprehensive set of domains [5, 7]. Moreover, the ICF was developed as a universal classification which can be applied to various cultures and health systems [5].

As a conceptual model, the ICF recognises that functioning and disability is a result of the interaction between components: body functions ("b"), body structures ("s"), activities and participation ("d") and contextual factors, namely, environmental factors ("e") and personal factors (Fig. 20.1). As a classification system, the ICF can serve as a basis for evaluating the breadth and complexity of VR services by providing a comprehensive list of functioning and disability domains in the form of alphanumeric-coded ICF categories that are arranged in a hierarchical manner [11]. Below is an illustration of this categorisation:

ICF component	d activities and participation
Chapter	d8 Major life areas
Second-level category	d850 Remunerative employment
Third-level category	d8500 Self-employment
	d8501 Part-time employment
	d8502 Full-time employment

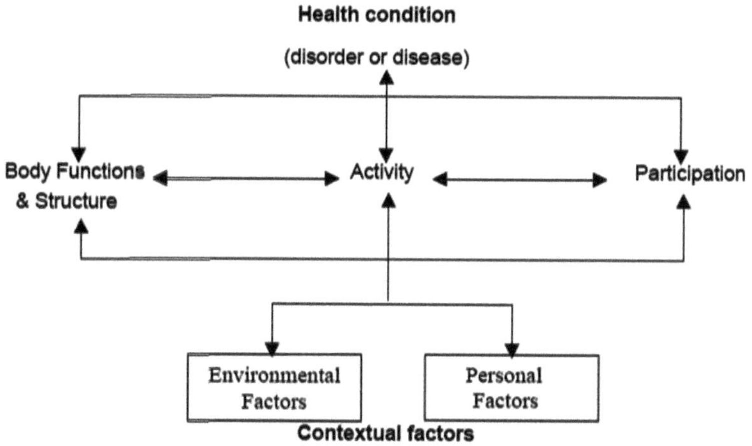

Fig. 20.1 International classification of functioning, disability and health (ICF) [11]

The ICF has 1,424 ICF categories, which make the utility of those categories not feasible. Hence, a brief and a comprehensive ICF Core Set (of domains) has been specifically developed for VR [12]. An ICF Core Set is a short list of ICF categories. The comprehensive version is lengthy, contains 90 categories (for a full list, see http://www.icf-research-branch.org). and is intended for multidisciplinary assessment, while the Brief ICF Core Set for VR consisting of 13 ICF categories (Table 20.1) serves as a minimum data set (i.e. list of functioning domains) that are to be reported in clinical studies or single-discipline clinical encounter within the context of VR to describe the impact of the disease on functioning [13]. The brief version can serve as a uniform data set because it identifies the essential issues experienced by patients in VR, which should be assessed, measured and evaluated.

The ICF Core Set essentially provides "what" to measure. "How" to measure an ICF category is possible by using a standard questionnaire, for example.

Hence, as part of the process in developing the ICF Core Set for VR, a systematic review was performed with linking of outcomes (including questionnaires) to the ICF [14]. The process basically involved linking of constructs found in the questionnaire items to the best fitting ICF category. This chapter will focus on patient-reported questionnaires (PRQ). Such questionnaires are commonly used in various fields of medicine and in VR [14] and are especially helpful when measuring constructs or latent variables. By providing a list of questionnaires that can assess the domains in the ICF Core Set, VR practitioners can now integrate the use of the ICF Core Set in their daily clinical practice by using those questionnaires.

The objective of this chapter is to present the PRQs that were linked to the 13 ICF categories of the brief version of the ICF Core Set for Vocational Rehabilitation.

Table 20.1 Title and description of ICF categories in the brief Core Set for Vocational Rehabilitation (total = 13 categories) [12]

ICF code	Title	Definition
d155	Acquiring skills	Developing basic and complex competencies in integrated sets of actions or tasks so as to initiate and follow through with the acquisition of a skill, such as manipulating tools or playing games like chess
d240	Handling stress and other psychological demands	Carrying out simple or complex and coordinated actions to manage and control the psychological demands required to carry out tasks demanding significant responsibilities and involving stress, distraction or crises, such as driving a vehicle during heavy traffic or taking care of many children
d720	Complex interpersonal interactions	Maintaining and managing interactions with other people, in a contextually and socially appropriate manner, such as by regulating emotions and impulses, controlling verbal and physical aggression, acting independently in social interactions and acting in accordance with social rules and conventions
d845	Acquiring, keeping and terminating a job	Seeking, finding and choosing employment; being hired and accepting employment; maintaining and advancing through a job, trade, occupation or profession; and leaving a job in an appropriate manner
d850	Remunerative employment	Engaging in all aspects of work, as an occupation, trade, profession or other form of employment, for payment, as an employee, full or part time or self-employed, such as seeking employment and getting a job, doing the required tasks of the job, attending work on time as required, supervising other workers or being supervised and performing required tasks alone or in groups
d855	Non-remunerative employment	Engaging in all aspects of work in which pay is not provided, full time or part time, including organised work activities, doing the required tasks of the job, attending work on time as required, supervising other workers or being supervised and performing required tasks alone or in groups, such as volunteer work, charity work, working for a community or religious group without remuneration and working around the home without remuneration
e310	Immediate family	Individuals related by birth, marriage or other relationship recognised by the culture as immediate family, such as spouses, partners, parents, siblings, children, foster parents, adoptive parents and grandparents
e330	People in positions of authority	Individuals who have decision-making responsibilities for others and who have socially defined influence or power based on their social, economic, cultural or religious roles in society, such as teachers, employers,

(continued)

Table 20.1 (continued)

ICF code	Title	Definition
		supervisors, religious leaders, substitute decision-makers, guardians or trustees
e580	Health services, systems and policies	Services, systems and policies for preventing and treating health problems, providing medical rehabilitation and promoting a healthy lifestyle
e590	Labour and employment services, systems and policies	Services, systems and policies related to finding suitable work for persons who are unemployed or looking for different work or to support individuals already employed who are seeking promotion
b130	Energy and drive functions	General mental functions of physiological and psychological mechanisms that cause the individual to move towards satisfying specific needs and general goals in a persistent manner
b164	Higher-level cognitive functions	Specific mental functions especially dependent on the frontal lobes of the brain, including complex goal-directed behaviours such as decision-making, abstract thinking, planning and carrying out plans, mental flexibility and deciding which behaviours are appropriate under what circumstances; often called executive functions
b455	Exercise tolerance functions	Functions related to respiratory and cardiovascular capacity as required for enduring physical exertion

This chapter can guide clinicians and researchers in choosing which PRQ measure to use to operationalise the ICF in VR.

20.2 Methods

20.2.1 Overview of Original Study

The current study is based on a previous systematic literature review (original study), which linked concepts found in measures and questionnaires to the specific ICF categories [14]. That review utilised the following search terms and keywords, "Vocational rehabilitation", "Return to work", "Occupational rehab*", "Work rehab*", "Work reintegration", "Job rehab*", "Job reentry", "Employ* rehab*" and "Employ* reentry", in multiple databases: CINAHL, PsycINFO, Medline, Global Health, Vocation and Career Collection.

20.2.2 Database of Questionnaire Items

A database was created in an Excel spreadsheet (Microsoft Corporation 2007, Redmond WA), showing the items of each questionnaire, which have been linked to the ICF categories in the VR Brief ICF Core Set. Definition for each ICF category is provided in Table 20.1. Only standard patient-reported questionnaires with items linked to the VR Brief Core Set were surveyed.

20.2.3 Survey of Questionnaires

An inventory of PRQs corresponding to each ICF category included in the ICF Core Set for VR was developed.

20.3 Results

20.3.1 Item Database

Based on the systematic review, 229 articles were selected. From these, 650 measures were identified (154 were questionnaires and clinical tests) [14]. Of those measures, there were 68 PRQs.

A database was created showing the items of all the questionnaires that addressed the ICF categories of the Brief ICF Core Set for VR. The database shows a wide range of questionnaires covering domains on mental health to physical health. Table 20.2 shows the acronyms and the corresponding full name of each PRQ. Table 20.3 contains a list of PRQs where concepts of a particular ICF category were found.

A total of 855 items from the 68 PRQs were linked to ICF categories of the Brief ICF Core Set for VR.

20.4 Discussion

Effective VR is essential in mitigating the growing burden of work disability. At the same time, VR is a complex process with a wide array of domains to consider and examine. The ICF presents a comprehensive language and reference framework with which we can utilise in VR practice. In an effort to increase the utility of the ICF by practitioners, ICF Core Sets have been developed. An ICF Core Set is a short extract of ICF categories from the entire ICF classification that are relevant and specific to a health condition or setting. To capture functioning within the

Table 20.2 Acronyms and names of PRQs. Some PRQs are copyrighted and require permission before they can be used. Make sure to check with individual developers

Acronym	Name of questionnaire
4DSQ	Four-Dimensional Symptom Questionnaire [15]
ADS	Activities Discomfort Scale [16]
ASI	Addiction Severity Index [17]
BDI	Beck Depression Inventory [18]
BIPQ	Brief Illness Perception Questionnaire [19]
BORRTI	Bell Objects Relations and Reality Testing Inventory [20]
BQ	Baecke Questionnaire (with work, sport and leisure time index) [21]
CAN-E	Camberwell Assessment of Needs-European short version [22]
CES-D	20-item Center for Epidemiologic Studies Depression scale [23]
COPM	Canadian Occupational Performance Measure [24]
CSQ-8	Client Satisfaction Questionnaire-8 [25]
CWPP	Work Personality Profile [26]
DASS	Depression Anxiety and Stress Scale [27]
DMQ	Dutch Musculoskeletal Questionnaire [28]
EQ- 5D	Euro QOL [29]
ES	Empowerment Scale [30]
FQOLS	Flanagan Quality of Life Scale [31]
GAS	Goal Attainment Scale [32]
GRWA	Graded Reduced Work Ability Scale [33]
GSES	General Self-Efficacy Scale [34]
HADS	Hospital Anxiety and Depression Scale [35]
HAQ-II	Revised Helping Alliance Questionnaire [36]
HAT-QOL	Holmes Quality of Life [37]
HDRS	Hamilton Depression Rating Scale [38]
HS	Hope Scale [39]
HSCL	Hopkins Symptoms Check List [40]
ISEL	Interpersonal Support Evaluation List [41]
JCQ	Job Content Questionnaire [42]
JSQ	Cooper Job Stress Questionnaire [43]
LBOS	Low Back Outcome Score [44]
LOT-R	Life Orientation Test-Revised [45]
LSI	Life Skills Inventory [46]
MHLC	Multidimensional Health Locus of Control questionnaire (Form A) [47]
MWHLCs	Modified Wallston's Health Locus of Control [48]
MSQ	Minnesota Satisfaction Questionnaire [49]
MZDI	Modified Zung Depression Index [50]
ODQ	Oswestry Low Back Pain Disability Questionnaire [51]
OMPQ	Örebro Musculoskeletal Pain Questionnaire [52]
OSQOL	Quality of Life Scale [53]
PANSS	Positive and Negative Syndrome Scale [54]
PAR-Q	Physical Activity Readiness questionnaire- revised 2002 [55]

(continued)

Table 20.2 (continued)

Acronym	Name of questionnaire
PCS	Pain Catastrophizing Scale [56]
PDI	Pain Disability Index [57]
PDQ	Pain Disability Questionnaire [58]
PSEQ	Pain Self Efficacy Questionnaire [59]
QD	Quick-DASH [60]
QOLQ	Quality of Life Questionnaire [61]
RDQ	Roland-Morris Disability 24 Questionnaire [62]
ROMI	Rating of Medication Influences Scale [63]
RPQ	Rivermead Post Concussion Symptoms Questionnaire [64]
SAS-SR	Social Adjustment Scale – Self Report version [65]
SCISCE	Stages of Change Interview for Seeking Competitive Employment [66]
SERS	Self-Esteem Rating Scale [67]
SF-36	Short Form 36-item health survey [68]
SF-12	Short Form 12-item health survey [69]
SHC	Subjective Health Complaint Inventory [70]
SOC	Sense of Coherence Scale -29 [71]
STAXI	State-Trait Anger Inventory [72]
URICA	University of Rhode Island Change Assessment scale [73]
VBBA	Need for Recovery Scale (in Dutch) [74]
WAI	Work Ability Index [75]
WAIV	Work Alliance Inventory [76]
WAPGAR	Work APGAR – modified [77]
WCQ	Ways of Coping Questionnaire [78]
WEJS	Work Experience and Judgment Scale [79]
WHO-DAS	WHO-DAS [80]
WHO-QOL	WHO Quality of Life Measure- BREF [81]
WLQ-16	16-item version of the Work Limitations Questionnaire [82]

context of work disability, the ICF Core Set for Vocational Rehabilitation has been developed. However, an ICF Core Set consists of only categories and as such it does not prescribe how to assess those categories, although it does state what domains of functioning needed to be assessed. Hence, there is a critical need to be able to identify the measures that can be used to assess an ICF category. To assist busy healthcare practitioners in VR in implementing the ICF into everyday practice.

This chapter contains a list of PRQs that correspond to and capture the ICF categories in the Brief ICF Core Set for VR. This list will be able to guide VR practitioners in choosing the appropriate questionnaire to operationalise the ICF in their daily practice and improve their interventions by targeting the domains found to be problematic using the PRQs.

Table 20.3 Identified PRQs for each ICF category of the brief ICF Core Set for Vocational Rehabilitation

ICF category code	PRQs containing the concept of the ICF category on the first column	
d155	COPM	QOLS
	CWPP	SERS
	DMQ	WEJS
d240	DMQ	STAXI
	ISEL	WEJS
	JSQ	WCQ
	OMPQ	
d720	BORRTI	PANSS
	CWPP	SERS
	LSI	STAXI
d845	COPM	MHLOC
	DMQ	OMPQ
	HAT-QOL	SAS-SR
	ISEL	SCISCE
	LSI	WAI
	MSQ	
d850	ADS	WEJS
	ASI	CWPP
	BDI	OMPQ
	BQ	PDQ
	COPM	PSEQ
	DMQ	QD
	EQ- 5D	QOLQ
	FQOLS	SCISCE
	GRWA	SF-12
	HAT-QOL	SF-36
	JCQ	WAI
	JSQ	WAPGAR
	LBOS	WHO-QOL
	LSI	WLQ-16
		VBBA
	MHLOC	
	MSQ	
d855	BDI	JCQ
	BQ	KAS
	COPM	PDI
	DMQ	PSEQ
	FQOLS	QD
	GRWA	RDQ
	HAT-QOL	WAI

(continued)

Table 20.3 (continued)

ICF category code	PRQs containing the concept of the ICF category on the first column	
e310	ASI	MHLC
	CAN-E	PANSS
	DMQ	PDQ
	HAT-QOL	PSEQ
	ISEL	WHO-DAS
	KAS	
e330	CWPP	OMPQ
	DMQ	PAR-Q
	JCQ	WAPGAR
	LSI	WEJS
	MSQ	
e580	ASI	LSI
	BIPQ	MHLOC
	CAN-E	ODQ
	CSQ-8	ROMI
	DMQ	URICA
	GAS	WAI
	HAQ-II	WAIV
	ISEL	WHO-QOL
	JSQ	
e590	ASI	JSQ
	DMQ	LSI
	JCQ	VBBA
b130	4DSQ	QOLQ
	BDI	OSQOL
	BQ	PANSS
	DASS	RDQ
	CAN-E	ROMI
	CES-D	RPQ
	DMQ	SCISCE
	FQOLS	SF-12
	GAF	SF-36
	GSES	SHC
	HADS	URICA
	HAT-QOL	VBBA
	HDRS	WCQ
	HS	WEJS
	HSCL	WHO-QOL
	LOT-R	

(continued)

Table 20.3 (continued)

ICF category code	PRQs containing the concept of the ICF category on the first column	
b164	BORRTI	MSQ
	CWPP	PANSS
	DMQ	PCS
	ES	SOC
	HDRS	URICA
	HS	WCQ
	KAS	WEJS
	LSI	
b455	BQ	OSQOL
	DMQ	RPQ
	MZDI	WEJS

Choosing the right questionnaire solely based on its contents is not as straightforward as it may seem. There are many questions that needed to be addressed first. Should users administer or apply the whole PRQ, although many of the other items in the PRQ probably are irrelevant? Or should the users only use a single corresponding category in the PRQ? But then, is that appropriate? What happens to the reliability of the PRQ when some items are taken out? If the whole PRQ is used for measuring one ICF Core Set category, will that not mean that several different probably extensive PRQs should be used to address other ICF categories?

From a pragmatic perspective, it is ultimately the decision of the vocational rehabilitation practitioner to pick and choose PRQs that aim to capture what the practitioner wants to capture. It must, however, be an informed decision with consideration to the concepts contained in the PRQ, the specific ICF category that needs to be prioritised, and efficiency.

The goal is to use only as few PRQs as possible to capture most, if not all, categories in the ICF Core Set for Vocational Rehabilitation given the limited amount of time in the clinics.

In a practical sense, although not advisable in research or when pooling data at patient group level, items from a PRQ can be selected that captures an ICF category. So, for example, for the 13 ICF categories of the ICF Core Set for Vocational Rehabilitation, one item can be obtained from one PRQ. Since some items might be linked to more than one ICF category, then in such a case, more than one ICF category can probably be addressed by only using one item. This is all about efficiency, which is necessary in vocational rehabilitation assessment with time as a limitation. One way to address efficiency while considering precision of measuring disability is through computer adaptive testing, where a clinician can have a precise assessment of disability yet the patient only answers less number of questions.

The list of PRQs suggests a diverse array of questionnaires, all of which assess functioning in VR at some level. The questionnaires assess common domains in the context of mental health, musculoskeletal conditions, general health and pain. This general finding emphasises the breadth of VR as a field of research and practice. PRQs are widely being used in VR practice. Hence, the emphasis on sound and robust outcome measurement is vital in facilitating adequate and appropriate return to work processes. There is an increasing focus on outcome measures in health and a growing need to improve healthcare measures, including those utilised in VR.

Our study has some limitations. First, we did not use the comprehensive version of the ICF Core Set for Vocational Rehabilitation which provides a comprehensive list of domains that covers the full spectrum of problems in functioning experienced by individuals undergoing vocational rehabilitation. With all the 90 ICF categories of the comprehensive version, however, this would also give a long list of questionnaires and again, loses feasibility. On the other hand, it is also possible that some of the PRQs have similar items due to conceptual overlap; hence some of them may be similar for some ICF categories. Second, we did not review the psychometric properties of the PRQs other than the face and content validity already provided by the ICF Core Set. The list of PRQs we provided here will benefit further from knowing the reliability properties such as test-retest and internal consistency and other aspects of validity such as construct validity and predictive validity. In return to work outcomes, it is also important that we know how responsive or sensitive a PRQ is to change in the status of the individual and to be able to answer whether the patient has truly recovered, deteriorated or remain unchanged. Third, while second-level ICF categories should be sufficient enough for general use, there are still various categories (third or fourth level) which have not been used as the basis for looking at PRQs. It may be difficult at times to exclusively claim that items of a PRQ measure specific categories, as they may measure only certain concepts within the categories. This refers particularly to those items measuring third-level categories which were then aggregated to second-level categories.

An interesting point to note was that the ICF category *d850 Remunerative employment* ($n = 31$) and the *d855 Non-remunerative employment* ($n = 14$) shared 11 PRQs. This shows the overlap between paid and nonpaid work-related activities and the importance of looking at both in VR [14]. Another interesting point was the relatively high number of PRQs on "quality of life" (QOL). The question arises why there are so many questionnaires, which were seemingly intended to measure the same construct. While this study is by no means a comprehensive description of why this may be the case, it might be that QOL while being a commonly used term amongst healthcare practitioners and has widespread recognised importance, the consensus on what it entails precisely is not so well defined [83].

20.5 Conclusion

The results of this study could act as a guide for healthcare practitioners in VR to integrate the ICF into everyday practice. By operationalising the ICF with PRQs, we are provided with a better understanding of assessing and evaluating patient needs based on a comprehensive biopsychosocial framework and informed care in VR.

The World Health Organization's ICF Core Set for Vocational Rehabilitation provides the "what" to measure in patients in vocational rehabilitation but does not specify "how" to measure them. This chapter can serve as a guide to clinicians in choosing which PRQs to use to operationalise the ICF in vocational rehabilitation fit for their purpose and setting.

References

1. Benítez-Silva H, Disney R, Jiménez-Martín S. Disability, capacity for work and the business cycle: an international perspective. Econ Policy. 2010;25:483–536.
2. Organisation for Economic Co-operation and Development Directorate for Employment, Labour and Social Affairs. Sickness, disability and work: keeping on track in the economic downturn (background paper). Stockholm: High-Level Forum; 2009.
3. Hoffman C, Rice D, Sung HY. Persons with chronic conditions: their prevalence and costs. JAMA. 1996;276:1473–9.
4. Lehman AF. Vocational rehabilitation in schizophrenia. Schizophr Bull. 1995;21:645–56.
5. Escorpizo R, Ekholm J, Gmuender HP, Cieza A, Kostanjsek N, Stucki G. Developing a core set to describe functioning in vocational rehabilitation using the international classification of functioning, disability, and health (ICF). J Occup Rehabil. 2010;20:502–11.
6. Clayton S, Barr B, Nylen L, Burström B, Thielen K, Diderichsen F, Dahl E, Whitehead M. Effectiveness of return-to-work interventions for disabled people: a systematic review of government initiatives focused on changing the behaviour of employers. Eur J Public Health. 2012;22(3):434–9.
7. Escorpizo R, Reneman MF, Ekholm J, et al. A conceptual definition of vocational rehabilitation based on the ICF: building a shared global model. J Occup Rehabil. 2011;21:126–33.
8. Patten SB, Williams JV, Wang J. Mental disorders in a population sample with musculoskeletal disorders. BMC Musculoskelet Disord. 2006;7:37.
9. Wang J, Adair CE, Patten SB. Mental health and related disability among workers: a population-based study. Am J Ind Med. 2006;49:514–22.
10. World Health Organization. The burden of musculoskeletal conditions at the start of the new millenium. Geneva: WHO Technical Report Series 919; 2003.
11. World Health Organization. International classification of functioning, disability and health. Geneva: World Health Organization; 2001.
12. Finger ME, Escorpizo R, Glassel A, et al. ICF core set for vocational rehabilitation: results of an international consensus conference. Disabil Rehabil. 2012;34:429–38.
13. Cieza A, Stucki G. The international classification of functioning disability and health: its development process and content validity. Eur J Phys Rehabil Med. 2008;44:303–13.
14. Escorpizo R, Finger ME, Glassel A, Gradinger F, Luckenkemper M, Cieza A. A systematic review of functioning in vocational rehabilitation using the international classification of functioning, disability and health. J Occup Rehabil. 2011;21:134–46.

15. Terluin B, Van Rhenen W, Schaufeli W, De Haan M. The four-dimensional symptom questionnaire (4DSQ): measuring distress and other mental health problems in a working population. Work Stress. 2004;18:187–207.
16. Turner JA, Robinson J, McCreary CP. Chronic low back pain: predicting response to nonsurgical treatment. Arch Phys Med Rehabil. 1983;64:560–3.
17. McLellan AT, Luborsky L, O'Brien CP, Woody GE. An improved diagnostic instrument for substance abuse patients: the addiction severity index. J Nerv Ment Dis. 1980;168:26–33.
18. Beck AT, Steer R, Brown G. Manual for the beck depression inventory-II. San Antonio: Psychological Corporation; 1996.
19. Broadbent E, Petrie KJ, Main J, Weinman J. The brief illness perception questionnaire. J Psychosom Res. 2006;60:631–7. doi:10.1016/j.jpsychores.2005.10.020.
20. Bell MD. Bell Object Relations and Reality Testing Inventory (BORRTI) manual. Los Angeles: Western Psychological Services; 1995.
21. Baecke JA, Burema J, Frijters JE. A short questionnaire for the measurement of habitual physical activity in epidemiological studies. Am J Clin Nutr. 1982;36:936–42.
22. Phelan M, Slade M, Thornicroft G, et al. The Camberwell assessment of need: the validity and reliability of an instrument to assess the needs of people with severe mental illness. Br J Psychiatry. 1995;167:589–95.
23. Radloff LS. The CES-D scale: a self report depression scale for research in the general population. Appl Psychol Meas. 1977;1:385–401.
24. Law M, Polatajko H, Pollock N, McColl MA, Carswell A, Baptiste S. Pilot testing of the Canadian occupational performance measure: clinical and measurement issues. Can J Occup Ther. 1994;61:191–7.
25. Attkisson CC, Zwick R. The client satisfaction questionnaire. Psychometric properties and correlations with service utilization and psychotherapy outcome. Eval Program Plann. 1982;5: 233–7.
26. Law CK, Siu AM, Lee JL, Lee SW. Prediction of work rehabilitation placements using the Chinese work personality profile. Psychiatr Rehabil J. 2006;30:120–8.
27. Lovibond SH, Lovibond PF. Manual for the depression anxiety stress scales. 2nd ed. Sydney: Psychology Foundation; 1995.
28. Hildebrandt VH, Bongers PM, van Dijk FJ, Kemper HC, Dul J. Dutch musculoskeletal questionnaire: description and basic qualities. Ergonomics. 2001;44:1038–55.
29. The EuroQol group. EuroQol–a new facility for the measurement of health-related quality of life. Health Policy. 1990;16(3):199–208.
30. Bulsara C, Styles I, Ward AM, Bulsara M. The psychometrics of developing the patient empowerment scale. J Psychosoc Oncol. 2006;24:1–16.
31. Burckhardt CS, Anderson KL. The quality of life scale (QOLS): reliability, validity, and utilization. Health Qual Life Outcomes. 2003;1:60.
32. Kiresuk TJ, Smith A, Cardillo JE, editors. Goal attainment scaling: applications, theory, and measurement. Hillsdale: Lawrence Erlbaum Associates; 1994.
33. Haldorsen EM, Indahl A, Ursin H. Patients with low back pain not returning to work. A 12-month follow-up study. Spine (Phila Pa 1976). 1998;23:1202–7; discussion 1208.
34. Schwarzer R, Jerusalem M. Generalized self-efficacy scale. In: Weinman J, Wright S, Johnston M, editors. Measures in health psychology: a user's portfolio, Causal and control beliefs. Windsor: NFER-NELSON; 1995. p. 35–7.
35. Zigmond AS, Snaith RP. The hospital anxiety and depression scale. Acta Psychiatr Scand. 1983;67:361–70.
36. Luborsky L, Barber JP, Siqueland L, et al. The revised helping alliance questionnaire (HAq-11) psychometric properties. J Psychother Pract Res. 1996;5:260–71.
37. Holmes WC, Shea JA. A new HIV/AIDS-targeted quality of life (HAT-QoL) instrument: development, reliability, and validity. Med Care. 1998;36:138–54.
38. Hamilton M. A rating scale for depression. J Neurol Neurosurg Psychiatry. 1960;23:56–62.

39. Snyder CR, Sympson SC, Ybasco FC, Borders TF, Babyak MA, Higgins RL. Development and validation of the state Hope scale. J Pers Soc Psychol. 1996;70:321–35.
40. Derogatis LR, Lipman RS, Rickels K, Uhlenhuth EH, Covi L. The Hopkins symptom checklist (HSCL): a self-report symptom inventory. Behav Sci. 1974;19:1–15.
41. Barrera M, Irvin NS, Ramsay TB. Preliminary development of a scale of social support: studies on college students. Am J Community Psychol. 1981;9:435–47.
42. Karasek R, Brisson C, Kawakami N, Houtman I, Bongers P, Amick B. The job content questionnaire (JCQ): an instrument for internationally comparative assessments of psychosocial job characteristics. J Occup Health Psychol. 1998;3:322–55.
43. Cooper CL, Rout U, Faragher B. Mental health, job satisfaction, and job stress among general practitioners. BMJ. 1989;298:366–70.
44. Greenough CG, Fraser RD. Assessment of outcome in patients with low-back pain. Spine (Phila Pa 1976). 1992;17:36–41.
45. Scheier MF, Carver CS, Bridges MW. Distinguishing optimism from neuroticism (and trait anxiety, self-mastery, and self-esteem): a reevaluation of the life orientation test. J Pers Soc Psychol. 1994;67:1063–78.
46. Brigance AH. Brigance diagnostic life skills inventory. North Billerica: Curriculum Associates, Inc.; 1994.
47. Wallston KA, Wallston BS, DeVellis R. Development of the multidimensional health locus of control (MHLC) scales. Health Educ Monogr. 1978;6:160–70.
48. Murphy GC, Young AE, Vo KM. Using locus of control to predict the return-to-work achievements of back-injured occupational rehabilitation clients. Aust J Rehabil Couns. 1995;1:83–92.
49. Weiss DJ, Dawis RV, England GW, Lofquist LH. Manual for the Minnesota satisfaction questionnaire, Minnesota studies in vocational rehabilitation, vol. 22. Minneapolis: University of Minnesota, Industrial Relations Center; 1967.
50. Main C, Wood P, Hillis S, et al. The distress and risk assessment method. A simple patient classification to identify distress and evaluate the risk of poor outcome. Spine. 1992;17:42–52.
51. Fairbank JC, Couper J, Davies JB, O'Brien JP. The Oswestry low back pain disability questionnaire. Physiotherapy. 1980;66:271–3.
52. Linton SJ, Boersma K. Early identification of patients at risk of developing a persistent back problem: the predictive validity of the Örebro musculoskeletal pain questionnaire. Clin J Pain. 2003;19:80–6.
53. Le Pen C, Levy E, Loos F, Banzet MN, Basdevant A. "Specific" scale compared with "generic" scale: a double measurement of the quality of life in a French community sample of obese subjects. J Epidemiol Community Health. 1998;52:445–50.
54. Kay SR, Fiszbein A, Opler LA. The positive and negative syndrome scale (PANSS) for schizophrenia. Schizophr Bull. 1987;13:261–76.
55. Thomas S, Reading J, Shephard RJ. Revision of the physical activity readiness questionnaire (PAR-Q). Can J Sport Sci. 1992;17:338–45.
56. Sullivan MJL, Bishop S, Pivik J. The pain catastrophizing scale: development and validation. Psychol Assess. 1995;7:524–32.
57. Tait RC, Chibnall JT, Krause S. The pain disability index: psychometric properties. Pain. 1990;40:171–82.
58. Anagnostis C, Gatchel RJ, Mayer TG. The pain disability questionnaire: a new psychometrically sound measure for chronic musculoskeletal disorders. Spine (Phila Pa 1976). 2004;29:2290–302.
59. Tonkin L. The pain self-efficacy questionnaire. Aust J Physiother. 2008;54:77.
60. Beaton DE, Wright JG, Katz JN, Upper Extremity Collaborative Group. Development of the QuickDASH: comparison of three item-reduction approaches. J Bone Joint Surg Am. 2005; 87:1038–46.
61. Boixadós M, Pousada M, Bueno J, Valiente L. Quality of life questionnaire: psychometric properties and relationships to healthy behavioral patterns. Open Psychol J. 2009;2:49–57.

62. Roland MO, Morris RW. A study of the natural history of back pain. Part 1: development of a reliable and sensitive measure of disability in low back pain. Spine. 1983;8(2):141–4.
63. Weiden P, Rapkin B, Mott T, et al. Rating of medication influences (ROMI) scale in schizophrenia. Schizophr Bull. 1994;20:297–310.
64. King NS, Crawford S, Wenden FJ, Moss NE, Wade DT. The Rivermead post concussion symptoms questionnaire: a measure of symptoms commonly experienced after head injury and its reliability. J Neurol. 1995;242:587–92.
65. Zweig RA, Turkel E. The social adjustment scale-self-report: psychometric properties for older adults. Psychol Rep. 2007;101:920–6.
66. Corrigan PW, McCracken SG, Holmes EP. Motivational interviews as goal assessment for persons with psychiatric disability. Community Ment Health J. 2001;37:113–22.
67. Nugent WR, Thomas JW. Validation of a clinical measure of self-esteem. Res Soc Work Pract. 1993;3:191–207.
68. Ware JE. SF-36 health survey. Manual and interpretation guide. Boston: The Health Institute, New England Medical Center; 1997.
69. Ware JE. SF-12; how to score the SF-12 physical and mental health summary scales. Boston: The Health Institute, New England Medical Center; 1995.
70. Eriksen HR, Ihlebaek C, Ursin H. A scoring system for subjective health complaints (SHC). Scand J Public Health. 1999;27:63–72.
71. Antonovsky A. The structure and properties of the sense of coherence scale. Soc Sci Med. 1993;36:725–33.
72. Spielberger CD, Gorsuch RL, Lushene RE. The state-trait anxiety inventory: test manual. Palo Alto: Consulting Psychologist Press; 1970.
73. DiClemente CC, Hughes SO. Stages of change profiles in outpatient alcoholism treatment. J Subst Abuse. 1990;2:217–35.
74. van Veldhoven M, Broersen S. Measurement quality and validity of the "need for recovery scale". Occup Environ Med. 2003;60:i3–9.
75. Tuomi K, Eskelinen L, Toikkanen J, Jarvinen E, Ilmarinen J, Klockars M. Work load and individual factors affecting work ability among aging municipal employees. Scand J Work Environ Health. 1991;17:128–34.
76. Horvath AO, Greenberg LS. The development and validation of the working alliance inventory. J Couns Psychol. 1989;36:223–33.
77. Bigos SJ, Battie MC, Spengler DM, et al. A prospective study of work perceptions and psychosocial factors affecting the report of back injury. Spine (Phila Pa 1976). 1991;16:1–6.
78. Folkman S, Lazarus RS, editors. Manual for the ways of coping questionnaire. Palo Alto: Consulting Psychologists Press; 1988.
79. Van Veldhoven M. Psychosociale arbeidsbelasting en werkstress [Psychosocial job demands and work stress]. Ph.D. thesis. The Netherlands: University of Groningen; 1996.
80. World Health Organization. Measuring health and disability – manual for WHO disability assessment schedule (WHODAS 2.0); 2010.
81. Skevington SM, Lotfy M, O'Connell KA, WHOQOL Group. The world health organization's WHOQOL-BREF quality of life assessment: psychometric properties and results of the international field trial. A report from the WHOQOL group. Qual Life Res. 2004;13:299–310.
82. Beaton DE, Kennedy CA. Beyond return to work: testing a measure of at-work disability in workers with musculoskeletal pain. Qual Life Res. 2005;14:1869–79.
83. Carr AJ, Thompson PW, Kirwan JR. Quality of life measures. Br J Rheumatol. 1996;35: 275–81.

Chapter 21
Clinician-Reported Outcome Measures: Experiences from Multicenter Follow-Up and an Overview of Commonly Used Measures in Vocational Rehabilitation and Disability Evaluation

Ingemar F Petersson, Birgitta Grahn, and Kjerstin Stigmar

21.1 Introduction

In 2001, the ICF was introduced as a conceptual framework, to provide a more comprehensive description of an individual's functioning in relation to health. The ICF is a complement to the medical diagnostic codes in the ICD-10 [1] and focuses on describing functioning both in positive and negative terms. The ICF framework describes two main areas: health conditions and contextual factors. These areas are divided in different *components*. The health conditions consist of the two components, body structure and function, and activity and participation. The contextual factors are divided in environmental factors and personal factors. Furthermore, the different components are subgrouped in *domains,* in order to offer a more specific description. Each domain is further divided in *categories.*

In the ICF, disability is described as *limitations* of body structure and function and *restriction* of activity and participation. The environmental factors are described as facilitators or barriers. The system not only offers an opportunity to describe which component, domain, or category that is affected. By using the qualifiers in ICF, it is also possible to state the severity of a problem concerning

I.F. Petersson (✉)
Epidemiology and Register Centre South, Skånes universitetssjukhus, Medicon Village, Tunavägen 22, 223 81 Lund, Sweden

Lund University, Lund, Sweden
e-mail: ingemar.petersson@med.lu.se; ingemar.petersson@skane.se

B. Grahn • K. Stigmar
Epidemiology and Register Centre South, Skånes universitetssjukhus, Medicon Village, Tunavägen 22, 223 81 Lund, Sweden

Lund University, Lund, Sweden

Department of Health Sciences, Division of Physiotherapy, Lund University, Lund, Sweden

R. Escorpizo et al. (eds.), *Handbook of Vocational Rehabilitation and Disability Evaluation*, Handbooks in Health, Work, and Disability, DOI 10.1007/978-3-319-08825-9_21

structural or functional limitations, activity, and participation restrictions and to what extent the environment is a facilitator or a barrier.

21.2 The Relevance of ICF in Vocational Rehabilitation and Work Disability Evaluation

Vocational rehabilitation and work disability evaluation are relevant in a diversity of fields in health care. In some areas the medical condition has obvious consequences on the individual's health and ability to work. The individual is just too sick and the discussion about work is not relevant, before the medical treatment has been successful. In other fields, vocational rehabilitation and disability evaluation are relevant early in the rehabilitation phase, maybe already from the very beginning. Such fields can be in primary health-care settings, in pain rehabilitation, and certainly in occupational health services.

> The goal for vocational rehabilitation is to enable an individual to return to working life, by reclaiming function, activity, and participation in combination with making necessary adjustments in the work environment.

This must not necessarily be to the present work, but can also be to adjusted work or different work tasks with the same employer, or with another employer, or with a vocational rehabilitation specialist. The individual may have the capacity to perform, but actual performance at work is very much dependent on contextual factors, i.e., environmental and personal factors. In the ICF, environmental factors can be seen as available opportunities, covering physical, mental, and social work demands, work organization, and work environment demands from a broad perspective. Compared to medical rehabilitation, environmental aspects are absolutely essential in vocational rehabilitation and must be paid as much attention as medical status. We also know that other factors, such as personal factors, are important when making prognosis of work ability and sick leave, and it is essential to consider them in vocational rehabilitation or work disability evaluations. This emphasizes the importance of using all components of the ICF. The ICF is not a theoretical model in the sense we usually mean, but can rather be seen as a foundation to how we make sure that we cover all relevant aspects when dealing with vocational rehabilitation and work disability evaluation. Some of these practical aspects will be further discussed in this chapter.

Another important aspect in the field of vocational rehabilitation and disability evaluation is that it is vital to pay attention not only to functional impairments, activity limitations, and participation restriction but also to the individual's resources in relation to work. The ICF offers the opportunity to state to what extent a domain is affected both in positive and negative terms.

Important concepts in vocational rehabilitation are *work ability* and *return to work (RTW)*. An individual can possess *specific* work ability, i.e., in relation to a specific work position where the individual is requested to perform specific work tasks. *General* work ability means having capacity to perform generally existent work. The concept of work ability is discussed within different contexts, such as medicine, social insurance, and philosophical contexts. Regardless of these discussions, most researchers agree that work ability is a relational concept and covers a broad spectrum of aspects that can be classified in all aspects of the ICF.

Closely related to work ability is the concept of *work productivity*. From an employer perspective, this concept is vital. An employee may have some work ability and can be present at work, but actually *performing* at work is another thing. In research, the terms *absenteeism* and *presenteeism* are sometimes used as outcome measures. Absenteeism means being off work due to some reason, usually ill health. Presenteeism means being at work but underperforming, due to ill health.

RTW is often discussed in relation to rehabilitation and after a period of sick leave. This is also an important outcome in research and often used as a dichotomy, RTW or not RTW. The term must be specified each time and described whether part-time RTW is included or not and also concerning time aspects. To RTW it is obviously important, but it is also necessary to gain sustainability in work ability.

In conclusion, the ICF offers a broad framework to describe and/or state he individual's capacity in relation to work environment. In addition, you can also describe personal factors that play an important role in work disability.

21.3 Clinician-Reported Outcome Measures: CROMs

In all parts of health care and rehabilitation, it is important to evaluate the results of different interventions. One way to categorize evaluations is to divide them into patient-reported outcome measures (PROMs) and clinician-reported outcome measures (CROMs). PROMs mainly cover self-reports in questionnaires.

CROMs are defined as measurements reported by a health professional. They cover a broad spectrum of methods, including observational methods, performance tests, and measurements.

More advanced CROMs are more expensive and time consuming.

When dealing with the results of vocational rehabilitation and disability evaluation, both the individual's capacity and the work environment, including different work demands, must be evaluated. Both PROMs and CROMs deal with the individual's capacities and work environmental aspects.

In this chapter, we will focus on CROMs that may be applicable in clinical rehabilitation, in particular in vocational rehabilitation and disability evaluation.

The intention is to stay close to a practical and clinical context. Furthermore, we will focus on CROMs that are valid for one patient group that is most commonly studied in sick leave: patients with musculoskeletal disorders (MSD). We will also give some examples on how ICF-based CROMs can be used in ordinary clinical practice on patients with MSD and mental disorders, in order to facilitate quality assurance and results on rehabilitation.

21.3.1 CROMs: Function

In order to perform an activity in a certain environment, different functions may be necessary. It is, however, also important to emphasize that a functional limitation can be compensated for with a supportive work environment. To evaluate only function is sometimes relevant in work disability evaluation, but often instruments cover both the function and activity components. Tests focusing on different functions can be conducted at the clinic and may require different equipment. If grading functional level from 0 to 4, which corresponds to no functional limitation to complete functional limitation, we give examples of some functional tests.

21.3.1.1 Functional Capacity Evaluations

Functional Capacity Evaluations (FCE) are not specific, validated tests, but rather umbrella terms for tests that can be applied in disability evaluation [2]. The tests can be related to a specific job, a specific disease, or can be generic. An FCE can be on mental functioning, on physical functioning, or on a combination of both.

One part of an FCE can be a traditional aerobic capacity test [3]. This requires a bike, a stopwatch, a pulse monitor, and a blood pressure cuff. In a recent study, aerobic capacity was strongly correlated to work ability [4]. Aerobic capacity is captured by the ICF category *b455 Exercise tolerance functions*.

21.3.1.2 Grip Strength

Manual material handling is common in many different occupations and work tasks. Grip strength is covered by the ICF category *b730 Muscle strength functions*. There are different ways to measure grip strength requiring some kind of device. A Jamar dynamometer can be used to measure maximal grip strength [5] and in rheumatology the GRIPPIT technique is frequently used [6]. The test is performed by asking the patient to press the dynamometer as hard as possible. Two tryouts are performed for each hand with a notification of the dominant hand. The two devices, Jamar dynamometer and GRIPPIT, cannot be used interchangeably, since they have different qualities [7].

21.3.2 CROMs: Activity and Participation

For the ICF component activity and participation, it is important to pay special attention to the fact that the qualifiers give us the opportunity to assess on different levels. Mainly, two levels are used: performance and capacity. It is also possible to go further by describing capacity with assistance and performance without assistance. Performance is in relation to the actual environment and can be related to specific work ability. Capacity is the highest possible functional level in standard environment with or without assistance. These aspects are highly relevant in vocational rehabilitation. First, it is important to decide if the individual's activity and participation are classified in relation to ordinary work or work in general. This is particularly important in sick leave and insurance medicine issues. Second, it is important to see activity and participation in relation to workplace adjustments, since they may increase the individual's capacity.

Below, some examples of tests are suggested. These tests are easy to perform at a clinic and are standardized, although the results can be related to other comparable environments and also to different work demands.

21.3.2.1 Six-Minute Walk Test

The six-minute walk test [8] is often used in the follow-up in rehabilitation programs, but also in disability evaluations. It refers to the ICF category *d450 to walk.* The test is easy to perform and requires only 30 m walking distance and a stopwatch. A track of 30 m is marked, and the patient is asked to walk as far as possible during 6 min. The patient is allowed to take breaks or to vary the walking speed. The six-minute walk test can be a prognostic factor for work ability in patients with low back pain (LBP) [9].

21.3.2.2 The PILE Test

The Progressive Isoinertial Lifting Evaluation (PILE) is available in cervical and lumbar versions [10]. The test is a standardized lifting test in a standard environment. In relation to ICF, it refers to the ICF category *d430 Lifting and carrying*. The test requires a bookshelf with standardized distance between the shelves, a stopwatch, weights, and a pulse monitor. The patient is asked to lift a carriage with weights from one level to another at a certain speed, four lifts in 20 s. Every 20th second, additional weight is added. The patient decides when he or she wants to stop the test and also what lifting technique that is used. The test leader is responsible for the patient's pulse and to ensure that the weights are not too heavy. There are different weight limits in different countries. The results of the test are maximal lifting weight and pulse when the test is accomplished.

21.3.2.3 Participative Methods

In vocational rehabilitation, a participative approach is suggested, although there is still need for further development of the research methodology in the field [11]. By using the patient's experiences, preferences, and perceptions, the results of an evaluation can become more valid. This can also be related to the component participation in the ICF, i.e., the patient is participating in her or his own disability evaluation and vocational rehabilitation.

There are different instruments and methods that include a participative approach. One example is Patient-Specific Functional Scale [12]. This instrument offers a structured model for the patient and the health professional to discuss what activities that offer difficulties in everyday life or at work. The scale covers physical, mental, and social restrictions.

21.3.3 CROMs: Environmental Factors

As described above, environmental factors are very important in vocational rehabilitation and disability evaluation. The aim of such rehabilitation is to support the individual in reclaiming the capacity that is needed, in order to RTW. This capacity must then be related to physical, mental, and social work demands. Just assessing the individual's capacity does not tell us very much about what the individual actually can perform in a certain environment or in certain work tasks. The environmental aspects must be described as rigorously as function, activity, and participation aspects.

In the ICF, environmental aspects are not explicitly developed for work environment, but rather for environmental aspects in general. They are qualified as obstacles or facilitators, from "no barrier" to "complete barrier" and from "no facilitator" to "complete facilitator."

21.3.3.1 Quick Exposure Check

The Quick Exposure Check (QEC) is an example of a combination of PROMs and CROMs. It is an observational method that is generic and is performed at the workplace during performance. The instrument is not strictly defined in relation to environmental aspects, since it includes functions and activities as well. The aim of the observation is to capture exposure for well-known risk factors for work disability. The instrument includes observations of different positions for the back, neck, shoulder and arm, wrist, and hand (CROMs) and the employees experience of weights handled, time spent on work task, one-hand force, visual demands, driving a vehicle, vibrating tools, work tempo, and stress (PROMs). The test is summed up in exposure scores that are related to exposure levels [13].

21.3.3.2 Assessment of Work Characteristics (AWC)

This instrument was developed in occupational therapy [14] and is based on the Model of Human Occupation [15]. The aim is to examine to what extent the work environment puts different demands on the individual's skills when performing. The method comprises demands on motoric, process, and communication and interactive skills.

21.3.4 CROMS: Personal Factors

In the ICF, personal factors are described but not classified. These factors are not regarded as a part of health, but rather as background factors that can contribute to the experience of health. The personal factors must be seen in a global, cultural context and may differ between different ethnic groups and citizens. They may have significant impact on the results of vocational rehabilitation and also when evaluating work disability, and therefore we need to be attentive to them and describe them. Although they are not qualified, they are closely related to personal factors that are classified in the area of function.

21.3.4.1 Age

Age is one of the major factors affecting the outcomes of vocational rehabilitation and must be considered in disability evaluation and in the rehabilitation planning process. We know from earlier studies that age is a predictor of RTW and also affects work ability [16]. First, there is a sociocultural aspect of age, related to retirement, which differs between cultures and contexts. The retirement age varies between countries and types of occupation. If an individual has reached a certain age and is close to retirement, RTW efforts will probably be less likely to succeed. This can be related to the individual and how he or she experiences age in relation to work, but also how the workplace includes older employees.

During the life span, an individual's physical capacity normally drops. The cardiorespiratory capacity tends to decrease significantly between 25 and 65 years of age. Muscle strength has almost the same decrease. Cardiorespiratory capacity is an important aspect of work ability. In some professions physical strength can play an important role in the individual's ability to perform work tasks. Although these aspects are affected by age, they are classified as functional limitations in the ICF. Since age is a factor that cannot be influenced, it is important to be aware of the fact that such age-related factors can be influenced to a certain level. CROMs on cardiorespiratory factors are used in the area of physical performance, such as fitness tests and different strength tests. These tests require special equipment and are often more expensive and time consuming.

21.3.4.2 Gender

Gender is not supposed to influence the planning of rehabilitation, but it is important to be aware of gender impact on sick leave. More women than men receive sick leave in European countries, and prognostic factors for RTW have been described differently for females and males [17]. As an example, in the health-care system in south Sweden, gender is paid special attention to in the sick-listing process and in disability evaluations, and since we know that women are asked other questions than men, they receive other diagnoses and are more sick-listed in general.

21.3.4.3 Lifestyle

Lifestyle factors are important for an individual's health and experience of well-being. The ICF does not provide a classification system for lifestyle factors, but it is still important to describe these factors, since they may contribute to the results of a vocational rehabilitation program and a disability evaluation. Important factors for work ability are smoking habits, physical activity [16], drug abuse, and eating habits [16]. No generally accepted CROMs seem to be available in this area.

21.3.4.4 Education and Profession

Educational level is closely related to the individual's experience of health. This is relevant from a global perspective. Also in relation to work ability, educational level is of importance [18]. There are other aspects of education as well, including teaching the patient about his or her disease and health condition. This can be exemplified by the Educational Needs Assessment Tool (ENAT) which is a PROM used in rehabilitation in rheumatology [19]. No generally accepted CROMs appear to be available in this area.

21.3.4.5 Health Literacy

In recent years, health literacy has been experienced as an important aspect of an individual's health. To be able to take responsibility and appropriate health decisions, and to follow instructions in rehabilitation, it is crucial to understand information concerning health and health care. In the follow-up of rehabilitation programs, PROMs are often used. Health literacy is especially important and needs special attention, when PROMs are used, in order to interpret the results of the questionnaire properly. When using CROMs, health literacy may play an important role, but not as obvious as in using PROMs.

21.3.4.6 Coping Strategies, Locus of Control, Motivation, and Self-Efficacy

In recent years, identifying an individual's coping strategies, locus of control, motivation, and self-efficacy has become more and more important. Rehabilitation research shows that these factors play a very important role for the results of rehabilitation programs and for the planning of them. Objections to the ICF have been raised in the area of motivation and will. The criticism has mainly concerned the fact that whether an individual is performing or not depends on the individual's actual willingness to perform to a large extent. Awareness of this fact and use of personal factors as a description can ensure that these aspects are properly covered.

There are several questionnaires, most of them self-reported, aiming at identifying coping strategies among individuals with disability. Self-efficacy has in a number of studies been able to predict RTW [20, 21] and was also lower among sick-listed persons [22]. To our knowledge, there are no CROMs available on self-efficacy.

21.4 CROMs Relating to ICF in Medical Conditions

For the majority of patients at working age, there is a wish to return to work if it by any means is possible in relation to the medical condition. About one third of all short- and long-term work disability is related to MSDs [23]. For most MSDs there is a tradition to relate outcomes of function to the ICF, both in pure clinical settings and in vocational rehabilitation settings.

This section will focus on clinician-reported outcomes (CROMs) from a practical and clinical point of view. It will give an informal overview of the role of environmental and personal factors, activities, and participation. It will also offer suggestions on test batteries that can be used in different medical conditions.

Clinician-reported questionnaires have by tradition been used in many different medical areas for evaluation in vocational rehabilitation. As MSDs in most countries are a major cause for work disability, the experiences from this area are more abundant than from other diagnostic groups. Some of the examples are taken from the evaluation of different rehabilitation programs for MSDs, including rheumatic diseases.

21.4.1 CROMs in Rheumatoid Arthritis (RA)

Several attempts have been made over the past decade to include ICF in the evaluation of RA patients. The ICF has been shown to be useful and responsive in RA clinical settings and clinical trials [24]. The most widely used CROM is the Signals of Functional Impairment (SOFI) test which includes standardized observational functional information for patients with RA. It has been used in several clinical studies [25].

Efforts to use clinician-reported/observational outcome measures for RA have been reported. These include complex daily activities such as walking and stair climbing [26]. They also include sports and recreational activities or more demanding daily activities such as running or jumping. Some tests have been used in RA patients with lower limb disability to account for changes over time in addition [27].

The more commonly used tests for lower limbs include:

- Timed walking
- Timed stair climbing
- Timed chair stand

The more commonly used tests for upper limbs include [28]:

- GRIPPIT (hand strength)
- Shoulder, arm, and hand test
- Signals of Functional Impairment (SOFI)

Composite tests for both upper and lower limbs include:

- SOFI.
- Also tests on aerobic capacity can be seen as a CROM in RA [28].

The most frequently used outcome measure for functional assessment in RA has been the PROM measure, the Stanford Health Assessment Questionnaire (HAQ) [29]. In the last decade it has also been validated for and used for other rheumatic diseases. Only a few studies try to relate this PROM in RA to CROMs in RA, so for clinical purposes they have to be separately related to the ICF depending on what you aim to measure and describe [28].

21.4.2 CROMs in Ankylosing Spondylitis (AS)

The most frequently used outcome measures for functional assessment in AS have been the PROM measures included in the Bath Ankylosing Spondylitis Indices, i.e., BASDAI (disease activity), BASFI (function), and BASG-1 and BASG-2 (global health) [30]. However, the Bath indices also include one CROM, the Bath Ankylosing Spondylitis Metrology Index (BASMI) focusing on axial range of movement. CROMs mainly used for RA have also been used in AS such as:

For upper limbs [28]:

- GRIPPIT (hand strength)
- Shoulder, arm, and hand test
- SOFI

Composite tests for both upper and lower limbs:

- SOFI. [28]
- Also test on aerobic capacity can be seen as a CROM [31].

21.4.3 CROMs in Osteoarthritis (OA)

The most frequently used outcome measures for functional assessment in knee OA has been the PROM measures Western Ontario and McMaster Universities Osteoarthritis Index (WOMAC). This index has been extended with sports- and knee-related quality-of-life measures in the Knee injury and Osteoarthritis Outcomes Score (KOOS) [32] and the Hip disability and Osteoarthritis Outcomes Score (HOOS) for the hip. For measuring hand functions, the AUSCAN has been used in clinical trials.

Some attempts have been made in the past decade to include ICF in the evaluation of OA patients [33]. The use of CROMs for OA has been reported, including complex daily activities such as walking and climbing [33]. CROMs for OA could also include sports and recreational activities or more demanding daily activities such as running or jumping [33]. In addition, some tests have been used in OA patients with lower limb disability to account for changes over time [33].

The more commonly used tests in knee pain and knee OA include [33]:

- One-leg raising test (*)
- One-leg hop for distance test
- Knee-bending strength (*)
- Toe raising (*)
- Lateral step-up
- Knee bending/30 s (*)
- Joint position sense

The tests more focused on clinical use are marked with a (*). These tests are not thoroughly evaluated in vocational rehabilitation settings.

21.4.4 CROMs in Low Back Pain (LBP)

In disability evaluation of LBP, it is important to assess if the patient is at risk for developing long-term disability. The Örebro Musculoskeletal Pain Screening Questionnaire (ÖMPSQ) is available in a full version and a short version. These instruments are PROMs and are widely used. Since risk assessment for the development of long-term disability is important, new instruments have been developed in order to supply clinical practice with valid, reliable, and feasible instruments. A new instrument, the Start Back Screening Tool, has been developed in the UK [34]. Other PROMs are also used, such as the Work Ability Index (WAI) and Work Ability Index-Single Item Question.

Practical guidelines for the management of LBP in occupational health services have been developed in 2013 [35]. They were developed among a group of occupational health professionals and researchers. They suggest both a methodology and some reliable tests that are easy to use and implement in clinical practice.

Table 21.1 Overview of CROMs linked to different ICF components

Structure and function	Activity and participation	Environmental factors	Personal factors
Functional Capacity Evaluations (FCE)	Six-minute walk test	Quick Exposure Check (QEC)	
Aerobic capacity test	The PILE test	Assessment of Work Characteristics (AWC)	
Grip strength	Timed walking		
Shoulder, arm, and hand test	Timed stair climbing		
Signal of Functional Impairment (SOFI)	Timed chair stand		
	Patient-Specific Functional Scale (PSFS)		

Both PROMs and CROMs are recommended. CROMs that can be relevant in LBP disability evaluation and vocational rehabilitation are:

- Six-minute walk test
- Aerobic capacity evaluation
- PILE test
- Patient-Specific Functional Scale
- Quick Exposure Check

These instruments were described in Sects. 21.3.1, 21.3.2, 21.3.3, and 21.3.4.

When categorizing different instruments in relation to the ICF, the ICF linking rules can be used. These rules provide the opportunity to group either on domain or category level. Below, we provide a table of CROMs presented in this chapter (Table 21.1). The CROMs are linked to different ICF components.

21.5 Using the ICF in Clinical Follow-Up: Examples from a National Rehabilitation Program

In Sweden, a national rehabilitation program was introduced in 2009 to develop primary health-care-based vocational rehabilitation to improve work ability in patients on sick leave or at risk for long-term sick leave. This was a national initiative from the government and fully tax funded [36]. The program was aimed at patients with MSD and/or mild to moderate mental illness, which were the two patient groups dominating the sickness compensation programs in Sweden. The program included multimodal rehabilitation for patients with MSD and cognitive behavioral therapy for patients with mental illness. It had its full focus on vocational-oriented interventions in primary health care.

In southern Sweden, comprehensive preparations were conducted before the rehabilitation program started, in order to enable follow-up on results, quality assurance, bench marking, and research. The aim was also to ensure that different patient-related aspects were covered in relation to the ICF. For this purpose, a new observational methodology was used as CROM. It was also important that outcomes were easy to assess and to report. The follow-up included both CROMs and PROMs.

Functioning was assessed by a health-care professional (occupational therapist, nurse, psychologist, physical therapist or physician). Functional limitations were graded on five levels, from no limitation (1) to total limitation (5). The health-care professionals were also supposed to state whether functional limitations were confirmed by objective measures and to make a prognosis of the function.

For patients with MSD, three function categories were chosen: *b280 Sensation of pain*, *b710 Mobility in joint functions*, and *b455 Exercise tolerance functions*. These categories were chosen from the Comprehensive ICF Core Set for Chronic Widespread Pain [37]. For patients with mental illness, function categories were chosen from the Comprehensive ICF Core Set for Depression, *b134 Sleep functions* and *b164 Higher-level cognitive functions* [38]. In addition, *d240 Handling stress and other psychological demands* was included since patients with mental disorders often had stress-related problems.

The follow-up for patients with MSD and mental illness included PROMs covering function, activity, and participation. Also, the EuroQOL five dimensions questionnaire (EQ-5D) was used to evaluate changes in health-related quality of life and to be used in health economic evaluations. This instrument covers several function and activity categories [39]. The patients were asked to rate how they perceived their own work ability.

21.5.1 Research Report from Follow-Up on Functioning Assessment in Pain Rehabilitation

In the scientific report on multimodal rehabilitation in the national rehabilitation program, 406 patients were included [40]. Several outcomes were reported. The CROMs on function, evaluated by health professionals, were reported at the start and after rehabilitation. In the analysis, the patients were divided in three groups, based on sick leave and/or disability pension records the year prior to the rehabilitation program, no sick leave, part-time sick leave, and full-time sick leave. Within all three groups, all functions (pain, mobility in joint functions, and exercise tolerance functions) improved between start and after rehabilitation.

At the start, there were significant differences in *b280 Sensation of pain* between the group with no sick leave and/or disability pension in the year prior to rehabilitation and the group with full-time sick leave before rehabilitation. After rehabilitation, there were differences in pain between the group with no sick leave and part-time sick leave and also between the group with no sick leave and full-time sick leave. In the group with no sick leave before rehabilitation, a larger part of the patients improved concerning *b280 Sensation of pain* and *b710 Mobility in joint functions*.

In *b455 Exercise tolerance functions*, there were no differences between the groups in improvement, even though there were differences both at rehabilitation start and after rehabilitation between the groups.

When evaluating *b710 Mobility in joint functions*, there were differences in how this function improved, but differences were also seen at rehabilitation start and after rehabilitation.

The function categories that were chosen in the follow-up of the Swedish national rehabilitation program were easy to evaluate, and they provided a broad description of the patient's functioning. Since they were chosen from the Comprehensive ICF Core Set for Chronic Widespread Pain, they were seen as relevant and valid.

21.5.2 Research Report from Follow-Up on Functioning Assessments in Rehabilitation of Mental Illness

In a report on the results of the national rehabilitation program on patients with mental illness, the ICF function categories were evaluated at baseline and after completed rehabilitation [41]. These functions were reported as CROMs. Patients with no sick leave at rehabilitation start were compared with patients with sick leave. *b134 Sleep functions* were reported as improved, within both groups, but there were no differences in improvement between patients with and without sick leave. The levels of *b164 Higher-level cognitive functions* were also reported as significantly improved within both groups, and here a difference was seen when the groups were compared. The group with no sick leave at baseline improved more. When looking at *d240 Handling stress and other psychological demands*, improvement was seen within both groups, but there were no differences between the groups. Among patients with mental disorders, the selection of three different function categories from the Comprehensive ICF Core Set for Depression was easy to evaluate.

21.6 Conclusions and Recommendations

In summary, it is important to ensure that different components of ICF are covered already in the planning process on follow-up of interventions.

> Regardless the type of evaluation measures used (CROMs and/or PROMs), it is necessary to map how these measures correspond to the ICF. This is especially important in vocational rehabilitation and work disability evaluation, since environmental and also personal factors may play such an important role.

In the Swedish national rehabilitation program, we gained valuable experience from evaluating different function categories, based on the Comprehensive ICF Core Sets. We have experienced these categories as feasible and convenient. We have also, as described in Sect. 21.5.1, experienced that they are sensitive to changes and differences in clinical practice in primary care. Still, there is a need for further evaluating reliability aspects as well as the value as long-term prognostic factors.

References

1. World Health Organization. International statistical classification of diseases and related health problems, 10th Revision 2010. Available at: http://www.who.int/classifications/icd/en/
2. Pransky GS, Dempsey LG. Practical aspects of functional capacity evaluations. J Occup Rehabil. 2004;14:217–29.
3. Åstrand P-O, Rodahl K, Dahl HA, Strømme SB. Textbook of work physiology: physiological of bases of exercise. Champaign: Human Kinetics; 2003.
4. Strijk JE, Proper KI, van Tralen MM, Wijngaard P, van Mechelen W, van der Beek AJ. The role of work ability in the relationship between aerobic capacity and sick leave: a mediation analysis. Occup Environ Med. 2011;68:753–8.
5. Mathiowetz V, Weber K, Volland G, Kashman N. Reliability and validity of grip and pinch strength evaluations. J Hand Surg Am. 1984;9(2):222–9.
6. Nordenskiöld UM, Grimby G. Grip force in patients with rheumatoid arthritis and fibromyalgia and in healthy subjects. A study with the Grippit instrument. Scand J Rheumatol. 1993;22(1):14–9.
7. Massy-Westropp N, Health M, Rankin W, Aern M, Krishnan J, Hearn TC. Measuring grip strength in normal adults: reference ranges and a comparison of electronic and hydraulic instruments. J Hand Surg. 2004;29(3):514–9.
8. American Thoracic Society. ATS statement: guidelines for the six-minute-walk-test. Am J Respir Crit Care Med. 2003;166:111–7.
9. Nordeman L, Gunnarsson R, Mannerkorpi K. Prognostic factors for work ability in women with chronic low back pain consulting primary health care; a 2-year prospective longitudinal cohort study. Clin J Pain. 2014;28(1):65–72.
10. Haldorsen EM, Kronholm K, Skouen JS, Ursin H. Predictors for outcome of a multi-modal cognitive behavioural treatment program for low back pain patients – a 12-month follow-up study. Eur J Pain. 1998;2:293–307.
11. Rivilis I, van Eerd D, Cullen K, Cole DC, Irvin E, Tyson J, Mahood Q. Effectiveness of participatory ergonomic interventions on health outcomes: a systematic review. Appl Ergon. 2008;39(3):342–58.
12. Gross DP, Battie MC, Asante AK. The Patient-Specific Functional Scale: validity in worker's compensation claimants. Arch Phys Med Rehabil. 2008;89:1294–9.
13. Reference guide to Quick Exposure Check. Cited: 14 Apr 2014. Available at: http://www.lni.wa.gov/Safety/Topics/Ergonomics/pdfs/QECReferenceGuide.pdf
14. Sandqvist JL, Gullberg MT, Henriksson CM, Gerdle BU. Content validity and utility of the Assessment of Work Performance (AWP). Work. 2008;30(4):441–50.
15. Kielhofner G. A model of human occupations. 5th ed. Baltimore: Lippincott Williams & Wilkins; 2008.
16. Van Den Berg TI, Elders LA, De Zwart BC, Burdorf A. The effects of work-related and individual factors on the Work Ability Index: a systematic review. Occup Environ Med. 2009; 66: 211–20.

17. Lidwall U, Bergendorff S, Voss M, Marklund S. Long term sickness absence: changes in risk factors and the population at risk. Int J Occup Med Environ Health. 2009;22(2):157–68.
18. Bevan S, McGee R, Quadrello T. Fit for work? Musculoskeletal disorders in Sweden. The work foundation. 2009. www.fitforworkeurope.eu
19. Ndosi M, Bremander A, Hamnes B, Horton M, Kukkurainen ML, Machado P, Marques A, Meesters J, Stamm TA, Tennant A, de la Torre-Aboki J, Vliet Vlieland TP, Zangi HA, Hill J. Validation of the educational needs assessment tool as a generic instrument for rheumatic diseases in seven European countries. Ann Rheum Dis. 2013. Aug 6. [Epub ahead of print].
20. Brouwer S, Franche RL, Hogg-Johnson S, Lee H, Krause N, Shaw WS. Return-to-work self-efficacy: development and validation of a scale in claimants with musculoskeletal disorders. J Occup Rehabil. 2011;21:234–58.
21. Richard S, Dionne CE, Nouwen A. Self-efficacy and health locus of control: relationship to occupational disability among workers with back pain. J Occup Rehabil. 2011;21:421–30.
22. Labriola M, Lund T, Christiensen KB, Albertsen K, Bultmann U, Jensen JN, Villadsen E. Does self-efficacy predict return-to-work after sickness absence? A prospective study among 930 employees with sickness absence for three weeks or more. Work. 2007;29:233–8.
23. Hubertsson J, Englund M, Hallgårde U, Lidwall U, Löfvendahl S, Petersson IF. Sick leave patterns in common musculoskeletal disorders – a study of doctor prescribed sick leave. BMC Musculoskeletal; May 24, 2014;15:176.
24. Uhlig T, Moe R, Reinsberg S, Kvien TK, Cieza A, Stucki G. Responsiveness of the International Classification of Functioning, Disability and Health (ICF) Core Set for rheumatoid arthritis. Ann Rheum Dis. 2009;68(6):879–84. doi:10.1136/ard.2008.088708. Epub 2008 Jul 14.
25. Eberhardt KB, Svensson B, Moritz U. Functional assessment of early rheumatoid arthritis. Br J Rheumatol. 1988;27(5):364–71.
26. Bremander AB, Petersson IF, Roos EM. Validation of the Rheumatoid and Arthritis Outcome Score (RAOS) for the lower extremity. Health Qual Life Outcomes. 2003;1(1):55.
27. Eurenius E, Stenström CH. Physical activity, physical fitness, and general health perception among individuals with rheumatoid arthritis. Arthritis Rheum. 2005;53(1):48–55.
28. Hagel S, Lindqvist E, Petersson IF, Nilsson JÅ, Bremander A. Validation of outcome measurement instruments used in a multidisciplinary rehabilitation intervention for patients with chronic inflammatory arthritis – linkage to the International Classification of Functioning, Disability and Health (ICF), construct validity and responsiveness to change. J Rehabil Med. 2011;43(5):411–9.
29. Fries J. The hierarchy of quality-of-life assessment, the Health Assessment Questionnaire (HAQ), and issues mandating development of a toxicity index. Control Clin Trials. 1991;12 (4 Suppl):106S–17.
30. Haglund E, Bergman S, Petersson IF, Jacobsson L, Strömbeck B, Bremander A. Differences in physical activity patterns in patients with spondyloarthritis. Arthritis Care Res (Hoboken). 2013;65:492
31. Hagel S, Lindqvist E, Bremander A, Petersson IF. Team-based rehabilitation improves long-term aerobic capacity and health-related quality of life in patients with chronic inflammatory arthritis. Disabil Rehabil. 2010;32(20):1686–96.
32. Paradowski PT, Bergman S, Sundén-Lundius A, Lohmander LS, Roos EM. Knee complaints vary with age and gender in the adult population. Population-based reference data for the Knee injury and Osteoarthritis Outcome Score (KOOS). BMC Musculoskelet Disord. 2006;7: 38.
33. Bremander AB, Dahl LL, Roos EM. Validity and reliability of functional performance tests in meniscectomized patients with or without knee osteoarthritis. Scand J Med Sci Sports. 2007; 17(2):120–7.
34. Hill JC, et al. Comparison of stratified primary care management for low back pain with current best practice (STarT Back): a randomised controlled trial. Lancet. 2011;378(9802): 1560–71.

35. Jensen I, Wåhlin C, Dahlgren M, Hjalmársson L, Ziemelis S, Blomquist P, Hagström R, Berndtsson A, Nordrup E, Ivarsson Walther R, McKeogh M, Carlstedt-Duke B, Stigmar K, Rahm L, Eden L. Riktlinjer vid ländryggsbesvär. En sammanställning från Företagshälsans riktlinjegrupp 1/2013. Cited: 2 Apr 2014. Available at: http://www.foretagshalsor.se/sites/default/files/fsf/Filer/riktlinjer_vid_landryggsbesvar_utgava_2.pdf (in Swedish).
36. Rehabiliteringsgarantin – En rapport från Inspektionen för socialförsäkringen. Rapport 2012: 17, Stockholm. 2012;17:10–11 (Summary in English). www.inspsf.se
37. WHO. Comprehensive ICF core set for chronic wide-spread pain. Cited: 11 Mar 2014. Available at: http://www.icf-research-branch.org/download/finish/8-musculoskeletal-conditions/169-comprehensive-icf-core-sets-for-chronic-widespread-pain
38. WHO. Comprehensive ICF core set for depression. Cited: 4 Mar 2014. Available at: http://www.icf-research-branch.org/images/stories/ICF%20Core%20Sets%20Download/Comprehensive_and_Brief_ICF_Core_Sets_Depression.pdf
39. Cieza A, Stucki G. Content comparison of health-related quality of life (HRQOL) instruments based on the international classification of functioning, disability and health (ICF). Qual Life Res. 2005;14(5):12225–37.
40. Stigmar KE, Petersson IF, Jöud A, Grahn B. Promoting work ability in a structured national rehabilitation program in patients with musculoskeletal disorders: outcomes and predictors in a prospective cohort study. BMC Musculoskelet Disord. 2013;14:57.
41. Busch H, Bonnevier H, Hagberg J, Lohela Karlsson M, Bodin L, Norlund A, Jensen I. En nationell utvärdering av rehabiliteringsgarantins effekter på sjukfrånvaro och hälsa. Slutrapport del1. Enheten för interventions- och implementeringsforskning, Institutet för miljömedicin (IMM), Karolinska Institutet. Stockholm 2011 (in Swedish).

Chapter 22
ICF-Based Tools in Rehabilitation Toward Return to Work: Facilitating Inter-professional Communication and Comprehensive Documentation

Melissa Selb, Andrea Glässel, and Reuben Escorpizo

22.1 Introduction

One of the most important overall goals of rehabilitation with regard to community integration is return-to-work, an outcome that has been associated with better health [1–3]. In spinal cord injury (SCI), employment is related to greater life satisfaction, higher level of activities, and health [1–4]. Employment and education are two of the main factors that determine outcome after SCI in terms of quality of life [5–7].

Vocational rehabilitation programs play a key role in bringing persons with a health condition back to work while encouraging employment retention. Escorpizo and colleagues defined vocational rehabilitation as a multi-professional evidence-based approach that is provided in different settings, services, and activities to working age individuals with health-related impairments, limitations, or restrictions with work functioning and whose primary aim is to optimize work participation [8]. In an earlier paper, Selander described vocational rehabilitation as "medical, psychological, social and occupational activities aiming to re-establish among

---

This chapter is an extended adaptation of the publication *Glässel A, Rauch A, Selb M, Emmenegger K, Lückenkemper M, and Escorpizo R. A case study on the application of the International Classification of Functioning, Disability, and Health (ICF)-based tools for vocational rehabilitation in spinal cord injury. Work. 2012; 41(4): 465–474* with permission from IOS Press.

M. Selb (✉) • A. Glässel
Swiss Paraplegic Research, Guido-Zäch-Strasse 4, 6207 Nottwil, Switzerland

ICF Research Branch, WHO CC FIC in Germany (DIMDI), Nottwil, Switzerland
e-mail: melissa.selb@paraplegie.ch

R. Escorpizo
Swiss Paraplegic Research, Guido-Zäch-Strasse 4, 6207 Nottwil, Switzerland

ICF Research Branch, WHO CC FIC in Germany (DIMDI), Nottwil, Switzerland

Department of Rehabilitation and Movement Science, The University of Vermont, Burlington, VT, USA

R. Escorpizo et al. (eds.), *Handbook of Vocational Rehabilitation and Disability Evaluation*, Handbooks in Health, Work, and Disability, DOI 10.1007/978-3-319-08825-9_22

sick or injured people with previous work history, their working capacity and prerequisites for returning to the labour market" [9].

Vocational rehabilitation programs including vocational reintegration aim to enhance adjustments to life following SCI by equipping the client with the skills and resources required for community life [1, 2]. SCI-specialized vocational rehabilitation programs address generic vocational exploration, evaluation, counseling, training, job placement and transportation options, accessibility, and overcoming architectural and financial barriers to gainful employment after the injury [5]. Clients with SCI benefit from these special vocational rehabilitation programs by improving functional independence and employment [10].

> Vocational rehabilitation helps persons with a health condition to return to work and stay on the job by optimizing the person's skills and resources required for vocational reintegration and community life.

Multiple factors were associated with successful vocational rehabilitation or return-to-work programs [11, 12]. To address the multiple factors in vocational rehabilitation, an inter-professional approach is needed to enable people with health conditions to achieve and maintain optimal functioning required for vocational integration or reintegration (e.g., in competitive employment) which could then facilitate participation in other aspects of life [13].

SCI is an example in which clients are faced with a multitude of health-related problems with respect to body functions and body structures, activities and participation, and environmental factors (barriers) [14] and where an inter-professional approach is important for optimizing vocational rehabilitation outcomes [15]. Hence, a comprehensive description of the client's functioning status is an essential element to sound client-oriented vocational rehabilitation management. Since the role of the individual client in the vocational rehabilitation process is important for successful job reintegration, the assessment of client expectations by an inter-professional team is the basis for planning vocational intervention [12, 16].

> An inter-professional approach and a comprehensive description of the client's functioning status are essential for successful client-oriented vocational rehabilitation management.

22.1.1 International Classification of Functioning, Disability, and Health (ICF)

As described in Chap. 2, the International Classification of Functioning, Disability, and Health (ICF) is the conceptual framework and reference classification developed by the World Health Organization (WHO) to describe "functioning and disability"

[17]. The ICF provides functioning domains in the form of 1424 ICF categories that are hierarchically organized under the ICF components of body functions and body structures, activities and participation, and environmental factors. Personal factors are yet to be classified in the ICF. The components are then further organized into chapters, e.g., Neuromusculoskeletal and movement-related functions (Chap. 7 *under body functions*), Structures related to movement (Chap. 7 *under body structures*), Mobility (Chap. 4 *under activities and participation*), and Products and technology (Chap. 1 *under environmental functions*). Each chapter consists of ICF categories with varying levels of categorization; when going from the second to the fourth level, the category's definition becomes more detailed.

The ICF framework offers rehabilitation professionals the possibility of building a common understanding across professional disciplines and settings based on a standardized language to describe the spectrum of domains of functioning and disability [17].

> The ICF facilitates inter-professional collaboration by offering rehabilitation professionals a common framework for exchanging information about a client's functioning.

22.1.2 ICF Core Sets

The implementation of the ICF in daily practice can pose a challenge for rehabilitation professionals [18, 19]. The ICF has been recommended as a useful framework to aid communication and structure rehabilitation plans; to clarify team roles, i.e., "who does what" within the team, to avoid redundancy in interventions; and to aid in clinical reasoning [20]. To facilitate the practical and feasible use of the ICF in daily practice, ICF Core Sets have been developed [21, 22]. An ICF Core Set refers to a short list of ICF categories that are considered relevant for describing individuals with a given health condition (e.g., SCI) or within a health-related context or setting (e.g., vocational rehabilitation) [23]. ICF Core Sets are developed following an established, evidence-based scientific process [24] that involves conducting four preparatory studies, i.e., a systematic literature review, a qualitative study (either focus groups and/or individual semi-structured interviews), a web-based expert survey, and an empirical multicenter study. Based on the results from these four studies as well as their knowledge and experience with the particular health condition or health-related context, experts, i.e., health and other professionals and clients themselves, decide during an international consensus conference which ICF categories to include in the ICF Core Set.

The comprehensive and brief versions of the ICF Core Set for vocational rehabilitation addresses the most relevant problems experienced by persons who are engaged in a vocational rehabilitation program irrespective of the health condition and setting in which vocational rehabilitation is provided [23].

The comprehensive set is generally designed for inter- and multidisciplinary settings and the brief set as a practical tool for single discipline clinical encounters and constitutes the minimum data set [23–26].

22.1.3 Using the ICF in Vocational Rehabilitation

The versatility of the ICF, specifically in the form of ICF Core Sets, is evident in how it can be employed in vocational rehabilitation. A Comprehensive ICF Core Set for vocational rehabilitation consisting of 90 ICF categories was developed in 2010. Out of the 90 Comprehensive ICF Core Set categories, 13 ICF categories were selected for the Brief ICF Core for vocational rehabilitation. These ICF Core Sets could serve as a guide on measures that help clinicians and researchers implement optimal rehabilitation programs for individuals of working age with limited or restricted work participation due to disease, injury, or health-related event [23]. For example, the 13 categories of the brief set provided the starting point for developing the Work Rehabilitation Questionnaire (WORQ), a questionnaire to assess and evaluate functioning in vocational rehabilitation settings (see Chap. 23 for more details). Another example of applying the ICF and ICF Core Sets in vocational rehabilitation is the use of the ICF-based documentation tools that correspond to the "Rehab-Cycle" model [27–29].

> The ICF's utility in vocational rehabilitation is enhanced by the Comprehensive and Brief ICF Core Sets for vocational rehabilitation, short lists of the most relevant ICF categories that can guide client assessment and rehabilitation plannning.

22.1.4 ICF-Based Documentation Tools

The rehabilitation cycle or "Rehab-Cycle" integrates the ICF in an inter-professional rehabilitation management approach that can help rehabilitation professionals to structure and coordinate their tasks from the identification of the problem to the planning of intervention. This iterative process includes four key elements (1) *assessment*, (2) *assignment*, (3) *intervention*, and (4) *evaluation*. For each element, ICF-based documentation tools have been developed taking into account the ICF Core Sets. These tools aim to facilitate the documentation and planning of rehabilitation services. The tools include the *ICF Assessment Sheet, ICF Categorical Profile, ICF Intervention Table,* and the *ICF Evaluation Display* (see Fig. 22.1) [18, 27] and are also available online (www.icf-casestudies.org) [30].

The *ICF Assessment Sheet* helps rehabilitation professionals to understand the client's functioning and to identify the needs to be addressed in rehabilitation. It provides an overview of the client's functioning state with input from both the client

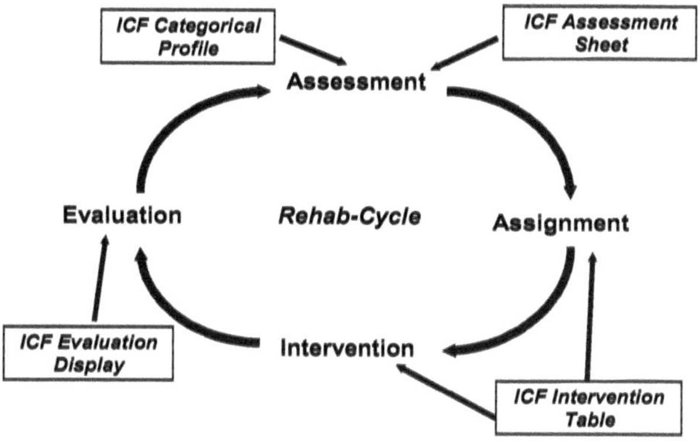

Fig. 22.1 Integration of ICF documentation tools into the Rehab-Cycle [17, 29]

and the rehabilitation professional [31]. Considering the client's own perspective of his/her functioning problems enriches the information provided by the rehabilitation professional and can later guide intervention planning [32]. See Table 22.1.

To facilitate the identification of intervention targets that are related to common goals identified by the client and the rehabilitation professional, an *ICF Categorical Profile* is generated. The ICF Categorical Profile serves as the central source of information for the rehabilitation team for intervention planning. It is generally set up using a suitable ICF Core Set in combination with a rating of the respective ICF categories using ICF qualifiers. ICF qualifiers are used to rate the extent of a problem for each ICF category by estimating the level of difficulties ("0" = no problem; "1" = mild problem; "2" = moderate problem; "3" = severe problem; "4" = complete problem). Environmental factors can be rated either as a barrier or as a facilitator, and in some cases an environmental factor can be rated as both a barrier and a facilitator [17], e.g., a spouse can be a facilitator by providing essential care but can also be a barrier if this care becomes too sheltering and prevents the person from becoming more independent. Although personal factors are not yet classified in the ICF, they have an influence on the client's functioning in terms of the rehabilitation process [33, 34], including vocational rehabilitation [35]. Thus, personal factors are rated as having a positive, neutral, or negative influence on the client's functioning. See Table 22.2.

To facilitate the coordination of interventions, roles, and resources within an interprofessional team in vocational rehabilitation, the *ICF Intervention Table* provides a comprehensive overview of all the intervention targets (represented by ICF categories), the interventions, and the corresponding rehabilitation professional who is assigned to address each intervention target. More than one rehabilitation professional may be assigned to one intervention target. The ICF Intervention Table also displays the expected goals (goal value) for each target. See Table 22.3.

The *ICF Evaluation Display* based on ICF Core Set categories illustrates the results of the assessment and reexamination of the client's functioning. It displays long-term and short-term goals and reflects the extent of a problem the client is experiencing in a particular ICF category as rated with ICF qualifiers before (first value) and after intervention (final value). A goal value is defined, in order to determine whether a goal has been achieved following an intervention (see Tables 22.2, 22.3, and 22.4).

Table 22.1 ICF assessment sheet

	Body functions/ structure	Activities and participation	
Client	I have some pain when moving my legs	I can't sit without using my arms to prop up	I used to go motorcycling, play golf
	I have spasticity, in particular when moving myself	Moving with the wheel-chair is improving, but I still have problems over-coming obstacles	I want to do some kind of sports
	I still get fungal skin infection	I am now able to dress my lower extremities	I like meeting my friends (at least once a week)
	I am able to manage my bladder and control defection well	I take care of my medica-tion and treatment schedule	I want to go home for the weekend
	I have problems with my body balance		I want to work again but I can't imagine working at the com-puter all day
			I am willing to learn a new profession
	Body functions/ structures	Activities and participation	
Health professionals	Power of isolated mus-cles (arms)	Changing basic body positions	Remunerative employment
	Power of muscles in the lower half of the body	Maintaining a sitting position	
	Power of muscles of the trunk	Moving around in different locations	
	Supportive functions of the arms	Moving around using equipment	
	Structure of areas of the skin – at risk	Driving motorized vehicles	
		Caring for the skin	
		Regulating urination	
		Regulating defection	
	Environmental factors	Personal factors	
Health pro-fessionals and client	Wheelchair does not fit ideally	26 years old, male	Is able to cope with health situation
	Car is not wheelchair adapted	Sharing a flat with a friend	Has a strong will to be able to walk again
	Accident insurance is paying for health services	Trained as a salesperson for home electronics, but worked as a mover before accident	Willing to learn a new profession
	Parents support him	Very motivated to clarify vocational future	
	Friends support him		
	Health professionals		

Table 22.2 ICF categorical profile

Goal definition and achievement for vocational rehabilitation		Assessment (5 months post-trauma)		
Goal achievement		0 1 2 3 4		
Client Goal: Vocational reintegration, engaging in a remunerative employment				0
Long-term Goal (LTG): Evaluation and decision on new employment prospect				0
Short-term Goal 1 (STG1): Employment-specific education or training				1
Short-term Goal 2 (STG2): Occupational stress tests in new workplace situation				1
ICF categories		**ICF Qualifier† (First value)**	**Goal Relation**	**Expected Goal value**
ICF Code	**ICF title**	+4 +3 +2 +1 0 1 2 3 4		
b130	Energy and drive functions		STG1/2	1
b280	Sensation of pain		STG1/2	0
b455	Exercise tolerance functions		STG1/2	0
b730*	Muscle power functions		STG1/2	1
b810*	Protective functions of the skin		STG1/2	0
d155	Acquiring skills		STG1/2	2
d177*	Making decisions		STG1/2	2
d240	Handling stress and other psychological demands		LTG	1
d410*	Changing basic body positions		STG1/2	1
d415*	Maintaining a sitting position		STG1/2	2
d430*	Lifting and carrying objects		STG1/2	1
d465*	Moving around using equipment		STG1/2	1
d475*	Driving		STG1/2	2
d720	Complex interpersonal interactions		--	--
d825*	Vocational training		LTG	1
d840*	Apprenticeship		STG1/2	1
d845	Acquiring, keeping and terminating a job		LTG	2
d850	Remunerative employment		LTG	0
d855	Non-remunerative employment		--	--
e115*	Assistive products and technology for personal use in daily living		STG1/2	+4
e120*	Assistive products and technology for personal mobility.		STG1/2	+2
e310	Immediate family		STG1/2	+3
e330	People in positions of authority		STG1/2	+3
e580	Health systems, services and policies		--	--
e590	Labour and employment services, systems and policies		LTG	+4
Influence of Personal Factors				
		positive neutral negative		
PF	Coping with health situation		STG 1/2	positive
PF	Motivated to clarify vocational situation		LTG, STG 1	positive
PF	Willing to learn new profession		LTG, STG 1	positive

*ICF categories added from the Comprehensive ICF Core Set for vocational rehabilitation. † ICF qualifiers ranged from 0 (no problem) to 4 (complete problem) in the body functions, body structures, and activities and participation and from 4 (complete barrier) to +4 (complete facilitator) in the environmental factors. In personal factors, the positive, neutral, or negative influence on the client's functioning is marked.

Table 22.3 ICF intervention table

	Intervention targets		Intervention	Psych	OT	SW	Voc trainer	Phys	PT	Nurse	First value	Goal value
Body function	b130	Energy and drive functions	Psychological therapy	x							2	1
	b280[a]	Sensation of pain	Medication					x			3	0
			Manual therapy						x			
	b455	Exercise tolerance functions	Movement training						x		3	0
	b730[a]	Muscle power functions	Training with equipment						x		3	1
	b810[a]	Protective functions of the skin	Instruction for skin control							x	1	0
Activities and participation	d155	Acquiring skills	Skill training		x		x				3	2
	d177[a]	Making decisions	Counseling	x		x					4	2
	d240	Handling stress and other psychological demands	Counseling	x							3	1
	d410[a]	Changing basic body positions	Training of changing body positions		x				x	x	3	1
	d415[a]	Maintaining a sitting position	Reaction training						x		3	2
	d430[a]	Lifting and carrying objects	Training with equipment						x		3	1
	d465[a]	Moving around using equipment	Wheelchair training						x		3	1
			Instruction of "Swiss trac®"		x							
	d475[a]	Driving	Counseling for adapted devices		x						4	2
			Driving lessons		x							
	d825[a]	Vocational training	Vocational training		x		x				2	1
	d840[a]	Apprenticeship	Counseling/instruction				x				3	1

	d845	Acquiring, keeping and terminating a job	Counseling/instruction				x				4	2
	d850	Remunerative employment	Vocational testing and training, coaching/liaison with former employer	x		x	x				4	0
Environmental factors	e115[a]	Assistive products and technology for personal use in daily living	Choice of assistive devices		x		x				2	+4
	e120[a]	Assistive products and technology for personal mobility …	Choice of wheelchair		x						2	+2
	e310	Immediate family	Counseling/ instruction	x				x		x	+2	+3
	e330	People in positions of authority	Coaching/Liaison with former employer			x	x				+2	+3
	e590	Labour and employment services, systems and policies	Counseling			x	x				+2	+4

Influence of personal factors

		Intervention targets	Intervention	Responsible Professional	First Value			Goal Value		
					Pos.	*Neutral*	*Neg.*	*Pos*	*Neutral*	*Neg.*
Personal factors	*PF*	Coping with health situation	Psychological therapy	Psych	x			x		
	PF	Motivated to clarify vocational situation	Counseling/instruction	Voc trainer, Psych	x			x		
	PF	Willing to learn new profession	Counseling/instruction Skill training	Voc trainer, OT	x			x		

[a]ICF categories added from the Comprehensive ICF Core Set for vocational rehabilitation

Abbreviations: *OT* occupational therapist, *Phys* physician, *PT* physical therapist, *Psych* psychologist, SW *social worker*, *Voc trainer* vocational trainer, *EF* environmental factors, *PF* personal factors

Table 22.4 ICF evaluation display comprises initial assessment

ICF Code	ICF title	Interventions	Assessment (5 months post-trauma): ICF Qualifier† (+4 +3 +2 +1 0 1 2 3 4)	Expected Goal value	Evaluation (7 months post-trauma): ICF Qualifier† (+4 +3 +2 +1 0 1 2 3 4)	Achieved Goal value
Goal definition and achievement for vocational rehabilitation						
Goal achievement						
Client Goal: Vocational reintegration, engaging in a remunerative employment				0		–
Long-term Goal: Evaluation and decision on new employment prospect				0		✓✓
Short-term Goal 1: Employment-specific education or training				1		✓✓
Short-term Goal 2: Occupational stress tests in new workplace situation				1		✓✓
	Long-term Goal					
d240	Handling stress and other psychological demands	Counseling		1		✓✓
d825*	Vocational training	Vocational testing & training		1		✓✓
d845	Acquiring, keeping and terminating a job	Counseling / instruction		2		–
d850	Remunerative employment	Vocational training, Coaching/ Liaison with former employer		0		–
e590	Labour and employment services, systems and policies	Counseling		+4		✓
	Short-term Goal 1/2					
b130	Energy and drive functions	Psychological therapy		1		✓✓
b280	Sensation of pain	Medication / Manual therapy		0		✓
b455	Exercise tolerance functions	Movement training		0		✓✓
b730*	Muscle power functions	Training with equipment		1		✓
b810*	Protective functions of the skin	Instruction for skin control		0		✓✓
d155	Acquiring skills	Skill training		2		✓✓
d177*	Making decisions	Counseling		2		✓✓
d410*	Changing basic body positions	Training of changing body positions		1		✓✓
d415*	Maintaining a sitting position	Reaction training		2		✓✓

d465*	Moving around using equipment	Wheelchair training / Instruction of 'Swiss trac®'		1		✓✓
d475*	Driving	Counseling for adapted devices / Driving lessons		2		✓✓
d840*	Apprenticeship	Counseling / instruction		1		✓✓
e115*	Assistive products and technology for personal use in daily living	Choice of assistive devices		+4		✓
e120*	Assistive products and technology for personal mobility.	Choice of wheelchair		+2		✓✓
e310	Immediate family	Counseling / instruction		+3		✓✓
e330	People in positions of authority	Coaching/ Liaison with former employer		+3		✓✓

Influence of Personal Factors														
Goal definition and achievement for vocational rehabilitation			Assessment (5 months post-trauma)						Evaluation (7 months post-trauma)					
			First value			Expected Goal value			Final value			Achieved Goal value		
			Pos.	Neutr	Neg	Pos.	Neutr	Neg	Pos.	Neutr	Neg	Pos.	Neutr	Neg
PF	Coping with health situation	Psychological therapy												
PF	Motivated to clarify vocational situation	Counseling / instruction												
PF	Willing to learn new profession	Counseling / instruction, Skill training												

*ICF categories added from the Comprehensive ICF Core Set for vocational rehabilitation.

† ICF qualifiers ranged from 0 (no problem) to 4 (complete problem) in the components of body functions, body structures, and activities and participation and from 4 (complete barrier) to +4 (complete facilitator) in the environmental factors. In personal factors, the positive, neutral, or negative influence on the individual's functioning is marked.

The following case vignette of a person with SCI illustrates the application of the ICF-based tools in a vocational rehabilitation program [30, 36].

22.2 Vignette

22.2.1 Case History

Martin was a 26-year-old male who sustained a traumatic SCI as a result of a motorcycle accident. The injury was classified as complete paraplegia, at the seventh thoracic vertebra. Prior to the injury, Martin worked as a mover, although he was originally trained as a salesman for home electronics. He shared an apartment located in the suburbs with a friend and spent his leisure time riding his motorcycle, playing golf, and socializing with his friends and family. After the accident and after Martin's spine was surgically stabilized, he was discharged to the early post-acute inpatient unit of an SCI center where an inter-professional rehabilitation program was initiated. After several months, Martin achieved a degree of independence with self-care, respiration and sphincter management, and mobility as reflected in an improved Spinal Cord Independence Measure (SCIM) score [37, 38]. Four months following his accident, Martin's vocational situation was still uncertain. It was clear, however, that he would be unable to go back to his pre-accident job as a mover. Planning for post-rehabilitation activities had begun, and Martin conveyed his concern [30, 36]:

> "The insecurity of my future situation is my biggest problem right now; it also defines my most important goals. When I think about leaving the rehabilitation centre, there is so much that is unclear – my work, my living situation. It's a real stress for me".

22.2.2 Assessment

The nature of the client's previous job, whether requiring mental or physical activity, and his acquired resources do not only help to determine the type and duration of the vocational rehabilitation program but also whether the client's return to work can be realized within the client's inpatient or outpatient care program. The first step in the Rehab-Cycle is usually the initial assessment that takes place shortly after admission to the SCI center using the ICF Assessment Sheet. However, in the case of Martin, the ICF Assessment Sheet displayed in Table 22.1 is the one that was completed 4 months after admission to the SCI center and that focuses on the relevant information for vocational rehabilitation. Table 22.1 shows statements made by Martin ordered according to the ICF components of body functions and structures, activities, and participation. Likewise the combined input from the rehabilitation ("health") professionals in the inter-professional vocational rehabilitation team (occupational therapist, physical therapist, nurse, vocational counselor, physician) is structured according to the same ICF components. Table 22.1 also shows information on the environmental and personal factors that were provided by Martin's vocational rehabilitation team that also encompassed the assessments of the social worker and psychologist involved and reflected Martin's statements related to environmental and personal factors.

The second step in the Rehab-Cycle's assessment phase is obtaining a comprehensive functioning profile using the ICF Categorical Profile. For Martin, the information from the ICF Assessment Sheet as well as results of clinical tests and measures were translated into the corresponding ICF categories from the Brief ICF Core Set for vocational rehabilitation as well as additional categories from the Comprehensive ICF Core Set. Categories from the Comprehensive ICF Core Set are added when the ICF categories of the Brief ICF Core Set do not completely reflect the results. For example, applying the client-oriented "Canadian Occupational Performance Measure" (COPM) [39, 40] limitations in *d430 Lifting and carrying objects* due to impaired muscle power functions (examined with Manual Muscle Testing [41] and Jamar Dynamometer for hand function [42]) were identified that may have an impact on Martin's vocational outcome. The category *d430* was added to the list of categories for the ICF Categorical Profile, since *d430* is included in the Brief ICF Core Set for vocational rehabilitation. To complete the functioning profile, the responsible team member then rated each ICF category using an ICF qualifier.

For a prognosis based on the assessment, the vocational rehabilitation team, together with Martin, defined several goals. Martin indicated that his primary goals are to work and live independently. The long-term goal (LTG) expected to be achieved at the end of the rehabilitation program was the evaluation and the decision to be made on a new employment prospect. In addition, the vocational rehabilitation team defined two short-term goals (STGs): STG1 focused on employment-specific education and STG2 on performance of several occupational stress tests in a new workplace situation. All three goals were then correlated to Martin's functioning status presented in each ICF category listed. Considering the functioning profile along with the identified goals, Martin and his vocational rehabilitation team defined the goal value or ICF qualifier for each of the ICF categories to target with interventions in his vocational rehabilitation program. For three categories of the Brief ICF Core Set for vocational rehabilitation (*d720 Complex interpersonal interactions, d855 Non-remunerative employment and e580 Health systems, services and policies*), no goal value was defined as they were seen as either non-problematic or minimally relevant to the vocational rehabilitation process and thus not targeted during Martin's vocational rehabilitation.

22.2.3 *Assignment and Intervention*

The next phase in the Rehab-Cycle is the assignment phase, during which the tasks and responsibilities are assigned to the rehabilitation team members. To facilitate this process, the ICF Intervention Table is created. The ICF Intervention Table in

Table 22.3 outlines Martin's intervention plan and the corresponding responsibilities of team members as defined by the vocational rehabilitation team. The use of the ICF Intervention Table makes overlapping interventions transparent. The ICF Intervention Table also included the assessment rating (first value) at 5 months post-admission and the goal value identified on Martin's ICF Categorical Profile.

Further education in STG1 encompassed an individually adapted vocational rehabilitation program that also included vocational counseling and testing *e590 Labor and employment services, systems and policies* aimed at identifying interests and transferable skills and strengthening Martin's ability to make concrete decisions about returning to work. Through STG2, various occupational stress tests conducted by the vocational counselor and occupational therapist exposed Martin to diverse job situations to test his physical, technical, intellectual, and communication skills as well as probe into his vocational interests.

Intensive training with the occupational and physical therapists enabled him to more optimally propel his wheelchair as described by the ICF category *d465 Moving around using equipment,* a prerequisite for accessing a workplace.

To address the intervention target *d475 Driving* – an activity that will facilitate Martin's access to a future workplace – a certified instructor under supervision of an occupational therapist was assigned to provide driving lessons using an adapted vehicle.

In a collaborative effort between occupational therapist and vocational counselor, a variety of activities (e.g., a typing course and computer training) were suggested to assist Martin in *d155 Acquiring skills.* Although he disliked working with computers, his past experience in these courses helped to promote Martin's self-motivation and self-confidence and to clearly define areas in which he had particular interest. The vocational counselor and social worker worked together with Martin's former employer (i.e., ICF category *e330 People in positions of authority*) to provide coaching in the workplace and discuss possible arrangements for return to work (*d825 Vocational training*; *d845 Acquiring, keeping and terminating a job;* and *d850 Remunerative employment*) including negotiating for financial support from the insurance company. In addition, psychological counseling focused on improving his interaction with persons in his environment such as his family (*e310 Immediate family*).

22.2.4 Evaluation

To identify changes in Martin's level of functioning, a reassessment of his functioning state corresponding to intervention goals was performed before his discharge from the SCI center. These results were rated again using the qualifier scale and entered into the ICF Evaluation Display. See Table 22.4.

Martin tested different alternatives for a new profession. His decision regarding a new employment prospect (LTG) was closely related with determining his interests and transferable skills and hands-on experiences during his individualized training program (STG1). The interventions contributed to expanding his skills like using a computer or improving his functioning, e.g., improving access to his future workplace by independently maneuvering his wheelchair. At the end of the vocational rehabilitation program, Martin achieved his LTG by deciding on a new career as a vocational coach. Not only did vocational counseling provide essential support in managing the vocational rehabilitation process, it helped Martin to organize all the information and experiences gained during his vocational rehabilitation in order to make a decision about his vocational future.

At the *personal factors* level, the psychologist identified ambition and strong coping abilities as Martin's strengths, which positively influenced *d240 Handling stress and other psychological demands*. According to the psychologist, Martin's steadfast interest in his future and his high motivation *b130 Energy and drive functions* enabled him to achieve personal and vocational goals. Having a clear job prospect was important for building his self-esteem and life satisfaction. With Martin's determination and positive attitude during his inpatient rehabilitation, the inter-professional team succeeded in helping him accept and cope with his situation.

22.3 Implications for Daily Use

Vocational rehabilitation is a key enabling process for individuals whose work participation may have been hampered by a health condition. We have illustrated the complex effects and multiple problems associated with SCI and the challenges they pose on return-to-work. Because of the complexity, multiple professionals are involved in facilitating effective vocational rehabilitation. In this case of Martin, we employed the ICF as a reference framework to better capture and address the complexities surrounding vocational rehabilitation and SCI.

22.3.1 Structure for Comprehensive Assessment and Intervention Planning

The case of a person with SCI engaged in vocational rehabilitation showed how client-oriented and comprehensive ICF-based documentation tools could be integrated within a vocational rehabilitation program following a systematic and comprehensive approach based on the Rehab-Cycle. The ICF was used to systematically structure the evaluation of the client and determine the appropriate care [18]. Moreover, the process as described in this chapter supports the use of existing standard measures to assess an ICF category. For example, established client-oriented measures such as the COPM are compatible with and complementary to the ICF [39, 40, 43, 44].

Although each of the ICF-based documentation tools addressed individual aspects of the Rehab-Cycle, the information provided on one documentation tool was instrumental in completing the other documentation tool. For example, the functioning profile and the goals set on the ICF Categorical Profile (one tool) was required to decide on the interventions and team roles indicated on the ICF Intervention Sheet (another tool). Likewise without the first value (or ICF qualifier rating) from the ICF Categorical Profile, the vocational rehabilitation team would not have been able to determine whether or not the client achieved the goals that were set.

The ICF Evaluation Sheet offers a snapshot of the changes in the client's functioning, thereby contributing to further intervention planning and decision-making regarding the next steps toward the ultimate goal of optimal vocational reintegration. Client-identified problems and factors are important for developing a problem-solving strategy for people with disabilities that can guide intervention and rehabilitation goals resulting in improved functioning [32].

While employing all four documentation tools would be the all-inclusive and most comprehensive approach to the Rehab-Cycle, depending on the purpose and time constraints for documentation, it might be of consideration to use only some of the documentation tools, for example, the ICF Intervention Table and the ICF Evaluation Display. The ICF Evaluation Display already encompasses essential information from the ICF Assessment Sheet and the ICF Categorical Profile [30], and the ICF Intervention Table displays the interventions and goals that are assigned to different team members.

22.3.2 Multidisciplinary and Inter-professional Communication

In client-oriented management, the conceptual framework of the ICF helps to facilitate and guide communication and care for the client, clarify roles of team members, and aid in clinical reasoning [20, 45]. In this case, the ICF-based documentation tools encouraged inter-professional communication in that they required the rehabilitation professionals involved to identify relevant functioning domains based on discipline-specific assessments (ICF Assessment Sheet), to decide on a mutual rating for each ICF category and set shared goals (ICF Categorical Profile), to determine the appropriate interventions and allocate the respective responsibilities for conducting the interventions (ICF Intervention Sheet), and to discuss and conclude goal achievement (ICF Evaluation Display). The set of ICF categories employed in the assessment, intervention planning, and reevaluation provides a common language for the various rehabilitation professionals involved.

In addition, the ICF-based tools facilitate transparent documentation and information exchange between the rehabilitation professionals in the team. Specifically, the ICF Intervention Table serves as an overview for the inter-professional vocational rehabilitation team, and clearly displaying where the responsibilities for an intervention target including the targets that are shared. For example, with *d465 Moving around using equipment*, the physical therapist is responsible for wheelchair training while the occupational therapist is responsible for instructing the client on using the "Swiss Trac®", a device that attaches to a wheelchair and pulls it over a variety of surfaces [46]. Having an overview also helps to avoid unnecessary redundancy of resources or gaps in services through miscommunication. Overall transparency in documentation and information exchange leads to a more manageable rehabilitation process [30].

Of course, applying the ICF in an inter-professional context like vocational rehabilitation can be time-consuming – all team members would have to learn the ICF framework and classification system and then adopt the ICF in patient management. This was a common experience of some neurorehabilitation clinics that implemented the ICF [47]. Although perhaps time-consuming, the implementation of the ICF in rehabilitation management or vocational rehabilitation should still be encouraged. An online open-access tool for learning the ICF is available [19, 48] that can offer a quick way to gain basic knowledge about the ICF framework and classification. ICF-based documentation tools can become attractive for daily practice only when the employment of these tools is seen as making administration and documentation procedures more efficient [19]. Escorpizo et al. proposed that the additional amount of time spent may also lead to realizing the added value of ICF-based documentation and evaluation, which will in turn favor the collaboration within an inter-professional team [19].

The Rehab-Cycle based ICF documentation tools – Assessment Sheet, Categorical Profile, Intervention Table and Evaluation Display – can help structure comprehensive assessment and rehabilitation planning, promote inter-professional communication and avoid redundancy by clarifying team roles and responsibilities and evaluate if rehabilitation goals have been achieved.

22.3.3 ICF for Training Rehabilitation Professionals

In addition to the aforementioned benefits for implementing the ICF and ICF-based tools in rehabilitation management, specifically for vocational rehabilitation, ICF-based tools can also be employed in teaching the structure and the various steps of the rehabilitation process to students of various health professions [49]. For students or beginners it can often be difficult to break down the complexity of the working steps on which an inter-professional rehabilitation setting is based. The ICF-based tools applied in each phase of the Rehab-Cycle can help students understand the process better. Moreover, the ICF-based tools can support students in strengthening their clinical decision-making skills by reminding them to ask the following questions: *What aspects of functioning are relevant to my patient or client? Which assessment instruments can measure these relevant aspects adequately? Which of these functioning aspects am I able to address alone and which require help from my supervisors or colleagues? What treatment goals can address these functioning aspects, and in addition to me who from an inter-professional team should work on these goals? Was my treatment successful or not? Do I have to work more on any of the agreed treatment goals?* Finally, *which treatment techniques and strategies have proven most effective for addressing these goals?*

The Rehab-Cycle based ICF documentation tools can be integrated in the training of rehabilitation professionals to help explain the working steps of the inter-professional rehabilitation process and give students reminders of what to consider in making clinical decisions.

There are already some inter-professional training programs that have integrated the ICF-based tools in their educational strategy for teaching physical, occupational and speech therapists in the ICF and in rehabilitation management, e.g., University of Applied Sciences and Arts HAWK Hildesheim, Germany [50–52].

22.3.4 Challenges in Using the ICF-Based Tools in Vocational Rehabilitation

The use of ICF qualifiers for rating a client's functioning as seen in the ICF Categorical Profile and ICF Evaluation Display generally provides comprehensive information about the severity of problems reflected in the ICF categories. However, since a standard guide on how to use ICF qualifiers to rate an ICF category is yet to be established, less-than-desired reliability and precision [53, 54] may result. Another confounding factor is that ICF Core Sets define only "what to measure and not how to measure" [19]. Future research in mapping measures and in the development of a robust scale for rating ICF categories will contribute to better measurement of a client's functioning status.

An ICF Core Set is not a measurement tool; it defines only what to measure and not how to measure.

22.3.5 Real-Life Experience Using ICF-Based Tools

The ICF-based tools described in this chapter have proven its utility in real life. One example is the Vocational Rehabilitation Fund or VIRK in Iceland [55, 56]. VIRK has developed an assessment tool based on a combination of the ICF Categorical Profile and a simplified version of the ICF Intervention Table. The assessment tool, containing the 20 categories of the EUMASS set [57] and ten additional ICF categories from the whole ICF, is used to measure an individual's ability to work. VIRK's vocational rehabilitation services as well as other professionals in Iceland use this assessment tool. The Icelandic experience will hopefully serve as a model for broader use of the ICF-based tools in vocational rehabilitation.

22.4 Summary

This case study illustrated how the ICF-based documentation tools, ICF Assessment Sheet, ICF Categorical Profile, ICF Intervention Table, and ICF Evaluation Display, following the framework of the Rehab-Cycle can be used in inter-professional vocational rehabilitation management, specifically in facilitating inter-professional communication and in ensuring comprehensive and transparent documentation. These tools can easily be combined with existing standard measures and incorporated in daily practice to benefit client care. Nevertheless, there is still a need for further research to optimize clinical utility and feasibility. Amidst the challenges, using the ICF-based tools presented in this chapter is a reasonable start in proving that the use of the ICF in documentation could be beneficial in the delivery of effective care in vocational rehabilitation settings and ultimately toward improving work or employment outcomes of individuals with disability.

Acknowledgments The authors would like to thank the client and the rehabilitation team at Swiss Paraplegic Center in Nottwil, Switzerland, as well as coauthors of the original publication, Alexandra Rauch, Karl Emmenegger, and Miriam Lückenkemper for their invaluable support.

Ethical Approval

The case study was approved by the Cantonal Ethics Commission of Lucerne, Switzerland, with project number 628/30 October 2006 and was performed in accordance with the Declaration of Helsinki.

Study Questions

1. What are ICF Core Sets?

   Answer: ICF Core Sets are short lists of ICF categories that are considered relevant for describing individuals with a given health condition or within a health-related context or setting.

2. What are the key elements of the Rehab-Cycle and their corresponding ICF-based documentation tools?

   Answer: The key elements of the Rehab-Cycle are assessment, assignment, intervention and evaluation. While the ICF Assessment Sheet and the ICF Categorical Profile can facilitate the assessment phase, the ICF Intervention Table can be used in the assignment and intervention phase, and the ICF Evaluation Display in the evaluation phase.

3. What is the purpose of the ICF Assessment Sheet, ICF Categorical Profile, ICF Intervention Table and ICF Evaluation Display?

   Answer:

   The ICF Assessment Sheet provides an overview of the client's functioning state with input from both the client and the rehabilitation professional.

   The ICF Categorical Profile facilitates the identification of intervention targets by defining long and short-term goals and outlining the client's functioning status in selected ICF categories.

   The ICF Intervention Table supports intervention planning by providing a comprehensive overview of all of the interventions targets (as represented by ICF categories), the interventions, and the corresponding rehabilitation professional assigned to address each intervention target.

   The ICF Evaluation Display indicates whether the shared goals set by the client and rehabilitation team were achieved based on the ICF Categorical Profile and the results of the re-examination of the client's functioning after intervention.

References

1. Krause JS. Employment after spinal cord injury. Arch Phys Med Rehabil. 1992;73(2):163–9.
2. Krause JS. Spinal cord injury and its rehabilitation. Curr Opin Neurol Neurosurg. 1992;5(5):669–72.
3. Schonherr MC, Groothoff JW, Mulder GA, Eisma WH. Participation and satisfaction after spinal cord injury: results of a vocational and leisure outcome study. Spinal Cord. 2005;43(4):241–8.
4. Scelza WM, Kirshblum SC, Wuermser LA, Ho CH, Priebe MM, Chiodo AE. Spinal cord injury medicine. 4. Community reintegration after spinal cord injury. Arch Phys Med Rehabil. 2007;88(3 Suppl 1):S71–5.
5. Gobelet C, Franchignoni F. Vocational rehabilitation. Paris: Springer; 2006.
6. Krause JS, Sternberg M, Maides J, Lottes S. Employment after spinal cord injury: differences related to geographic region, gender, and race. Arch Phys Med Rehabil. 1998;79(6):615–24.
7. Krause JS, Anson CA. Adjustment after spinal cord injury: relationship to participate in employment or education activities. Rehabil Couns Bull. 1997;40:202–14.
8. Escorpizo R, Reneman MF, Ekholm J, Fritz J, Krupa T, Marnetoft SU, et al. A conceptual definition of vocational rehabilitation based on the ICF: building a shared global model. J Occup Rehabil. 2011;21(2):126–33.

9. Selander J. Unemployed sick-leavers and vocational rehabilitation – a person-level study based on a national social insurance material. Stockholm: Karolinska Institutet, Department of Rehabilitation Medicine; 1999.
10. Wang RY, Yang YR, Yen LL, Lieu FK. Functional ability, perceived exertion and employment of the individuals with spinal cord lesion in Taiwan. Spinal Cord. 2002;40(2):69–76.
11. Sheikh K, Mattingly S. Employment rehabilitation: outcome and prediction. Am J Ind Med. 1984;5(5):383–93.
12. Schonherr MC, Groothoff JW, Mulder GA, Schoppen T, Eisma WH. Vocational reintegration following spinal cord injury: expectations, participation and interventions. Spinal Cord. 2004;42(3):177–84.
13. D'Amour D, Ferrada-Videla M, San Martin Rodriguez L, Beaulieu MD. The conceptual basis for interprofessional collaboration: core concepts and theoretical frameworks. J Interprof Care. 2005;19 Suppl 1:116–31.
14. Biering-Sorensen F, Scheuringer M, Baumberger M, Charlifue SW, Post MW, Montero F, et al. Developing core sets for persons with spinal cord injuries based on the International Classification of Functioning, Disability and Health as a way to specify functioning. Spinal Cord. 2006;44(9):541–6.
15. Kirshblum SC, Priebe MM, Ho CH, Scelza WM, Chiodo AE, Wuermser LA. Spinal cord injury medicine. 3. Rehabilitation phase after acute spinal cord injury. Arch Phys Med Rehabil. 2007;88(3 Suppl 1):S62–70.
16. Selander J, Marnetoft SU, Bergroth A, Ekholm J. Return to work following vocational rehabilitation for neck, back and shoulder problems: risk factors reviewed. Disabil Rehabil. 2002;24(14):704–12.
17. World Health Organization. International Classification of Functioning, Disability and Health: ICF. Geneva: World Health Organization; 2001.
18. Rauch A, Cieza A, Stucki G. How to apply the International Classification of Functioning, Disability and Health (ICF) for rehabilitation management in clinical practice. Eur J Phys Rehabil Med. 2008;44(3):329–42.
19. Escorpizo R, Stucki G, Cieza A, Davis K, Stumbo T, Riddle DL. Creating an interface between the International Classification of Functioning, Disability and Health and physical therapist practice. Phys Ther. 2010;90(7):1053–63.
20. Tempest S, McIntyre A. Using the ICF to clarify team roles and demonstrate clinical reasoning in stroke rehabilitation. Disabil Rehabil. 2006;28(10):663–7.
21. Üstün TB, Chatterji S, Kostanjsek N. Comments from WHO for the Journal of Rehabilitation Medicine Special Supplement on ICF Core Sets. J Rehabil Med. 2004;Suppl. 44:7–8.
22. Stucki G, Cieza A, Ewert T, Kostanjsek N, Chatterji S, Üstün TB. Application of the International Classification of Functioning, Disability and Health (ICF) in clinical practice. Disabil Rehabil. 2002;24(5):281–2.
23. Finger ME, Escorpizo R, Glässel A, Gmunder HP, Lückenkemper M, Chan C, et al. ICF Core Set for vocational rehabilitation: results of an international consensus conference. Disabil Rehabil. 2012;34(5):429–38.
24. Selb M, Escorpizo R, Kostanjsek N, Stucki G, Üstün B, Cieza A. A guide on how to develop an international classification of functioning, disability and health core set. Eur J Phys Rehabil Med. 2014; in press.
25. Cieza A, Ewert T, Üstün TB, Chatterji S, Kostanjsek N, Stucki G. Development of ICF Core Sets for patients with chronic conditions. J Rehabil Med. 2004;Suppl. 44:9–11.
26. Stucki G, Kostanjsek N, Üstün TB, Cieza A. ICF-based classification and measurement of functioning. Eur J Phys Rehabil Med. 2008;44(3):315–28.
27. Steiner WA, Ryser L, Huber E, Uebelhart D, Aeschlimann A, Stucki G. Use of the ICF model as a clinical problem-solving tool in physical therapy and rehabilitation medicine. Phys Ther. 2002;82(11):1098–107.
28. Stucki G, Sangha O. Principles of rehabilitation. In: Klippel John DP, editor. Rheumatology. 2nd ed. London: Mosby Elsevier; 1997. p. 1–11.

29. Stucki G, Kroeling P. Principles of rehabilitation. In: Hochberg S, Smolen JS, Weinblatt ME, Weisman MH, editors. Rheumatology. 3rd ed. Edinburgh: Mosby Elsevier; 2003. p. 517–30.
30. Swiss Paraplegic Research. Implementation of the International Classification of Functioning, Disability and Health (ICF) in rehabilitation practice. ICF case studies. 2007 [cited 2013 Accessed Sept. 2013.]; Available from: http://www.icf-casestudies.org
31. Rauch A, Escorpizo R, Riddle DL, Eriks-Hoogland I, Stucki G, Cieza A. Using a case report of a patient with spinal cord injury to illustrate the application of the International Classification of Functioning, Disability and Health during multidisciplinary patient management. Phys Ther. 2010;90(7):1039–52.
32. Rothstein JM, Echternach JL, Riddle DL. The Hypothesis-Oriented Algorithm for Clinicians II (HOAC II): a guide for patient management. Phys Ther. 2003;83(5):455–70.
33. Geyh S, Peter C, Müller R, Stucki G, Cieza A. Translating topics in SCI psychology into the International Classification of Functioning, Disability and Health. Top Spinal Cord Inj Rehabil. 2011;16(3):104–30.
34. Geyh S, Peter C, Müller R, Bickenbach JE, Kostanjsek N, Üstün TB, et al. The personal factors of the International Classification of Functioning, Disability and Health in the literature – a systematic review and content analysis. Disabil Rehabil. 2011;33(13–14):1089–102.
35. Chamberlain MA, Fialka Moser V, Schuldt Ekholm K, O'Connor RJ, Herceg M, Ekholm J. Vocational rehabilitation: an educational review. J Rehabil Med. 2009;41(11):856–69.
36. Glässel A, Rauch A, Selb M, Emmenegger K, Lückenkemper M, Escorpizo R. A case study on the application of International Classification of Functioning, Disability and Health (ICF)-based tools for vocational rehabilitation in spinal cord injury. Work. 2012;41(4):465–74.
37. Catz A, Itzkovich M, Agranov E, Ring H, Tamir A. SCIM–spinal cord independence measure: a new disability scale for patients with spinal cord lesions. Spinal Cord. 1997;35(12):850–6.
38. Catz A, Itzkovich M, Steinberg F, Philo O, Ring H, Ronen J, et al. The Catz-Itzkovich SCIM: a revised version of the Spinal Cord Independence Measure. Disabil Rehabil. 2001;23(6):263–8.
39. Law M, Baptiste S, McColl M, Opzoomer A, Polatajko H, Pollock N. The Canadian occupational performance measure: an outcome measure for occupational therapy. Can J Occup Ther. 1990;57(2):82–7.
40. Baptiste S, Law M, Pollock N, Polatajko H, McColl MA, Carswell A. The Canadian occupational performance measure. World Federation of Occupational Therapy Bulletin. 1993;28:47–51.
41. Kendall H, McCreary E, Provence P. Muscles, testing and function. Baltimore: Williams & Wilkins; 1993.
42. Sisto SA, Dyson-Hudson T. Dynamometry testing in spinal cord injury. J Rehabil Res Dev. 2007;44(1):123–36.
43. Bodiam C. The use of the Canadian Occupational Performance Measure for the assessment of outcome on a neurorehabilitation unit. Br J Occup Ther. 1999;62(3):123–6.
44. Stamm TA, Cieza A, Machold KP, Smolen JS, Stucki G. Content comparison of occupation-based instruments in adult rheumatology and musculoskeletal rehabilitation based on the International Classification of Functioning, Disability and Health. Arthritis Rheum. 2004;51 (6):917–24.
45. Jette AM, Haley SM. Contemporary measurement techniques for rehabilitation outcomes assessment. J Rehabil Med. 2005;37(6):339–45.
46. ATEC Ingenieurbüro AG. Webpage of Swiss Trac. 2009 [September 2013]; Available from: http://www.swisstrac.ch/en/swisstrac.html
47. Rentsch HP, Bucher P, Dommen Nyffeler I, Wolf C, Hefti H, Fluri E, et al. The implementation of the "International Classification of Functioning, Disability and Health" (ICF) in daily practice of neurorehabilitation: an interdisciplinary project at the Kantonsspital of Lucerne. Switzerland Disabil Rehabil. 2003;25(8):411–21.
48. World Health Organization (WHO). ICF eLearning tool. 2008 [cited 2013 September 2013]; Available from: http://p.ideaday.de/104.2/icf/en/index.html

49. Jones LE. Introducing the ICF: the development of an online resource to support learning, teaching and curriculum design. Physiotherapy. 2011;97(1):55–8.
50. REHADAT Informationssystem zur beruflichen Rehabilitation BfReV, Deutsche Vereinigung für Rehabilitation, Deutsche Rentenversicherung Bund. Rehabilitation Scientists in Germany (In German: Rehabilitationswissenschaftlerinnen und Rehabilitationswissenschaftler in Deutschland). 2013 Contract No.: Internet version.
51. Borgetto B, Max S. Optimization of communication and cooperation in rehabilitation through an ICF-supported interdisciplinary documentation system (ICF-DokuSys) (In German: Optimierung der Kommunikation und Kooperation in der Rehabilitation durch ein ICF-gestütztes interdisziplinäres Dokumentations-System (ICF-DokuSys)). 7. ICF-Anwenderkonferenz der DGRW; Münster, Germany 2009.
52. University of Applied Sciences and Arts HAWK (Hochschule für angewandte Wissenschaft und Kunst) Hildesheim/Holzminden/Göttingen FoSWaH. Module handbook for occupational therapy, speech and language therapy, physical therapy. Module description: Multiprofessional knowledge and skills (In German: Modulhandbuch Bachelor-Studiengang Ergotherapie, Logopädie, Physiotherapie. Modulbeschreibung: Multiprofessionelle Kompetenzen). 2 Sept 2010.
53. Uhlig T, Lillemo S, Moe RH, Stamm T, Cieza A, Boonen A, et al. Reliability of the ICF Core Set for rheumatoid arthritis. Ann Rheum Dis. 2007;66(8):1078–84.
54. Starrost K, Geyh S, Trautwein A, Grunow J, Ceballos-Baumann A, Prosiegel M, et al. Interrater reliability of the extended ICF core set for stroke applied by physical therapists. Phys Ther. 2008;88(7):841–51.
55. Konráðsdóttir A. The Icelandic model – new rehabilitation scheme using ICF. Rehabiliteringsforum Danmark – 2nd Nordic conference on work-oriented rehabilitation; Grenå, Denmark 2012.
56. Fund VVR. VIRK – Vocational Rehabilitation Fund: summary from the annual report for 2011–2012.
57. Brage S, Donceel P, Falez F. Development of ICF core set for disability evaluation in social security. Disabil Rehabil. 2008;30(18):1392–6.

Chapter 23
Development and Testing of an ICF-Based Questionnaire to Evaluate Functioning in Vocational Rehabilitation: The Work Rehabilitation Questionnaire (WORQ)

Monika Elisabeth Finger, Robert De Bie, Dennis Nowak, and Reuben Escorpizo

23.1 Introduction

The identification of clients in need for work or vocational rehabilitation, the provision of adequate support, and the access to vocational rehabilitation interventions vary worldwide widely across countries [1]. These differences are largely due to differences in disability and insurance policies and services as well as in cultural differences and attitudes toward people with disabilities [2]. In OECD countries about 6 % of the working-age population received a disability benefit in 2008 [3]. Some of these people are undoubtedly unable to work, but many could work given the right kind of help and they want to work [1]. To have such a large slice of the working-age population economically inactive represents not only a significant waste of human resources. The payment of benefits is also continuously increasing

M.E. Finger (✉)
ICF Unit, Swiss Paraplegic Research, Guido-Zäch-Strasse 4, 6207 Nottwil, Switzerland

ICF Research Branch, WHO CC FIC in Germany (DIMDI), Nottwil, Switzerland

Caphri Research School, Maastricht University, Maastricht, The Netherlands
e-mail: monika.finger@paraplegie.ch

R. De Bie
Department of Epidemiology and Institute for Education, Maastricht University, Maastricht, The Netherlands

D. Nowak
Institute and Outpatient Clinic for Occupational, Social and Environmental Medicine, Clinical Center, Ludwig-Maximilians-University, Munich, Germany

R. Escorpizo
ICF Unit, Swiss Paraplegic Research, Guido-Zäch-Strasse 4, 6207 Nottwil, Switzerland

ICF Research Branch, WHO CC FIC in Germany (DIMDI), Nottwil, Switzerland

Department of Rehabilitation and Movement Science, The University of Vermont, Burlington, VT USA

R. Escorpizo et al. (eds.), *Handbook of Vocational Rehabilitation and Disability Evaluation*, Handbooks in Health, Work, and Disability, DOI 10.1007/978-3-319-08825-9_23

the financial burden for the social security systems and, in addition, disability is a major cause of income poverty.

Since the 1980s, evidence has been growing for the fact that it is important to support workers to stay at their workplace or to return early to work after enduring injuries or sickness to diminish the risk and level of disability [4, 5]. This has led to an increasing interest in vocational rehabilitation and the return-to-work process on different levels; disability policy and economy on the macro level, health-care and work service provider, payer, and work provider on the meso level; and down to the individual health professional providing vocational rehabilitation interventions on a micro level [6]. Nevertheless, in practice few common standards for identifying, evaluating, and monitoring work-related abilities and problems are used at any specific level. This lack of a common understanding of functioning is not only hampering the exchange of information within a specific level, e.g., between health professionals and vocational counselors, or service providers and payers, on the same level, but also hinders an efficient communication between levels [7–9].

The rising awareness of health and work professionals to support the client's integration or reintegration to work as timely as possible has led to the development of a wide range of interventions and vocational rehabilitation programs. These programs are mostly designed to meet the needs of a specific health condition or setting [10–12]. In addition, a wide range of context or health condition-specific assessment instruments have been taken on from other fields of rehabilitation or have been developed to meet the needs of work intervention. Examples are the SF-36 [13] to evaluate health-related quality of life, the Beck Depression Inventory [14] to evaluate depression, and the Oswestry Low Back Pain Disability Questionnaire [15] to quantify disability for low back pain.

Despite the growing use of these disease- or symptom-specific assessment and outcome measures that are mostly used in specific health disciplines, there is still a lack of standardization in assessing and documenting problems and abilities. In the course of the vocational rehabilitation process, this variability may cause misconceptions and redundancies between professionals and settings. In addition, a comprehensive description that is understandable for the client and all professionals involved of the functional abilities and limitations of a client in daily life, at home, or at the workplace would be an essential part for the successful recognition of clients with a high need for vocational rehabilitation.

The International Classification of Functioning, Disability, and Health (ICF) provides a reference frame to describe and measure human functioning in the context of health in a standardized way [16]. In recent studies the ICF has proved to be a valid framework in the context of vocational rehabilitation [17–20]. It therefore provides a suitable base for developing standardized instruments to assess and document functioning throughout return-to-work processes.

The International Classification of Functioning, Disability and Health (ICF) provides a common reference frame and language to describe, assess and document human functioning in vocational rehabilitation and may therefore provide a suitable base for developing standardized assessment instruments.

23.2 The International Classification of Functioning Disability, and Health and the ICF Core Sets for Vocational Rehabilitation

The ICF was endorsed by the World Health Assembly in May 2001 as a reference framework and language to describe and measure functioning and disability of individuals whose *Body Function, Body Structure, Activities, and Participation* may be impaired, limited, or restricted due to a health condition [16, 21]. The classification was developed to be used by health professionals, clients, and other stakeholders in the field of health and disability, independent of the setting, culture, and context [21]. The classification contains 1,424 categories. Since its approval by the WHO, several studies have been conducted supporting the use of the ICF in the context of work or vocational rehabilitation.

To enhance the usability of the ICF in clinical practice, carefully selected short lists of ICF categories, so-called ICF Core Sets, were developed by the WHO in collaboration with the ICF Research Branch. The included categories are chosen to cover the most influential functioning properties of a health condition or a specific setting. Following a defined methodology [22], the development of ICF Core Sets incorporates a structured set of processes with four preparatory studies: a systematic review of the literature, an expert survey, a cross-sectional study, and qualitative patient focus groups or interviews. The final selection of ICF categories for inclusion in the ICF Core Set is done in a multistage consensus process involving experts from all WHO regions.

In an additional process, a "Generic Set" was developed on a statistical basis. The Generic Set contains a list of seven ICF categories that depicts the core functioning of persons with any health condition and setting [23].

In 2010 the ICF Core Set for vocational rehabilitation was developed as the first setting-specific ICF Core Set. Its aim was to provide the users with a list of relevant ICF categories that can be used to describe and document the functioning of individuals who are undergoing vocational rehabilitation. The Core Set for vocational rehabilitation consists of a comprehensive list of 90 and a brief list of 13 ICF categories [17].

The Brief ICF Core Set for vocational rehabilitation, supplemented by the seven categories of the Generic Set, represents the minimal number of domains that should be evaluated or report on in any field of vocational rehabilitation. The Comprehensive ICF Core Set for vocational rehabilitation, on the other hand, can

Table 23.1 Categories of the Brief ICF Core Set for vocational rehabilitation and the generic set

ICF code	ICF text	Source of categories	
		Brief set	Generic set
b130	Energy and drive functions	✓	✓
b152	Emotional functions		✓
b164	Higher-level cognitive functions	✓	
b280	Sensation of pain		✓
b455	Exercise tolerance functions	✓	
d155	Acquiring skills	✓	
d230	Carrying out daily routine		✓
d240	Handling stress and other psychological demands	✓	
d450	Walking		✓
d455	Moving around		✓
d720	Complex interpersonal interactions	✓	
d845	Acquiring, keeping and terminating a job	✓	
d850	Remunerative employment	✓	✓
d855	Non-remunerative employment	✓	
e310	Immediate family	✓	
e330	People in positions of authority	✓	
e580	Health services, systems and policies	✓	
e590	Labour and employment services, systems and policies	✓	

be seen as a pool of domains from which additional categories can be chosen to construct a list that is adapted to the needs of the specific health-care setting, program, or even to the needs of an individual client (Table 23.1).

The development of the ICF Core Set for vocational rehabilitation was a first attempt toward the integration of the ICF in clinical vocational rehabilitation practice. However, it was a challenge to use it in daily practice.

The categories of the ICF essentially indicate what to assess when evaluating functioning [24]. By employing the "WHO ICF qualifiers," one might also be able to assess the magnitude of a problem in functioning. However, the lack of reliability and sensitivity of the WHO ICF qualifiers and the lack of guidelines on how the ICF categories can be assessed pose a difficulty in interpreting change [25, 26] in the context of intervention. Another challenge when using ICF categories in clinical practice is given by their broad definitions and nonprofessional-specific language. Using the ICF classification requires an extent of training of stakeholders that should not be underestimated. Although more and more professionals rely on the ICF when they design new intervention programs or assessment instruments, the implementation of the ICF remains nonuniform and mostly setting specific [27–29]. To alleviate the use of the ICF in vocational rehabilitation, ICF-based instruments that are easy to administer and interpret by all involved professionals and the clients may therefore lead to improved interdisciplinary communication and common understanding of functioning abilities and problems across vocational rehabilitation settings [30–32].

ICF Core Sets are evidence based short lists of ICF categories, selected to cover the most relevant functioning properties of a health condition or specific health setting. ICF Core Sets were intended to enhance the usability of the ICF in clinical practice.

23.3 Development of the ICF-Based Work Rehabilitation Questionnaire WORQ

After a review of instruments currently used in vocational rehabilitation, we found none that was designed to capture the functioning domains relevant in vocational rehabilitation given the diverse health conditions and return-to-work (RTW) settings. The need for such an instrument expressed by clinicians and researchers led us to the development of the Work Rehabilitation Questionnaire (WORQ).

The key to an effective measurement instrument design is to know exactly what it should measure. The measure has to be designed and then performed for a predetermined purpose [33, 34].

We defined the purpose of the new measurement as follows: WORQ should be an instrument that:

1. Assesses work functioning in individuals participating in vocational rehabilitation, and it should be based on ICF.
2. Is used and understood in any vocational rehabilitation setting or by any responsible professional and by the clients.
3. Is used independently of any health condition.
4. Can be administered at any time point within the continuum of the return-to-work process.

As a consequence of these conditions, the use of our instrument had to be independent of any specific professional skills or clinical tests. It would become a generic instrument to gain a fast and comprehensive overview of the functioning problems that an individual experiences during his or her return-to-work processes. Therefore, we decided to design a questionnaire that is client rated and interviewer administered.

The first version of WORQ was developed in three phases:

1. First, the relevant domains to assess functioning in the context of vocational rehabilitation, represented by ICF categories, were identified.
2. Questions to assess the selected ICF categories were worded in English. The scaling for the response options was decided on. The WORQ was cognitively tested.
3. Finally, the WORQ was cross-culturally translated from English to German.

23.3.1 First Phase of the WORQ Development: Identifying Functioning Domains

To start with, we decided to base the selection of domains represented in WORQ on the Comprehensive ICF Core Set for vocational rehabilitation, because this core set represents the most comprehensive and agreed on list of domains that are relevant to assess functioning in vocational rehabilitation. However, we also realized that the Comprehensive ICF Core Set with its 90 categories would lead to a very long questionnaire with many questions relevant to only a small proportion of clients in vocational rehabilitation and thus it would be totally impractical to use in clinical practice. Therefore, we based our selection on the 13 categories from the Brief ICF Core Set for vocational rehabilitation. This core set contains the least number of categories that are essential to describe the typical spectrum of limitations in functioning and in the environment. As this selection was not sufficient to create a satisfactory functioning profile of the clients, we decided to select additional categories from the Comprehensive ICF Core Set. The selection was based on two additional sources of information – results of a statistical analysis of the Comprehensive ICF Core Set for vocational rehabilitation and the literature.

First we used a statistical approach by conducting an explorative Rasch analysis on the whole Comprehensive ICF Core Set for vocational rehabilitation [35, 36]. We used a data set with 152 participants from a previous study [19].

See additional information: Frame 23.1: The Rasch Model.

Based on this explorative Rasch analysis, 28 ICF categories from *Body Functions* and *Activities and Participation* were added to the categories of the Brief ICF Core Set. As the scope of the questionnaire was to assess functioning by providing a functioning profile, no further environmental factors were added. The 28 categories were chosen using the following criteria: 13 categories that fit the Rasch model and showed no local dependency with other categories were directly selected. Seven more categories that fit the Rasch model and where local dependencies with other categories could be eliminated were also added. Since a study based on expert consensus gave higher weight to *Activities and Participation* within the context of work disability, the rule was that when a category from F*unctions* showed local dependency with a category from *Activities and Participation,* the *Activities and Participation* category was selected [17]. Another eight categories were added for further testing if (1) two categories from the same component, either *Body Functions* or *Activities and Participation*, showed local dependency; (2) item fit showed no preference for one category; and (3) a meaningful clinical decision based on evidence from the literature could not be made. Finally, in addition to the 28 statistically selected categories, we added another three categories, *b280 Sensation of pain*, *b730 Muscle power functions*, and *d430 Lifting and carrying objects.* Although these categories did not fit the Rasch model, they were included because they were judged to be important for gaining a comprehensive understanding of functioning in vocational rehabilitation based on the literature and clinical expert opinion [37, 38].

This process ended with a pool of 44 ICF categories; 13 belonged to the Brief ICF Core Set for vocational rehabilitation, 28 were identified from statistical testing (Rasch analysis), and 3 were identified from the literature. Four of the categories came from the ICF component *Environmental Factors*, 15 from *Body Functions*, and 25 from *Activities and Participation.*

Based on the selection process described above, it could be presumed that WORQ represents a multidimensional scale. As a consequence it would not be appropriate to compare subjects or groups using item sum scores of this first version of WORQ [39].

23.3.2 Second Phase of the WORQ Development: Formulating the Questionnaire

When formulating questions, it is essential to consider that a questionnaire is only as good as the questions it contains. Studies have shown that respondents are executing four steps when answering questions. First, they have to understand and interpret the question. Second, they must search their memories for relevant information, and third, integrate all the information. Finally, they must translate their judgment into a response, by selecting one of the response options offered by the question [34, 39].

23.3.2.1 Wording of the Questionnaire

Taking these considerations into account, we used simple, familiar words in lay language when wording the WORQ to enhance the understandability of the WORQ questions. In addition, we based the wording on items and questions that had already been used and tested for its distinctness in two other ICF-based questionnaires. These instruments were the WHO Disability Assessment Schedule 2.0 (WHODAS 2.0) [40] and the World Health Survey Instrument (WHS) [41].

See additional information: Frame 23.2: WHODAS 2.0 and WHS.

To inform the client about the content and the benefit of WORQ, the questionnaire starts with a short introduction text which should be read to the client. The questionnaire is structured in two sections. Section one contains 17 sociodemographic and work-related questions. This section is intended to gain basic data of the person, such as age, sex, and civil status, and an overview of work-relevant factors. Information on the four environmental categories from the Brief ICF Core Set, namely, *e310 Immediate family*; *e330 People in positions of authority*; *e580 Health services, systems and policies*; and *e590 Labour and employment services, systems and policies*, are included in this part. In addition, proxy questions are formulated to evaluate the six categories from *activities and participation* that describe vocational education or work situations, namely, *d825 Vocational training*; *d830 Higher education*; *d840 Apprenticeship (work preparation)*; *d845 Acquiring, keeping and terminating a job*; *d850 Remunerative employment*; and *d855 Non-remunerative employment.* These categories are assessed using proxy questions to learn about the current work or vocational rehabilitation situation of the client and not to rate the amount of problems that the client experiences in these activities. The amount of problems a client was facing in training, education, or work was not assessed, because in the preliminary testing of the questions, the results showed that the amount of problems was more related to the type of work, the work setting, or the vocational intervention rather than providing reliable information on the functioning of the client.

Section two of the WORQ contains questions to assess functioning. To begin with, a stem question was developed: "Overall in the past week, to what extent did you have problems with..." A recall period of 1 week was chosen, because this time period is long enough to enable the client to experience the activity or function addressed in the respective question, but also short enough to measure change in a rehabilitation program lasting on average 4–6 weeks.

Thirty six questions, representing 34 categories, were phrased to assess functioning in the context of vocational rehabilitation. 34 questions were worded to be rated by the client. Two questions [35, 36] of the WORQ, which evaluate the ICF categories *b117 Intellectual functions* and *b126 Temperament and personality functions*, respectively, were worded to be rated by the interviewer due to the challenge in rating them as client reported.

Multiple sources were used to word and phrase the questions. If no appropriate question from the two WHO questionnaires, WHODAS 2.0 and the World Health Survey Instrument (WHS), was found, the WORQ questions were formulated based on the original text of the ICF category [16], and on questions from measurement instruments identified in a systematic review, previously linked to the ICF (see Table 23.2).

23.3.2.2 Scaling of the Questionnaire

As response options for Section two of the WORQ, a visual-analogue scale from 0 to 100 (VAS-100) with anchor points of 0 (no problem) and 100 (complete problem) was chosen to rate the functioning questions [42, 43]. This scale was chosen to obtain scores that could be used to look at changes within subjects and could be displayed easily as functioning profiles by translating them into the ICF qualifiers. It was also important to find a scale that was easy to understand and enabled the clients a free rating of their problems. Although VAS is widely used as a type of response options for multiple item scales, it has to be taken into consideration that the VAS has no true unit of measurement and, accordingly, is ordinal only [44]. VAS scores should always be analyzed as noncontinuous data using statistical methods for ordinal data [45].

Table 23.2 Selection criteria and phrasing of WORQ-SR- items

ICF category being measured	Included how?	Wording based on:	Addressed in WORQ question nr:
Part I: Sociodemographics and background information			
d850 Remunerative employment	Brief Core Set for VR	ICF text: definition of category	Question nr. 4
d825 Vocational training	Statistics based	ICF text: definition of category	Question nr. 4
d830 Higher education	Statistics based	ICF text: definition of category	Question nr. 4
d840 Apprenticeship	Statistics based	ICF text: definition of category	Question nr. 4
d845 Acquiring, keeping and terminating a job	Brief Core Set for VR	ICF text: definition of category	Question nr. 6
e590 Labour and employment services, systems and policies	Brief Core Set for VR	ICF text: definition of category	Question nr. 10
e580 Health services, systems and policies	Brief Core Set for VR	ICF text: definition of category	Question nr. 12
e590 Labour and employment services, systems and policies	Brief Core Set for VR	ICF text: definition of category	Question nr. 14
e310 Immediate family	Brief Core Set for VR	ICF text: definition of category	Question nr. 15
e330 People in positions of authority	Brief Core Set for VR	ICF text: definition of category	Question nr. 16
Part II: Functioning			
b117 Intellectual functions	Statistics based	ICF text: definition of category	Question nr. 6
b126 Temperament and personality functions	Statistics based	ICF text: definition of category	Question nr. 7
b126 Temperament and personality functions	Statistics based	ICF text: definition of category	Question nr. 8
b130 Energy and drive functions	Brief Core Set for VR	WHS question nr. Q2081	Question nr. 1
b134 Sleep functions	Statistics based	WHS question nr. Q2080	Question nr. 2
b144 Memory functions	Statistics based	WHO-DAS 0.2 question nr D1.2	Question nr. 3
b152 Emotional functions	Statistics based	WHS question nr. Q2090	Question nr. 4
b152 Emotional functions	Statistics based	WHS question nr. Q2091	Question nr. 5
b160 Thought functions	Statistics based	ICF text: definition of category	Question nr. 9
b164 Higher-level cognitive functions	Brief Core Set for VR	WHO-DAS 0.2 question nr D1.3	Question nr. 10
b230 Hearing functions	Statistics based	ICF text: definition of category	Question nr. 11

(continued)

Table 23.2 (continued)

ICF category being measured	Included how?	Wording based on:	Addressed in WORQ question nr:
b235 Vestibular functions	Statistics based	ICF text: definition of category	Question nr. 12
b280 Sensation of pain	Generic ICF Set	WHS question nr. Q2030	Question nr. 13
b455 Exercise tolerance functions	Brief Core Set for VR	ICF text: definition of category	Question nr. 14
b730 Muscle power functions	Clinical importance	ICF text: definition of category	Question nr. 15
b810 Protective functions of the skin	Statistics based	ICF text: definition of category	Question nr. 16
d155 Acquiring skills	Brief Core Set for VR	WHO-DAS 0.2 question nr S3	Question nr. 17
d160 Focusing attention	Statistics based	ICF text: definition of category	Question nr. 18
d166 Reading	Statistics based	ICF text: definition of category	Question nr. 19
d177 Making decisions	Statistics based	ICF text: definition of category	Question nr. 20
d210 Undertaking a single task	Statistics based	ICF text: definition of category	Question nr. 21
d230 Carrying out daily routine	Statistics based	ICF text: definition of category	Question nr. 22
d240 Handling stress and other psychological demands	Brief Core Set for VR	ICF text: definition of category	Question nr. 23
d315 Communicating with – receiving – nonverbal messages	Statistics based	ICF text: definition of category	Question nr. 24
d350 Conversation	Statistics based	WHO-DAS 0.2 question nr D1.6	Question nr. 25
d360 Using communication devices and techniques	Statistics based	ICF text: definition of category	Question nr. 26
d430 Lifting and carrying objects	Clinical importance	ICF text: definition of category	Question nr. 27
d430 Lifting and carrying objects	Clinical importance	ICF text: definition of category	Question nr. 28
d440 Fine hand use	Statistics based	ICF text: definition of category	Question nr. 29
d450 Walking	Expressed patients' needs and generic ICF set	ICF text: definition of category	Question nr. 30
d450 Walking	Expressed patients' needs and generic ICF set	WHO-DAS 0.2 question nr S7	Question nr. 31

(continued)

Table 23.2 (continued)

ICF category being measured	Included how?	Wording based on:	Addressed in WORQ question nr:
d455 Moving around	Statistics based	ICF text: definition of category	Question nr. 32
d470 Using transportation	Statistics based	ICF text: definition of category	Question nr. 33
d475 Driving	Statistics based	ICF text: definition of category	Question nr. 34
d540 Dressing	Statistics based	WHO-DAS 0.2 question nr S9	Question nr. 35
d570 Looking after one's health	Statistics based	ICF text: definition of category	Question nr. 36
d720 Complex interpersonal interactions	Brief Core Set for VR	ICF text: definition of category	Question nr. 37
d870 Economic self-sufficiency	Statistics based	ICF text: definition of category	Question nr. 38
b210 Seeing functions	Statistics based	WHS question nr. Q2071	Question nr. 39
b210 Seeing functions	Statistics based	WHS question nr. Q2072	Question nr. 40

Abbreviations: *WHS* World Health Survey, *WHO-DAS II* WHO Disability Assessment Schedule 2.0

23.3.2.3 Cognitive Testing of WORQ

After wording a draft version of the questionnaire, it was an important next step in the development to obtain feedback from a small but representative sample of potential responders. The purpose of this test was to determine the relevance of the questions, the potential uncertainty in the wording, and the extent to which there might be problems in obtaining response. In addition, it might be determined that responders are likely to be offended by a certain question or that responders misunderstand what the question is asking [34].

The draft version of WORQ was sent to three health professionals and two nonclinicians to be carefully reviewed. The five participants first answered the WORQ just as if they were research subjects. In addition, they filled in a questionnaire addressing understandability of the questions, suitability of response options, and appropriateness of length of the questionnaire. Based on their responses, the wording of the questions 4, 5, and 9 was slightly modified. The length of the questionnaire was considered satisfactory, and the response options were assessed to be adequate and easy to understand. In addition, the questions were found to cover all the essential aspects of functioning to be considered for vocational rehabilitation.

23.3.3 Third Phase of the WORQ Development: Cross-Cultural Translation of WORQ

As WORQ was first developed in English and the testing of its psychometrics was planned in a German-speaking population, the questionnaire had to be translated from English to German.

It is widely recognized that if measures are to be used across cultures, the items must not only be translated well linguistically but also must be adapted culturally to maintain the content validity of the questionnaire, as the cultural differences may lead to differences in the valuation of phrases, questions, and included examples. For example, in Europe, it is the norm to shake hands to welcome a person in a formal way. In other parts of the world, people are bowing to each other or hugging a visitor at the first meeting. A person with hand problems may avoid shaking hands with strangers. This behavior may be perceived as not following social rules and may hamper creating new relationships in one culture, but have no relevance in another one.

To ensure the quality of the WORQ translation, a cross-cultural adaptation was performed according to the recommendations of Beaton [46]. In our case the English version of the WORQ was the source questionnaire for all future developments with English as our source language.

In a first step, WORQ was translated to German. Two bilingual translators with German and Swiss German as native languages conducted a forward-translation from English to German; the two worked independently of each other. The first translator was familiar with the WORQ concepts and had a background in physiotherapy. The second was not familiar with the WORQ concepts and had a background in psychology and communications. The translated versions were compared and analyzed in a group meeting, including an additional bilingual person that knew the cultural situation of Germany and the German speaking part of Switzerland. Different wordings were discussed until consensus was reached on the final translation. Three German-speaking nonclinicians that were not involved in the development of WORQ tested the German version. Based on their input, a first German version of WORQ was finalized.

Two bilingual translators back translated this first version to English independently. The first translator was a native English speaker who was familiar with the concept of WORQ. The second translator was a German native speaker who was a certified English translator. She was not familiar with the concept of WORQ. None of them had participated in the previous development phases. The results of the back translation were evaluated and discussed in a group consisting of the four translators, one developer of the questionnaire, and a research psychologist who is experienced in the cross-cultural translation of measurement instruments. Discrepancies in the wording of WORQ were identified, discussed, and resolved in a group consensus. A first version of WORQ in both German and English was obtained.

The Work Rehabilitation Questionnaire (WORQ) provides an example for the development of an ICF based instrument to assess functioning in vocational rehabilitation, independent of the underlying health condition and throughout return-to-work processes.

23.4 Usability and Psychometrics of the WORQ

The usability and psychometrics (test-retest reliability, internal consistency, and construct validity) of WORQ-German were evaluated in a rehabilitation center in Switzerland in a department offering various types of vocational rehabilitation, such as work-related physical or cognitive training, skills training, workplace evaluation and adaptation, and support in changing the profession.

The inclusion criteria for the participants in the psychometric study were phrased to capture clients with as many health conditions and diverse states of their rehabilitation as possible, to test if WORQ was able to capture their main problems in functioning. Clients of working age (18–65 years) that participated in a vocational rehabilitation intervention or program due to a health condition were eligible. In addition, they had to understand and write German to be able to answer the questionnaires and they had to be able to give informed written consent.

The health and work professionals of the vocational rehabilitation department, occupational therapists, vocational counselors, and work reintegration specialists were introduced to the WORQ and to the study protocol. Nine professionals, who volunteered to participate as interviewers in the study, were further trained to administer the WORQ and, if needed, to support the client in answering an additional client questionnaire.

The secretary of the department was instructed to contact all clients that fulfilled the inclusion criteria at admission. After giving written informed consent, the participants were asked to fill in a client case record form containing sociodemographics and work-specific information and information concerning their health, functioning, and pain. In addition the case record form contained four other questionnaires to assess construct validity: the EuroQol-5D-single index (EQ-5D) [47], the Medical Outcome Study Short Form 36 (SF-36) [13], Beck's Depression Inventory II (BDI II) [14], and the World Health Organization Quality of Life Questionnaires (WHOQoL) [48].

Finally WORQ was tested in a sample ($n = 74$) of clients with musculoskeletal and neurological disorders [49] (Table 23.3).

After returning the case record form, the responsible professional administered the first WORQ interview and a date for the second interview was agreed on. A researcher (physiotherapist) from the study center during her first contact with the client administered the second interview.

Table 23.3 Characteristics of respondents

Characteristics	First interview $n=74$ (%)	Second interview $n=52$ (%)
Age, mean ($^{\perp}$SD), years	37.68 (12.7 SD)	36.75 (12.4 SD)
Male	62 (83.8)	45 (86.5)
More than high school education	43 (58.1)	32 (61.5)
Work experience, median ($^{\pm}$IQR), years	16.0 (5–28)	17.0 (5–27)
Married	28 (37.8)	19 (36.5)
Type of vocational rehabilitation		
Work-related physical training/intervention	46 (62.2)	33 (63.5)
Work-related cognitive training/intervention	54 (73.0)	38 (73.1)
Return to work to the same employer	29 (39.2)	19 (36.5)
Looking for/change to a new profession	16 (21.6)	12 (23.1)
Type of disorders		
Neurological	34 (45.9)	24 (46.2)
Musculoskeletal	33 (44.6)	24 (46.2)
Internal/psychiatric	9 (9.5)	4 (7.7)
Number of comorbidities (SCQ)		
0 comorbidity	16 (21.6)	11 (21.2)
1 comorbidity	26 (35.1)	18 (34.6)
$\geq$ 2 comorbidities	32 (43.2)	23 (44.2)
Duration of sickness absence, median (IQR), month	10.0 (4.0–22.25)	8 (4.0–21.25)

Abbreviations: $^{\perp}$*SD* standard deviation, ±*IQR* interquartile range, *SCQ* the self-administered comorbidity questionnaire [50]

23.4.1 Usability

After administering the second WORQ interview, the researcher asked the first 25 clients and the nine professionals that had administered the first interviews, to comment on the usability of WORQ. How easily the wording could be understood was rated as "no difficulty" by 8 out of 9 professionals (89 %) and by 23 out of 25 clients (92 %). Two clients argued the questions were at times too generic, e.g., concerning having problems with strength or lifting ability. One work reintegration specialist argued that having to repeat the stem question "Overall in the past week, to what extent did you have problems with..." when reading out the questions to the client was laborious and cumbersome. The response options of the VAS were rated as "good" by six professionals (67 %) and 21 clients (84 %). The length of the questionnaire and the 26 min (SD ± 11.55) that were needed to administer WORQ in the first interview were rated as "good" by all clients but as being too long by two vocational counselors and one work reintegration specialist (33 %). In addition three professionals (33 %) found it difficult to rate the client's problem in questions 35 and 36 on intellectual and temperament functions. This corresponded with the experience of the rater of the second interview, since she reported an inability to rate questions 35 and 36 due to a lack of information.

Looking at usability, the WORQ was mostly appreciated by the clients as they felt that the questionnaire allowed them to reflect upon their daily problems in functioning and express the full range of problems they considered as barriers for a successful return to work. Although the professionals valued the information gained through WORQ, the average time of 26 min to administer WORQ was reported to be a major obstacle to integrating WORQ in daily practice.

23.4.2 Reliability

Due to the inability of the second interviewer to administer question 35 and 36, test-retest reliability of section two of the WORQ was performed on only 34 items. Spearman correlation was used because the data was not normally distributed and the score was based on VAS ratings [51, 52]. The test-retest agreement was 0.789. The internal consistency of WORQ was measured by Cronbach's alpha which is a general coefficient of homogeneity between items. Values for the coefficient can range from 0 (no internal consistency) to 1 (perfect internal consistency), where a value above 0.8 is considered acceptable [53]. A calculation on data of all 74 clients of the first interview showed a Cronbach's alpha of 0.883 for the full 36 items and a Cronbach's alpha of 0.887 when item 35 and 36 were deleted. When looking at the average correlation between items, only 23 of the 36 items showed a correlation-fit of at least 0.3. One item, question 32 "...having sufficient money to cover your cost of living?" was even inversely correlated with an inter-item correlation of −0.132. These analyses supported the assumption from the selection process that functioning in VR, as measured by the WORQ, consists of more than one underlying concept. The WORQ may be used to document a functioning profile of individuals in vocational rehabilitation and as an outcome measure on an individual basis [54]. It may not be appropriate to compare sum scores across groups of individuals, at this point in time.

23.4.3 Validity

Validity of the WORQ was explored from three perspectives: content validity, face validity, and criterion validity. Content validity of the WORQ in the context of vocational rehabilitation was assumed due to the fact that the items in the questionnaire were derived in a carefully designed selection process from the ICF Core Set for vocational rehabilitation. The ICF Core Set was rigorously developed using input from patients, clinicians, experts, and the literature and can be seen as the reference standard to assess and describe the relevant factors concerning functioning in vocational rehabilitation, independent of the health condition, or vocational rehabilitation setting.

To evaluate face validity, the involved professionals and the clients were asked as how complete they perceived the functioning profile for individuals in vocational rehabilitation was, when it was assessed with the WORQ. Professionals rated

WORQ as a comprehensive instrument concerning functioning. However, they missed additional contextual factors, including environmental factors such as work place descriptions, and personal factors such as coping strategies. The clients on the other hand appreciated the breadth of coverage of WORQ. They felt that the questionnaire allowed them to reflect upon their daily problems in functioning in a broad way, not restricted to their primary injury or body region directly affected by their disease. The clients felt that WORQ allowed them to address not only their physical functioning problems but also psychological or social issues and needs. Three patients (12 %) mentioned that they missed an item related to "walking," although question 26 asks for "... to what extent did you have problems with moving around including crawling, climbing, and running?"

To assess criterion validity, the WORQ was compared to EuroQol-single index, BDI II, SF-36, and WHOQoL using Spearman correlation. Interestingly the correlation coefficient between WORQ and SF-36 (which assesses general health) was fairly low (−0.353), whereas the correlation between WORQ and quality of life assessed by WHOQoL and EuroQoL (which assesses current health) was moderate (−0.439 and −0.419, respectively). These findings appear to acknowledge that the perception of general health and quality of life, as measured by SF-36, EuroQoL and WHOQOL, represents concepts that are only partially related to work functioning and therefore should be evaluated independently. The highest correlation coefficient was found between WORQ and BDI II that assesses depression (0.548). Psychological functioning, in particular emotional functions related to sadness, worries, or being depressed, may play a major role in self-perceived functioning in vocational rehabilitation. The influence of psychological functioning might be underestimated in clients in vocational rehabilitation without psychiatric diagnosis. These assumption is also supported by the fact that none of the clients in our study population reported psychiatric conditions as primary health condition, but more than 75 % of the clients in our sample reported at least one comorbidity and indicated to experience periods of being depressed or anxious concerning their future – a finding that is consistent with the literature [55].

In our inpatient-study population WORQ showed good face validity. The question remains if these findings can be generalized to other populations and especially to clients in an outpatient setting. Therefore, the validity of WORQ in other populations and in other settings has to be proved in further studies. Nevertheless, WORQ was developed to be used independently of the vocational rehabilitation setting, along the whole continuum of the return-to-work process. Preliminary findings in the follow-up of the inpatients after the discharge into an outpatient setting are promising.

23.5 Further Development of WORQ

Based on the findings of the usability interviews and the psychometric data, the study group decided to further develop WORQ to expand its usability in clinical practice. Three major developmental areas were defined: first, to design a self-reported version of WORQ to meet the time needs of the professionals; second, to establish sensitivity to change of WORQ and its predictive validity of return to work status; and third, to investigate further the scale of the second section of WORQ and to look into its dimensionality and possibly develop unidimensional subscores. Such subscores would enable us to look deeper into functioning patterns and to compare scores across individuals, health conditions, and vocational rehabilitation settings.

23.5.1 WORQ Self-Reported Version (WORQ-SR)

To convert the WORQ interviewer-administered version 1 (WORQ-IA1) into a self-reported version, we carefully reviewed the introductory text and the questions. The introductory text was adapted to address the client directly. The questions 35 and 36 that were capturing the ICF categories *b117 Intellectual functions* and *b126 Temperament and personality functions* were primarily rated by a professional in the interviewer-administered version and had to be reformulated to a self-rated format. The challenge in this was to ensure that the concepts of the underlying ICF categories in the context of vocational rehabilitation were still evaluated properly. The question on intellectual functions now reads: "Overall in the past week, to what extent did you have problems with...being irritable?" The question on temperament and personality functions was split into two questions. They read: "Overall in the past week, to what extent did you have problems with...your temper?" and "....your self-confidence."

To gain more specific information, as suggested in the usability interviews by the clients, the question 4 of WORQ-IA on Lifting and Carrying objects was split into two, now reading: "Overall in the past week, to what extent did you have problems with ... lifting and carrying objects weighing up to 5 kg?" and "... lifting and carrying objects weighing more than 5 kg?" This distinction was made due to the physical demand definitions from the Dictionary of Occupational Titles that defines 5 kg (10 lb) as a prerequisite for sedentary work [56]. Based on the newly developed Generic ICF Set and the recommendation of the clients, two questions evaluating the ICF category *d450 Walking* were also added. Finally, based on expert consensus, two further questions evaluating the time burden that the clients face due to their health condition were added. They read: "Overall in the past week, how long did it take you... in the morning to get up and get ready (washed, dressed, have breakfast) to leave the house?" and "... to do all the necessary things required throughout the whole week for your health, such as attending therapy, or medical consultations, or doing your exercises?" The current versions of WORQ-SR and WORQ-IA can be freely accessed under www.myworq.org.

A longitudinal study to evaluate further psychometrics and to identify the underlying concepts of WORQ is ongoing. Statistical methods as explorative factor or Rasch analysis will thereby be applied to evaluate and test identified subscales.

23.6 Use of WORQ in Clinical Practice: Generic Versus Condition- or Symptom-Specific Instruments

As described in Sect. 25.3, it is necessary to define the purpose of a measurement instrument, in order to assess and obtain accurate information when the measure is applied in practice. WORQ was developed to evaluate and document functioning in the context of vocational rehabilitation, independent of the health condition, or setting [49]. This means that WORQ was designed as a generic instrument and can be used across the wide field of vocational rehabilitation. It can be looked at as an instrument for the use at a meso level to inform service providers and payers as well as a screening tool and outcome measure on the micro level to identify problematic areas of relevance in functioning in a client and to monitor its changes over time. Since WORQ reflects the severity of functioning problems from the client perspective, it may potentially quantify the overall burden in functioning in a way that can be understood by any professional or client as well as by the employers or payers. An instrument like WORQ may therefore enhance interdisciplinary understanding and simplify communication across the continuum of vocational rehabilitation [32]. In the future, if the scaling problem will be solved, WORQ may also provide basic data on functioning in vocational rehabilitation to compare functioning patterns across health conditions or clients.

On the other hand, after identifying the most relevant functioning problems, a "condition-specific" approach that quantifies or analyzes specific functioning aspects of a single disease, for example, the Oswestry Low Back Pain Disability Questionnaire, or a "symptom-specific" approach, as a Rotation tests in vertigo, may be indispensable. The information gained from such an instrument is designed to be more detailed than information from a generic measure and therefore be of great importance for specialized professionals to guide their clinical reasoning process and choice of treatment. Such symptom- or condition-specific instruments or tests usually require specific expertise to be administered and analyzed and are therefore bound to a specific professional group.

In summary it has to be remembered that measurement must be performed for a predetermined purpose and the appropriate instrument has to be chosen accordingly. Both generic and condition-specific instruments correspond to different objectives and should be considered as complementary [57].

23.7 The Role of Environmental and Personal Factors in Assessment of Functioning Problems in Vocational Rehabilitation

The biopsychosocial approach of the ICF puts the concepts of functioning and disability in a new light, as functioning is defined as an umbrella term encompassing all *Body Functions, Activities, and Participation.* Similarly, disability serves as an umbrella term for impairments, activity limitations, and participation restrictions [16]. A person's functioning and disability is seen as a dynamic interaction between a health condition and the contextual factors, namely, environmental factors and personal factors.

23.7.1 The Role of Environmental Factors

Environmental factors represent the physical, social, and attitudinal surrounding in which a person lives. They can interact with functioning as facilitators or barriers. Their influence may widely vary between persons, and in clinical practice they often have to be determined individually for the clients. In vocational rehabilitation, an increasing amount of research has been conducted in recent years to identify environmental factors that are relevant for vocational rehabilitation and to decode their impact on functioning and on return-to-work in specific. For example, in a recent review Streibelt et al. [58] identified the labor market situation and the social support and social attitudes in the family and at the workplace as the most relevant environmental factors [59]. In addition, specific work demands [60], case management by the treating physician, and administrative behavior of insurers [61] were also identified to be relevant. Identifying environmental barriers is a first step to remove them and may therefore be an essential step to facilitate and sustain return to work.

When looking at WORQ-IA and WORQ-SR, we realize that in both versions the clients are asked to rate their problems in functioning during the last week. The wording of this stem question implicitly asks the client to take the influence of the environment into account. We can further see that environmental factors considered as relevant for vocational rehabilitation, such as the support of the family, the employer, and the social system, as well as factors direct linked to the actual and future work of the clients, are registered in section one. It may be essential to know these factors when analyzing and interpreting the functioning problems that the client has rated in section two, because the environment may influence the client's rating in different ways. First, in the stem question the client is asked to rate the problems encountered during the last week. Depending on his or her environment, the demands on certain abilities or activities may vary. As an example, a client in an inpatient rehabilitation setting may experience only minor problems when driving, since there is a need for a car only once or twice a week to go shopping. After discharge, however, the client has to drive more than 40 min in heavy traffic twice a day to work and home, and that will cause severe problems in driving.

23.7.2 The Role of Personal Factors

Personal factors are the particular background of an individual's life and living. They may include sociodemographic factors, such as gender, race, age, and civil status. They may also include, health-related factors, such as comorbidities, fitness, and lifestyle, and behavioral factors and characteristics, such as habits, upbringing, coping styles, social background, education, profession, past and current experience, and overall behavior pattern. All of these may interact with functioning and therefore modify any level of disability. Personal factors are not classified in ICF yet because of the large social and cultural variance associated with them [16].

In vocational rehabilitation personal factors are identified to be major predictors and modifiers of return-to-work outcome. Age, gender, civil status, and ethnicity were identified to be predictors for return to work with higher age, being female, and being single were negatively correlated. Low job satisfaction, poor social networks, and a sense of powerlessness, having no control over the vocational rehabilitation process, no control over number and content of medical examinations and interventions, and the personal belief if one would return to work within 6 month were also strongly associated with the work outcome [61, 62].

Even though WORQ itself is not assessing personal factors except of some sociodemographic factors, the comprehensiveness in which the client's functioning is addressed conveyed the clients that they were looked at as whole individuals. Such an understanding may enable the professionals and representatives from the payer side to approach personal beliefs and behavioral patterns of clients in a more empathic way as a basis for a personalized and supportive guidance of the client [61, 63].

In summary, environmental factors and personal factors are constantly interacting with the functioning of a client. The specific influence of an environmental factor or a personal characteristic of a person has to be determined individually. Therefore, environmental factors and personal factors should be administered along with information on functioning. To enhance comparability and communication across professions and settings as well as to structure documentation and to improve interventions and rehabilitation management, it might be beneficial in the future to develop generic instruments on environmental and personal factors for the use in vocational rehabilitation.

Environmental factors and personal factors constantly interact with functioning. Hence environmental factors and personal factors should be administered along with the functioning information and taken into consideration when analyzing functioning problems.

Frame 23.1: Statistics – The Rasch Model

A Rasch model can be used for checking whether or not tested ICF categories are measuring the same construct, e.g., functioning in the context of work.

In a unidimensional Rasch model, aspects of functioning with varying levels of difficulty that measure the same underlying construct are expected to differentiate levels of functioning in clients, e.g., *walking*, *moving around*, and *using transportation* as aspect of the construct "mobility in vocational rehabilitation." This relation is referred to as the item fit between the data and the model.

A further assumption of the Rasch model is the absence of local dependencies, in which items in a test should not be related to close to each other.

The classical level of significance ($\alpha \leq 0.05$) in determining the model fit is usually Bonferroni corrected to reduce the probability of type one error. Measure for the strength of the local dependencies is usually expressed in a Spearman correlation and set at $r = 0.3$.

Measuring the same construct in a questionnaire is crucial when intending to sum the scores on the items. A Rasch analysis can be used to check the degree to which this scoring and summing is defensible.

Frame 23.2: WHO Disability Assessment Schedule 2.0 (WHODAS 2.0) and the World Health Survey (WHS)

WHODAS 2.0

Conceptually WHODAS 2.0 was developed by WHO, as a generic assessment instrument to produce standardized information on disability levels of individuals across cultures, in clinical setting as well as for the general population. It is based on the International Classification of Functioning, Disability, and Health (ICF) and can be used across all diseases, including mental, neurological, and addictive disorders.

WHODAS 2.0 covers six domains:

1. Cognition – understanding and communicating
2. Mobility – moving and getting around
3. Self-care – hygiene, dressing, eating and staying alone
4. Getting along – interacting with other people
5. Life activities – domestic responsibilities, leisure, work, and school
6. Participation – joining in community activities [REF:http://www.who.int/classifications/icf/whodasii/en/]

World Health Survey Instruments

The World Health Survey Instruments (WHS) were developed as self-reported questionnaires, tested, and translated to numerous languages to be used in the World Health Survey. This was initiated by WHO to strengthen

(continued)

Frame 23.2 (continued)
national capacity to monitor critical health outcomes and health systems by using valid, reliable, and comparable household survey instruments. It was designed as a real-life data-collection platform for obtaining information on the health of populations and health systems. It was first implemented in 2002–2004 in partnership with 70 countries. WHS contain nine sections:

1. Sociodemographic characteristics
2. Health state descriptions
3. Health state valuations
4. Risk factors
5. Mortality
6. Coverage
7. Health system responsiveness
8. Health goals and social capital
9. Interviewer observations

For the wording of WORQ, section 3000 "Health state valuation" of the long version of the Individual WHS questionnaire was looked at. [http://www.who.int/healthinfo/survey/instruments/en/].

Study Questions

1. Why does the ICF provide a suitable base for developing standardized instruments to assess and document functioning in individuals in vocational rehabilitation?

   Answer: The ICF was developed by the WHO as a reference framework and language to describe and measure functioning and disability of individuals with problems in functioning due to a health condition and has proven to be a valid framework in vocational rehabilitation. As vocational rehabilitation involves multiple stakeholder and diverse health care and work settings a common understanding of functioning, and a common language as provided by the ICF may enhance efficient communication between the client, professionals and across settings and therefore facilitate efficient return-to-work management.

2. What is the first and most important step, when developing a new assessment instrument like WORQ for example?

   Answer: The first step, when developing a new instrument is to clarify its purpose. Therefore three major questions have to be answered:

   1. What specific construct should be measured: WORQ was designed to measure functioning based on the ICF of individuals participating in vocational rehabilitation.

2. In which context should the respective instrument be used: WORQ was designed to be used in any vocational rehabilitation setting throughout the continuum of the return-to-work process.
3. Who should use the instrument: WORQ was designed to be administered by any health- or work professional and answered by a client in vocational rehabilitation.
4. In which population or health condition should an instrument be used: WORQ was designed to be used independent of any health condition.

3. Why should environmental factors and personal factors be administered along with information on functioning, when evaluating clients in vocational rehabilitation?

Answer: Environmental factors and personal factors constantly interact with the functioning of a client, yet the influence of a specific environmental factor or a personal characteristic may differ greatly between clients and therefore has to be determined individually. Obtaining information on environmental and personal factors would enhance comparability of data on functioning and may lead to a better interprofessional understanding of the client's needs.

References

1. OECD High-Level Forum. Sickness, disability and work; keeping on track in the economic downturn. Background paper, Stockholm; 14–15 May 2009. www.oecd.org/dataoecd/42/15/42699911.pdf. Accessed 1 Aug 2013.
2. De Boer WE, Besseling JJ, Willems JH. Organisation of disability evaluation in 15 countries. Prat et Organ des Soins. 2007;38(3):205–17.
3. OECD, editor. Sickness, disability and work: breaking the barriers. Paris: OECD; 2010.
4. Suva (Swiss accident insurance), editor. Medizinische Mitteilungen, Nr.79. Luzern: Suva; 2008.
5. Marnetott SU, Selander J, Bergroth A, Ekholm J. Factors associated with successful vocational rehabilitation in a Swedish rural area. J Rehabil Med. 2001;33(2):71–8.
6. Kapiriri L, Norheim FO, Martin DK. Priority setting at the micro-, meso- and macro-levels in Canada. Norway and Uganda. Health Policy. 2007;82(1):78–94.
7. Coutu MF, Legare F, Durand MJ, Corbiere M, Stacey D, Loisel P, et al. Fostering shared decision making by occupational therapists and workers involved in accidents resulting in persistent musculoskeletal disorders: a study protocol. Implement Sci. 2011;6:22-5908-6-22.
8. van der Weide WE, Verbeek JH, van Dijk FJ, Doef J. An audit of occupational health care for employees with low-back pain. Occup Med (Lond). 1997;47(5):294–300.
9. Brunarski D, Shaw L, Doupe L. Moving toward virtual interdisciplinary teams and a multi-stakeholder approach in community-based return-to-work care. Work. 2008;30(3):329–36.
10. Guzman J, Esmail R, Karjalainen K, Malmivaara A, Irvin E, Bombardier C. Multidisciplinary bio-psycho-social rehabilitation for chronic low back pain. Cochrane Database Syst Rev. 2002;1(1):CD000963.
11. Hoving JL, Broekhuizen ML, Frings-Dresen MH. Return to work of breast cancer survivors: a systematic review of intervention studies. BMC Cancer. 2009;9:117.

12. Kissinger DB. Traumatic brain injury and employment outcomes: integration of the working alliance model. Work. 2008;31(3):309–17.
13. Ware JE. SF-36 health survey. Manual and interpretation guide. Boston: The Health Institute, New England Medical Center; 1997.
14. Beck AT, Steer R, Brown G. Manual for the Beck depression inventory-II. San Antonio: Psychological Corporation; 1996.
15. Fairbank JC, Couper J, Davies JB, O'Brien JP. The Oswestry low back pain disability questionnaire. Physiotherapy. 1980;66(8):271–3.
16. World Health Organization. International classification of functioning, disability and health. Geneva: World Health Organization; 2001.
17. Finger ME, Escorpizo R, Glassel A, Gmunder HP, Luckenkemper M, Chan C, et al. ICF Core Set for vocational rehabilitation: results of an international consensus conference. Disabil Rehabil. 2012;34(5):429–38.
18. Escorpizo R, Finger ME, Glassel A, Cieza A. An international expert survey on functioning in vocational rehabilitation using the international classification of functioning, disability and health. J Occup Rehabil. 2011;21(2):147–55.
19. Finger ME, Glassel A, Erhart P, Gradinger F, Klipstein A, Rivier G, et al. Identification of relevant ICF categories in vocational rehabilitation: a cross sectional study evaluating the clinical perspective. J Occup Rehabil. 2011;21(2):156–66.
20. Saltychev M, Kinnunen A, Laimi K. Vocational rehabilitation evaluation and the International Classification of Functioning, Disability, and Health (ICF). J Occup Rehabil. 2013;23 (1):106–14.
21. World Health Organization (WHO), editor. How to use ICF: a practical manual for using the International Classification of Functioning, Disability and Health. Exposure draft for comment. Geneva: World Health Organization; 2013.
22. Selb M, Escorpizo R, Kostanjsek N, Stucki G, Üstün B, Cieza A. A guide on how to develop an International Classification of Functioning, Disability and Health Core Set. Eur J Phys Rehabil Med. 2014. [Epub ahead of print] April 1.
23. Cieza A, Oberhauser C, Bickenbach J, Chatterji S, Stucki G. Towards a minimal generic set of domains of functioning and health. Eur J Phys Rehabil Med. 2014;14(1):218.
24. Stucki G, Cieza A, Ewert T, Kostanjsek N, Chatterji S, Ustun TB. Application of the International Classification of Functioning, Disability and Health (ICF) in clinical practice. Disabil Rehabil. 2002;24(5):281–2.
25. Okochi J, Utsunomiya S, Takahashi T. Health measurement using the ICF: test-retest reliability study of ICF codes and qualifiers in geriatric care. Health Qual Life Outcomes. 2005;3:46.
26. Jette AM, Norweg A, Haley SM. Achieving meaningful measurements of ICF concepts. Disabil Rehabil. 2008;30(12–13):963–9.
27. Rentsch HP, Bucher P, Dommen Nyffeler I, Wolf C, Hefti H, Fluri E, et al. The implementation of the 'International Classification of Functioning, Disability and Health' (ICF) in daily practice of neurorehabilitation: an interdisciplinary project at the Kantonsspital of Lucerne. Switz Disabil Rehabil. 2003;25(8):411–21.
28. Hollenweger J. Developing applications of the ICF in education systems: addressing issues of knowledge creation, management and transfer. Disabil Rehabil. 2013;35(13):1087–91.
29. Jacob T. The implementation of the ICF among Israeli rehabilitation centers – the case of physical therapy. Physiother Theory Pract. 2013;29(7):536–46.
30. Glassel A, Rauch A, Selb M, Emmenegger K, Luckenkemper M, Escorpizo R. A case study on the application of International Classification of Functioning, Disability and Health (ICF)-based tools for vocational rehabilitation in spinal cord injury. Work. 2012;41(4):465–74.
31. Rauch A, Cieza A, Stucki G. How to apply the International Classification of Functioning, Disability and Health (ICF) for rehabilitation management in clinical practice. Eur J Phys Rehabil Med. 2008;44(3):329–42.

32. Finger M, Selb M, Escorpizo R. Using ICF in physiotherapy in multidisciplinary vocational rehabilitation: a case study of low back pain. Physiother Res Int. 2014. [Epub ahead of print] April 15.
33. Finch E, Brooks D, Stratford PW, Mayo NE. Physical rehabilitation outcome measures: a guide to enhanced clinical decision making. 2nd ed. Hamilton: BC Decker; 2002.
34. Krosnick JA, Presser S. Question and questionnaire design. In: Marsden PV, Wright JD, editors. Handbook of survey research. 2nd ed. Bingley: Emerald Group Publishing Limited; 2010. p. 263–313.
35. Linacre J. Sample size and item calibration stability. Rasch Meas Trans. 1994;7:328.
36. Linacre JM. Sample size and item calibration [or person measure] stability. Available at: www.rasch.org/rmt/rmt74m.htm. Accessed 28 Mar 2013.
37. Lydell M, Grahn B, Mansson J, Baigi A, Marklund B. Predictive factors of sustained return to work for persons with musculoskeletal disorders who participated in rehabilitation. Work. 2009;33(3):317–28.
38. Soer R, van der Schans CP, Geertzen JH, Groothoff JW, Brouwer S, Dijkstra PU, et al. Normative values for a functional capacity evaluation. Arch Phys Med Rehabil. 2009;90(10):1785–94.
39. Leung W. How to design a questionnaire. Stud Br Med J. 2001;9:187–9.
40. Üstün TB, Kostanjsek N, Chatterji S, Rehm J, editors. Measuring health and disability: manual for WHO Disability Assessment Schedule (WHODAS 2.0). Geneva: World Health Organization; 2010.
41. World Health Organization. World Health Survey instruments and related documents: long version: individual questionnaire. Available at: http://www.who.int/healthinfo/survey/whslonghouseholdhigh.pdf. Accessed 25 Jan 2012.
42. Wewers ME, Lowe NK. A critical review of visual analogue scales in the measurement of clinical phenomena. Res Nurs Health. 1990;13(4):227–36.
43. Hjermstad MJ, Fayers PM, Haugen DF, Caraceni A, Hanks GW, Loge JH, et al. Studies comparing Numerical Rating Scales, Verbal Rating Scales, and Visual Analogue Scales for assessment of pain intensity in adults: a systematic literature review. J Pain Symptom Manag. 2011;41(6):1073–93.
44. Forrest M, Andersen B. Ordinal scale and statistics in medical research. Br Med J (Clin Res Ed). 1986;292(6519):537–8.
45. Kersten P, Kucukdeveci AA, Tennant A. The use of the Visual Analogue Scale (VAS) in rehabilitation outcomes. J Rehabil Med. 2012;44(7):609–10.
46. Beaton DE, Bombardier C, Guillemin F, Ferraz MB. Guidelines for the process of cross-cultural adaptation of self-report measures. Spine (Phila Pa 1976). 2000;25(24):3186–91.
47. The EuroQol Group. EuroQol – a new facility for the measurement of health-related quality of life. Health Policy. 1990;16(3):199–208.
48. The WHOQOL Group. Development of the WHOQoL: rationale and current status. Int J Ment Health. 1994;23:24–56.
49. Finger M, Escorpizo R, Bostan C, De Bie R. Work Rehabilitation Questionnaire (WORQ): development and preliminary psychometric evidence of an ICF-based questionnaire for vocational rehabilitation. J Occup Rehabil. 2013;24(3):498–510.
50. Sangha O, Stucki G, Liang MH, Fossel AH, Katz JN. The Self-Administered Comorbidity Questionnaire: a new method to assess comorbidity for clinical and health services research. Arthritis Rheum. 2003;49(2):156–63.
51. Field A. Discovering statistics using SPSS. 3rd ed. London: Sage; 2009.
52. Hinkle D, Wiersma W, Jurs S, editors. Applied statistics for the behavioral sciences. 5th ed. Boston: Houghton Mifflin; 2003.
53. George D, Mallery P. SPSS for Windows step by step: a simple guide and reference. 11.0 update. 4th ed. Boston: Allyn and Bacon; 2003.
54. Bickenbach J, Cieza A, Selb M, Emmenegger K, Lückenkemper M, Escorpizo R, editors. ICF core sets: manual for clinical practice. 1st ed. Göttingen: Hogrefe; 2012.

55. Linder J, Ekholm KS, Jansen G, Lundh G, Ekholm J. Long-term sick leavers with difficulty in resuming work: comparisons between psychiatric-somatic comorbidity and monodiagnosis. Int J Rehabil Res. 2009;32(1):20–35.
56. Official Social Security Website, USA. Code of federal regulations § 404.1567. Physical exertiooon requirements. Available at: http://www.ssa.gov/OP_Home/cfr20/404/404-1567.htm. Accessed 20 Jan 2014.
57. Le Pen C, Levy E, Loos F, Banzet MN, Basdevant A. "Specific" scale compared with "generic" scale: a double measurement of the quality of life in a French community sample of obese subjects. J Epidemiol Community Health. 1998;52(7):445–50.
58. Streibelt M, Egner U. A systematic review of the predictors of return to work following vocational retraining. Rehabilitation (Stuttg). 2013;52(2):111–8.
59. Bergström G, Hagberg J, Busch H, Jensen I, Björklund C. Prediction of sickness absenteeism, disability pension and sickness presenteeism among employees with back pain. J Occup Rehabil. 2013. doi:10.1007/s10926-013-9454-9.
60. Zoer I, de Graaf L, Kuijer PP, Prinzie P, Hoozemans MJ, Frings-Dresen MH. Matching work capacities and demands at job placement in employees with disabilities. Work. 2012;42 (2):205–14.
61. Vocational Rehabilitation Task Group, Industrial Injuries Advisory Council, Waddell G, Burton AK, Kendall NA. Vocational rehabilitation – what works, for whom, and when? 1st ed. London: TSO (The Stationery Office); 2008.
62. Iles RA, Davidson M, Taylor NF. Psychosocial predictors of failure to return to work in non-chronic non-specific low back pain: a systematic review. Occup Environ Med. 2008;65 (8):507–17.
63. Nicholas MK, Linton SJ, Watson PJ, Main CJ, "Decade of the Flags" Working Group. Early identification and management of psychological risk factors ("yellow flags") in patients with low back pain: a reappraisal. Phys Ther. 2011;91(5):737–53.

Chapter 24
Applying the Work Rehabilitation Questionnaire WORQ: A Case Illustrating Its Use in Evaluating Functioning of a Person After a Traumatic Brain Injury in an Interprofessional Vocational Rehabilitation Setting

Melissa Selb, Monika Elisabeth Finger, and Reuben Escorpizo

24.1 The Impact of Traumatic Brain Injury on a Person's Vocational Situation

Irrespective of the nature of injury or level of functioning, traumatic brain injury (TBI) impacts on all aspects of the injured person's lived experience including work participation. Considering that a majority of persons who survive a TBI are of working age, the person with TBI still has many years to fulfill his vocational potential. In Chap. 10 Leonardi et al. referred to studies that indicate a low employment rate of persons following a TBI; the most recent findings showed an approximate return-to-work (RTW) rate of 40 % after injury and many persons included in the studies were unable to return to their former job or successfully maintain the job long-term [1]. Therefore, it would be important to answer the question: *What factors contribute to an increased or reduced potential for work participation?*

Despite the difficulty in defining indicators for accurate prediction of RTW outcomes in persons following TBI [2], there are some factors that seem to contribute to an increased potential for RTW. Among the most notable factors

M. Selb (✉) • M.E. Finger
Swiss Paraplegic Research, Guido-Zäch-Strasse 4, 6207 Nottwil, Switzerland

ICF Research Branch, WHO CC FIC in Germany (DIMDI), Nottwil, Switzerland
e-mail: melissa.selb@paraplegie.ch

R. Escorpizo
Swiss Paraplegic Research, Guido-Zäch-Strasse 4, 6207 Nottwil, Switzerland

ICF Research Branch, WHO CC FIC in Germany (DIMDI), Nottwil, Switzerland

Department of Rehabilitation and Movement Science, The University of Vermont, Burlington, VT, USA

R. Escorpizo et al. (eds.), *Handbook of Vocational Rehabilitation and Disability Evaluation*, Handbooks in Health, Work, and Disability, DOI 10.1007/978-3-319-08825-9_24

include self-awareness, pre-injury work situation, education level, functioning status and involvement in vocational rehabilitation [2, 3]. Accurate self-awareness seems to be related to a more positive long-term employment outcome following TBI, specifically with regard to a person's motivation toward interventions (treatment or rehabilitation) and appropriate goal-setting [2, 4, 5]. In addition to self-awareness, persons with a higher education level or those who had worked in a skilled or professional occupation before injury were more likely to return to work. Pre-injury employment is also related to higher RTW rates than those who were not employed before the TBI [2, 3]. Compared to the factors already mentioned, functional status, e.g., "physical disability, cognitive impairment, independence, psychosocial adjustment, and adaptation to the community", as assessed at discharge from rehabilitation, seems to be a more reliable and consistent predictor of RTW outcome of persons following TBI [3, 5]. Moreover, there is support for the prognostic value of mental functioning such as "concept formation, divided and selective attention, mental flexibility, mental programming, and planning." Last but not least involvement in vocational rehabilitation (VR) or utilization of rehabilitation services seems to improve vocational outcome [2, 3]. Shames et al. also emphasized that the coordinated effort between the vocational rehabilitation staff, client/patient, and when possible the employer is essential for a successful RTW [2, 4].

Although it is valuable to recognize the individual factors that contribute to increasing vocational potential in persons following a TBI, it is equally important or perhaps even more important to understand the complex interaction between them. Understanding the dynamic interaction of these influencing factors can facilitate the planning and implementation of strategies and interventions accordingly.

The biopsychosocial model of the International Classification of Functioning, Disability and Health (ICF) reflects this dynamic interaction between the health condition, e.g., TBI, body functions and structures, activities and participation, and environmental and personal factors [6].

The ICF can help to better understand the complex interactions between various factors that influence the vocational potential of persons with a health condition.

24.2 The Work Rehabilitation Questionnaire or WORQ

Since its endorsement by the World Health Assembly in May 2001, the ICF has become an internationally accepted standard for describing functioning of individuals experiencing impairments in their body functions and structures, limitations in carrying out activities, and restrictions in participating in vocational, social and community life due to a health condition. In an effort to make the ICF more practical for use in daily clinical practice, ICF Core Sets (ICF-CS) or short lists of ICF categories using an evidence-based scientific, multi-method process were developed [7–9]. The process includes four studies – a systematic literature review, an expert survey, a cross-sectional study, and a qualitative study that may include focus groups and individual interviews – all of which provides evidence for an iterative, consensus, and decision-making process that takes place during a conference of experts. The experts then decide the final selection of ICF categories for inclusion in the two types of ICF-CS, the comprehensive and the brief versions.

In 2010 the Comprehensive and Brief ICF-CS for VR were developed [7]. These shortlists of relevant ICF categories that can be used to describe and document the functioning of individuals who are participating in a VR program not only provide "functioning domains in an effort to examine VR outcomes and the multiple factors associated with VR", they served as the first step toward developing an ICF-based instrument for measuring functioning throughout the continuum of VR across various settings. All 13 categories of the Brief ICF-CS for VR served as the basis for the development of the Work Rehabilitation Questionnaire or WORQ [10–13]. WORQ also contains questions that reflect 31 categories from the comprehensive set and *d450 Walking* (since this category is part of the Generic Set) [14, 15]. See Chap. 23 for a detailed description of WORQ including information about its development.

WORQ consists of two parts. Part 1 consists of sociodemographic and work-related questions, and part two employs a visual analogue scale ranging from 0 to 100 (VAS-100) with anchor points of 0 (no problem) and 100 (complete problem). WORQ is intended to be patient-reported in two forms: interviewer-administered and self-reported and is applicable in any setting that provides VR. In this chapter, the self-report version (WORQ-SR) was used. Both forms of WORQ are described in more detail in Chap. 23.

> To facilitate the exploration of VR outcomes and the multiple factors associated with VR, the Brief and Comprehensive ICF-CS for VR served as the basis for developing WORQ.

24.3 Case History

This hypothetical case example is based on clinical experience and was constructed solely to demonstrate the use of WORQ-SR together with the ICF-CS for TBI in an interprofessional setting.

Tom, a 28-year-old single man, was in a car accident 7 months ago during which he incurred a brain injury. While waiting at a traffic light, another car hit his car from behind. At the time of the accident, he seemed to be uninjured although quite shaken. It was only a week post-accident that he went to seek medical attention due to nausea, recurring severe headache, some concentration problems, and periodic spatial disorientation. His general practitioner referred him to a neurologist. Although two MRIs showed no clear brain damage, the neurologist, who had considerable experience treating patients following a TBI, diagnosed Tom with mild TBI (*ICD-10: S06.0 Concussion*) [16] based on Tom's persistent symptoms. In addition, other symptoms, such as memory problems and fatigue as well as increased irritability, showed up in the time period before the diagnosis was made. The neurologist referred Tom to 3 months of rehabilitation.

At the time of the accident Tom had been working as a warehouse clerk with some personnel responsibilities for a large international furniture and home decorating store chain. His main tasks included processing incoming deliveries of goods using a designated computer program, unloading, stacking and storage of the goods using a forklift, supervising warehouse apprentices/trainees, and assisting customers to find products in the self-pickup warehouse. Tom had completed 2 years of university studies in business administration before deciding to work full time and stop his studies. Tom regularly worked for this store chain as entry-level warehouse worker during his university holidays. Since Tom was a "regular" temporary worker, a diligent employee, and a quick learner, he increasingly received additional responsibilities. After 2 years of working in the warehouse, he accepted a full-time job as a warehouse clerk and terminated his university studies. He had been working for this store chain full time for 5 years when the accident occurred. Following the accident, he was only able to work a few days. After his diagnosis, the neurologist put Tom on sick leave until after rehabilitation.

24.4 Setting and the RTW Program

One month post-injury, Tom was admitted to an interprofessional rehabilitation facility that also included an RTW program. Since the rehabilitation facility with a brain injury unit is far away from Tom's home, he had to be admitted as an inpatient. The brain injury unit team includes physicians, nurses, physical and occupational therapists, speech-language pathologists, a respiratory therapist, neuropsychologists, a behavioral psychologist, neuropsychiatrists, social workers, and a dietician. The rehabilitation facility's RTW program staff, i.e., vocational rehabilitation counselors or occupational therapists working as vocational specialists, collaborate closely with the brain injury unit as well as with the other units in the facility. The main objectives of the rehabilitation program are as follows: (1) community integration including return to work and (2) improved physical, cognitive, and behavioral functioning.

During the first 2 weeks of rehabilitation, patients undergo a battery of assessments in order to gain a baseline of patient functioning. The responsible vocational specialist also conducts an assessment for each patient in coordination with the brain injury unit. At the end of the 2 weeks, the rehabilitation team including the vocational specialist meets to discuss the assessment results and decide on a goal-oriented rehabilitation/intervention plan that can be discussed and decided together with the patient (and if appropriate with the patient's family). This chapter will focus on the activities of the RTW program. However, since the RTW program staff harmonizes assessments and interventions with those of the brain injury unit staff, the RTW program for each patient should also reflect the decisions and rehabilitation efforts of the brain injury unit.

24.5 Assessing Functioning with WORQ-SR and Brief ICF-CS for TBI

24.5.1 Gathering Information

Part of the initial assessment conducted by the vocational specialist is the use of WORQ-SR. The patient is asked to complete the WORQ-SR [11, 12], and the responsible vocational specialist briefly discusses the results with the patient. Discussing the results with the patient gives the vocational specialist the opportunity to reconfirm that the patient understood the questions and responded accurately, as well as gather additional information as needed, possibly building from work-related findings of the assessments conducted by the brain injury unit staff.

Since WORQ-SR is not health condition-specific, it is advisable to gather additional information that captures TBI-related aspects of a person's functioning that may impact on the person's work potential. This information can be drawn from the assessment findings from the brain injury unit by using the Brief ICF-CS for TBI [8]. The Brief ICF-CS for TBI is a set of 23 ICF categories that provides the minimal international standard for describing the functioning of a person following a TBI irrespective of severity or nature of the TBI. See Table 24.1. The ICF-CS for TBI, like the other ICF-CSs, is not itself a measurement instrument. It can, however, indicate aspects of functioning that should be measured and can be used for creating a functioning profile by rating the person's level of functioning in each of the categories included in the ICF-CS using *ICF qualifiers* [6]. The generic qualifier scale ranges from 0 to 4, with 0 = no problem, 1 = mild problem, 2 = moderate problem, 3 = severe problem, and 4 = complete problem. ICF qualifiers are explained in detail in Chap. 2 of this book.

> To acquire a comprehensive functioning profile that also reflects a person's experience with a specific health condition, WORQ can be used together with a health condition-specific ICF-CS.

Table 24.1 Overview of the ICF categories included in WORQ and the brief ICF Core Set for traumatic brain injury (ICF-CS for TBI)

		WORQ	Brief ICF-CS for TBI
Body functions (N = 18)		*N = 15*	*N = 8*
b110	Consciousness functions		X
b117	Intellectual functions	X	
b126	Temperament and personality functions	X	
b130	**Energy and drive functions (G)**	**X**	**X**
b134	Sleep functions	X	
b140	Attention functions		X
b144	**Memory functions**	**X**	**X**
b152	**Emotional functions (G)**	**X**	**X**
b160	Thought functions	X	
b164	**Higher-level cognitive functions**	**X**	**X**
b210	Seeing functions	X	
b230	Hearing functions	X	
b235	Vestibular functions	X	
b280	**Sensation of pain (G)**	**X**	**X**
b455	Exercise tolerance functions	X	
b730	Muscle power functions	X	
b760	Control of voluntary movement functions		X
b810	Protective functions of the skin	X	
Body structures (N = 1)		*N = 0*	*N = 1*
s110	Structure of brain		X
Activities and participation (N = 29)		*N = 26*	*N = 9*
d155	Acquiring skills	X	
d160	Focusing attention	X	
d166	Reading	X	
d177	Making decisions	X	
d210	Undertaking a single task	X	
d230	**Carrying out daily routine (G)**	**X**	**X**
d240	Handling stress and other psychological demands	X	
d315	Communicating with – receiving – nonverbal messages	X	
d350	**Conversation**	**X**	**X**
d360	Using communication devices and techniques	X	
d430	Lifting and carrying objects	X	
d440	Fine hand use	X	
d450	**Walking (G)**	**X**	**X**
d455	Moving around (G)	X	
d470	Using transportation	X	
d475	Driving	X	
d5	Self-care		X
d540	Dressing	X	
d570	Looking after one's health	X	

(continued)

Table 24.1 (continued)

		WORQ	Brief ICF-CS for TBI
d720	**Complex interpersonal interactions**	X	X
d760	Family relationships		X
d825	Vocational training	X	
d830	Higher education	X	
d840	Apprenticeship (work preparation)	X	
d845	**Acquiring, keeping and terminating a job**	X	X
d850	Remunerative employment (G)	X	
d855	Non-remunerative employment	X	
d870	Economic self-sufficiency	X	
d920	Recreation and leisure		X
Environmental factors (N = 8)		*N = 4*	*N = 6*
e115	Products or substances for personal use in daily living		X
e120	Products and technology for personal indoor and outdoor mobility and transportation		X
e310	**Immediate family**	X	X
e320	Friends		X
e330	People in positions of authority	X	
e570	Social Security services, systems and policies		X
e580	**Health services, systems and policies**	X	X
e590	Labour and employment services, systems, and policies	X	

ICF categories in bold are those that are included in both WORQ and Brief ICF-CS for TBI; (G) = category is part of the Generic Set

24.5.2 Electronic Version of WORQ and Brief ICF-CS for TBI

To ease and speed up the completion of WORQ-SR, an electronic version is available through the website www.myworq.org [12]. The electronic version allows the user to complete WORQ-SR for a particular patient, and a functioning profile can be produced. Since www.myworq.org is not supported by a secure database, the entered data must be saved on the user's own computer. The data can be reloaded for an additional assessment, e.g., a reassessment after a VR intervention. Ideally, the facility in which VR is offered within an interprofessional team should have an electronic documentation system in place, allowing all members of the interprofessional team, including the vocational specialist, to access the patient's medical, therapy, and VR documentation, e.g., WORQ-SR. Such an electronic documentation system will be incorporated in the hypothetical case example in this chapter. In addition to the electronic version of WORQ-SR, an electronic ICF-based documentation form is available that allows the user to select the Brief ICF-CS for TBI, or in combination with other ICF-CSs, to create a functioning profile for a specific person. The electronic ICF-based documentation form can be found on

◆◆
◆WORQ

Work Rehabilitation Questionnaire
Self-Report

Date **01/05/2013**
Day Month Year

Full Name **Tom XXX**
ID Number (if applicable) 1234

The Work Rehabilitation Questionnaire (WORQ) is a questionnaire that has been developed to better understand the extent of problems in functioning that people may have due to their health condition(s) and who are undergoing work or vocational rehabilitation. Part 1 of WORQ will ask for sociodemographics and background information. Part 2 will ask you a series of questions concerning your functioning. When answering part 2, think about your ***past week,*** *considering both your good and bad days and the extent of your problem on average in the past week.*

PART 1: SOCIODEMOGRAPHICS AND BACKGROUND INFORMATION

1. **Age (in years)** 28 years old   2. **Sex** ☐ female ☑ male

3. **Civil status** ☑ never married ☐ married ☐ separated ☐ divorced ☐widowed ☐ cohabiting/living with somebody

4. **Which best describes your current work status, or if currently not working your last work status?**
☑ Employed ☐ Self-employed ☐ Non-paid work such as volunteer
☐ Student or in training ☐ Homemaker ☐ Retired ☐ *Not applicable*

5. **Which of the following describes your current work status best?**
a. If currently working, are you? ☐ Full time ☐ Part time ☐ On modified or light duty
Or, if currently not working, are you? ☑ Not working due to health reason
☐ Not working due to participation in vocational rehabilitation
☐ Not working due to other reasons: Please specify

b) If currently not working, since when have you been off from work? 15/03/2013
Day Month Year

6. **When thinking about your work or vocational rehabilitation program: Are you currently:** (Check all that apply)
☐… Engaging in vocational training activities such as in acquiring knowledge and skills for a job, including school training
☐… Engaging in programs related to preparation for employment such as apprenticeship or internship
☑… Engaging in activities to secure or maintain your current job
☐… Looking for a (new) job or work

7. **What is the highest level of education that you have completed?**
☐ No formal schooling ☐ Less than primary school ☐ Primary school ☐ Secondary school
☑ College / university ☐ Post-graduate degree

8. **What is your current job or profession or if currently not working, what is the last job or profession you worked in (job title)?** ***Warehouse Clerk with personnel responsibilities***

9. **What kind of business, industry or service is (or was) your job in?**
(e.g., cardboard box manufacturing, road maintenance, retail shoe store, secondary school, dairy farm, municipal government) ***Retail***

Fig. 24.1 (continued)

10. What kind of work are (or were) you doing?
(e.g., driving trucks, operating machines, writing letters, answering telephone calls)

Processing incoming deliveries of goods, use of SAP, unloading and storing goods, driving a forklift, responsible for warehouse trainee, assisting customers to find goods

11. If a change of job is planned, what future job are you aiming for?

____________________ ☑ *Not applicable*

12. Are you in medical or therapeutic treatment? ☑ Yes ☐ No ☐ *Not applicable*
(e.g. with physician, therapists, etc.)?

If yes, please specify: ***In brain injury unit – doctors, occupational therapist, physical therapist, neuropsychologist, psychologist***

13. Do you have current restrictions? ☑ Yes ☐ No ☐ *Not applicable*
(e.g. lifting limited to 5kg, limited weight bearing on your leg or arm)

If yes, please specify: ***short-term memory (often forget things after only a few minutes), sometimes get lost and am unsure where I have to go, get tired very quickly, get frustrated easily – never had these problems before my accident. I am not myself.***

14. What kind of work or vocational intervention are you receiving now? (list all you know)
(e.g. physical training, cognitive training, case management, vocational training, work place adaptation, work evaluation etc.)

Interventions: ***Cognitive training, memory training, no direct vocational intervention***

15. In your current situation, do you get the support you need from your family ☑ Yes ☐ No ☐ *Not applicable*

If yes, please specify what kind of support you get:
Before rehab, my mother drove me to appointments and shopping, because I could not remember how to get to where I had to go. She and dad also give me moral support. My girlfriend and I talk every morning and evening. She motivates me and gives me hope.

16. If still employed, do you get the support you need from your supervisor or boss? ☑ Yes ☐ No ☐ *Not employed*

If yes, please specify what kind of support you get: ***My boss, also a friend of mine, said that after rehab, I can go back to my old job if everything is Ok again. He said that I changed a bit after the accident. I was an easy guy to work with. Afterwards I got irritated quickly.***

17. *Outside of your current work or vocational rehabilitation program,* do you get the support you need from government or private employment agencies to find suitable work, or looking for different work?

☐ Yes ☐ No ☑ *Not applicable*

If yes, please specify what kind of support you get:

____

Fig. 24.1 (continued)

PART 2: MAIN SECTION

Based on the scale below rate your level of problem in the past week for each question from 0 = no problem to 100 = complete problem. You are allowed to rate your problem using any number from 0 to 100. The higher the number you give, the more problem you experience for that question. You can look at the 0-100 scale again if you need to refresh your mind on how to answer the question. If you think that a question is not applicable to you, you can check "Not Applicable" in the rightmost column. Please answer all questions as accurately and completely as possible. *Make sure that your answer refers to your ability to function or do an activity without any help from anybody or without any assistive device.*

No Problem 0 — 10 — 20 — 30 — 40 — 50 — 60 — 70 — 80 — 90 — 100 **Complete Problem**

	Overall in the past week, to what extent did you have problems with...	No Problem Complete Problem 0...100	*Not Applicable*
1	... not feeling rested and refreshed during the day?	80	☐
2	... sleeping, such as falling asleep, waking up frequently during the night or waking up too early in the morning?	80	☐
3	... remembering to do important things?	70	☐
4	... your usual daily activities because you felt sad or depressed?	20	☐
5	... your usual daily activities because you felt worried or anxious?	20	☐
6	... being irritable?	70	☐
7	... your temper?	70	☐
8	... your self-confidence?	80	☐
9	... thinking clearly?	85	☐
10	... analyzing and finding solutions to problems in day to day life?	40	☐
11	... hearing?	0	☐
12	... keeping your balance while maintaining a position or during movement?	0	☐
13	... bodily aches or pains?	80	☐
14	... general endurance when performing physical activities?	80	☐
15	... muscle strength?	0	☐
16	... skin problems, such as broken skin, ulcers, bedsores and thinning of skin?	0	☐
17	... learning a new task (e.g., learning a new game, learning how to use the computer, learning how to use a tool, etc.)?	0	☐
18	... focusing attention on a specific task or e.g. filtering out distractions such as noise?	75	☐
19	... reading?	40	☐
20	... making decisions?	25	☐
21	... starting and completing a single task such as making your bed or cleaning up your desk or workplace?	0	☐

Fig. 24.1 (continued)

	Overall in the past week, to what extent did you have problems with...	No Problem Complete Problem 0...100	Not Applicable
22	... carrying out your daily routine or day to day activities?	70	☐
23	... handling stress, crises, or conflict?	70	☐
24	... understanding body gestures, symbols and drawings?	0	☐
25	... starting and maintaining a conversation?	0	☐
26	... using communication devices such as using a telephone, telecommunication devices, and computers?	65	☐
27	... lifting and carrying objects weighing up to 5kg?	0	☐
28	... lifting and carrying objects weighing more than 5kg?	0	☐
29	... fine hand use such as handling objects, picking up, manipulating and releasing objects using the hand, fingers, and thumb?	0	☐
30	... walking a short distance (less than 1 km)?	0	☐
31	... walking a long distance (more than 1 km)?	0	☐
32	... moving around including crawling, climbing, and running?	0	☐
33	... using transportation as a passenger ?	0	☐
34	... driving a car or any form of transportation?	20	☐
35	... getting dressed?	0	☐
36	... looking after your health such as maintaining a balanced diet, getting enough physical activity, and seeing your doctor as needed?	0	☐
37	... your relationships with people?	25	☐
38	... having sufficient money to cover your cost of living?	0	☐

>> Do you wear glasses or contact lenses? Yes ☐ / No ☑

	Overall in the past week, to what extent did you have problems with...	No Problem Complete Problem 0...100	Not Applicable
39	... seeing and recognizing an object at arm's length?	0	☐
40	... seeing and recognizing a person you know across the road (distance of about 20 meters or 66 feet)?	0	☐

	Overall in the past week, how long did it take you...	Hours needed	Not Applicable
41	... in the morning to get up and get ready (washed, dressed, have breakfast) to leave the house?	1	☐
42	... to do all the necessary things required throughout the whole week for your health, such as attending therapy, or medical consultations, or doing your exercises?	35	☐

-End-

Thank you for your participation!

Finger ME, Escorpizo R, Bostan C, De Bie R. Work Rehabilitation Questionnaire (WORQ): Development and Preliminary Psychometric Evidence of an ICF-Based Questionnaire for Vocational Rehabilitation. J Occup Rehabil. 2014;24(3): 498-510.

Fig. 24.1 Work Rehabilitation Questionnaire

www.icf-core-sets.org [13]. Like the electronic version of WORQ-SR, the data entered on the electronic ICF-based documentation form must be saved on the user's own computer and reloaded for an additional assessment.

The electronic version of WORQ, available at www.myworq.org and the electronic ICF-based documentation form, available at www.icf-core-sets.org, can ease and speed up the documentation on functioning status.

24.5.3 *Creating a Functioning Profile Based on WORQ-SR and the Brief ICF-CS for TBI*

Upon Tom's completion of WORQ-SR, the vocational specialist met with him to discuss the results. See Fig. 24.1 for the completed WORQ-SR.

The discussion between Tom and the vocational specialist enabled them to clarify comprehension issues related to some WORQ-SR questions. For example, Tom understood that question 13 "*Do you have current restrictions?*" required him to list the functioning problems he was experiencing at the time of the assessment. This question, however, refers to recommendations provided by the doctor or another health professional for restricting a patient's activities in consideration of the patient's current health status and recovery process. Based on this, Tom changed his response to "no" restrictions. Moreover, the vocational specialist had the opportunity to gather additional information about Tom's work situation before and after his TBI including his relationships with his supervisor and co-workers, what he enjoyed and disliked about his job, and details about his work tasks. Tom also clearly indicated that his goal for rehabilitation is to restore his functioning to the level that he is able to return to work full time at his pre-TBI job. In response, the vocational specialist informed Tom of various options for facilitating his returning to work with the help of vocational counseling and coaching. See Chaps. 5 and 8 for a description of vocational counseling and job placement, respectively.

WORQ can support client/patient-health professional communication by providing an opportunity to discuss the client/patient's experience in completing WORQ as well as the results.

Based on Tom's responses to WORQ, additional information gathered in the bilateral discussion including his expressed long and short-term goals, as well as work-related information derived from the assessment findings from the brain injury unit, the vocational specialist created a functioning profile specifically for Tom.

The functioning profile generated using the electronic ICF-based documentation form on www.icf-core-sets.org is a simplified version of the *Categorical Profile* described in Chap. 22. In addition to enabling the user to rate a patient's functioning based on information gathered from various sources like the case history, patient-reported questionnaires like WORQ, clinical examination reports, clinical/diagnostic tests, etc., the Categorical Profile requires the user to state long and short-term goals, link the ratings to these goals, and identify a target rating for each ICF category defined.

In the case of Tom, the categories defined were derived from WORQ and the Brief ICF-CS for TBI. To the 56 ICF categories of the combined set, *coping with health condition* and *motivated to return to work* were added to account for personal factors that were revealed as having an impact on RTW during the meeting between Tom and the vocational specialist as well as from the psychologist's assessment report. See Table 24.2.

Several of the categories were rated with 8 "not specified" or 9 "not applicable." For example, *s110 Structure of brain*, a category derived from the Brief ICF-CS for TBI, was rated with an ICF qualifier of 8, since none of the brain injury unit reports pinpointed a definite lesion on the brain. The categories of education and employment (*d825 Vocational training, d830 Higher education, d840 Apprenticeship, d845 Acquiring, keeping and terminating a job, d850 Remunerative employment, and d855 Non-remunerative employment*) were rated with 9, since Tom was not engaged in any of these education/employment situations at the time of assessment. Moreover, the developers of WORQ, as explained in Chap. 23, intended these categories to provide insight into the type of work, work setting, or vocational intervention in which the patient is involved rather than reflect the patient/client's functioning status in these categories. The environmental factor *e590 Labour and employment services, systems, and policies* was also rated with 9, since Tom was intending to return to his pre-TBI employer and not receiving any employment services.

The functioning profile can also be helpful in highlighting aspects of functioning that may require additional assessment and testing for selected disciplines within the rehabilitation team. For example, on WORQ-SR Tom rated his problem in *d475 Driving* with a VAS of 20, equivalent to an ICF qualifier of 1 or mild difficulty. In the discussion about this WORQ-SR result, Tom clarified that his problem is less the act of driving but rather the orientation to the streets during driving. Since one of Tom's main tasks at the store chain is driving a forklift around a large warehouse with many numbered corridors and sections, the vocational specialist recommended to the occupational therapist and neuropsychologist that they consider conducting additional tests addressing the execution of driving. Driving is also important for Tom's RTW potential, since his workplace is more accessible by car than by public transport.

Table 24.2 Functioning profile

Goal definition for vocational rehabilitation		Assessment (1.5 months post-trauma) 0 1 2 3 4		
Long-term Goal (LTG): Return to work at pre-trauma employer				0
Short-term Goal 1 (STG1): Develop strategies to better handle stress and react in a constructive manner				1
Short-term Goal 2 (STG2): Learn strategies/techniques to organize thoughts better and compensate for memory problems				1
ICF categories		**ICF Qualifier[†] (First value)**	**Goal Relation**	**Expected Goal value**
ICF Code	**ICF title**	+4 +3 +2 +1 0 1 2 3 4		
b110	Consciousness functions *		--	--
b117	Intellectual functions		--	--
b126	Temperament and personality functions		STG1/2	1
b130	Energy and drive functions		LTG, STG1	1
b134	Sleep functions		LTG, STG1/2	1
b140	Attention functions *		STG2	1
b144	Memory functions		STG2	1
b152	Emotional functions		LTG	0
b160	Thought functions		STG2	1
b164	Higher-level cognitive functions		STG2	1
b210	Seeing functions		--	--
b230	Hearing functions		--	--
b235	Vestibular functions		--	--
b280	Sensation of pain		LTG, STG1/2	1
b455	Exercise tolerance functions		LTG, STG1	1
b730	Muscle power functions		--	--
b760	Control of voluntary movement functions *		--	--
b810	Protective functions of the skin		--	--
s110	Structure of brain *	8	--	--
d155	Acquiring skills		--	--
d160	Focusing attention		STG 2	1
d166	Reading		LTG	1
d177	Making decisions		LTG	1
d210	Undertaking a single task		--	--
d230	Carrying out daily routine		LTG	0
d240	Handling stress and other psychological demands		LTG, STG1	0

d315	Communicating with – receiving – nonverbal messages		--	--
d350	Conversation		--	--
d360	Using communication devices and techniques		LTG, STG2	1
d430	Lifting and carrying objects		--	--
d440	Fine hand use		--	--
d450	Walking		--	--
d455	Moving around		--	--
d470	Using transportation		--	--
d475	Driving		LTG	0
d5	Self-care *		--	--
d540	Dressing		--	--
d570	Looking after one's health		--	--
d720	Complex interpersonal interactions		LTG, STG1	0
d760	Family relationships *		--	--
d825	Vocational training	9	--	--
d830	Higher education	9	--	--
d840	Apprenticeship (work preparation)	9	--	--
d845	Acquiring, keeping and terminating a job	9	--	--
d850	Remunerative employment	9	-	--
d855	Non-remunerative employment	9	--	--
d870	Economic self-sufficiency		--	--
d920	Recreation and leisure *		Not targeted	Not targeted
e115	Products or substances for personal use in daily living *		STG2	+4
e120	Products and technology for personal indoor and outdoor mobility and transportation *	9	--	--
e310	Immediate family		LTG, STG1	+4
e320	Friends *		LTG, STG1	+4
e330	People in positions of authority		LTG, STG1	+4
e570	Social Security services, systems and policies *		STG2	+4
e580	Health services, systems and policies		Not targeted	Not targeted
e590	Labour and employment services, systems and policies	9	--	--
Influence of Personal Factors				
		positive / neutral / negative		
PF	Coping with health situation	positive	STG 1/2	positive
PF	Motivated to return to work	positive	LTG	positive

*ICF categories added from the Brief ICF Core Set for Traumatic Brain Injury that are not included in WORQ.

† ICF qualifiers ranged from 0 (no problem) to 4 (complete problem) in the body functions, body structures, and activity and participation and from 4 (complete barrier) to +4 (complete facilitator) in the environmental factors. In personal factors, the positive, neutral, or negative influence on the patient's functioning is marked.

24.6 Implications for Goal-Setting and Intervention Planning

With the conclusion of the initial assessments, the rehabilitation team including the vocational specialist met to discuss the assessment results. During this meeting, the functioning profile, among other reports, was reviewed and considered toward deciding on a rehabilitation intervention plan that could be proposed to Tom. The *ICF Intervention Table* that was introduced in Chap. 22, could be employed at this point in the rehabilitation-planning phase for outlining the interventions and the respective team member(s) responsible for each intervention. The use of the ICF Intervention Table will not be detailed in this case example.

Since the role of the individual in the VR process is important for successful RTW [17, 18], getting Tom's feedback on the rehabilitation intervention plan proposed by the interprofessional team is essential for appropriately planning the work-oriented rehabilitation interventions.

The information gathered using the results from WORQ and the rating of the selected condition-specific ICF-CS can serve as the basis for a person's functioning profile as well as inform the planning and evaluation of work-oriented interventions.

24.7 Evaluating Functioning After Interventions

In addition to determining specific assessments, identifying goals, and planning interventions, WORQ in combination with the Brief ICF-CS in the form of a functioning profile as described above can be used to document a person's functioning over time [9–11, 14, 19]. Since the functioning profile is only a snapshot of a person's functioning at one time point, the functioning profile has to be adapted to reflect the person's functioning at a later point in time. Rauch et al. proposed an ICF-based documentation sheet called *Evaluation Display* [19] to document the change over time. Since the Evaluation Display requires the user to re-rate the ICF categories from the first functioning profile, the Evaluation Display enables the user to see whether the person has achieved the goals set at the time of the previous assessment. Along with the Categorical Profile and Intervention Sheet, the Evaluation Display is also described in more detail in Chap. 22. See Table 24.3 for the Evaluation Display created for Tom.

Table 24.3 ICF evaluation display comprises initial assessment

Goal definition and achievement for vocational rehabilitation			Assessment (1.5 months post-trauma)		Evaluation (4 months post-trauma)	
Goal achievement			0 1 2 3 4		0 1 2 3 4	
Long-term Goal (LTG): Return to work full-time at pre-trauma employer				0		✓
Short-term Goal 1 (STG1): Develop strategies to better handle stress and react in a constructive manner				1		✓✓
Short-term Goal 2 (STG2): Learn strategies/techniques to organize thoughts better and compensate for memory problems				1		✓✓
ICF categories			**ICF Qualifier**†	**Expected** Goal value	**ICF Qualifier**†	**Achieved** Goal value
ICF Code	**ICF title**	**Interventions**	+4 +3 +2 +1 0 1 2 3 4		+4 +3 +2 +1 0 1 2 3 4	
b126	Temperament and personality functions	Psychological counseling		1		✓✓
b130	Energy and drive functions	Psychological counseling		1		--
b134	Sleep functions	Medical, Psychological counseling		1		✓✓
b140	Attention functions *	Cognitive training		1		--
b144	Memory functions	Cognitive training		1		✓✓
b152	Emotional functions	Psychological counseling		0		--
b160	Thought functions	Cognitive training		1		✓✓
b164	Higher-level cognitive functions	Cognitive training		1		✓✓
b280	Sensation of pain	Medication, Psychological		1		✓✓
b455	Exercise tolerance functions	Endurance training		1		✓✓
d160	Focusing attention	Cognitive training		1		✓✓
d166	Reading	Cognitive training		1		✓✓
d177	Making decisions	Psychological counseling		1		✓✓
d230	Carrying out daily routine	Occupational therapy		0		✓
d240	Handling stress and other psychological demands	Psychological counseling		0		✓✓
d360	Using communication devices and techniques	Occupational therapy, Voc. Coaching		1		✓✓
d475	Driving	Occupational therapy, Voc. Coaching		0		--
d720	Complex interpersonal interactions	Psychological counseling		0		✓✓
e115	Products or substances for personal use in daily living *	Occupational therapy		+4		✓✓
e310	Immediate family	Psychological counseling		+4		✓✓

(continued)

Table 24.3 (continued)

e320	Friends *	Psychological counseling		+4		–
e330	People in positions of authority	Vocational counseling Liaison with employer		+4		✓✓
e570	Social Security services, systems and policies *	Social work counseling		+4		–

Influence of Personal Factors												
Goal definition and achievement for vocational rehabilitation			Assessment (5 months post-trauma)						Evaluation (7 months post-trauma)			
			First value			Expected Goal value			Final value			Achieved Goal value
			Pos.	Neutr	Neg	Pos.	Neutr	Neg	Pos.	Neutr	Neg	
PF	Coping with health situation	Psychological therapy										✓✓
PF	Motivated to return to work	Vocational counseling										✓✓

✓= partly achieved
✓✓=achieved completely
-- = not achieved

*ICF categories added from the Brief ICF Core Set for Traumatic Brain Injury that are not included in WORQ.

† ICF qualifiers ranged from 0 (no problem) to 4 (complete problem) in the body functions, body structures, and activity and participation and from 4 (complete barrier) to +4 (complete facilitator) in the environmental factors. In personal factors, the positive, neutral, or negative influence on the patient's functioning is marked.

The ICF Evaluation Display can be used to document change over time, and assess whether the shared goals set by the client/patient and rehabilitation team at the time of the previous assessment were achieved.

Tom's Evaluation Table completed 2 weeks before discharge from rehabilitation revealed that he achieved most of his goals. Since some goals were not achieved (b130 Energy and drive functions and b140 Attention functions) Tom was only able to return to work part-time at the time of discharge. Accordingly, his long-term goal of returning to work full time at his pre-trauma employer was only partly achieved.

24.8 Value of Employing WORQ in the VR Process

This case example has shown that the value of employing WORQ in combination with the respective condition-specific ICF-CS (in this case the Brief ICF-CS for TBI) in the VR process is manifold.

First, WORQ can serve as a *standardized and comprehensive way of information gathering*. In Chap. 8 Homa and DeLambo emphasized that a comprehensive and accurate evaluation of the client/patient from the start is key to a well-planned VR program and could ultimately facilitate an appropriate RTW decision. WORQ was designed to provide the VR specialist and other professionals involved in the VR process with a tangible guide for acquiring a comprehensive overview of physical, mental, cognitive, and social aspects as well as sociodemographics and work-related information that could influence the VR process. WORQ in combination with the respective condition-specific ICF-CS can drive the work-oriented assessment process and help evaluate the patient's overall progress in the program. Moreover, initial validation and testing have shown that WORQ and WORQ-SR are reliable, consistent, and easy to be administered by health professionals, vocational specialists, case managers, and patients alike [10, 11] – thus increasing the potential for its implementation in practice.

WORQ, in combination with a selected condition-specific or context-specific ICF-CS, can be useful in driving the VR process, by providing a guide for gathering relevant information in a standardized and comprehensive way.

Second, WORQ and the functioning profile derived from WORQ can *facilitate interprofessional communication*. In several chapters of this book, specifically Chaps. 5 and 8, the authors promote the notion that transdisciplinary exchange [20] between professionals involved in the VR is essential for the success of the VR process. In this case example, the transdisciplinary communication was supported through the use of the WORQ- and ICF-CS-based functioning profile in both the assessment phase and in planning the rehabilitation interventions. In addition, WORQ itself proved to be an "ice-breaker," that is, a tool that opens up the discussions for several topics. The vocational specialist used WORQ to gather additional information that contributed to the quality of the individualized and goal-oriented functioning profile.

WORQ can facilitate interprofessional communication that can, in turn, contribute to the success of the VR process.

Lastly, WORQ is the starting point for setting VR goals. WORQ provides the foundation for a RTW-oriented functioning profile. In this case example, the functioning profile/Categorical Profile generated from the ICF categories of WORQ and the ICF-CS for TBI facilitated goal-setting in the VR plan by explicitly asking the user to indicate the expected goal value in relation to the patient/client's level of functioning as represented by the bar diagram. Moreover, the bar diagram of the patient/client's level of functioning helps users to visualize the patient/client's functioning status, presumably making the overall goal-setting task easier.

24.9 Next Steps

Since the case example described here is hypothetical, albeit based on real-life experiences, there is a need to longitudinally test the real-life utility of WORQ in various VR settings involving diverse stakeholders.

In conclusion, WORQ seems to offer a user-friendly ICF-based instrument for assessing work-oriented functioning in VR, and that would additionally support interdisciplinary planning of the VR process with the ultimate goal of work participation.

Study Questions

1. What information do the questions in WORQ cover?

   Answer: In addition to sociodemographics and work-related questions, WORQ contains questions that reflect all 13 categories of the Brief ICF-CS for VR, 31 categories of the Comprehensive ICF-CS and d450 Walking.

2. In the case example, why was the category s110 Structure of brain (please make the ICF category italics) was rated with the ICF qualifier of 8 and e590 Labour and employment services, systems and policies (please make the ICF category italics) with 9?

Answer: An ICF qualifier of 8 is defined as "not specified". Since none of the assessment reports received from brain injury unit pinpointed a definite lesion on the brain, s110 was considered not specified. An ICF qualifier of 9 is defined as "not applicable". Since Tom, the person in the case study, intended to return to work to his pre-injury employer and was not receiving employment services, e590 was considered not applicable.

3. List at least three (3) benefits of using WORQ in the VR process

   Answer:
   At least three of the following:

   1. Can serve as a standardized and comprehensive way of gathering information
   2. Facilitate interprofessional communication
   3. Facilitate client/patient-health professional communication
   4. Can be the basis for developing a functioning profile
   5. Can serve as a starting point for setting and evaluating VR goals

References

1. Van Velzen JM, Van Bennekom CA, Edelaar MJ, Sluiter JK, Frings-Dresen MH. How many people return to work after acquired brain injury?: a systematic review. Brain Inj. 2009;23 (6):473–88.
2. Shames J, Treger I, Ring H, Giaquinto S. Return to work following traumatic brain injury: trends and challenges. Disabil Rehabil. 2007;29(17):1387–95.
3. Ownsworth T, McKenna K. Investigation of factors related to employment outcome following traumatic brain injury: a critical review and conceptual model. Disabil Rehabil. 2004;26 (13):765–83.
4. Sherer M, Bergloff P, Levin E, High Jr WM, Oden KE, Nick TG. Impaired awareness and employment outcome after traumatic brain injury. J Head Trauma Rehabil. 1998;13(5):52–61.
5. Wehman P, Targett P, West M, Kregel J. Productive work and employment for persons with traumatic brain injury: what have we learned after 20 years? J Head Trauma Rehabil. 2005;20 (2):115–27.
6. World Health Organization. International Classification of Functioning, Disability and Health (ICF). Geneva: World Health Organization; 2001.
7. Finger ME, Escorpizo R, Glassel A, Gmunder HP, Luckenkemper M, Chan C, et al. ICF Core Set for vocational rehabilitation: results of an international consensus conference. Disabil Rehabil. 2012;34(5):429–38.
8. Laxe S, Zasler N, Selb M, Tate R, Tormos JM, Bernabeu M. Development of the International Classification of Functioning, Disability and Health core sets for traumatic brain injury: an International consensus process. Brain Inj. 2013;27(4):379–87.
9. Selb M, Escorpizo R, Kostanjsek N, Stucki G, Üstün TB, Cieza A. A guide on how to develop an International Classification of Functioning, Disability and Health Core Set. Eur J Phys Rehabil Med. 2014; in press.
10. Finger ME, Escorpizo R, Bostan C, De Bie R. Work Rehabilitation Questionnaire (WORQ): development and preliminary psychometric evidence of an ICF-based questionnaire for vocational rehabilitation. J Occup Rehabil. 2014; 24(3): 498–510.

11. Portmann Bergamaschi R, Escorpizo R, Staubli S, Finger ME. Content validity of the Work Rehabilitation Questionnaire-Self-Report Version WORQ-SELF in a subgroup of spinal cord injury patients. Spinal Cord. 2014; 52(3): 225–30.
12. Finger ME, Escorpizo R. Work Rehabilitation Questionnaire Self-Reported version (WORQ-SR). Swiss Paraplegic Research ICF Research Branch [cited 2014]. Available from: http://www.myworq.org/
13. ICF Research Branch in cooperation with the World Health Organization Family of International Classifications collaborating centre in Germany (at DIMDI), Swiss Paraplegic Research. Electronic ICF-based documentation [cited 2014]. Available from: http://www.icf-core-sets.org
14. Bickenbach JE, Cieza A, Rauch A, Stucki G, editors. ICF core sets. Manual for clinical practice. Göttingen: Hogrefe; 2012.
15. Cieza A, Oberhauser C, Bickenbach JE, Chatterji S, Stucki G. Towards a minimal generic set of domains of functioning and health. BMC Public Health. 2014;14(1):218.
16. World Health Organization. International statistical classification of diseases and related health problems (ICD). Geneva: World Health Organization; 2010.
17. Schonherr MC, Groothoff JW, Mulder GA, Schoppen T, Eisma WH. Vocational reintegration following spinal cord injury: expectations, participation and interventions. Spinal Cord. 2004;42(3):177–84.
18. Selander J, Marnetoft SU, Bergroth A, Ekholm J. Return to work following vocational rehabilitation for neck, back and shoulder problems: risk factors reviewed. Disabil Rehabil. 2002;24(14):704–12.
19. Rauch A, Cieza A, Stucki G. How to apply the International Classification of Functioning, Disability and Health (ICF) for rehabilitation management in clinical practice. Eur J Phys Rehabil Med. 2008;44(3):329–42.
20. Cartmill C, Soklaridis S, David Cassidy J. Transdisciplinary teamwork: the experience of clinicians at a functional restoration program. J Occup Rehabil. 2011;21(1):1–8.

Part IV
The Way Forward

Chapter 25
Challenges and Opportunities

Reuben Escorpizo, Soren Brage, Debra Homa, and Gerold Stucki

25.1 Global Perspective

A landmark convention by the United Nations (UN) that is likely to have the most impact on persons with disability in recent history is the United Nations Convention on the Rights of Persons with Disabilities (UNCRPD) [1]. The UN adopted the UNCRPD in 2006 with the intent to change the attitudes and approaches to persons with disability, including children. The convention is premised on providing the foundation of human rights for all persons with disability regardless of their disability; it puts persons with disability in equal position to those persons without disability in terms of their rights of access to services and opportunities. This is a critical piece to current efforts by the community advocating for persons with disability whether in the realm of vocational rehabilitation or return-to-work and

R. Escorpizo (✉)
Department of Rehabilitation and Movement Science, The University of Vermont, Burlington VT 05405, USA

Swiss Paraplegic Research, Nottwil, Switzerland

ICF Research Branch, WHO CC FIC in Germany (DIMDI), Nottwil, Switzerland
e-mail: escorpizo.reuben@gmail.com

S. Brage
Research Unit, Directorate for Labour and Welfare, Oslo, Norway

D. Homa
Department of Rehabilitation and Counseling, University of Wisconsin-Stout, Menomonie, WI, USA

G. Stucki
Swiss Paraplegic Research, Nottwil, Switzerland

ICF Research Branch, WHO CC FIC in Germany (DIMDI), Nottwil, Switzerland

Department of Health Sciences and Health Policy, University of Lucerne, Lucerne, Switzerland

R. Escorpizo et al. (eds.), *Handbook of Vocational Rehabilitation and Disability Evaluation*, Handbooks in Health, Work, and Disability, DOI 10.1007/978-3-319-08825-9_25

social security and disability evaluation. The guiding principles of the UNCRPD emphasize the rights of persons with disability with regard to nondiscrimination, full and effective participation and inclusion in society, acceptance of persons with disability as part of humanity, and having equal opportunity, and accessibility [1]. These are essential principles when assessing persons with disability and will need to be integrated in health and health-related policy by the government and organizations that provide services and care for persons with disability so as to optimize their functioning and mitigate their disability. As a major life area of participation for most individuals, work is an integral part of life and everyday living and can seriously be impacted with the presence of a health condition. Hence, our ability to capture disability and work disability in particular is critical.

Published in 2011, the World Report on Disability's [2] definition of "disability" is mainly predicated on the World Health Organization's International Classification of Functioning, Disability and Health (ICF) [3] where disability is defined as an umbrella term for impairment of bodily structures and bodily functions, activity limitations, and participation restrictions. Furthermore, disability occurs when there is negative interaction between the health condition and contextual factors such as environmental factors and personal factors that may impact the body and the societal role of a person [3]. The adoption of this broad definition of disability is the first step towards a common understanding of disability and coordinating efforts so as to mitigate disability at the level of the individual while also taking into account the public health perspective.

The United Nations Convention on the Rights of Persons with Disabilities (UNCRPD) emphasizes the rights of persons with disability with regard to nondiscrimination, full and effective participation and inclusion in society, acceptance of persons with disability as part of humanity, and having equal opportunity, and accessibility. The International Classification of Functioning, Disability and Health (ICF) is a framework by the World Health Organization (WHO) to understand disability based on impairment of bodily structures and bodily functions, activity limitations, and participation restrictions of a person.

25.2 Vocational Rehabilitation and Disability Evaluation

The ICF provides a comprehensive framework, a consistent classification, and relevant ICF Core Sets for disability evaluation and vocational rehabilitation. The relational concepts of illness and functioning and the emphasis on personal and environmental factors are in concordance with recent advances in social security. An integrative biopsychosocial model is increasingly being considered and used in social security institutions in many countries in the world. The ICF also provides an understanding of the multifocal aspects of functioning that could be used easily in vocational rehabilitation settings and social security systems.

Helping individuals find jobs that are aligned with their interests and abilities is a key task of job development, and vocational assessment should help individuals select suitable occupational goals and services needed to promote their success. Thus, vocational rehabilitation professionals need to assess the correspondence or "fit" between the individual's interests and abilities and the needs and requirements of the individual's current or prospective work environment. Where the "fit" is less than optimal, they may determine how to improve it through various types of interventions, such as job accommodations, skills training, and counseling. The ICF framework is ideally suited in providing a holistic approach to vocational rehabilitation that is sufficiently comprehensive for purposes of vocational rehabilitation planning and service provision. Ultimate employment success often depends on the result of variables interacting at both micro (individual) and macro (societal) levels; the ICF can help vocational rehabilitation professionals identify the multiple factors at these levels that have an impact on employment. Identification of these factors can then provide the basis of vocational rehabilitation strategies that are more precisely calibrated to address problems and improve the likelihood of success. A particularly important advantage of the ICF framework is that it helps vocational rehabilitation professionals be more aware of the environmental factors that have an impact on individuals' ability to perform successfully at school and/or work, as research suggests that environmental variables are likely to be overlooked, while personal characteristics are given more attention.

The ICF provides a comprehensive framework and classification, and relevant ICF Core Sets for disability evaluation and vocational rehabilitation. The ICF is ideally suited in providing a holistic approach to vocational rehabilitation for purposes of vocational rehabilitation planning and service provision.

25.3 Challenges

The full integration of the ICF in social security will take some time. While the framework and to some extent the classification have been adopted in many social security organizations to support and clarify the assessment of the individual's functional ability and disability, the classification is not widely used. The uptake and progress in implementation might be slow, since social security organizations by tradition act slowly. Changes in policy and working methods have to be channeled through political procedures and could take a long time to prepare, discuss, and decide. An overall general challenge is to make this process as quick and efficient as possible.

Social security organizations need to change their approach to disability evaluation. Many have retained a disease-oriented approach, and there is a need to change to a strong focus on functioning. This indeed requires a paradigm shift and progressive approach in social security. Many countries have started this process. There is a need for functioning assessment and evaluation of work ability in two settings that can be seen in a continuum. One setting is vocational rehabilitation where we need assessments to guide the return-to-work processes; another is the need for assessments to determine the right to benefits. We need to develop ICF-based instruments for these two settings.

It is also a challenge to clarify, define, and describe the link between functioning (as represented by ICF) and disease (as represented by International Classification of Diseases [4]) in the evaluation of rights to disability benefits. One way to address this challenge is by using disease-specific ICF Core Sets. That, however, would add another layer of complexity given the frequent comorbidities that we see in disability evaluations. With the upcoming 11th revision of the ICD, we will see a more integrated biomedical and biopsychosocial approach [5].

The ICF framework is well suited for describing and assessing the individual's functional capacity and has gained increasing acceptance. However, disability evaluations in social security have to take into consideration several more elements than functional ability, e.g., sociomedical history, prognosis, and causal links. A single classification cannot capture all of these, and the ICF cannot provide a framework for all the questions that need an answer, nor was it ever intended to be a one-size-fit all approach. Rather, the strength of the ICF lies in its inherent role in lending an integrative approach to understanding and measuring functioning and disability alongside other health-related approaches and models.

It could be said that a classification of functioning also should be able to describe changes in functioning given the proper measurement. Change in functioning is an essential part of disability evaluation in social security. This book pointed out that one way to meet this challenge is to do consecutive measurements and assessments on the individual; an approach that is standardized, robust, and reliable. This would then give an assessor a series of snapshots to estimate as accurately as possible the changes in a person's functioning.

> There is a need for functioning assessment and evaluation of work ability in two settings that can be seen in a continuum. One setting is vocational rehabilitation where we need assessments to guide the return-to-work processes. The other setting is the need for assessments to determine the right to benefits. We need to develop ICF-based instruments for these two settings.

The vocabulary and definitions of terms provided by the ICF have been assimilated into social security organizations in Europe to some extent. The classification is also receiving more acceptance as a language independent of professions. From the view of social security, there remain challenges related to environmental and personal factors. The environmental factors are at the moment not precise enough for use in social security and would need further development and "granularization" so those factors can be operationalized in a sensible and practical manner. The evaluation of work ability usually requires a more precise description of work demands, work situations, and work environment than the ICF can currently provide. There is a strong need to expand the ICF classification in this dimension in the coming years. Anner et al. [6] have also suggested further development of the environmental factors in order for us to better capture disability and identify the environmental influencers [6]. In the ICF, there is no obvious place to classify vocational rehabilitation interventions of various types. One way of doing this could be to classify them as environmental factors. That would, however, require that a new type of qualifier – interventions – be introduced into the classification, with the possibility to qualify both for positive and negative effects.

The lack of classification of personal factors is one limitation in using the ICF. Other inventories or instruments are necessary if one wants to describe personal factors, like motivation or sense of coherence, in a standardized way in disability evaluations in social security. At present, this standardization is carried out depending on the country, setting, or national policy.

Nevertheless, by taking into account factors of the individual and the environment, the ICF even in its current form brings about a comprehensive overview of the different factors that may impact disability. Without these contextual factors such as social support and type of health services or peer support and access for work productivity, it will be quite difficult to put disability into context as some of those factors can minimize, strengthen, or neutralize the effects of rehabilitative intervention [7, 8]. There are instances when personal factors such as age together with the mental health status may be significantly associated, and which may in turn affect the level of disability at work [9].

The complexity and length of the ICF has hindered its acceptance in some vocational rehabilitation settings. The ICF Core Set for Vocational Rehabilitation [10] should help expedite its use in clinical settings. However, the ICF Core Set for vocational rehabilitation needs further research to assess its further validity and utility in real-life settings. This research could also help identify the areas that are not yet specifically coded in the ICF, particularly for relevant and work-specific environmental factors and categories of activities/participation. Currently, the ICF does include codes for many variables that are known to have an impact on employment outcomes, such as various forms of social support and assistive technology. However, there appears to be a need for additional categories that identify items of importance during the vocational rehabilitation process, including specific items relevant to the job placement process, such as job-seeking skills training, on-the-job support, and job coaching. More precise codes and definitions are also needed in the area of work and employment (Activities and Participation) which can be potentially be mapped to existing job classification systems like the International Standard Classification of Occupations by the International Labour Organization (http://www.ilo.org/public/english/bureau/stat/isco/), or O*NET (http://www.onetonline.org). In addition, there is a need for more clear-cut strategies for identifying vocational rehabilitation interventions when using the ICF. A current problem in job placement research is the lack of consistency in research methodology. The ICF has the potential to address this problem, but without sufficient and precise inclusion of vocational rehabilitation interventions, its potential may be reduced.

Within the ICF, the contextual factors, namely, environmental factors and personal factors would need to be further developed in terms of conceptualization and classification. The more precise clarification of these factors will enhance our understanding of interventions targeted towards disability.

Several authors have pointed out that the ICF is too comprehensive to be used in toto. The use of short list – ICF Core Sets – is one way to develop the use of the ICF further. ICF Core Sets for specific diseases were the first to be created according to a defined methodology, and they have been followed by Core Sets for specific settings. The EUMASS Core Set for disability assessment in social security is one example [11], and the development of the ICF Core Set for vocational rehabilitation is another [10]. In social security, the use of disease-specific or setting specific- Core Sets should be discussed and tested. Some European countries have a strong medical influence on the decision process in social security, with a corresponding emphasis on diagnosis. In these countries, modified disease-specific ICF Core Sets might be useful. There are shortcomings with disease-specific ICF Core Sets, and perhaps the most important in social security is the high prevalence of comorbidity in benefit claimants. In many cases there is a combination of somatic and mental conditions that together could limit activity. In such cases, there would be a need for several ICF Core Sets, and that is undoubtedly a complex and cumbersome task to do. Hence, using setting-specific Core Sets would be more cost-effective when several comorbidities exist.

Whatever type of ICF Core Sets are used in social security, it should be remembered that instruments and protocols based on ICF Core Sets have a dual purpose. Guiding the individual back to work is the primary objective and, if that is not successful, to evaluate the need for financial support. The instruments will be different in scope, scaling, and content depending on the situation.

The ICF needs a robust and feasible operationalization to be "useable" in practice. The ICF Core Sets are merely the framework and classification for the gathering of information on clients. There is a need for concrete tools, instruments, or questionnaires that can be used in clinical practice and in research.

In this book, we have given several examples of the development of ICF-based tools and questionnaires. Other chapters have also shown how the ICF can be linked to already existing clinical instruments. There is a need for further development and continuous improvement of tools and questionnaires in clinical vocational rehabilitation in line with these examples. In social security, this development process has just begun and work has started to link the ICF to existing and newly developed instruments in disability evaluation.

An interesting challenge is how to select the proper tools and ICF Core Sets for clinical work and work in social security evaluation.

An ICF-based system in vocational rehabilitation and disability evaluation can refer to the use of ICF Core Sets and ICF-based or ICF-compatible tools. With this approach, however, the purpose of the evaluation needs to be carefully focused to the needs of the client and the assessor and must be specific to the context, health condition, or setting.

In order for us to be able to capture and measure disability, it is imperative that we define disability and its different components. At a glance, disability as a terminology can be simple and straightforward, but more often than not, defining disability can be a daunting and complex task depending on which stakeholder is being asked. For a patient, disability depends on the chronicity and severity of the health condition and how it impacts their activities of daily living, for example, walking, recreation, and self-care such as putting on socks and shoes [12]. For a payor, defining disability depends on the value of a particular intervention that can be determined by the relationship (ratio) between positive outcomes over cost. For a healthcare provider, it might depend mainly on clinical outcomes with limited input from the patient. Furthermore, the understanding and knowledge of disability can have regional differences and scope likely due to legislation differences among countries [13].

As an integrative biopsychosocial model, the ICF [3] sheds light into the multidimensionality and nonlinearity of disability in a structured way that shows different aspects of functioning such as those related to body functions, body structures, and activities and participation of an individual that define disability, for example, the ability to make a distinction between mental and physical forms of disability to inform intervention [14].

One benefit to using the ICF is that the model promotes seeing disability through a multidisciplinary lens, hence breaking down silos between health professions. Multidisciplinary care is becoming more and more important as to how persons with disability are being assessed and treated and provides the benefit of multiple perspectives on the disability, especially with regard to setting of also diverse rehabilitation goals for patients [15]. However, the notion of multidisciplinary care has been challenged and found to be non-evident in terms of its effectiveness [16]. One major caveat to this matter though is the specificity of the population and health condition. However, the patient population in disability evaluation and vocational rehabilitation settings are diverse and hence, would benefit from multidisciplinary care.

Disability can also be seen from an economic perspective highlighting the role of cost associated with the health condition. This cost can be direct costs or indirect costs, both of which burden the individual, their families and caregivers, and the society in general. There is a lack of a standard health metric that can be applied in strategic decision-making concerning disability and burden of disease [17], and this lack of metric contributes further to our challenge in examining the economics of disability or work disability using a common standard.

For us to be able to measure whether or not we are mitigating the effects of disability and addressing its adverse effects, we ought to know what we are measuring and to have the necessary and appropriate disability tools or measures. Many sophisticated methods of capturing or measuring disability have been presented in the literature such as Rasch analysis for reducing a list of items into an essential list of domains, for example, efficiently and precisely quantifying disability for low back pain patients [18] or employing computer adaptive testing in the clinic. However, the question is which method works and for what purpose?

Different stakeholders see disability differently. This diversity in the perception of disability challenges people involved in disability research and practice to measure disability taking into account the population where the measurement is taking place, the frequency of measurement, and the impact of knowing the outcomes.

25.4 Opportunities

The critical importance of vocational rehabilitation has been gaining ground in health conditions never thought of before like cancer [19] and in developing sophisticated ways of delivering a consumer-centered telemedicine [20].

We need to review what we know about commonly administered functional capacity evaluation measures as to whether or not they provide us with comprehensive biopsychosocial aspects rather than the physical aspects alone [21]. We also need to do a better job with patients who have mental health conditions like depression and whose disability would not be readily apparent compared to a physical form of disability [22]. We need to be able to look at applications relating to the cross-cultural applicability of the ICF, for example, in indigenous people with their unique experiences [23].

In clinical work, tools developed from the ICF have been used to follow the rehabilitation process in vocational rehabilitation. Similar tools can be developed in social security, where they can provide us with the necessary, structured, and transparent information for multi-professional evaluation of disability.

This book demonstrates how ICF Core Sets can be linked to existing patient-reported outcomes by providing principles on how to choose, implement, and operationalize the ICF Core Set for vocational rehabilitation. Also in social security, client-reported outcomes are used. By linking these to the ICF, they can be matched to outcomes reported by the assessor.

Clinician-reported outcomes on functioning have always been a key step to disability evaluation in social security. There is a need to further develop this area and to assure the reliability and validity of these measures across different health conditions and healthcare settings.

In social security, there is a challenge to find a balance between the concern for an individual's uniqueness and the need for general policy on disability. The adoption of ICF-based instruments would make it easier to standardize tools, questionnaires, and protocols. In such a situation it might be tempting, and natural, to overlook the unique experience of the individual hence, prudence is advised.

> Health and disability are always evolving in terms of how they are conceptualized and measured. Upward trends in chronic diseases and telemedicine are gaining emergence in clinical practice and research that can impact how vocational rehabilitation and disability evaluation are performed and delivered. With the advancement in modern outcomes measurement, our ability to capture functioning and disability has vastly improved compared to decades ago.

The ICF is a standardized framework and classification for studies on individuals' functioning and the relation between functioning and the environment. It may be possible to match individual functioning with demands at the work place and this should be one focus of national and international studies.

The component of personal factors in the ICF needs to be developed. In social security, some of these factors have more importance than others, and in particular motivation for return to work has been claimed as essential both to describe, to assess, and, if possible, to influence the course of the return-to-work process. There must be an effort towards the testing of scales and questionnaires. There is also a need to follow how individual clinical cases in vocational rehabilitation develop over time and with the use of ICF-based tools this is possible. There is also a need for further research on ICF-based tools and instruments with the aim of having optimal clinical utility and feasibility of these instruments and tools.

In social security, the ICF can support efforts to reach greater transparency and fairness of decisions. The framework and classification, as well as recent developments in Core Sets, have been taken into use in social security institutions. The ICF meets the need for a stronger emphasis on return-to-work processes and on the individual's functioning and work ability in disability claims.

The ICF is necessary to measure functional capacity of the claimant in social security, but it should be emphasized that the functioning assessment only constitutes a part of the whole disability evaluation process.

For social security, there is a strong need to develop the environmental factors of the ICF and start working on further developing the personal factors.

For both vocational assessment and job placement, applying the ICF model can alert practitioners to those areas where clients need to improve or develop a skill in or where environmental supports and modifications are needed. Often the types of interventions that are needed fall into two main categories: those directed to changing the individual through some type of remediation, such as establishing or improving a skill (e.g., skills training, job-seeking skills training, etc.) or those targeted to changing the environment, often in the form of support (e.g., providing job coaching, assistive technology). In the vocational rehabilitation setting, when an individual's potential skill level is low, this often means the person needs more support in the environment. For individuals with severe disabilities, a combination of skill development and environmental supports and/or modifications is often needed.

Tools based on the ICF would be useful for gathering client information in vocational assessment and job placement. Vocational assessment should be holistic and take into account all aspects that are relevant to the person's work functioning, including personal, social, cultural, medical, and psychological factors [24]. The ICF provides a comprehensive framework that can help organize, integrate, and interpret a vast amount of information from multiple sources, including interview data, medical reports, and test results. It should be possible to link many existing assessment instruments to the coding structure of the ICF [25]. The ICF framework can also help vocational assessment professionals develop individualized recommendations for services that help eliminate or minimize barriers to employment.

The comprehensive classification of the ICF provides a foundation for vocational rehabilitation planning, both in vocational assessment and job placement. It can help prevent vocational rehabilitation professionals from overlooking important areas of functioning and opportunities for interventions by ensuring consideration of multiple factors that are important for success, such as social aspects of the workplace and the impact of stigma.

During job placement, the ICF framework could also help organize information in a way that helps expedite planning and problem-solving. The ICF highlights the role of functioning, rather than diagnosis or disability type, which is what is needed for determining appropriate job accommodations and other interventions at the job site that will promote a successful outcome.

A number of studies have tried to identify variables associated with successful vocational rehabilitation outcomes, both in terms of client characteristics and service variables. There is a need to link services to outcomes and to find out what works, what is most effective, and for whom. Much of the research in job placement is hampered by a lack of consistency in methodologies that allow cross-comparisons among studies. In addition, multiple variables are not consistently defined. The ICF conceptual framework could address this inconsistency, which is needed for evidence-based practice.

Job placement research also suggests that approaches that are tailored to meet the needs of individuals with specific types of disabilities are more effective than a one-size-fits-all approach. The Individual Placement and Support model [26] is an example of an evidence-based approach that is individualized to meet client needs within the actual work setting to reduce the impact of vocational barriers and functional limitations. Research examining the ICF framework in relation to employment outcomes has thus far been limited to a handful of studies. The few studies that have been published suggest that the ICF has potential as a useful tool in identifying factors that are related to work participation. However, more research in this area is needed.

The ICF provides a foundation for vocational rehabilitation planning, both in vocational assessment and job placement. It can help prevent vocational rehabilitation professionals from overlooking important areas of functioning and opportunities for interventions by ensuring consideration of multiple factors that are important for a successful program.

Evidence-based practice in job placement should include examination of environmental factors that can act as barriers or facilitators. Research indicates that successful placement outcomes in vocational rehabilitation are associated with multiple interventions that go beyond the focus on the workplace and include those that can enhance independent functioning more broadly, such as agency collaboration, an effective working alliance between the client and rehabilitation counselor, and services to families [27]. ICF-based tools can provide vocational rehabilitation professionals with precisely defined functional strengths and limitations; ideally, this information could be linked to occupational information databases.

More research is needed to match existing instruments with the appropriate ICF categories. New instruments could also be developed, based on the Core Set for Vocational Rehabilitation. Questions have also been raised about the validity of the ICF qualifiers [28] and how to apply the ICF codes and qualifiers in a consistent manner [29]. There is a need for developing methods to make use of the ICF coding in a more streamlined and less time-consuming manner for vocational rehabilitation professionals, such as through computerized adaptive testing or related tools. With broader acceptance of the ICF, especially by public vocational rehabilitation programs, it should ultimately be possible to track individuals' progress and outcomes to determine what works, what is effective, and with which individuals, given their unique combination of strengths, barriers, and environmental contexts.

References

1. United Nations. Convention of the rights of persons with disabilities and optional protocol. Geneva: United Nations; 2006.
2. World Health Organization. World report on disability. Geneva: World Health Organization; 2011.
3. World Health Organization. International classification of functioning, disability and health. Geneva: World Health Organization; 2001.
4. International classification of diseases (ICD-10) [Internet]. Available from: http://www.who.int/classifications/icd/en/
5. Escorpizo R, Kostanjsek N, Kennedy C, Nicol MM, Stucki G, Ustun TB, et al. Harmonizing WHO's international classification of diseases (ICD) and international classification of functioning, disability and health (ICF): importance and methods to link disease and functioning. BMC Public Health. 2013;13:742, 2458-13-742.
6. Anner J, Schwegler U, Kunz R, Trezzini B, de Boer W. Evaluation of work disability and the international classification of functioning, disability and health: What to expect and what not. BMC Public Health. 2012;12:470, 2458-12-470.
7. Forslund MV, Roe C, Arango-Lasprilla JC, Sigurdardottir S, Andelic N. Impact of personal and environmental factors on employment outcome two years after moderate-to-severe traumatic brain injury. J Rehabil Med. 2013;45(8):801–7.
8. Berzina G, Paanalahti M, Lundgren-Nilsson A, Sunnerhagen KS. Exploration of some personal factors with the international classification of functioning, disability and health Core Sets for stroke. J Rehabil Med. 2013;45(7):609–15.
9. Wilkie R, Blagojevic-Bucknall M, Jordan KP, Pransky G. Onset of work restriction in employed adults with lower limb joint pain: individual factors and area-level socioeconomic conditions. J Occup Rehabil. 2013;23(2):180–8.
10. Finger ME, Escorpizo R, Glassel A, Gmunder HP, Luckenkemper M, Chan C, et al. ICF core set for vocational rehabilitation: results of an international consensus conference. Disabil Rehabil. 2012;34(5):429–38.
11. Brage S, Donceel P, Falez F. Development of ICF core set for disability evaluation in social security. Disabil Rehabil. 2008;30(18):1392–6.
12. Heiberg KE, Ekeland A, Mengshoel AM. Functional improvements desired by patients before and in the first year after total hip arthroplasty. BMC Musculoskelet Disord. 2013;14:243, 2474-14-243.
13. Coomer K, Houdmont J. Occupational health professionals' knowledge, understanding and use of work ability. Occup Med (Lond). 2013;63(6):405–9.
14. Pekkanen L, Neva MH, Kautiainen H, Dekker J, Piitulainen K, Wahlman M, et al. Disability and health-related quality of life in patients undergoing spinal fusion: a comparison with a general population sample. BMC Musculoskelet Disord. 2013;14:211, 2474-14-211.
15. Meesters J, Hagel S, Klokkerud M, Stovgaard I, Bremander A, Grotle M, et al. Goal-setting in multidisciplinary team care for patients with rheumatoid arthritis: an international multi-center evaluation of the contents using the international classification of functioning, disability and health as a reference. J Rehabil Med. 2013;45(9):888–99.
16. Metzelthin SF, van Rossum E, de Witte LP, Ambergen AW, Hobma SO, Sipers W, et al. Effectiveness of interdisciplinary primary care approach to reduce disability in community dwelling frail older people: cluster randomised controlled trial. BMJ. 2013;347:f5264.
17. Longfield K, Smith B, Gray R, Ngamkitpaiboon L, Vielot N. Putting health metrics into practice: using the disability-adjusted life year for strategic decision making. BMC Public Health. 2013;13 Suppl 2:S2, 2458-13-S2-S2. Epub 17 Jun 2013.
18. Lu YM, Wu YY, Hsieh CL, Lin CL, Hwang SL, Cheng KI, et al. Measurement precision of the disability for back pain scale-by applying Rasch analysis. Health Qual Life Outcomes. 2013;11:119, 7525-11-119.

19. Hubbard G, Gray NM, Ayansina D, Evans JM, Kyle RG. Case management vocational rehabilitation for women with breast cancer after surgery: a feasibility study incorporating a pilot randomised controlled trial. Trials. 2013;14:175, 6215-14-175.
20. Martinez-Alcala CI, Munoz M, Monguet-Fierro J. Design and customization of telemedicine systems. Comput Math Methods Med. 2013;2013:618025.
21. Lakke SE, Soer R, Geertzen JH, Wittink H, Douma RK, van der Schans CP, et al. Construct validity of functional capacity tests in healthy workers. BMC Musculoskelet Disord. 2013;14:180, 2474-14-180.
22. Schellart AJ, Zwerver F, Anema JR, Van der Beek AJ. The influence of applying insurance medicine guidelines for depression on disability assessments. BMC Res Notes. 2013;6:225, 0500-6-225.
23. Alford VM, Remedios LJ, Webb GR, Ewen S. The use of the international classification of functioning, disability and health (ICF) in indigenous healthcare: a systematic literature review. Int J Equity Health. 2013;12:32, 9276-12-32.
24. Breeding R. The utility of proactive vocational assessment in advancing consumer empowerment. Vocat Eval Career Assess Prof J. 2006;2(2):39–56.
25. Chan F, Keegan J, Sung C, Drout M, Pai CH, Anderson E. The world health organization ICF model as a framework for assessing vocational rehabilitation outcomes. J Rehabil Adm. 2009;33(2):91–112.
26. Campbell K, Bond GR, Drake RE. Who benefits from supported employment: a meta-analytic study. Schizophr Bull. 2011;37(2):370–80.
27. Fleming AR, Del Valle R, Kim M, Leahy MJ. Best practice models of effective vocational rehabilitation service delivery in the public rehabilitation program: a review and synthesis of the empirical literature. Rehabil Couns Bull. 2012;56:146–59.
28. Glassel A, Rauch A, Selb M, Emmenegger K, Luckenkemper M, Escorpizo R. A case study on the application of international classification of functioning, disability and health (ICF)-based tools for vocational rehabilitation in spinal cord injury. Work. 2012;41(4):465–74.
29. Reed G, Lux J, Bufka L, Trask C, Peterson DB, Stark S, et al. Operationalizing the international classification of functioning, disability and health in clinical settings. Rehabil Psychol. 2005;50(2):122–31.

Index

R. Escorpizo et al. (eds.), *Handbook of Vocational Rehabilitation and Disability Evaluation*, Handbooks in Health, Work, and Disability, DOI 10.1007/978-3-319-08825-9

W

MIX
Papier aus verantwortungsvollen Quellen
Paper from responsible sources
FSC® C105338

If you have any concerns about our products,
you can contact us on
ProductSafety@springernature.com

In case Publisher is established outside the EU,
the EU authorized representative is:
Springer Nature Customer Service Center GmbH
Europaplatz 3, 69115 Heidelberg, Germany

Printed by Libri Plureos GmbH
in Hamburg, Germany